Developmental Physical Education for Today's Children

As always, To the Sunshine of My Life:
Ellie, David Lee, Jennifer, and Dan
and to
Margie Hanson
in Recognition of a Lifetime of Commitment to Children

CONTENTS IN BRIEF

PART I
The Learner

1 Developmental Physical Education: An Overview *4*
2 Childhood Growth and Motor Development *17*
3 Movement Skill Acquisition *35*
4 Fitness Enhancement *56*
5 Cognitive Learning *72*
6 Affective Growth *84*
7 Children with Disabilities *100*

PART II
The Program

8 The Developmental Curriculum *124*
9 Planning Skill Themes *147*
10 The Content Areas *167*
11 Assessing Progress *181*

PART III
The Teacher

12 Effective Teaching *200*
13 Positive Discipline *219*
14 Teaching Styles *230*
15 Safety Considerations and Legal Liability *243*

PART IV
The Skill Themes

16 Fundamental Stability Skill Themes *258*
17 Fundamental Locomotor Skill Themes *278*
18 Fundamental Manipulative Skill Themes *315*
19 Stunts and Tumbling Skill Themes *354*
20 Large and Small Equipment Skill Themes *374*
21 Disc Sport Skill Themes *399*
22 Basketball Skill Themes *411*
23 Soccer Skill Themes *434*
24 Softball Skill Themes *458*
25 Volleyball Skill Themes *480*

PART V
The Program Strands

26 The Vigorous Activity Strand for Fit Movers *500*
27 The Perceptual-Motor Strand for Multisensory Learners *515*
28 The Creative Dance Strand for Expressive Movers *539*
29 The Folk Dance Strand for Cooperative Social Learners *563*

Appendixes

CONTENTS

Preface *xxi*

PART I

The Learner

1 Developmental Physical Education: An Overview

Key Concept *4*
Chapter Objectives *4*
Terms to Remember *4*
The Aims and Goals of Physical Education *6*
Developmental Physical Education
  Defined *7*
The Components of Developmental Physical
  Education *9*
  Motor Development *9*
  Cognitive Learning *11*
  Affective Growth *14*

Summary *16*
Complementary Readings *16*
Supplementary Readings *16*
Videos *16*

2 Childhood Growth and Motor Development

Key Concept *17*
Chapter Objectives *17*
Terms to Remember *17*

Growth *18*
  Early Childhood (Ages Three to Eight) *18*
  Later Childhood (Ages Eight to Twelve) *21*
Factors Affecting Growth *22*
  Nutrition *22*
  Exercise *22*
  Illness *23*
  Lifestyle *23*
Development *24*
The Dynamics of Development *24*
Factors Affecting Motor Development *25*
  Developmental Sequence *25*
  Developmental Variability and Readiness *28*
  Differentiation and Integration *29*
  Sensitive Learning Periods *29*
Early Childhood Development *29*
  Motor Characteristics *31*
  Cognitive Characteristics *32*
  Affective Characteristics *32*
Later Childhood Development *32*
  Motor Characteristics *33*
  Cognitive Characteristics *33*
  Affective Characteristics *34*

Summary *34*
Complementary Readings *34*
Supplementary Readings *34*

3 Movement Skill Acquisition

Key Concept *35*
Chapter Objectives *35*
Terms to Remember *35*
The Importance of Developing Children's
  Movement Skills *36*

Movement Skills and Movement Patterns   *36*
The Categories of Movement   *37*
   Stability Movement Skills   37
   Locomotor Movement Skills   40
   Manipulative Movement Skills   40
   Movement Phrases   40
Environmental Factors that Influence Movement
   Skill Acquisition   *41*
   Opportunity for Practice   42
   Encouragement   42
   Instruction   43
   Ecological Setting   43
The Fundamental Movement Skill Phase   *43*
   Initial Stage   43
   Elementary Stage   43
   Mature Stage   44
The Specialized Movement Skill Phase   *45*
   Transition Stage   45
   Application Stage   46
   Lifelong Utilization Stage   46
Types of Movement Performance   *46*
   Externally Paced and Internally Paced Movement   46
   Gross and Fine Movement   46
   Discrete, Serial, and Continuous Movement   47
The Levels of Movement Skill Learning   *47*
   Beginning/Novice Level   47
   Intermediate/Practice Level   49
   Advanced/Fine-Tuning Level   49
Movement Skill Homework   *50*
Implications for Teaching Developmental Physical
   Education   *54*

Summary   54
Complementary Readings   55
Supplementary Readings   55
Videos   55

Health-Related Fitness   58
Performance-Related Fitness   58
Health-Related Components of Fitness   *58*
   Muscular Strength   61
   Muscular Endurance   62
   Cardiovascular Endurance   62
   Joint Flexibility   63
   Body Composition   63
Performance-Related Components of
   Fitness   *64*
   Balance   64
   Coordination   64
   Agility   64
   Speed of Movement   64
   Power   65
Informed Movers Defined   *65*
   Independent Exercisers   65
   Nutritious Eaters   66
Principles of Fitness Development   *66*
   Overload   66
   Specificity   66
   Progression   66
   Frequency/Intensity/Timing/Type (FITT)   67
   Individuality   68
Fitness Homework   *68*
Eager Movers Defined   *68*
   Active Movers   69
   Playful Movers   69
   Partners with Parents   69
Implications for Teaching Developmental Physical
   Education   *70*

Summary   70
Complementary Readings   71
Supplementary Readings   71
Videos   71

4   Fitness Enhancement

Key Concept   56
Chapter Objectives   56
Terms to Remember   56
The Challenge   *57*
Fit Movers Defined   *58*

5   Cognitive Learning

Key Concept   72
Chapter Objectives   72
Terms to Remember   72
Active Learners Defined   *73*
   Cognitive Mapmaking   73

Critical Thinking   73
The Cognitive Concept Components   75
Skill Concepts   75
Movement Concepts   76
Activity Concepts   77
Fitness Concepts   77
Academic Concepts   77
Multisensory Learners Defined   78
Perceptual-Motor Learning   78
The Perceptual-Motor Components   79
Body Awareness   79
Spatial Awareness   79
Directional Awareness   81
Temporal Awareness   81
The Importance of Perceptual-Motor
    Learning   81
Implications for Teaching Developmental Physical
    Education   82

Summary   82
Complementary Readings   83
Supplementary Readings   83
Videos   83

6   Affective Growth

Key Concept   84
Chapter Objectives   84
Terms to Remember   84
The Importance of Self-Esteem in Becoming a
    Self-Discovering Learner   85
Components of a Positive Self-Concept   86
Belonging   86
Perceived Competence   86
Worthiness   87
Acceptance of Self   87
Uniqueness   88
Virtue   89
The Importance of Developing Children's
    Self-Concept   89
Security   89
Status   90
Cooperative Learners Defined   91
Working Together   91

Social Decision Makers   92
Reasons for Fostering Positive Socialization   92
Group Affiliation   92
Attitude Formation and Character Education   92
Moral Growth   94
Factors That Influence Affective
    Development   94
Encouragement   95
Goal Setting   96
Self-Assessment   96
Moral Dilemmas   96
Implications for Teaching Developmental Physical
    Education   97

Summary   98
Complementary Readings   99
Supplementary Readings   99
Videos   99

7   Children with Disabilities

Key Concept   100
Chapter Objectives   100
Terms to Remember   100
The Physical Education Program   102
The Adapted Program   102
The Remedial Program   102
The Developmental Program   103
Inclusion   104
Categories of Developmental Disabilities   104
Children with Physical Disabilities   104
Children with Mental Disabilities   110
Children with Emotional Disabilities   113
Children with Learning Disabilities   115
Other Disabilities   117
The Individual Education Program (IEP)   118
Special Needs of Children with
    Disabilities   118
Social Adjustment   118
Body Image Enhancement   118

Summary   119
Complementary Readings   119
Supplementary Readings   119

The Program

8   The Developmental Curriculum

Key Concept   124
Chapter Objectives   124
Terms to Remember   124
Steps in Planning the Curriculum   125
    Establish a Value Base   125
    Develop a Conceptual Framework   127
    Determine Objectives of the Program   128
    Design the Program   131
    Establish Assessment Procedures   135
    Implement the Program   135
The Developmental Curricular Model   136
    Preschool and Primary Grades   137
    Intermediate and Upper Elementary Grades   137
The Extended Curriculum   139
    Recess and Noon-Hour Programs   139
    Daily Fitness Programs   141
    Intramural Programs   141
    Club Programs   142
    Interscholastic Programs   142
Special Programs   142
    Special Days   143
    Gym Shows and Public Demonstrations   143
Tournaments   144
    Round-Robin Tournament   144
    Ladder Tournament   144

Summary   146
Complementary Readings   146
Supplementary Readings   146

9   Planning Skill Themes

Key Concept   147
Chapter Objectives   147
Terms to Remember   147

Steps in Planning a Movement Skill Theme   148
    Preplanning   148
    Assessing Entry Levels   149
    Specific Planning   149
Sequencing the Daily Lesson   153
    Introduction   154
    Review   155
    Body   155
    Lesson Summary   155
Implementing the Daily Lesson   156
    Putting It All Together   156
    Successful Lessons   156
    Evaluating the Daily Lesson   157
    Moving On   158
    Revisiting   158
Organizing Facilities   158
    Indoor Facilities   159
    Outdoor Facilities   160
Organizing Equipment   160
    Equipment Selection   160
    Equipment Placement and Use   161
Preparing Instructional Aids   161
    Task Cards   161
    Bulletin Boards   162
    Visual Aids   162
Organizing Student Helpers   162
    Squads and Squad Leaders   162
    Gym Helpers   166

Summary   166
Complementary Readings   166
Supplementary Readings   166
Videos   166

10   The Content Areas

Key Concept   167
Chapter Objectives   167
Terms to Remember   167
Games   168
    Types of Games   168
    Selecting Appropriate Game Activities   171
Dance   172
    Rhythm and Types of Dance   173
    Selecting Appropriate Rhythmical Activities   176

Self-Testing   *176*
   Types of Self-Testing Activities   177
   Selecting Appropriate Self-Testing Activities   178

Summary   179
Complementary Readings   179
Supplementary Readings   180
Videos   180

11   Assessing Progress

Key Concept   181
Chapter Objectives   181
Terms to Remember   181
Motor Assessment   *183*
   Process Assessment   183
   Guidelines for Observational Assessment   183
   Product Assessment   184
   Guidelines for Performance Assessment   184
   Motor Assessment Tests   184
Fitness Assessment   *190*
   When to Assess   190
   What to Assess   191
   Fitness Assessment Tests   191
Computer Applications for Assessment   *194*
   Computerized Motor Assessment   194
   Computerized Fitness Assessment   194

Summary   194
Complementary Readings   195
Supplementary Readings   195

PART III

The Teacher

12   Effective Teaching

Key Concept   200
Chapter Objectives   200

Terms to Remember   200
Responsibilities of the Teacher   *201*
   Planning the Curriculum   201
   Organizing the Learning Environment   201
   Planning and Implementing the Lesson   201
   Assessing Pupil Progress   202
   Counseling Students   202
   Acting as Community Representative   202
   Professional Growth   203
Stages in Becoming an Effective
   Teacher   *204*
   Concern for Personal Success   204
   Concern for Self   205
   Concern for Students   205
Characteristics of Effective
   Teachers   *206*
   Personal Traits   206
   Traits in the Classroom   207
   Assessment Traits   208
Verbal Communication   *208*
   Getting Attention   209
   Maintaining Attention   209
   Providing Clarity   209
   *Checking for Understanding and
      Retention   210*
   Providing Feedback   210
   Changing Well-Learned Techniques   211
Nonverbal Communication   *212*
   Postures   212
   Gestures   213
   Facial Expressions   213
Conveying Enthusiasm   *213*
   Interest in Your Subject Matter   214
   Interest in Your Students   214
Improving Communication Skills   *214*
   Respect Physical Distance   214
   Observe Children   215
   Self-Study   215
Listening to Children   *216*
   Children's Verbal Messages   216
   Children's Nonverbal Messages   216
   Knowing the Learner   216

Summary   217
Complementary Readings   218
Supplementary Readings   218
Videos   218

●

13   Positive Discipline

Key Concept   219
Chapter Objectives   219
Terms to Remember   219
Discipline Defined   220
Techniques for Imposing Teacher
    Control   220
    Nonverbal Responses   221
    Verbal Responses   221
    Time Out   221
Punishment   222
Techniques for Developing Self-Control   223
    Establish Routines and Rules   224
    Reduce the "Don'ts"   224
    Be Reasonable   224
    Follow Through   224
    Be Consistent   224
    Praise Others   225
    Be Assertive   225
    Demonstrate Trust   226
Requirements for Positive Discipline   226
    Be a Positive Role Model   226
    Plan Efficiently   226
    Communicate Effectively   227
    Self-Assess   228

Summary   228
Complementary Readings   228
Supplementary Readings   229

●

14   Teaching Styles

Key Concept   230
Chapter Objectives   230
Terms to Remember   230
Factors That Influence Selection of Various
    Teaching Styles   231
    Movement Skill Learning Factors   231
    Student Comprehension and Compliance Factors   223
Styles of Teaching   235
    Direct Styles   236

    Indirect Styles   238
    Combining Direct and Indirect Styles   240

Summary   242
Complementary Readings   242
Supplementary Readings   242

●

15   Safety Considerations and Legal Liability

Key Concept   243
Chapter Objectives   243
Terms to Remember   243
Conditions of Legal Liability   244
    Negligence   244
    Contributing to an Attractive Nuisance   245
    Malpractice   246
    Defenses against Negligence   246
Frequent Conditions Leading to Legal Action   247
    Ignoring Mandated Legislation   247
    Improper Instruction   248
    Inadequate Supervision   248
    Failure to Provide a Safe Environment   249
Minimizing Legal Liability   249
    Record-Keeping   249
    Written Policies   252
    Insurance Coverage   253

Summary   253
Complementary Readings   254
Supplementary Readings   254
Videos   254

PART IV

The Skill Themes

●

16   Fundamental Stability Skill Themes

Key Concept   258
Chapter Objectives   258

Terms to Remember   258
Stability Skill Sequencing   259
Dynamic and Static Balance   259
   Beam Walk   261
   One-Foot Balance   261
Body Rolling   265
   Forward Roll   265
   Dodging   267
Skill Development Activities   270
   Exploratory Activities   270
   Guided-Discovery Activities   271
Skill Application Activities   271
   Stability Games   272
Assessing Progress   277

Summary   277
Complementary Readings   277
Supplementary Readings   277
Videos   277

17   Fundamental Locomotor Skill Themes

Key Concept   278
Chapter Objectives   278
Terms to Remember   278
Locomotor Skill Sequencing   279
Running and Leaping   279
   Running   280
   Leaping   282
Jumping and Hopping   283
   Horizontal Jumping   283
   Vertical Jumping   285
   Jumping from a Height   286
   Hopping   288
Galloping, Sliding, and Skipping   289
   Galloping and Sliding   289
   Skipping   291
Skill Development Activities   292
   Exploratory Activities   292
   Guided-Discovery Activities   292
Skill Application Activities   308
   Locomotor Games   309
Assessing Progress   312

Summary   312
Complementary Readings   314
Supplementary Readings   314
Videos   314

18   Fundamental Manipulative Skill Themes

Key Concept   315
Chapter Objectives   315
Terms to Remember   315
Manipulative Skill Sequencing   316
Throwing and Catching   317
   Throwing   317
   Catching   319
Kicking and Trapping   320
   Kicking   321
   Trapping   322
Dribbling and Ball Rolling   324
   Dribbling   324
   Ball Rolling   325
Striking and Volleying   327
   Horizontal Striking   327
   Volleying   329
Skill Development Activities   330
   Exploratory Activities   330
   Guided-Discovery Activities   330
Skill Application Activities   346
   Manipulative Games   347
Assessing Progress   350

Summary   353
Complementary Readings   353
Supplementary Readings   353
Videos   353

19   Stunts and Tumbling Skill Themes

Key Concept   354
Chapter Objectives   354
Terms to Remember   354
Skill Sequencing   355
Safety Considerations   356
Spotting   356

Body-Rolling Skills   356
   Sideways Rolling   357
   Forward Rolling   357
   Backward Rolling   359
Springing Skills   360
   Upright Springing   360
   Inverted Springing   362
Upright Support Skills   362
   Individual Supports   364
   Partner Supports   366
Inverted Support Skills   367
   Headstand Skills   367
   Transitional Supports   369
   Handstand Skills   370
Assessing Progress   371

Summary   372
Complementary Readings   372
Supplementary Readings   372
Videos   373

20   Large and Small Equipment Skill Themes

Key Concept   374
Chapter Objectives   374
Terms to Remember   374
Skills With Large Equipment   375
   Balance-Beam Skills   376
   Rope-Climbing and Cargo Net Skills   378
   Horizontal Ladder Skills   380
   Inner Tube and Springboard Skills   382
   Springboard and Vaulting Skills   384
   Turning Bar Skills   386
   Parachute Skills   387
Skills With Small Equipment   390
   Balance Boards and Stilts Activities   390
   Balloon Activities   390
   Ball Activities   391
   Beanbag Activities   392
   Hoop Activities   393
   Jump Rope Activities   394
   Stretch Rope Activities   395
   Wand Activities   397
Assessing Progress   397

Summary   397
Complementary Readings   398
Supplementary Readings   398
Videos   398

21   Disc Sport Skill Themes

Key Concept   399
Chapter Objectives   399
Terms to Remember   399
Disc Skill Sequencing   400
Disc Throwing   400
   Backhand Throw   401
   Forehand Throw   401
   Overhand Throw   403
   Teaching Tips   403
   Concepts Children Should Know   404
Disc Catching   404
   Two-Handed Sandwich Catch   404
   Two-Handed Clap Catch   404
   One-Handed Catch   405
   Teaching Tips   405
   Concepts Children Should Know   406
Fitness and Skill Development
   Activities   406
   Warm-up Activities   406
   Skill Drills   407
Basic Rules for Ultimate   408
Assessing Progress   408

Summary   409
Complementary Readings   410
Supplementary Readings   410
Videos   410

22   Basketball Skill Themes

Key Concept   411
Chapter Objectives   411
Terms to Remember   411
Developing a Basketball Skills Theme   412
Basketball Skill Sequencing   412

Passing and Catching *413*
  Chest Pass 413
  Bounce Pass 414
  One-Handed Overarm Pass 414
  Two-Handed Overarm Pass 415
  Catching 415
  Teaching Tips 415
  Concepts Children Should Know 416
Dribbling and Pivoting *417*
  Stationary Dribble 417
  Moving Dribble 417
  Crossover Dribble 418
  Pivoting 418
  Teaching Tips 418
  Concepts Children Should Know 419
Goal Shooting *419*
  One-Handed Push Shot 420
  Jump Shot 420
  Lay-up Shot 420
  Free Throw Shooting 421
  Teaching Tips 421
  Concepts Children Should Know 422
Fitness and Skill Development Activities *422*
  Warm-up Activities 423
  Skill Drills 423
  Basketball Lead-up Games 426
Basic Rules for Basketball *429*
Assessing Progress *430*
  Process Assessment 430
  Product Assessment 430

Summary 430
Complementary Readings 433
Supplementary Readings 433
Videos 433

23 Soccer Skill Themes

Key Concept 434
Chapter Objectives 434
Terms to Remember 434
Soccer Skill Sequencing *435*
Kicking Skills *435*
  Instep Kick 435
  Push Pass 438

  Inside-of-Foot Kick 438
  Punting 439
  Teaching Tips 439
  Concepts Children Should Know 440
Trapping Skills *441*
  Shin Trap 441
  Sole-of-Foot Trap 441
  Inside-of-Foot Trap 442
  Inside-of-Thigh Trap 442
  Chest Trap 443
  Teaching Tips 443
  Concepts Children Should Know 444
Dribbling Skills *444*
  Inside-of-Foot Dribble 444
  Outside-of-Foot Dribble 444
  Teaching Tips 445
  Concepts Children Should Know 445
Volleying Skills *446*
  Juggling 446
  Heading 446
  Teaching Tips 446
  Concepts Children Should Know 447
Fitness and Skill Development Activities *447*
  Warm-up Activities 447
  Skill Drills 448
  Soccer Lead-up Games 450
Basic Rules for Soccer *453*
Assessing Progress *453*
  Process Assessment 453
  Product Assessment 454

Summary 456
Complementary Readings 456
Supplementary Readings 457
Videos 457

24 Softball Skill Themes

Key Concept 458
Chapter Objectives 458
Terms to Remember 458
Developing a Softball Skills Theme *459*
Softball Skill Sequencing *459*

Throwing   *460*
  Overhand Throw   461
  Sidearm Throw   462
  Underhand Throw   462
  Pitching   463
  Teaching Tips   463
  Concepts Children Should Know   464
Fielding   *464*
  Fly Ball   464
  Line Drive   465
  Ground Ball   465
  Teaching Tips   465
  Concepts Children Should Know   466
Hitting   *466*
  Batting   466
  Bunting   467
  Teaching Tips   467
  Concepts Children Should Know   468
Fitness and Skill Development Activities   *468*
  Warm-up Activities   468
  Skill Drills   469
  Softball Lead-up Games   471
Basic Rules for Softball   *475*
Assessing Progress   *476*
  Process Assessment   476
  Product Assessment   476

Summary   476
Complementary Readings   478
Supplementary Readings   478
Videos   478

25   Volleyball Skill Themes

Key Concept   480
Chapter Objectives   480
Terms to Remember   480
Developing a Volleyball Skills Theme   *481*
Volleyball Skill Sequencing   *481*
Volleying   *483*
  Overhead Pass   483
  Bump Pass   483
  Set   484
  Dig Pass   484

Teaching Tips   485
  Concepts Children Should Know   486
Serving   *486*
  Underhand Serve   486
  Overhead Serve   487
  Teaching Tips   487
  Concepts Children Should Know   488
Fitness and Skill Development Activities   *488*
  Warm-up Activities   489
  Skill Drills   489
  Volleyball Lead-up Games   490
Basic Rules for Volleyball   *494*
Assessing Progress   *494*
  Process Assessment   494
  Product Assessment   494

Summary   497
Complementary Readings   497
Supplementary Readings   497
Videos   497

The Program Strands

26   The Vigorous Activity Strand for Fit Movers

Key Concept   500
Chapter Objectives   500
Terms to Remember   500
Aerobic Activities   *501*
Muscular Strength and Endurance
  Activities   *505*
  Arm and Shoulder Activities   507
  Abdominal Activities   507
  Lower Back Activities   508
  Leg Activities   508
  Combative Activities   508
Joint Flexibility Activities   *510*
  Back and Trunk Stretching Activities   510

Arm and Shoulder Stretching Activities   512
Leg Stretching Activities   513

Summary   513
Complementary Readings   514
Supplementary Readings   514
Videos   514
Recordings   514
Comprehensive Fitness Education Programs   514

27 The Perceptual-Motor Strand for Multisensory Learners

Key Concept   515
Chapter Objectives   515
Terms to Remember   515
Body Awareness Activities   *516*
Spatial Awareness Activities   *519*
Directional Awareness Activities   *522*
Temporal Awareness Activities   *525*
Visual Perception Activities   *527*
   Depth Perception   527
   Form Perception   528
   Figure-Ground Perception   529
Auditory Perception Activities   *530*
   Listening Skills   531
   Auditory Discrimination   532
   Auditory Memory   533
Tactile/Kinesthetic Perception Activities   *534*
   Tactile Discrimination and Matching   534
   Tactile/Kinesthetic Memory   536

Summary   536
Complementary Readings   537
Supplementary Readings   537
Recordings   537

28 The Creative Dance Strand for Expressive Movers

Key Concept   539
Chapter Objectives   539
Terms to Remember   539
Rhythmic Fundamentals   *540*
   Understanding the Elements of Rhythm   540
   Discovering Rhythm   541
   Applying Rhythm   543
Singing Rhythms   *545*
   Finger Plays   546
   Rhymes and Poems   549
   Singing Dances   551
Creative Dance   *555*
   Creative Rhythmic Expression   555
   Imitative Dances   556
   Interpretative Dances   558
   Dance Making   559

Summary   561
Complementary Readings   561
Supplementary Readings   561
Videos   561
Audio Resources   561

29 The Folk Dance Strand for Cooperative Social Learners

Key Concept   563
Chapter Objectives   563
Terms to Remember   563
Preparing to Teach a Dance   *564*
Basics of Folk Dance   *564*
   Steps   565
   Terms   566
   Formations   567
Ethnic Dances   *567*
Square Dances   *573*
Line Dances   *578*

Summary   584
Complementary Readings   584
Supplementary Readings   585
Videos   585
Audio Resources   585

APPENDIX A: Total Body Fundamental Movement Pattern: Observational Assessment Form   *587*

**APPENDIX B: Segmental Fundamental
Movement Pattern: Observational
Assessment Form** *588*

**APPENDIX C: Individual Motor Assessment
Progress Report for Fundamental
Movement Skills** *589*

**APPENDIX D: Sport Skill Observational
Assessment Forms** *590*

**APPENDIX E: Relevant Position Papers and
Guidelines of National
Associations** *594*

SUBJECT INDEX *595*

ACTIVITY INDEX *601*

**DEVELOPMENTAL MOVEMENT SKILLS
INDEX** *607*

Developmental Physical Education for Today's Children, Third Edition, is written for both undergraduate and graduate students in physical education, early childhood education, and elementary education. It is especially designed for those taking a first course in children's physical education, although it is also used by many colleges and universities for more advanced courses because of its comprehensive and in-depth coverage of important topics.

The most distinguishing feature of this text is that it is written from a developmental perspective. Children are, therefore, viewed first, and foremost, from where they *are* in terms of their motor, cognitive, and affective development (e.g., individual appropriateness), rather than where they *should* be (age-group appropriateness). To that end, the more traditional activity orientation to children's physical education and the "newer" movement education perspective are merged and cooperatively applied. Our knowledge of children's motor development, movement skill learning, and fitness enhancement serves as the conceptual framework for the developmental approach advocated here. This is done in a manner that is in harmony with the cognitive and affective development of children and congruent with a broad spectrum of educational philosophies.

This third edition of *Developmental Physical Education for Today's Children* has been completely updated and extensively revised. The book maintains its integrity as being much more than a "cookbook" or bland text void of a consistent philosophical approach. A number of new learning aids have been added to help readers focus on essential concepts and practical pointers. The developmental approach advocated here attempts to apply our knowledge of children's growth and motor development in a comprehensive manner that recognizes the essential concept of the individuality of the learner—individuality in terms of motor, cognitive, and affective development.

In this new edition each chapter opens with a **Key Concept, Chapter Objectives,** and **Terms to Remember.** These represent the essential points covered in the chapter and are intended to focus the reader on the critically important information to follow. In the chapters

there are two primary learning aids entitled **Teaching Tips** and **Concepts.** Teaching Tips boxes provide the reader with quick and easy reference tools for making practical application to the information being discussed. The Concept boxes distill the discussion into its essential concepts. At the end of each chapter is a brief **Summary** that capsulizes the information contained in the just completed chapter. **Key Terms** appear in boldface in the text and are followed closely by a definition or explanation. **Complementary Readings** and **Supplementary Readings** conclude each chapter and represent the most up-to-date information available at press time. The Complementary Reading section contains the sources referred to in the chapter and additional recommended readings. Supplementary Readings are additional up-to-date readings for the student desiring more in-depth coverage of the topic. Each entry has been selected for its focus on the topic, overall quality, and general reader accessibility. Whenever possible, a final section on **Videos** has been included. The number and quality of video resources have increased dramatically in the past several years. Their use can greatly enhance the quality of your classroom instruction.

Developmental Physical Education for Today's Children is organized so teachers can easily use the text in its entirety in a single course or divide the chapters for use in two separate courses. Parts I, II, and III (*The Learner, The Program,* and *The Teacher*) center on essential background information for successful teaching. These fifteen chapters can be effectively incorporated into a full semester methods course. Parts IV and V (*The Skill Themes* and *The Program Strands*), the last fourteen chapters, can easily be used in a course focusing on developmental movement experiences for preschool and elementary school children.

Part I, *The Learner,* focuses on the child from a developmental perspective. Chapter 1, "Developmental Physical Education: An Overview," is critically important to making maximum use of the rest of the text. The aims and goals of children's physical education are discussed, followed by a thorough definition of *developmental* physical education.

Next, the motor, cognitive, and affective components of developmental physical education are briefly introduced as are the movement skill theme and program strand approaches to teaching children's physical education.

Chapter 2 introduces factors that affect children's growth patterns and motor development. In addition, this chapter outlines motor, cognitive, and affective characteristics during the periods of early and later childhood in an attempt to help the reader form a generalized, age-appropriate view of the mythical "average" child.

Chapters 3 and 4, "Movement Skill Acquisition" and "Fitness Enhancement," clearly focus on these two topics as the unique and primary outcomes of the developmental physical education program. Chapter 3 contains the categories of movement, phases and stages of motor development, and levels of learning a new movement skill. Chapter 4 discusses how the components of physical fitness, principles of fitness development, and fitness homework enhance children's physical behaviors.

Chapters 5 and 6, "Cognitive Learning" and "Affective Growth," deal with important additional outcomes of quality physical education. Chapter 5 centers on the cognitive concept and perceptual-motor outcomes of children's physical education. Self-concept development, positive socialization, and character education are included in Chapter 6.

Chapter 7, "Children with Disabilities," which concludes Part I, focuses on the physical activity needs of children with disabilities and describes for teachers categories of limiting conditions that affect these children. A wealth of Teaching Tips can be found in this chapter.

Part II, *The Program,* combines what we know about the learner and the teacher and operationalizes it in a manner that is both developmentally appropriate and practical. Chapters 8, 9, and 10 deal with "The Developmental Curriculum," "Planning Skill Themes," and "The Content Areas," respectively. Chapter 8 focuses on the steps in planning the curriculum and the developmental curricular model. Attention is also given to the extended curriculum and special programs. Chapter 9 describes the steps in planning a skill theme, sequencing the daily lesson, and implementing the lesson. This chapter also offers tips on organizing facilities and equipment, preparing instructional aids, and organizing student helpers. Chapter 10 looks at the content areas of games, dance, and self-testing experiences and provides many suggestions for selecting appropriate activities from each area.

Chapter 11, "Assessing Progress," concludes Part II and centers on motor assessment and fitness assessment as the two primary evaluative responsibilities of the physical education teacher. Various types and purposes of assessment are discussed, along with a brief presentation of several motor and fitness assessment tests.

Part III, *The Teacher,* contains four chapters that provide the reader with a realistic view of both the art and the science of teaching. Chapters 12 and 13, "Effective Teaching" and "Positive Discipline," are essential to understanding the role of the teacher. Chapter 12 discusses the teacher's responsibilities, stages in becoming an effective teacher, characteristics of master teachers, and effective verbal and nonverbal communication techniques. Chapter 13 takes a close look at class control and suggests ways to help lead children to improved self-control.

Chapter 14, "Teaching Styles," is a critical element of this text. This chapter discusses important factors to consider when utilizing a particular teaching style, as well as a variety of direct and indirect methods. No amount of reading, however, will show students how to use the spectrum of teaching styles effectively. It is therefore critically important to follow up this chapter by having students observe master teachers at work and, most important, experience actual teaching situations.

Chapter 15, "Safety Considerations and Legal Liability," concludes Part III and centers on legal liability, actions that frequently result in lawsuits, and precautions to take to minimize legal liability. Students must recognize the risks involved in children's education and take positive steps to minimize their exposure to harmful conditions, while at the same time maximizing children's learning.

Part IV, *The Skill Themes,* contains ten chapters that form the core of the developmental movement skill theme approach. Chapters 16, 17, and 18, "Fundamental Stability Skill Themes," "Fundamental Locomotor Skill Themes," and "Fundamental Manipulative Skill Themes," focus on the acquisition of mature patterns of fundamental movement. Each chapter outlines the recommended steps for developing a movement skill theme and describes a wide variety of fundamental movement skills. Each fundamental movement skill is also accompanied by a *Visual Description, Verbal Description, Common Developmental Difficulties* that children encounter in progressing to the mature stage, and *Recommended Teaching Tips* for helping children overcome these developmental difficulties. These are followed by discussion of the *Concepts Children Should Know,* including a variety of Skill Concepts (how the body should move), and *Movement Concepts* (how the body can move). A variety of *Skill Development Activities* are provided in the form of exploratory and guided-discovery experiences. This section will prove especially helpful to those new to the indirect movement exploration and guided-discovery teaching styles. *Skill Application Activities* conclude the chapter with a sampling of traditional game activities. These activities have been selected because they can be easily modified, promote inclusion rather than exclusion, and are fun.

Chapters 19 and 20, "Stunts and Tumbling Skill Themes" and "Large and Small Equipment Skill Themes," provide the reader with a wealth of valuable information. Chapter 19 centers on body rolling, springing, and upright support and inverted support skills. Safety considerations and spotting are also included in this chapter. A special feature of this chapter and the skill theme chapters that follow is the inclusion of *Teaching Progression Charts.* These unique charts are the result of careful task analysis, and they list activities in increasing order of complexity. Activities are grouped into Beginning, Intermediate, and Advanced levels. Effective teachers will use these charts to guide them in selecting activities that are developmentally appropriate for their students. Chapter 20 describes many large and small apparatus activities ranging from the balance beam and the parachute to the use of balloons, stretch ropes, and wands. Again, activities are presented in a task-analyzed sequence from simple to complex, and from beginning through advanced level activities.

Chapters 21 through 25, "Disc Sport Skill Themes," "Basketball Skill Themes," "Soccer Skill Themes," "Softball Skill Themes," and "Volleyball Skill Themes," provide a sampling of sport skill themes generally appropriate for upper elementary children. Each chapter shows a recommended sequence for developing a sport skill theme and describes a wide variety of developmentally appropriate sport skills. Each skill is accompanied by a *Verbal Description* and *Visual Description* of correct technique, followed by *Teaching Tips* and *Concepts Children Should Know.* These are followed by a section on *Fitness and Skill Development Activities,* including sport specific warm-up activities and skill drills. Lead-up games and basic rules of the game are also found in each chapter. Once again, the activities included in each chapter are presented from simple to complex and highlighted in *Developmental Activities Charts,* along with specific guidance for when to introduce and refine specific sport skills. Each chapter concludes with a section on *Assessing Progress.* Samples of practical process and product assessment techniques applied to each sport are presented.

Part V, *The Program Strands,* is the final section. Although this text emphasizes the acquisition of fundamental movement skills and sport skills, it is recognized that effective teaching involves considerably more than movement skill learning. Throughout each lesson a variety of specifically stated learning objectives that focus on fitness acquisition, cognitive learning, and affective growth are included as strands throughout the curriculum. Chapter 26, "The Vigorous Activity Strand for Fit Movers," describes aerobic activities, muscular strength and endurance activities, and joint flexibility activities appropriate for children. Chapter 27, "The Perceptual-Motor Strand for Multisensory Learners," deals with perceptual-motor, visual, auditory, and tactile/kinesthetic perception activities. Chapter 28, "The Creative Dance Strand for Expressive Movers," focuses on fundamental rhythm, singing rhythm, and creative dance activities for children. Creative rhythmic expression, imitative dance, and interpretative dance are also included. Chapter 29, "The Folk Dance Strand for Cooperative Social Learners," includes information ranging from preparing to teach a dance to basic steps, dance terms, and formations. A variety of ethnic, square, and line dances appropriate for children are also included. Finally, the Appendixes provide assessment forms that can be used to track students' progress, and a list of relevant position papers and guidelines from national associations.

SUPPLEMENTARY RESOURCES

Please note that a variety of supplementary resources are available to help students and their instructors more effectively use this text. They include:

Carlisle, C., and S. Cole. (1996). *Skillful Movers.* Dubuque, IA: Brown & Benchmark. (A unique lesson plan manual that compliments *Developmental Physical Education for Today's Children* and is much more than a generic age-appropriate cookbook of lessons. *Skillful Movers* assists teachers in designing developmentally appropriate lessons for the *real* children that they teach.)

Gallahue, D. L., and J. O. Ozmun. (1995). *Understanding Motor Development: Infants, Children, and Adults.* Dubuque, IA: Brown & Benchmark. (An excellent resource for in-depth learning about motor development. This text serves as the scientific basis for the information contained and developmental approach advocated in *Developmental Physical Education for Today's Children.*)

Ignico, A. (1994). *Assessment of Fundamental Motor Skills.* Videotapes. Dubuque, IA: Brown & Benchmark. (These instructional videos permit learners to observe fundamental movement skills at each developmental stage found in *Developmental Physical Education for Today's Children*. They are an excellent instructional aid of significant value to serious students of fundamental movement.)

Ignico, A. (1995). *Assessment of Sport Skills.* Videotapes. Dubuque, IA: Brown & Benchmark. (These instructional videos permit learners to observe sport skills for basketball, softball, and volleyball found in *Developmental Physical Education for Today's Children*. This set of eight tapes is an excellent instructional aid.)

ACKNOWLEDGMENTS

In the development of any project of this magnitude, many individuals deserve particular thanks. For preparation of the manuscript I am especially grateful to **S**uper **S**ecretary **S**andy **S**mith, affectionately known as S[4.] Sandy has been a competent, positive "can do" force in completing this edition. I am also grateful to the photographers of this edition of the text: Renee McFarland and Tami Benham-Deal. Special thanks to Julie Nizamoff for the line drawings contained in the skill theme chapters.

A long list of colleagues and former students deserve credit for helping me think through topics, for helping me crystallize my philosophy of developmental physical education, and for serving as models of excellence in teaching. There are too many to mention here, but please be assured that I am forever grateful to each and everyone of you. My gratitude and fond appreciation are also expressed to Scott Spoolman and Megan Rundel of Brown & Benchmark—Scott for his confidence in my abilities, and Megan for her patience and helpful assistance in getting this edition in print.

A very special thank you is extended, once again, to my very special mate, Ellie. Thanks, Ellie, for accepting my need to write and for putting up with the many, many hours that it has taken from our life together. Also, thank you to my children, David Lee and Jennifer, now grown and adults on their own, who served as willing subjects and inspired their father to learn more about the twin topics of motor development and developmental physical education. Finally, I thank God who makes all things possible; who sustains me; who helps me see through new eyes.

David L. Gallahue
Bloomington, IN

Developmental Physical Education for Today's Children

PART I

The Learner

1 Developmental Physical Education: An Overview

2 Childhood Growth and Motor Development

3 Movement Skill Acquisition

4 Fitness Enhancement

5 Cognitive Learning

6 Affective Growth

7 Children with Disabilities

Developmental Physical Education: An Overview

—•—

Key Concept

In gaining motor control and movement competence, the individuality of the learner (**I**), goal of the task (**T**), and conditions of the environment (**E**) must be accommodated in order to maximize learning (**ITE**)

—•—

Chapter Objectives

The purpose of this chapter is to provide you with the tools to:

• Discuss what is meant by the terms *learning to move* and *learning through movement* as they relate to the aims and goals of developmentally appropriate physical activity.
• Define the term *developmental physical education* and illustrate how it incorporates the concepts of both *individual appropriateness* and *age appropriateness.*
• Distinguish between the skill themes and the program strands of the developmental physical education curriculum.
• Provide a generic definition for the term *physical fitness* and list the components of both health-related and performance-related fitness.
• Discuss the concept of the "natural" athlete in terms of movement skill acquisition.
• Discuss the role of developmental physical activity in children's cognitive learning.
• Explain how physical activity plays an important role in children's affective growth.

—•—

Terms to Remember

Aim	Movement Skill
Learning-to-Move Aim	Physical Fitness
Learning-Through-Movement Aim	Health-Related Fitness
Physically Educated	Performance-Related Fitness
Goal	Cognitive Learning
Objective	Concept Learning
Developmental Physical Education	Perceptual-Motor Learning
Individual Appropriateness	Affective Growth
Age-Group Appropriateness	Self-Concept
Motor Development	Positive Socialization

Finally, after years of concentrated effort by professional organizations, health professionals, concerned educators, and parents, many North Americans have recognized the vital importance of vigorous physical activity and the necessity for providing children with quality physical education experiences. In fact, the American Academy of Pediatrics, the American Medical Association, the National Education Association, the National Association of Elementary School Principals, the American Alliance for Health, Physical Education, Recreation and Dance (AAHPERD), and several other national professional organizations have all endorsed Resolution 97 of the U.S. Congress (1987) stating: "That the Congress encourages State and local governments and local educational agencies to provide high quality daily physical education programs for all children in kindergarten through grade 12." Furthermore, the U.S. Department of Health and Human Services (1990) has included daily physical education and increased physical activity as two of its top physical activity and fitness priorities for the nation to achieve by the year 2000. These goals strive to:

1. Increase to at least 50 percent the proportion of children and adolescents in 1st through 12th grade who participate in daily school physical education.
2. Increase to at least 50 percent the proportion of school physical education class time that students spend being physically active, preferably engaged in lifetime physical activities.

CONCEPT 1.1

Many national organizations are actively promoting the goals of *quality* physical education programs offered *daily.*

Despite an act of Congress, the Healthy People 2000 Objectives, and the admonishments of the American Heart Association, no federal law exists mandating physical education in our nation's public schools. Each state is left to decide for itself concerning whether and how much time should be devoted to physical education. Based on the *Shape of the Nation Survey* (NASPE, 1993), Illinois is still the only state that requires daily physical education for all students K–12. The state of Washington requires daily physical education for all students K–8, and Alabama requires it for all students K–6. Moreover, only thirteen states currently require physical education specialists to teach physical education at the elementary school level. There is still much work to be done in realizing the elusive goal of quality, daily physical education for all.

The AAHPERD, through the National Association for Sport and Physical Education (NASPE), and the President's Council on Physical Fitness and Sports are the primary groups spearheading the quest for *daily* physical education and, with others, working to ensure *quality* programs for all. It is important that you recognize the significance of the terms *daily* and *quality.* Quality physical education uses the gymnasium or playing field as a learning laboratory, has measurable objectives, and seeks to attain these objectives in a systematic manner. Quality physical education is within the reach of all teachers who are truly dedicated to children's learning. It is not a "throw out the ball" program or some form of glorified recess period. On the other hand, daily physical education is still an unfulfilled goal in the majority of North American schools. If children are to realize the full potential of physical education, then we must continue to strive for daily and quality physical education. Convincing evidence indicates that American children are frequently unable to take advantage of the many benefits of vigorous

---

The American Heart Association (1992) has labeled physical inactivity as a fourth risk factor for coronary heart disease, along with smoking, high blood pressure, and high cholesterol levels. Additionally, in the Statement on Exercise from the American Heart Association published in *Circulation* (1992), the committee stated that:

Children should be introduced to the principles of regular physical exercise and recreational activities at an early age. Schools at all levels should

develop and encourage positive attitudes toward physical exercise, providing opportunities to learn skills and to perform physical activities, especially those that can be enjoyed for many years. The school curriculum should not overemphasize sports and activities that selectively eliminate children who are less skilled. Schools should teach the benefits of exercise and the development and maintenance of exercise conditioning throughout life.

physical activity because of poor or nonexistent physical education programs, sedentary lifestyles, and the erroneous assumption that children, by the very nature of being children, get plenty of vigorous physical activity. As a result, low levels of fitness and movement skill development among our nation's youth are all too common. Movement should be at the very center of children's lives, permeating all facets of their development, whether in the motor, cognitive, or affective domains of their behavior. To deny children the opportunity to reap the many benefits of regular vigorous physical activity is to deny them the opportunity to experience the joy of efficient movement, the health benefits of vigorous physical activity, and a lifetime as confident and competent movers.

This chapter will provide you with an overview of the many benefits of a quality physical education that is sensitive to the needs and interests of children and is based on the developmental level of the individual. But first, we must clearly outline the aims and goals of physical education and define the term *developmental physical education.*

THE AIMS AND GOALS OF PHYSICAL EDUCATION

An **aim** is the overarching purpose or intent of what we do. The aims of physical education have been stated by many authors and leaders in the profession. Lofty ideals and flowery platitudes have often clouded the fact that the basic aim of physical education may be simply and succinctly stated as follows: to set aside a portion of every school day for large-muscle activities that encourage and develop *learning to move* and *learning through movement*.

The **learning-to-move aim** of physical education is based on acquiring movement skills and enhancing physical fitness. The **learning-through-movement aim** of physical education is based on the fact that effective physical education can positively affect both the cognitive and affective (social-emotional) development of children. Becoming **physically educated** by learning to move and learning through movement has been defined by NASPE (1992). "A physically educated person HAS learned skills necessary to perform a variety of physical activities, IS physically fit, DOES participate regularly in physical activity, KNOWS the implications of and the benefits from involvement in physical activities, VALUES physical activity and its contributions to a healthful lifestyle."

Students learning to move and moving to learn.

CONCEPT 1.2
Learning to move and learning through movement are the broad-based aims of all quality physical education programs.

A **goal** is generally viewed as something toward which we continually expend effort and which we strive to achieve. In education, goals are long-term purposes measured through the attainment of a series of objectives. An **objective** is the means used to achieve a goal. Objectives are the observable, measurable, and quantifiable statements that guide the teacher to select appropriate educational strategies that help students attain their goals. Quality physical education programs establish clearly defined objectives, and the content of the program reflects constant effort toward their attainment.

Movement skill acquisition: the heart of the developmental physical education program.

AIMS: Overarching intent

Learning to move Learning through movement

GOALS: Long-term purposes

Movement skill acquisition Fitness enhancement Cognitive learning Affective growth

FIGURE 1.1 *The aims and goals of developmental physical education.*

The acquisition of movement skills is a primary goal of developmental physical education. This goal focuses on helping children become skillful movers, knowledgeable movers, and expressive movers in a wide variety of fundamental and specialized movement skills. The goal of fitness enhancement focuses on helping children become fit movers, informed movers, and eager movers by promoting an active way of life. The cognitive learning goals of developmental physical education center on helping children become more effective multisensory learners and active learners. As such, movement is a viable medium for both perceptual-motor and cognitive concept learning. Similarly, affective development can be fostered by helping children achieve the affective behavior goals of becoming self-discovering learners and cooperative learners. By promoting these goals, teachers can use movement as an effective tool to enhance self-esteem, encourage positive socialization, and character education. Figure 1.1 diagrams the aims and goals of developmental physical education.

CONCEPT 1.3

Physical education should be viewed from a developmental perspective and taught in instructionally appropriate ways.

DEVELOPMENTAL PHYSICAL EDUCATION DEFINED

Children's development is frequently studied from a compartmentalized standpoint focusing on one domain (cognitive, affective, *or* psychomotor) of human behavior to the exclusion of the others. This has led to an unbalanced view of the developmental process and resulting educational practice. It is crucial that those interested in **developmental physical education** *not* compound the errors of compartmentalization and instead view the child as a total integrated being (cognitive, affective, *and* psychomotor). This is a root cause of the physical education profession's historical difficulty in establishing itself as a legitimate aspect of the school curriculum. Only when educators in general, and school boards in particular, recognize and respect the fact that children are multifaceted individuals, with a wide range of backgrounds, and that becoming physically educated involves complex interaction of the cognitive, affective, and psychomotor domains will physical education take its place in North American schools as a legitimate and respected force in the total school curriculum.

In addition to recognizing the vital interactive importance of each domain of human behavior, developmental physical education recognizes that there is a complex relationship among the individual's biological makeup, his or her own unique environmental circumstances, and the specific objective of the learning task being engaged in by the child. See Figure 1.2 for a visual representation of this important concept. Such a transactional model implies that factors within the task, the individual, and the environment are equally important in the learning process and are not only influenced by one another (interaction) but have the capabilities of being modified (transaction) by each other.

Therefore, developmental physical education is physical education that emphasizes the acquisition of motor control and movement competency based on the unique developmental level of the individual. It recognizes and incorporates the many contributions that systematic, sensitive teaching can make to both the cognitive and affective development of the individual. Developmental physical education encourages the uniqueness of the individual and is based on the fundamental proposition that although motor development is age-related, it is *not* age-dependent. As a result, teacher decisions concerning what to teach, when to teach it, and how to teach are based primarily on the appropriateness of the activity for the individual and only secondarily on the appropriateness of the activity for a certain age group.

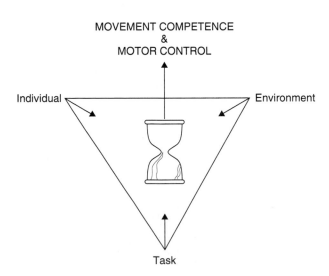

FIGURE 1.2 *Developmental Physical Education recognizes the relationship among the specific requirements of the task, the biology of the individual, and the conditions of the learning environment in promoting motor control and movement competence.*

TEACHING TIPS

For developmental physical education to be valid it must:

- Focus on the relationship among the specific requirements of the task, the biology of the individual and the conditions of the learning environment.
- Recognize that age-group appropriateness provides only general guidelines for activity selection.
- Focus on movement skill acquisition and fitness enhancement.
- Insist on the individual appropriateness of developmental movement experiences.
- Utilize learning mediums that are fun.
- Emphasize moving and learning rather than sitting, waiting, and watching.
- Promote individual standards of success and achievement that minimize failure.

Individual appropriateness, the key concept of developmental physical education, is based on the central proposition that each child has his or her unique timing and pattern of growth and development (see Chapter 2). Therefore, the movement activities engaged in by children in developmentally based physical education programs are geared to their stage of motor development and level of movement skill learning (see Chapter 3). Additionally, the inclusion of specific movement experiences is considerably influenced by personal levels of physical fitness (see Chapter 4), cognitive development (see Chapter 5), and affective development (see Chapter 6).

CONCEPT 1.4
Developmental physical education utilizes instructional strategies and learning experiences that are individually appropriate as well as age-group appropriate.

Age-group appropriateness is of secondary importance in the developmental physical education program. The developmental curriculum is *not* based on chronological age or grade level but is influenced by both. The process of development proceeds from simple to complex and from general to specific as individuals strive to increase their competence in the motor, cognitive, and affective domains of human behavior. As a result, patterns of behavior emerge that may help to guide the selection of movement experiences that are typically appropriate for specific age groups. All children diverge from typically expected age-group patterns of behavior at one time or another. Some have special needs that require significant modifications to the program (see Chapter 7), whereas others can be successfully accommodated through careful attention to the concept of individual appropriateness. Children are not miniature adults. Their needs, interests, and capabilities are considerably different from those of adolescents and adults. Likewise, the developmental capabilities, expectations, and appropriateness of movement activities included in any physical education program vary considerably among preschool, primary grade, intermediate, and upper elementary grade children. The developmental physical education program is not a recess or play period. It is, however, a learning laboratory in which children learn to move and learn through movement by having activities based on sound principles of child development and grounded in the needs, interests, and unique abilities of the individuals being served.

THE COMPONENTS OF DEVELOPMENTAL PHYSICAL EDUCATION

Developmental physical education has motor, cognitive, and affective components. Each is briefly discussed in the following paragraphs.

Motor Development

The motor domain is the basis for the movement skill themes of the developmental program. Fitness enhancement and cognitive and affective development form the important program strands that are woven throughout each skill theme (see Figure 1.3). The unique contribution of developmental physical education is in the realm of motor development. **Motor development** is the progressive change in one's movement behavior brought about by interaction of the individual with the environment and the task. In other words, one's unique hereditary makeup, combined with specific environmental conditions (e.g., opportunities for practice, encouragement, and instruction) and the requirements of the movement task itself,

determines the rate and extent of one's movement skill acquisition and fitness enhancement.

CONCEPT 1.5
Developmental Physical Education focuses on the fact that children's motor development involves progressive change in their motor behavior brought about by interaction among the requirements of the learning task, the biology of the individual, and the conditions of the environment.

Movement Skill Acquisition.   Movement skill acquisition is at the very core of the developmental physical education program. The term **movement skill** refers to the development of motor control, precision, and accuracy in the performance of both fundamental and specialized movements. Movement skills are developed and refined to a point that children are capable of operating with considerable ease and efficiency within their environment. As children mature, the fundamental (or basic) movement skills developed when they were younger are applied as specialized (or complex) skills to a wide variety of games, sport, dance, and recreational activities. For example, the fundamental movement skill of striking an object in an underhand, sidearm, or overarm pattern is progressively refined and later applied in sport and recreational pursuits such as golf, tennis, and baseball.

Movement skills may also be categorized into broad and sometimes overlapping categories (see Figure 1.4). The movement categories of locomotion, manipulation, and stability represent the primary focus for movement skill theme development. Chapter 3, "Movement Skill Acquisition," examines these categories more closely in terms of movement skill development and movement skill learning.

Fitness Enhancement.   The critical fitness objectives of developmental physical education focus on enhancing the ability and motivation of children to function in an environment that both requires and promotes the development of fitness. Physical fitness may be viewed as possessing the elements of both health-related fitness and performance-related fitness. Agreement on a suitable definition of physical fitness is often difficult, and the term is generally broadly described because the level of fitness required of one individual may not be the same as that required of another. Hence, a generic definition of **physical**

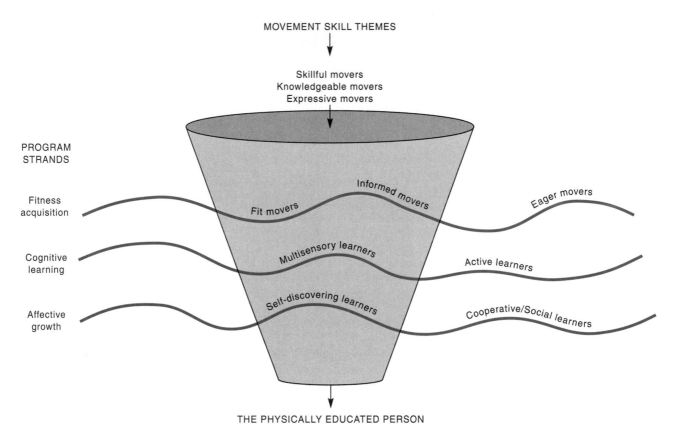

MOVEMENT SKILL THEMES

Skillful movers
Knowledgeable movers
Expressive movers

PROGRAM
STRANDS

Fitness
acquisition   Fit movers   Informed movers   Eager movers

Cognitive
learning   Multisensory learners   Active learners

Affective
growth   Self-discovering learners   Cooperative/Social learners

THE PHYSICALLY EDUCATED PERSON

FIGURE 1.3 *Movement skill themes are at the core of the developmental physical education program and their accompanying fitness, cognitive, and affective strands.*

fitness is considered to be the ability to perform daily tasks without undue fatigue and to possess ample reserves of energy for recreational pursuits and emergency needs. Muscular strength, muscular endurance, cardiovascular endurance, and joint flexibility are universally considered to be **health-related fitness** components. Body composition is also considered by most to be a health-related component.

C O N C E P T   1 . 6
The core of the developmental physical education program centers on movement skill acquisition and fitness enhancement through means appropriate to the individuals being taught.

The concept of **performance-related fitness** (also known as skill-related, or motor, fitness) is an elusive term that has been studied extensively over the past several years and is classified by some experts as an aspect of physical fitness. Balance, coordination, agility, speed of movement, and power are among the most frequently cited components of performance-related fitness. The generality and specificity of these components have been debated and researched for years, with the bulk of the evidence in favor of their specificity. For years proponents of the general nature of motor fitness (i.e., those who believe in the concept of the "natural" athlete) believed that individuals who excelled in certain sports had corresponding abilities that automatically carried over to other activities. Although this often does occur, it is now considered to be a result of the individual's personal motivation,

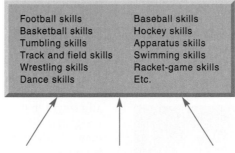

SELECTED SPECIALIZED
SPORT-RELATED
MOVEMENT SKILLS

Football skills	Baseball skills
Basketball skills	Hockey skills
Tumbling skills	Apparatus skills
Track and field skills	Swimming skills
Wrestling skills	Racket-game skills
Dance skills	Etc.

SELECTED FUNDAMENTAL
MOVEMENT SKILLS

LOCOMOTION	MANIPULATION	STABILITY
1. Basic (one element): a. Walking b. Running c. Leaping d. Jumping e. Hopping 2. Combinations (two or more elements): a. Climbing b. Galloping c. Sliding d. Skipping	1. Propulsive: a. Ball rolling b. Throwing c. Kicking d. Punting e. Striking f. Volleying g. Bouncing 2. Absorptive: a. Catching b. Trapping	1. Axial: a. Bending b. Stretching c. Twisting d. Turning e. Swinging 2. Static and Dynamic Postures: a. Upright balances b. Inverted balances c. Rolling d. Starting e. Stopping f. Dodging

FIGURE 1.4 *Fundamental movement skills must be developed and refined prior to the introduction of specialized sport skills.*

participation in many fitness activities, and several specific sport aptitudes rather than any direct carryover of motor abilities from one activity to another. Simply stated, the components of performance-related fitness are "traits," not abilities, and the notion of the "natural" athlete is not supported by the bulk of the research on the topic. Children's health-related and performance-related fitness play an important role in the development of total

fitness. Figure 1.5 provides an overview of the components of physical fitness. Each will be discussed in further detail in Chapter 4, "Fitness Enhancement."

Cognitive Learning

Although the unique contribution of developmental physical education is in acquisition of movement skills and fitness enhancement, many important contributions are also made to cognitive aspects of children's development. **Cognitive learning** is progressive change in the ability to think, reason, and act. Because children are both multisensory learners and active learners, an important strand of the developmental physical education program focuses on concept learning and perceptual-motor learning. Chapter 5, "Cognitive Learning," focuses in greater detail on this topic.

Fitness enhancement can be both fun and challenging.

Concept Learning.   Movement can be used to enhance the understanding and application of cognitive and academic learning. With regard to movement, **concept learning** is a permanent change in one's motor behavior brought about by experiences designed to foster understanding of the movement concepts, skill concepts, fitness concepts, and activity concepts of the developmental physical education program. Cognitive learning can, and does, occur in the gymnasium and on the playing field. Moreover, many important academic concepts traditionally taught in the classroom can be effectively learned in the gymnasium. In fact, several authors have described how specific types of activities may reinforce concept learning of language arts competencies, basic mathematical operations, and social studies and science concepts (Buschner, 1994; Pellegrini and Boyd, 1993).

There are many reasons that cognitive concept learning can be effectively taught through movement. Among them is the fact that active participation is fun. Movement often meets the needs and interests of children more than less active classroom activities. Active participation in a game in which academic concepts are being taught makes it difficult for the child's attention to be diverted by extraneous stimuli. Also, many of today's children undervalue academic achievement but highly regard physical performance. Using active games as a learning medium pairs pleasurable and highly regarded play with less valued

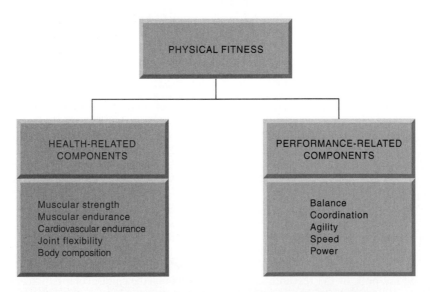

FIGURE 1.5 *The health-related and performance-related components of physical fitness.*

academic activity and thus increases children's interest in practicing the academic skill. Active learning through movement activities also enables children to deal with their world in concrete terms rather than in the abstract. Children generally regard movement as fun, not to be equated with the routine "work" of the classroom. It should be noted, however, that not all children benefit academically through active participation in movement activities. On the contrary, there is overwhelming evidence that the sedentary academic activities in traditional classrooms are quite effective for many individuals. The point is that some children benefit greatly from a program that integrates movement activities with academic concept development and that most children will probably realize at least some improvement. Figure 1.6 illustrates the components of cognitive concept learning found in the developmental physical education program. Each is discussed further in Chapter 5.

Perceptual Motor Learning.   Learning is a process involving both maturation and experience. Not all children entering school are at the same ability level. Although little can be done to speed up the maturational component of this process, parents and teachers can influence the experiential component. **Perceptual-motor learning** involves the establishment and refinement of sensory sensitivity to one's world through movement. This sensory sensitivity involves developing and refining an adequate spatial and temporal world. All movement occurs in space and involves an element of time. Developing these structures is basic to efficient functioning in a variety of other areas. It is possible to enhance children's knowledge of their spatial world by involving them in movement activities that contribute to their body awareness, directional awareness, and spatial awareness. Children's awareness of their temporal world may be increased through activities that focus on the synchrony, rhythm, and sequencing of movements. Selected visual, auditory, and tactile abilities may also be reinforced through movement in carefully selected activities.

Many motor-training programs have been developed, claiming to enhance the cognitive functioning of children. To date, there is little scientific research to support the hypothesis that certain movement activities directly impact the cognitive functioning of children. This does not mean that movement experiences engaged in by children during physical education programs cannot be effectively used as a medium for learning through movement. On the contrary, educators now recognize the importance of movement skill learning to enhance children's learning. In other words, through good teaching, movement can be effectively used to increase children's awareness of themselves and the world around them. The proper use of the "teachable moment" and an emphasis on developing the concepts of *why, what, how,* and *when* in relation to one's movement are important in helping children learn by reinforcing information in the traditional setting of the classroom. Figure 1.7 outlines the perceptual-motor components dealt with in the developmental physical education program. Each is discussed in greater detail in Chapter 5.

CONCEPT 1.7
Important cognitive and affective competencies can be effectively reinforced through the developmental physical education program.

CONCEPT
LEARNING

Skill concepts
Movement concepts
Activity concepts
Fitness concepts
Academic concepts

FIGURE 1.6 *The components of concept learning dealt with in the developmental physical education program.*

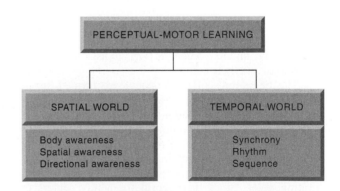

FIGURE 1.7 *The perceptual-motor components dealt with in the developmental physical education program.*

Affective Growth

An important outcome of any quality physical education program is enhancement in the affective domain. **Affective growth** is learning that increases the ability of children to act, interact, and react effectively with other people as well as with themselves. It is often referred to as "social-emotional development" and is vitally important to children. A good or poor parent, an affluent or culturally deprived environment, and the quality and quantity of stimulation largely determine whether children view their world as one that they can control or as one that controls them.

The movement experiences engaged in by children play an important role in how they view themselves as individuals and how they relate to their peers and use their free time. Astute parents and teachers recognize the vital importance of balanced social-emotional development. They understand the affective development of children and use this knowledge to enhance children's self-esteem and positive socialization and to encourage and structure meaningful movement experiences that strengthen children's emotional and social development. Chapter 6, "Affective Growth," explores children's self-esteem and childhood socialization and examines how this information may be incorporated into the developmental physical education program.

Self-Concept Enhancement. Being good at games, sports, and vigorous physical activities contributes greatly to the development of a positive, stable self-concept in children. Although it is by no means the only way in which self-concept is established, movement plays an important role for most children. **Self-concept** may be defined as one's personal perception of his or her competence in physical, cognitive, and social settings. It is a value-free description of self that impacts on all that we do. Children are active, energetic, emerging beings who use play and movement as ways to learn more about themselves and their bodies.

The beginnings of self-concept are formed during childhood. Children often view themselves on one end of two extremes—good or bad—in all that they do. Because their egocentric natures do not permit them to view their particular strengths and weaknesses objectively, some children frequently cannot fully grasp the concept that their abilities to act lie somewhere between these self-limiting poles. Since their world frequently centers on play and vigorous activity, the successes they experience in these areas are important in establishing their positive self-concept. Figure 1.8 provides an overview of the components of a positive self-concept. Each component is discussed in detail in Chapter 6.

Positive Socialization. **Positive socialization** in a physical education, recreation, or sports setting generally occurs in the form of fair play, cooperative behavior, or good sportsmanship, all indicators of positive moral behavior. Participation in physical activities usually occurs in a social setting, a setting that requires children to make decisions about both cooperative and competitive behaviors. Physical activity, then, has tremendous potential to promote positive moral behavior and to teach the virtues of honesty, teamwork, loyalty, self-control, and fair play. Responsible teachers can take advantage of the

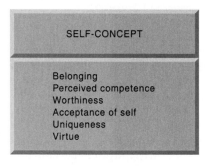

FIGURE 1.8 *Components of a positive self-concept.*

Boys and girls interacting cooperatively—part of the process of positive socialization.

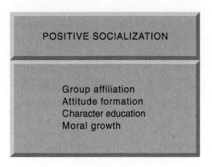

FIGURE 1.9 *The components of positive socialization.*

moral dilemmas—real or manufactured—that arise during play and games to foster moral growth among their students. In short, the child who is positively socialized into his or her culture is one who acts morally, is concerned about the welfare of others, and is willing to work cooperatively toward achieving common goals. Sports and movement activities offer teachers many opportunities to model and encourage positive socialization in children.

Figure 1.9 illustrates the components of positive socialization. Each is discussed in further detail in Chapter 6.

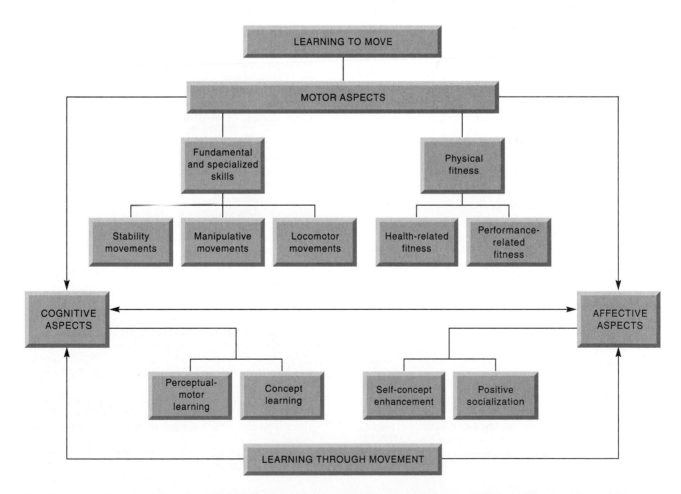

FIGURE 1.10 *The aspects of the child's development dealt with in the developmental physical education program.*

SUMMARY

This chapter examined the general aims and goals of physical education. Developmental physical education was defined in terms of individual appropriateness and age-group appropriateness. The potential outcomes of quality physical education experiences were also discussed. Remember, the movement activities engaged in by children play an important role in their total development. Children are involved in the important and exciting task of learning to move effectively and efficiently through their world. They are developing a variety of fundamental and specialized movement skills and enhancing their individual levels of physical fitness. In short, they are learning to move with joy, efficiency, and control.

Children are also learning through movement. Movement is the vehicle by which they explore all that is around them. It enhances their perceptual-motor and concept learning and promotes the development of a positive self-concept and positive socialization. The interrelated nature of the motor, cognitive, and affective aspects of developmental physical education is readily apparent and is summarized in Figure 1.10.

COMPLEMENTARY READINGS

Bredenkamp, S. (1992). What is "developmentally appropriate" and why is it important? *JOPERD* 63:31–32.

Buschner, C. A. (1994). *Teaching Children Movement Skills and Concepts.* Champaign, IL: Human Kinetics.

Grineski, S. (1992). What is a truly developmentally appropriate physical education program for children? *JOPERD* 63:33–35.

National Association for Sport and Physical Education. (1994). *Developmentally Appropriate Practice in Movement Programs for Young Children.* (A *COPEC* Position paper.) Reston, VA: AAHPERD.

National Association for Sport and Physical Education. (1992). *Developmentally Appropriate Physical Education Practices for Children: A position statement of Council on Physical Education for Children (COPEC).* Reston, VA: AAHPERD

National Association for Sport and Physical Education. (1992). *The Physically Educated Person.* Reston, VA: AAHPERD.

National Association for Sport and Physical Education. (1990). *Fit to Achieve: Educational Information.* Reston, VA: AAHPERD.

Seefeldt, V., ed. (1987). Justifying physical education. *JOPERD* 58:42–72.

U.S. Department of Health and Human Services. (1990). *Healthy People 2000: National Health Promotion and Disease Prevention Objectives.* (stock number 017-001-00474-0).

U.S. Congress. (1987). *H. Con. Res.97: To Encourage State and Local Governments and Local Educational Agencies to Provide High Quality, Daily Physical Education Programs for All Children in Kindergarten Through Grade 12.* (100th Congress, 1st session). Washington, DC: U.S. Government Printing Office.

Weiller, K. H. (1992). The social-emotional component of physical education for children. *JOPERD* 63:50–53.

SUPPLEMENTARY READINGS

American Heart Association. (1992). *A.H.A Labels Physical Inactivity as a Fourth Risk Factor for Coronary Heart Disease.* A news release of the American Heart Association National Center, 7320 Greenville Avenue, Dallas, TX.

American Heart Association. (1992). Policy statement for health professionals by the Committee on Exercise and Cardiac Rehabilitation. *Circulation* 86, 1.

Gallahue, D. L. (1990). Moving and learning: Linkages that last. In W. Stinson, ed., *Moving and Learning and the Young Child.* Reston, VA: AAHPERD.

Giles-Brown, E. (1993). Teach administrators why physical education is important. *Strategies* 6:23–25.

National Association for Sport and Physical Education. (1994). *Sport and Physical Education Advocacy Kit.* Reston, VA: AAHPERD.

Pellegrini, A. D., and B. Boyd. (1993). The role of play in early childhood development and education: Issues in definition and function. In B. Spodek, ed., *Handbook of Research on the Education of Young Children.* New York: Macmillan (pp.105–121).

VIDEOS

Curriculum in Head Start. Washington, DC: Head Start Bureau, Department of Health and Human Services. (15 min.).

Individualizing in Head Start. Washington, DC: Head Start Bureau, Department of Health and Human Services. (17 min.).

Let's Move Let's Play! Developmentally Appropriate Movement and Classroom Activities for Preschool Children. (1993). Reston, VA: NASPE, and KinderCare. (15-min. staff training video).

Making the Case for Quality Daily Physical Education. Reston, VA: AAHPERD/NASPE. (12 min.).

CHAPTER 2

Childhood Growth and Motor Development

●

Key Concept

The Processes of Growth and Motor Development Proceed in a Predictable Sequence but at Varying Rates Among Children

●

Chapter Objectives

The purpose of this chapter is to provide you with the tools to:
- Describe the normal, orderly process of growth during both the early childhood and later childhood periods.
- Discuss the roles of nutrition, exercise, chronic illness, and lifestyle factors on the process of childhood growth.
- Discuss the dynamics of development in terms of the self-organizing nature of the task, the individual, and the environment.
- Distinguish between the cephalocaudal and proximodistal principles of development and demonstrate how they influence movement skill acquisition.
- Discuss what is meant by the self-regulatory process of growth.
- Explain what is meant by the terms *differentiation* and *integration* with regard to the process of development. Give examples of each.
- Speculate on the role of individual variability, readiness, and sensitive learning periods in the process of motor development.
- List and describe typical motor, cognitive, and affective characteristics of children during the early and later childhood periods.
- Propose specific implication for developmental teaching based on the typical characteristics of children.

●

Terms to Remember

Physical Growth	Secular Trends	Developmental Sequence
Myelin	Motor Development	Cephalocaudal
Otitis Media	Dynamic Systems	Proximodistal
Growth Retardation	Nonlinear	Developmental
Hypertrophy	Discontinuous Process	Variability
Atrophy	Self-Organizing	Readiness
Self-Regulatory	Transactional Model of	Differentiation
Growth	Development	Integration
Lifestyle Factors	Development	Sensitive Period

There has been a surge of interest in the growth and motor development of children. No longer are educators content with the vague notion that children somehow "magically" increase their abilities to function as they advance in age. Physicians, psychologists, physiologists, educators, and coaches have become more aware of the need for accurate information concerning the process of growth and motor development and its influence on the developing child.

Several questions must be answered before sound developmental physical education programs can be formulated. First, what is the normal, orderly process of growth? Second, what factors affect growth in children? Third, what are the influences of both maturation and experience on the process of motor development? Fourth, what are the typical motor, cognitive, and affective characteristics of children? Fifth, what factors affect the motor development and movement skill learning of children?

GROWTH

Physical growth, a process associated with increases in structure size, is marked by steady increases in height, weight, and muscle mass during childhood. Growth is not as rapid during childhood as during infancy, and it gradually decelerates throughout childhood until the preadolescent growth spurt. It is important to understand the process of physical growth throughout childhood and the factors that affect children's growth if you are to be truly effective in promoting movement skill acquisition and fitness enhancement. Figure 2.1 illustrates the weight for stature (height) of girls from ages two through ten. Figure 2.2 shows the weight for stature of boys from ages two through eleven-and-a-half. It should be noted, however, that height-weight charts like those depicted do not take body type differences into consideration. Care, therefore, should be taken in their interpretation and use.

CONCEPT 2.1
Growth occurs in an orderly and predictable sequence throughout childhood, but with considerable individual variation.

Early Childhood (Ages Three to Eight)

The annual height gain from the early childhood period to puberty is about two inches per year, with weight gains averaging five pounds per year. At this stage of growth, some differences may be seen between boys and girls in terms of height and weight, but they are minimal. The physiques of male and female preschoolers and primary grade children are remarkably similar when viewed from a posterior position, with boys being only slightly taller and heavier. Both boys and girls have similar amounts of muscle and bone mass, and both show a gradual decrease in fatty tissue as they progress through the early childhood period.

Body proportions change markedly during early childhood because of the various growth rates of the body. The chest gradually becomes larger than the abdomen, and the stomach gradually protrudes less. By the time children reach their sixth birthday, their body proportions more closely resemble those of older children in the elementary school.

Bone growth during early childhood is dynamic, and the skeletal system is particularly vulnerable to malnutrition, fatigue, and illness. The bones ossify (harden) at a rapid rate during early childhood unless there has been severe, prolonged nutritional deprivation.

The development of **myelin,** a fatty substance around the neurons (commonly referred to as the process of myelination), permits the transmission of nerve impulses and is not complete at birth. At birth many nerves lack myelin, but with advancing age greater amounts of it encase the nerve fibers. Myelination is largely complete by the end of the early childhood period, thus allowing for efficient transference of nerve impulses throughout the nervous system. It is interesting to note that increased complexity in children's movement skills is possible following myelination. As the cortex matures and becomes progressively more organized, children are able to perform at higher levels both motorically and cognitively.

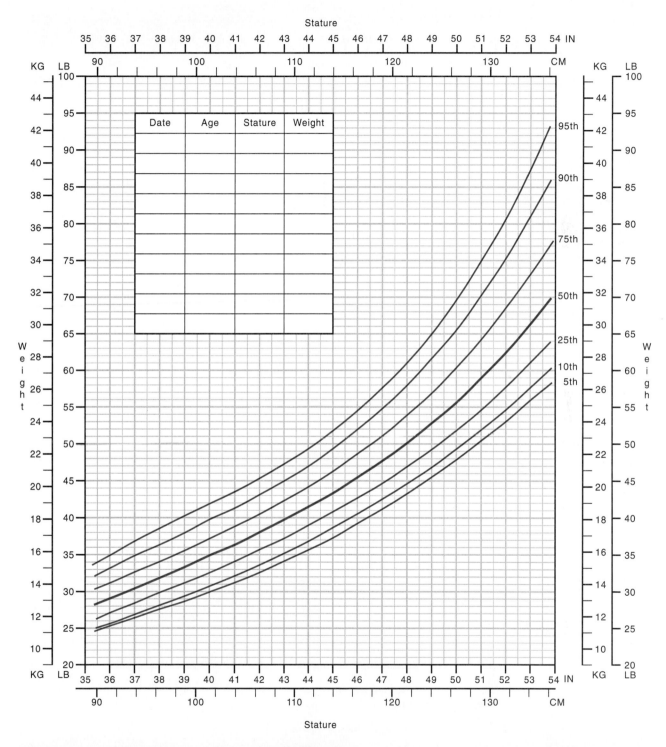

FIGURE 2.1 *Prepubertal girls: 2 to 10 years. Weight for stature.*

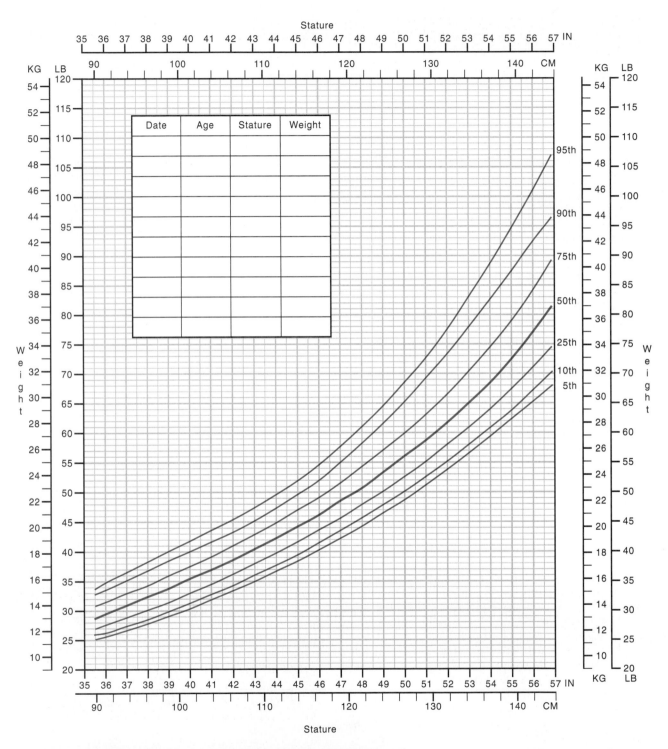

FIGURE 2.2 *Prepubertal boys: 2 to 11½ years. Weight for stature.*

Growth is rapid throughout infancy and slows during early childhood.

The sensory apparatus is still developing during the early childhood years. The eyeball does not reach its full size until about twelve years of age. The macula of the retina is not completely developed until the sixth year, and young children are generally farsighted. This is one important reason why young children have difficulty fixating on and intercepting moving objects.

Young children have more taste buds than adults, and they are generously distributed throughout the insides of the throat and cheeks as well as on the tongue, causing greater sensitivity to taste. This results in profound likes and dislikes for certain types of foods.

Because of the flat angle of the eustachian tube connecting the middle ear with the throat, young children are also more sensitive to infections of the ear. **Otitis media,** inflammation of the inner ear, is quite common among young children and may influence their balancing abilities.

Later Childhood (Ages Eight to Twelve)

The period of later childhood, from about the eighth to the twelfth year of life, is typified by slow but steady increases in height and weight and by progress toward greater organization of the sensory and motor systems. Changes in body build are slight during these years. Later childhood is more a time of lengthening and filling out prior to the prepubescent growth spurt that occurs around the eleventh year for girls and the thirteenth year for boys. Children make rapid gains in learning during later childhood and are capable of functioning at increasingly sophisticated levels in the performance of movement skills. This period of continued slow growth in height and weight gives children time to get used to their bodies. This is an important factor in the typically dramatic improvement seen in coordination and motor control in the later childhood years. The gradual change in size and the close relationship maintained between bone and tissue development are important factors in increased levels of motor functioning.

CONCEPT 2.2
Both the rate and extent of growth are influenced by a variety of environmental and genetic factors.

Growth during childhood is highly variable.

Differences between the growth patterns of boys and girls are minimal during later childhood. Both have greater limb growth than trunk growth, but boys tend to have longer legs, arms, and standing height during this period. Likewise, girls tend to have greater hip width and thigh size during this period. Because there is relatively little difference in physique or weight exhibited until the onset of the preadolescent period, girls and boys can participate effectively together in most activities.

During later childhood very slow growth occurs in brain size. The size of the skull remains nearly the same, although there is a broadening and a lengthening of the head toward the end of this period.

Perceptual abilities become increasingly refined. The sensorimotor apparatus works in ever greater harmony, so that by the end of this period, children can perform numerous sophisticated skills. The ability to strike a pitched ball, for example, improves with age and practice because of improved visual acuity, tracking abilities, reaction time, movement time, and sensorimotor integration. A key to maximum development of more mature growth patterns in children is utilization. In other words, if children have, through the normal process of maturation, improved perceptual abilities, they must be experimented with and integrated more completely with the motor structures through practice. Failure to have abundant opportunities for practice, instruction, and encouragement during this period prevents many individuals from acquiring the perceptual and motor information needed to perform skillfully.

FACTORS AFFECTING GROWTH

Growth is not an independent process. Although heredity sets the limits of growth, environmental factors help determine whether these limits are reached. The degree to which these factors affect motor development is not entirely clear and needs further study. However, it is clear that factors such as nutrition, exercise, illness, and lifestyle play a significant role in the process of physical growth.

Nutrition

Numerous investigations have provided clear evidence that dietary deficiencies can delay growth during childhood. The extent of **growth retardation** depends on the severity, duration, and time of onset of undernourishment. For example, if severe, chronic malnutrition occurs during the first four years of life, there is little hope of catching up to one's age mates in terms of mental development, because the critical period of brain growth has passed.

The physical growth process can be interrupted through malnutrition at any time between infancy and adolescence. Malnutrition may also contribute to the development of certain diseases that affect physical growth. For example, lack of vitamin D in the diet can result in rickets, vitamin B-12 deficiencies may cause pellagra, and the chronic lack of vitamin C results in scurvy. These diseases are now relatively rare in our society, but the effects of kwashiorkor, a debilitating disease resulting from protein malnutrition that retards growth, are seen in many parts of the world where there is a general lack of food and good nutrition. Children suffering from chronic malnutrition, particularly during infancy and early childhood, may never completely reach the growth norms for their age levels. Evidence of this is shown in developing nations where adult height and weight norms are considerably lower than those for industrialized nations.

Dietary excesses may also affect the growth of children. In affluent countries obesity is a major problem. The causes of childhood obesity and its influences on motor development are of considerable concern. The constant barrage of television commercials loudly extolling one junk food or another, the "fast food" addiction of millions, and the use of edibles as a pacifier, or bribery for good behavior, all may have an effect on the nutritional health of children. The individual nature of children, with their own unique biochemical compositions, makes it difficult to pinpoint where adequate nutrition ends and malnutrition begins.

Exercise

One of the principles of physical activity is that of use and disuse. Stated simply, a muscle that is used will **hypertrophy** (increase in size) and a muscle that is not used will **atrophy** (decrease in size). In children, activity definitely promotes muscle development. Although the number of muscle fibers does not increase, the size of the fibers does, and muscles respond and adapt to increased amounts of stress. Maturation alone will not account for increases in muscle mass. An environment that promotes vigorous physical activity on the part of the child will do much to promote muscle development. Further, active children tend to have less body fat in proportion to lean body mass.

Growth slows during later childhood.

Although physical activity generally has positive effects on the growth of children, it can have negative effects if carried to an extreme. The increasing popularity of youth sports and the intensity of training that often accompanies it may be contributing to this problem, but the critical point separating harmful and beneficial activity is not clear. It seems reasonable to assume, however, that strenuous activity carried out over an extended period of time may injure children's muscle and bone tissue. "Swimmer's shoulder," "tennis elbow," and "runner's knees" are but a few of the ailments plaguing children who have exceeded their developmental limits. To help avoid such problems, teachers and parents should carefully supervise children's exercise and activity programs. The potential benefits of exercise to growth are great, but the limits of the individual must be carefully considered.

CONCEPT 2.3

Development proceeds in a predictable manner but varies greatly in rate and individual readiness.

Illness

While the standard acute childhood illnesses (chicken pox, colds, measles, and mumps) do not have a marked effect on growth, the extent to which other illnesses and diseases retard growth depends on their duration, severity, and timing. Often the interaction of malnutrition and illnesses in children makes it difficult to determine accurately the specific cause of growth retardation. The combination of conditions, however, puts the child at risk and greatly enhances the probability of measurable growth deficits.

Interruption of the normal pace of growth is compensated for by a still unexplained **self-regulatory growth** process that helps children catch up to their age-mates. For example, although a severe illness may temporarily retard a child's gain in height and weight, there is a definite tendency to catch up with one's age-mates upon recovery from the illness. This self-regulatory process can compensate for minor deviations in the growth process, but it is unable to make up for major deviations. Restricted opportunities for movement and deprivation of experience have been shown to interfere with children's abilities to perform movement tasks that are characteristic of their age level. The extent to which children are able to catch up to their age-mates depends on the duration and severity of deprivation, the age of the child, and the level of motivation to make improvements.

Lifestyle

Lifestyle factors, or **secular trends,** as they are sometimes called, refer to the tendency for children to be both taller and heavier, age for age, and to mature at an earlier age than children several generations ago. The trend for secular increases is not universal. Increases in growth, maturation, and physical performance levels have been demonstrated in most developed countries. However, some developing nations have not demonstrated secular increases and in some cases have even shown secular decreases in stature. The changes in secular trends are largely caused by changes in lifestyle and nutritional habits from one generation to another.

The influence of secular trends in size and maturation in North America and other developed nations appears to have stopped. There has been little indication of secular increases in height and maturation in these countries in the past several years. There has, however, been a definite secular trend in children's weight. Recent studies have clearly revealed that today's children and adults are significantly heavier than their age-mates of ten to twenty years ago.

DEVELOPMENT

Development is the continuous process of change over time beginning at conception and ceasing only at death. **Motor Development,** therefore, is progressive change in movement behavior throughout the life cycle. Motor development involves continuous adaptation to changes in one's movement capabilities in the never ending effort to achieve and maintain motor control and movement competence. Such a perspective does not view development as being domain specific, nor does it view development as being stage-like or age dependent. Instead, this perspective suggests that *some* aspects of one's development can be conceptualized into domains, as being stage-like or age-related, while others cannot. Furthermore, the concept of achieving and maintaining competence encompasses all developmental change—change that is both positive and negative.

Currently, Dynamical Systems Theory is popular among developmentalists as an explanatory means for better understanding the process of development. On the other hand, the Phases of Motor Development (Gallahue and Ozmun, 1995) serve as a descriptive means for better understanding and conceptualizing the product of development. The dynamics of development are discussed here and in the chapter that follows along with the phases of motor development.

CONCEPT 2.4
Both descriptive and explanatory views of the process of development are essential for understanding children's motor behavior.

THE DYNAMICS OF DEVELOPMENT

It is important to know about the products of development in terms of what children are typically like during particular age periods (description). It is equally important, however, to know what causes these changes to occur (explanation). Many developmentalists are looking at explanatory models in conjunction with descriptive models in an attempt to understand more about the underlying processes that actually govern motor development. A **dynamic systems** explanation is currently popular among many (Gallahue and Ozmun, 1995).

In brief, the term *dynamic,* or *dynamical* as it is sometimes called, conveys the concept that developmental change is nonlinear and discontinuous, rather than linear and continuous. Because development is viewed as **nonlinear,** it is seen as a **discontinuous process.** That is, individual change over time is not necessarily smooth and hierarchical and does not necessarily involve moving toward ever higher levels of complexity and competence in the motor system. Individuals, particularly those with disabling conditions, are encumbered by impairments that tend to impede their motor development. For example, children with spastic cerebral palsy are frequently delayed in learning to walk independently. When independent walking is achieved, the gait patterns will be individualized and achieved at a point in time appropriate for each. Although, by definition, development is a continuous process, it is also a discontinuous process. In other words, from a dynamical perspective, development is viewed as a "continuous-discontinuous" process. The dynamics of change occur over time, but in a highly individual manner influenced by a variety of critical factors within the system.

The term *systems* conveys the concept that the human organism is self-organizing and composed of several subsystems. It is **self-organizing** in that by their very nature humans are inclined to strive for motor control and movement competence. It is the subsystems, namely, the task, the individual, and the environment, operating separately and in concert that actually determine the rate, sequence, and extent of development. In other words, there is not some preprogrammed universal plan that unfolds on an inflexible schedule. Using our example of children with spastic cerebral palsy, it is clear that they will, as self-organizing systems, develop their individually unique gait pattern in response to their capabilities in terms of meeting the achievement demands of the walking task.

Developmentalists have for years recognized the interactive role of two primary systems on the developmental process: heredity and environment. Many now, however, have taken this view one step further in recognizing that the specific demands of the movement task itself actually transact with the individual (i.e., hereditary or biological factors) and the environment (i.e., experience or learning factors) in the development of stability, locomotor, and manipulative movement abilities. Such a **transactional model of development** implies that factors within various subsystems of the task, the individual, and the environment not only interact with one another but also have the potential for modifying and being modified by each other as one strives to gain motor control and movement competence (Figure 2.3).

Both the processes and the products of motor development should constantly remind us of the individuality of the learner. Each individual has his or her own unique

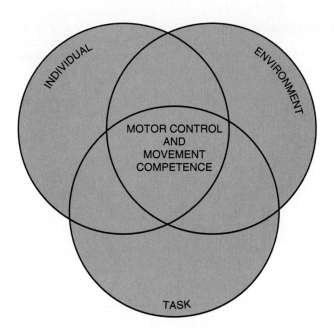

FIGURE 2.3 *Interaction among the task, the individual and the environment.*

timetable for the development and extent of acquisition of abilities. Although our "biological clock" is rather specific when it comes to the sequence of movement skill acquisition, the rate and extent of development is individually determined and dramatically influenced by the specific performance demands of the individual task itself. Typical age periods of development are just that: typical, and nothing more. Age periods merely represent approximate time ranges during which certain behaviors may be observed for the mythical "average" individual. Overreliance on these time periods would negate the concepts of continuity, specificity, and individuality in the developmental process and are of little practical value when working with individuals with developmental disabilities.

FACTORS AFFECTING MOTOR DEVELOPMENT

Development is a change in functional capability. We generally view development in children to be an upward process leading toward increased capabilities. Development as a lifelong process, however, also concerns the

diminishing of capabilities in middle age and gradual regression with advancing age. The process of motor development depends on a variety of developmental factors. Teachers must be aware of the tremendous complexity of the process of motor development and must objectively view their role as catalysts for change in this process.

As a child develops, gradual shifts or increments in level of functioning occur in the stability, locomotor, and manipulative categories of movement behavior. During infancy, children gain the very simplest controls over their movements in order to survive at the lowest level of motoric functioning. Preschool and primary-grade children are involved in developing and refining their fundamental movement skills. The many complex movements found in sport and dance are little more than highly elaborated forms of these fundamental movements.

The unique genetic inheritance that accounts for our individuality can account for our similarity in many areas. One of these similarities is the trend for human development to proceed in an orderly, predictable fashion. A number of factors that affect motor development tend to emerge from this predictable pattern. Table 2.1 illustrates the sequence of emergence of selected stability, locomotor, and manipulative abilities during childhood.

 CONCEPT 2.5
Several biological factors explain, in part, both the sequence and rate of motor development in childhood.

Developmental Sequence

Developmental sequence refers to the orderly, predictable sequence of motor control. **Cephalocaudal** development refers specifically to the gradual progression of increased control over the musculature, moving from the head to the feet. The tendency of young children to be clumsy and to exhibit poor control over the lower extremities may be due to incomplete cephalocaudal development.

Proximodistal development refers specifically to progression in control of the musculature from the center of the body to its most distant parts. Young children, for example, are able to control the muscles of the trunk and shoulder girdle sooner than they can gain control over the muscles of their wrist, hand, and fingers. Teachers of primary-grade children are recognizing this principle of development when they teach the less refined elements of manuscript printing before they introduce the more complex and refined movements of cursive writing.

TABLE 2.1 *Sequence of Emergence of Selected Locomotor/Manipulative/Stability Abilities*

Movement Pattern	Selected Abilities	Approximate Age of Onset
Walking		
Walking involves placing one foot in front of the other while maintaining contact with the supporting surface	Rudimentary upright unaided gait	13 months
	Walks sideways	16 months
	Walks backward	17 months
	Walks upstairs with help	20 months
	Walks upstairs alone—follow step	24 months
	Walks downstairs alone—follow step	25 months
Running		
Running involves a brief period of no contact with the supporting surface	Hurried walk (maintains contact)	18 months
	First true run (nonsupport phase)	2–3 years
	Efficient and refined run	4–5 years
	Speed of run increases, mature run*	5 years
Jumping		
Jumping takes three forms: (1) jumping for distance; (2) jumping for height; and (3) jumping from a height. It involves a one- or two-foot takeoff and landing on both feet	Steps down from low objects	18 months
	Jumps down from object with one foot lead	2 years
	Jumps off floor with both feet	28 months
	Jumps for distance (about three feet)	5 years
	Jumps for height (about one foot)	5 years
	Mature jumping pattern*	6 years
Hopping		
Hopping involves a one-foot takeoff with a landing on the same foot	Hops up to three times on preferred foot	3 years
	Hops from four to six times on same foot	4 years
	Hops from eight to ten times on same foot	5 years
	Hops distance of fifty feet in about eleven seconds	5 years
	Hops skillfully with rhythmical alteration, mature pattern*	6 years
Galloping		
The gallop combines a walk and a leap with the same foot leading throughout	Basic but inefficient gallop	4 years
	Gallops skillfully, mature pattern*	6 years
Skipping		
Skipping combines a step and a hop in rhythmic alteration	One-footed skip	4 years
	Skillful skipping (about 20 percent)	5 years
	Skillful skipping for most*	6 years

TABLE 2.1 *(continued)*

Movement Pattern	Selected Abilities	Approximate Age of Onset
Reach, Grasp, Release		
Reaching, grasping, and releasing involves making successful contact with an object, retaining it in one's grasp and releasing it at will	Primitive reaching behaviors	2–4 months
	Coralling of objects	2–4 months
	Palmar grasp	3–5 months
	Pincer grasp	8–10 months
	Controlled grasp	12–14 months
	Controlled releasing	14–18 months
Throwing		
Throwing involves imparting force to an object in the general direction of intent	Body faces target, feet remain stationary, ball is thrown with forearm extension only	2–3 years
	Same as above but with body rotation added	3.6–5 years
	Steps forward with leg on same side as the throwing arm	4–5 years
	Boys exhibit more mature pattern than girls	5 years and over
	Mature throwing pattern*	6 years
Catching		
Catching involves receiving force from an object with the hands, moving from large to progressively smaller balls	Chases ball; does not respond to aerial ball	2 years
	Responds to aerial ball with delayed arm movements	2–3 years
	Needs to be told how to position arms	2–3 years
	Fear reaction (turns head away)	3–4 years
	Basket catch using the body	3 years
	Catches using the hands only with a small ball	5 years
	Mature catching pattern*	6 years
Kicking		
Kicking involves imparting force to an object with the foot	Pushes against ball; does not actually kick it	18 months
	Kicks with the leg straight and little body movement (kicks *at* the ball)	2–3 years
	Flexes lower leg on backward lift	3–4 years
	Greater backward and forward swing with definite arm opposition	4–5 years
	Mature pattern (kicks *through* the ball)*	5–6 years
Striking		
Striking involves sudden contact to objects in an overarm, sidearm, or underhand pattern	Faces object and swings in a vertical plane	2–3 years
	Swings in a horizontal plane and stands to the side of the object	4–5 years
	Rotates the trunk and hips and shifts body weight forward	5 years
	Mature horizontal pattern with stationary ball	6–7 years

Continued

TABLE 2.1   *(continued)*

Movement Pattern	Selected Abilities	Approximate Age of Onset
Dynamic Balance		
Dynamic balance involves maintaining one's equilibrium as the center of gravity shifts	Walks one-inch straight line	3 years
	Walks one-inch circular line	4 years
	Stands on low balance beam	2 years
	Walks on four-inch wide beam for a short distance	3 years
	Walks on same beam, alternating feet	3–4 years
	Walks on two- or three-inch beam	4 years
	Performs basic forward roll	3–4 years
	Performs mature forward roll*	6–7 years
Static Balance		
Static balance involves maintaining one's equilibrium while the center of gravity remains stationary	Pulls to a standing position	10 months
	Stands without handholds	11 months
	Stands alone	12 months
	Balances on one foot three to five seconds	5 years
	Supports body in basic three-point inverted positions	6 years
Axial Movements		
Axial movements are static postures that involve bending, stretching, twisting, turning, and the like	Axial movement abilities begin to develop early in infancy and are progressively refined to a point where they are included in the emerging manipulative patterns of throwing, catching, kicking, striking, trapping, and other activities	2 months–6 years

Source: David L. Gallahue and J. C. Ozmun, *Understanding Motor Development* (Dubuque, IA: Wm. C. Brown & Benchmark, 1995).

*The child has the developmental "potential" to be at the mature stage. Actual attainment will depend on environmental factors.

Developmental Variability and Readiness

Although children's development follows a characteristic developmental sequence that is universal and resistant to major changes, the rate at which children acquire these traits and abilities is quite variable. **Developmental variability** refers to age variations in the rate of movement skill acquisition. For example, children progress at differing rates in attaining the mature fundamental manipulative skills of throwing and catching or the baseball sport skills of batting and fielding a ground ball. Such variability is entirely understandable when we

consider the complex interaction among the cognitive, affective, and motor aspects of children's development. This variability is further coupled with their unique hereditary makeup and specific environmental circumstances, all of which ensure that children will develop at varying rates. Developmental variability is the most important concept to consider in designing and implementing the developmental curriculum with an emphasis on individual appropriateness.

Readiness refers to conditions within both the individual and the environment that make a particular task appropriate for the child to master. As used today, the concept of readiness extends beyond biological maturation and includes environmental factors that can be modified or manipulated to encourage or promote learning. Some children simply are not ready for the experiences that we are prepared to provide them. For example, your students certainly will not be ready to learn how to do a handstand if they have not mastered the progression of skills leading from a tripod to a tip-up, headstand, and finally a handstand. To ensure that we are on target with our instructional strategies and the content of our program we need to be certain that children have the prerequisite skills.

It is critically important for us to recognize and respect the concepts of developmental variability and individual readiness both among groups of children and within individual children. We simply cannot consider children solely on the basis of their chronological age or grade level and expect to be successful in movement skill acquisition and fitness enhancement.

Differentiation and Integration

A developing child's motor control is marked by the coordinated, progressive, and intricate interweaving of neural mechanisms of opposing muscle systems into an increasingly mature relationship. Two different but related processes are associated with this increase of functional complexity: differentiation and integration. **Differentiation** is the gradual progression from the gross globular (overall) movement patterns of infants to the more refined and functional movements of children as they mature. **Integration** refers to the coordinated interaction of opposing muscle and sensory systems. For example, the young child gradually progresses from ill-defined corralling movements when attempting to grasp an object to more mature and visually guided reaching and grasping behavior. This differentiation of movements of the arms, hands, and fingers followed by integration of the use of the eyes with the movements of the hand to perform rudimentary eye-hand coordination tasks is crucial to normal development.

Sensitive Learning Periods

Basically, a **sensitive period** is a broad time frame or window of opportunity when the learning of specific new skills is easier and quicker. For example, there appear to be sensitive periods for learning how to speak a foreign language, play a musical instrument, and perform a host of gross motor skills ranging from swimming and bicycle riding to gymnastic and baseball skills.

CONCEPT 2.6
Childhood represents an important sensitive period for movement skill acquisition.

Children, especially young children, are generally fearless in terms of risking physical injury and fearless in terms of risking personal failure and peer ridicule. Additionally, they are eager learners unencumbered by a history of negative learning experiences, feelings of incompetence, and the fear of injury, ridicule, or peer rejection. The entire period of childhood may be viewed as a sensitive period for mastering fundamental movement skills and being introduced to a wide variety of sport skills. More specifically, the period of early childhood, roughly from ages three to eight, is especially important. The development of mature fundamental movement is a prerequisite to the learning and mastery of sport skills. Failure to take advantage of this sensitive movement skill learning period of childhood makes it difficult for the child to attain higher levels of skill later on.

Normal development in later periods may be hindered if children fail to receive proper stimulation during a sensitive period. For example, the presence of inadequate nutrition, prolonged stress, inconsistent mothering, or lack of appropriate learning experiences early in life may have a more negative impact on development than if these factors were present at a later age.

The concept of sensitive periods does have a positive side. It suggests that appropriate intervention during a sensitive period tends to facilitate more positive forms of subsequent development than if the same intervention occurs later. The concept of sensitive periods rejects the notion that there are highly specific time frames in which one must develop movement skills. There are, however, broad periods during which development of certain skills is most easily accomplished.

EARLY CHILDHOOD DEVELOPMENT

Play is what young children do when they are not eating, sleeping, or complying with the wishes of adults. Play occupies most of their waking hours, and it may literally be viewed as the child's equivalent of work as performed by adults. Children's play is the primary means by which they learn about their bodies and movement capabilities. Play also facilitates cognitive and affective growth in the young child and provides an important means of developing both fine and gross motor skills.

The preschool years are a period of important cognitive development. Preschool children are actively involved in enhancing their cognitive abilities in a variety of ways. During this time they develop cognitive functions that eventually result in logical thinking and concept formulation. Young children are incapable of thinking from any point of view other than their own. Their perceptions dominate their thinking, and what they experience at a given moment has great influence on them. During this preconceptual phase of cognitive development, seeing is, literally, believing. In the thinking and logic of preschool children, their conclusions need no justification. Even if they did, the children would be unable to reconstruct their thoughts and show others how they arrived at their conclusions.

Affective development is also dramatic during the preschool years. During this period children are involved in the two crucial social-emotional tasks of developing a sense of autonomy and a sense of initiative. Autonomy is expressed through a growing sense of independence, which may be seen in children's delight in responding with the word *no* to almost any direct question. The answer will often be *no* to a question such as "Do you want to play outside?" even when the child clearly would like to. This behavior can be viewed as the child's expression of a newfound sense of independence and an ability to manipulate some factors in the environment rather than always as an expression of sheer disobedience. One way to avoid this natural autonomous reaction to a question is to form a positive statement instead, for example, "Let's go play outdoors." In this way the child is not confronted with a direct yes-or-no choice. Care must be taken, however, to give children abundant situations in which an expression of their autonomy is reasonable and proper.

Young children's expanding sense of initiative is also seen through their curious exploring and their very active behavior. Children begin to engage in new experiences such as climbing, jumping, running, and throwing objects

---

TEACHING TIPS

Implications for teaching developmental physical education based on typical *early childhood characteristics*:

- Emphasize the process (qualitative aspects) of movement prior to the product (quantitative aspects).

- Focus on movement skill learning, remembering that skill learning takes time, practice, and repetition.

- Teach fewer things well rather than doing a mediocre job with too many objectives.

- Provide plenty of opportunity for gross motor activities in both undirected and directed settings.

- Include plenty of positive reinforcement to encourage the establishment of a positive self-concept and to reduce the fear of failure.

- Stress developing a variety of fundamental stability, locomotor, and manipulative skills, first alone and then as movement phrases.

- Teach boys and girls together (it's the law); at this stage their interests and abilities are quite similar.

- Promote perceptual-motor learning through movement skill acquisition.

- Take advantage of the child's great imagination through the use of drama and imagery.

- Provide a wide variety of experiences that improve object handling skills and promote eye-hand coordination.

- Incorporate bilateral skills such as skipping, galloping, and hopping with alternate foot leading after unilateral movements have been fairly well established.

- Encourage children to take an active part in the program by "showing" and "telling" others what they can do to promote social interaction.

- Provide for individual differences and allow children to progress at their own rate.

- Establish standards for acceptable behavior and abide by them.

- Provide wise guidance in establishing a sense of doing what is right and proper for its own sake.

- Personalize instruction based on individual readiness.

for their own sake and for the sheer joy of sensing and knowing what they are capable of doing. Failure to develop a sense of initiative and autonomy at this stage frequently leads to feelings of shame, worthlessness, and guilt. Establishment of stable self-concept in preschoolers is crucial to proper affective development because it directly affects both cognitive and psychomotor functions.

Through the medium of play, preschoolers develop a wide variety of fundamental stability, locomotor, and manipulative abilities. If they have a stable and positive self-concept, the gain in control over their musculature is a smooth one. The timid, cautious, and measured movements of the two- to three-year-old gradually give way to the confident, eager, and often reckless abandon of the four- and five-year-old. Preschoolers' vivid imaginations make it possible for them to jump from "great heights," climb "high mountains," leap over "raging rivers," and run "faster" than an assorted variety of "wild beasts."

Children of preschool age are rapidly expanding their horizons, asserting their individuality, developing their abilities, and testing their limits (as well as testing the limits of their family and others around them). In short, young children are pushing out into the world in many complex and wondrous ways. It is critical, though, to understand their developmental characteristics and their limitations as well as their potentials. Only in this way can we effectively structure movement experiences for them that truly reflect their needs and interests and are within their levels of ability.

CONCEPT 2.7
Children exhibit a variety of motor, cognitive, and affective characteristics that are, in a broad sense, age appropriate.

Primary-grade children take the first big step into their expanding world when they enter first grade. For many, first grade represents the first separation from the home for a regularly scheduled, extended block of time. It is the first venture out of the secure play environment of the home and into the world of adults. Entering a school represents the first time that many children are placed in a group in which they are not the center of attention. It is a time when sharing, concern for others, and respect for the rights and responsibilities of others are established. Kindergarten is a readiness time in which to begin making the gradual transition from an egocentric, home-centered play world to the group-oriented world of adult concepts and logic. In the first grade the first formal demands for cognitive understanding are made. The major cognitive milestone of the first and second grader is learning how to read at a reasonable level. The child is involved in developing the first real understanding of time and money and numerous other cognitive concepts. By the second grade children should be well on their way to meeting and surmounting the ever broadening array of cognitive, affective, and psychomotor tasks that are placed before them.

The following selected developmental characteristics represent a synthesis of findings from a wide variety of sources and are presented here to provide a more complete view of the "typical" child during the early childhood years.

Children can be challenged through imagery during the early childhood period.

Motor Characteristics

1. Growth proceeds at a slow but steady pace, with annual height gains of about two inches and annual weight gains of approximately five pounds.
2. Perceptual-motor abilities are rapidly developing, but confusion often exists in body, directional, temporal, and spatial awareness.

3. Good bladder and bowel control are generally established by the end of this period, but accidents sometimes occur with younger children.
4. Children during this period are rapidly developing and refining fundamental movement abilities in a variety of skills. Cross-lateral movements such as skipping, however, often present more difficulty than unilateral movements.
5. Children are active and energetic and would often rather run than walk.
6. Gross motor control is developing rapidly and generally occurs sooner than fine motor control.
7. Fine motor control develops to the point that children can dress themselves, color, stack blocks, and write with reasonable skill.
8. The body functions and processes become well regulated. A state of physiological homeostasis (stability) becomes well established.
9. The physiques of boys and girls are remarkably similar. A posterior view of boys and girls reveals no readily observable structural differences.
10. Because children at this stage are farsighted, their eyes are not generally ready for extended periods of close work.

Cognitive Characteristics

1. Children at this stage are increasingly able to express their thoughts and ideas verbally.
2. A fantastic imagination enables children to imitate both actions and symbols with little concern for accuracy or the proper sequencing of events.
3. Children continuously investigate and discover new symbols that have a primarily personal reference.
4. Children learn the "how" and "why" of their actions through active play.
5. Early childhood is a preoperational phase of development, resulting in a period of transition from self-satisfying behaviors to fundamental socialized behaviors.

Affective Characteristics

1. During early childhood children are generally egocentric and assume that everyone thinks the way they do. As a result, they often seem to be quarrelsome and exhibit difficulty in sharing and getting along with others.
2. They are often fearful of new situations, shy, self-conscious, and unwilling to leave the security of what is familiar.

3. They are learning to distinguish right from wrong and are beginning to develop consciences.
4. Children at the beginning of this period are often nonconforming and irregular in their behavior, whereas older children are often viewed as more stable and conforming.
5. The self-concept is rapidly developing. Providing children with success-oriented experiences and positive reinforcement is especially important during these years. These experiences help to build children's senses of competence.

LATER CHILDHOOD DEVELOPMENT

Children in the upper elementary grades are generally happy, stable, and able to assume responsibilities and cope with new situations. They are eager to learn more about themselves and their expanding world; they enthusiastically test their developing skills and typically have a wide range of interests.

The following is a listing of selected developmental characteristics typical of children during later childhood.

Hero worship is common during later childhood.

Motor Characteristics

1. Growth is slow but steady, from about age eight to the end of this period.
2. The body begins to lengthen out with an annual gain of only one to two inches and an annual weight gain of only three to six pounds.
3. The cephalocaudal (head-to-toe) and proximodistal (center-to-periphery) principles of development are evident at this stage. Children's larger muscles are considerably better developed than their small muscles.
4. Girls are generally about a year ahead of boys in physiological development. Separate interests begin to develop during this period.
5. Hand preference is firmly established, with about 90 percent preferring the right hand and about 10 percent preferring the left.
6. Reaction time improves. Difficulty with eye-hand and eye-foot coordination is evident at the beginning of this period, but by the end it is generally well established.
7. Both boys and girls are full of energy but often possess low endurance levels. Responsiveness to training is, however, great.
8. Visual-perceptual abilities are fully developed by the end of this period.
9. Fundamental movement skills should be well developed by the beginning of this period, and children are ready to be introduced to a variety of sport skills.
10. Competence develops rapidly if children have ample opportunities for practice, quality individualized instruction, and positive encouragement.

Cognitive Characteristics

1. Children's attention span is often very focused, especially for activities that are of great personal interest. They are intellectually curious and are eager to know "why."
2. Children are eager to learn and to please adults, but they need assistance and guidance in decision making.

TEACHING TIPS

Implications for teaching developmental physical education based on typical *later childhood characteristics*:

- Provide experiences that help children make the transition from mature fundamental movement skill acquisition to sport skill learning.

- Provide remedial opportunities for children to refine and combine fundamental movement skills to the point that their movements are fluid and efficient.

- Assure children that they are accepted and valued so they know they have a stable and secure place in the school.

- Offer plenty of encouragement and positive reinforcement to promote continued development of a positive self-concept.

- To help promote self-reliance, expose children to experiences in which they have progressively greater amounts of responsibility.

- Help children adjust to the rougher ways of the school playground and neighborhood without being rough or crude themselves.

- Introduce children to individual, dual, and team activities as their competence develops.

- Children at this level often learn best through active participation. Integration of academic concepts with movement activities provides an effective way to reinforce concepts in science, mathematics, social studies, and the language arts.

- Discuss play situations involving such topics as taking turns, fair play, cheating, and good sportsmanship in an effort to establish a more complete sense of right or wrong.

- Encourage children to "think" before engaging in an activity. Help them recognize potential hazards as a means of reducing their sometimes reckless behavior.

- Opportunities should be provided for participation in youth sport activities that are developmentally appropriate and geared to the needs and interests of children.

3. Children have good imaginations and display extremely creative minds, but self-consciousness often predominates.
4. Children at the beginning of this period are limited in their abstract thinking abilities and learn best with concrete examples. More sophisticated abstract cognitive abilities are evident by the end of this period.

Affective Characteristics

1. Interests of boys and girls are similar at the beginning of this period but soon begin to diverge. Both enjoy self-testing activities as a means of trying out and testing their developing skills.
2. During the primary grades children are generally self-centered and play poorly in large groups although they handle small-group situations well. Effective large-group interaction improves.
3. Children are often aggressive, boastful, self-critical, and overreactive; they accept victory as well as defeat poorly without effective adult interaction.
4. Children are responsive to authority and critically conscious of what is "fair."
5. Children are adventurous and eager to be involved with friends in "dangerous" or "secret" activities.

SUMMARY

Childhood growth and motor development is a process that is predictable in terms of universal principles and sequential progressions as children develop higher levels of functioning. There is, however, considerable individual variation in the rate and extent of acquisition of these higher levels of functioning. Consideration of these factors must be paramount as we select specific experiences and utilize specific teaching behaviors. We must consider the *individual*

appropriateness of the movement activities we employ in a developmental physical education program.

Teachers of developmental physical education must also learn about the typical motor, cognitive, and affective characteristics of early childhood and later childhood. This knowledge will provide you with important guidelines for selecting movement experiences and applying teaching behaviors that are sensitive to the concept of *age-group appropriateness*.

COMPLEMENTARY READINGS

Barnett, B. E., and W. Merriman. (1991). Misconceptions in motor development. *Strategies* 5(3):5–7.

Boucher, A., ed. (1988). Early childhood physical education. *Journal of Physical Education, Recreation, and Dance* 59(7):42–72 (series of articles).

Gallahue, D. L., and J. C. Ozmun. (1995). *Understanding Motor Development.: Infants, Children, Adolescents, Adults.* Dubuque, IA: Brown & Benchmark (Chapter 3, Factors affecting motor development).

SUPPLEMENTARY READINGS

Cook-Shumway, A. and Woollacott, M. H. (1995). *Motor Control Theory and Practical Applications.* Baltimore, MD: Williams & Wilkins.

Gabbard, C. (1996). *Lifelong Motor Development.* Dubuque, IA: Wm. C. Brown.

Haywood, K. M. (1993). *Life Span Motor Development.* Champaign, IL: Human Kinetics.

Malina, R.M., and C. Bouchard. (1991). *Growth, Maturation, and Physical Activity.* Champaign, IL: Human Kinetics.

Payne, V. G., and L. D. Isaacs. (1995). *Human Motor Development: A Lifespan Approach.* Mountain View, CA: Mayfield.

CHAPTER 3

Movement Skill Acquisition

●

Key Concept

The Core of the Developmental Physical Education Program is in Helping Children Become: *Skillful Movers, Knowledgeable Movers, Expressive Movers*

●

Chapter Objectives

The purpose of this chapter is to provide you with the tools to:
- Provide examples of stability, locomotor, and manipulative movements at the fundamental and specialized movement skill phases.
- Describe and give examples of movement phrases, using each category of movement.
- List and describe four primary environmental factors that influence movement skill development.
- Identify and discuss characteristics of the underlying stages of fundamental movement phase and the specialized movement phase.
- Give examples of internally paced and externally paced, gross and fine, and discrete, serial, and continuous movement activities.
- Provide guidelines for teaching individuals at the beginning, intermediate, and advanced levels of movement skill learning.
- Propose means for incorporating movement skill homework into the physical education program.

●

Terms to Remember

Skillful Movers
Fundamental Movement Skill
Specialized Movement Skill
Movement Pattern
Categories of Movement
Stability Movement
Locomotor Movement
Gross Motor Manipulation
Fine Motor Manipulation
Movement Phrases
Ecological Setting

Fundamental Movement Phase
Initial Stage
Elementary Stage
Mature Stage
Specialized Movement Phase
Transition Stage
Proficiency Barrier
Application Stage
Lifelong Utilization Stage
Externally Paced
Internally Paced

Gross Motor
Fine Motor
Discrete Movement
Serial Movements
Continuous Movements
Beginning/Novice Level
Intermediate/Practice Level
Advanced/Fine-Tuning Level
Movement Skill Homework

The unique contribution of children's physical education is in the area of movement skill acquisition. In this chapter we will look at how children become skillful movers. **Skillful movers** are those individuals who move with control, efficiency, and coordination in the performance of fundamental or specialized movement tasks. The topics of knowledgeable movers and expressive movers will be dealt with separately in later chapters. In this chapter we will first discuss the importance of developing children's movement skills, the categories of movement, the factors that influence how children acquire movement skills, and the phases and stages of motor development. After a brief discussion of the types of movement skills, we will examine the levels and stages of learning a new movement skill. A discussion of movement skill homework and implications for teaching developmental physical education conclude the chapter.

THE IMPORTANCE OF DEVELOPING CHILDREN'S MOVEMENT SKILLS

Failure to develop and refine fundamental and specialized movement skills during the crucial preschool and elementary school years often leads children to frustration and failure during adolescence and adulthood. Failure to develop mature patterns in throwing, catching, and striking, for example, makes it quite difficult for them to succeed in and enjoy even a recreational game of softball. Children cannot take part, with success, in an activity if they have not learned the essential movement skills contained within that activity.

This does not mean that if they do not learn skills during childhood they cannot develop them later in life. However, it is easiest to develop these skills during childhood. If children don't develop the skills early, they too often remain unlearned. Several factors contribute to this situation. One is an accumulation of bad habits from improper learning. It is much more difficult to "unlearn" faulty movements than to learn to do them correctly in the first place. Self-consciousness and embarrassment is a second factor. "I have two left feet," "I'm all thumbs," or "What a klutz" are all derogatory phrases that children may use to describe poor performance. A third factor causing many movement skills to remain unlearned is fear. Fear of being injured and being ridiculed by peers are very real anxieties that often contribute markedly to

The mature fundamental movement skill of throwing overhand.

difficulty in learning movement skills later in life. Therefore, it is crucial that children fully develop their fundamental movement abilities and a variety of basic sport skills during childhood.

MOVEMENT SKILLS AND MOVEMENT PATTERNS

Although often used interchangeably, the terms *movement skill, fundamental movement skill, specialized movement skill,* and *movement pattern* have important differences. A *movement skill,* which may be either a fundamental movement skill or a specialized skill, is a series of movements performed with accuracy and precision. In a movement skill, control of movement is stressed and extraneous movement is therefore limited. Striking a ball with an implement is a movement skill.

A **fundamental movement skill** is an organized series of basic movements that involve the combination of movement patterns of two or more body segments. Fundamental movement skills may be categorized as stability, locomotor, or manipulative movements. Twisting and turning, running and jumping, and striking and throwing are examples of fundamental movement skills from each of these categories.

A **specialized movement skill** is a fundamental movement skill or combination of fundamental movement skills that have been applied to the performance of a specific sport, recreational or daily living activity. Therefore, the fundamental movement skills of twisting the body and striking an object may be applied, in their horizontal form, to batting in a game of baseball or, in their vertical forms, to playing golf or serving a tennis ball.

A **movement pattern** is an organized series of related movements. More specifically, a movement pattern involves the performance of an isolated movement that in and of itself is too restricted to be classified as a fundamental movement skill or a sport skill. For example, the sidearm, underarm, or overarm patterns of movement alone do not constitute the fundamental movement skills of throwing or striking or the sport skills of pitching or batting in baseball. They merely represent an organized series of movements in which movement is stressed but accuracy, control, and precision are limited.

C O N C E P T   3 . 1
A variety of terms may be used to describe the various forms, levels, and types of movement skill.

Developmental physical education recognizes the need to focus on the "process," or mechanics of movement skill acquisition, prior to the "product," or performance aspects of movement skill development. Physical educators who recognize the validity of this developmental movement skill learning focus their teaching efforts on helping children to become skillful movers by acquiring fundamental movement skills and sport skills in a variety of stability, locomotor, and manipulative movements.

Skillful movers.

THE CATEGORIES OF MOVEMENT

Movement skills, whether fundamental movement skills or specialized movement skills, may be subdivided into categories. The three **categories of movement** are *stability, locomotor,* and *manipulative* movements. These three categories and resulting movement phrases can further be organized according to the sports skills themes (such as soccer or volleyball, for example) in which these movement skills are most emphasized. Figure 3.1 summarizes these categories, and Table 3.1 provides a list of selected sport skill themes from the developmental physical education curriculum.

Stability Movement Skills

Stability movement skills form the basis for all locomotor and manipulative skills, because all movement involves an element of stability. **Stability movement skills** are those in which the body remains in place but moves around its horizontal or vertical axes. In addition, they are also dynamic balance tasks in which a premium is placed on gaining or maintaining one's equilibrium against the force of gravity. For example, the forward roll in tumbling and dodging a ball are both considered to be stability skills because of the strong emphasis placed on maintaining equilibrium throughout each task. Axial movements such as reaching, twisting, turning, bending, and stretching are fundamental stability abilities, as are

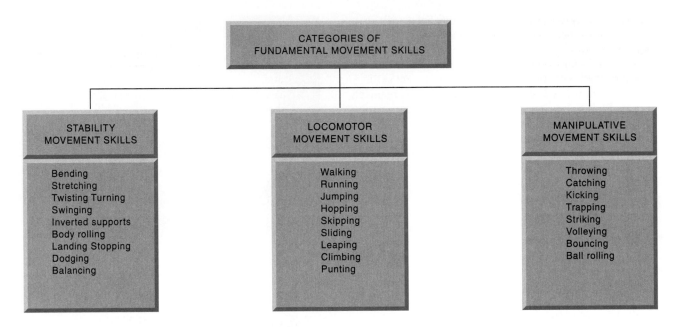

FIGURE 3.1 *Selected fundamental movement skill themes.*

TABLE 3.1 *Selected Sport Skill Themes and the Movement Skills Most Emphasized in Each*

Sport Skill Themes	Stability Movement Skills	Locomotor Movement Skills	Manipulative Movement Skills
Basketball skills	Selected axial movement skills: Pivoting Dodging Guarding Picking Blocking Cutting Faking	Running Sliding Leaping Jumping	Passing Catching Shooting Dribbling Tipping Blocking Rebounding
Combative skills	All axial movement skills Dodging and feinting Static balance skills Dynamic balance skills	Stepping Sliding Hopping (karate)	Dexterity (fencing) Striking (kendo)
Dance skills	All axial movement skills Static balance postures Dynamic balance postures	Running Leaping Jumping Hopping Skipping Sliding Stepping	Tossing Catching

TABLE 3.1   *(continued)*

Sport Skill Themes	Stability Movement Skills	Locomotor Movement Skills	Manipulative Movement Skills
Disc sport skills	All axial movement skills Static balance postures Dynamic balance postures	Stepping Running Jumping	Tossing Catching
Football skills	Blocking Tackling Dodging Pivoting	Running Sliding Leaping Jumping	Passing Catching Carrying Kicking Punting Centering
Gymnastic skills	Inverted supports: Rolling, landing All axial movement skills Static balance moves Dynamic balance moves	Running Jumping Skipping Leaping Hopping Landing	

Implement striking skills
  (tennis, squash, racquetball,
  hockey, lacrosse, golf)
	Dynamic balance skills:
	Turning
	Twisting
	Stretching
	Bending
	Dodging
	Pivoting
		Running
		Sliding
		Leaping
		Skating
		Walking
			Forehand
			Backhand
			Striking
			Driving
			Putting
			Chipping
			Lobbing
			Smash
			Drop
			Throwing
			Trapping
			Poling

Skiing skills	All axial movement skills Dynamic balance skills Static balance skills	Stepping Walking Running Sliding	
Soccer skills	Tackling Marking Dodging Feinting Turning	Running Jumping Leaping Sliding	Kicking Trapping Juggling Throwing Blocking Passing Dribbling Catching Rolling

Continued

TABLE 3.1   *(continued)*

Sport Skill Themes	Stability Movement Skills	Locomotor Movement Skills	Manipulative Movement Skills
Softball/baseball skills	Selected axial movement skills: Dynamic balance skills Dodging	Running Sliding Leaping Jumping	Throwing Catching Pitching Batting Bunting
Target sport skills	Static balance skills		Aiming Shooting
Track and field skills	All axial movement skills: Dynamic balance skills	Running Hopping Vertical jumping Horizontal jumping Leaping Starting	Shot put Discus Javelin Hammer Pole vault Baton passing Throwing
Volleyball skills	Dynamic balance skills Selected axial movements	Running Sliding Jumping Diving Sprawling Rolling	Serving Volleying Bump Dig Spike Dink Block

lifting, carrying, pushing, and pulling. Other fundamental stability skills involve a variety of positions involving inverted support, such as the tripod and headstand. Still others involve transitional postures, such as body rolling and springing movements. Stability skills emphasize static (stationary) balance or dynamic (moving) balance. Sport skill abilities in tumbling and gymnastics, as well as in diving and figure skating, all depend on stability.

Locomotor Movement Skills

Locomotor movement skills are those in which the body is transported in a horizontal or vertical direction from one point to another. Activities such as running, jumping, hopping, leaping, and skipping are considered to be fundamental locomotor movements. When these fundamental skills become elaborated and further refined, they can be applied to specific sports. For example, the fifty-yard dash, running the bases in softball, the high jump in track, and running a pass pattern in football are all specialized, sport-related locomotor skills.

Manipulative Movement Skills

These skills refer to either gross motor or fine motor movements. **Gross motor manipulation** refers to movements that involve giving force *to* objects or receiving force *from* objects. Throwing, catching, kicking, trapping, and striking are considered to be fundamental gross motor manipulative skills. Manipulative sport skills are an elaboration and further refinement of these basic skills. For example, hitting a tennis ball, throwing the javelin, catching a baseball, and playing the game of soccer all involve numerous manipulative skill abilities that are refinements of the fundamental tasks of striking, throwing, catching, and kicking, respectively.

The term **fine motor manipulation** refers to object-handling activities that emphasize motor control, precision, and accuracy of movement. Tying one's shoes, coloring, and cutting with scissors are all examples of fundamental fine motor manipulative skills. Target archery, violin playing, and the popular game of darts all have essential fine motor aspects and are considered to be fine motor, specialized movement skills. Physical educators are concerned primarily with the acquisition of gross motor manipulative skills and, to a somewhat lesser extent, with fine motor manipulative skills.

C O N C E P T   3 . 2

Stability, locomotor, and manipulative movements and the combination of these into movement phrases serve as the *categories* of movement into which fundamental and specialized movement skills may be classified.

Knowledgeable movers.

Movement Phrases

Movement phrases are combinations of stability, locomotor, and manipulative movements. They are introduced *after* children have mastered the basic elements of a single fundamental movement. For example, rather than being content with jumping off the springboard and landing in a bent-knee position, children now want to jump off, land, and do a forward roll. Or they may want to jump with a half-turn followed by a backward roll. As their skills develop, these movement phrases become longer, more complex, and more refined.

Participating successfully in most games and sports involves the combination of movements into sequences. For example, striking and running are combined into a phrase in baseball batting and base running, as are running, reaching, catching, and throwing in a typical baseball fielding sequence. Movement skills, whether they are fundamental or specialized, are generally learned best when focused on singularly. However, after the skill has been reasonably well mastered, it should be combined with others and used in dynamic gamelike situations. Purposeful movement in the real world is a series of coordinated phrases, not isolated, unconnected movements.

ENVIRONMENTAL FACTORS THAT INFLUENCE MOVEMENT SKILL ACQUISITION

Historically, many educators have erroneously assumed that children somehow "automatically" develop their movement skills as they mature. Therefore, the physical education period, particularly during the primary grades, was often viewed as little more than a glorified recess period, in which an endless variety of games were played with little more reason than that they were fun or that they contributed to other social-emotional objectives. Little serious consideration was given to using the early grades as a time for helping children master their fundamental movement abilities or using the upper grades to introduce children to a wide variety of sport skills. Children's physical education was instead viewed as a time to get away from the confines of the classroom, to have fun, and to "blow off steam."

It is now widely recognized that many environmental factors play an important role in movement skill acquisition and that children need encouragement, frequent opportunities for practice, and quality instruction in an ecologically sound environment to develop and refine their movement abilities. The preschool and early elementary years are recognized as the critical time for mastering fundamental movement skills. Maturation alone will not account for this development. Children who have mastered these skills are then ready to begin the exciting process of developing specialized skills and applying them to a wide variety of game, sport, dance, and recreational activities for a lifetime of vigorous movement.

CONCEPT 3.3

Environmental factors, including opportunities for practice, encouragement, instruction, and the ecological setting of the environment itself, significantly influence the development of movement skills.

Opportunity for Practice

Three factors play a crucial role in children's opportunities to practice developing their movement skills—facilities, equipment, and time.

Many children live in congested cities in high-rise apartments, cramped housing complexes, or sprawling suburbs—all of which frequently lack sufficient facilities to meet their needs to move. They may lack the facilities to play ball, fly a kite, or play a game of tennis. Even in areas where facilities have been set aside for public use, children must share their use with adolescents and adults. All too often, the needs and interests of children are preempted by older individuals. As a result, children are left to fend for themselves in the pursuit of vigorous movement experiences.

Opportunities for practice are also frequently limited by a lack of proper equipment. The cost of basketballs, baseball gloves, and hockey sticks, for example, is high. Parents and community centers often find it prohibitively expensive to purchase sufficient amounts and varieties of equipment for children to use.

A third factor, time, may be the most important determiner of opportunities for practice. Many children simply do not have the time to develop their movement skills. Their day is so highly programmed with school, television, computer games, and homework that little time is left for active movement.

Ample facilities, equipment, and time are all critical to fundamental movement skill development. Parents and teachers who fail to provide numerous opportunities for

fundamental movement skill learning are substantially limiting children's developmental potential and their eventual success with the specialized sport skills of later childhood, adolescence, and adulthood.

Practice opportunities should first be introduced under internally paced, or static, conditions. In this way, the learner can focus on one skill requirement at a time and therefore maximize opportunities for success. As the skill develops it should then be practiced, when appropriate, under externally paced, or dynamic, conditions in which the environmental conditions are flexible and constantly changing. Such an approach to sequencing practice promotes a learning environment focused on adaptability, movement variability, and motor creativity. Please refer to the "Teaching Tips" sections later in the chapter for specific ideas on how to structure opportunities for practice based on the type and level of movement skill being learned.

If children do in fact need ample opportunities for practice in order to develop their movement skills, then we must try to provide appropriate facilities, equipment, and time. The school physical education program provides the best avenue of ensuring learning opportunities for all children. The need first for *quality* and then for *daily* physical education is obvious. Quality daily physical education is absolutely essential if we are serious about our goals of developing skillful movers and providing ample practice opportunities for all.

Encouragement

Many children do not receive sufficient encouragement to develop their movement abilities. In many families today both parents are employed outside the home. In other families a single parent is trying to raise the children. A frequent result of such situations is that the time and energy required to involve children in physical activities is missing. Too often children are quick to imitate the adults in their lives in their pursuit of the "good life"— the "workaholic" ethic that leaves little time for family activities, leisure, and purposeful recreational pursuits. On the other hand, some children are part of a family in which the cares of the workday are left behind only to be replaced by a mind-dulling escape to television or other passive activities. This failure to stimulate, encourage, and motivate children to become actively involved in physical activity because of a lack of time, energy, interest, or personal example results in the failure of many children to develop their movement abilities.

Instruction

The quality of the instruction given to children is perhaps the most crucial factor influencing development of their movement skills. Opportunities for practice and encouragement alone will not bring about the development of skillful movement in most children. You, the teacher, are the necessary ingredient. Without you, many children will never develop mature fundamental movement skills or acquire related sport skills. The school physical education program, whether at the preschool or elementary school level, is the *only* place where children can be guaranteed to receive the encouragement, opportunities for practice, and quality instruction so vital to movement skill acquisition.

Ecological Setting

The **ecological setting** refers to the immediate environmental surroundings in which children are attempting to learn. It includes object props, such as the use of available facilities, equipment, and supplies, and behavior settings in terms of the number of students in the class and their ability to attend to the instructional cues that are provided by the instructor.

It is important to recognize that the ecological setting of the learning environment has a dramatic impact on movement skill learning. For example, ample numbers of balls are essential if we want children to be maximally active. It is not enough, however, simply to have the proper quantity. It is critically important to have a sufficient variety of balls in terms of varying sizes, shapes, colors, and textures if we are serious about helping children become skillful ball handlers. So, too, it is of critical importance that the class size be appropriate in terms of student numbers in order that all children can be given ample opportunities for practice, encouragement, and instruction by a knowledgeable, caring teacher—a teacher who is able to cope realistically with the number of students in the class. Take, for example, my daughter's sixth grade physical education class, in which there were 110 students and only one teacher. The ecological setting of that learning environment in terms of the teacher-to-student ratio made it essentially impossible for progress to be made in their ball-handling skills. Under these circumstances, the teacher was able to do little more than maintain a semblance of order, resulting in lots of sitting, waiting, and watching while a few students were active.

THE FUNDAMENTAL MOVEMENT SKILL PHASE*

The period ranging from about two to seven years of age is generally considered to be the **fundamental movement phase** of movement skill acquisition. This young age is the ideal time for children to master basic stability, locomotor, and manipulative skills. These movement skills may be viewed as developing along a continuum of stages within this phase, progressing from the initial to the elementary and finally to the mature stage (Figure 3.2). A wide variety of fundamental stability, locomotor, and manipulative skills are described and pictured in Chapters 16 through 18.

Initial Stage

At the **initial stage** of developing a fundamental skill, children make their first observable and purposeful attempts at performing the task. This stage is characterized by relatively crude, uncoordinated movements. The child may make valid attempts at throwing, catching, kicking, or jumping, but major components of the mature pattern are missing, and movements are either grossly exaggerated or inhibited. Rhythmically coordinated execution of the movement is also absent. Two- and three-year-olds typically function at the initial stage.

Elementary Stage

The **elementary stage** of fundamental movement skill development is typical of the performance of three- to five-year-old children. The elementary stage of development appears to depend primarily on maturation. In this transitional period between the initial and mature stages, coordination and rhythmical performance improve, and children gain greater control over their movements. However, movements at this stage still appear somewhat awkward and lacking in fluidity.

---

*The phases of motor development are classified as the Reflexive, Rudimentary, Fundamental, and Specialized Movement Phases (see Figure 3.2). The reflexive and rudimentary phases are characteristic of infancy and toddlerhood. They form critical building blocks for the fundamental and specialized phases of early childhood and beyond. For a detailed discussion of each of these phases see: D. L. Gallahue and J. C. Ozmun, *Understanding Motor Development* (Dubuque, IA: Wm. C. Brown & Benchmark, (1995).

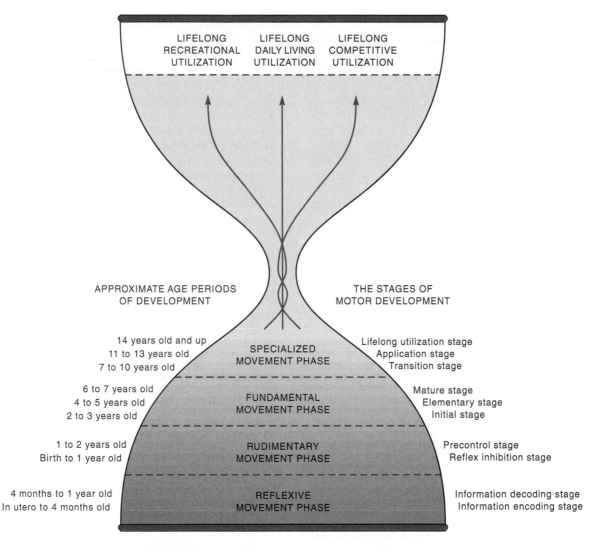

FIGURE 3.2 *A descriptive view of the phases and stages of motor development.*

Many adults are only at the elementary stage in such basic activities as throwing, striking, and catching. They have progressed to this stage primarily through maturation but, because of insufficient practice, encouragement, and instruction, they have failed to achieve the mature stage. The central core of the developmental physical education program for preschool and primary grade children should be focused on helping them progress from the elementary to the mature stage in a wide variety of fundamental movements.

Mature Stage

The **mature stage** of fundamental movement skill development is characterized by the integration of all the component parts of a pattern of movement into a well-coordinated, mechanically correct, and efficient act. From this stage, performance improves rapidly. For example, children are able to throw farther, run faster, and jump higher after the mature stage has been attained. A mature fundamental skill may be continually

An overhand throwing pattern at the initial stage.

refined, combined with other movement skills, and utilized in a variety of specialized movements.

The mature stage can be attained in most fundamental movements by age six or seven. Children frequently, however, reach this stage at varying rates. Some may be delayed, or they may fail to achieve the mature stage in certain skills. Others may be advanced and reach this stage more rapidly. If development is delayed over a period of years, certain skills may never be attained in their mature form without considerable effort and outside influence. Failure to develop mature patterns of fundamental movement will limit children in acquiring specialized sport skills in later childhood, adolescence, and adulthood. Mature fundamental movement skills form the basis for all sport skills, and they must be learned. Failure to do so will result in a cycle of frustration and failure.

CONCEPT 3.4
Movement skill development may be described as a series of age-related, but not age-dependent, phases which, in turn, are made up of identifiable stages of movement skill acquisition.

THE SPECIALIZED MOVEMENT SKILL PHASE

The **specialized movement phase** typically begins around age seven. Most children begin to develop a keen interest in sports. Boys and girls alike select their favorite sports heroes, don football jerseys and baseball caps, select their favorite running shoes, and frequently carry a basketball or a baseball glove to school. They are eager to learn new skills and apply them to a wide variety of sport activities. Efficient sports skill development is based on proper development of fundamental movement abilities. Although it begins in childhood, sport skill development frequently continues through adolescence and into adulthood. The specialized movement skill phase of development may be subdivided into three stages—transition, application, and lifelong utilization (Figure 3.2). A wide variety of sport-related movement skills are described and illustrated in Part IV, *The Skill Themes.*

Transition Stage *grade 2-5*

The **transition stage** of specialized movement skill development generally begins around age seven and extends to about age ten. Children at this stage usually express a high degree of interest in many sports but possess little actual ability in any. If they have not developed mature skills during the fundamental movement phase, they will be hampered in sport skill acquisition. This has been termed the **"proficiency barrier"** by Haubenstricker and Seefeldt (1986), and it presents a very real dilemma for the individual (child or adult) interested in learning sport skills but possessing insufficient fundamental movement skills to do so.

Children are eager to learn a variety of sports, and the physical education program should introduce sport skills and the basic elements of many sport-related activities, but only after the mature stage has been reached in corresponding fundamental movement skills. Children should be given opportunities during the transition stage to further refine specific fundamental movements and to use them as sport skills in a variety of skill drills and lead-up activities. For example, the fundamental movement skill of kicking may be applied to the sport skill of using the instep kick in soccer. This skill may be practiced in drill situations and then applied to a lead-up activity such as line soccer, circle soccer, or six-on-a-side soccer. At the transition stage children should not play the official sport as part of the instructional physical education program. Rather, they should be exposed to the basic skills, rules, and strategies of several sports through skill drills and a variety of lead-up activities.

Application Stage *grades 6-8*

The **application stage** is typified by the middle school or junior high school student, from about eleven to thirteen years of age. However, with the surge of participation throughout North America in youth sport programs, this stage may actually begin much earlier for many. Many children are applying their movement skills to organized sports participation as early as age six or even sooner. The key element at the application stage is that children have developed sufficient skill and knowledge of the game to apply the activity meaningfully to competitive or recreational settings.

Children at the application stage have begun to select types of sports that they prefer. Preferences are based primarily on previously successful experiences, body type, geographic location, and emotional, social, and cultural factors. Some may prefer individual sports, whereas others may prefer team sports. Some may enjoy contact sports, whereas others may prefer noncontact sports. Some may particularly enjoy water sports; others, court sports; and still others, dance activities. The narrowing of interests at this stage is accompanied by an increased desire for competence. Form, precision, accuracy, and standards of good performance are all especially important to the learner at the application stage. Therefore, more complex skills are practiced, and strategies and rules take on greater importance.

Lifelong Utilization Stage

The **lifelong utilization stage,** the final stage within the specialized movement phase, is based on previous sport and fundamental skill stages and continues throughout life. It is a period during which individuals select activities they particularly enjoy and pursue them throughout their lifetime for fun, fitness, and fulfillment. At this stage, high interest in specific activities is evidenced through active participation on a regular basis, whether on a competitive or recreational level.

TYPES OF MOVEMENT PERFORMANCE

Movement may be classified in a variety of ways. One popular classification scheme uses the terms *externally paced*, or *open motor skill,* for movement skill performance that is governed by the conditions of the immediate environment, and *internally paced*, or *closed motor skill,* for an environment that waits to be acted upon by the performer (Magill, 1993). These two terms serve as descriptors of both the nature of the movement and the intent of the activity itself. Movement may also be classified as *gross motor* or *fine motor,* and as either *discrete, serial,* or *continuous.* A brief discussion of each follows.

Externally Paced and Internally Paced Movement

Externally paced movement activities involve making responses to constantly changing and unpredictable environmental cues. An example would be bringing a soccer ball upfield or dribbling a basketball against a defensive player. As a result, rapidity and flexibility in decision making are required of the performer. The racquet sports and most aspects of the games of basketball, football, baseball, and soccer are externally paced. Both the physical education teacher and the coach need to recognize the nature of dynamic activities and provide opportunities that promote rapid decision making and adaptive behaviors in a variety of gamelike situations.

Internally paced movement activities require a fixed performance in a given set of environmental conditions. The performer is permitted the luxury of moving at his or her own pace through the activity and has time to recognize and respond to the static conditions of the environment. Internally paced activities generally emphasize accuracy, consistency, and repetition of performance. Bowling, golf, archery, and weight lifting are considered to be internally paced activities, as are swimming, basketball free throw shooting, and most track and field events. The teacher in these activities needs to provide ample opportunities for children to repeat the activity under environmental conditions that duplicate as nearly as possible the actual performance environment.

CONCEPT 3.5
Initial learning of a new movement skill, whether gross or fine, discrete, serial, or continuous, frequently occurs best under internally paced conditions.

Gross and Fine Movement

There is not a clear delineation between the terms *gross* and *fine,* but movements are often classified as one or the other. A **gross motor** movement involves movement of the large muscles of the body. Most sport skills are classified

For both internally and externally paced movement activities:

- Identify whether the activity is externally or internally paced.

- Establish a learning and practice environment consistent with the dynamic or static nature of the activity.

- Introduce dynamic activities under static conditions first (that is, control the environment and conditions of practice).

- Introduce situations that require responses to sudden and unpredictable cues in dynamic activities as the skill develops.

- Strive for greater consistency, duplication, and reduction of environmental cues for static activities as the skill develops.

- Encourage the learner to "think through" the activity in the early stages of learning.

- Encourage the learner to screen out unnecessary cues.

as gross motor in nature, with the exception perhaps of target shooting, archery, and a few others. **Fine motor** movements involve limited movements of parts of the body in the performance of precise movements. The manipulative movements of sewing, writing, and typing are generally thought of as fine motor movements.

Discrete, Serial, and Continuous Movement

On the basis of its temporal aspects, movement may also be classified as discrete, serial, or continuous. A **discrete movement** has a very definite beginning and ending. Throwing, jumping, kicking, and striking a ball are examples of discrete movements. **Serial movements** involve the performance of a single, discrete movement several times in rapid succession. Rhythmical hopping, basketball dribbling, and a soccer or volleyball volley are typical serial tasks. **Continuous movements** are movements that are repeated for a specified period of time. Running, swimming, and cycling are common continuous movements.

THE LEVELS OF MOVEMENT SKILL LEARNING

Fitts and Posner (1967), Adams (1971), and Gentile (1972) were the first to propose models for movement skill learning—whether at the fundamental or specialized phase, internally or externally paced, gross or fine, discrete, serial, or continuous—occurring in a hierarchical sequence of learning that may be classified into broad levels or stages. Since then considerable research has supported the concept that movement skill learning does occur in identifiable stages (Magill, 1993; Schmidt, 1991; Shea et al., 1993).

The terms used throughout this text to represent these levels are *beginning* (novice), *intermediate* (practice), and *advanced* (fine-tuning). Each level refers to a period during which both the learner and the teacher have specific, identifiable tasks and responsibilities. The three levels in learning a movement skill are briefly discussed in the following sections. Figure 3.3 illustrates how these three levels correspond with the phases and stages of motor development. Keep in mind that in the real world you will encounter students at differing levels of skill development both within and between skills.

CONCEPT 3.6
Characteristic levels of movement skill learning, independent of age, typify the learning of a new movement skill.

Beginning/Novice Level

The **beginning/novice level** is the first level in learning a movement skill. At this level the movements of the learner are generally uncoordinated and jerky. The learner begins to construct a mental plan of the activity and is actively trying to understand the skill. Because of the conscious attention that the learner gives to every detail of the task itself, performance is poor. The learner may experience fatigue early in the activity, which is caused more by the mental requirements of the task than by performing the task itself. At this level the learner tends to pay attention to all the information that is available but is unable to "screen out" what is irrelevant. The learner is attracted as much by what is *not* important as by what is. Teachers of students at the beginning level of learning a movement skill need to be aware of the conscious cognitive requirements of this level and

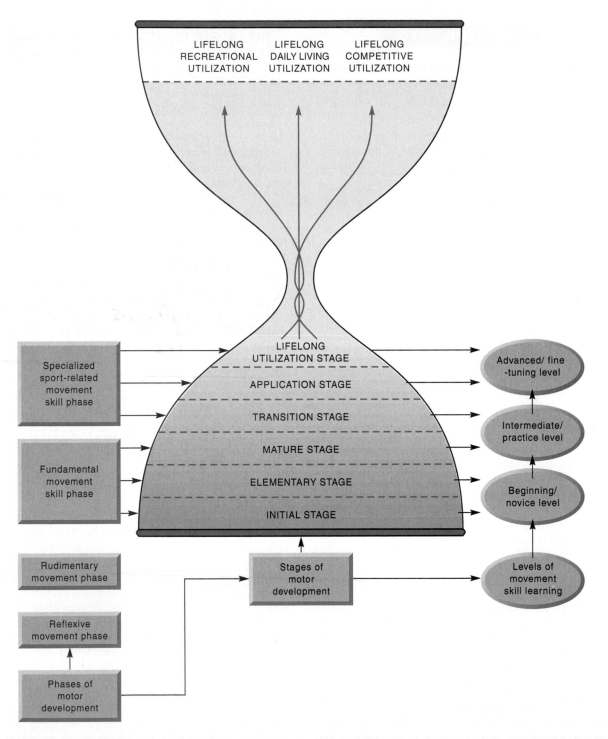

FIGURE 3.3 *The interrelationship between the phases and stages of motor development and the levels of movement skill learning.*

For learners at the *beginning/novice level* of learning a new movement skill:

- Introduce the major aspects of the skill only. Be brief.

- Provide for a demonstration of the skill to help the learner form a mental picture.

- Permit the learner to try out the skill.

- Provide plenty of opportunity for exploration of the skill itself and self-discovery of general principles of the skill.

- Recognize that the beginning/novice level is primarily a cognitive phase and that the learner needs only to understand the general idea.

- When possible, compare the new skill to similar skills that the learner may be familiar with.

- Provide immediate, precise, and positive feedback concerning the skill.

- Avoid situations that emphasize the product of one's performance during this phase. Focus, however, on the process.

Close attention to the task is characteristic of the beginning/novice level of learning a new skill.

understand that the instructional intent during this period should be only to provide the learner with a general idea of the skill or activity.

Intermediate/Practice Level

The **intermediate/practice level** of learning a new movement skill begins after the learner understands the skill in general and is able to perform it in a manner approximating the final skill. The learner at this level has a better understanding of the skill, and a mental plan for performing it becomes more fully developed. The skill at this level has utility and is practiced repeatedly. Conscious attention to the elements of the task diminishes. The learner begins to devote more attention to the goal or product of the skill than to the process itself. The poorly coordinated, jerky movements so evident at the beginning level gradually disappear. The learner gains a "feel" for the skill as kinesthetic sensitivity becomes more highly attuned. As a result, the learner relies less on verbal and visual cues and more on muscle sense.

Teachers at the intermediate level recognize that students understand the skill and set up practice sessions that generally focus on refining the skill and maximizing learner feedback.

Advanced/Fine-Tuning Level

The **advanced/fine-tuning level** is the third and final level in learning a movement skill. The learner at this level has a complete understanding of the skill. The mental plan for the skill is highly developed, and the learner pays very little attention to the cognitive aspects of the task. In fact, individuals at this level often have difficulty describing how they perform the activity. They often resort to a "let me show you" or a "do it like this" statement, followed by actual performance of the skill. The

For learners at the *intermediate/practice level* of learning a new movement skill:

- Provide numerous opportunities for practice and skill application.

- Provide opportunities for skill refinement in a supportive, nonthreatening environment.

- Devise practice situations that progressively focus on greater and greater skill refinement.

- Provide short, fast-paced practice sessions with frequent breaks prior to longer sessions with few breaks.

- Be able to analyze skills and provide constructive criticism.

- Structure practice sessions that focus on quality performance ("perfect practice makes perfect").

- Provide frequent, precise, immediate, and positive feedback.

- Allow for individual differences in the rate of skill learning.

- Focus attention on the whole skill whenever possible.

- Practice at the rate and in the manner that the skill will be used during "real-life" performance of the skill.

✳ *Practice is the key element of the intermediate level of learning a new movement skill.*

learner at this level is refining and fine-tuning skills. In activities where movement is the key element, it is smooth, fluid, and highly coordinated. In activities where the absence of movement is most highly valued, there is a general appearance of ease, mastery, and control. The performer is able to ignore irrelevant information and is not bothered by distractions. The learner has excellent timing and anticipation of movements and appears to act automatically, although in reality the skill is finely tuned and requires only minimum conscious control.

At the elementary school level there are generally few performers at the advanced level of learning a movement skill. However, with the increased tendency to specialize in sport skill development at an early age, this may change. Teachers of students at the advanced level should focus on further refining and maintaining the skill and on

providing selected feedback. Figure 3.4 illustrates the levels and stages of learning a new movement skill.

Each level in the process of learning a new movement skill requires concerned, knowledgeable, and sensitive guidance by the teacher. It is imperative that the teacher understand the characteristics of the learner at each level so that the physical education period may be effectively structured for maximum learning and performance. Acquiring a movement skill is a process that takes time, so providing organized, quality instructional sessions geared to the learner's skill level and developmental level is crucial to helping a child realize his or her full potential.

MOVEMENT SKILL HOMEWORK

Based on the just concluded discussion of the phases and stages of motor development and the levels of movement skill learning, it now becomes important to consider the

For learners at the *advanced/fine-tuning level* of learning a new movement skill:

- Structure practice sessions that promote intensity and enthusiasm.
- Be available to provide encouragement, motivation, and positive support.
- Offer suggestions and tips on strategy.
- Structure practice sessions that duplicate gamelike situations.
- Help the performer anticipate his or her actions in gamelike situations.
- Know the performer as an individual and be able to adjust methods to meet individual needs.
- Provide feedback that focuses on specific aspects of the skill.
- Avoid requiring the performer to think about detailed execution of the skill, which may result in overattention to the cognitive elements of the task (sometimes referred to as "analysis paralysis").

At the advanced or fine-tuning level of learning, a movement skill performance is "automatic," with little conscious attention given to the elements of the task.

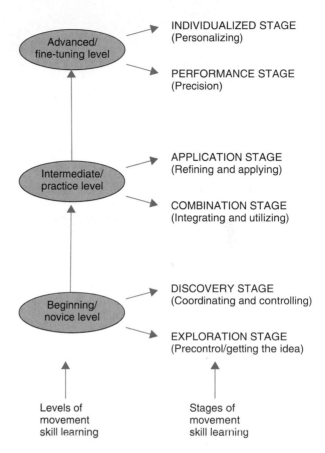

FIGURE 3.4 *Levels and stages of learning a new movement skill.*

curricular reality with which teachers are often faced. All too frequently teachers have too many students and too little time to maximize learning. **Movement skill homework** is a partial answer to this dilemma. If children are given tasks to work on at home, they can utilize the help of a parent or older sibling to practice the skills currently being stressed during the physical education period. To this end, the author, working with Fitness Finders Inc., has developed a series of homework packets called "Skill-A-Week" (1994). Skill-A-Week (see Figure 3.5) is designed to be implemented at home in ways that are easy, effective, and fun. Individual take-home sheets containing the initial, elementary, and mature stages for several fundamental movement skills are sent with children to encourage further activity for all children, or just for those needing additional help. Each take-home sheet

Take-Home Sheet

Your child is learning how to throw overhand in physical education. It is necessary to learn the mechanics of the overhand throw in order to properly catch or strike an object. All children can learn to throw correctly with proper instruction and practice. So, grab a ball and try one of the activities provided on the back of this sheet.

OVERHAND THROW

One-hand overhand throw as used in softball/baseball.

Stage 1
The child faces the target. The throw is more like a push than a throw.

Stage 2
The child moves the feet, but usually steps with the same side leg as the throwing arm.

Stage 3
The shoulders point toward the object. The elbow comes forward before the ball. The child steps forward with the leg opposite the throwing arm.

Note: Some stage 3 skills can be seen by age 7, but a child will *not* refine the movement without sufficient practice and time.

FIGURE 3.5 *Sample Skill-A-Week™ take-home sheet for movement skill homework (Fitness Finders Inc., Box 160, Spring Harbor, MI. 49283, 517–750–1500).*

Go and Throw

Proper throwing techniques develop with practice. Use the following suggestions to help your child develop good overhead throwing techniques.

Stand with one shoulder toward the target, the throwing arm reaching back.

Bring the elbow "behind" the head.

Say "left" when you step, "right" when you throw.

(Opposite for a left-handed throw.)

As you say "right," bring the elbow forward first.

Reach for the target.

Throwing for Fun Activities

Hoop It!
   Hang a tire or hoop in a place where throwing will be safe. Have your child try to throw a ball through the hoop. Once skills develop, swing the hoop slightly to increase the difficulty and skill.

No Catch
   Have your child try to throw the ball to you so you can catch it. However, do not require him/her to catch it when you return it. Simply roll it back so he/she can concentrate on throwing.

FIGURE 3.5 *(continued)*

On the 10th anniversary of becoming the NBA's all-time leading scorer, **Kareem Abdul-Jabbar** thinks about teaching basic skills to a new generation of basketball players. "If you had asked me three years ago, I'd have said, 'Forget it. Are you out of your mind?'" Abdul-Jabbar said.

"Now, it's not quite like that. There's a great need for people to teach the game. I don't think a lot of the young players, especially the front line players, are learning the fundamentals."

—from *USA Today*, 1994

provides visual and verbal information about the key elements of the particular skill. Teaching tips and suggested activities are also included. The information contained in Skill-A-Week is based on the information found in the fundamental Skill Theme chapters (Chapters 16–18) found later in this text. Currently, Skill-A-Week packets are available for the fundamental skills of running, leaping, horizontal jumping, overhand throwing, hopping, vertical jumping, jumping from a height, and sliding/galloping.

IMPLICATIONS FOR TEACHING DEVELOPMENTAL PHYSICAL EDUCATION

The knowledge that fundamental and sport skill development depends on environmental factors such as practice, encouragement, and quality instruction has vital implications for the physical education of children. For the vast majority of children, personalized, developmentally appropriate instruction is essential. Teachers must allow for sufficient time in practicing the skill and must use positive reinforcement techniques to continually encourage the learner.

CONCEPT 3.7
Teaching for movement skill acquisition requires adoption of strategies that recognize the interaction among the requirements of the learning task, the biology of the individual, and the conditions of the environment, in a manner that is both individually appropriate and age-group appropriate.

As stated earlier, the development of movement skills is age-related; it is not age-dependent. Skill acquisition is highly individualized because of the unique hered-

ity and experiences of each child. Therefore, it is inappropriate to classify movement activities solely by age or by grade level; such a procedure violates the principle of individual appropriateness. Physical education teachers should select movement experiences based on the ability level of children and on their phase of movement skill development and level of movement skill learning. The use of approximate ages for the phases of motor development and their corresponding stages provide only age-appropriate guidelines to the functioning of most children. Many children may be significantly ahead or behind this schedule.

Frequently there are differences in movement skill development within the same child. For example, it is entirely possible for an eight-year-old to be highly skilled and functioning at the application stage in swimming or gymnastics, two popular age-group sports, and still be only at the initial or elementary stage in fundamental manipulative skills such as throwing, catching, and running. Although we should continue to encourage accelerated behavior in one area, we should ensure that the individual develops at least an acceptable level of proficiency in all aspects of movement. The developmentally based physical education program provides for the balanced movement skill development of all children.

SUMMARY

This chapter dealt with the core of the developmental physical education program: movement skill acquisition. The term *movement skill* and its variations (*fundamental movement skill, specialized movement skill,* and *movement pattern*) were defined. The categories of movement were examined, and an effort was made to classify all movements as stability, locomotor, or manipulative in nature or to combine these categories into movement phrases. The importance of developing children's movement skills was also discussed, along with the environmental factors that significantly influence the acquisition of movement skill.

We described how the phases and stages of motor development relate to children's motor behavior. Remember that although these stages tend to be sequential, predictable, and age-related, they are neither age-dependent nor maturationally determined. In other words, environmental factors such as opportunities for practice, encouragement, quality instruction, and the ecological setting help determine the extent to which one's movement skills are developed. Care must be taken to view the child both individually and developmentally in the acquisition of movement skill. The learning of a new movement skill was described as occurring at predictable levels or stages, from the beginning or novice level, to the intermediate or practice level, and finally to the advanced or fine-tuning level. Remember, movement skill learning is age-independent. All of us—whether child, adolescent, or adult—progress through these levels when learning a new movement skill. By carefully attending to the motor development and movement skill learning of children, first as individuals (individual appropriateness) and only secondarily as a group (age-group appropriateness), teachers can better provide effective instruction. Failure to do so will negate the foundations of developmental physical education.

COMPLEMENTARY READINGS

Ainsworth, J., and C. Fox. (1989). Learning to learn: A cognitive processes approach to movement skill acquisition. *Strategies* 3:20–22.

Fitness Finders Inc. (1994). *Skill-A-Week.* Box 160, Spring Arbor, MI 49283 (517–750–1500).

Gallahue, D. L., and J. C. Ozmun. (1995). *Understanding Motor Development: Infants, Children, Adolescents, Adults.*

Dubuque, IA: Wm. C. Brown & Benchmark (Chapter 4, Motor development: A theoretical model).

Magill, R. A. (1993). *Motor Learning: Concepts and Applications.* Dubuque, IA: Wm. C. Brown (Chapter 1, Introduction to motor skills and motor learning research).

Milne, D. C., J. Hubenstricker, and V. D. Seefeldt. (1991). Remedial motor education: Some practical suggestions. *Strategies* 4:15–18.

Shea, C. H., W. L. Shebilske, and S. Worchel. (1993). *Motor Learning and Control.* Englewood Cliffs, NJ: Prentice-Hall.

Tjeerdsma, B. L. (1991). Imagery in elementary physical education. *Strategies* 4:25–28.

SUPPLEMENTARY READINGS

Adams, J. (1971). A closed-loop theory of motor learning. *Journal of Motor Behavior* 3:111–149.

Fitts, P. M., and M. I. Posner. (1967). *Human Performance.* Belmont, CA: Brooks-Cole.

Gentile, A. M. (1972). A working model of skill acquisition with application to teaching. *Quest*, Monograph XVII, 3–23.

Haubenstricker, J., and V. Seefeldt. (1986). Acquisition of motor skills during childhood. In *Physical Activity and Well-Being,* ed. V. Seefeldt, Reston, VA: AAHPERD.

Schmidt, R. A. (1991). *Motor Learning and Performance.* Champaign, IL: Human Kinetics.

VIDEOS

Introduction to Coaching Kids. 391 El Portal Road, San Mateo, CA: Distinctive Home Video Productions. (30 min.).

Learning to Be Active: First Lessons in Sports Participation. 200 N. Castlewood Dr., North Palm Beach, FL: The Athletic Institute. (43 min.).

Teaching Sport Skills to Young Athletes. 391 El Portal Road, San Mateo, CA: Distinctive Home Video Productions. (20 min.).

CHAPTER 4

Fitness Enhancement

Key Concept

A Primary Strand of the Developmental Physical Education Program Centers on Helping Children Become *Fit Movers, Informed Movers,* and *Eager Movers*

Chapter Objectives

The purpose of this chapter is to provide you with the tools to:
• Discuss the current status of children's fitness.
• Provide a concise but specific definition of the term *physical fitness.*
• Distinguish between the terms *health-related fitness* and *performance-related fitness,* identify the components of each and how they are measured.
• Debate the pros and cons of including body composition as an aspect of physical fitness.
• List and describe the basic principles of fitness development and illustrate how each may be applied in a physical education setting.
• Discuss the concepts of fitness homework and fitness breaks and illustrate how they may be successfully implemented.
• List several useful techniques for motivating children to be active movers.

Terms to Remember

Physical Fitness
Fit Movers
Health-Related Fitness
Performance-Related
    Fitness
Muscular Strength
Isotonic Strength
Isokinetic Strength
Isometric Strength
Muscular Endurance
Relative Endurance
Dynamic Endurance
Static Endurance
Cardiovascular
    Endurance

Aerobic Exercise
Anaerobic Exercise
Joint Flexibility
Body Composition
Proprioceptors
Balance
Static Balance
Dynamic Balance
Coordination
Agility
Speed
Reaction Time
Movement Time
Power
Informed Movers

Principle of Overload
Principle of Specificity
Principle of Progression
Threshold of Training
Target Zone
FITT Principle
Hypertrophy
Atrophy
Principle of
    Individuality
Fitness Homework
Fitness Training
Fitness Education
Eager Movers
Fitness Breaks

That physical fitness is a topic of continuing interest throughout the world is evidenced by the considerable coverage of the fitness status of children and youth in professional and lay literature. Studies comparing the physical fitness of youth over the past thirty years reveal that American boys and girls are less fit than their counterparts of ten, twenty, or even thirty years ago. Although the validity of these studies in terms of the generalizations made from them has been challenged by some people, it is clear that much needs to be done to improve youth fitness and to heighten public awareness of its vital role in children's total development. The popular belief that children get plenty of regular, vigorous physical activity as a normal part of their everyday routine is no more than a myth for millions of youngsters. Although many adults have a heightened awareness of the benefits of vigorous physical activity, only a limited awareness of this need has trickled down to children. This disgraceful situation can be eliminated if we make the improvement of youth fitness a national priority.

This chapter examines the challenge of helping children become *fit movers, informed movers,* and *eager movers.* We will define the term *physical fitness* and discuss the importance of fitness development in children, the factors that influence the level of fitness, fitness homework, and how to motivate children to become active. A section on implications for developmental physical education concludes the chapter.

THE CHALLENGE

Much of the news about children's fitness is not encouraging. Results of the National Children and Youth Fitness Study (Ross and Gilbert, 1985; Ross and Pate, 1987) reveal that over one-third of the children tested were insufficiently active in their daily lives to derive aerobic benefits. The same study and a ten-year study of the AAU Physical Fitness test data (Updyke, 1994) reports that children are fatter and heavier than their counterparts of twenty or even just ten years ago.

Despite these gloomy reports, however, there is hope for the future. Several experts argue that today's children and youth are no less fit now than in previous years (Corbin and Pangrazi, 1992). Pangrazi and Corbin (1993, p.14) noted that: "Over the last 40 years, the media have reinforced the idea that our children are unfit. *Are* American children and youth unfit? Recent research suggests that they are more fit than previously reported." Clearly there is a need for better data before comparisons can be made (Blair, 1992). As parents become more concerned about healthful living and begin to improve their personal level of physical fitness, they tend to become more concerned about the fitness levels of their children. Additionally, considerable public attention is being drawn to children's fitness levels. Consequently, there has been considerable grassroots action in local communities across North America that has had a positive impact on raising fitness levels. Moreover, a concerted effort is underway by the American Alliance for Health, Physical Education, Recreation and Dance (AAHPERD), the National Association for Sport and Physical Education (NASPE), and the President's Council on Physical Fitness and Sports to achieve the important goals of improving children and youth fitness levels and providing quality daily physical education. This may well be our last best chance to truly make fitness and quality physical education a reality for all. In fact, the U.S. Department of Health and Human Services (1990) has declared physical activity and fitness as the first of twenty-two priority public health goals for the nation to achieve by the year 2000. Two of the twelve objectives of these goals deal specifically with school physical education programs (see chapter 1, page 5):

Furthermore, too many Americans are seriously overweight and out-of-shape. According to recent federal government statistics:

- An estimated 33 percent of Americans were overweight in 1991—up from 25 percent in 1980.
- Today, 32.1 percent of white females, 48.5 percent of African-American females, 47.2 percent of Hispanic females, and 32 percent of men of all races were overweight.
- Childhood obesity has increased dramatically in the past two decades, with 21 percent of all 12 to 19-year-olds (one in five teenagers) now overweight (C. Everett Koop Foundation, 1994).

CONCEPT 4.1
Adoption of long-term healthy lifestyle behaviors is the primary goal of the fitness portion of the developmental physical education program.

We need to be realistic, however, in the attempt to implement these objectives. Koslow (1988) noted that in order to achieve the health-related objectives of enhancing aerobic endurance, muscular strength and endurance, and joint flexibility, 150 to 200 minutes of activity time would be required per week. Unfortunately, few North American elementary schools have that amount of time

"Perhaps we should rethink the fitness objective for physical education. Obviously the limitation in instructional time is a factor for consideration. Of greater importance is the question, 'What are we trying to accomplish with the fitness objective?' The primary objective is to equip children and youth with knowledge, attitudes, and skills for making healthy lifestyle choices—not only as children, but also as adults. . . . The most important fitness objective for physical education is to help students establish consistent exercise behavior patterns that will be maintained into adulthood."

available to achieve fitness objectives, let alone the important skill objectives of physical education. It is time to critically reexamine what it is that we are trying to achieve in meeting the fitness objectives of physical education. Blair and Meredith (1994, p.17) say it best:

By becoming knowledgeable movers and eager movers, as well as fit movers, we are helping children establish the important basis for healthy lifestyle choices and for being active movers as adolescents and adults. Fitness is an important objective of the developmentally based physical education curriculum. It is a strand throughout the entire curriculum, not just a unit or single theme. It is a thread present in all that is done in the developmental movement program. Fitness is enhanced through vigorous active participation in games and sports, dance and rhythmic activities, and gymnastics and self-testing activities.

FIT MOVERS DEFINED

A generic definition of physical fitness was provided in Chapter 1. More specifically, **physical fitness** is further defined as a positive state of well-being influenced by regular vigorous physical activity, genetic makeup, and nutritional adequacy. The health status of the individual suggests the upper and lower limits of physical fitness that can be reasonably expected. One's nutritional status can greatly inhibit or enhance the level of physical functioning, and one's genetic structure limits the level of fitness that can be attained. All three factors should be considered in the development and maintenance of children's fitness. **Fit movers** enhance their physical fitness in two broad areas: health-related fitness and performance-related fitness.

CONCEPT 4.2
Physical fitness is a positive state of well-being influenced by regular vigorous physical activity, genetic makeup, and nutritional adequacy.

Health-Related Fitness

Health-related fitness is a relative state of being, not an ability, skill, or capacity. Health-related fitness is transient, genetically interdependent, and not directly related to athletic skill. The development and maintenance of health-related fitness is a function of physiological adaptation to increased overload. Therefore, it can be readily altered with use or disuse. Children who are fit movers strive for, obtain, and maintain personal standards of health-related fitness that are optimal for their individual levels of development.

Performance-Related Fitness

Performance-related fitness is genetically dependent in terms of absolute potential, relatively stable, and closely related to athletic skill. The development and maintenance of performance-related fitness is a function of practice and skill development within broadly defined genetic limits. Children who are fit movers strive for, achieve, and maintain personal standards of performance-related fitness that are appropriate to their individual levels of development.

HEALTH-RELATED COMPONENTS OF FITNESS

Muscular strength, muscular endurance, cardiovascular endurance, and joint flexibility are the universally accepted health-related components of physical fitness. Body composition is also considered by many to be an aspect of health-related fitness. Important information about both the health-related and performance-related components of physical fitness is summarized in Tables 4.1 and 4.2, respectively, and is discussed further in the following paragraphs.

TEACHING TIPS

The following list includes national organizations that promote fitness enhancement.

Federal Resources:

- **National Diabetes Information Clearinghouse;** Box NDIC, Bethesda, MD 20892. Collects and distributes information about diabetes and patient education materials, including sports and exercise. Also provides consumer publications on exercise.

- **National Diffusion Network;** Department of Education, 555 New Jersey Avenue NW., Room 510, Washington D.C. 20208–1525. Makes programs available and provides funds for exemplary educational programs for adoption by schools, colleges, and other institutions. A number of programs are health-related.

- **National Heart, Lung, and Blood Institute; Education Programs Information Center;** 4733 Bethesda Avenue, Suite 530, Bethesda, MD 20814. Services include dissemination of public education materials, information for health professionals, materials on work site health, and response to specific information requests. Distributes consumer materials on a variety of topics, including exercise and the heart.

- **Office of Minority Health Resource Center;** P.O. Box 37337, Washington, D.C. 20013. Responds to inquiries about major health problems among minority populations, including physical activity.

- **U.S. Department of Health and Human Services; Office of Disease Prevention and Health Promotion (ODPHP);** P.O. Box 1133, Washington, D.C. 20013–1133. Copies of the "Health Objectives of the Nation—Year 2000" and articles and pamphlets promoting health and physical activity are available through this office.

Private Resources

- **American Alliance for Health, Physical Education, Recreation and Dance (AAHPERD);** 1900 Association Drive, Reston, VA 22091. AAHPERD through its six affiliated associations has developed programs in several areas, including fitness for children, youth, and adults. Exercise programs for the elderly and persons with special needs are also available. NASPE promotes daily quality physical education and quality sport experiences for children and youth. Materials are available.

- **American College of Sports Medicine (ACSM);** P.O. Box 1440, Indianapolis, IN 46206. Publishes a variety of materials, including position statements on the use of anabolic steroids, prepubescent strength training, fitness, and quality physical education experiences.

- **American Heart Association;** 7320 Greenville Avenue, Dallas, TX 75231–4599. Distributes a full range of educational materials, both print and audiovisual, addressing all aspects of cardiovascular health, including physical activity and exercise. Promotes the popular Jump Rope For Heart Program. A master catalog of materials is available through local chapters or affiliates.

- **National Fitness Leaders Association (NFLA);** 7929 Westpark Drive, Suite 200, McLean, VA 22102. The NFLA is composed of previous winners—the alumni—of the Healthy American Fitness Leaders Award. Promotes fitness and health in America. Materials available.

- **National Handicapped Sports and Recreation Association;** 1145 19th Street NW, Suite 717, Washington, D.C. 20208. Provides sports and recreational activities for persons with orthopedic, spinal cord, neuromuscular, and visual challenges through 56 community-based chapters.

- **National Recreation and Park Association;** 3101 Park Center Drive, Alexandria, VA 22302. Strives to increase public awareness of the role of physical fitness in health, encourages recreation, and establishes standards for recreation services. Materials available for a fee.

- **YMCA of the USA;** National Director, Health and Physical Education, 101 North Wacker Drive, Chicago, IL 60606. YMCA physical fitness and health programs include fitness training, conditioning, and group fitness programs for all ages. A variety of brochures are available from over 2,000 local YMCAs. Materials available for a fee.

TABLE 4.1

Common Measures of Children's Health-Related Fitness and a Synthesis of Findings

Health-Related Fitness Components	Common Tests	Specific Aspect Measured	Synthesis of Findings
Cardiovascular endurance	Step test	Physical work capacity	VO_2 max estimates are tenuous with young children. Children can achieve maximum VO_2 values similar to adults when corrected for body weight. Maximal heart rates decrease with age. Trend for improved VO_2 max values in both boys and girls with age. Girls level off after age 12 or so. Boys continue to improve.
	Distance run	Aerobic endurance	
	Treadmill stress test	Max VO_2	
	Bicycle ergometer	Max VO_2	
Muscular strength	Hand dynamometer	Isometric grip strength	Annual increase for boys from age 7 on. Girls tend to level off after age 12. Boys slow prior to puberty, then gain rapidly throughout adolescence. Boys superior to girls at all ages.
	Back and leg dynamometer	Isometric back and leg strength	
	Cable tensiometer	Isometric joint strength	
Muscular endurance	Push-ups	Isotonic upper body endurance	Similar abilities throughout childhood, slightly in favor of boys on most items. Lull in performance prior to age 12. Large increases in boys from 12 to 16, then a leveling off. Girls show no significant increases without special training after age 12.
	Sit-ups	Isotonic abdominal endurance	
	Flexed arm hang	Isometric upper body endurance	
	Pull-ups	Isotonic upper body endurance	
Flexibility	Bend and reach	Hip joint flexibility	Flexibility is joint specific. Girls tend to be more flexible than boys at all ages. Flexibility decreases with reduced activity levels.
	Sit and reach	Hip joint flexibility	
Body composition	Hydrostatic weighing	Percent body fat	Children at all ages have higher percentages of fat then their age-mates of 20 years ago. Active children are leaner than obese children at all ages. Obese children are less active than non-obese children
	Skinfold calipers	Estimate of percent body fat	
	Body mass index	Estimate of percent body fat	
	Electrical impedance	Estimate of percent body fat	

Source: David L. Gallahue and J. C. Ozmun, *Understanding Motor Development* (Dubuque, IA: Wm. C. Brown & Benchmark, 1995).

TABLE 4.2

Common Measures of Children's Performance-Related Fitness and a Synthesis of Findings

Motor Fitness Component	Common Tests	Specific Aspect Measured	Synthesis of Findings
Coordination	Cable jump	Gross body coordination	Year by year improvement with age in gross body coordination. Boys superior from age 6 on in eye-hand and eye-foot coordination.
	Hopping for accuracy	Gross body coordination	
	Skipping	Gross body coordination	
	Ball dribble	Eye-hand coordination	
	Foot dribble	Eye-foot coordination	
Balance	Beam walk	Dynamic balance	Year by year improvement with age. Girls often outperform boys, especially in dynamic balance activities until about age 8. Abilities similar thereafter.
	Stick balance	Static balance	
	One-foot stand	Static balance	
Speed	20-yard dash	Running speed	Year by year improvement with age. Boys and girls similar until age 6 or 7, at which time boys make more rapid improvements. Boys superior to girls at all ages.
	30-yard dash	Running speed	
Agility	Shuttle run	Running agility	Year by year improvement with age. Girls begin to level off after age 13. Boys continue to make improvements.
	Side straddle	Lateral agility	
Power	Vertical jump	Leg strength and speed	Year by year improvement with age. Boys outperform girls at all age levels.
	Standing long jump	Leg strength and speed	
	Distance throw	Upper arm strength and speed	
	Velocity throw	Upper arm strength and speed	

Source: David L. Gallahue and J. C. Ozmun, *Understanding Motor Development* (Dubuque, IA: Wm. C. Brown & Benchmark, 1995).

Muscular Strength

Muscular strength may be defined as the ability of the body to exert a maximum force against an object external to the body. In its purest sense, it is the ability to exert one maximum effort. Children engaged in daily active play do much to enhance their leg strength by running and bicycling. Their arm strength is developed through such activities as lifting and carrying large objects, handling tools, and swinging on monkey bars.

Children need ample opportunity to increase strength in the upper arms and shoulder girdle.

Muscular strength may be increased through isotonic, isokinetic, and isometric means. **Isotonic strength** is the ability of a muscle or group of muscles to perform a maximal or near-maximal effort once or for a limited number of repetitions, in which the muscles alternately shorten and lengthen. Free weights, pulley weights, sit-ups, and push-ups are commonly used to increase isotonic strength.

Isokinetic strength is the same as isotonic strength in that the muscles alternately shorten and lengthen, but they are also required to accommodate to variable resistance throughout the process. In isokenetic strength activities the resistance is equal to the force applied throughout the range of motion. Variable resistance devices and Nautilus-type machines are commonly used to increase isokinetic strength.

Isometric strength is the ability of a muscle group to maintain a contracted state over a period of several seconds. A flexed arm hang or static push-up where the arms are flexed to a ninety degree angle and the body weight supported for eight to twelve seconds is an example of an isometric strength-building activity. Isometric activities do not require special equipment but are generally viewed as less effective than either isotonic or isokinetic strength activities.

Muscular Endurance

Muscular endurance is the ability to exert force against an object external to the body for several repetitions. Muscular endurance is similar to muscular strength in terms of

the activities performed but differs in emphasis. Strength-building activities require overloading the muscle or group of muscles to a greater extent than endurance activities. Endurance-building activities require less overload on the muscles but require a greater number of repetitions. Boys and girls performing several sit-ups, pull-ups, or push-ups are performing muscular endurance activities.

When we speak of relative strength or **relative endurance,** we are referring to the child's fitness level adjusted for his or her body weight. It stands to reason that an adult's gross level of fitness is greater than that of a child, but when one's body weight is divided into the total fitness score, the differences are much less pronounced.

Muscular endurance may be viewed as both a dynamic and a static phenomenon. **Dynamic endurance** is the muscle's ability to flex and extend repeatedly and is increased through progressive resistance training. This training should use light to moderate resistance with a moderate to high number of repetitions. On the other hand, **static endurance** is the muscle's ability to stay flexed for a long period of time and is increased through progressive resistance training using light to moderate resistance also. However, the length of time this contracted muscle state is maintained is more crucial than the number of repetitions.

CONCEPT 4.3
Health-related fitness is multifaceted, is influenced by a variety of factors, and is able to be improved through vigorous physical activity.

Cardiovascular Endurance

Cardiovascular endurance is specific to the heart, lungs, and vascular system. It is generally considered to be the single most important aspect of fitness. Cardiovascular endurance refers to the ability to perform numerous repetitions of an activity requiring considerable use of the circulatory and respiratory systems. It is difficult to measure accurately the volume of oxygen used in aerobic activities with children without using sophisticated scientific equipment and causing considerable stress to the child. We do know, however, that children are generally not as active as they need to be to develop good cardiovascular endurance. Cardiovascular endurance is dependent, in large part, on the lifestyle of the individual child. The keys to developing cardiovascular endurance are frequency, duration, and intensity. The greater the frequency, the longer the duration, the more intense the

Swimming is an excellent aerobic endurance activity.

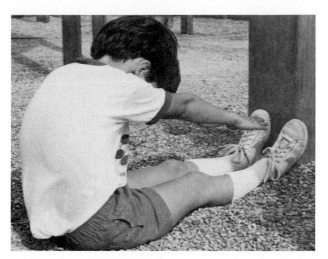

Static stretching of the lower back and hamstring muscles.

workout, the greater the impact will be on improving cardiovascular endurance. Activities such as running, pedaling a bicycle, and swimming are all aerobic in nature and should be a part of children's daily life.

Cardiovascular endurance may be improved by performing aerobic and anaerobic exercise. **Aerobic exercise** involves participation in vigorous physical activities in which the heart rate is elevated above a threshold level (approximately 140 to 180 beats per minute) and maintained at that level for an extended period of time (approximately fifteen minutes or more). Distance running, cycling, and swimming are all aerobic in nature. **Anaerobic exercise,** on the other hand, is high-intensity exercise of short duration that does not depend on the body's ability to supply oxygen. Sprint events in track and swimming are typical anaerobic activities. Children need to be involved in both aerobic and anaerobic exercise. Both contribute measurably to a healthy heart, lungs, and vascular system.

Joint Flexibility

Joint flexibility, another aspect of health-related fitness, is the ability of the various joints of the body to move through their full range of motion. Flexibility is joint-specific and can be improved with practice. Most children are involved in numerous flexibility developing activities. Their constant bending, twisting, turning, and stretching, along with the natural elasticity of their bodies, account for much of their flexibility. One needs only to look at the contorted positions that children sit in while watching television or listening to a story to realize that they have a good deal of flexibility in the hip and knee joint. All too often, however, the range of motion diminishes in later childhood and adolescence because of lack of activity.

Body Composition

Body composition is defined as the proportion of lean body mass to fat body mass. It is one's relative fatness or leanness adjusted for height. Although not universally agreed upon as a component of health-related fitness, body composition is viewed by many as an important aspect of physical fitness. Basically, those who oppose the inclusion of body composition as a measure assert that fitness is for *every body*—the slim and lean as well as the overweight and obese (Updyke, 1994). Furthermore, they claim that one's body type largely depends on heredity and, as a result, is very difficult to alter to any great extent. Moreover, there are problems in assessing body composition, which require using fat assessment techniques that are frequently unreliable, embarrassing, and socially objectionable to some.

On the other hand, proponents of body composition as a component of health-related fitness point out that it is an important aspect of overall health and fitness. They argue that being *overfat* is the issue, not being *overweight,* as determined by traditional height-weight tables.

CONCEPT 4.4
Reliable field assessment of body composition is not only difficult but questioned by some as being a valid component of physical fitness.

Furthermore, they assert that obesity is at epidemic levels among children and youth and is measurably greater today than twenty or even ten years ago. Moreover, they make the telling point that obesity contributes to degenerative diseases, health problems, and reduced longevity. For these reasons they advocate the inclusion of body composition as a component of health-related fitness (Ross and Gilbert, 1985; Ross and Pate, 1987).

Both sides of the issue present interesting arguments. Popular fitness tests include or exclude body composition as a health-related fitness component depending on the philosophy of the developer of the test. Your selection and use of one test over another will be determined by your position on this issue. The decision is yours.

PERFORMANCE-RELATED COMPONENTS OF FITNESS

Performance-related fitness is an aspect of physical fitness related to the quality of one's movement skill. The performance-related components of physical fitness are generally considered to be balance, coordination, agility, speed of movement, and power. Children who display skill in several activities such as bicycling, swimming, throwing, catching, and climbing are said to have good skill-related fitness. The performance-related components are emphasized with children in this order because of their developmental basis. In other words, emphasis is placed first on enhancing children's balance skills, followed by promoting coordination and agility activities. Activities that promote speed and power are the last to be emphasized in the developmentally based physical education program. It is important to emphasize that movement control (balance, coordination, and agility) should be developed prior to force production (speed, power).

CONCEPT 4.5
The components of performance-related fitness are closely related to movement skill and its qualitative aspects.

Balance

Balance is a complex part of one's motor fitness, which is influenced by vision, the inner ear, the cerebellum, the **proprioceptors** (nerve endings) in muscles, joints, and tendons, and the skeletal muscles. **Balance** is the ability to maintain one's equilibrium in relation to the force of gravity and to make minute alterations in one's body position when it is placed in various positions. Balance may be subdivided into static and dynamic balance. **Static balance** is the ability to maintain one's equilibrium in a fixed position, such as when standing on one foot or on a balance board. **Dynamic balance** is the ability to maintain one's equilibrium while the body is in motion, such as when walking on a balance beam or bouncing on a trampoline. In actuality, all movement involves an element of either static or dynamic balance, because balance is a basic aspect of all movement. As such, it is important for children to begin developing their balancing abilities at an early age.

Coordination

Coordination is the ability to integrate separate motor systems with varying sensory modalities into efficient movement. The harmonious working together of the synchrony, rhythm, and sequencing aspects of one's movements is crucial to coordinated movement. Various parts of the body may be involved, such as eye-foot coordination, as in kicking a ball or walking upstairs. Eye-hand coordination is evident in fine motor activities such as bead stringing, tracing, and clay modeling or in gross motor activities such as catching, striking, or volleying a ball.

Agility

Agility is the ability to change direction of the entire body quickly while moving from one point to another. This ability may be enhanced in children through participation in chasing and fleeing games and through certain dodging activities. Working through mazes and obstacle courses also aids agility development.

Speed of Movement

Speed is the ability to move from one point to another in the shortest time possible. It is influenced by one's **reaction time** (the amount of time elapsed from the signal *go* to the first movement of the body) and **movement time** (the time elapsed from the initial movement to completion of the activity). Reaction time is generally considered to be

Training for increased speed.

Speed, agility, and coordination combined.

innate, but movement time may be improved with practice. Children's speed of movement may be seen in activities such as running, climbing, and playing tag. Speed of movement may be improved by providing ample opportunities for practice and open spaces in which to run and play.

Power

Power, the ability to perform one maximum effort in as short a period as possible, is sometimes referred to as *explosive strength* and represents the product of strength times speed. This combination of strength and speed is exhibited by children when jumping, striking, or throwing for distance. The speed of contraction of the muscles involved, as well as the strength and coordinated use of these muscles, determines the degree of power.

INFORMED MOVERS DEFINED

Children need to be **informed movers** when it comes to knowing about and being able to apply fitness concepts to their own lives (Petray, 1994). Vigorous physical activity is important in childhood because exercise enhances the components of physical fitness. As a result, exercise stimulates bone growth, develops lung capacity, aids in

blood circulation, lowers blood pressure, and reduces cholesterol levels. Physical fitness also contributes to a heightened self-concept, improved body image, a sense of personal accomplishment, and self-discipline. It may further contribute indirectly to academic achievement; children are more alert and tend to pay more attention to their classwork when they are physically fit. Furthermore, physical fitness helps children prepare for physical and emotional emergencies and aids in weight control.

Independent Exercisers

Children who are informed movers have the essential fitness knowledge and concepts to become independent exercisers. Although daily physical education and daily fitness breaks are a goal to strive for, the reality is that most North American children have an average of only two physical education lessons per week. Based on what we know about principles of fitness training (refer to the FITT principle discussed in the following section), it is essentially impossible to make real fitness gains in such a limited amount of time. Therefore, it is important to adopt a philosophy of educating children in terms of physical fitness, rather than simply training them. As they become educated into the knowledge and value outcomes of physical fitness children then have the tools to become independent and motivated exercisers.

One way of helping children become independent exercisers is through the use of activity calendars. Activity records are distributed to parents by letter, or a handout at a school-wide fitness fair. Explanations of requirements for various grade and developmental levels are provided. Personal activity records are posted on the refrigerator at home. Students, with parental assistance, maintain a log of their vigorous activities for the month. At the end of each month the activity records are submitted to the physical education teacher. Certificates of participation or other appropriate means of positive reinforcement may be given at the end of each semester.

Nutritious Eaters

Obesity and weight problems in children should concern parents and teachers. Because inactivity is a more relevant factor than overeating in childhood obesity, physical activity plays an important role in controlling weight. An obese child has less energy for vigorous activity and leads a more sedentary life. Although the total number of calories consumed by obese children may be no more (and may be even less) than that eaten by non-obese children, they actually gain weight because of their low level of physical activity. Children who are informed movers are also nutritious eaters. They have the knowledge concepts embodied in the Food Pyramid and are able to translate this knowledge into action in their daily life eating habits.

Nutrition records are an excellent means of helping children become more aware of the foods that they consume. Like activity records, daily food records may be sent home and with parent assistance serve as a valuable means for educating both children and adults on the essentials of healthful eating.

PRINCIPLES OF FITNESS DEVELOPMENT

Certain basic principles play a major role in the improvement and maintenance of physical fitness. The following factors should be taken into consideration when determining the type of fitness program to establish and the amount of activity for children to perform.

CONCEPT 4.6
Specific training principles play a crucial role in the development and maintenance of physical fitness.

Overload

The **principle of overload** is the basis for fitness enhancement. To increase fitness, a person must perform more work than he or she is generally accustomed to doing. This may be accomplished by either increasing the amount of work done or by reducing the period of time in which the same amount of work is accomplished. An overload of the specific system enhances one's level of fitness. The amount of overload must be progressively increased to promote continual fitness improvement.

Doing one's usual amount of physical activity will maintain a certain level of fitness. However, only when muscles are overloaded will strength, endurance (both muscular and cardiovascular), and joint flexibility be increased.

Specificity

The **principle of specificity** deals with improvement in the various aspects of fitness that are specific to the type of training engaged in and to the muscles being exercised. Overload must be specific for the particular fitness component and muscle group being exercised. Even though the components of fitness and the systems of the body are related, specific types of training develop specific qualities of fitness and produce greater amounts of change in the parts exercised. Strength activities, for example, will not have much influence on improving muscular or cardiovascular endurance. Coordination is not markedly improved through performance of push-ups, and the shoulder-girdle muscles are not measurably strengthened by running or playing a game of soccer. Because of the needs of the total child, the fitness training program should contain several types of exercises.

Progression

The **principle of progression** is based on the concept that overload of a specific muscle group must be increased systematically over time. Too often children and some adults believe that they can begin to enhance their fitness at levels that far exceed their present capability. Progression is tied to concepts commonly known as the threshold of training and target zone.

The **threshold of training** is the minimum amount of exercise required to produce fitness gains. Those new to a fitness training program can begin at or near the threshold level and gradually increase their activity in frequency, intensity, and time (FIT). The goal, therefore, is to increase gradually these three components until the target zone is reached. The **target zone** is the point at

Children need to understand and appreciate the benefits of regular vigorous physical activity if we are serious about them becoming both informed movers and eager movers:

Increased Muscular Strength and Endurance

- Stimulates bone growth
- Increases bone mineralization
- Reduces susceptibility to injury
- Enhances self-concept
- Improves body image
- Enhances physical appearance

Improved Levels of Cardiovascular Endurance

- Improves lung capacity
- Strengthens the heart muscle
- Improves circulation
- Reduces cholesterol levels (LDL)
- Lowers heart rate
- Increases oxygen carrying capacity (VO$_2$ max)
- Aids in stress reduction and promotes relaxation
- May reduce susceptibility to the common cold

Greater Joint Flexibility

- Helps prevent injury
- Increases work/play efficiency
- Improves motor performance
- Increases range of motion
- Promotes fluidity of movement

Individually Optimum Body Composition

- Improves circulatory efficiency
- Reduces respiratory distress
- Reduces susceptibility to some diseases
- Enhances self-concept

Improved Performance-Related Fitness

- Improves game, sport, and dance performance
- Aids in weight control
- Provides the tools for enhancing health-related fitness
- Helps reduce number of injuries
- Encourages regular, active participation

---

which maximum benefits are obtained for one's individual level of fitness. Clearly, following the principle of progression is essential if real gains are to be made in fitness levels.

Frequency/Intensity/Timing/Type(FITT)

The **FITT principle** of frequency, intensity, timing (duration), and type of exercise is closely associated with overload, specificity, and progression principles. The frequent use of a body part in vigorous physical activities will either improve its efficiency (above threshold) or help it remain at about the same state. Failure to use the body part will diminish its efficiency. Muscles that are used regularly will **hypertrophy,** or increase in size, and muscle tone will be improved, whereas muscles that are not used regularly will **atrophy,** or decrease in size and tone. Exercise must be regular to be effective. Most

experts agree that a minimum of three days and a maximum of six days per week is required for improvement.

Exercise intensity means that physical exertion must be beyond that required for daily living to produce fitness gains. The specific muscle or system must be overloaded above the threshold level and progressively approach the target zone.

Exercise time must be of sufficient duration to be effective. As a rule of thumb, a minimum of fifteen minutes is required. Remember, however, that both the threshold of training and one's target zone increase as improved levels of fitness are attained. Conversely, as fitness levels decline, the training threshold and target zone decrease.

Exercise type refers to the fact that in order to get the benefits of vigorous physical activity exercise may take many forms. Exercise type covers a full range of activities focusing on enhancing one or more of the various components of fitness in a variety of play, game, and sport activities, as well as in traditional exercise settings such as calisthenics and jogging. Careful consideration of exercise type is vitally important when working with children. Most children are not sufficiently self-motivated to voluntarily take part in calisthenic exercises or to run a mile on a regular basis. Turn the activity into a game, however, and it becomes much easier to motivate them to become active participants.

Individuality

The **principle of individuality** means that each person improves in level of fitness at his or her own rate. Several factors such as age, body type, nutritional status, body weight, health status, and level of motivation determine one's individual level of fitness. No criteria exist for individual rates of trainability, and each child responds in a manner peculiar to his or her own particular environmental circumstances and hereditary characteristics. Therefore, overreliance on normative standards of fitness and comparing children with one another are not advised. Remember that one of the primary goals of the fitness strand is to enhance fitness behaviors and to help children become eager movers, that is, to motivate children to be physically active and achieve personal standards of fitness.

FITNESS HOMEWORK

Recognize that because of the principles of fitness training, the reality of making measurable contributions to children's fitness thorugh the in-school physical education program is frequently quite limited. Why? Simply because of time. Insufficient time to attain a training effect from vigorous physical activity is the single greatest deterrent to children's fitness enhancement. Therefore, the concept of assigning **fitness homework** is a valid way to minimize the negative impact of insufficient time. Fitness homework may be "assigned" by the teacher for children to do during recess, at home while watching television, before bedtime, or after school with a parent or friend.

Fitness homework may take many forms. Students may simply be assigned fitness tasks to complete during commercial breaks of their television watching time. Later they may be asked to informally report to you on their progress and frequency of compliance. Fitness homework may also take the form of a home fitness chart sent to parents with an explanation of various fitness activities, their purpose, and supervisory hints. Parents can then help children with proper performance and exercise compliance and perhaps even exercise with them.

 CONCEPT 4.7
Fitness homework and fitness breaks are valid means of enhancing the impact of fitness education.

Fitness homework is an effective motivational tool that assumes that children are knowledgeable about how to work for higher levels of fitness and are eager to do so. Remember, the fitness strand of the developmental physical education program is intended not only to develop fit movers but also to create informed movers and to motivate eager movers. The developmental program goes beyond fitness "training" and recognizes the importance of fitness "education." **Fitness training** can occur with little or no enthusiasm or cognitive comprehension of why it is essential or how to go about it. **Fitness education,** on the other hand, recognizes that it is vitally important for children to

1. know why fitness enhancement is personally important,
2. know how to go about it in a safe and healthful manner, and
3. be sufficiently motivated to participate with little or no outside prodding.

EAGER MOVERS DEFINED

During their early years, children are usually **eager movers,** willing to participate in vigorous physical activity. Too often it is assumed that, because children frequently participate in play activities during their spare time, they do not need an instructional program of skill and fitness development. When this attitude is taken, the teacher often neglects to teach movement skills that are necessary for participation in vigorous physical activities. Children will participate in such activities only when they have developed

 CONCEPT 4.8
A variety of motivational techniques must be used to sustain children's interest and participation in physical fitness activities.

TEACHING TIPS

Techniques for *motivating children* to achieve greater fitness include:

- Make it fun by giving the fitness activity a name and making it a game.
- Develop an all-school, fifteen- to twenty-minute, daily fitness break in addition to the instructional physical education program.
- Stress individual standards of achievement and personal progress.
- Emphasize the why and how of fitness.
- Avoid comparing children with one another and overreliance on norms.
- Add music to the workout session.
- Develop fitness bulletin boards.
- Vary distances, activities, repetitions, and time.
- Publish fitness information in the school newspaper.
- Develop graphs and charts of individual progress.
- Incorporate obstacle courses into the program.
- Try timed circuits, varying the circuit regularly.
- Try treasure hunts with younger children and orienteering skills with older students.
- Participate in the American Heart Association/AAHPERD Jump Rope For Heart Program.
- Form a running club, jump rope club, or aerobics club for daily activities before school or during recess time.
- Get involved yourself and exercise with the children.

sufficient skills to enjoy participation. By developing their movement skills, children have the "tools" for gaining and maintaining improved levels of fitness.

In addition to providing challenging experiences, teachers need to provide a great range of activities. By getting to know students and assessing their interests and abilities, you can plan activities that appeal to children, which is important in preventing experiences that are unsuccessful, frustrating, and not enjoyable. A positive attitude toward participation in vigorous physical activities is essential if children are to remain motivated toward an active way of life (Whitehead, 1994).

Children are generally positively motivated to engage in physical activity when they see someone they look up to being active. To this end, incorporating a "Principal's Weekly Fitness Walk" into your school may help children become more eager movers. Students through good behavior, outstanding performance, or some other form of achievement earn the opportunity to take a power walk with the building principal. This serves as a novel but effective means of helping convey the concept that fitness is for everybody. It also serves as a means of promoting habitual physical activity.

Active Movers

Physical fitness is accomplished through regular, systematic, intense participation in vigorous activities. Some activities contribute more to one aspect of fitness than others. Therefore, it is important to provide a variety of activities that interest children and motivate them to exercise regularly. Have a planned program and do not leave physical activity to chance. Activities that can be performed for a few minutes or for a long period of time, with others or alone, are all important in planning fitness-building activities that children can do at home. It is helpful to give the children fitness challenges that they can practice or perform after school hours.

Playful Movers

With children, it is essential that you minimize the mind-dulling and often boring repetition of physical exercise. The more fun and gamelike the activities are, the easier it will be to motivate children. Remember that with children, "give it a name and make it a game." In other words, modify the fitness activity to resemble a game or vigorous play activity to maximize participation and encourage compliance. For example, with younger children you may take advantage of their vivid imaginations and turn your fitness activities for the day into a story play such as a bear hunt, trip to the moon, or day at the circus. With older children you will be successful if you introduce personal record keeping; cooperative and vigorous, gamelike fitness sessions; and aerobic dance activities.

Partners with Parents

Another area in which you can have an influence is that of parent education. Many parents are concerned when their child is not physically active, but they frequently do not know what to do to help. Also, many parents have lost or have never developed habits of regular, vigorous physical activity. A trained physical educator can establish programs in which interested parents attend sessions to learn more about children's physical development, how to develop a family fitness program, and helpful fitness-building activities. Operating alone, the school can have only limited success. Fitness is a year-round, lifelong objective. Therefore, there must be cooperative efforts between the home and the school to develop and maintain the physical fitness of children. The activity calendars and food records discussed earlier are effective means of involving parents in the fitness and nutrition education of their children.

IMPLICATIONS FOR TEACHING DEVELOPMENTAL PHYSICAL EDUCATION

Lifelong habits of activity or inactivity are established during childhood. Creating positive attitudes toward gaining and maintaining an acceptable level of physical fitness and providing opportunities to develop the components of fitness are important objectives of the physical education program.

Traditionally, schools have placed children in environments that demand rigid conformity to inactivity. The scheduled physical education class and recess periods are frequently the only times children have an opportunity to be physically active during the school day. Although potentially helpful, the instructional physical education program generally is not capable of enhancing fitness levels to a significant degree because of insufficient duration and frequency. Similarly, recess is often a time of inactivity or relatively sedentary play. Because of these problems, many schools are incorporating daily **fitness breaks** of fifteen to twenty minutes into the school program. The fitness break is an all-school activity, engaged in by students, faculty, and staff *in addition* to the instructional physical education period. The emphasis is on continuous vigorous physical activity. Some schools use hallways, the gymnasium, the cafeteria, or outdoor facilities for mass participation. Other schools have self-contained breaks, led by the teacher in the classroom or on the playground. Improved fitness results from participation in vigorous activities that require skill and are interesting to children. Ensuring that movement skills are developed so that avenues are opened for recreational pursuits is an important responsibility of the teacher. Schools must offer opportunities for children to develop and apply movement skills that are essential for self-direction in vigorous physical activities.

SUMMARY

This chapter dealt with the importance of fitness acquisition in helping children become fit movers, informed movers, and eager movers. Today's children live in the midst of a fitness boom that has permeated all facets of North American society. Unfortunately, however, only limited information has trickled down from this movement to children. The results of several recent national surveys of children's fitness clearly reveal that much more needs to be done. Recent encouraging signs point to a surge of interest in children's fitness, and there is hope for the future.

We defined the elusive term *physical fitness* and discussed other health-related and performance-related components of fitness. Examples of each component were given to personalize their meaning in terms of children's fitness enhancement. We discussed basic principles of fitness enhancement and gave examples of each principle in action. It is essential that children understand these principles of training and that they be adhered to for balanced and healthful fitness attainment. It is important, too, that you convey these fitness concepts to children in developmentally appropriate ways, so that they will possess the essential tools for their own fitness enhancement.

The notions of fitness homework and fitness breaks were discussed as ways to extend and maximize the impact of fitness education among children. Time limitations placed on physical education teachers frequently make it exceedingly difficult, if not impossible, to demonstrate measurable improvements in children's fitness levels. Limitations in terms of insufficient frequency, intensity, and duration of training directly violate basic principles of fitness enhancement.

You will need to devise techniques for motivating children to engage eagerly in positive fitness behaviors as part of their chosen lifestyle. Fun, variety, and peer group identification are important motivational tools that you will want to include in your fitness training programs.

The fitness strand of the developmental physical education program is aimed not only at fitness training to develop fit movers but also includes fitness education and fitness motivation for developing informed movers and eager movers. Physical fitness is an important quality linked to a positive state of health and is within reach of all. Developmental physical education has the opportunity to provide children with the essential tools to attain and maintain a healthy lifestyle that includes regular vigorous physical activity.

COMPLEMENTARY READINGS

Blair, S. N. (1992). Are American children and youth fit? The need for better data. *Research Quarterly for Exercise and Sport* 63:120–23.

Elsey, S. C. (1991). Extracurricular fitness. *Strategies* 5:13–18.

Fox, K. (1991). Motivating children for physical activity: Toward a healthier future. *JOPERD* 62:34–38.

Franks, B. D. (1989). *YMCA Youth Fitness Test Manual.* Champaign, IL: Human Kinetics.

Haywood, K. M. (1991). The role of physical education in the development of active lifestyles. *Research Quarterly for Exercise and Sport* 62:151–56.

Koslow, R. R. (1988). Can physical fitness be a primary objective in a balanced PE program? *JOPERD* 59:75–77.

McSwegin, P. J., ed. (1989). Fitting in fitness. *JOPERD* 60:30–45.

Morrow, J. R., ed. (1992). RQES forum: Are American children and youth fit? *Research Quarterly for Exercise and Sport* 63:95–136.

Pangrazi, R. P., and C. B. Corbin. (1993). Physical fitness: Questions teachers ask. *JOPERD* 64:14–19.

Pangrazi, R. P., and C. B. Corbin. (1994). *Teaching Strategies for Improving Youth Fitness.* Reston, VA: AAHPERD.

Ratliffe, T., and L. McCravey Ratliffe. (1994). *Teaching Children Fitness.* Champaign, IL: Human Kinetics.

Ross, J. G., and G .G. Gilbert. (1985). The national children and youth fitness study: A summary of findings. *JOPERD* 56:45–50.

Ross, J. G., and R. R. Pate. (1987). The national children and youth fitness study II. *JOPERD* 58:49–96.

Ross, J. G., et al. (1987). What's going on in the elementary physical education program? *JOPERD* 58:32–34.

Thomas, D. Q., and J. R. Whitehead. (1993). Body composition assessment: Some practical answers to teacher's questions. *JOPERD* 64:16–19.

U.S. Department of Health and Human Services. (1990). *Healthy People 2000: National Health Promotion and Disease Prevention Objectives.* (Stock Number 017-001-00474-0). Washington, D.C.: U.S. Government Printing Office.

Whitehead, J. R. (1994). Enhancing fitness and activity motivation in children. In R. R. Pate and R. C. Hohn, eds., *Health and Fitness Through Physical Education,* Champaign, IL: Human Kinetics.

SUPPLEMENTARY READINGS

Blair, S. N., and M. D. Meredith. (1994). The exercise-health relationship: Does it apply to children and youth? In R. R. Pate and R. C. Hohn, eds., *Health and Fitness Through Physical Education,* Champaign, IL: Human Kinetics.

Corbin, C. B., and R. P. Pangrazi. (1992). Are American children and youth fit? *Research Quarterly for Exercise and Sport* 63:96–106.

Gallahue, D. L., and J. C. Ozmun. (1995). Physical development of children. In *Understanding Motor Development,* Dubuque, IA: Wm. C. Brown & Benchmark (Chapter 12: *Physical development of children*).

Hawkes, S. R., and P. Richins. (1994). Toward a new paradigm for the management of obesity. *Journal of Health Education* 25:147–53.

Morrow, J. R. ed. (1991). RQES forum: Physical education and the public health. *Research Quarterly for Exercise and Sport* 62:123–56.

Petray, C. K. (1994). Physical fitness education and assessment: Addressing the cognitive domain. In R. R. Pate and R. C. Hohn, eds., *Health and Fitness Through Physical Education,* Champaign IL: Human Kinetics.

Sallis, J. F., and T. L. McKenzie. (1991). Physical education's role in public health. *Research Quarterly for Exercise and Sport* 62:124–37.

Updyke, W. F. (1994). Fitness trends in a large population of 6–10-year-old children. *Summary Report of the Chrysler-AAU Physical Fitness Testing Program.* Poplars Building, Bloomington, IN: AAU.

VIDEOS

Childhood Obesity: Learning to Lose Weight. Films for the Humanities and Sciences. (1994). PO Box 2053, Princeton, NJ 08543. (28 min.).

Herschel Walker's Fitness Challenge for Kids. Walker, H. (1989). Charleston, WV: Cambridge Physical Education and Health. (40 min.).

Shape Up America. C. Everett Koop Foundation. (1994). 6707 Democracy Blvd., Suite 107, Bethesda, MD 20817–1129.

Teaching Children Fitness Video. Ratliffe, T., and L. McCravey Ratliffe. (1994). Champaign, IL: Human Kinetics. (30 min.).

Cognitive Learning

CHAPTER 5

Key Concept

An Important Strand of the Developmental Physical Education Program Is Helping Children Become *Active Learners* and *Multisensory Learners*

Chapter Objectives

The purpose of this chapter is to provide you with the tools to:
• Describe what is meant by the terms *critical thinking, cognitive mapmaking* and *divergent movement ability* and discuss how each may be facilitated through physical activity.
• List and describe the various components of cognitive concept learning.
• Demonstrate understanding of the concept that children become knowledgeable movers by being both active learners and multisensory learners.
• Define the term *perceptual-motor* and diagram the perceptual-motor process.
• List and describe the perceptual-motor components and give examples of each.
• Discuss the role of perceptual-motor learning in cognitive development.
• Distinguish between readiness and remediation in perceptual-motor learning and discuss the proposed role of each.

Terms to Remember

Cognitive Concept
   Learning
Cognitive Maps
Critical Thinking
Sensorimotor Phase
Preoperational Phase
Concrete Operations
   Phase
Skill Concept Learning
Movement Concept
   Learning
Activity Concept
   Learning

Fitness Concept
   Learning
Academic Concept
   Learning
Learning
Multisensory Learning
Perception
Perceptual-Motor
Perceptual-Motor Process
Body Awareness
Spatial Awareness
Subjective Localization
Objective Localization

Self Space
General Space
Restricted Space
Shape
Level
Pathways
Directional Awareness
Relationships
Laterality
Directionality
Temporal Awareness
Learning Readiness
Remediation

The study of cognitive concept learning and perceptual-motor learning attempts to answer the age-old question of how we come to know our world. From the moment of birth, children begin to learn how to interact with their environment. This interaction is a cognitive process, as well as a motor process. Sherrill (1993, p. 306) notes that: "Perception is functionally inseparable from movement, cognition, and language. Voluntary, conscious thought and action are rooted in meanings derived from the environment. In normal development perceptual-motor learning is spontaneous."

The view taken in this chapter is that perceptual-motor learning and concept development are both aspects of cognitive learning that are especially important during the period of childhood. We will, therefore, focus on the interactive nature of these processes. Multisensory learning and its component parts are discussed along with the importance of concept learning and perceptual-motor learning through movement.

It should be noted that the term *cognitive concept learning* is not to be confused with *academic concept learning*. Academic concept learning deals specifically with the traditional subject matter areas of math, language arts, science, and the like. Cognitive concept learning is a much more inclusive term that includes academic learning as only *one* of its several components.

ACTIVE LEARNERS DEFINED

Cognitive concept learning, through cognitive mapmaking and critical thinking, is a viable outcome of the developmentally based physical education program. It takes into account children's level of cognitive development as well as their motor development and recognizes that the motor and cognitive domains are indeed intertwined. **Cognitive concept learning** is, therefore, defined as the process by which information is organized, put into memory, and made available for recall and application to a variety of settings. Cognitive concept learning provides children with the tools for critical thinking. It uses movement activities to aid in retention, recall, decision making, and application.

Movement skill learning, whether it is learning fundamental or specialized movement skills, is an active learning process intricately interrelated with cognition. Movement skill learning cannot occur without the benefit of higher thought processes. All voluntary movement requires an element of cognition. The more complex the movement task, the more complicated the cognitive processing involved.

Cognitive Mapmaking

As movement skills are learned, **cognitive maps,** or mental images, are formed. This image is retained in memory, ready to be recalled and re-created on split second notice. As skill continues to improve, performance appears to be almost automatic, with little or no conscious thought involved. Although movement skill performance is not automatic in the true sense of the word, the skill becomes so thoroughly learned that it appears to be so. For example, when walking from place to place we give scant attention to how, when, and exactly where we place one foot in front of the other. We do not consciously think about how our arms swing in opposition to our leg action, or that we are striding forward in an alternating heel-to-toe fashion. All of these processes have been so thoroughly learned that they appear to be automatic because they do not require our conscious attention. Try, however, walking on ice, in sand, or with a heavy backpack. The different set of conditions under which the task is performed will cause you, for a short while, to attend consciously to the modified requirements of the task until a new cognitive map has been formed and put into memory. Therefore, it is critically important that we help children learn both the skill concepts and the movement concepts associated with how their bodies should move and how their bodies can move, respectively. By doing so, we materially aid them in forming cognitive maps of fundamental and specialized movement skills.

Critical Thinking

Lipman (1988, p. 39) first defined **critical thinking** as "skillful, responsible thinking that facilitates good judgment because it (1) relies upon criteria, (2) is self-correcting, and (3) is sensitive to context." Critical thinking, therefore, is a form of cognitive accountability based on concept formation, in which the learner notes relationships and makes conscious decisions based on established criteria. The constant knowledge explosion that today's children are immersed in demands that they become critical

CONCEPT 5.1
Cognitive concept learning in physical education involves children in the processes of critical thinking and cognitive mapmaking.

Children are critical thinkers.

thinkers in order to be able to bring personal meaning and clarity to what is happening around them.

With regard to critical thinking in the motor domain, McBride (1992, p. 115) was the first to define it as "reflective thinking that is used to make reasonable and defensible decisions about movement tasks and challenges." To this end, McBride proposed a four-phase model linking critical thinking with physical education instruction that includes the necessity for the learner to engage in (1) cognitive organization, (2) cognitive action, (3) cognitive outcomes, and (4) psychomotor outcomes. The use of indirect teaching styles that involve children in the important process of "learning to learn" has a positive impact on critical thinking skills in a physical education setting. If you used teaching behaviors in a ball-throwing skill theme, for example, that required students to (1) reflect and make conscious decisions about essential aspects of throwing a ball for distance (cognitive organization), (2) demonstrate implementation of these decisions in a variety of throwing activities (cognitive action), and (3) personally judge their success in terms of how far and accurately the ball travels (cognitive and psychomotor outcomes), you would be promoting critical thinking skills among your students. If, on the other hand, you chose to use a command style of teaching in which you essentially did all of the organization, dictated the throwing behaviors to use, and told your students about the cognitive and psychomotor outcomes of the task, you would be doing little to promote critical thing among your students.

If we subscribe to the Piagetian (i.e., cognitive) view of learning, we then become interested in children going beyond *replicating* ideas and/or movements based on the decisions of others and become interested in them *producing* new ideas and/or movements based on the results of their own decisions.

Recent experiments in the area of divergent movement ability (that is, the ability to produce different fundamental movement skills when performing locomotor, manipulative, or stability tasks) have demonstrated that children's divergent movement abilities are the combined product of several critical thinking processes (Cleland and Gallahue, 1993; Cleland, 1994).

Jean Piaget (Peterson and Felton-Collins, 1986) was among the first developmentalists to demonstrate a link between motor processes and cognitive learning. Piaget's work highlighted the important role that movement plays in the cognitive development of infants and young children. His **sensorimotor phase** involves coordination of the infant and young child's motor activities and perceptions into a tenuous whole. This phase of development, and the corresponding stages within that phase, clearly illustrates the link between movement and cognition. The **preoperational phase** encompasses the early childhood years and is characterized by egocentric behaviors. The **concrete operations phase** is typical of the elementary school years and is typified by increasing curiosity. The achievement of competence within the preoperational and the concrete operations phases is considerably aided, according to Piaget, through the process of movement.

An important outgrowth of Piaget's work has been a cognitive theory of learning that emphasizes the *process* aspects of learning and not simply the product. Cognitive learning theory views learning as a process that involves experimentation, exploration, and individual decision making; it is a process that necessitates the reconstruction of incorrect events into a new, correct, whole. Subscribing to a Piagetian view of learning lends considerable support to the importance of indirect, exploratory, guided-discovery, and problem-solving approaches to learning, particularly for those at the beginning/novice level of learning a new movement skill.

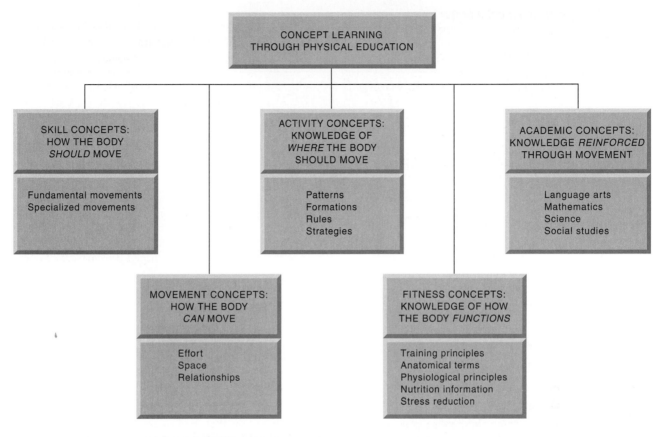

FIGURE 5.1 *The components of cognitive concept learning.*

THE COGNITIVE CONCEPT COMPONENTS

Several aspects of cognitive concept learning relate to movement (Figure 5.1). Each is briefly discussed in the following paragraphs, and suggestions for using them in the developmentally based physical education curriculum are offered.

CONCEPT 5.2
It is essential for children to learn the skill concepts, movement concepts, activity concepts, and fitness concepts of developmental physical education if they are to be knowledgeable movers as well as skillful movers.

Skill Concepts

Skill concept learning deals specifically with how the body *should* move. Teachers and coaches must recognize that problems associated with insufficient instructional time, large classes, the immaturity of some children, or simply the complexity of the task itself frequently make it difficult to attain the goal of developing skillful movers within the confines of the instructional class. Therefore, it is essential that children learn about how their bodies are supposed to move in the performance of fundamental and specialized movement skills. For example, children are frequently unable to kick, throw, or dribble a ball at the mature stage. Unfortunately, the instructional portion of the school day fails, for one or more of the reasons just mentioned, to adequately help them become skillful in these fundamental movements. Similarly, older children often have trouble mastering many of the sport skills

TABLE 5.1   *The Movement Concepts*

EFFORT (How the Body Moves)	SPACE (Where the Body Moves)	RELATIONSHIPS (Moving with Objects/People)
Body Movement with Varying:	Body Movement at Varying:	Body Movement in Relation to:
Force	**Levels**	**Objects**
strong	high/medium/low	over/under
light	**Directions**	in/out
Time	forward/backward	between/among
fast	diagonally/sideward	in front/behind
slow	up/down	lead/follow
medium	various pathways (curved, straight,	above/below
sustained	zigzag, etc.)	through/around
sudden	**Ranges**	**People**
Flow	body shapes (wide, narrow, curved,	mirroring
free	straight, etc.)	shadowing
bound	body spaces (self space and general space)	in unison
	body extensions (near/far, large/small,	together/apart
	with and without implements)	alternating
		simultaneously
		partner/group

presented during the regular instructional portion of the class. If, however, these same children are provided with the vital skill concepts about how their bodies should move when kicking, throwing, dribbling a ball, or performing specific sport skills, they will have the necessary tools for learning outside the confines of the gymnasium—on the playground, at home, or on the youth sport team. Part IV, *The Skill Themes,* provides a wide variety of skill concepts for both fundamental and specialized movement skills.

Movement Concepts

Movement concept learning deals with how the body *can* move. Seldom in the real world does movement occur under the same conditions time after time. Most movement tasks in games, sport, and dance are dynamic in nature, mandating fluidity and flexibility in one's movement patterns. Furthermore, the ecology of the environment itself is dynamic. Changes in the playing surface, facilities, equipment, and number of participants make it virtually impossible to address all of these possibilities. The dynamic nature of movement, the ever-changing environment, and the situational requirements

of the task make it absolutely essential for children to learn about how their bodies can move.

Certainly, we should introduce a new movement skill first under static conditions in which the environment and the task itself are maintained as nearly as possible in an invariant form. This procedure is essential at the beginning/novice level of new movement skill learning. We must, however, be mindful that this same movement skill will seldom be performed in isolation or under the same static conditions in which it was originally learned. Hence, we must recognize the importance of movement concept learning as an essential aid to learning the many and varied ways in which the body is capable of moving in performing a single fundamental movement skill or a group of skills chained together as specialized sport skills.

Because our environment is constantly changing, we must develop plasticity (that is, adaptability) of movement in order to move with control and efficiency. Therefore, to help young learners develop the ability to move in a variety of ways under a variety of circumstances, we need to ensure that they have ample opportunities to experiment with and explore the movement concepts of *effort, space,* and *relationships* (see Table 5.1). By experiencing how the body can move (effort), where the body can move (space), and with whom and with what the body can move (relationships), children become versatile dynamic movers—movers capable of responding with skill, precision, and plasticity to the variety of movement circumstances in which they move every day. Part IV, *The Skill Themes,* provides examples of numerous movement concepts for both fundamental and specialized movement skills.

Activity Concepts

Activity concept learning deals with *where* the body should move. Activity concepts center on the learning of patterns, formations, rules, and strategies for effective participation in game, sport, and dance activities. Developmental physical education recognizes the importance of activity concept learning as a way to provide children with a knowledge base for effective participation—participation that will occur most frequently in recreational and competitive settings outside of the physical education class. Therefore, when we help children learn the activity concepts involved in six-on-a-side soccer, kickball, or the Boot Scootin' Boogie, we are providing them with the essential knowledge of where they should position themselves, how to respond to elements of the activity, and how to follow the rules and strategies for successful participation. Activity concepts must be geared to children's levels of motor, cognitive, and effective development. They must be both age-group appropriate and individually appropriate.

Care should be taken to recognize that although activity concepts can and should be taught systematically, they should not be the main focus of the lesson. The primary focus of the developmental lesson is on learning new movement skills and enhancing fitness. Activity concepts should be included during the skill application portion of the lesson, but they should not serve as an excuse for promoting a physical education program that stresses "playing the game" rather than first learning the skills that enable a child to play the game successfully. Activity concepts are important in that they provide the learner with the tools for effective participation—participation that occurs primarily outside of the instructional physical education program.

Fitness Concepts

Fitness concept learning deals with *what* one needs to do to gain and maintain a healthy lifestyle. Because of the physiological requirements for achieving a training effect, fitness enhancement is not a reality in many physical education programs. Certainly, children's fitness enhancement is a laudable goal that should be sought, but it is an elusive one in programs that do not provide sufficient frequency, intensity, and time for a training effect to occur. Children must, however, learn essential fitness concepts for healthful living and be shown how they can incorporate these concepts into their daily lives (Petray, 1994).

It is essential that children learn about and have opportunities to apply the principles of fitness training. They need to know not only the components of health-related and performance-related fitness but how each may be enhanced. It is essential that children begin to learn and apply basic anatomical terms such as *abdominals, biceps,* and *triceps* and physiological terms such as *target heart rate, threshold of training,* and *static stretching.* They should also learn about the link between proper nutrition, fitness, and good health. Because of the stressful nature of many children's lives, it is becoming increasingly important to teach children about basic principles of relaxation and stress reduction.

Fitness concepts can be effectively integrated into the fitness strand of the developmental physical education program. They must, however, be integrated in a manner that is both developmentally sound and curricularly valid. In other words, it is important to recognize the cognitive comprehension level of your students and to tailor fitness concepts to that level of understanding. Also, a curricular sequence that builds concept upon concept should be adopted. This step avoids the trap of teaching children the same thing year after year with little or no consideration given to curricular progression.

Academic Concepts

Academic concept learning deals with using movement activities as a means of *reinforcing* knowledge concepts in language arts, mathematics, science, and social studies—concepts traditionally covered exclusively in the classroom. Movement activities have repeatedly been shown to be an effective way to help children grasp—through the use of additional sensory modalities (primarily the tactile and kinesthetic modes)—concepts that were once taught only in the two-dimensional, auditory-visual environment of the classroom.

CONCEPT 5.3
Movement can be used effectively to reinforce many of the academic concepts dealt with in the traditional classroom.

If academic concept learning is to be effective in the gymnasium, two things must be done. First, you must take time to talk with classroom teachers and, when possible, to visit the classroom. You can then see firsthand what is being taught, when it is being presented, and how the children respond. You will need to discuss with the classroom teacher in specific terms what you can do to supplement and reinforce the classroom curriculum. Such a procedure has an added bonus in garnering support for your program. Classroom teachers who know that you are interested in their instructional goals tend to be more receptive to *your* instructional goals. You will gain an ally in the support and promotion of your program when you show interest in the classroom teacher's program.

Second, you must teach for transfer of skills. In other words, you must help children link what is being taught in the classroom to its application in the gymnasium. You cannot assume that children will make this link themselves. When teaching for transfer it is important to use the gymnasium as a way to demonstrate the relevancy of academic concepts. For example, the importance of learning fractions can easily be demonstrated when teaching how to compute batting averages or win-loss percentages. The ethnic heritage of cultures from around the world can be brought alive through games and folk dances characteristic of various cultures. Story writing can be expressed through small group mini-plays that emphasize the movement components of the story. Academic concept learning that is reinforced in the gymnasium should be a by-product of good teaching that is aware of, and sensitive to, the needs of the whole child.

Children are active learners.

MULTISENSORY LEARNERS DEFINED

Learning is a process that culminates in a relatively permanent change in behavior as a result of experience or practice. By its very nature, learning is a process that relies on both sensory and motor information. Learning is multisensory in nature because it is dependent on what we see, hear, feel, taste, touch, and smell. **Multisensory learning** is a process of change brought about by the

C O N C E P T   5 . 4
Because children are multisensory learners, all voluntary movement involves an element of perception.

internalization and integration of sensory stimuli that results in a perception or a perceptual-motor response.

Perceptual-Motor Learning

The word **perception,** which means to know or to interpret information, is the process of organizing and synthesizing information that we gather through the various sense organs with stored information or past data, which leads to a modified response pattern.

When we consider the term **perceptual-motor,** then, we know that the first part of the term signifies the dependency of voluntary movement activity on some form of sensory information. All voluntary movement involves an element of perceptual awareness resulting from sensory stimulation. The second part of the term *perceptual-motor* indicates that the development of one's perceptual abilities depends, in part, on movement. Perceptual abilities are learned abilities and, as such, use movement as an important medium for this learning. The reciprocal relationship between sensory input and motor output enables both perceptual and motor abilities to develop in harmony.

It has long been recognized that the quality of one's movement performance depends on the accuracy of perception and the ability to interpret these perceptions into a series of coordinated movement acts. The terms *eye-hand coordination* and *eye-foot coordination* have been used for years to express the dependency of efficient movement on the accuracy of one's sensory information. The individual in the process of shooting a basketball free throw has numerous forms of sensory input that must be sorted out and expressed in the final act of shooting the ball. If the perceptions are accurate and if they are expressed in a coordinated sequence, the basket is made. If not, the shot misses. All voluntary movement involves the use of one or more sensory modalities to a greater or lesser degree, depending on the movement act to be performed.

CONCEPT 5.5
The quality of one's movement performance is significantly influenced by the accuracy of one's perceptions.

As multisensory learners, children use their visual, auditory, tactile, and kinesthetic senses to learn about the spatial and temporal aspects of their expanding world. The **perceptual-motor process** is a process of attaining increased skill and improving the ability to function. This process involves the following steps:

1. *Sensory input:* receiving various forms of stimulation by way of specialized sensory receptors (visual, auditory, tactile, and kinesthetic) and transmitting this stimulation to the brain in the form of neural energy.
2. *Sensory integration:* organizing incoming sensory stimuli and integrating it with past or stored information (memory).
3. *Motor interpretation:* making internal motor decisions (recalibration) based on the combinations of sensory (present) and long-term memory (past) information.
4. *Movement activation:* executing the actual movement (observable act) itself.
5. *Feedback:* evaluating the movement act using various sensory modalities that feed back information into the sensory input aspect of the process, thus beginning the cycle again (KR, Knowledge of Results; and KP, Knowledge of Performance).

Figure 5.2 illustrates the perceptual-motor process. Take a few minutes to review this figure to fully appreciate the importance of perception in the process of movement.

THE PERCEPTUAL-MOTOR COMPONENTS

Although the movement experiences found in the regular physical education program are by definition perceptual-motor activities, some programs emphasize perceptual-motor quality rather than gross motor quality. In remedial and readiness training programs, for example, the emphasis is on improving specific perceptual-motor components. Therefore, movement activities are grouped according to the perceptual-motor qualities they enhance. One common grouping includes body awareness, spatial awareness, directional awareness, and temporal awareness (Figure 5.3). Activities designed to enhance these qualities are used in the regular instructional physical education program, but with the primary objective of movement skill acquisition rather than perceptual-motor learning.

CONCEPT 5.6
The development of children's spatial and temporal world is aided through practice in perceptual-motor activities.

Body Awareness

Body awareness activities are designed to help children better understand the nature of their bodies and the functions of the parts. There are three aspects of body awareness: (1) knowledge of the body parts, (2) knowledge of what the parts can do, and (3) knowledge of how to make the parts move. Movement experiences that draw attention to one or more of these components contribute positively to the development of children's awareness of their bodies and movement capabilities.

Spatial Awareness

Spatial awareness activities are designed to enhance children's awareness of the orientation of their bodies in space and the amount of space that they occupy. Spatial awareness is developmentally based and progresses from subjective to objective localization as the child matures and gains new experiences. **Subjective localization** refers to a period when children are able to locate objects in space relative to

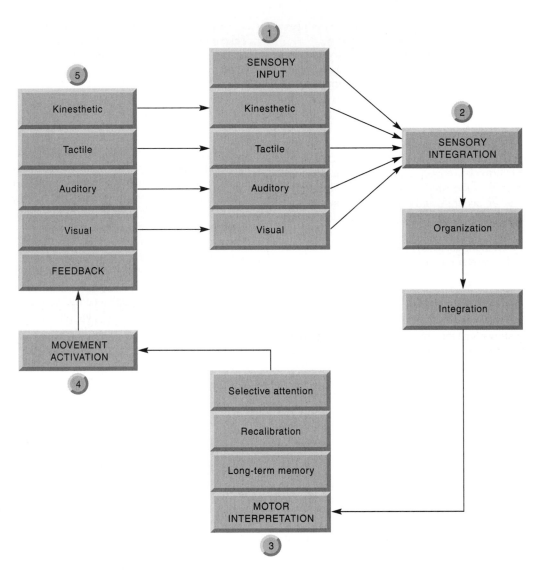

FIGURE 5.2 *The perceptual-motor process.*

themselves, but frequently with an erroneous perception of the amount of space their bodies occupy. **Objective localization** refers to the period when children are able to function independently of their bodies when making spatial and locational judgments. Movement experiences that focus on making spatial judgments relative to body location and how much space it occupies may contribute positively to the child's awareness of space. "My body is to the left of the hoop" is a statement denoting subjective localization.

"The hoop is in front of the cone," in turn, typifies the concept of objective localization.

Children need to understand that they can move in space in a variety of ways. Their **self space,** or personal space as it is often called, is the area immediately surrounding their bodies. **General space** is the total available space in the room, gymnasium, or on the playground. **Restricted space** is a specifically prescribed or limited area in which they may move. Additionally, movement serves as

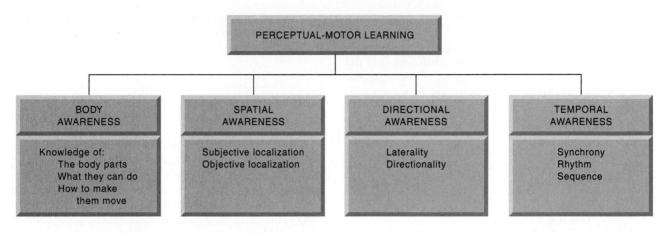

FIGURE 5.3 *The components of perceptual-motor learning.*

a primary means for children to learn how their bodies may take on different shapes and move at different levels and in a variety of pathways as they move through space. **Shape** is represented through the body assuming positions such as ones that are wide, narrow, curved, and straight. **Level** is achieved by the body moving at a high, medium, or low level. **Pathways** take the form of movement through space in ways that are curved, straight, zigzag, and so forth.

Directional Awareness

Directional awareness activities enhance awareness of the body as it is projected into external space. Directional awareness gives dimension to objects in space and implies that one is moving in relationship to something else. The concept of **relationships** as used in movement implies that one is moving in conjunction with other objects, props, or people. You may, for example, move in relationship to the hoop, the rope, or the cones. You may also move in relationship to your partner, teammate, or opponent.

The concepts of left, right, up, and down take on meaning in a relationship context when the child has established directional awareness. **Laterality** is the term used for an internal "feel" for direction. Simply "knowing" left from right, without having to give conscious attention to external cues such as the watch on your right wrist and the ring on your left hand, is evidence of a well-developed internal sense of laterality. **Directionality,** the *name* given to the actual meaning of directions, usually develops prior to the internal sense of laterality. Therefore, being aware that you have a left and a right but not

being able to consistently and internally apply that concept would be considered to be directionality *without* laterality. When we link movement activities to the verbal cues of in/out, up/down, over/under, left/right, between/among, and so forth, we help children develop a sense of directional awareness that encompasses both laterality and directionality.

Temporal Awareness

Temporal awareness refers to the child's development of an internal time structure. Temporal awareness enables the efficient coordination of movements of the eyes and limbs. The terms *eye-hand coordination* and *eye-foot coordination* refer to the result of fully developed temporal awareness. Children who are developing their temporal awareness are in the process of learning how to synchronize movements in a rhythmical manner and to put them into the proper sequence. Rhythmical running, dancing, and juggling all require varying degrees of temporal awareness.

THE IMPORTANCE OF PERCEPTUAL-MOTOR LEARNING

The study of the influence of perceptual-motor development falls into two broad categories: (1) the influence of perceptual-motor experiences on non-impaired children (**learning readiness**), and (2) the influence of perceptual-motor training among groups containing some form of sensory, intellectual, physical, neurological, or emotional disability (**remediation**).

The primary concern of the physical educator interested in the study of perceptual-motor behavior is in the potential influence of planned programs of specific movement experiences on this behavior. Readiness programs are preventive and geared toward preschool and primary-grade children. Research supports the claim that practice in perceptual-motor activities does enhance children's abilities in this area (Davis and Burton, 1991; Gibson, 1979; Kavale and Mattson, 1983).

CONCEPT 5.7
There is little scientific support for the notion that practicing perceptual-motor activities has a direct effect on improving academic achievement.

Remedial training programs are directed at those children in the regular classroom who, for unexplained reasons, are failing to keep pace with their classmates. They do not have apparent physical, neurological, or intellectual disabilities, but they fail to reach their potential. Some of these children may have perceptually based learning difficulties. Although speculative evidence suggests that perceptual-motor training programs may improve performance in the classroom by some of these children, in fact, the Association for Childhood Learning Disabilities (1989) has categorically denied the hypothesized benefits of perceptual-motor training on the remediation of learning disabilities and has encouraged its members, through a position paper, to refrain from such claims.

There are no panaceas in remedial or readiness training. A physical education program that emphasizes perceptual-motor learning must be viewed as only one avenue by which the perceptual abilities of children may be enhanced. We simply do not have sufficient evidence to support the claim that improved perceptual-motor abilities will directly affect children's academic performance. It could be argued, however, that one positive result of perceptual-motor oriented physical education programs may be improved self-esteem for children.

CONCEPT 5.8
Practicing perceptual-motor activities may help improve some aspects of young children's learning readiness.

Improved perceptions of oneself as being capable and competent may carry over to the classroom work of some children.

IMPLICATIONS FOR TEACHING DEVELOPMENTAL PHYSICAL EDUCATION

Developmental physical education enhances perceptual-motor learning and cognitive concept learning by encouraging children to participate in gross motor activities that involve them in the use of the various sensory modalities and the process of learning to learn. Not all children are at the same level of cognitive development upon entering school. Cognition is a process influenced by both maturation and experience and, as such, proceeds at the child's individual rate. Because readiness is prerequisite to success in school, perceptual and cognitive readiness are important aspects of children's total readiness for learning.

The percentage of perceptually based learning difficulties is great enough to initiate readiness programs for some preschool and primary-grade children. Even though the research is not conclusive that this training directly affects later learning, empirical evidence strongly supports the notion. Deprivation of experiences hinders learning, especially during the early formative years. Therefore, a well-planned developmentally based physical education program that incorporates a variety of movement activities provides many of the experiences that help children develop perceptual-motor and cognitive concept learning. As educators we need to continue to devise additional opportunities for movement experiences that are often absent from the lives of children. Providing supplementary experiences that children are unable to create, receive, or fully utilize on their own will have a positive effect on the development of cognitive concepts and perceptual-motor skills.

SUMMARY

This chapter dealt with children as both active learners and multisensory learners. Cognitive concept learning was discussed from the standpoint of children being active learners. Cognitive concepts, namely skill concepts, movement concepts, activity concepts, fitness concepts, and academic concepts can be effectively taught in the gymnasium. Perceptual-motor learning was examined, and the role of movement in the perceptual-motor process was discussed and illustrated. Also presented were the spatial and temporal aspects of perceptual-motor learning, namely, body awareness, spatial awareness, directional awareness, and temporal awareness. Although the focus of developmental physical education is primarily movement skill learning and fitness enhancement, it must remain open to and plan for opportunities to reinforce both perceptual-motor learning and cognitive concept learning.

COMPLEMENTARY READINGS

Buschner, C. A. (1994). *Teaching Children Movement Concepts and Skills.* Champaign, IL: Human Kinetics.

Cleland, F. E. (1994). Young Children's Divergent Movement Ability: Study II. *Journal of Teaching Physical Education* 13:228–241.

Cleland, F., and D. L. Gallahue. (1993). Young Children's Divergent Movement Ability. *Perceptual & Motor Skills,* 77:535–544.

Elliot, M. E. (1990). Concept learning in elementary physical education. *Strategies* 3:8–10.

McBride, R. E. (1992). Critical thinking—An overview with implications for physical education. *Journal of Teaching Physical Education* 11:112–125.

Petray, C. K. (1994). Physical fitness education and assessment: Addressing the cognitive domain. In R. R. Pate and R. C. Hohn, eds., *Health and Fitness Through Physical Education,* Champaign, IL: Human Kinetics.

Schwager, S., and C. Labate. (1993). Teaching for critical thinking in physical education. *JOPERD* 64:24–26.

Thompson-Chepyator, J. R. (1995) Critical thinking in K–12 physical education: conceptual frameworks. *ICHPER•SD Journal* 31;2:10–15.

SUPPLEMENTARY READINGS

ACLD. (1987). The Childhood Learning Disabilities position statements: Measurement and training of perceptual and perceptual-motor functions. *Journal of Learning Disabilities* 20:349–50.

Davis, W. E., and A. W. Burton. (1991). Ecological task analysis: Translating movement behavior into practice. *Adapted Physical Activity Quarterly* 8:154–177.

Gibson, J. J. (1979). *The Ecological Approach to Visual Perception.* Boston: Houghton Mifflin.

Gredler, M. E. (1994). Principles of cognitive learning in physical education. In R. R. Pate and R. C. Hohn, eds., *Health and Fitness Through Physical Education,* Champaign, IL: Human Kinetics.

Kavale, K., and P. D. Mattson. (1983). One jumped off the balance beam: Meta-analysis of perceptual-motor training. *Journal of Learning Disabilities* 16:165–73.

Lipman, M. (1988). Critical thinking—What can it be? *Educational Leadership,* 46:38–43.

Peterson, R., and V. Felton-Collins. (1986). *The Piaget Handbook for Teachers and Parents.* New York: Teachers College Press.

Sherrill, C. (1993). Perceptual-motor learning: An ecological approach. In *Adapted Physical Activity, Recreation and Sport,* Dubuque, IA: Wm. C. Brown & Benchmark.

VIDEOS

Teaching Children Movement Concepts and Skills Video. Buschner, C. (1994). Champaign, IL: Human Kinetics. (30 min.).

Education through the Physical. Orange County Department of Education, P.O. Box 9050, Costa Mesa, CA 92028. (Two tapes: 9 min., 20 min.).

CHAPTER 6

Affective Growth

Key Concept

An Important Strand of the Developmental Physical Education Program Involves Helping Children Become *Self-Discovering Learners* and *Cooperative Learners*

Chapter Objectives

The purpose of this chapter is to provide you with the tools to:
• Define *self-concept* and *positive socialization* as they relate to children becoming self-discovering learners and cooperative learners.
• List and discuss the components of a positive self-concept.
• Provide examples of how physical education experiences can help to enhance self-esteem.
• Discuss how children's self-concept development can be enhanced by improving their sense of personal security and status.
• Discuss the influence of status, roles, and cultural norms on children's socialization into society.
• Speculate how children's socialization into their culture is affected by group affiliation, character education, and moral growth.
• List a variety of factors that influence affective development.
• Describe how developmental physical education can make real and lasting contributions to children's affective development in terms of both "me" and "we."
• Discuss the implications of children's affective development on teaching developmental physical education.

Terms to Remember

Self-Concept	Status	Moral Growth
Self-Esteem	Cooperative Learning	Moral Reasoning
Belonging	Cultural Socialization	Moral Behavior
Competence	Role	Moral Dilemma
Perceived Competence	Cultural Norms	Moral Dissonance
Self-Confidence	Group Affiliation	Self-Encouragement
Worthiness	Attitudes	Encouraging Others
Self-Acceptance	Character	Goal Setting
Uniqueness	Compliance	Self-Assessment
Virtue	Identification	
Security	Internalization	

Teachers play an important role in children's affective development through positive encouragement, help with realistic goal setting and self-assessment, and using moral dilemmas as a positive learning medium. Learning in the affective domain is an important strand of the developmental physical education program. By their very nature, children are self-discovering learners and cooperative learners. They are intricately engaged in the process of learning about themselves and how to interact with others in their world. They are learning about their unique abilities and are forming the basis for their self-concepts. They also are in the process of being socialized into a democratic society, a society that has certain behavioral requirements and expectations.

This chapter focuses on the twin affective topics of self-concept and positive socialization in and through the physical education setting. We will discuss what is meant by the terms *self-concept* and *positive socialization* and examine the components of both. Factors influencing self-concept development and positive socialization are also covered along with specific instructional implications for the developmentally based physical education program.

Children are self-discovering learners.

THE IMPORTANCE OF SELF-ESTEEM IN BECOMING A SELF-DISCOVERING LEARNER

As self-discovering learners, children's sense of personal worth is at the very core of their existence. Children's self-concept is influenced by all aspects of their daily life and affects how they approach their world. Our self-perceptions may be quite accurate or quite different from reality. However, all self-perceptions are important because they determine whether our self-concept is positive or negative.

William James, one of the early students of self-concept, considered an individual's self-perceptions to be an important variable in understanding human behavior. He once remarked that when two people meet, there are really six persons present. There is each person as he or she is, each as the other sees him or her, and each as seen by himself or herself.

Self-concept is a personal judgment of worthiness that is expressed in the attitudes one holds toward oneself. It is a value-free description of self. On the other hand, the term **self-esteem,** although frequently used interchangeably with self-concept, is our self-description influenced by how we think others view us. Taken together, self-concept and self-esteem represent the total of our perceptions of our worthiness and competence. Our everyday experiences dictate whether we view ourselves as competent or incompetent, worthy or unworthy. However, in turn, our self-concepts determine in large part how we act in and react to those experiences. Therefore, in many ways our self-concepts determine what we expect to happen. People whose performances do not match their personal aspirations tend to evaluate themselves as inferior no matter how high their attainments may be. They are likely to feel inadequate, guilty, shameful, and even depressed. Conditions that threaten to expose personal inadequacies are a major cause of anxiety. Belief in ourselves and the conviction that we can impose order on a segment of our universe are basic prerequisites for a stable, positive self-concept. Both children and adults with low esteem tend to be more conforming than those who have high esteem. They may have suffered dominance, rejection, or severe punishment, all of which have a negative impact on self-esteem. But the result is often the same—neither children nor adults can function effectively as self-discovering and cooperative learners if they lack esteem and confidence.

CONCEPT 6.1
Self-concept and self-esteem are learned behaviors significantly influenced by children's experiences in vigorous physical activity.

COMPONENTS OF A POSITIVE SELF-CONCEPT

Positive self-concept has many components. Among the most important are a sense of belonging, the development of competence, a sense of worthiness, self-acceptance, recognizing and accepting one's uniqueness, and virtuous behavior. Figure 6.1 illustrates these components. Although no universal pattern or set of conditions seems to be absolutely required to produce a positive self-concept, recent longitudinal evidence indicates that children must have the consistent, long-term presence of at least one significant person in their lives (Hamburg, 1992). This significant person helps nurture the following components.

CONCEPT 6.2
Self-concept development is influenced by many factors that can be manipulated through sensitive, caring teaching.

Belonging

Belonging is the positive feeling that an individual experiences when acting as part of a group and feeling accepted and valued by the members of that group. Not only is it necessary for the group to regard the individual as belonging, but it is also essential that the individual regard himself or herself as belonging. A sense of belonging is an important aspect of a positive self-concept. Teachers can do many things in the classroom to help children feel that they belong.

Learning and using each child's first name, as well as recognizing something unique about each child, is an excellent way to help children develop a sense of belonging. Being a contributing member of a class, club, or team also fosters a sense of belonging, as does wearing identity symbols such as tee shirts, certain hairstyles, and certain types of gym shoes. As the teacher, you are in an excellent

position to help children feel that they are an important part of what makes their class, group, or team "the greatest." Try to work constantly to include each student and to foster a group sense of "we" and "us." Reject the notion of exclusion and overidentification with the words *me* and *I* when encouraging a sense of belonging.

Insist that the number of students in physical education classes be no larger than the number of students in the classroom. Small classes foster a sense of belonging. Keep practice groups and teams as small as reasonably possible. Remember, it is generally better to have too few in a group activity than too many. Constantly work for group sizes that maximize the participation and contributions of all to the success of the activity.

Perceived Competence

Competence refers to how efficiently we accomplish a given task. **Perceived competence** is a personal self-evaluation of one's competence in comparison to others and previous personal experience. Perceived competence increases when one achieves personal goals or demonstrates individual improvement, and it is situation specific. For example, one may perceive herself as competent in baseball and basketball but incompetent in swimming and gymnastics. Additionally, perceived competence is relative to one's personal frame of reference. For instance, a Little League baseball player may perceive himself as being an "all-star" player, his frame of reference being parents, coaches, teammates, and other players in the league. Seldom, however, does he extend his perception of baseball competence beyond to players in the Little League World Series, at the local high school, or at the professional level. Instead, he sees himself as being competent in the context of his world.

Competence is closely linked to **self-confidence,** which is an inner feeling of belief in oneself. If a child has low self-confidence and perceived competence, then his or her feelings about the past are likely to be negative. It is the child's perception of these past experiences that a teacher may be most able to change. Potential for change is important for self-concept development. One of the steps teachers need to take to improve children's self-concept is to help them reinterpret the meaning of past experiences to put negative thoughts into their proper perspective. Children need to see themselves as competent. Quality instruction in movement skill acquisition and fitness enhancement contributes greatly to a sense of perceived competence in children.

Perceived competence tends to encourage increased mastery attempts and leads to higher levels of actual competence. Competence promotes self-confidence, which in

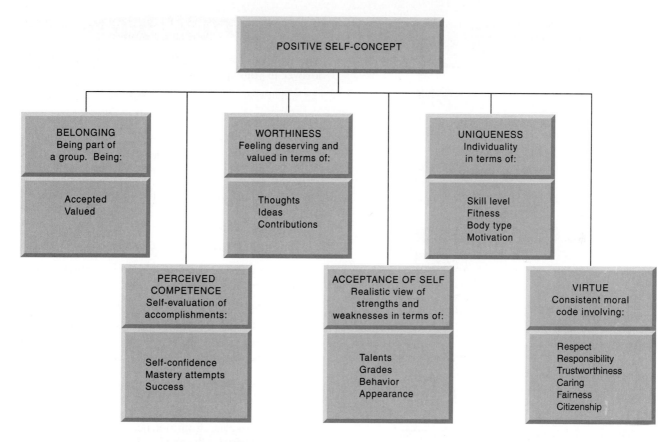

FIGURE 6.1 *Components of a positive self-concept.*

turn leads to improved self-esteem and a more positive self-concept (Figure 6.2).

Worthiness

A sense of **worthiness** develops out of seeing yourself as deserving and valued because of the kind of person you are, and because you see yourself as worthwhile in the estimation of others. To know that your thoughts, ideas, and contributions are valued by others is to feel worthwhile.

Too often, teachers convey the message that children's questions, answers, or performance levels are inadequate. Such behavior does not promote a sense of being valued. On the other hand, actions that are meant to express love and concern are not always pleasant (as in disciplining a child). It is, therefore, crucial for children's sense of worth that actions meant to express concern are perceived as such and are not viewed as an affront to a child's sense of worth as an individual.

The use of "magic words" such as "please," "thank you," "awesome," "good job," and "you can be proud of . . ." convey the message to children that they are worthwhile and respected for who they are, not for what they are. Magic words serve to encourage children to compliment each other during activities, promote socially appropriate responses, and improve self-esteem. Also, taking photos or making a videotape of children involved in activities individually or as a group promotes personal and corporate identity, and the notion that "I am someone, and I count."

Acceptance of Self

Self-acceptance involves recognizing and accepting that we have weaknesses as well as strengths, limitations as well as abilities, and display incompetence as well as competence. To achieve self-acceptance it is crucial to view both these negative and positive aspects in their

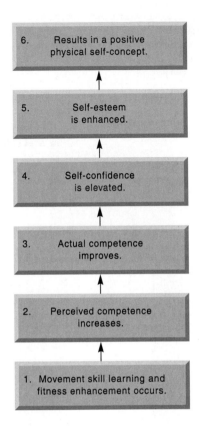

FIGURE 6.2 *A hierarchical view of self-concept enhancement through increased competence in the motor domain.*

TEACHING TIPS

Ten ways to avoid saying "no" or "wrong" to a child's answer to your question:

- "That's an interesting point of view."
- "Perhaps I didn't make myself clear."
- "Let me rephrase my question."
- "You've got the general idea."
- "That's part of the answer."
- "Good thinking, but not quite what I was looking for."
- "Are you saying that . . ."
- "Now there's an interesting perspective."
- "That's a good beginning, can anyone else help Jennifer finish the answer?"
- "You sure have your thinking cap on, but . . ."

totality and to learn how to deal with them positively. For children, this is frequently a difficult process. Their right–wrong, good–bad view of the world (characteristic of the concrete operations level of cognitive development) and unrealistic expectations from significant others make it hard for many children to accept themselves on the basis of who they are rather than for what they have achieved. Acceptance of self has its roots in acceptance by others.

Accepting teachers are concerned about children and are willing to exert themselves on their behalf. They are loyal sources of affection and support. They exhibit their acceptance in a variety of ways, with expressions of interest and concern being perhaps the major underlying features of their behaviors. Their actions convey an attitude of unconditional acceptance of individuals for *who* they are, not for *what* they are. For example, accepting teachers refrain from behaviors that give the impression that a child's behavior, appearance, grades, or talents determine their view of the child. They instead accept each and every child for his or her uniqueness and innate value and worth. Accepting teachers make a clear distinction between the choices that a child makes and who the child is. For example, the choice of throwing the ball at another student was poor, but the teacher shows that she still cares for the thrower and trusts that he or she will learn from the situation.

One of the most potent ways of teaching children to be accepting of themselves is to demonstrate personal self-acceptance. Permitting children to see some of your weaknesses and how you deal positively with them can be a very useful technique. For example, when repeatedly missing a basketball free throw you may say, "I never was very good at making free throws, but I really love the game of basketball." Teachers are significant others in the lives of children, and their demonstration of personal self-acceptance serves as a positive role model for children to emulate and aids them to view themselves in a more positive light.

Uniqueness

Recognizing, respecting, and celebrating one's personal **uniqueness** is a hallmark of a positive self-concept. The entire premise of developmental teaching—in the gymnasium or in the classroom—is based on the concept of individualization through developmentally appropriate experience. It is vitally important that we help children recognize and accept their unique qualities. Teachers who are attentive to students recognize children's uniqueness and structure their worlds appropriately. They allow for individual differences in experience, skill level, body type, fitness, and motivation.

Teachers are then able to permit relatively great freedom within the structure they have established, because all children recognize that they have a legitimate place in the class or group. Limits need to be reasonable and appropriate to the developmental level of children, not inflexible or arbitrary. The uniqueness of the individual must be respected, encouraged, and celebrated.

Virtue

A frequently forgotten component of a positive self-concept is virtue. **Virtue** is the sense that one is operating with consistency in accordance with an established moral code, a moral code that is consistent with the expectations of one's culture. In a physical education setting, that moral code may take the form of sharing, taking turns, good sportsmanship, fair play, or other forms of cooperative behavior. Children need to know that a basic requirement of a civilized society involves virtuous behavior. Teachers who both expect and help children to see themselves as acting in such a manner are making an important contribution to positive self-concept development.

The group settings of the classroom, gymnasium, and playground are excellent places to foster children's sense of virtue. Clearly defined and fairly enforced rules for acceptable behavior provide children with a clear view of adult expectations. Catching children being good, rather than only catching them being bad, is another effective technique of fostering a sense of virtue among children.

THE IMPORTANCE OF DEVELOPING CHILDREN'S SELF–CONCEPT

It is universally agreed that one's self-concept is learned. In the preschool and the elementary school years, parents, teachers, and caregivers are the primary models for the developing behavior of children. They provide children's primary feedback; through them children learn how their behavior is influencing others. Parents and teachers are also the primary evaluators of behavior. They give "moral" or "worth" meanings to the activities of children.

The Greatest Gift

As parents, teachers, and coaches we have the greatest gift to give to children—a positive self-concept.
We can do this by
treating them as though they were already what they could only hope to become:
letting them, through our eyes, see themselves as competent, worthy, and in control of their destiny;
giving them direction to their longings and leaving them with the conviction that their fate can be molded by their hopes and deeds, that their lives need not be shaped by accident, that their happiness does not depend on happenstance;
introducing them to themselves;
allowing them to learn who they are and what they can be.
If this is accomplished, they will no longer be strangers to themselves.
They will feel at home in the world.

David L. Gallahue

As the self-concept develops, children act in ways consistent with that concept. Significant others who serve as models and mediators in children's lives play a crucial role in determining the results of learning. Self-esteem develops only in the presence of others and is believed by many to be largely formed and stabilized by about age eight or nine. One of our tasks as adults working with children is to ensure that a profound sense of respect for the self is nurtured through our teaching and that children develop a sense of both security and status through quality, sensitive, caring teaching.

 CONCEPT 6.3
A positive view of self is vitally important in helping to provide children with a sense of security and status.

Security

The security of children comes from their identification with significant others, primarily parents and teachers. **Security** is identification with significant others and knowing that you are loved, valued, and accepted unconditionally for who you are—not what you are—in spite of personal weaknesses, inadequacies, or limitations.

This fact has several important implications for self-concept development. First, identification provides a sense of belonging. Children begin to shape their selves to become more like a revered adult. Second, having a sense of security provides an inner place where children know they are safe; they can operate from this safe base without fear of rejection. Third, security gives children a measure of what they perceive to be power, since the wishes of parents and teachers tend to become the wishes that they adopt. Finally, security provides children with a sense of control over their environment. It provides them with the knowledge that their life is not shaped by fate or luck; that their destiny does not depend on happenstance. It provides children with the security of knowing that they control their future and are unconditionally supported by parents, teachers, and coaches as they do so.

Status

Children are incompetent in most tasks in the early years of life, but considerable learning occurs during childhood, and a concept of personal status begins to emerge. **Status** refers to one's perceived position in a particular group—in the family, in the classroom, on the playing field, or with the peer group. The struggle throughout life is not so much between being competent or incompetent, but between perceiving oneself in a positive way in spite of incompetencies that exist. Children seek status and must look at incompetencies as learning tasks rather than as personal defects. The response of adults should be, "You may not be able to do it now, but with practice you will!"

Just as children receive considerable feedback about their incompetence, they need to receive positive feedback about their newly developing competencies. As school-age children spend more time with their peers, competencies are evaluated by age-mates. Their sense of perceived competence or incompetence is likely to be enlarged or diminished by the peer group. This is a time when children frequently face harsh criticism from age-mates because their peers may not be mature enough to temper criticism on the basis of other people's feelings.

Competence frequently becomes enmeshed with competition during the elementary school years, and judgments begin to be made on the basis of how well children do in comparison with others rather than in comparison with past personal performances. The nature of our competitive society makes it difficult to avoid competition

Security and status are important outcomes of a positive self-concept.

entirely, whether it is in games and sport or for good grades and personal recognition. As children venture more into the world, it is, however, possible for their sense of competence to expand without overreliance on competition as the means.

As children develop, they have a larger set of evaluators and feedback agents, so there is the possibility of more negative as well as positive evaluations. They become increasingly aware of themselves as members of a group and enjoy their growing independence as they try to take care of their own needs in routine activities and in play. Their developing skills in gross motor activities help them play on equal terms with their peers. But when competition is used to measure competence, the increased possibility of failure becomes a reality. Failure may result in the lowering of one's status in the eyes of others and in one's personal self-evaluation. Success, on the other hand, tends to have the opposite effect and plays an important role in enhancing self-concept.

Children are cooperative learners.

Teachers concerned with children's personal sense of status can devise ways for them to demonstrate competence through means other than competition. They recognize that the gymnasium, like the classroom, is a learning laboratory where the focus is on enhancing competence, not competing with one's peers. There are many opportunities for healthy competition in most communities, but it should never be a focal point of the instructional physical education program if we are truly interested in promoting children's sense of security and status.

COOPERATIVE LEARNERS DEFINED

Simply stated, **cooperative learning** is a process of positive socialization that involves working with others to achieve a common goal. Commonly referred to by children as "working together," cooperative learning requires effective communication, mutual compromise, individual honesty, fair play, and teamwork. These values and skills can be taught effectively in the developmentally based physical education program and should be primary goals of the cooperative learning strand of the curriculum. Cooperative learning promotes children's positive socialization into their culture.

CONCEPT 6.4
Movement skill learning and fitness enhancement generally occur in a group setting requiring cooperative behaviors for successful participation.

Working Together

Much of what children do occurs in the company of others, necessitating a variety of cooperative behaviors in both a cultural and a social context. This interaction takes many forms, and children adopt several social roles in their daily encounters with parents, caregivers, teachers, schoolmates, friends, teammates, and coaches. **Cultural socialization** is a process whereby one modifies his or her behaviors to conform to the expectations of an individual or group. It is a process through which children learn the rules and skills of functioning in their cultural milieu, which in turn enables them to be integrated into and participate as contributing members of society.

Children's socialization is largely dependent upon three things; namely, status, roles, and norms. Status refers to one's position in society as well as to one's position in a family or other group. Children have many positions. They have different levels of status conferred upon them as sons or daughters, students, playmates, or athletes. As a result, they learn to play a role that is associated with the level of status identified for each position. A **role** is an individual behavior used to carry out a particular status. For example, parents frequently remark about how much more mature their son or daughter acts at school than at home. Similarly, classroom teachers often observe vastly different behaviors on the playground or during the physical education class than in the classroom. In other words, the child's "job description" (status) in different social settings interacts with his or her "interpretation of the job" (role) and produces behaviors that are frequently different from one setting to another. These behaviors are governed by certain norms or standards of behavior. **Cultural norms** are acceptable standards of behavior that are expected of all members of society no matter what their status or their perceived role in acting out that position. Cultural norms may, however, vary from one social setting to another. For example, commonly accepted behaviors in the gymnasium such as running, tagging, and throwing objects are not generally viewed as acceptable in the confines of the classroom. As children become socialized into their culture they learn what is acceptable and unacceptable behavior in a variety of settings.

Social Decision Makers

Socialization is a process that goes beyond the mere internalization of status, roles, and norms in a nonthinking and conforming manner. It is a dynamic interactive process between society and the individual, a process that depends on and requires both reasoning and decision making. One of the goals of developmental physical education, as well as of all good teaching, is to influence the process of children's socialization. This can be done by helping them learn about, experience, and adopt socially appropriate behaviors. Cooperative behavior is not automatically conferred upon children. It is learned behavior that can be modified and improved, especially during childhood.

REASONS FOR FOSTERING POSITIVE SOCIALIZATION

Children's development does not occur in a vacuum but in multicultural social settings that are dynamic and require cooperative interaction with others. Because of the many and varied roles that physical activity takes—in free play, in the physical education class, in intramural activities or competitive sport—its role in developing positive socialization in children is undeniably important. The desire for group affiliation is frequently cited as a primary reason for children's tremendous interest in recreational and competitive sport activities. Similarly, attitudes, character, and moral growth are fostered in social settings. What better place than the social setting of the gymnasium, playground, or athletic field to internalize the normative behaviors required for meaningful group affiliation, positive attitude formation, character development, and moral growth?

CONCEPT 6.5
Positive socialization experiences contribute to improved group affiliation, positive attitude formation, character education, and moral growth.

Group Affiliation

One of the most compelling forces of childhood is the need to belong. **Group affiliation,** the need to be accepted and identified as a member of a particular group, is quite powerful. In fact, the need for group affiliation tends to increase through the elementary years, peaking in the strong peer group influences of the junior high school and high school years. A sense of belonging, as discussed earlier, is an important component of a positive self-concept, and its value must not be underestimated. The importance of the peer group, youth sports, clubs, and even gangs is tied to the need for identity through peer group affiliation. Children who have developed their movement skills to the point where they are viewed by others (as well as by themselves) as competent are generally among the first to be included as part of the group. On the other hand, children who have failed to develop a reasonable level of movement competence in games and sports are frequently excluded from the group, or at best only marginally tolerated.

Attitude Formation and Character Education

A major function of positive socialization is the transference of the attitudes and values of one's culture from one generation to the next. Basically, **attitudes** are opinions about something or someone that are evidenced in one's behavior. An attitude is a learned behavior—based on knowledge or ignorance and positive or negative experiences—that results in a value being placed on something or someone. **Character** is how we live in response to what we hold to be important, meaningful, and worthwhile. Our character tends to reflect the values that we hold and is an outgrowth of our attitudes. For example, children who do not like (value) vigorous physical activity and try to be excused from their physical education classes are frequently accused of having a "bad attitude." For whatever reason, they have developed a negative attitude toward vigorous activity that has culminated in failure to value it as part of their lifestyle. As a result, they will go to great lengths to avoid active participation.

CONCEPT 6.6
Attitudes are learned behaviors acquired in a social context and they can be shaped, modified, or changed.

Attitudes and the personal meaning attached to activities, places, events, and people are learned behaviors acquired in a social context. As a result, they may be shaped, modified, or changed. To personally acquire an attitude that culminates in a value, three things must occur: compliance, identification, and internalization. **Compliance** is associated with doing something in the hope that it will result in a favorable response from someone

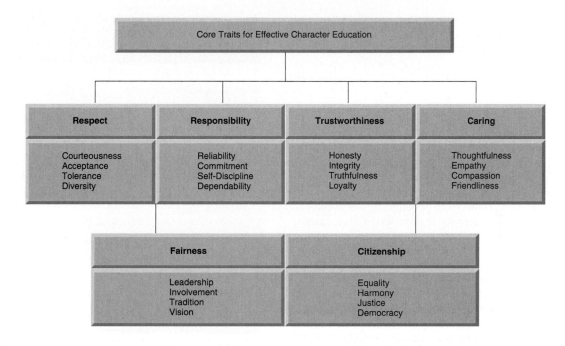

FIGURE 6.3 *Core traits for character education and their related components that can be effectively integrated into the school curriculum.*

else. For example, David Lee shares his jump rope with a playmate in the hope of getting a favorable response from the teacher. **Identification,** on the other hand, is a process that requires one to adopt the attitude or value of another. In our example, David Lee now shares his jump rope with a playmate because he knows that is what the teacher would do. Finally, **internalization** means taking on a particular behavior as part of one's own value system. Using our example of David Lee, he now shares his jump rope because it is his own desire to do so. David Lee has finally internalized what most of us would consider to be a positive character trait, sharing.

 CONCEPT 6.7
Character education is a valid, worthwhile, and essential endeavor to be engaged in by all concerned teachers.

The developmental physical education program has both the opportunity and the responsibility for shaping positive attitudes and helping children value participation

in vigorous physical activity. Of importance also is the responsibility, shared with all other teachers, of helping children internalize standards of proper behavior and conduct such as honesty, tolerance, acceptance, and empathy. It is important that you not shrink from these responsibilities under the misguided notion that it is not your job, or on the assumption that someone else will teach these important lessons. Oftentimes, you, the teacher, are the only person in the lives of the children you touch who can take responsibility for forming wholesome attitudes and developing positive character traits in your students. In many communities, rich and poor, large and small, teachers are the only significant others left in the child's life who are capable of imparting this information. The traditional triad of the home, the church, and the school has in many cases eroded so completely that the school is the only avenue left to teach many of life's important lessons. Forgive me if I appear to be preaching, but it is essential to recognize the importance of positive attitude formation and character development as a daily function of all good teaching as we work toward the goal of positive socialization. Figure 6.3 depicts core traits for effective character education that cut across virtually all social strata. Take a few minutes to study each. Reflect on how you might infuse these in your teaching as you strive to build character in your students.

Moral Growth

The concept of **moral growth** recognizes that the individual has both the potential and the need for higher levels of moral reasoning and moral behavior. **Moral reasoning** involves making intelligent decisions about what is right and wrong. **Moral behavior,** on the other hand, is one's ability to operate consistently within a value system that has reasoned right from wrong. It is commonly believed that physical activity in the form of play, games, and sports participation has the potential for fostering moral growth. This is probably due to the variety of emotions raised and the unpredictable situations that come up in both cooperative and competitive activities. Free play, games, and sports participation provide ideal settings for teaching the qualities of honesty, loyalty, self-control, teamwork, fair play, and good sportsmanship. Refraining from lying, cheating, and intimidating opposing players are moral decisions governed by concern for the physical and psychological welfare of others.

C O N C E P T   6 . 8
Core character traits of respect, responsibility, trust, caring, fairness, and citizenship are central to physical activity and sport, thereby making the physical education class a unique setting for promoting moral growth.

In most states children under the age of nine are, by law, considered to be amoral and not responsible for their actions. That is, their sense of what is right and wrong has not been fully developed and internalized. Young children tend to be self-centered and operate on the basis that "if it feels good, just do it." Therefore, they need to encounter social settings that provide them with opportunities for moral growth.

Moral growth can be encouraged through the creation of moral dilemmas. A **moral dilemma** is a situation, real or manufactured, that offers an opportunity for moral reasoning and moral decision making under the careful supervision of the teacher. For example, moral dilemmas frequently occur in children's races, kickball games, and self-report fitness scores. When these dilemmas arise, the

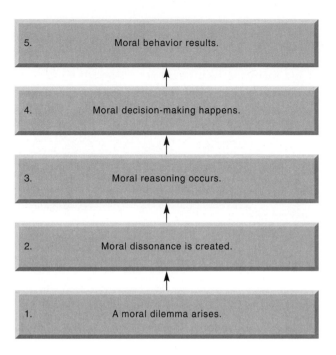

FIGURE 6.4 *The steps leading to moral behavior.*

teacher has an excellent opportunity to call attention to them, thus promoting moral growth by helping students sort through what is good, right, and fair.

Free play, physical education, and sports provide ideal settings where various levels of moral behavior can be observed and improved. Remember, however, that unless children's thought processes are stimulated, moral dissonance is not likely to occur. **Moral dissonance** is personal questioning brought about by attention given to moral dilemmas that arise from good versus bad, right versus wrong, or fair versus unfair. If dissonance fails to occur, it is unlikely that moral reasoning, decision making, and growth will result. Figure 6.4 highlights the steps leading to moral behavior.

FACTORS THAT INFLUENCE AFFECTIVE DEVELOPMENT

Many factors contribute to affective development of children. Among them are giving praise and encouragement, setting realistic goals, encouraging realistic self-assessment, and using moral dilemmas to teach fair play.

Children need to clearly understand the definitions of the following terms and how they are manifested through sportsmanship.

- *Fair Play:* To play according to the rules and to apply them equally to all.
- *Teamwork:* To work cooperatively with one or more persons toward a common goal.
- *Loyalty:* To be consistent and faithful to an individual, group, or team.
- *Self-control:* To be in control of and responsible for one's actions.
- SPORTSMANSHIP: The combined result of fair play, teamwork, loyalty, and self-control in both victory and defeat.

Try the "sandwich" approach when encouraging children.

- *First,* find something good about the effort or the performance and tell the child. ("Your wind-up and arm action are looking much better.")
- *Second,* provide an instructional cue. ("Remember, follow through in the direction that you want the ball to go.")
- *Third,* encourage the performer with a positive statement. ("Keep up the good work: you're making real progress.")

Encouragement

Encouragement takes many forms and ranges from self-encouragement to encouraging others. It is often difficult for adults to say nice things about themselves, but children must learn that it is all right to feel good about oneself. Children learn from models and from imitation. To teach **self-encouragement,** teachers can encourage themselves verbally in front of students. This is difficult to do because most of us have learned not to "brag" or to draw attention to ourselves for fear of being considered conceited or prideful. You can begin self-encouragement by expressing self-satisfaction in minor accomplishments. You might, for example, say how you feel about something you have done or made, like "I really felt good when I made that foul shot," or "It made me feel good to know that I made that bulletin board display." If someone in the class responds with, "I don't think it's so great," it is appropriate to say, "I didn't say it was great, but things don't have to be perfect for us to feel good about them." Teachers should regard this self-reinforcement and positive self-referent language as a teaching activity.

The purpose of self-encouragement is not to enhance your self-concept but to teach children that it is okay to feel good about themselves. You can begin by praising your own work and then move to praising personal qualities. Begin with things that are not highly personal. It might be easier to use group encouragement first, such as

"The team did a great job" or "Our class can do it" before using individual self-praise. Question-asking is one of the tools that can be used to get children to praise themselves. A question such as "Don't you think you did well on that?" gives children a chance to say something positive about themselves. It is, however, important at some point to move into more personal qualities so that children begin to see that it is okay to say nice things about themselves as individuals. It may be helpful to tell your students what you are doing. This helps them to know it is all right to say nice things when they feel good about what they have done and that one of the joys of life is to share our good feelings with one another.

 CONCEPT 6.9
Encouragement helps students see themselves as having the potential for success, and, with work, capable of achieving great things.

Self-encouragement and **encouraging others** are positively related. Learning to encourage is a skill that is applied to others as well as to oneself. Learning how to encourage others permits each child to become a reinforcer for other children. Both children and teachers need to be taught how to encourage others and how to receive encouragement from others.

Teachers should give positive reinforcement in specific small areas of good and poor performance. Children need to be given statements that cushion failure with success—"You will do better next time," "You didn't get a hit this time, but you probably will next time up," "Wow! What a super effort; you're really getting the idea." This helps to connect the failure with hope for the future.

Goal Setting

Goal setting must be individual, must be made in relation to past performance, and must have an end in view. If children are to have a commitment to reach a goal, it is important that they have some part in setting the goal. The goal should be slightly higher than that reached by previous performance. This may be far below the eventual performance toward which the child is striving or toward which the teacher is aiming, but the lower level is reasonable in the sense that it is attainable. This gives positive reinforcement for the achievement of a near goal on the way to achieving a larger goal.

Self-Assessment

Teaching children **self-assessment,** or how to evaluate themselves and others realistically, is an important factor influencing affective development that is sometimes ignored. Children do not have a natural basis for realistic evaluation and self-assessment. They tend to be overly harsh with themselves and give themselves fewer "strokes" than adults would deem appropriate. To maintain a positive outlook, the evaluation of self must be accurate and realistic. If you are dealing with true failure, look at it from the standpoint of learning. Improvement and learning extend the possibility of turning the experience of personal or team failure into one that can build up the individual's self-concept and the group's sense of identity and cohesiveness. It is true that failure is a fact of life, and it must be faced by all of us. But is it really necessary for it to be such a big part of the lives of so many children? Failure must be minimized and put into its proper perspective if we are serious about using physical activity as a way to enhance self-concept and promote positive socialization.

CONCEPT 6.10
Children frequently need help in making realistic self-assessments and forming appropriate goal-directed behaviors.

Every child should be able to find some degree of success and accomplishment in the physical activities of the gymnasium or athletic field. As teachers we must structure experiences in such a way that each individual can succeed. For some, success may simply be getting into the game, making a hit, or catching a fly ball. For others, it may be hitting a home run, making a double play, or being on the all-star team. Success should never be measured solely by one's win–loss record or coming in first place. We must help children make realistic assessments of their efforts and find additional means of measuring success. This is a difficult process, but we must help children learn how to evaluate themselves on the basis of improvement and learning and not simply on being the "best."

Unrealistic evaluations by self and others only compound the problems of real failure. The purpose of realistic assessment is not to have children completely avoid negative evaluations. Some realistic assessments may be negative. However, a negative evaluation that is realistic provides a basis for change that will allow positive performance and, therefore, positive self-assessment.

Moral Dilemmas

As mentioned earlier, a moral dilemma is a behavior situation, real or manufactured, that requires moral reasoning and moral decision making based on that reasoning. Moral behavior goes beyond the socially acceptable conventions of shaking hands or congratulating an opponent. It involves making decisions about one's personal code of conduct, decisions that look out for the rights of others, in play, game, and sport settings. Physical education teachers and coaches are in a unique position to foster real moral growth. The demands for cooperation, sharing, turn-taking, courteous behavior, fair play, and good sportsmanship must all be expected and followed for successful participation.

Structuring moral dilemmas in the gymnasium and encouraging children to work through them in a thinking and caring manner promotes a sense of moral virtue. For example, in a competitive ball game where the score is tied, time is running out, and one team must first get the ball in order to have a chance of winning, you might stop the activity, sit the class down, and present the dilemma: Is it okay to intentionally foul your opponent or fake an injury in order to have a time-out called? This will result in a variety of responses, both for and against intentional fouling and feigning injury, and provide you with the opportunity to promote moral reasoning and moral growth.

Steps that lead to *moral growth* include the following:

- Create or take advantage of an existing moral dilemma. (For example, discuss student cheating in self-reporting scores on a standardized fitness test.)

- Ask those involved to *describe* the dilemma. ("What happened?" "Why did it happen?" "How did it happen?")

- Help students *focus* on the specific word or term describing the dilemma. ("This is an issue involving _____." The word might be honesty, fair play, communication, cooperation, teamwork, or sportsmanship.)

- Work with students to *define* the meaning of the word and its consequences if ignored. ("Honesty is being truthful, trustworthy and fair. Failure to be honest leads to, or results in, _____."

- *Operationalize* the meaning of the word and its importance to the current situation. ("Why is it important to be honest when recording our fitness scores?")

- *Apply* the concept implied by the word first to other relevant topics in the same setting and then to other areas. ("What are other areas in games and sports where honesty is very important?" followed by: "Why is honesty important in all that we do?")

- *Reinforce* positive moral behaviors whenever possible. ("I'm sure pleased with the accurate and honest reporting of your fitness scores.")

Successful participation implies that the "bottom line" is more than winning or losing; it concerns giving your all, while at the same time providing others with the respect and dignity that they deserve. Placing children in contrived situations where they have to think about, make decisions, and act on moral issues provides a training environment for moral growth. Also, taking advantage of "teachable moments" where situations spontaneously arise that provide an opportunity for moral decision making can also enhance moral growth. Additionally, the behaviors that you, the teacher, model for children play a vital role in chldren's learning to recognize and respond to moral issues.

IMPLICATIONS FOR TEACHING DEVELOPMENTAL PHYSICAL EDUCATION

Considerable speculation, theory, and research have revealed the unique contribution of vigorous physical activity to the affective development of children (Coakley, 1987; Bredemeier and Shields, 1987; Harter, 1982; Weiss, 1987). Because the number of variables influencing such research is formidable, it is difficult to establish conclusively whether the relationship between physical activity and improvements in self-concept and positive socialization is causal or only casual. In other words, do specific types of experiences in physical activity measurably affect specific aspects of affective development (that is, a causal relationship)? Or, does physical activity in general influence, among other things, one's affective development (that is, a casual relationship)?

This does not mean that quality developmental physical education programs cannot or do not have a significant impact on self-concept development and positive socialization. It simply means that at this time a precise measurement of the specific variables and extent of this influence is not possible. Child development specialists, psychologists, and educators are quick to recognize that affective development is difficult to measure objectively. It is, however, relatively easy to subjectively observe positive changes in children who have been involved in a quality physical education program that is success oriented, developmentally appropriate, oriented toward reasonable goals, challenging, individualized in instruction, and full of positive reinforcement.

The movement skill levels of children are often controlled by factors outside of their influence. Things such as physical stature, health-related conditions, lack of experience, and poor instruction make it impossible for many children to meet their own personal standards of performance or those of the peer group. Movement is not the only influence on children's affective development, but it is an important one. If movement skills are poorly developed, the chances are good that this will negatively affect children's perceived movement competence. If children begin to feel they are not able to do things, they tend to become less willing to participate. Also, if other children show that they do not regard the child highly because of lack of ability, the child is more apt to feel negative and encounter problems of group affiliation and positive socialization.

It is important that children develop a proper perspective on success and failure. Children must experience success. Using teaching approaches that emphasize the individuality of the learner is an excellent way to help all children find a measure of achievement. Using exploratory, guided-discovery, and problem-solving approaches to learning, especially during the beginning/ novice level of learning a new movement skill, is an excellent way to permit a variety of "correct" solutions and helping to ensure success. It is vitally important that children feel they are making progress, especially at the early stages of learning a new movement skill. Success has a tendency to increase effort and the number of mastery attempts. Perceptions of failure, however, tend to discourage the learner, heighten anxiety, reduce effort, and decrease the number of attempts at learning the new skill.

The ratio of success to failure that children experience should emphasize success to the point that they are conditioned to expect further and greater success. Persons of low self-esteem wish for success just as much as others, but they do not believe they have the necessary qualities or the "right stuff" to achieve success. Children will gain little by repeating a task for which their responses are inappropriate, their ability inadequate, or their information insufficient. Children need to have some sense that eventually they will be able to master the task; otherwise, they will not be willing to continue trying. This suggests the importance of analyzing the movement situations children are engaged in and the resources at their disposal for accomplishing movement tasks successfully.

Individualizing instruction is important in programming for success. Try to design individualized activities in accordance with each child's motor, cognitive, and affective level of functioning. There will be some stretching and growing, but the steps forward are small enough and individualized enough that the child can be assured of finding success. Individually appropriate movement experiences are necessary for the balanced and wholesome development of all children.

Because children often respond to scary or daring challenges, adventure activities may lure them to perform new and more challenging feats. You will need to consider what is developmentally appropriate in the challenge and

to sequence the task according to difficulty. This is of crucial importance in determining a child's sense of success or failure. Competition should not be introduced until children have developed a sufficient degree of movement competence and can appreciate cooperative behavior in a competitive setting.

Adults working with children need to be accepting. There is no place for teasing, scaring, or criticizing. Each of these can negatively affect self-concept and positive socialization. The person who works with children in movement skill acquisition and fitness enhancement needs to be a warm, caring adult, because children need more than anything else the trust and endorsement of significant others. Caring teachers who are interested in helping children develop to their fullest potential should look seriously at the levels of movement skill and fitness children have attained. Although developmental physical education is not a panacea for all educational problems, it can, through good teaching, make positive contributions to a stable, positive self-concept and the components of positive cultural socialization.

SUMMARY

In this chapter we discussed the child as both a self-discovering learner and a cooperative learner and defined terms important to the developing self—*self-concept, self-esteem,* and *self-confidence.* We described several components of a positive self-concept and how physical education teachers can enhance each one. The importance of a positive self-concept was discussed in terms of developing personal security and status. All good teachers, parents, and coaches make positive contributions to children's self-esteem, and all can help to enhance children's senses of belonging, competence, worthiness, self-acceptance, appreciation for personal uniqueness, and virtue. Teachers of physical education and coaches are frequently in an especially good position to influence the development of the self because of the high positive value that most children place on being good at games, sports, and other physical activities and because of the social settings in which most physical activities occur.

Because children are also cooperative learners, their positive socialization, or their cooperative interaction with others in both social and cultural settings, is particularly important. Some of the reasons for encouraging positive socialization include group affiliation, positive attitude formation, character development, and moral growth. We concluded the chapter with factors that influence children's affective development and ended with a detailed discussion of the implications of self-concept enhancement and positive socialization for the developmental physical education program.

COMPLEMENTARY READINGS

Bowyer, G. (1993). Helping students think positively. *Strategies* 6:8–12.

Deline, J. (1991). "Why can't they get along?" Developing cooperative skills through physical education. *JOPERD* 62:21–26.

Hellison, D., and N. Georgiadis. (1992). Teaching values through basketball. *Strategies* 5:5–8.

Kretchmer, R. S. (1992). Getting it right. *Strategies* 5:9–11.

Kretchmer, R. S. (1991). The ethics gap. *Strategies* 5:15–18.

Levitt, S. L. (1991). Professional practice: A lesson in empathy. *Strategies* 5:11–12.

Sage, G. H. (1986). Social Development. In V. Seefeldt, ed., *Physical Activity and Well-Being,* Reston, VA: AAHPERD.

Seagren, S., and T. Sharpe. (1993). Promoting cooperation in the gym. *Strategies* 6:8–9.

Thomson-Chepyator, J. R., ed. (1994). Multicultural Education: Culturally Responsive Teaching. *JOPERD* 65:31–74 (Part of feature issue with several helpful articles).

Thomson-Chepyator, J. R., ed. (1995). Multicultural Education: Culturally Responsive Teaching Part II. *JOPERD* 66:41–53.

Tomme, P. M., and J. C. Wendt. (1993). Affective teaching: Psychosocial aspects of physical education. *JOPERD* 64:66–69.

SUPPLEMENTARY READINGS

Bredemeier, B. J., and D. L. Shields. (1987). Moral growth through physical activity: A structural/developmental approach. In D. Gould and M. R. Weiss, eds., *Advances in Pediatric Sport Sciences, Volume 2: Behavioral Issues,* Champaign, IL: Human Kinetics.

Coakley, J. J. (1987). Children and the sport socialization process. In D. Gould & M. R. Weiss, eds., *Advances in Pediatric Sport Sciences, Volume 2: Behavioral Issues,* Champaign, IL: Human Kinetics.

Coakley, J. J. (1994). *Sport in Society: Issues and Controversies.* St. Louis, MO: Mosby.

Hamburg, D. (1992). *Today's Children: Creating a Future for a Generation in Crisis.* New York: Times Books.

Harter, S. (1982). Developmental perspectives on self-esteem. In E. M. Hetherington, ed., *Handbook of Child Psychology, Volume IV: Socialization, Personality and Social Development,* New York: Wiley.

Lumpkin, A., and S. K. Stoll. (1994). *Sport Ethics: Applications for Fair Play.* Reston, VA: AAHPERD.

Weiss, M. R. (1987). Self-esteem and achievement in children's sport and physical activity. In D. Gould and M. R. Weiss, eds., *Advances in Pediatric Sport Sciences, Volume 2: Behavioral Issues,* Champaign, IL: Human Kinetics.

VIDEOS

Youth Sports: Is Winning Everything? 391 El Portal Road, San Mateo, CA: Distinctive Home Video Productions. (29 min.).

Sports Psychology for Youth Coaches. 391 El Portal Road, San Mateo, CA: Distinctive Home Video Productions. (30 min.).

CHAPTER 7

Children with Disabilities

Key Concept

Children with Disabilities Are Faced with a Wide Variety of Challenges, Many of Which Can Be Successfully Integrated into the Developmentally Based Physical Education Program

Chapter Objectives

The purpose of this chapter is to provide you with the tools to:
- Identify essential aspects of Public Laws 94–142 and 99–457 and discuss their implications for teaching physical education.
- Distinguish among various types of programs designed to physically educate children with disabilities.
- Identify and discuss the basic elements of a variety of physical, mental, emotional, and learning disabilities.
- Suggest ways that the physical education program might be modified to accommodate children with various physical, mental, emotional, and learning disabilities.
- Identify and discuss the unique social and personal needs of children with disabilities.

Terms to Remember

Individualized Education
   Program (IEP)
Adapted Physical Education
Remedial Physical
   Education
Developmental Physical
   Education
Physical Disability
Sensory Impairment
Visual Impairment
Auditory Impairment
Cardiovascular Limitations
Neuromuscular Limitations
Cerebral Palsy
Spasticity

Athetosis
Ataxia
Rigidity
Tremor
Epilepsy
Grand Mal Seizure
Jacksonian Seizure
Petit Mal Seizure
Psychomotor Seizures
Asthma
Cystic Fibrosis
Musculoskeletal Limitation
Osgood-Schlatter's
   Condition
Arthritis

Postural Deviations
Scoliosis
Lordosis
Kyphosis
Mental Disabilities
Mild Retardation
Moderate Retardation
Severe Retardation
Profound Retardation
Brain Damage
Environmental Retardation
Genetic Retardation
Classic Emotional Disorder
Autism
Rhythmical Stereotypes

Echolalia
Learning Disability
ATLO Children
Attention Deficit Disorder
   (ADD)
Inattention
Impulsivity
Hyperactivity
Other Health Impairments

Every school contains some children with physical, mental, emotional, or learning disabilities. Their challenges may range from the mild to the severe, and they may be single or multiple, temporary or permanent. However, each of these children is limited in some measurable way in the ability to participate in or benefit fully from the physical activities characteristic of their peers.

The Education for All Handicapped Children Act of 1975 (PL 94–142) ensures that *all* children from ages three to twenty-one are provided an "appropriate education."* Additionally, the Education of the Handicapped Amendments Act of 1986 (PL 99–457) became effective in 1991 and extends previous legislation to include infants, toddlers, and preschoolers from birth to age five. These important federal laws, which have dramatically influenced how individuals with disabilities are treated in the United States, are of particular importance to physical educators. Physical education is the only subject area specifically identified in the definition of an "appropriate education." The provisions of Public Law 94–142 mandate that all children with diagnosed disabilities must be provided with an appropriate physical education program and that this program must be offered in the "least restrictive environment." Therefore, children with special physical, mental, or emotional needs must be given the opportunity to take part in the regular physical education program unless their needs can only be met through a specially designed program as prescribed by their **Individualized Education Program (IEP).** Physical education contributes to the growth and development of children with special needs through the medium of movement. This fact has been wisely recognized in Public Law 94–142, which mandates a policy of inclusion ("mainstreaming") whenever and wherever possible.

---

*Although PL 94–142 and 99–457 frequently use the term *handicapped,* it is viewed as degrading by many. The terms *disability, challenged, special needs,* and *limiting condition* are generally viewed as more appropriate and are strongly encouraged. In fact, PL 101–476, the Individuals with Disabilities Education Act (IDEA), enacted in 1990, finally officially discarded the term *handicapped* and replaced it with the term *disability.*

CONCEPT 7.1

All children have a right to an education appropriate to their motor, cognitive, and affective level of development.

KEY FEDERAL LEGISLATION FOR CHILDREN WITH DEVELOPMENTAL DISABILITIES

Legislation	Target Group	Key Concepts
PL 94–142 (Education for All Handicapped Children Act of 1975)	Shall serve 6–18-year-olds with handicaps	1. Free, appropriate public education 2. Least restrictive environment 3. Individualized Program Plan (IPP) 4. Individualized Education Program (IEP)
PL 99–457 (Amendments to PL 94–142, 1986)	Shall serve 0–2 and 3–5-year-olds with developmental delays or "at risk" as defined by each state	1. Public education services at no cost to the family 2. Coordinated child find 3. Mandates state policy for 3–5-year-olds 4. Extends PL 94–142 provisions to 3–5-year-olds 5. Mandates early identification and programming
PL 101–476 (Individuals with Disabilities Education Act, revision of PL 94–142, 1990)	May serve 3–5 and 19–21-year-olds	1. Autism added as a separate category 2. Brain injury added as a separate category 3. Eliminates term *handicapped* and replaces it with *disability*

This chapter looks at several disabilities and examines the role of physical education in the education of children with disabilities. The problems of social adjustment faced by children with disabilities are also considered. Furthermore, several practical teaching strategies are included, in the "Teaching Tips" boxes, throughout the chapter for the regular physical education program that includes children with disabilities.

THE PHYSICAL EDUCATION PROGRAM

Children cannot be excluded from a physical education program because of a disability, whether temporary or permanent, mild or severe, single or multiple. Whenever possible, they must be mainstreamed into the regular physical education class. When the disability prohibits participation in the regular physical education class, as determined by their IEP, a specialized program must, by law, be offered.

Children need to be included in the regular physical education program whenever possible to learn how to interact effectively with their environment, develop movement skills, enhance fitness levels, and learn how to use leisure time wisely. Children who do not have a disability are given an opportunity to learn tolerance and acceptance and to be unencumbered by the notion that someone is "different."

CONCEPT 7.2
Public school children with disabilities must be integrated into the developmental physical education program in the least restrictive manner.

At first, physical education teachers often feel overwhelmed by the fact that they must provide appropriate educational experiences for children with disabilities. They often feel ill-prepared and frustrated by this requirement. Remember, however, that children with disabilities are children first. Although they may have some unique needs, they are much more like children who do not have a disability than they are unlike them. Avoid the trap of classifying your students as "handicapped" and "normal." The normal child is a mythical average from which all children deviate to some degree. Some children deviate from this norm more than others. Because of this, they have special needs that must be met somewhat differently than the needs of their peers. These needs may be met

through one or more of the following types of physical education programs: the adapted program, the remedial program, or the developmental program (see Figure 7.1).

The Adapted Program

The **adapted physical education** program provides for physical activities that are modified according to the physical, mental, and emotional limitations of a challenged individual or group. The aim of the adapted physical education program is to permit each child to function within his or her range of abilities. In this sense, regular physical education programs that make real and constant efforts at individualizing instruction are in fact "adapting" their instruction to the needs of all children. These teachers are constantly modifying the learning goals and movement experiences based on the unique needs and current abilities of the children they teach.

The Remedial Program

The **remedial physical education** program differs from the adapted program in that it is corrective in nature and includes specific exercises and physical activities designed to improve body mechanics. Improvement in such basic movement tasks as standing, sitting, and moving through space are important learning goals of the remedial program, as is improvement in perceptual-motor functioning.

Specialized training is required in the area of remedial physical education. The remedial program should be conducted under the supervision of a physician and may incorporate suggestions from a physical therapist or school psychologist. Most elementary schools do not have the physical facilities and specialized equipment often recommended for carrying out an effective remedial program. Consequently, teachers are frequently required to improvise and use what is available in the school and community. Furthermore, remedial programs that do exist frequently promote exclusion and separate classes for children with disabilities, thereby undermining the important concepts embodied in mainstreaming and inclusion. In any case, complete records must be kept for each child in the program. These records should include a health history, an IEP, and an updated physician's report with a clear description of appropriate physical activities to be engaged in by the child. It should be reemphasized that specialized training is necessary to conduct an effective remedial physical education program and that these programs must be conducted under the supervision of a physician.

THE ADAPTED PROGRAM

A modified program of movement activities that maximizes the potential of persons with disabilities through an individualized education program.

THE REMEDIAL PROGRAM

A program of specific exercises and activities for correcting errors in body mechanics and perceptual-motor functioning.

THE DEVELOPMENTAL PROGRAM

An individualized program of movement activities based on personal needs and designed to improve movement, fitness, and social-emotional skills.

FIGURE 7.1 *The relationships among the adapted, remedial, and developmental programs.*

The developmental physical education program is sensitive to the needs of all children.

The Developmental Program

The **developmental physical education** program contains elements of both the adapted and remedial programs. It is concerned specifically with individual improvement in movement skill acquisition, fitness enhancement, and cognitive and affective development. The developmental physical education program is concerned with all children, those with disabilities and those without. Its primary goals are improvement in movement control, emotional control, and learning enjoyment. The developmental program is similar to the adapted program in that it strives to individualize learning and modify movement experience based on the unique physical, mental, and emotional abilities of each child. The developmental program is similar to the remedial physical education program in that it shares the goals of improved body mechanics and perceptual-motor functioning.

C O N C E P T   7 . 3
An essential tenet of developmental physical education is the need for individual appropriateness in the selection of movement experiences for *all* children.

The developmental physical education program can be implemented effectively with all children. It does, however, require the assessment of movement abilities prior to planning a specific program of activities. Assessment may take many forms. It may be subjective or objective, process-based or product-based, individual or group. It must, however, be regular and systematic and occur before as well as after a program of activities is engaged in. Chapter 11 focuses on assessing progress.

Inclusion

The philosophy of *inclusion* of children with mild to severe disabilities is currently very popular in the United States, and an outgrowth of the Individuals with Disabilities Education Act of 1990. Basically, full inclusion refers to fully integrating children with severe disabilities, as well as those with lesser disabilities, into the regular classroom and physical education class with their nondisabled peers. Schools that practice a philosophy of full inclusion involve children with a wide range of severe disabilities into all aspects of the class, not just as special visitors at certain times during the day. This places special demands on the physical education teacher and is viewed by many as an impossible task (Craft, 1994).

Inclusion *is* possible if your curriculum is developmental in more than name only. If your curriculum is developmental, it should be able to incorporate the broad range of abilities that are found among today's children. Careful analysis of the learning tasks incorporated into the lesson makes it possible, with practice, to devise appropriate learning outcomes for all students. Inclusion *is* possible if you have additional help. The use of teacher aides, parent helpers, and peer student helpers is essential. Inclusion *is* possible if you have the active support of parents, school administration, and health care workers. The physical education teacher's job has become more demanding because of the focus on inclusion, but it can be successful if it is developmentally based, realistic in terms of student to teacher ratios, and actively supported.

CONCEPT 7.4
A philosophy of inclusion of children with mild to severe disabilities into all aspects of the educational process has been adopted by many school corporations and is supported by law.

CATEGORIES OF DEVELOPMENTAL DISABILITIES

Children with developmental disabilities are generally classified into four broad and sometimes overlapping categories: children with physical disabilities, mental disabilities, emotional disabilities, and learning disabilities. A brief look at several specific conditions that are frequently encountered in the public schools follows.

Children with Physical Disabilities

PL 94–142 defines a **physical disability** as any physical condition that interferes with the child's educational performance and includes disabilities caused by disease, congenital factors, and other unspecified causes. About 3 percent of the school-age population has physical impairments. Children with physical disabilities are characterized by faulty functioning of their sensory receptors or their musculature that limits or restricts their ability to function in some manner. Children with a physical impairment may suffer from one or more disabling conditions. These conditions restrict their movement and mandate modifications in the physical activities in which they engage. For purposes of our discussion, physical disabilities have been subdivided here into sensory impairments and cardiovascular, neuromuscular, musculoskeletal disorders, and pulmonary limitations (see Figure 7.2).

CONCEPT 7.5
Children with physical disabilities may exhibit sensory, cardiovascular, neuromuscular, or orthopedic limitations that can be successfully compensated for through developmentally appropriate physical activity.

Sensory Impairments.   **Sensory impairment** is one in which the sensory receptors are unable to transmit or interpret stimuli in a manner conducive to educational performance. By far the most common sensory impairments are visual limitations and auditory limitations.

Visual Impairments.   The child with a **visual impairment** is defined as one whose educational performance is adversely affected even when corrective lenses are worn. PL 94–142 specifically states that the child does not have to be blind or even near blind to qualify as having a visual limitation. The physical education program for visually

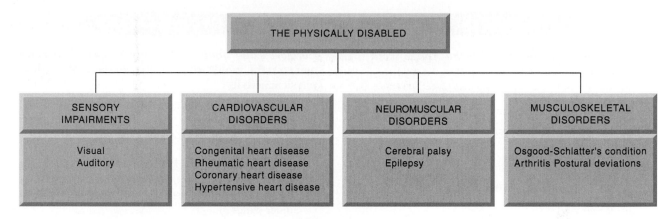

FIGURE 7.2 *Common physical limitations found among children.*

Visually impaired children **may range from the legally blind to the partially sighted:**

- Use a whistle or verbal cue to signal the class to move or to stop.
- Clearly mark field dimensions and safety hazards in bright colors.
- Use a "buddy" system for all activities.
- Use many auditory cues to help the student gain a quicker understanding of space and distances.
- Set definite goals and objectives to be reached.
- Use music often, both for relaxation and for motivation.
- Include strenuous big-muscle activities.
- Modify activities that require quick directional changes.
- Provide structure, routine, and consistency.

impaired children may be modified to provide additional tactile, kinesthetic, and auditory stimulation for less severe impairments. Severe visual impairments may require substitution of other sensory modalities for sight. Verbal directional guidance, tactile stimulation, and the use of specialized sound-emitting devices can all be very helpful in the physical education program for the visually impaired.

Auditory Impairments.   Children with **auditory impairment** have difficulty processing verbal information with or without amplification, and this interferes with their educational performance. Auditory impairments are one of the most common limiting conditions found in children and adults. Hearing loss may range from partial to complete. Children with hearing impairments that have gone unattended are frequently mistaken for being mentally retarded, slow learners, or behavioral problems. The following is a list of possible signs of hearing impairment:

1. Faulty speech patterns; faulty pitch, tone, or volume.
2. Holding the head to one side, inattentiveness, excessive daydreaming, inability to follow directions.
3. Inability to detect who is speaking and what is being said.
4. Emotional instability; hostility or extreme withdrawal.
5. Failure in school.
6. Difficulty in maintaining balance.
7. Inability to join class discussions and group games.
8. Feelings of social inferiority.

Children with auditory impairments that can be corrected through the use of hearing aids should be able to take part in most of the activities of the regular physical

Children with *auditory impairments* range from the hard of hearing to the totally deaf:

- Establish and maintain good eye contact.

- Place students where they can easily see the teacher.

- Use visual cues in conjunction with auditory cues whenever possible.

- Speak clearly and concisely.

- Encourage working with a "buddy" to aid learning.

- Make liberal use of visual aids.

- Be aware that children with auditory impairments frequently have problems with balance and require extra spotting in many balance-based activities.

- Do not yell in an attempt to make yourself heard. Instead, speak slowly and clearly, using visual prompts, demonstration, or signing when possible.

- Be consistent and patient, and be sure to follow through.

- Do not take failure to respond or apparent disinterest as a personal affront.

***Cardiovascular limitations* require special attention and careful monitoring of the amount of vigorous physical activity:**

- Work within the guidelines clearly established by the child's physician.

- Watch closely for signs of undue stress.

- Provide frequent rest periods.

- Incorporate nonvigorous physical activities into the program, including archery, golf, and bowling for older children.

- Provide opportunities for less strenuous activities such as dance, simple games, and basic tumbling skills for younger children.

- Work for increased fitness and skill levels at a slower, more relaxed pace than with nonimpaired children.

- Require a periodic medical clearance for participation.

- Listen to students, be sensitive to their requests to rest, and watch for signs of fatigue.

- Use lightweight equipment when possible.

- Require a physician's clearance after the student has been absent due to illness.

---

education program. In those activities that necessitate removal of the aids (such as swimming and gymnastics), the student should be accompanied by a "buddy," and the teacher should be certain that he or she speaks clearly, distinctly, and directly toward the student. Children with severe auditory impairments that cannot be corrected (deafness) will require special attention. Greater attention will need to be given to visual input than verbal input. Demonstrations, written descriptions, wall charts, and videotape replays are all effective teaching tools for use with the deaf child.

Cardiovascular Limitations.   Cardiovascular limitations include congenital heart disease, rheumatic heart disease, coronary heart disease, and hypertensive heart disease. Although often thought of as a major health problem only in adults, cardiovascular disorders are also quite prevalent in children.

Depending on the specific nature of the disorder, children may be severely or only moderately restricted in the type, amount, and duration of physical activity in

which they may take part. It is of utmost importance to work closely with the child's physician concerning the degree of involvement permitted and to be alert for signs of undue physical stress. Most children with cardiovascular disabilities can benefit from a modified physical education program that works within the limits of their abilities and is sensitive to their special needs.

Neuromuscular Limitations.   Children with neuromuscular limitations are characterized by damage to the brain or spinal cord. Cerebral palsy and epilepsy are the most common neurological disorders.

Cerebral Palsy.   **Cerebral palsy** is a nonprogressive, permanent condition caused by damage to the motor area of the cortex. It results in paralysis, weakness, tremor, or uncoordinated movement, depending on the severity and

Children with neuromuscular limitations can still experience success in physical education.

Children with *cerebral palsy* present a special challenge to the physical education teacher:

- Work in conjunction with the physical therapist to provide appropriate activities.

- Stress socialization and acceptance by peers rather than skill perfection.

- Focus on movement skills that have a high carryover value for later life and for present leisure-time activities.

- Concentrate on throwing balls to promote controlled releasing.

- Practice catching bounced balls rather than ones that are tossed. Have students kick or strike stationary balls. These movements are easier and promote greater success.

- Encourage rhythmic activities to promote increased motor control.

- Encourage aquatic activities as an excellent way to promote relaxation.

- Initiate sustained, flowing-movement activities for children with spasticity.

- Give students with athetosis extra help with relaxation.

- Avoid balance and fine motor-coordination activities with children who have ataxia.

location of the brain damage. Cerebral palsy is classified into five categories:

Spasticity is typified by limited voluntary control of movement as a result of hypertonia of the muscles. An exaggerated stretch reflex causes the arms and legs to contract rapidly when passively stretched and results in an inability to perform precise movements. The legs are often rotated inward, the arms stiff and flexed at the elbows. Body movements are characteristically jerky and uncertain. Spasticity is the most common form of cerebral palsy, occurring in about 60 percent of all cases. Mental retardation, speech disorders, and perceptual problems are also frequently associated with spastic cerebral palsy.

Athetosis accounts for approximately 25 percent of all cerebral palsy and is characterized by involuntary, jerky movements. Movement is uncontrollable, random, and almost constant. Facial grimaces are common, as are hearing, speech, and visual impairments.

Ataxia represents about 10 percent of all cerebral palsy and is typified by very poor balance and coordination. Movements are deliberate but awkward and wobbly. Perceptual abilities are generally diminished, especially in the proprioceptive and vestibular areas. Speech disorders are common.

Rigidity is characterized by extreme body stiffness and absence of the stretch reflex. Mental retardation is common with rigidity, as well as restricted movement and hyperextension. About 3 percent of all cases of cerebral palsy are classified as rigidity.

Tremor is the least frequent form of cerebral palsy, occurring in only about 2 percent of the cerebral palsy population. It is characterized by rhythmic, involuntary movements. When voluntary movement is attempted, the tremor tends to increase. Tremors are often mixed with muscle rigidity. Mental retardation is common. The degree of involvement of cerebral palsy and other neurological impairments may be classified by location:

1. Monoplegia—involvement of only one limb (rare)
2. Paraplegia—involvement of both legs only
3. Hemiplegia—involvement of one arm and one leg on the same side of the body
4. Triplegia—involvement of three limbs (rare)
5. Quadriplegia—involvement of all four limbs

In all cases of cerebral palsy—whether mild, moderate, or severe—the individual will benefit from a program of modified physical activities. The physical educator can do much, working in conjunction with the physician, to improve the child's level of physical functioning. Social integration with one's peers is of special importance. The development of social skills and improved peer-group relationships is an important goal of the developmental-adapted physical education program.

Epilepsy.   **Epilepsy,** a condition caused by an electrochemical imbalance in the brain, is typified by seizures that may be mild or severe. Seizures may, in many cases, be effectively controlled with a variety of drugs. Persons with epilepsy may exhibit one or more of the following seizures when uncontrolled by medication.

Grand mal seizures are accompanied by an aura phase, characterized by a sinking feeling or a vague feeling of uneasiness. This is followed by a tonic phase in which there is a loss of consciousness and rapid, involuntary, writhing contraction of the muscles. The clonic phase follows, typified by intermittent contractions. This is followed by a deep, relaxed sleep phase.

Jacksonian seizures are similar to grand mal seizures but without the aura and tonic phases. They are characterized by intermittent contraction and relaxation of the muscles beginning in one part of the body and spreading outward. The seizures are also accompanied by loss of consciousness.

Petit mal seizures are characterized by a momentary loss of consciousness. The child will suddenly stop all activity, appear dazed, and then resume regular activity.

Psychomotor seizures are characterized by short-term changes in normal behavior, in which there is no memory of the atypical behavior. Temper tantrums, incoherent speech, and aggressive behaviors are frequent symptoms.

Most children with epilepsy should be encouraged to take part in the regular physical education program. However, because excessive sensory stimulation or trauma to

---

TEACHING TIPS

Children with *epilepsy* frequently take part in the regular program with few restrictions. Be certain, however, to

- Work with the child's physician to outline a program of physical activities.

- Remember that children with epilepsy are in all other ways like their peers except for occasional seizures, and these seizures are generally controlled effectively through medication.

- In the event of a seizure, remain calm and administer appropriate first aid. Help the other children to understand what is happening and to be accepting of the condition.

- Focus on activities requiring concentration, such as rhythmic activities.

- Promote inclusion rather than exclusion.

- Request that the classroom teacher alert you to any abnormal behavior the child may have displayed prior to the physical education class.

- Avoid climbing activities when the child's condition is doubtful.

---

the head frequently trigger epileptic seizures, care should be taken to avoid both situations.

Pulmonary Limitations.   Two primary pulmonary limitations are encountered by teachers in the elementary school; asthma, and cystic fibrosis. Both are briefly discussed.

Asthma.   **Asthma** is a pulmonary condition affecting the bronchial tubes. It interferes with normal breathing and may range from mild to severe. Physical activity can be beneficial for children with asthma. Low fitness is not inherent to the disease. In fact, fitness levels range from that acquired by Olympic athletes to the very poor levels found in sedentary children. Fitness levels do, however, tend to decrease as the severity and number of asthma attacks increases. In designing activity programs for asthmatic children it is important to find activities that do not provoke an exercise-induced asthma attack. A warm-up period is especially important prior to vigorous activity in order to accustom the air passage to exercise. Activities such as swimming, team games, and circuit training are generally recommended. Avoid exercise in cold and dry air whenever possible.

Cystic Fibrosis.

Cystic Fibrosis is a progressive noncurable disease in which the lungs gradually fill with mucus, causing difficulty in breathing and eventually death. The primary limiting factor in children with cystic fibrosis is ventilation, thereby limiting aerobic endurance. Instructors must seek the written advice of the child's physician prior to beginning an activity program. Activities that permit frequent rest periods, such as swimming, circuit training, walking, and team sports with short bouts of exercise, are generally recommended.

Musculoskeletal Impairments.

A wide variety of musculoskeletal limiting conditions including Osgood-Schlatter's condition, arthritis, and postural deviations are frequently encountered in the physical education class. A **musculoskeletal limitation** is a disease or condition of the bones or muscles that affects the child's ability to move effectively and efficiently.

Osgood-Schlatter's Condition.

Osgood-Schlatter's condition is common in prepubescent boys and girls, typified by pain and swelling around the knee joint. It is completely curable with medical treatment and frequently disappears after a few years without medical intervention. Osgood-Schlatter's condition is caused by separation of the patellar ligament from the tibia. It is frequently the result of undue tendon strain, improper alignment of the leg, or direct injury to the knee. Repeated jarring activities, such as improper running technique or landing heavily, seem to contribute to this condition.

For treatment, some authorities recommend complete immobilization of the leg for a minimum of six weeks, followed by restricted physical activity for up to one year. Others recommend a continued program of regular physical activities limited only by the individual's pain tolerance. Teachers at the upper elementary and junior high school levels encounter frequent cases of Osgood-Schlatter's condition. Be prepared to modify or restrict activities as required by the child's physician.

Arthritis.

Arthritis is frequently thought of as a disease of the aged, but a significant number of children also suffer from the disease, which currently has no cure. Basically, **arthritis** is a painful condition caused by inflammation of the joints. Rheumatoid arthritis, the most common form of arthritis found in children, attacks the entire skeletal system and results in inflammation, stiffness, and

---

TEACHING TIPS

The wide variety of *musculoskeletal impairments* makes it essential that all physical activity be individually based and medically approved:

- Conduct a medically approved program within the guidelines established by the child's physician.
- Provide activities that promote inclusion and maximum participation.
- Teach proper techniques of falling from wheelchairs, crutches, and standing postures.
- Provide activities suited to the level of ambulation of the child.
- For children with Osgood-Schlatter's condition, avoid activities involving jumping, landing, and other activities that stress the knee.
- Encourage and practice proper posture and body mechanics in the performance of activities.
- Equalize the skill levels of your teams so that all have an opportunity to win.
- Promote aquatic activities for relaxation, control, and less muscular stress.
- Encourage sustained stretching movements for children with arthritis.
- Work closely with the physician and physical therapist in providing an individualized program of adapted physical activities.

---

acute pain in the joints. Rheumatoid arthritis varies greatly in severity, but in all cases movement of the affected joints is recommended.

Children with arthritis should be included in the regular physical education program whenever possible. They should be encouraged to take part in sustained stretching activities to promote joint flexibility. Some activities may need to be modified during periods when the condition is particularly painful.

Postural Deviations.

Postural deviations are common among elementary school-age children. They may be classified as either functional or structural. Functional **postural deviations** are the result of faulty muscular development, which is frequently caused by habitual

Obesity is a frequently occurring limiting condition.

postures and overdevelopment of certain muscle groups. Children who habitually carry their books on one side of the body or who consistently sit on the floor with their knees forward and their feet behind are likely to develop functional postural deviations.

Structural postural deviations involve structural abnormalities of the skeletal system itself. These abnormalities may be caused by congenital defects, uncorrected functional deviations, or skeletal injuries that have not healed properly. Structural impairments require surgery for correction, whereas functional impairments are correctable through a program of proper activities to strengthen identified muscle groups.

Postural problems are common among school-age children. Among the most common are scoliosis, lordosis, and kyphosis.

Scoliosis, or lateral curvature of the spine, may be structural but is most often functional. If left untreated, the characteristic C curve of the spine may develop into an S curve. If scoliosis is detected in the young child, a program of corrective exercises should begin immediately. If it is not detected until late adolescence, little can be done, and the condition will probably not develop further. To modify the condition at this time a back brace must be worn for several years.

Lordosis, or swayback, as it is sometimes called, is typified by an exaggerated curve of the lower back. This exaggerated lumbar curve results in a forward tilt of the pelvis

and weak abdominal muscles. Corrective activities at the early stages of lordosis include making the individual aware of his or her posture and helping the child to develop the habit of consciously tucking the hips under the spine. Activities designed to strengthen the abdominal muscles and to stretch the muscles of the lower back are also helpful.

Kyphosis, or hunchback, as it is frequently called, is a condition characterized by an exaggerated curve in the thoracic region of the spine. Round shoulders, winged scapula, and a forward head tilt are frequently found in conjunction with kyphosis. A program of exercises designed to stretch the chest muscles and strengthen the back muscles will help alleviate this condition.

Children with Mental Disabilities

Children with **mental disabilities** are generally said to have mental retardation. Mental retardation is a condition that generally results in below-normal functioning in motor development as well as in intellectual development. The lack of motor development is due, in part, to problems these children have with cognition (a part of all physical activity) and to their frequent lack of opportunity for activity. This statement should not be viewed as simply another means of demonstrating the vast differences between these children and their chronological peers. It should, however, point out that, to a large degree, this lack of development is caused by the gross neglect that individuals with mental retardation have suffered for years. What more can be expected if one's life is spent in endless hours of boredom brought about by constant inactivity? Human beings need physical activity to continue functioning at their optimum level, no matter what their intellectual capabilities are. We cannot expect children with mental retardation to approach their chronological counterparts in terms of physical functioning if they do not have sufficient movement experiences and sound guidance in their motor development. Although we must recognize that the ability of the child's mind to function establishes outer limits on the potential functioning of his or her body, we must not let this distract us from striving for maximal performance.

Physical education and therapeutic recreation programs can aid greatly in reducing the "halo" of physical inadequacies that contributes negatively to one's mental retardation. There is an ever expanding circle of artificial disability that forms around the original and unalterable mental disability. This is evidenced by performance scores on numerous tests of physical status by children with mental retardation. A well-planned program of movement activities will help. This is not to say that

TEACHING TIPS

Children with *mild mental retardation* will benefit from the following suggestions:

- Stress gross motor activities focusing on fundamental stability, locomotor, and manipulative skills.
- Work for higher levels of fitness in a consistent and progressive manner.
- Be sure all instruction builds skill upon skill and is success-oriented.
- "Show" more and explain less.
- Include routine and structure in each session.
- Keep rules simple.
- Provide for many kinds of rhythmical activities.
- Stress the element of fun in physical activity.

- Provide manual assistance in certain activities for the children as needed.
- Reduce skills to their simplest components.
- Name the movement or skill being taught to help develop a movement vocabulary.
- Be sure that practice periods are short, with frequent changes in activities to reduce frustration.
- Let children repeat their successes several times to enjoy the feeling of accomplishment.
- Reward approximations of the skill with frequent verbal praise.
- Avoid activities in which individuals are eliminated.
- Set standards of acceptable behavior by praising good behavior rather than focusing on the negative.

---

physical education is a panacea for "curing" mental retardation. It is true, though, that the halo effect can be significantly reduced through a quality physical education program and that children with mental retardation can often progress at a rate similar to those without mental retardation, even though they may still be unable to perform at the same level.

CONCEPT 7.6
The needs of children with mental, emotional, and learning disabilities can be served effectively, at some level, through the developmental physical education program.

Many with mental retardation do well in simple games and tumbling and such sports as track and field, soccer, basketball, swimming, and bowling. The Special Olympics has aptly demonstrated that those with mental disabilities can find success, fitness, and fulfillment through physical activity. Moreover, the Special Olympics training program is developmentally sequenced and contains activity progressions appropriate for individuals with mental retardation.

Physical educators can do much to help children with mental retardation approach their chronological peers in terms of skill mastery by providing them with a well-planned, individualized program of activities that gradually increase in complexity and require greater movement control. Thus, simple games and skills, when mastered, should be continually replaced by others that are more fun, challenging, and satisfying.

Mental disabilities are typified by faulty development of intelligence to a point that it interferes with the ability to learn. The following classifications, adopted by the American Association on Mental Deficiency, are the most widely used and universally accepted categorization of levels of mental retardation. Children with mild and moderate retardation are generally mainstreamed into the regular physical education class. Those with severe and profound mental retardation are generally not.

1. **Mild retardation** (50 to approximately 70 I.Q.)
2. **Moderate retardation** (40–49 I.Q.)
3. **Severe retardation** (25–39 I.Q.)
4. **Profound retardation** (unmeasurable)

Children with mild or moderate mental retardation are considered to be in the educable range and may be expected to take part in the developmental physical education program. Educationally, children with severe or profound retardation are considered to be at the trainable and custodial levels, respectively. They will benefit most from a special program of adapted physical activities geared to their particular needs.

Children with mild and *moderate mental retardation* will benefit from the following suggestions:

- Permit more time for learning to occur.
- Shorten sentences, using fewer verbal cues and more visual and tactile cues.
- Teach only one skill at a time.
- Reinforce and praise all accomplishments, no matter how small.
- Praise attempts as well as accomplishments.
- Simplify instructions and repeat them frequently.
- Use frequent demonstrations of the task to be learned and actual hands-on physical manipulation through the skill as necessary.
- Use visual prompts and color coding as necessary.
- Stress compliance with basic rules of safety.
- Treat each individual with dignity, respect, and a sincere display of caring.

Down's syndrome is a frequent type of mental retardation.

It is generally assumed that roughly 3 percent of the total population meets the criteria for mental retardation. Of this 3 percent, approximately 95 percent are in the mild to moderate range. Only about 5 percent of the entire mentally challenged population is in the severe or profound range.

The causes of mental retardation are numerous and varied. The vast majority of retardation is caused by brain damage that occurs prior to, during, or after birth; environmental retardation caused by infections or drugs; and genetic retardation caused by chromosomal abnormalities (Figure 7.3).

Brain Damage.   **Brain damage,** the primary cause of mental retardation, is characterized by damage to the central nervous system before birth (prenatal), during birth (perinatal), or after birth (postnatal). Prenatal factors that have been linked with mental retardation include poor maternal nutrition, the use of chemical agents (drugs, alcohol, and tobacco), and maternal illnesses. Perinatal factors include the use of drugs to aid in the birth process itself and the manner and type of delivery. Postnatal factors range from infant accidents and injuries to infant nutrition and chemical imbalances.

Environmental Retardation.   **Environmental retardation,** caused by factors such as infections and intoxicants to the expectant mother, the infant, or the young child, is a secondary cause of mental retardation. For example, the expectant mother who contracts rubella (German measles) during the first trimester of her pregnancy, or uses crack cocaine or other mind-altering drugs, runs the risk of damaging her unborn child. The syphilitic mother transmits her condition to her child, a frequent cause of retardation. Rh incompatibility, infant poisoning, and other diseases that occur during infancy also contribute to mental retardation.

Genetic Retardation.   **Genetic retardation** is the third and least frequent cause of mental retardation. Genetic retardation is brought about by chromosomal abnormalities. Deviations in the structure or number of chromosomes are related to gene mutations or the effects of certain drugs, viruses, and ionizing radiation. Down's syndrome, one of the most frequently encountered forms

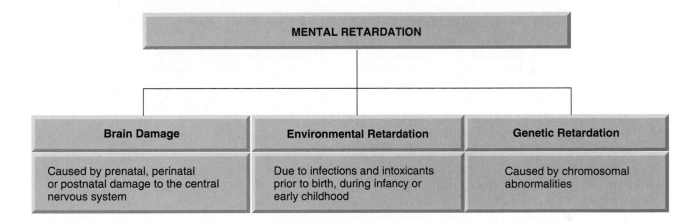

```
                        MENTAL RETARDATION
```

Brain Damage	Environmental Retardation	Genetic Retardation
Caused by prenatal, perinatal or postnatal damage to the central nervous system	Due to infections and intoxicants prior to birth, during infancy or early childhood	Caused by chromosomal abnormalities

FIGURE 7.3 *The three primary causes of mental retardation.*

of genetic retardation, is caused by chromosomal damage and results in mental retardation, cardiovascular impairments, and the characteristic mongoloid appearance.

Children with Emotional Disabilities

Children with emotional disorders are characterized by behavior patterns that have a detrimental effect on their adjustment and interfere with the lives of others. The causes of emotional disorders are not completely understood, nor is it clear why some individuals react in a negative emotional way while others with equivalent backgrounds do not. Emotional disorders are generally classified as being either classic emotional disturbance or autism. Both are briefly discussed in the following paragraphs.

Classic Emotional Disturbance. As defined by PL 94–142, a child with **classic emotional disorder** is one who has an inability to learn that cannot be explained by sensory problems, health factors, or intellectual deficits; is unable to make and maintain satisfactory interpersonal relationships with peers and adults; demonstrates inappropriate behaviors; is generally unhappy or depressed; or develops physical symptoms in response to school or personal problems. A child with an emotional disorder may be characterized by extremes in behavior, chronic unacceptable behavior, or persistent problems at home or school. It has been variously estimated that the number of children with classic emotional disorders ranges from only 2

Children with emotional disabilities are a reality in today's classroom and gymnasium.

TEACHING TIPS

Although the behaviors displayed by children with *emotional disorders* **range from prolonged withdrawal to extreme disruption and hostility, there are basic guidelines that, if followed, will be helpful:**

- Understand that children with an emotional disability need someone stable and orderly to serve as an example of steadiness.

- Structure the learning environment so that the child knows exactly what is expected. Using a teacher-centered teaching approach often works best.

- Learn to expect the unexpected. You can count on children with emotional disabilities to overreact to new or potentially threatening situations.

- Set limits on what the child can and cannot do. Clearly define what is acceptable and unacceptable behavior. The process of limit-setting should be done in the spirit of helpful authority. Children feel safer when they know the boundaries in which they may operate.

- Set limits in such a way that they arouse little resentment.

- Limits should be phrased in language that does not challenge the child's self-respect. For example, say "Time to put the balls away" instead of "Don't shoot another time, John. Put the ball away immediately!"

- Accept the fact that there may be little progress in the first month or two. Their progress will depend on the severity of their disturbance. A sense of trust and rapport must develop between teacher and child.

- Nonverbal reactions and facial expressions often give away your thoughts. The child with an emotional disability may depend a great deal on nonverbal clues of acceptance, resignation,

disappointment, pride, and so forth. Learn to attend to the signs you communicate to the child as well as to the signs conveyed to you.

- Help the child express feelings and vent hostilities through socially acceptable channels.

- Be firm and consistent in your discipline, but discipline in a manner that conveys an attitude of helpfulness, not authority.

- Learn each child's name and let them know yours. Refer to them by name.

- Structure activities for success. Every child should be able to achieve an element of success to help them overcome a sense of failure and lack of confidence.

- Immediately reinforce and praise the child for desired behavior.

- Avoid imposing standards or limits that are not within the child's capabilities.

- Be cognizant of individual differences and modify activities to meet these needs.

- Avoid elimination activities that exclude children from even part of the lesson.

- Use competitive activities sparingly, and ease children into competitive situations very carefully.

- Activities should be within the individual's capabilities but must be challenging. If they are too easy, the child will not perform. If they are too hard, the child will not perform or will quit.

- Do not let small incidents "snowball." The child must know who is in charge and respect that position.

- Be thoroughly prepared and try to anticipate problems before they occur.

- Be patient, understanding, and quick to forgive.

---

to over 20 percent of the total population, with boys outnumbering girls 4 to 1 (Sherrill, 1993). Even using the conservative figure of 2 percent results in a school-age population of over one million children who are considered to have serious emotional disorders, a fact that warrants the attention of all educators.

Severe, prolonged emotional disorders have been shown to be linked to a variety of psychological, sociological, and physiological factors. Psychological factors are the result of constant frustration and arise from the child's inability to cope with the real or imagined pressures of society. The results are feelings of anxiety, fear,

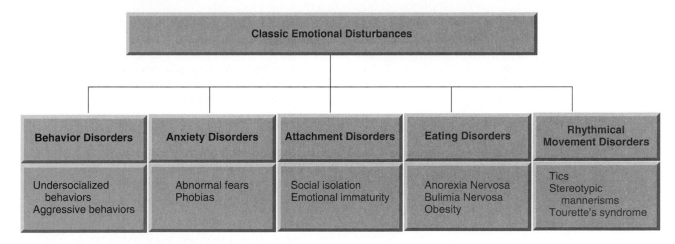

FIGURE 7.4 *Common emotional disorders found among children and typical associated behaviors.*

hostility, or insecurity, which are manifested in inappropriate behavior patterns. Sociological factors include early home experiences and socioeconomic aspects of the home environment. Child abuse, ranging from physical and verbal abuse to sexual abuse and neglect, is an important sociological contributor to severe emotional disturbances. Likewise, physiological factors such as heredity, neurological disorders, and chemical imbalances may contribute to emotional disabilities. Figure 7.4 lists a variety of classic emotional disturbances that you are likely to encounter.

Children with emotional disorders may exhibit unusual anxiety reactions, atypical frustrations, fears and phobias, and impulsive behaviors. The following signs and symptoms may help in identifying these children in the classroom:

1. A tendency to have accidents
2. Hyperactivity
3. Imaginary fears and phobias
4. Regressive, immature behavior
5. Aggressive, hostile behavior
6. Withdrawal into a fantasy world
7. Abnormal fear of failure and criticism
8. Unexplained poor school achievement
9. Frequent disciplinary visits to the principal's office
10. Inability to relate appropriately with the peer group

Autism.   Officially, autism is no longer considered to be a form of emotional disturbance. The Individuals with Disabilities Education Act (IDEA, 1990) calls for autism to be recognized as a separate diagnostic category. The fact is, however, that children with autism are generally grouped with those who are classified as having an emotional disability and those who have significant problems requiring behavior management. **Autism** is a developmental disability that manifests itself prior to age three, persists throughout life, and is characterized by significant delays in both language and social development. Autism is a disorder that affects the central nervous system. Although its origin is unknown, it may, among other things, be associated with chemical exposure during the fetal period, nutritional imbalances, or untreated phenylketonuria (PKU). There is little support for claims that autism is psychological in nature and associated with poor parenting.

Individuals with autism range in intelligence from severely retarded to above average, although most have some degree of retardation (Davis, 1990). Children with autism are seldom included in the regular physical education program because of the frequent tendency for muteness or peculiar speech patterns, bizarre behaviors, lack of social responsiveness and withdrawal, unusual **rhythmical stereotypes** (that is, rocking and head banging), and **echolalia** (that is, repetition of the words of others).

Children with Learning Disabilities

A fourth classification of children with disabilities is the learning disabled. PL 94–142 defines the child with a **learning disability** as one who is restricted in the ability to read, write, think, speak, spell, or do mathematical

⬤━━━━━━━━━━━━━━━━━━━━━ TEACHING TIPS ━━━━━━━━━━━━━━━━━━━━━⬤

When working with children who have *learning disabilities* it will be helpful to:

- Know and understand the specific nature of the child's learning difficulty.

- Structure personalized activities that work within the child's present level of abilities.

- Help the child find an element of success during each lesson.

- Progress from simple to more complex activities in small increments, being sure to use positive encouragement.

- Provide numerous opportunities for reinforcing academic concepts through movements that are normally dealt with in a classroom setting.

- Remember that children with specific learning disabilities have generally experienced a great deal of frustration and failure. Therefore, it is very important to create an atmosphere of challenge and success.

- Promote a "yes I can" attitude.

- Help the child gain a better understanding of his or her body, the space it occupies, and how it can move.

- Help the child establish a sense or feel for direction through carefully sequenced movement activities.

- Make frequent use of rhythmic activities and stress the rhythmical element to all coordinated movement.

---

operations due to the inability to fully utilize basic psychological processes involved in using spoken or written language. The term *learning disability* excludes problems in learning that may be traced to physical (visual, auditory, or motor) disabilities and mental retardation. It also excludes learning disabilities brought about primarily by cultural, economic, or environmental conditions. Children with a specific learning disability are sometimes referred to as **ATLO children,** an acronym for "All Those Left Over."

Children with specific learning disabilities are frequently difficult to detect. They often appear quite normal in their physical, social, and mental development, but for some unexplained reason they fail to achieve at an acceptable level in school. The discrepancy between potential and performance often results in peer-related problems and considerable emotional upheaval. The learning impairment itself may be relatively minor and specific to motor, perceptual, writing, or speaking difficulties; or it may be quite complex and involve the intricate interaction of several or all of these processes. Although perceptual-motor training programs have been advocated for years as an effective way to remediate learning disabilities, the area is too diverse and too complex to merit such simple solutions. The effects of perceptual-motor programs on the academic achievement and cognitive processes of children with

learning disabilities is highly speculative. The fact is that quality physical education programs do produce positive changes in personal, social, and motivational response patterns of children. It may be that these factors have an indirect influence on the acquisition of skills and abilities necessary for academic success (Figure 7.5).

Attention Deficit Disorder. Many children with learning disabilities have an **attention deficit disorder (ADD).** ADD is characterized by three factors: inattention, impulsivity, and hyperactivity. Characteristic displays of **inattention** include not paying attention; failing to finish what they start; having difficulty concentrating on schoolwork; and having trouble sticking with play activities. **Impulsivity** is characterized by acting before thinking; having trouble getting organized; needing lots of supervision; frequent calling out in class; impatience in waiting one's turn in game and group situations. **Hyperactivity** is typified by constant difficulty in sitting still; excessive fidgeting; and running about with little aim or purpose. All of these may be symptoms of ADD and warrant expert diagnosis.

Hyperactivity. Children with Attention Deficit Disorder (ADD) are hyperactive as well as impulsive and distractable. The truly hyperactive child, however, may not

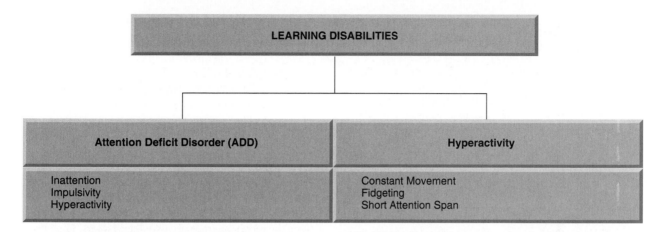

FIGURE 7.5 *Two common learning disabilities encountered in the regular physical education program.*

possess the ADD characteristics of impulsive behaviors and easy distractability. Hyperactivity is typified by extreme difficulty in sitting still long enough to complete a task. Hyperactive children are always on the move, fidgeting, moving their feet, tapping their fingers, constantly talking, and in perpetual motion. Hyperactive children tend to wear teachers out, because there is seldom a pause in their constant movement. This is frequently reflected in poor behavior reports, failing grades, and exhausted parents and teachers.

Children with hyperactivity are frequently quite bright and outgoing but need patient understanding help in slowing down, calming down, and simply relaxing. Although medications can be prescribed, a supportive, calm, caring, and structured environment can be of significant benefit. The physical education teacher can be of assistance by providing ample opportunities for vigorous physical activity in a structured setting.

Other Disabilities

The category of "other disabilities" includes a variety of health restrictions that may not be as easily observed as those discussed earlier but that adversely affect the child's educational performance. PL 94–142 defines **other health impairments** as any condition that results in limited strength, vitality, or alertness. These conditions may be caused by health problems such as asthma, diabetes, obesity, hemophilia, anemia,

The developmentally based physical education program is adapted through the IEP.

tuberculosis, or leukemia. In each of these cases it is important for the physical education teacher to work closely with the physician, parents, rehabilitation specialists, and other school officials to provide appropriate educational opportunities in the least restrictive environment.

THE INDIVIDUALIZED EDUCATION PROGRAM (IEP)

Appropriate identification, assessment, programming, and evaluation of the child's disabilities must be a team approach. Identification is the procedure by which children with special needs are located. Assessment is the means by which they are examined and their present status is determined. Motor assessment includes the initial screening, frequently by the regular physical education teacher, and a more extensive evaluation by the special physical education teacher or other educator with advanced training in special education. Once the child has been identified and his or her present level of abilities has been determined, it is possible to program appropriate learning activities.

Programming involves development of an IEP, which is individualized, need-based, and must be implemented in the least restrictive environment. In a team approach the physical education teacher should be involved in formulating the IEP, because it is he or she who will be responsible for its implementation and evaluation. The final aspect of the team process is evaluation, which refers to the procedures used to determine the degree to which the objectives established in the IEP have been met.

SPECIAL NEEDS OF CHILDREN WITH DISABILITIES

The needs and interests of children with physical, mental, or emotional disabilities are essentially the same as for all other children. They generally profit most when mainstreamed into the regular physical education program. Children with disabilities need to be accepted for who they are and treated with respect as contributors to the group, class, and society as a whole. They need challenging movement experiences that are within the limits of their abilities. They need ample opportunities to solve problems for themselves and to develop a greater sense of independence rather than dependence. Children with physical, mental, or emotional disabilities need to experience a wide variety of movement activities designed to break down the artificial limitations that are often built up around their disabilities. Like all children, they need ample opportunities for practice, sincere encouragement, and skilled instruction if they are to be expected to improve their movement competence and level of fitness. Children

need especially to adjust socially to their disability and to establish a realistic body image.

C O N C E P T   7 . 7
Children with disabilities often face body image and social adjustment problems that can be dealt with through developmentally appropriate physical activity.

Social Adjustment

A major problem encountered by children with disabilities is social adjustment (Krementz, 1992). This problem is often the result of external or societal factors. Historic attitudes toward the treatment of exceptional individuals have had a tremendous negative impact on our modern society and its attitudes. In the past, those with physical, mental, and emotional disabilities were treated as freaks, feared as being sent by Satan, cursed, given improper medical care and treatment, beaten, and even killed. Only relatively recently has the emphasis shifted away from a person's disabilities to his or her abilities. This more enlightened view has had a great effect on their education, as reflected in federal and state legislation, and has vastly improved their self-acceptance and social integration.

The physical education program in which children with disabilities are included makes a profound positive impact on the social adjustment of both those with disabilities and those without. The physical education program that is developmentally based, individualized, and personalized is geared to the needs and abilities of all children. As such, it influences the acceptance of these children by society and hence the individual's acceptance of herself or himself. The nondisabled population must understand that persons with disabilities are not looking for concessions or sympathy but want to be treated like others within their individual limits. Inclusion leads to acceptance. Inclusion promotes understanding, encourages favorable attitudes, and leads to both public- and self-acceptance.

Body Image Enhancement

We each possess some sort of awareness of our own body and its possibilities for movement and performance. This quality, or body image, as it is commonly called, is a learned concept that results from observation of the movements of parts of our body and the relationship of these different parts to each other and to external objects in space.

A well-developed body image is important because we do not deal in absolutes in our perceptions of ourselves or the world about us. If children fail to form a reasonably satisfactory body image, their self-concept is likely to be distorted, and they will be limited in their emotional and social development. The extent to which our body image is developed depends largely on movement experiences. Both the quality and the quantity of these movement activities are important. Movement experiences lead to a better orientation in space and provide information about the body that one would be unable to obtain otherwise. Movement enables us to gain sensory information concerning changes in muscle tone. The more information received, the better the quality of the information, and the more the body image is developed. The movement experiences and diverse gross motor activities inherent in a well-planned physical education program contribute a great deal to the development of a stable body image, which in turn influences self-esteem.

Children with disabilities who are either restricted from taking part in vigorous activities or whose performance is atypical fail to form a complete body image or may develop one that is distorted. This imperfect image further affects their perceptions of themselves and their external world. Distorted perceptions tend to undermine self-assurance and often lead to social and psychological difficulties.

Being able to perform a movement task in an acceptable manner contributes to one's confidence and self-assurance. When children with disabilities are given an opportunity to develop their movement abilities and to improve their body images, their confidence and self-assurance increase. Then the personality is reinforced, and the likelihood of problems of social adjustment is diminished.

All children, including those who have physical, mental, emotional, or learning disabilities, must be given the opportunity to engage in vigorous physical activity. The adjustments that must be made by exceptional children may be modified by the environment in which they live. The physical educator is a part of that environment. Working as a team, parents, teachers, and rehabilitation workers can contribute to children's physical and psychological development.

SUMMARY

The aim of the special program of physical education is to help each individual child to reach his or her potential physical, social, and emotional level of functioning in a well-planned, progressive program built around his or her unique needs, interests, and abilities. Teachers of children with disabilities must realize that the objectives they set and the outcomes they seek are often quite different from those sought by the child. Avoid the pitfall of selecting activities to satisfy program objectives based on your own abilities, interests, and feelings.

Success in teaching children with disabilities depends on the teacher's positive acceptance of each child and a genuine willingness to assimilate them into the regular physical education program. The ability to individualize and personalize instruction to meet children's unique needs and interests is also essential for long-term success. It is the teacher's responsibility to establish a climate conducive to learning, a climate in which children feel free to learn, to probe, and to explore. The key to success is in establishing freedom within limits. These limits should serve as guidelines rather than restraints and produce a nonthreatening environment that enables the teacher to accept children at whatever level they are functioning, encourage their enjoyment of movement activities, and motivate them to become as skilled as they can be within their special situations.

COMPLEMENTARY READINGS

Craft, D., ed. (1994). Inclusion: Physical education for all. *JOPERD* 65:23–61 (series of articles).

Dunn, J. M., ed. (1991). PL 99–457 Challenges and opportunities for physical education. *JOPERD* 62:33–48 (series of articles).

Fulsom-Meek, S. (1993). Preschoolers with disabilities: Programming considerations. *TEPE* 4:4–6.

Gross, S. (1990). How safe are your mainstreamed students? *Strategies* 4:11–13.

Gross, S., and D. Thompson. (1994). *Play and Recreation for Individuals with Disabilities: Practical Pointers.* Reston, VA: AAHPERD.

Krementz, J. (1992). *How It Feels to Live with a Disability.* New York: Simon.

Milne, D. C., J. L. Haubenstricker, and V. D. Seefeldt. (1991). Remedial motor education: Some practical suggestions. *Strategies* 4:15–18.

Miller, S. E. (1994). Inclusion of children with disabilities; Can we meet the challenge? *The Physical Educator* 51:47–52.

Stein, J. U. (1994). Total Inclusion or Least Restrictive Environment. *JOPERD* 65:21–25.

SUPPLEMENTARY READINGS

Aarons, M. and T. Gittens. (1992). A handbook of autism: a guide for parents and professionals. London: Routledge.

Auxter, D., J. Pyfer, and C. Huettig. (1993). *Adapted Physical Education and Recreation*. St. Louis: Mosby.

Block, M. E. (1995). Americans with Disabilities Act: Its impact on youth sports. *JOPERD* 66:28–32.

Block, M. E. and K. Etz. (1995). The pocket reference: a tool for fostering inclusion. *JOPERD* 66:47–51.

Davis, K. (1990). *Adapted Physical Education for Students With Autism*. Springfield, IL: Charles C. Thomas.

Eichstaedt, C. D., and B. W. Lavay. (1992). *Physical Activity for Individuals with Mental Retardation*. Champaign: IL: Human Kinetics.

Hamill, J., ed. (1992). The physically challenged child. *Pediatric Exercise Science,* 4 (3) (series of articles).

Harris, S. L. and J. L. Handleman. (1994). *Preschool Education Programs for Children with Autism*. Austin, TX: Pro-Ed.

Sherrill, C. (1993). *Adapted Physical Activity, Recreation and Sport*. Dubuque, IA: Wm. C. Brown & Benchmark.

Varnes, P., ed. (1994). *Youth at Risk: Targeting in on Prevention*. Reston, VA: AAHPERD.

Winnick, J. P., ed. (1995). *Adapted Physical Education and Sport*. Champaign, IL: Human Kinetics.

The Program

8   The Developmental Curriculum

9   Planning Skill Themes

10   The Content Areas

11   Assessing Progress

The Developmental Curriculum

Key Concept

Curriculum Is an Organized Process of Bringing Meaning, Scope, Sequence, and Balance to the Goals and Objectives of the Program In a Manner That Reflects the Values and Mission of Those Charged with Its Implementation.

Chapter Objectives

The purpose of this chapter is to provide you with the tools to:
- Outline the steps in curriculum construction.
- Discuss the ingredients of an effective mission statement.
- Succinctly state your philosophy of physical education.
- Distinguish among aims, goals, general objectives, and specific objectives.
- Discuss what is meant by the term *conceptual framework* and outline a conceptual framework for the developmental curriculum.
- Discuss the merits and requirements of behavioral objectives.
- List and describe a variety of teaching conditions that will influence the content of your curriculum.
- Demonstrate knowledge of what is meant by *scope, sequence,* and *balance* in terms of curriculum construction.
- Discuss the role of assessment in the total curricular process.
- Diagram the anatomy of the developmental physical education curriculum.
- Discuss the many and varied aspects of the extended curriculum.
- Describe special programs that are frequently included as an extension of the physical education curriculum.

Terms to Remember

Values
Mission Statement
Goals
Conceptual Framework
General Objectives
Conditions for
  Implementation
Specific Objectives

Behavioral Objectives
Terminal Objectives
Benchmark Objectives
Scope and Sequence
  Chart
Scope
Sequence
Curricular Balance

Developmental Curricular
  Model
Extended Curriculum
Recess
Noon–Hour Programs
Daily Fitness Programs
Intramurals
Club Programs

Interscholastic Program
Play Day
Sports Day
Field Day
Gym Shows
Public Demonstration
Round-Robin Tournament
Ladder Tournament

The elementary school physical education curriculum is an integral part of the total school program. As such, it incorporates a broad series of movement experiences that help children acquire movement skills and enhance fitness, along with promoting their cognitive and affective growth. An elementary school physical education curriculum that is well planned, well taught, and based on the developmental level of children is not a frill or appendage to the school program. It is a positive force in the education of the total child.

To achieve the goals of physical education, many movement activities from the various content areas of physical education (see Chapter 10) are used to achieve the objectives of the program. The specific activities from each of the content areas are viewed as activity tools and not as an end in themselves. The teacher's role is to teach children through activities. The focal point must always be the child, not the activity. If the goals of physical education are to have any real meaning, then curricular models must be congruent with these goals. Curricular models serve as "blueprints" for action; they make up the basic structure around which the daily lesson is planned and carried out by the teacher in the gymnasium or on the playing field. The information discussed in the preceding chapters is of little value if you cannot organize it and practically apply it to the lives of children. The value of theory and research that fail to foster models for implementation is limited at best. Conversely, curricular models not based on sound research and theory are also of limited value. It is, therefore, the intent of this chapter to outline the steps in constructing a curriculum and to propose a developmentally based curricular model for implementing the physical education program during the preschool and elementary school years. Noon-hour, after-school, recess, and extracurricular programs are also discussed as part of the extended curriculum.

CONCEPT 8.1
Curriculum planning is an essential aspect of any successful educational program.

STEPS IN PLANNING THE CURRICULUM

Six basic steps should be followed in developing a curriculum in any subject matter area, whether that subject is math, science, physical education, or basketball coaching:

(1) establish a value base for the program, (2) develop a conceptual framework, (3) determine the objectives of the program, (4) design the program, (5) establish assessment procedures, and (6) implement the program. A discussion of each step follows.

Establish a Value Base

A necessary first step in all curricular planning is to establish the value base on which the curriculum is to be built. Your **values** represent, in list form, what you hold near and dear in terms of children's physical education. Your list of values forms a working framework for the important mission statement that comes next.

The Mission Statement.   The **mission statement** represents what your curriculum attempts to do. The mission statement should be clearly and concisely stated, and it should be an outgrowth of your working list of values. The statement should be broadly based and represent the best thinking of the curriculum committee. Hammering out a mission statement as a group effort is often a difficult task. It is, however, a necessary first step because it sets the stage for all that follows and will serve as the cornerstone for outlining the broad general goals of curriculum.

CONCEPT 8.2
The content of the curriculum should directly reflect the values, mission, and goals of the curriculum.

The mission statement should be brief, generally consisting of a few concise paragraphs. The first paragraph introduces the reader to the broad, general aims of the program, and the next paragraph contains terse statements about the overall goals of the curriculum. These statements are sufficiently broad to cover the scope of the area being emphasized but are concise. The final paragraph generally summarizes what has been stated and reemphasizes the value of the program to the individual, community, or society. Refer to Table 8.1 for a sample school-wide mission statement.

Goals.   A list of the goals of the program follows the mission statement. **Goals** are generally considered to be broad areas of continuing interest and importance. Goals should directly reflect your values and mission statement.

◗ TEACHING TIPS ◗

The physically educated person *has, is, does, knows,* and *values* the following:

HAS Learned Skills Necessary to Perform a Variety of Physical Activities

1. . . . moves using concepts of body awareness, space awareness, effort, and relationships.
2. . . . demonstrates competence in a variety of manipulative, locomotor, and nonlocomotor skills.
3. . . . demonstrates competence in combinations of manipulative, locomotor, and nonlocomotor skills performed individually and with others.
4. . . . demonstrates competence in many different forms of physical activity
5. . . . demonstrates proficiency in a few forms of physical activity.
6. . . . has learned how to learn new skills.

IS Physically Fit

7. . . . assesses, achieves, and maintains physical fitness.
8. . . . designs safe, personal fitness programs in accordance with principles of training and conditioning.

DOES Participate Regularly in Physical Activity

9. . . . participates in health-enhancing physical activity at least three times a week.
10. . . . selects and regularly participates in lifetime physical activities.

KNOWS the Implications of and the Benefits from Involvement in Physical Activities

11. . . . identifies the benefits, costs, and obligations associated with regular participation in physical activity.
12. . . . recognizes the risk and safety factors associated with regular participation in physical activity.
13. . . . applies concepts and principles to the development of motor skills.
14. . . . understands that wellness involves more than being physically fit.
15. . . . knows the rules, strategies, and appropriate behaviors for selected physical activities.
16. . . . recognizes that participation in physical activity can lead to multicultural and international understanding.
17. . . . understands that physical activity provides the opportunity for enjoyment, self-expression, and communication

VALUES Physical Activity and Its Contributions to a Healthful Lifestyle

18. . . . appreciates the relationships with others that result from participation in physical activity.
19. . . . respects the role that regular physical activity plays in the pursuit of lifelong health and well-being.
20. . . . cherishes the feelings that result from regular participation in physical activity.

Source: From *The Physically Educated Person,* National Association for Sport and Physical Education, 1992, Reston, VA: NASPE.

TABLE 8.1

Sample School-wide Mission Statement

Education is democracy's medium for transmitting fundamental knowledge, skills, culture, and values. Developing these qualities in children is essential in fulfilling the personal and social responsibilities that such a society and culture place on its members.

The mission of our school is to exert continuous effort in developing and refining children's knowledge and abilities through breadth and depth of learning in all subject areas. This will enable pupils to acquire the critical skills of judgment, problem-solving, and decision-making required of participating citizens in contemporary society, as well as in the society of the future.

Social, physical, and emotional development must be emphasized to give pupils opportunities to gain experience and develop a positive sense of value concerning themselves and their place in society.

Our teachers' role is to facilitate, nurture, and advance learning. As educators, we are committed to better understanding the process of learning and the nature of children's development. As new methods and techniques of organization and instruction emerge, it is essential for our teachers to promote and implement innovations that reflect new knowledge.

In achieving its goals, the elementary school must foster cooperative efforts and shared responsibility among all participants in the educational process—learners, parents, teachers, administrators, and the community.

TEACHING TIPS

A sample *mission statement* for a developmental physical education curriculum might read like this:

>   *The mission of our physical education curriculum is to involve students in culturally relevant and developmentally appropriate movement experiences that focus on learning to move and learning through movement. Movement skills and fitness levels, thinking and reasoning abilities, and social-emotional skills are all enhanced by engaging children in a comprehensive program of fundamental movement, sport skill, physical fitness, and dance experiences. Systematic and realistic self-assessment of one's own progress aids in building on individual strengths and enables the curriculum to be adapted to individual needs.*
>
>   *The principles and values behind movement skills and lifetime fitness are taught in an atmosphere that promotes student understanding and appreciation. Through a child-centered developmentally based approach to teaching that is responsive to the safety and welfare of students, the physical education curriculum contributes to self-esteem enhancement, responsible behavior, creative expression, and group cooperation. This is accomplished in an environment that both values and provides opportunities for social growth, increased emotional maturity, and responsible citizenship.*
>
>   *The value of each child is recognized by striving for individual excellence in a caring and nurturing environment—an environment that promotes learning to move and learning through movement for all children.*

TEACHING TIPS

The *goals* of the developmental physical education curriculum include the following:

I. Motor Development Goals

- To assist children in becoming *skillful movers.*
- To aid children in becoming *knowledgeable movers.*
- To promote children's development as *expressive movers.*
- To provide children with opportunities to become *fit movers.*
- To educate children with the fitness knowledge to be *informed movers.*
- To create an environment that encourages children to be *eager movers.*

II. Cognitive Development Goals

- To foster an environment that encourages children to be *multisensory learners.*
- To stimulate children's interest in being *active learners.*

III. Affective Development Goals

- To assist children in becoming positive *self-discovering learners.*
- To create an environment that helps children become *cooperative learners.*

Develop a Conceptual Framework

A conceptual framework should undergird any curriculum. The **conceptual framework**—a basic, but often overlooked, aspect of curriculum building—represents the essential concepts on which your curriculum is based. It is the necessary link between your values, mission, and goals and the actual design of the program. The conceptual framework clarifies, defines, and classifies terms and concepts as they are used in the curriculum.

CONCEPT 8.3
Establishing the conceptual framework is an important, but frequently overlooked, step in the curricular process.

In the developmental physical education curriculum, the conceptual framework is composed of the following areas: (1) categories of movement, (2) content areas of

◄ TEACHING TIPS ►

All curricula require a *conceptual framework* to establish common ground and terminology for implementing the program. The conceptual framework of the developmentally based physical education curriculum includes these areas:

1. **Categories of Movement**
   a. Stability movements (e.g., static and dynamic balance)
   b. Locomotor movements (e.g., running, hopping, jumping, and leaping)
   c. Manipulative movements (e.g., throwing, catching, and kicking)
   d. Movement phrases (e.g., movement combinations)
2. **Content Areas of Physical Education**
   a. Games (e.g., low-level games, lead-up games, and sports)
   b. Dance (e.g., fundamental, creative, and folk and square dance)
   c. Self-testing (e.g., stunts, tumbling, and apparatus)
3. **Movement Concepts**
   a. Effort (i.e., force, time, and flow)
   b. Space (i.e., level, direction, and range)
   c. Relationships (i.e., objects and people)

4. **Phases and Stages of Motor Development**
   a. Fundamental phase (initial, elementary, and mature stages)
   b. Specialized phase (transition, application, and lifelong utilization stages)
5. **Levels and Stages of Movement Skill Learning**
   a. Beginning/novice level (awareness, exploration, and discovery stages)
   b. Intermediate/practice level (combination and application stages)
   c. Advanced/fine-tuning level (performance and individualized stages)
6. **Components of Physical Fitness**
   a. Health-related components (muscular strength, muscular endurance, cardiovascular endurance, joint flexibility, and body composition)
   b. Performance-related components (balance, coordination, agility, speed, and power)
7. **Styles of Teaching**
   a. Direct teaching styles (command and task methods)
   b. Indirect teaching styles (exploratory and guided-discovery methods)
   c. Combining teaching styles (limitation method)

physical education, (3) movement concepts, (4) phases and stages of motor development, (5) levels and stages of movement skill learning, (6) components of physical fitness, and (7) styles of teaching. All areas are central to the design and implementation of the program. Take a few minutes to study the Teaching Tips outline of the conceptual framework of the developmental physical education curriculum above.

Determine Objectives of the Program

Once the value base of the curriculum has been stated and the conceptual framework that will govern its structure has been determined, it is possible to state the general objectives of the program. **General objectives** begin to flesh out the goals of the program in terms that are more descriptive. Once these have been determined, it is essential to describe the **conditions for implementation,** that is, the terms under which the program will be conducted.

This should be done before determining the specific objectives of the program.

 CONCEPT 8.4
General objectives are universal, but the specific objectives that are derived from them can be stated only after the conditions under which the program is to be implemented have been determined.

General Objectives. General objectives are broad, desired outcomes that are established for the learner to achieve. These objectives might well be stated in terms of the motor, cognitive, and affective areas of development. The physical education program that is developmentally based, properly planned, and carefully implemented can

A sampling of *general objectives* from the developmental curriculum includes the following:

I. **Motor Area** (Skillful mover and fit mover goals translated into general objectives)
    A. Movement Skill Objectives
       1. To achieve mature levels in a variety of fundamental stability skills.
       2. To develop mature patterns in a variety of fundamental locomotor skills.
       3. To attain mature skill development in a variety of fundamental manipulative skills.
       4. To develop an acceptable level of skill in a variety of individual, dual, and team sports.
       5. To enhance skillful rhythmic movement in a variety of fundamental, creative, and folk and square dance activities.
    B. Physical Fitness Objectives
       1. To foster improved levels of health-related fitness.
       2. To promote improved performance-related fitness.

II. **Cognitive Area** (Knowledgeable mover, active learner, and multisensory learner goals translated into general objectives)
    A. To improve perceptual-motor learning in body, spatial, directional, and temporal awareness.
    B. To develop knowledge and understanding in a variety of activities including rules, strategies, fitness concepts, healthful living, and responsible decision making.
    C. To reinforce a variety of academic concepts in mathematics, science, social studies, and language arts.

III. **Affective Area** (Expressive mover, self-discovering learner, and cooperative learner goals translated into general objectives)
    A. To encourage self-expression, motor creativity, and aesthetic appreciation of movement.
    B. To contribute to a positive self-concept, self-confidence, and perceived physical competence.
    C. To develop positive socialization skills through cooperative play.

achieve a variety of general objectives. The degree to which they are achieved will depend on the developmental level of the students, the philosophy and expertise of the teacher, and the teaching styles used.

Conditions for Implementation.   Before establishing the specific objectives of the program, a thorough survey must be conducted of factors that may affect the program's content. Conditions that will affect the specific design of the program should be concisely stated to assess the boundaries within which the program must be conducted. If, for example, one of your general objectives is "to develop a variety of team sport skills," you will need to determine if you have ample space, equipment, and high enough ceilings before you translate it into the specific volleyball skill objective of "to be able to perform the overhead pass to a partner." Space, time, equipment, and facilities will play an important role in determining the specific objectives of your program. Additionally, the size and experience level of your classes, the number of times you meet per week, and the length of lessons will influence your specific objectives.

Only you know the conditions under which you must try to achieve the objectives of your program. Therefore, only you can determine what the specific objectives should be. The conditions under which physical educators are required to implement their programs vary greatly. In fact, there is frequently tremendous variation among schools in the same school district. Taking the time to realistically assess the teaching and learning environment will enable you to establish specific objectives that are reasonable and obtainable. Failure to do so will only lead to considerable frustration and failure.

Specific Objectives.   Once the general objectives have been established and the conditions under which the curriculum will be carried out have been stated, it is possible to determine the **specific objectives** of the program.

The developmental curriculum is based on the needs, interests, and developmental level of the students served, not *on age or grade criteria.*

Before determining the *specific objectives* of *your* program you must have the following information:

- facilities available (both school and community),
- equipment available,
- number of class periods per week,
- length of class periods,
- average number of pupils per class,
- pupils' entry level assessment,
- geographic location,
- typical weather conditions,
- community mores, and
- educational goals of the school system and community.

The specific objectives that you establish may be stated in process terms (behavioral terms), or in product terms (terminal objectives), both of which may be reflected in benchmark (marker) objectives throughout the program.

C O N C E P T   8 . 5
Specific objectives may be stated as behavioral objectives, terminal objectives, or benchmark objectives.

Each of the *specific objectives* that follow is directly related to the *general objectives* of "Developing mature patterns in a variety of fundamental locomotor (as well as manipulative and stability) skills." This general objective is in turn directly related to the curricular *goal:* "To assist children in becoming skillful movers." Moreover, this goal is also directly related to the *mission* of the program which includes "learning to move," which is directly related to one of the *values* of the developmental physical education program, namely, "increased movement competency."

Behavioral objectives are a form of specific objectives. They have three important characteristics: (1) they are observable, (2) they are measurable, and (3) they establish the criterion for performance. Behavioral objectives are valuable and quite worthwhile, but they are time-consuming to write and are frequently redundant. They are, however, valuable in that they clearly identify what is to be learned and how it is to be assessed. The following are samples of specific objectives stated in behavioral terms that may be appropriate for elementary school children.

The student will:

1. Perform two consecutive forward rolls beginning from a squat position and finishing in a squat position.
2. Demonstrate use of the instep kick in soccer by kicking it directly to a partner stationed twenty feet away in a drill situation.
3. Distinguish the difference between an even and an uneven beat in a musical composition and demonstrate the use of both using two different locomotor movements.
4. Make seven of ten basketball free throws from behind the foul line.

Terminal objectives are frequently used by physical education teachers rather than writing out each objective in behavioral terms. Terminal objectives are simply a listing of the specific motor, cognitive, and affective objectives to be achieved in the program. They are not listed by age or grade level but rather by progression from simple to complex and from general to specific. It is recommended that you become familiar with writing behavioral objectives before using terminal objectives as the focus for stating lesson objectives. Examples of terminal objectives follow. Students will increase competency in:

1. Stunts and Tumbling Skills
    a. Log roll
    b. Forward roll
    c. Backward roll
    d. Tripod
    e. Headstand
    f. Handstand
2. Soccer Skills
    a. Instep kick
    b. Push pass
    c. Outside-of-foot pass
    d. Punting
3. Rhythmic Interpretation of
    a. Accent
    b. Tempo
    c. Intensity
    d. Rhythmic pattern

Benchmark objectives are a sampling of specific marker objectives that are intended to be achieved by a certain time. Grades two, four, six, and eight are frequently used as marker years for determining which specific objectives have been achieved. The Outcomes Committee of the National Association for Sport and Physical Education (NASPE, 1992, p. 5) has identified examples of benchmark objectives based on their definition of a physically educated person being one that:

> HAS learned skills necessary to perform a variety of physical activities. IS physically fit. DOES participate regularly in physical activity. KNOWS the implications of and the benefits from involvement in physical activities. VALUES physical activity and its contributions to a healthful lifestyle.

Sample benchmark objectives have been established for kindergarten as well as grades 2, 4, 6, 8, 10, and 12. Figure 8.1 provides an example of benchmarks to be achieved by the end of the fourth grade.

Design the Program

Once the objectives of the program have been determined, it is time to make a **scope and sequence chart,** which outlines the scope, sequence, and curricular balance necessary to satisfy the specific objectives of the program from unit to unit and from year to year. Each of these aspects of the program design is discussed. Figure 8.2 illustrates a sample scope and sequence chart. It provides a general view of the objectives throughout the school year (scope) for each grade level (sequence) reflecting a broad range of activities (curricular balance).

CONCEPT 8.6
The actual design of the curriculum is reflected in a scope and sequence chart that is both balanced in content and age appropriate.

Scope.   The term **scope** as used in curriculum building refers to the content of the program in terms of its breadth or range throughout the academic year. The actual variety of units of work and skill through the year at any grade level represents the scope of the program for that grade level. For a curriculum to be effective, it must demonstrate sufficient scope. Its breadth should be enough to encompass a multitude of skills, activities, and ability levels.

In the developmental curriculum the scope and sequence chart is the point of contact between the program goals, general and specific objectives, and the actual learning activities of the program. The scope and sequence chart is constructed in such a manner that it reflects content that is age-group or grade appropriate, but it is the specific learning activities taken from these content areas and applied to the actual children being taught that determine the developmental appropriateness of the program. This important concept is discussed further and amply illustrated in Chapter 9, "Planning the Lesson."

NASPE PHYSICAL EDUCATION
OUTCOMES PROJECT

EXAMPLES OF BENCHMARKS—FOURTH GRADE

As a result of participating in a quality physical education program it is reasonable to expect that the student will be able to:

HAS	4	1. While traveling, avoid or catch an individual or object.
HAS	4	2. Leap, leading with either foot.
HAS	4	3. Roll, in a backward direction, without hesitating or stopping.
HAS	4	4. Transfer weight, from feet to hands, at fast and slow speeds using large extensions (e.g., mulekick, handstand, cartwheel).
HAS	4	5. Hand dribble and foot dribble a ball and maintain control while traveling within a group.
HAS	4	6. Strike a softly thrown, lightweight ball back to a partner using a variety of body parts, and combinations of body parts (e.g., the bump volley as in volleyball, the thigh as in soccer).
HAS	4	7. Consistently strike a softly thrown ball with a bat or paddle demonstrating an appropriate grip, side to the target and swing plane.
HAS	4	8. Develop patterns and combinations of movements into repeatable sequences.
HAS	4	9. Without hesitating, travel into and out of a rope turned by others.
HAS	4	10. Balance, with control, on a variety of moving objects (e.g., balance boards, skates, scooters).
HAS	4	11. Jump and land for height, and jump and land for distance using a mature motor pattern.
HAS	4	12. Throw, catch, and kick using mature motor patterns.
HAS	4	13. Demonstrate competence in basic swimming strokes and survival skills in, on, and around the water.
IS	4	14. Maintain continuous aerobic activity for a specified time.
IS	4	15. Maintain appropriate body alignment during activity (e.g., lift, carry, push, pull).
IS	4	16. Support, lift, and control body weight in a variety of activities.
DOES	4	17. Regularly participate in physical activity for the purpose of improving skillful performance and physical fitness.
KNOWS	4	18. Distinguish between compliance and noncompliance with game rules and fair play.
KNOWS	4	19. Select and categorize specialized equipment used for participation in a variety of activities.
KNOWS	4	20. Recognize fundamental components and strategies used in simple games and activities.
KNOWS	4	21. Identify ways movement concepts can be used to refine movement skills.
KNOWS	4	22. Identify activities that contribute to personal feelings of joy.
KNOWS	4	23. Describe essential elements of mature movement patterns.
KNOWS	4	24. Describe healthful benefits that result from regular and appropriate participation in physical activity.
KNOWS	4	25. Analyze potential risks associated with physical activities.
KNOWS	4	26. Design games, gymnastics, and dance sequences that are personally interesting.
VALUES	4	27. Appreciate differences and similarities in others' physical activity.
VALUES	4	28. Respect persons from different backgrounds and the cultural significance they attribute to various games, dances, and physical acitivities.
VALUES	4	29. Enjoy feelings resulting from involvement in physical activity.
VALUES	4	30. Celebrate personal successes and achievements and those of others.

Source: From *Outcomes of Quality Physical Education Programs*. National Association for Physical Education and Sport. 1992. Reston, VA: NASPE. Reprinted with permission.

FIGURE 8.1 *Sample benchmark objectives to be achieved by the end of the fourth grade.*

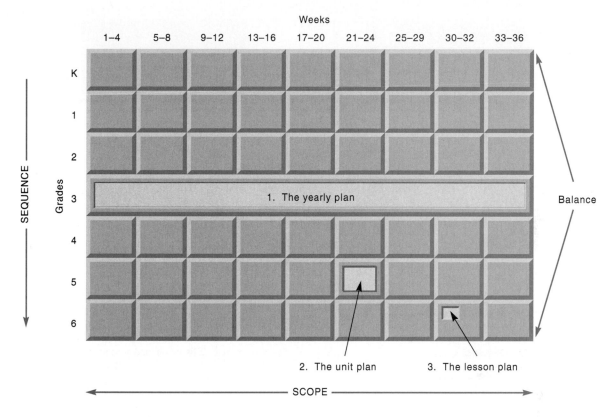

FIGURE 8.2 *The scope and sequence chart.*

Sequence.   When using the term **sequence,** we are referring to progression in terms of the year-to-year ordering of skills taught in the curriculum. In other words, the sequence of the program reflects the timing and depth of the program from grade to grade. For the curriculum to be effective, there must be clear evidence of progressive skill development from year to year. This is reflected in the sequence of the curriculum.

Curricular Balance.   The term **curricular balance** refers to the relative emphasis of the curriculum in terms of the time spent on specific content areas and the variety inherent in the program. Figure 8.3 provides suggested approximate yearly time percentages for the various content areas of the physical education program based on age-group appropriateness. More importantly, however, the "Teaching Tips" that follow present specific criteria for selecting or designing learning experiences that are developmentally appropriate.

TEACHING TIPS

Criteria for selecting appropriate learning experiences:

- Select activities that match the developmental level of the participants.

- Select activities that are both physically and psychologically safe and emphasize learning and cooperative participation instead of winning and making value judgments of comparative worth.

- Select activities that promote real learning, active participation, and learning enjoyment rather than activities that require little challenge or require waiting, watching, and general inactivity.

- Select activities that are relevant to the lives of your children and that have the potential of being applied to lifelong activities.

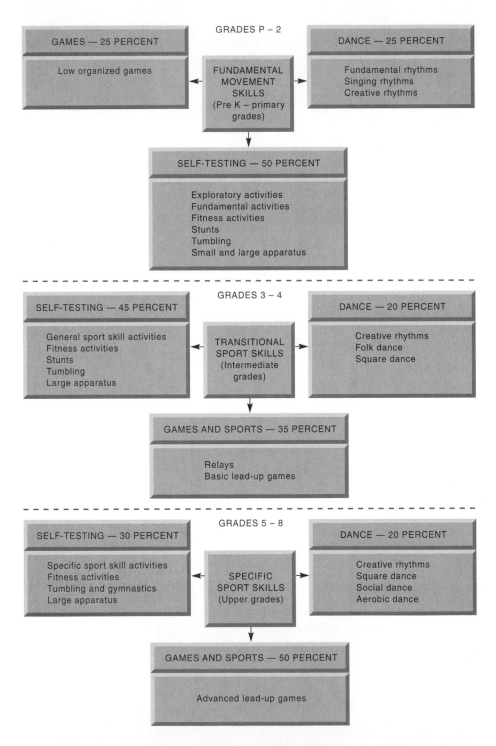

FIGURE 8.3 *Suggested approximate division of time for activities based on age-group appropriateness.*

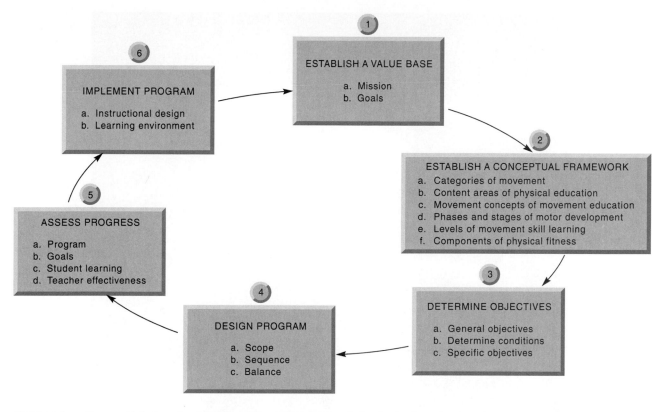

FIGURE 8.4 *Sequential steps in designing the developmental physical education curriculum.*

Any physical education curriculum that is to be of real value to children must endeavor to achieve harmony among scope, sequence, and curricular balance. Doing so helps to ensure that the activities engaged in by the children will be broad-based (scope), age-group appropriate (sequence), and of continuing interest (curricular balance).

Establish Assessment Procedures

Assessment, the fifth step in planning the curriculum, is an important part of the total process, because only through assessment can it be determined if the students have achieved the objectives of the program. Evaluation is a method of determining the strong and weak points of your program and your teaching. It may take many forms and be either subjective (process) or objective (product) in nature. Chapter 11, "Assessing Progress," discusses both process and product assessment. The important thing to remember in planning the curriculum is that each step is directly related to the preceding one and that

curriculum building is a sequential, orderly process. (See Figure 8.4.)

C O N C E P T   8 . 7
Assessment is the primary means of determining if the objectives of the curriculum have been achieved; assessment serves as a basis for curricular revision.

Implement the Program

Implementing the program is the sixth and final step in the curricular process. Implementation is the critical transition between planning and action (also known as: where the "rubber meets the road"). A careful reading of the five steps in the planning process should alert you to the extent and scope of planning that goes into the curricular

The developmental curriculum strives to make learning personally meaningful, active, and fun.

process. Failure to go through this planning process will result in considerable frustration on your part, and on the part of your students, as you attempt to implement your program. It is vitally important that as you prepare to implement a skill theme you: (1) preplan, (2) observe and assess, (3) plan and implement, and (4) evaluate and revise your lessons. Each of the chapters in Part IV: *The Skill Themes,* contains a "Teaching Tips" box at the beginning of the chapter to assist you with this process.

THE DEVELOPMENTAL CURRICULAR MODEL

The **developmental curricular model** for children's physical education is based on the concept that the development of one's movement abilities occurs in distinct but

often overlapping phases of motor development in each of the categories of movement. This is achieved through participation in activities that are applied to the traditional content areas of physical education and the movement concepts of movement education. These activities are geared to the learner's appropriate level of movement skill learning and level of physical fitness, and the activities are implemented through a variety of teaching styles. See Figure 8.5 for an illustration of this conceptual framework.

CONCEPT 8.8
Developmental curricular models incorporate into their conceptual framework emphasis on understanding the learner as an individual.

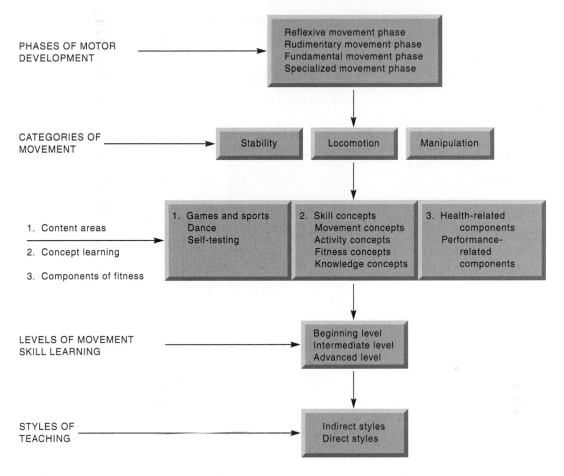

FIGURE 8.5 *Outline of the conceptual framework for the developmental physical education program.*

Preschool and Primary Grades

Developmental teaching recognizes that preschool and primary-grade children are generally involved in developing and refining their fundamental movement skills. These skills serve as the themes of the curriculum and the basis for the formation of units of instruction at this level. During this period more emphasis is placed on indirect styles of teaching because children tend to be at the beginning level of learning many movement skills. Exploratory and guided-discovery activities involving effort, space, and relationships, as well as games, rhythms, and self-testing activities, facilitate the use, practice, and mature development of fundamental movement skills (Figure 8.6).

Intermediate and Upper Elementary Grades

When the developmental model is applied to the intermediate and upper elementary grades, the focus of the curriculum changes from the fundamental movement phase to the specialized movement phase of development. During this phase, children are constantly combining and using stability, locomotor, and manipulative skills in a wide variety of sport-related activities. At this phase, units of instruction are viewed in the context of the activity to which they are being applied. The game of softball, for example, becomes a sports skill unit and involves combinations and elaborations of fundamental stability abilities (twisting, turning, and stretching), locomotor abilities (base running and sliding), and manipulative skills

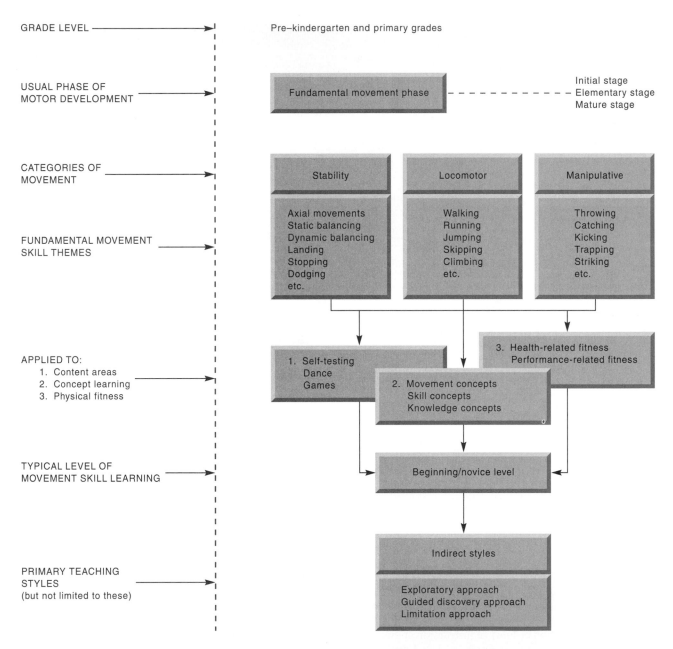

FIGURE 8.6 *Implementing the developmental model at the pre-kindergarten and primary grade level.*

(throwing, catching, striking). Teachers now focus their attention on developing the movement skills related to particular sport activities. These skills serve as the lesson themes within any given unit of instruction and are applied to the various content areas and knowledge concepts (rules, strategies, understandings, and appreciations) of physical education. Children's characteristic level of movement skill learning at this phase is the intermediate level. Therefore, emphasis is placed on the combination of skills and their practice in a variety of static drills and dynamic games. As a result, emphasis is generally placed on more direct teaching approaches (see Figure 8.7).

THE EXTENDED CURRICULUM

The physical education teacher is frequently responsible for conducting programs in addition to the basic instructional program. This is frequently referred to as the **extended curriculum,** or the hidden curriculum. Recess and noon-hour programs, daily fitness programs, intramural and club sport programs, and interscholastic programs are all logical extensions of the instructional program. Each can make positive contributions to various aspects of children's development, but none should be viewed as a substitute or replacement for a quality instructional program in physical education.

CONCEPT 8.9
The extended curriculum has the potential for being an important addition to the instructional physical education program.

Recess and Noon-Hour Programs

Recess is a North American tradition. Practically every elementary school in North America has some form of daily recess. The recess period generally takes the form of a midmorning or midafternoon break from the normal academic routine. Recess generally lasts from ten to twenty minutes and is held outdoors whenever possible so that children can play and have an opportunity to "let off steam" in acceptable ways. The theory behind the recess period is that this break from the relatively inactive routine of the classroom will enable children to refocus their energies and attention on their schoolwork. There is sufficient empirical evidence to warrant continuation of quality recess programs.

Noon-hour programs are an outgrowth of busing. In many school systems, children remain at school rather than go home during the lunch hour. The noon-hour program follows the lunch period and allows children to take part in free-choice activities on the playground or in the gymnasium. Children should not be permitted to gulp down their lunch in an effort to get more time on the playground or in the gymnasium. Approximately twenty minutes should be set aside for eating lunch. Early finishers should be required to wait the full twenty minutes.

Both the recess and the noon-hour programs are, by tradition, loosely structured. Children are generally allowed free choice in their activity selection. Most children select vigorous play activities, but some choose more quiet and sedentary activities. The keys to a successful recess and noon-hour program are proper facilities, ample equipment, and adequate supervision. The physical education teacher is frequently assigned responsibility for ensuring all three.

The facilities, whether indoors or out, are important to the success of the program. They should be free of safety hazards and regularly checked to eliminate unsafe conditions. The outdoor area should have ample space so that primary-grade children may play in areas separate from older children. The play area should contain hanging and climbing apparatus when possible. Large grassy and asphalt areas for a variety of activities are ideal. Markings for line and circle games such as four-square and hopscotch are helpful stimulators of purposeful, vigorous activity. Similarly, the indoor facility, whether the gymnasium or a multipurpose room, should be set up to allow for free choice and encourage vigorous activity.

The availability of equipment for the recess and noon-hour programs is the second key to success. There should be enough equipment (balls, frisbees, ropes, and so forth) so that all who want to play may. In many schools, classroom teachers keep a "fun box" with equipment to be used for recess. Children check out the equipment and are responsible for returning it to the box at the end of their play period.

Supervision is the third key to a successful recess or noon-hour program. Teachers frequently dread recess duty because of the mass chaos that often seems to accompany this responsibility. Such chaos is minimized if (1) one teacher is assigned to supervise no more than two classes at one time, (2) the supervisor can see all children at all times, (3) there is ample space and equipment for meaningful activity, and (4) the children are given instruction in appropriate playground activities.

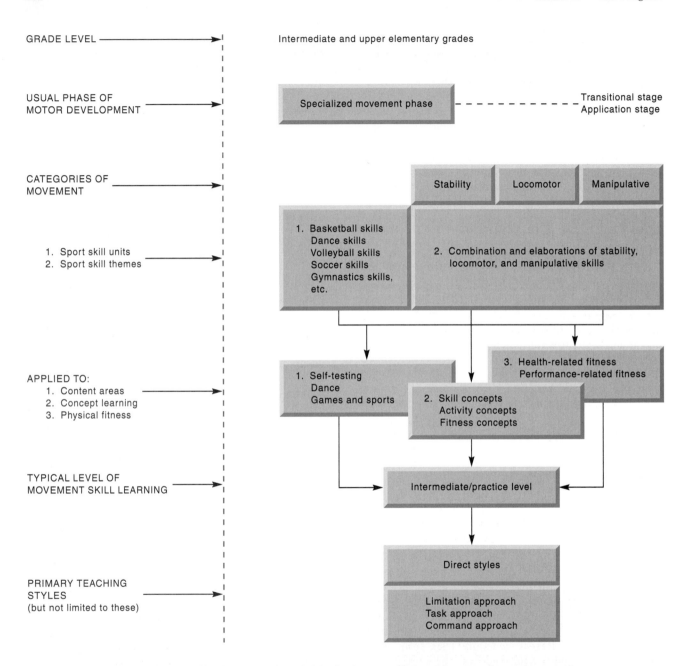

FIGURE 8.7 *Implementing the developmental model in the intermediate and upper elementary grades.*

The physical education teacher can play an important role in helping make the recess and noon-hour programs worthwhile to children and easy for classroom teachers to supervise. Taking the time to instruct children in how to organize a game of kickball, soccer, or four-square works wonders. Ensuring that the supervising teacher knows the basic rules of several appropriate games and has the proper equipment to help get them started is helpful. Finally, a behavior code for play on the playground or in the gymnasium will help reduce problems and maximize the educational potential of the recess and noon-hour programs.

Daily Fitness Programs

In recent years many school districts in Canada and the United States have introduced **daily fitness programs** into the total school program. Daily fitness programs frequently replace a recess period or are conducted during the last twenty minutes of the school day. Fitness programs are conducted in addition to the instructional physical education program and are frequently engaged in by the entire student body, faculty, and staff.

The daily fitness program is frequently conducted with the entire school population taking part during a specific fifteen- to twenty-minute portion of the day. Hallways may be used for stationary jogging or aerobic exercise to music. The gymnasium or multipurpose room may serve as a station for rope-jumping activities, and the classroom may be used for flexibility and vigorous strength- and endurance-building exercises. Trained students and teachers can act as fitness leaders. Daily fitness programs strive for total, active involvement for the entire time that has been set aside. People perform at their individual level of ability and are encouraged to do their best.

As the physical education teacher, you may be responsible for the daily fitness program. In schools where it does not yet exist, it will be your responsibility to develop a solid rationale to convince the administration, faculty, and students of the need for such a program. Once they are convinced, you will need to train teachers and students as fitness leaders. It will be important to keep interest in the program high and to demonstrate improved levels of fitness.

Intramural Programs

The intramural sports program is a logical extension of a quality physical education program, but it should never be a substitute for physical education. Intramurals are

Because of the sedentary nature of our society, many children do not get sufficient regular, vigorous physical activity. The instructional physical education program generally does not have adequate amounts of time or the regularity of a daily program to positively influence fitness levels to a significant degree. The realization that children are not as physically active as they need to be, coupled with the results of recent research linking the positive benefits of vigorous physical activity to human wellness, has caused many school corporations to add daily fitness activities to the total school curriculum in *addition* to the instructional physical education class.

generally conducted before school, during the noon hour, or after school. The intramural program should include all students who desire to participate, regardless of their skill level. In the elementary school, intramurals are special-interest programs for boys and girls who want to use the skills they have learned in the physical education class. **Intramurals** are physical activity programs conducted between groups of students within the same school. Greater emphasis is placed on playing the game in the intramural program than on instruction, although there is often an instructional component in terms of rules and the application of strategies.

The physical education teacher is frequently responsible for conducting a varied intramural program throughout the school year. Activities may be seasonal and may last four to six weeks. Popular intramural activities with elementary students include floor hockey, basketball, touch football, kickball, soccer, dodgeball, and volleyball. Players may be grouped into teams in a variety of ways. No matter what procedure is selected, the teacher's primary consideration should be the equalization of teams. All teams should have as near an equal chance to win as possible. Remember, emphasis in the intramural program should be on skill application and fun in a wholesome recreational setting.

For the intramural program to be successful, written policies regarding parental approval, eligibility, first aid, medical care, and awards should be available to all participants. The program should be evaluated on a regular basis in terms of the stated goals and objectives of the

TEACHING TIPS

Bill of Rights for Young Athletes*

All young athletes have the right to:

- participate in sports,
- participate at a level commensurate with each child's maturity and ability,
- have qualified adult leadership,
- play as a child and not as an adult,
- share in the leadership and decision-making of their sport participation,
- participate in safe and healthy environments,
- proper preparation for participation in sports,
- an equal opportunity to strive for success,
- be treated with dignity, and
- have fun in sports.

*From R. Martens and V. Seefeldt, *Guidelines for Children's Sports* (Reston, VA: AAHPERD, 1979).

---

program. Because participation is voluntary, the number of participants is often a good barometer of the program's success in terms of student interest.

Club Programs

The **club programs** are similar to intramural programs in that they are held before, during, or after school. However, the emphasis of the club program is on further instruction in specific activities and is little concerned with competing against one's classmates. Elementary school children frequently enjoy being members of a gymnastics club, fitness club, bicycle club, or leaders club.

Club programs are an extension of the regular physical education class in that they permit children with specific activity interests to get additional practice and instruction. They are especially enjoyable for the teacher because they permit work with small groups of students who are highly motivated to learn more about the activity.

Club participants frequently make good gym helpers. With training, they can be given some special responsibilities in the regular physical education class. This not only provides leadership experiences for these students, but gives the teacher much needed assistance and freedom to work with others needing additional instruction.

Interscholastic Programs

The extramural or **interscholastic program** provides children an opportunity to compete against boys and girls from other schools. The interscholastic program can be of great value to the children it serves, but it should be included in the curriculum only after both quality physical education and intramural sports programs are in place. Interscholastic activities should never replace or disrupt these basic programs.

Interscholastic athletic programs are intended to provide children with opportunities to develop into more complete and competent individuals. They are not intended to be an entertainment medium for parents, and they do not exist for the glorification of the coach. A win-at-all-cost attitude in any youth sport program should not be tolerated. Providing individuals the opportunity to pit their skills against others is the lifeblood of sports. Winning is important, but it must not be regarded as the primary reason for competition in the elementary school youth sport program.

SPECIAL PROGRAMS

The physical education teacher is frequently asked to conduct various special programs. Unlike extended curricular activities, special programs generally last from less than an hour to a full day. Whether they are long or short, special programs generally involve extensive planning and preparation. Special activities in the form of play days, sports days, and field days, along with gym shows and public demonstrations, are frequently encountered at the elementary school level.

Guidelines for a successful *gym show:*

- Involve all grades and every child in the show.

- Keep the program short. Forty-five minutes to one hour should be sufficient.

- Select activities that are part of the regular physical education program.

- Select activities that can be easily learned and performed by all.

- Do not worry about polished performances. Work for an acceptable standard.

- Do not use physical education class time for extended practices.

- Provide the audience with a printed program that outlines the sequence of performances and the objectives they achieve in the program.

- Use scarves, sashes, or hats as simple costumes to enhance the general appearance of the performances.

- Use appropriate musical accompaniment whenever possible to add to the general effect.

- Props such as parachutes, flashlights, streamers, and hoops also enhance the performance.

- Send an announcement home concerning the gym show along with a permission slip allowing participation.

- Allow for a complete run-through of the program before the big night.

- Take photos for use in a bulletin board display.

- Enlist the help of classroom teachers for supervision on the night of the performance.

CONCEPT 8.10
A variety of special events that heighten interest and add variety may be incorporated into the physical education curriculum.

Special Days

At the elementary school level there are frequently three types of special-day activities: the play day, sports day, and field day.

The **play day** is a special day of activities involving children from the same school or from two or more schools playing together on the same team. Play days among schools are frequently held at a central location in the community. Activities might include softball, soccer, basketball, and volleyball games. Children are randomly assigned to teams, and they do not compete as a class or as a school.

The **sports day** is similar to the play day except that classes or schools *do* compete against others as a team in a tournament-like atmosphere. More emphasis is placed on competition and awards. Sports days should emphasize participation by everyone. All children should have

an opportunity to play on a team representing their class or school.

The **field day** focuses on a variety of activities and is generally held within a single school, usually near the end of the school year. Track and field days are popular in many elementary schools. The field day is generally held during school hours, and children from each class compete. An important feature of the field day is that total scores are not kept. Emphasis is on pitting one's skills against other children, making new friends, and having fun.

Gym Shows and Public Demonstrations

Many experienced physical education teachers promote their programs with an annual gym show or public demonstration. These special programs may be held after school, during the early evening hours, or on a weekend. They are frequently held in conjunction with a PTA meeting or a local service club program or as a special event at a shopping mall.

Gym shows often focus on the highlights of the year's program, but this should not be the goal. The goal of the gym show is to provide children with an opportunity to demonstrate what they have learned in physical education class. These shows may also serve as a subtle means of getting maximum attendance at a PTA meeting or parents' night. In any case, the gym show can effectively showcase your program and build faculty and community support. Be certain to take advantage of the opportunity to conduct an annual gym show. Although it takes extra time, the dividends will be well worth the effort.

The **public demonstration** is different from the gym show in that it generally involves a smaller number of students and is sponsored by service organizations and shopping malls. The public demonstration might involve members from one or more of the club sport programs sponsored by the school. The gymnastics club, for example, may be asked to demonstrate their skills. The public demonstration is generally polished; practice is provided outside of the physical education period; and those who participate have special interests and abilities in the activity. When planning a public demonstration, follow the same guidelines as for the gym show. Be certain, however, to arrange for transportation to and from the demonstration site and to provide for ample adult supervision at all times.

Gym shows and public demonstrations are excellent promotional devices for the physical education program. Although they are time-consuming and often nerve-wracking, they are an important part of the extracurricular program because they inform the public about physical education and broaden the base of support for quality programs.

TOURNAMENTS

Tournaments are a common aspect of the extracurricular program. They may be conducted during recess or the noon hour, or they may be part of the intramural or club sport program. Tournaments can be beneficial to the physical education of children if the competitive element is not overemphasized and winning is not overly glorified. Tournaments permit the testing of one's skills against others and may be held for individual or group activities. Single elimination and double elimination tournaments are of questionable value in the developmental curriculum if the primary goal of competition is to promote skill improvement and enhance learning enjoyment. Therefore, only the round-robin and ladder tournaments are recommended for use and reviewed here. Both permit maximum participation by all participants.

TEACHING TIPS

Guidelines for conducting a *ladder tournament:*

- A player may challenge only the player one or two rungs above.
- The winner of a game remains on the higher rung if he or she was already there or exchanges positions from a lower rung.
- Once a challenge has been made, a deadline must be set by which the game must be played or canceled (within two or three days).
- Set a completion date for the tournament.
- Position players randomly to begin the tournament or, if skill abilities are known, place the most skilled on the bottom.

Round-Robin Tournament

The **round-robin tournament** permits every individual or team to play every other individual or team. This type of tournament takes the longest amount of time but is preferred if time permits. The player with the greatest number of wins is the winner in a round-robin tournament. Figure 8.8 depicts a double round-robin tournament for eight participants. By shading in the lower half of the score sheet, a single round-robin tournament is created.

Ladder Tournament

In the **ladder tournament,** players are arranged vertically. Any player may challenge another directly above. If that player wins, his or her name replaces the defeated player, who in turn moves down one rung on the ladder. A ladder tournament is a form of continuous competition limited only by time. The object is to climb to the top of the ladder and remain there until the tournament is over. Ladder tournaments work especially well for individual activities and can be conducted with a variety of skills for an extended period of time. They take little time to set up and can be easily run by the children themselves. Use of a grease pencil to record names on 3 × 5 cards placed in a slotted board works well, along with a simple set of rules placed next to the tournament board. Figure 8.9 depicts a typical ladder tournament.

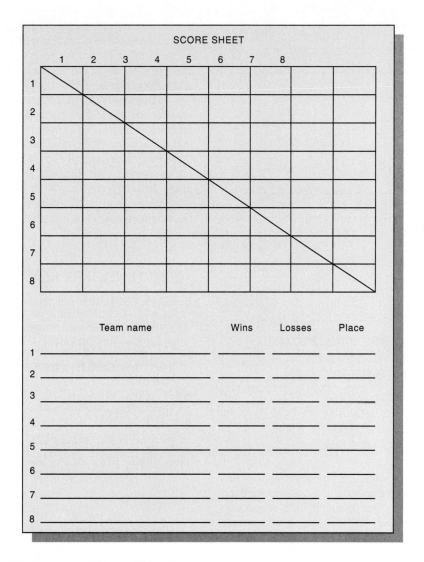

FIGURE 8.8 *Round-robin tournament for eight teams.*

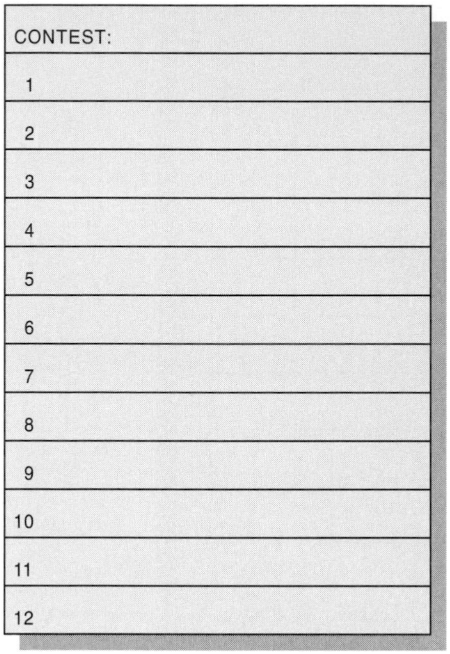

CONTEST:
1
2
3
4
5
6
7
8
9
10
11
12

FIGURE 8.9 *Format for a ladder tournament.*

SUMMARY

Curricular planning is essential if you are planning for success as a teacher. A broad-based, six-step procedure applies to all subject areas, including physical education: (1) establish a value base, (2) develop a conceptual framework, (3) determine objectives, (4) design the program, (5) implement the program, and (6) assess progress. Care should be taken to update your curriculum continually to maximize the effectiveness and relevancy of your program.

A curriculum is a blueprint for action geared to age-group appropriateness and subject to modification based on its individual appropriateness. The developmental physical education curriculum model takes into consideration both age-group appropriateness and individual appropriateness in the formation of specific objectives and individualized assessment procedures.

A frequently "hidden" aspect of the physical education curriculum is the extended program, which includes recess and noon-hour programs, fitness programs, intramurals, activity clubs, and interscholastic athletics. Plan these programs carefully so that they complement but do not overshadow the instructional physical education program. Special programs such as play days, field days, gym shows, and public demonstrations are also part of the extended curriculum in physical education.

COMPLEMENTARY READINGS

Bain, L. S. (1988). Curriculum for critical reflection in physical education. In R. S. Brandt, ed., *Content of the Curriculum, 1988 ASCD Yearbook,* Washington, DC: Association for Supervision and Curriculum Development.

Jackson, B. and F. Rokosz. (1995). Super kids day classic games: two field days for elementary schools. *JOPERD* 66:56–72.

NASPE. (1992). *The Physically Educated Person: Outcomes of Quality Physical Education Programs.* Reston, VA: NASPE.

Rokosz, F. M. (1993). *Procedures for Structuring and Scheduling Sports Tournaments.* Springfield, IL: Charles C. Thomas.

Siedentop, D., C. Mand, and A. Taggert. (1987). *Physical Education: Teaching and Curriculum Strategies for Grades 5–12.* Mountain View, CA: Mayfield.

SUPPLEMENTARY READINGS

Hellison, D. (1985). *Goals and Strategies for Teaching Physical Education.* Champaign, IL: Human Kinetics.

Hopple, C. (1995). *Teaching for Outcomes in Elementary Physical Education.* Champaign, IL: Human Kinetics.

Vickers, J. N. (1990). *Instructional Design for Teaching Physical Activities.* Champaign, IL: Human Kinetics.

CHAPTER 9

Planning Skill Themes

—

Key Concept

Successful Lessons Are the Result of Systematic Planning and Careful
Organization Geared to Both the Age-Group and Individual Appropriateness
of the Learner

—

Chapter Objectives

The purpose of this chapter is to provide you with the tools to:
• Describe the steps in planning a skill theme.
• List several examples of preplanning that should occur prior to developing the lesson.
• Provide examples of techniques for pre-assessing student entry levels to a skill theme.
• Distinguish among and give examples of the yearly plan, unit plan, and lesson plan as applied to movement skill themes.
• Outline and describe the anatomy of the daily lesson plan.
• Discuss several factors to take into consideration when implementing the daily lesson.
• Provide examples of various techniques for evaluating the lesson.
• Discuss the concept of "moving on" to a new skill theme and list factors to consider.
• Discuss the concept of "revisiting" a skill theme and list factors to be considered.
• List several suggestions for organizing indoor and outdoor facilities and equipment.
• Discuss the importance of planning ahead in terms of equipment placement and use.
• Provide examples of several instructional aids that may help implement the lesson.
• Describe how student helpers can be an asset to the lesson.
• Illustrate a variety of activity formations and discuss the purpose and advantages of each.

—

Terms to Remember

Developmental Skill Theme	Daily Lesson Plan	Skill Development	Videotaped Performances
Program Preplanning	Lesson Introduction	Teaching Episode	Skill Charts
Entry Level Assessment	Set Induction	Skill Application	Squads
Specific Planning	Anticipatory Set	Lesson Summary	Squad Leaders
Scope and Sequence Chart	Cognitive Set	Revisiting	Gym Helpers
Yearly Plan	Lesson Review	Task Cards	
Unit Plan	Body of the Lesson	Bulletin Boards	

The thematic approach to teaching has become popular in recent years. A **developmental skill theme** is a movement skill or group of related movement skills on which a lesson or unit of study is based to achieve the aims of learning to move and learning through movement. Developmental skill themes center on specific movement skills (either fundamental or specialized skills) that are to be developed and refined as the major focus of the lesson. What makes them developmental is that they incorporate what we know about children's motor development (see Chapter 2, "Childhood Growth and Motor Development"), the phases and stages of motor development and levels of movement skill learning (see Chapter 3, "Movement Skill Acquisition"), children's health-related and performance-related fitness (see Chapter 4, "Fitness Enhancement"), and their cognitive and affective development (see Chapters 5 and 6, "Cognitive Learning," and "Affective Growth") in the planning and implementing of lessons that are individually appropriate, meaningful, and fun. Activities from the content areas of physical education (games, dance, and self-testing) are incorporated into the skill theme approach as means of achieving these curricular objectives. For example, children who are at the fundamental movement phase of development take part in lessons designed to advance them to a more mature stage in running, jumping, throwing, or catching. Those at the specialized phase take part in skill themes that enhance sport skills in track and field, soccer, and softball.

This chapter examines the actual steps involved in planning the developmental physical education program at the grassroots level. Planning the daily lesson, formatting the lesson itself, evaluating its effectiveness, deciding when to move on and revisiting a skill theme are discussed. Suggestions for organizing facilities, equipment, and children are given, and guidelines for preparing instructional aids are also discussed.

> The central intent of the developmental skill theme approach is to help children achieve the curricular goals of becoming skillful movers, knowledgeable movers, and expressive movers.

CONCEPT 9.1
Teachers must plan specifically for learning to occur and avoid the trap of simply keeping children quiet, happy, and good.

STEPS IN PLANNING A MOVEMENT SKILL THEME

Planning is a crucial element in the success of any educational program. Without careful planning, the physical education class ends up being little more than a glorified recess period. Experience has shown that teachers who fail to plan are really in essence planning to fail. They delude themselves with the notion that they are too competent, too busy, or somehow above planning. As a result, they invariably run into difficulties and unwittingly encourage a series of disasters that are unnecessary, unfulfilling, and educationally unsound. The following represents an effective approach to planning and implementing developmental movement skill themes.

CONCEPT 9.2
Planning involves a number of specific steps that must be followed to maximize the impact of the physical education curriculum.

Preplanning

Once the basic parameters of the physical education curriculum have been established, you may begin the important and challenging process of **program preplanning** for your unique teaching situation. A first step in the preplanning process is to inventory the actual facilities, equipment, and supplies that are available to you. The number of times classes meet per week, the length of each class, and whether or not the children "dress" for gym will need to be determined. This important general information, along with other considerations such as class size, alternative facilities during inclement weather, and community mores, provides necessary facts about the actual teaching-learning environment.

The exact amount of time to be spent on any one skill theme should remain somewhat flexible. With younger children two to four class periods on some themes is appropriate, revisiting them later on in the school year. With older children you may wish to spend as long as three or four weeks on a specific unit of instruction.

Although it is suggested that near-equal balance be given to skill themes during the course of the school year, the specific amount of time you spend on particular skill themes will change as the abilities of individuals or the class change. For example, it may be helpful to children to focus more heavily on stability skill themes during the early periods of learning and gradually reduce this amount as they progress on to more mature stages of ability. Emphasis on some skill themes, particularly in the manipulative areas, should be increased from year to year. Others may remain constant.

CONCEPT 9.3

Planning involves a number of specific steps that must be followed to maximize the impact of the physical education curriculum.

Assessing Entry Levels

After the initial preplanning, observe your students and informally assess their current movement abilities. This is known as **entry level assessment.** (The chapters that follow in Part IV, *The Skill Themes,* describe the characteristics of numerous fundamental movement and sport skills. Read these chapters carefully and study the accompanying illustrations for each stage.)

To assess your students' present abilities in the movement skills on which you intend to focus, use simple checklists. (Keep in mind, too, that it is virtually impossible to conduct detailed formal assessments in a timely manner without the assistance of a trained teacher's aide.) Based on this observational assessment, you can then classify individuals or the group according to their level of movement skill learning (beginning, intermediate, or advanced). With this information, you can then make specific plans for lessons, taking care to use methods and techniques designed to move the class on to more skillful performance.

CONCEPT 9.4

Entry level assessment is an essential aspect of planning the developmentally appropriate physical education lesson.

The skill themes presented in the activity sections of this text contain *Developmental Teaching Progression Charts.* By referring to these charts, you will be able to locate appropriate activities geared to the assessed entry level of your students.

It is crucial to the concept of developmentally appropriate teaching that you observe and assess students *before* beginning the specific planning and implementation phase. Teachers have often been guilty of planning and implementing lessons and entire programs on age-related criteria alone. Diagnostic teaching requires that we carefully observe and assess the entry level of children before formulating and implementing specific strategies to advance them to the next stage of development.

The needs of the child should come first in planning movement skill themes.

Specific Planning

Once the preplanning and observational assessment of the entry level of ability has been completed, specific planning may begin. In **specific planning,** the teacher develops an age-appropriate scope and sequence chart (see Figure 9.1). The **scope and sequence chart** will provide you with an overview of the content of the curriculum in terms of age-group appropriateness. Based on the

Number of Lessons	PRIMARY GRADES			Number of Lessons	INTERMEDIATE GRADES		
	Kindergarten	First Grade	Second Grade		Third Grade	Fourth Grade	Fifth Grade
5	Organization and pre-assessment	Organization and pre-assessment	Organization and pre-assessment	5	Organization and pre-assessment	Organization and pre-assessment	Organization and pre-assessment
5	Skill/fitness testing	Skill/fitness testing	Skill/fitness testing	5	Skill/fitness testing	Skill/fitness testing	Skill/fitness testing
5	Introduction to body awareness	Beginning body awareness	Intermediate body awareness	20	Beginning ball skills I	Beginning soccer skills	Intermediate soccer skills
15	Introduction to locomotor skills I	Beginning locomotor skills I	Intermediate locomotor skills I				
15	Introduction to upper limb manipulative skills	Beginning upper limb manipulative skills	Intermediate upper limb manipulative skills	15	Beginning strength training	Intermediate strength training	Beginning football skills
10	Introduction to body handling skills I	Beginning body handling skills I	Intermediate body handling skills I	20	Beginning ball skills II	Beginning basketball skills	Intermediate basketball skills
10	Introduction to lower limb manipulative skills I	Beginning lower limb manipulative skills	Intermediate lower limb manipulative skills				
15	Introduction to rhythmics	Beginning creative rhythmic skills	Intermediate creative rhythmic skills	15	Advanced creative rhythmic skills	Beginning folk and square dance	Intermediate folk and square dance
10	Introduction to flexibility and body control	Beginning flexibility and body control skills	Intermediate flexibility and body control skills	20	Beginning ball skills III	Beginning volleyball skills	Intermediate volleyball skills
10	Introduction to upper body propelling skills	Beginning upper body propelling skills	Intermediate upper body propelling skills				
10	Introduction to body handling II	Beginning body handling skills II	Intermediate body handling skills II	20	Upper and lower limb striking skills	Beginning field hockey skills	Intermediate field hockey skills
10	Introduction to locomotor skills II	Beginning locomotor skills II	Intermediate locomotor skills II				
15	Introduction to upper limb manipulative skills II	Beginning upper limb manipulative skills II	Intermediate manipulative skills II	15	Advanced rhythmic skills	Beginning rhythmic aerobics	Intermediate rhythmic aerobics
15	Introductory dance	Beginning rhythmic skills	Intermediate rhythmic skills	15	Introduction to lifetime skills I	Beginning disc sport skills	Intermediate disc sport skills
15	Introduction to upper limb striking skills	Beginning upper limb striking skills	Beginning track and field skills	15	Introduction to lifetime skills II	Beginning softball skills	Intermediate softball skills
15	Introduction to lower limb manipulative skills II and post-assessment	Beginning lower limb manipulative skills II and post-assessment	Intermediate lower limb manipulative skills II and post-assessment	15	Beginning track skills and fitness testing	Individual track and field skills and fitness testing	Advanced individual track and field skills and fitness testing

FIGURE 9.1 *A sample scope and sequence chart (K–5) geared to age-group appropriateness.*

outline of the scope and sequence chart, preplanning information, and the observed performance of the children, you can begin to formulate more detailed yearly plans, unit plans, and daily lesson plans.

CONCEPT 9.5
Specific planning starts with the scope and sequence chart and ends with the daily lesson plan.

The Yearly Plan.   The **yearly plan** represents the scope of activities to be included in the curriculum at any one grade level for an entire school year. It is more detailed than the total curriculum outline and often reflects a seasonal influence that is based either on climatic conditions, which permit or prevent conducting classes outdoors, or the time of year for particular activities. The yearly plan should provide an outline of the skills to be engaged in by the class in each unit of instruction, geared closely to developmental appropriateness (see Figure 9.2).

The Unit Plan.   A **unit plan** is developed after the yearly plan has been outlined. It represents the themes of instruction (such as fundamental throwing and catching skills, stunts and tumbling skills, or soccer skills) to be covered in a block of time. The unit plan is broken down into the specific skill themes that will be covered each week and the activities that will be used to develop these skills.

The Lesson Plan.   A **daily lesson plan** enables teachers to make the best use of each class period, is an energy and time saver, and assures progression in the program. Each lesson should be a meaningful experience through which the pupils learn something new and refine previously learned materials and skills.

Maximum active participation by all should be the goal of every lesson. This can be accomplished by providing, when possible, individual pieces of equipment for each child. When this is not feasible you may want to use a station concept in which children rotate in small groups from one activity station to another. Another key to maximum activity is to predetermine the fewest number of participants required for success of the activity, forming several small groups instead of one or two large groups.

Lesson plans enable teachers to review and relate to the overall program objectives. They help in the preparation of the coming lesson, providing an organized and progressive procedure that aids in class interest and individual motivation and often helps prevent disciplinary

TEACHING TIPS

Unit plans **can be organized in numerous ways, but should contain the following information:**

- Title of the unit.
- Specific objectives to be achieved by the learner.
- Skills to be taught, in the appropriate sequence.
- Specific activities to be used to develop these skills.
- The equipment needed.
- The methods of evaluating the students' achievement of the objectives.
- Sources of information for teachers and students.

problems. Lesson plans help the teacher emphasize important points and skill elements. They aid in evaluating teacher as well as pupil progress.

CONCEPT 9.6
The daily lesson plan is the critical point at which the planning process and *real* children meet.

The lesson plan is more specific than the unit plan and is the primary means of clarifying exactly what you intend to do during a specific lesson with *"your"* children. Lesson planning, which is essential for success in any curricular area, helps to ensure that the teacher devises specific strategies for implementing the objectives of the lessson that are geared to the actual children being taught. Lesson planning in developmental physical education is essential because it is the focal point of planning for individual appropriateness.

Many formats can be used for writing a lesson plan, ranging from highly detailed ones required by college professors in methods courses to "off-the-top-of-the-head" plans made by some teachers on their way to school each day. Neither of these extremes is satisfactory, for obvious reasons. Remember that the primary purpose of the lesson plan is to help you think through your lesson so that it is maximally efficient in terms of the actual children you teach. Therefore, it is recommended that you consider writing brief lesson plans on a 5″ × 8″ index card, or on your personal computer. In these ways, you

GRADE 1

Weeks	1–2	3–6	7–10	11–14	15–18
Unit	Class pre-planning and assessment	Fundamental locomotor skills I	Fundamental manipulative skills I	Fundamental stability skills I	Fundamental rhythmic skills
Specific Skill Themes to Be Stressed	Skill and fitness testing Review of skills from previous year	Running Starting Stopping Changing direction Tagging Dodging Pivoting	Overhand throw Underhand throw Catching Vertical toss Object manipulation	Static balance Dynamic balance Rolling	Movement to varying: Accents Tempos Intensities Rhythmic patterns Application of rhythmic fundamentals

	19–22	23–26	27–30	31–34	35–36
	Fundamental locomotor skills II	Fundamental stability skills II	Creative dance skills	Fundamental manipulative skills II	Review, evaluation, and summary
	Hopping Skipping Galloping Leaping Jumping	Static balance Dynamic balance Rolling Body supports Inverted supports	Singing dances Simple dance forms	Kicking Bouncing Ball rolling Striking Dribbling	Skill and fitness testing Review of skills taught during the year

GRADE 5

Weeks	1–2	3–6	7–10	11–14	15–18
Unit	Class pre-planning	Touch football skills	Soccer skills	Rhythmic skills	Gymnastics skills
Specific Skill Themes to Be Stressed	Skill and fitness testing Review of skills from previous year	Passing Catching Centering Blocking Defense Rules Strategy	Kicking Trapping Dribbling Passing Tackling Rules Strategy	Creative rhythmics Dances without partners Folk dances Square dance	Apparatus Tumbling Pyramids Free exercise

	19–22	23–26	27–30	31–34	35–36
	Basketball skills	Volleyball skills	Softball skills	Track and field skills	Review, evaluation, and summary
	Dribbling Shooting Pivoting Passing Rules Strategy	Serving Bumping Setting Rotating Rules Strategy	Batting Pitching Throwing Fielding Catching Rules Strategy	Long jump High jump Dashes Distance run Hurdles Relays	Skill and fitness testing Review of skills taught during the year

FIGURE 9.2 *A sample yearly plan for a first grade and a fifth grade class based on developmental appropriateness.*

A well-planned lesson provides for:

- maximum participation in meaningful activities for all;

- opportunities for each class member to acquire new skills in accordance with the stated objectives;

- participation in, appreciation of, and enthusiasm for vigorous physical activity;

- a variety of carefully selected activities that have motor, cognitive, and affective value;

- opportunities to correlate and integrate physical education with other subject areas in the curriculum;

- opportunities for personal and social growth; and

- opportunity for self-evaluation of daily accomplishments.

FRONT

Lesson Objectives	Introduction	Review Activity	Lesson Focus		Summary/ Dismissal
			Skill Development	Skill Application	
Motor:					Review:
					Preview:
Cognitive:					Homework:
Affective:					Dismissal:

UNIT: _____ SKILL THEME: _____
GRADE: _____ CLASS: _____ DAY/WEEK/MONTH: _____

BACK

EQUIPMENT NEEDED:

RESOURCES:

Class Evaluation	Self-Evaluation

Safety Considerations:

FIGURE 9.3 *Sample format for a daily lesson plan on a 5″ × 8″ index card.*

can keep lesson plans in a file for easy reference for the following year when you may wish to use parts of the lesson again. You can make notations concerning the effectiveness of the lesson and suggestions for modifications. Figure 9.3 presents an outline for a sample daily lesson plan.

SEQUENCING THE DAILY LESSON

Once the objectives of the lesson have been determined, it will be necessary to focus on the actual content of the lesson. The lesson generally consists of four parts when there is ample time for all to be included: introduction, review, body, and lesson summary (see Figure 9.4).

Sometimes teachers are required to implement a lesson as short as fifteen to twenty minutes in length. If this is the case, meticulous planning is absolutely essential. You can not afford to waste even one minute. Furthermore, the review portion and skill development portion of the body of the lesson should remain intact, as much as possible. You may be able to incorporate the introductory portion of the lesson into the review, and you may need to sharply curtail or eliminate the skill application portion of the body of the lesson. With encouragement, children can apply the skill themselves during recess, at the noon hour, or after school. The lesson summary will have to be quite brief, perhaps occurring on the way back to the classroom.

CONCEPT 9.7
Effective lessons follow a logical, time-effective sequence.

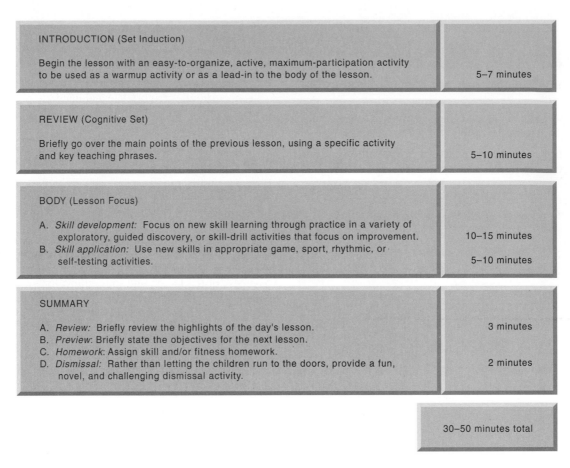

INTRODUCTION (Set Induction)

Begin the lesson with an easy-to-organize, active, maximum-participation activity to be used as a warmup activity or as a lead-in to the body of the lesson.

5–7 minutes

REVIEW (Cognitive Set)

Briefly go over the main points of the previous lesson, using a specific activity and key teaching phrases.

5–10 minutes

BODY (Lesson Focus)

A. *Skill development:* Focus on new skill learning through practice in a variety of exploratory, guided discovery, or skill-drill activities that focus on improvement.

10–15 minutes

B. *Skill application:* Use new skills in appropriate game, sport, rhythmic, or self-testing activities.

5–10 minutes

SUMMARY

A. *Review:* Briefly review the highlights of the day's lesson.
B. *Preview:* Briefly state the objectives for the next lesson.
C. *Homework:* Assign skill and/or fitness homework.

3 minutes

D. *Dismissal:* Rather than letting the children run to the doors, provide a fun, novel, and challenging dismissal activity.

2 minutes

30–50 minutes total

FIGURE 9.4 *Suggested format and time frame for implementing the lesson.*

You will frequently need to reduce your expectations of students and decrease the number of objectives for each lesson when class meets only once or twice a week for twenty to thirty minutes. Adoption of an attitude of doing fewer things, but doing them well, is advised. Avoid "throwing in the towel" and resorting to endless game playing with the excuse that "there just isn't enough time to teach." We must make maximum quality use of the time currently allotted us, while making a real effort to increase the frequency and number of minutes for each lesson. Our goal should be at least thirty minutes of daily instructional physical education for all. Remember, you are not alone in trying to achieve this goal. This is also the expressed goal of the U.S. Congress, the American Medical Association, the U.S. Department of Health and Human Services, the National Association for Sport and

Physical Education, and the President's Council on Physical Fitness and Sports (NASPE, 1994).

Introduction

The **lesson introduction** is sometimes referred to as **set induction, anticipatory set,** or **cognitive set** because it *sets* the tone for the lesson to come and provokes students' interest and enthusiasm. It is short, lasting only about five minutes, and establishes the tone for the activities to come. It is closely related to the focus of the day's lesson, designed to get the children organized and quickly involved and frequently has a vigorous fitness component. The introductory activity may serve as a warm-up or as a lead-in activity for the lesson to follow. Ideally, it will do both. The keys to successful introductory activities are total participation, vigorous activity, and ease of organization. The introductory activity is often an important way to prepare children to focus their attention on the lesson to come and to understand its purpose. Two examples of set induction follow:

- "When you're playing basketball with your friends, do you sometimes have trouble dribbling the ball up court without getting it stolen from an opposing player? Well, today we're going to learn two ways to prevent that from happening."

- "Have you ever tried putting three simple locomotor movements together: a hop, a step, and a jump? Today, we're going to begin doing just that by learning how to do what is called the triple jump." But first let's get with a partner and see how far we can do each one separately."

Review

The **lesson review** comes after the introduction. It generally lasts from five to ten minutes and provides a brief time to focus on the highlights of the previous lesson. Lengthy explanations and discussions of the previous lesson should be avoided. Rather, an appropriate activity, coupled with strategic teacher comments, should be the major aspect of this portion of the lesson. Remember, the reason for review is to help the child make the link between the material that was covered in the previous lesson and what will be presented as new material in the present lesson. Two examples of the review portion of the lesson follow:

- "Remember last lesson when several of us had trouble doing chin-ups and we discussed how our body weight played an important part? Why is it that some can do more chin-ups than others? What muscles do we use? What can we do to build strength in that area? Today our lesson will focus on several ways to build more strength in our arm and chest muscles."

- "Last lesson we worked on individual movement phrases on the mats that used rolls, turns, and springs. What were three important things that we learned about each? What kinds of rolls, turns, and springs did you use in your routine? Let's take a few minutes to try them again. Now, today, we are going to discover two new ways to travel down the mat using rolls, turns, and springs, and we're also going to add one more element to our personal movement phrases."

Body

The **body of the lesson** is the central focus of the daily lesson, and the greatest amount of time is devoted to it. The body of the lesson may range from fifteen to twenty-five minutes in length, depending on the total time allotted for class. It contains two sections: skill development and skill application. <u>**Skill development** is the single most important part of the entire lesson and may be divided into one or more teaching episodes.</u> A **teaching episode** is one that focuses on a particular aspect of skill development and incorporates use of a particular teaching style (see Chapter 14, "Teaching Styles" for a detailed discussion). In the skill development portion of the lesson there may be more than one teaching episode as skill upon skill is built and you move from one teaching style to another in your quest to maximize learning. It is here that the new material to be learned that day is taught. **Skill application** follows skill development and enables students to use newly learned skills in appropriate game, dance, or self-testing activities.

Care, however, should be taken to focus on the developmental aspect of the skill, with efforts concentrated on progressing to higher levels of ability rather than playing games for their own sake. Remember, only after the skill has been reasonably mastered should it be incorporated into gamelike activities.

The body of the lesson centers on skill development through practice, using a variety of teaching approaches that are selected depending on the developmental level of the class. Children at the fundamental movement skill phase benefit from a variety of exploratory, guided-discovery, and basic skill development activities. Boys and girls at the sport skill phase benefit more from activities that stress application of these skills, focusing on improved performance.

Lesson Summary

The **lesson summary,** which includes the lesson review and class dismissal, is the last portion of the lesson and is an important part of the lesson, even though it may last only two or three minutes. The summary provides the instructor with an opportunity to bring closure to the lesson by helping the children review what was stressed during the lesson and why they took part in certain activities. This also permits time to highlight what will be presented in the next lesson, assign fitness and skill practice "homework," and to arrange for orderly dismissal.

IMPLEMENTING THE DAILY LESSON

It is easy to read about a variety of teaching styles and to gain a textbook knowledge of how and when each method can be appropriately applied. Such textbook knowledge, however, is no substitute for actual experience. Therefore, it is the purpose of this section to offer practical suggestions for implementing the movement lesson. The reader is cautioned to recognize that textbook knowledge will not make you a good teacher. This knowledge must be coupled with frequent practice with children and critical self-analysis to have real and lasting benefit.

Putting It All Together

The primary objectives of the developmental physical education lesson are to help children acquire movement skills and enhance fitness. Additional objectives in a variety of cognitive and affective competencies are also an important part of the total curriculum. These objectives may be simply stated in terms of expected learner outcomes, but it is important that these outcomes be suitable for the child's developmental level. For example, the lesson objective may be "to improve jumping ability in the jump for distance" or "to be able to catch a small ball with greater efficiency."

Once the learning outcome has been established, the teacher proceeds to formulate the movement challenges to be presented in the lesson. Initially, the tasks may be open-ended and exploratory, followed by guided discovery and then progressive problem-solving. The progressive problem-solving or limitation portion of the lesson should lead to refinement of the desired skill by ensuring that each succeeding challenge or question given the learner is more narrowly defined. You should attempt to anticipate a broad range of possible responses before presenting the challenges in the lesson. It takes practice to structure meaningful movement challenges that lead to progressive skill refinement. Be prepared for solutions other than those you anticipate and recognize the necessity for restructuring problems that initially are not clearly understood.

You will need to consider whether, and at what point, to intervene with more direct styles of teaching. Following the movement challenge portion of the lesson, you may decide to use the task or command approaches.

The teacher must next determine which specific game, dance, or self-testing activities to use. These activities should use the movement skills that earlier were incorporated into the lesson. You may decide, for example, to have the children play a circle or tag game to reinforce the running skills worked on in the lesson; or you may select a rhythmical activity with a fast tempo to permit rhythmical running.

The last part of lesson planning concerns the summary and review. It is important for you to sit down for a few minutes with your students at the end of the lesson to review the movement skills that were stressed, thus reinforcing the lesson's concepts and crystallizing them in the children's thinking and action. The lesson summary is an excellent time to encourage students to do skill or fitness "homework" at home or with their friends.

Successful Lessons

To implement a successful movement lesson, the teacher needs to recognize several factors. First, the teacher must be certain that children are in fact making progress toward accomplishing the specifically stated objectives of the lesson. It is not enough that each child is active. Activities must be designed to achieve the lesson objectives, and objectives must be clearly stated in terms of their intended motor (movement skill acquisition and fitness enhancement), cognitive (perceptual-motor and concept learning), and affective (personal and social) outcomes. Remember, it is your responsibility to actively teach toward the stated objectives of your lesson. It is not enough to assume that learning occurs simply through participation in physical activities.

Second, it is important to understand the basic body mechanics of each skill. To foster efficient development of movement skills, you must understand the principles of movement involved and how to apply them.

A third requirement of a successful lesson is safety. The teacher must constantly anticipate potential dangers and ensure that proper safety precautions are being followed. For example, a return to more direct teaching approaches may be necessary during certain portions of the lesson to remedy an unsafe situation quickly and efficiently.

Fourth, the teacher should circulate throughout the class during the lesson and structure movement challenges in a variety of ways. Challenges may take the form of questions, problems, discussions, or verbal cues and should be varied so that none are used to the exclusion of the others. Phrases such as "Who can . . . ?" "How can you . . .?" "Let's try . . . ," "Find a way . . . ," "Let's see if . . . ," and "Is there another way to . . .?" are helpful. Care must be taken not to over-verbalize at the expense of active involvement on the part of the children.

TEACHING TIPS

Helpful hints for implementing a successful lesson include:

- Be thoroughly prepared; overplan.
- Maximize activity time and time-on-task for all.
- Insist on complete attention from the class at all times.
- Have all necessary equipment and supplies readily available prior to the lesson.
- Stand where everyone can see and hear you.
- Do not "talk down" to students, but use a vocabulary that is warm, friendly, and understandable to them.
- Begin class with a vigorous warm-up activity focusing on the fitness strand of the lesson.
- Teach by objectives; center your lesson on a specific movement skill theme geared to the developmental level of your students.
- Constantly observe and informally assess pupil progress; modify the lesson content accordingly.

- Be certain to incorporate the cognitive and affective strands into the lesson.
- Summarize, using key words or phrases.
- When asking for questions from the class, be specific.
- Emphasize body mechanics (process) prior to the results (product).
- Never let an activity drag. Change activities *before* children lose interest.
- Be observant of individual differences; structure the lesson so that all feel challenged and can find a measure of success.
- Use the final few minutes for reviewing the lesson, self-evaluation, and assigning "homework" in preparation for the next lesson.
- Incorporate dismissal techniques that are novel, fun, and orderly.
- Evaluate each lesson in terms of achievement of the objectives.

A fifth and final factor to consider in implementing a successful lesson is time-on-task and the amount of activity itself. Children have a great need to be active. Thus, the lesson should be one of active learning, not learning with little or no activity. Similarly, the amount of actual learning time spent on the objectives of the lesson is critical to the lesson's success. Time spent on class control problems, getting equipment, reorganizing groups, or taking attendance is time wasted because it detracts measurably from achieving the objectives of the lesson.

Successful lessons depend on careful adherence to the factors discussed previously. In addition, your genuine interest, enthusiasm, experience, ingenuity, and imaginative use of teaching approaches are also essential to the successful lesson.

Evaluating the Daily Lesson

Each step outlined in the preceding paragraphs is important to successful teaching of the physical education lesson. Carefully plan all aspects of the lesson to

maximize its impact. The effectiveness of your lessons should be evaluated periodically and adjustments made in the methods, techniques, and approaches used. Without periodic evaluation, it is impossible to know whether students have improved their abilities or how to plan effectively for subsequent lessons. Therefore, it is suggested that the teacher regularly assess pupil progress. At the preschool and elementary school levels, the key to successful evaluation is simplicity. As long as you are familiar with the developmental characteristics of both fundamental and specialized skills, simple observational assessment (process assessment) will generally suffice. Based on your informal evaluation of progress, you will need to modify your lessons. Constant monitoring of pupil progress provides the teacher with information necessary to plan effective, challenging, and developmentally appropriate lessons. Chapter 11, "Assessing Progress," deals with both process assessment and product assessment of movement skill learning.

TEACHING TIPS

It is time to move on to a new skill theme when:

- a high percentage of students have achieved the objectives of the skill theme,
- a high percentage of children have shown a reasonable degree of improvement beyond their entry level,
- active interest in the lesson has decreased, and
- the amount of time the children spend on task has decreased.

Effective teachers recognize the need for a scope and sequence chart that provides an age-appropriate blueprint for their program. As an effective teacher you must also recognize the vital need for developmental appropriateness achieved through observational assessment and detailed, but flexible, individual planning. A constant process of evaluating and reassessing pupil progress, interest, and needs will enable you to be flexible and able to refocus and revisit lessons to create the most effective learning environment.

Moving On

Probably the most crucial but least scientific aspect of the entire planning process is knowing when to move on to another skill theme. It is impossible to provide anything more than general guidelines on how much time should be spent on a particular skill theme. No two groups, classes, or individuals are exactly alike. Experienced teachers, however, sense when it is time to move on to another theme.

Ideally, every teacher wants all children to achieve a 100 percent success rate throughout the entire curriculum. This, of course, is not possible given the normal variation in natural abilities, learning styles, and other factors. Experienced teachers, however, continue to strive for 100 percent success, being fully aware that they will have to individualize their teaching to try to reach this elusive goal. Do not be discouraged with less than perfection. It is important to adopt an attitude that success is equal to improvement and that improvement is relative to the individual's entry level. For example, if you determine at the onset of the unit that children are at the initial stage in volleying and striking, and they have "only" achieved the elementary stage after several lessons, there has been improvement, even though the mature stage has not yet been reached. To maximize success, the movement challenges must be challenging but not overwhelming. Therefore, you need to carefully

and continually observe and refocus the lesson to achieve a balance between success, challenge, and failure.

Revisiting

Revisiting is based on developmental principles of physical and cognitive maturation and involves coming back to skill themes at different times throughout the school year. Subtle clues of frustration, boredom, inattention, and general off-task behavior are good indicators that it is time to refocus your lessons or move on to another skill theme. As a general rule of thumb, it is better to spend two or three lessons on a skill theme with preschool and primary-grade children and revisit it once or twice during the school year than it is to focus all your attention on it at one time. Children in the upper elementary grades tend to benefit from longer periods of time on a particular skill theme but also benefit from revisiting. It is suggested that you not spend more than a maximum of eight to ten lessons on any one unit of instruction at one time. Remember, however, to be flexible and responsive to the needs of your students and to revisit when appropriate. Figure 9.5 provides an overview of the cyclic nature of the steps in planning and implementing the lesson.

ORGANIZING FACILITIES

Particular attention needs to be given to the actual indoor and outdoor facilities that serve as teaching stations. Indoor facilities should be clean, free from safety hazards, and have proper flooring, lighting, and acoustics. Similarly, outdoor facilities need to be free from safety

CONCEPT 9.8
Knowing when to move on to another skill theme, and when to revisit a previous skill theme, is based on developmental considerations frequently masked in behavioral indicators.

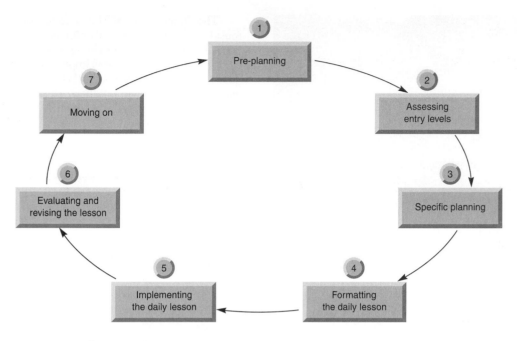

FIGURE 9.5 *Steps in planning and implementing the lesson.*

hazards, located away from occupied classrooms, and have clearly defined physical boundaries.

Indoor Facilities

The gymnasium is a classroom, a learning laboratory in which children use their entire bodies in the process of learning. Therefore, it is of utmost importance that the gymnasium be free from potential safety hazards. In many elementary schools the gymnasium also serves as the school cafeteria or as a multipurpose room. Frequently lunch tables are stored against walls or shoved into a corner. Special care should be taken to store tables and other equipment elsewhere. If this is not possible, it is important that they be secured and that the boundaries of the gymnasium are clearly redefined to exclude the area in which tables or other equipment are stored. The space that is used by your students must be free of obstacles if it is to be safe.

The flooring used for the indoor learning environment is also important. Tiled, wooden, or carpeted floors all have important implications for the type of activities that can be safely included in the lesson and the type of footwear children should wear. The manner in which the floor is marked should receive your careful attention. Pressure-sensitive tape can easily be applied for temporary markings. Be certain, though, that this tape is removed when you are finished. If permitted to remain on the floor for several months, it often becomes difficult to remove. In no case should masking tape be used for floor markings unless it is removed weekly. Masking tape dries out quickly and is extremely difficult to remove. A limited number of permanent markings is suggested for the gym floor in the preschool and elementary school. Too many lines tend to be confusing to children.

The acoustics of many gymnasiums may be difficult for some teachers to deal with. The large size of the gymnasium, the use of equipment, and a lack of sound-baffling devices such as carpeting or ceiling tile often result in poor acoustics. Be certain that you are familiar with the acoustics of your indoor teaching station. If the acoustics are bad, you will need to adjust your voice and use nonverbal cues accordingly. Failure to do so will result in considerable frustration and voice strain.

The gymnasium should be well lighted and free from shadows. All lights should be covered with protective grids to prevent breakage. The ceiling height and location of the lights will determine whether certain activities can

Facilities, equipment, and supplies must be organized for maximum meaningful participation.

be included or excluded. Volleyball, for example, should be prohibited if the lights are not covered or if the ceiling is too low to permit proper play.

Gymnasium floors should be cleaned at least twice each day. Remember, much of the children's time is spent on the floor; therefore, it needs to be free from dirt and debris. A large push broom or mop should be kept close by for frequent use. Gymnasium mats should be neatly stored and periodically cleaned with mild soap and water. Blindfolds, bandannas, and other cloth devices should be laundered frequently and stored properly.

Outdoor Facilities

You should inspect the outdoor physical education facility daily for potential safety hazards. Be certain that the area is free from obstacles, broken glass, and holes. Frequently, the outdoor facility is used after school hours by nonschool groups, so it is important that the daily inspection of the outdoor facility be made immediately prior to conducting classes. This takes only a few minutes and helps reduce potential hazards.

The surface area on which outdoor physical education classes are conducted should be level, dry, and free from stones and other debris. It should be far enough away from classrooms that it does not interfere with other classes. The outdoor facility should be located on school property as far from parking lots and city streets as possible. It should, however, be close enough to the school to permit easy access to equipment and shelter in case of a sudden change in the weather.

The boundaries of the outdoor instructional area must be clearly defined and enforced. The feeling of freedom that often comes with being outdoors must not hamper conduct of the class. It is important to be able to maintain visual and verbal contact with each member of the class at all times when outdoors. Defining, clearly marking, and enforcing boundaries will make your outdoor teaching job much easier.

CONCEPT 9.9
Effective lessons make maximum use of the time available through careful organization of facilities, equipment, instructional aids, and student helpers.

ORGANIZING EQUIPMENT

The selection, placement, and use of equipment are important aspects of effective organization of the lesson. To encourage maximum class participation and to minimize disruptive behavior, all members of the class should be actively involved throughout the lesson. Waiting in long lines or sharing equipment among several children can invite restlessness, boredom, and behavioral problems. On the other hand, if gymnasium equipment is properly selected, placed, and used, the learning objectives of the lesson can be maximized.

Equipment Selection

When purchasing equipment, it is wise to buy quality goods. Although quality equipment often costs more in the short run, it is generally less expensive to maintain in the long run. Purchasing quality equipment through reputable companies often affords longer, more effective use of the equipment and an opportunity for returns or exchanges when necessary.

It is helpful to keep a complete inventory of all gymnasium equipment. A listing of all bats, balls, beanbags, hoops, mats, and gymnastic apparatus is a must. The condition of the equipment should be noted on the inventory checklist, and faulty or broken equipment should be immediately repaired or replaced. An equipment inventory should be conducted at least twice a year—once at the beginning of the school year and again at the end. This will provide a complete accounting of the equipment available for use and an indication of what is needed. A copy of the inventory and list of defective or missing equipment should be given to the building principal or other appropriate school officials.

Equipment Placement and Use

The actual placement and use of equipment has a dramatic effect on the lesson. Whenever possible, provide for maximum participation by all members of the class. When using small apparatus such as balls, hoops, beanbags, and wands, it will be helpful to have an implement for each child. The manner in which this equipment is distributed to the class and returned to its proper place is worthy of attention. Simply giving the command "get a ball" will not do. A predetermined system must be devised to minimize confusion, pushing, and other disruptive behavior. Equipment may be passed out to students by the teacher, squad leaders may hand out equipment, or it may be obtained in small groups. Whatever methods you choose, be sure that they are quick and efficient and that they cause a minimum of disruption.

When large apparatus is being used, the physical layout should be such that each piece of equipment is free from obstacles and can be easily viewed by the teacher from any part of the room. Mats should be placed under each piece of apparatus, and the equipment itself should be safe for use. The equipment should be visually inspected and tested before its use. Safety hazards should be immediately corrected or repaired. In no case should you continue to use a piece of equipment that you know to be defective.

The use of large apparatus sometimes poses another problem. Setting up climbers, mats, balance beams, and the like is time-consuming. Therefore, it is generally advisable to have as few large equipment changes as possible from class to class. Be certain, however, to have all of the equipment out in its proper place, inspected, and ready for use before the class enters the gymnasium. Failure to do so only wastes time and creates unnecessary confusion. If equipment changes are necessary, students can be taught how to move certain pieces of apparatus under direct supervision.

Remember, the balls, bats, hoops, mats, and other equipment available to you represent the "tools" of your profession. Considerable care should be taken to ensure that it is in ample supply and good condition. There is little excuse for a physical education program with little or no equipment. Just as children cannot be expected to learn to read without books, they cannot be expected to develop their movement abilities without the proper equipment. The physical education program must have an annual budget that provides for equipment purchase,

To make maximum effective use of the allotted time, inspect all equipment and have it ready for distribution prior to class. Small equipment that is neatly stored on racks, in utility bags, or in containers can be quickly and easily put to use. Be certain, however, that after the equipment has been used, it is returned immediately to its proper location. This will ensure easy access for the next class.

replacement, and repair. Insufficient funds can be supplemented, to a degree, through the use of homemade equipment. However, teachers cannot be expected to develop and implement first-rate programs using only homemade equipment. Money-raising projects sponsored by the PTA or other interested groups can supplement the equipment budget. Much of the gymnasium and playground equipment found in elementary schools is obtained through fund-raising projects and donations by parent and teacher organizations.

PREPARING INSTRUCTIONAL AIDS

Another aspect of organizing the learning environment is the preparation and use of instructional aids. Successful teachers use various devices to enhance understanding and appreciation of the subject and to clarify instructions. The use of task cards, bulletin boards, and other visual aids can be an important aspect of the lesson.

Task Cards

A **task card** is a written description of what skill or movement activity should be performed. It clearly indicates acceptable individual levels of achievement and may provide the child with a verbal and or visual description of the task. Task cards are an effective visual technique to use with station teaching, individual pacing, and during open gym time. They provide students with information about what is to be done, how it is to be done, and what the standards of acceptable performance are. Using task cards enables members of the class to work on one or more activities at the same time. They provide maximum participation and promote individual standards of achievement.

Bulletin boards can be informational and educational.

Bulletin Boards

The use of bulletin boards in the elementary school physical education program should not be overlooked. **Bulletin boards** can be used to create interest, impart knowledge, and record information. Whether they are located in the gymnasium or in the hallway, they should be neat and attractive and should reflect your creative talents. To be most effective, they should be changed frequently during the school year.

Bulletin boards featuring upcoming units of work can heighten interest. Using magazine photos and drawings that show outstanding performers executing the same skills that you will be focusing on tends to create an atmosphere of anticipation for the lessons to come.

Bulletin boards can also be used effectively to impart knowledge. For example, the major muscle groups of the body may be illustrated on a bulletin board throughout the school year. Their location and appropriate activities for strengthening them may be highlighted. A nutrition bulletin board depicting the nutrition pyramid might also be displayed. You might post a list of all students who have achieved a certain standard on a skills test. The various components and standards of The President's Challenge, the AAU Physical Fitness Test, or Fitnessgram might also be the theme of an effective bulletin board.

Visual Aids

Videotaped performances can be effectively used in the physical education program to show children a visual model of the skills or sports to be learned. A videotape of outstanding performers in gymnastics or soccer, for example, helps to create a mental image of the level of skill that is possible. Care, however, must be taken when using this technique to be certain that the children are reminded that attaining such high levels of skill takes considerable time, effort, and practice. The approach should be, "You may not be able to do this now, but if you work hard you will be able to do many of these skills later." Using videotapes of skilled athletes helps motivate students to learn, to do their best, and to provide a purpose for skill learning and practice. Don't overlook the opportunity to videotape your own students. It will provide you and them with a useful learning tool as well as being fun and highly motivational.

Skill charts, another effective visual aid used by many teachers, may be purchased commercially or they may be homemade. The major advantage of a skill chart is that it provides students with a visual representation of the various elements of a particular skill. For example, the key elements in a soccer kick, an overhand throw, or a forward roll may be illustrated in photos, line drawings, or even stick figures. This is particularly important during the early stages of skill learning when the learner is attempting to form a conscious mental image of the task.

ORGANIZING STUDENT HELPERS

The very nature of the physical education program lends itself to the use of helpers. Large classes, varying facilities, and the use of many different types and amounts of equipment all highlight the importance of helpers in the physical education program. Also, the teacher is sometimes unable to demonstrate certain tasks or needs several extra hands to assist with spotting. Squad leaders and gym helpers can be of valuable assistance.

Squads and Squad Leaders

Squads are a useful technique for organizing groups of children. It is generally advisable to have an even number of squads so that they may be easily combined for various activities. The number of students per squad should be an even number and as small as possible to ensure maximum participation. Small squad sizes of six or eight students

TEACHING TIPS

Organizing Groups of Children

Each formation used in the gymnasium and on the playground is used for specific purposes. Avoid selecting activities that require frequent formation changes.

Single Circle Formation

- Frequently used for circle games and dances.
- Used for parachute activities.
- Good formation for discussions.
- Keep groups small for maximum participation (six to eight maximum).
- Stand at the edge of the circle when talking, never in the center.

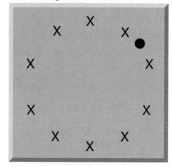

Single circle formation

Double Circle Formation

- Often used for circle partner activities.
- Used for numerous circle dances and mixers.
- Used for some circle games.
- Use floor markings to designate places.
- Change partners often.

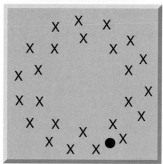

Double circle formation

File Formation

- Frequently used for locomotor and ball-dribbling activities.
- Used for numerous skill drills.
- Keep groups small (no more than eight to a group).
- Be sure the number of students in a group is an even number.
- Clearly explain and enforce rules.

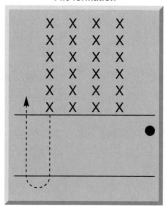

File formation

(continued)

TEACHING TIPS

(continued)

Shuttle Formation

- Used for numerous locomotor, throwing, and catching activities.
- Used for some skill drills.
- Explain and enforce a definite travel procedure.
- Stand where all can see you.
- Be sure students wait behind the restraining line until their turn.

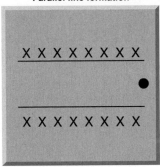

Parallel line formation

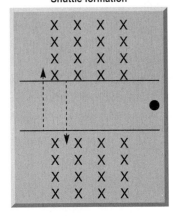

Shuttle formation

Parallel Line Formation

- Used for throwing, catching, and kicking skills.
- Used for basketball skill relays.
- Provide a restraining line to keep lines straight.
- Keep groups small with a maximum of six to eight per line.
- Be sure that lines are sufficiently apart to promote proper execution of the skill.

Scatter Formation

- Used for movement exploration and problem-solving activities.
- Great for creative expression activities.
- Be sure to set geographical boundaries before scattering.
- Be sure that each child has ample personal space for moving.
- Do not stand in one place. Move throughout the class.

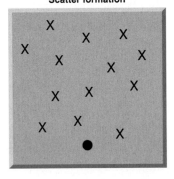

Scatter formation

(continued)

TEACHING TIPS

(continued)

Half-Circle Formation

- Frequently used for leader demonstrations.
- Use existing circle markings whenever possible.
- Avoid joining hands for extended periods when forming a half circle.
- The leader stands slightly outside the half circle so that all can see.

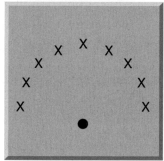

Half-circle formation

Checkerboard Formation

- Excellent formation for structured activities and with large groups.
- Provides maximum use of space.
- Avoid standing at one end of the formation for long periods. Move around its perimeter.

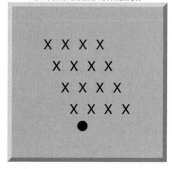

Checkerboard formation

Station Formation

- Excellent formation for promoting maximum participation and lesson variety.
- Permits teacher to be at the point of greatest need.
- Each station is frequently accompanied by a task card detailing the activity to be practiced.
- Various attainment levels (Level I, Level II, Level III) can be posted at each station to promote time on task and personalized mastery attempts.

---

are preferable to larger groups of ten or more. The placement of students in squads should be teacher-directed to ensure balance in ability levels. Squads should never be chosen in a manner that is embarrassing or humiliating to children.

Once the class has been divided into squads, have them select an appropriate squad name. Naming, numbering, or color-coding squads makes it easier for organization and regrouping throughout the lesson. It also helps to create group identity and to promote group pride. A des-ignated location for each squad to go upon entering the gymnasium is a helpful organizational technique.

Squad leaders should be selected for each group. The honor and responsibility of being a squad leader should be given to each child sometime during the course of the school year. Squad leaders should be changed frequently, generally at the beginning of a new unit of work. The composition of the squads themselves should be changed at least three or four times during the school year.

Squad leaders can perform many valuable functions such as taking roll, obtaining equipment, keeping records, moving their group, or leading exercises. Squad leaders should be praised for a job well done. Be sure to encourage them to have pride in the responsibilities of being a leader.

Gym Helpers

Physical education teachers are often permitted to incorporate gym helpers into their program. **Gym helpers** may be older students interested in working with youngsters. They may be high school students interested in a career in physical education. Some school systems provide funds for hiring adult paraprofessionals to serve as gym helpers. In any case, their presence in the program can be invaluable. Gym helpers can be assigned many of the routine chores of the physical education program such as organizing equipment, assisting with record keeping, officiating, leading activities, and helping with assessment. Remember, the use of gymnasium helpers is intended to provide you more time for personalized instruction; be sure to make maximum effective use of your time. Gym helpers should never be left in charge of the entire class. They should always be used in a professional manner to assist in providing the best program possible.

SUMMARY

At the very core of the teacher's responsibilities are planning, organizing, and implementing the lesson. Preplanning and entry level assessment set the stage for the progressively more specific steps in the planning process, namely developing yearly plans, unit plans, and daily lesson plans.

The sequence of presentation of the daily lesson is important if maximum effective use of the time available is to be achieved. A brief introductory activity followed by a review of the previous lesson begins the lesson. After that, the bulk of the lesson is spent on the body of the lesson and skill development, followed by skill application. The lesson concludes with a brief summary of the lesson and a novel dismissal activity.

A number of useful hints for implementing successful lessons were discussed, ranging from practical pointers on pulling the lesson together to evaluating the effectiveness of the lesson and knowing when to move on to a new skill theme. Efficient and effective techniques for organizing equipment, facilities, helpers, and groups of children were discussed in terms of their importance to implementing the lesson.

COMPLEMENTARY READINGS

Aicinena, A. (1991). Formal class closure—an effective instructional tool. *JOPERD* 62:72–73.

Arbogast, G. W., D. L. Kizer, and M. J. Mackey. (1995). Post-it: Use physical eduction bulletin boards. *Strategies* 8:9–11.

Arbogast, G., and J. Misner. 1990. Homework "how-to's." *Strategies* 4:12–15.

Docheff, D. (1990). Homework—In physical education? *Strategies* 4:10–11.

Kelly, L. E. (1989). Instructional time: The overlooked factor in P.E. curriculum development. *JOPERD* 60:29–32.

Metzler, M. W. (1990). *Instructional Supervision for Physical Education.* Champaign, IL: Human Kinetics.

National Association for Sport and Physical Education. (1994). *Sport and Physical Education Advocacy Kit.* Reston, VA: NASPE.

SUPPLEMENTARY READINGS

Graham, G., S. Holt-Hale, and M. Parker. (1993). *Children Moving.* Mountain View, CA: Mayfield.

Kirchner, G. (1995). *Physical Education for Elementary School Children.* Dubuque, IA: Wm. C. Brown.

Wall, J., and N. Murray. (1990). *Children and Movement.* Dubuque, IA: Wm. C. Brown.

VIDEOS

AMPT Pedagogy Course Self–Study Video. American Master Teacher Program. (1993). Champaign, IL: Human Kinetics. (60 min.).

CHAPTER 10

The Content Areas

—

Key Concept

Games, Dance, and Self-Testing Experiences Represent the Primary Content Areas of Physical Education and Are a Means for Achieving Increased Competency in the Motor, Cognitive, and Affective Domains of Human Behavior

—

Chapter Objectives

The purpose of this chapter is to provide you with the tools to:
• Discuss the role of game, dance, and self-testing (educational gymnastics) activities in the process of becoming a physically educated individual.
• List and give examples of each of the content areas and their subdivisions.
• Demonstrate how the content areas of physical education can and should be related to the specific objectives of the developmental curriculum.
• Provide guidelines for selecting appropriate activities for students.

—

Terms to Remember

Low-Level Games
Familiarization Games
Discovery Games
Cooperative Games
Group Initiatives
Group Problem-Solving
Trust Activities
Lead-Up Games
Skill Challenge Games
Formal Games
Official Sport Games
Rhythm
Rhythmic Fundamentals

Elements of Rhythm
Underlying Beat
Tempo
Accent
Intensity
Rhythmical Pattern
Singing Rhythms
Creative Dance
Folk Dance
Country/Western Dance
Social Dance
Aerobic Dance
Low Impact Aerobics

Skill Element
Social Element
Self-Testing
Educational
   Gymnastics
Fundamental
   Movement
Sport Skill
Movement Challenges
Perceptual-Motor
   Activities
Large Apparatus
Small Apparatus

ames, dances, and self-testing activities (frequently referred to as educational gymnastics activities) are part of the cultural heritage of all children. Although environmental conditions and standards of living change, the urge to play games, dance dances, and test one's skills remains a constant characteristic of every culture. Geographic location does not alter the age-old urges to run, jump, hop, chase and flee, hide and seek, hunt, guess, and dodge. One may find hundreds of variations on these themes, with as many different names, but the original theme remains the same.

This chapter focuses on game, dance, and self-testing activities as the three primary content areas of the physical education curriculum. We will look at the subdivisions of each content area and suggest ways to include effective activities in the physical education program.

Games are an important part of the educational process.

CONCEPT 10.1
Game, dance, and self-testing activities may serve many purposes, but all go beyond the basic objective of fun and extend to defensible educational objectives.

GAMES

When used properly, games are an important educational tool of the physical education program. Games may be static, dynamic, predesigned, teacher-designed, or student-designed. The predesigned games found in the

following chapters are merely sample activities to help get you started. These activities can easily be modified to suit your needs. Designing your own games is also a worthwhile task. After all, who knows your students' needs and interests better than you do? Furthermore, games designed by the students themselves can be of significant value, although this generally takes additional time and a gymnasium atmosphere conducive to creative problem-solving. The activities you select and the methods you use to teach games will depend on several factors: the objectives of the lesson, the ability of your students, the size of the class, and availability of time, equipment, and facilities.

CONCEPT 10.2
Games, in the developmental approach to teaching physical education, are viewed as a means of reinforcing and applying the results of movement skill learning.

Game, dance, and self-testing activities can be of value in preschool and elementary school physical education if they are used properly and for the right reasons. However, some physical education programs have become little more than play periods in which activities are engaged in simply for fun. Although fun is a worthy by-product of any good educational program, it should not be the primary purpose of the physical education program. Game, dance, and self-testing activities are a means to an end, rather than an end in themselves.

Types of Games

Games may be classified in a variety of ways, depending on their purpose and nature. The developmental approach to teaching children's physical education views games primarily as a tool for applying, reinforcing, and implementing a variety of fundamental movement and sport skills. Games are *not* viewed as a primary means of learning

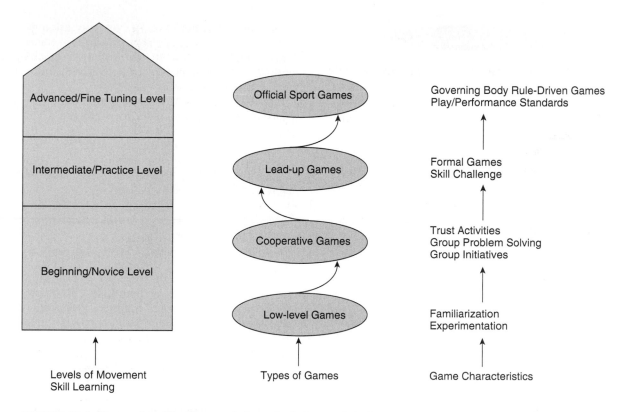

FIGURE 10.1 *Game classifications and characteristics,* **and** *their relationship to the levels of movement skill learning.*

new movement skills. Although movement skill acquisition is a primary objective of the movement lesson, games serve primarily as a means for applying and utilizing present skill levels. Other important objectives can, however, still be achieved through proper game selection and good teaching. Games are frequently classified as low-level type games, cooperative games, lead-up games, and official sports (see Figure 10.1).

Low-Level Games.   The term **low-level games** describes activities that are easy to play, have few and simple rules, require little or no equipment, and may be varied in many ways. Low-level games may be viewed as **familiarization games,** that is, ones that help the learner become acquainted with the basic skills involved in an activity. They may also be viewed as **discovery games** because the learner is establishing an awareness of the spatial requirements of the game while at the same time experimenting with how the game is played. Both familiarization

or discovery games are particularly appropriate for learners who are at the beginning/novice level of learning the skills being used in the game.

Low-level game activities, whether they are familiarization or discovery game activities, may be easily modified to suit the objectives of the lesson, the size of the room, and the number of participants. Because they are easy to learn and can be enjoyed by both children and adults, they are often used as an educational tool primarily during the preschool and primary grades. When viewed from a skill reinforcement and application perspective, low-level games are classifed as fundamental stability, fundamental locomotor, or fundamental manipulative games. That is, low-level games are classified according to the primary category of movement skill that they promote. Additionally, games are sometimes classified according to their (1) theme (tag, holiday, and seasonal games), (2) formation (mass, circle, and line games), (3) special space requirements (limited-space

When selecting and presenting a game for the first time:

- Choose games that are appropriate to the time, space, class size, available equipment, and specific objectives of the lesson.

- Plan in advance. Think through the games and have lines drawn, equipment ready, and other preplanning procedures completed.

- Make explanations clear, brief, and simple.

- When possible, demonstrate the activity or combine demonstrations with explanation.

- Place groups in the game formation when explaining how it is played.

- Correct outstanding faults, but avoid fine details in the beginning in order to get the game going.

- Avoid stopping the game too frequently to make corrections.

- Make suggestions in a positive way.

- Demonstrate interest by occasionally taking part.

- Do not overplay the game. Stop at the height of interest to maintain enthusiasm for the activity at a later date.

---

and classroom games), and (4) activity level (active and passive games).

Cooperative Games.   **Cooperative games** have become popular in recent years because they emphasize group interaction and positive socialization in a cooperative setting that de-emphasizes competition. Cooperative game activities are frequently classified as group initiatives, group problem-solving activities, and trust activities.

Group initiatives center on working cooperatively to accomplish a given task. For example, the lap sit is a popular group initiative with children and adults alike. Participants line up close behind one another and, on a signal, sit down on the lap of the person directly behind them.

Group problem-solving activities are similar to group initiatives except that they involve an element of creative problem-solving on the part of the participants, with possible alternative solutions to the problem posed by the instructor. For example, you may ask a group of four or five to get from point A to point B in contact with one another, but without their feet ever touching the ground. The several possible solutions to the problem all require the group to work cooperatively.

Trust activities are activities that require the participants to work cooperatively to overcome a challenge involving an element of danger. Trust falls, body passing, and pyramids are typical trust activities. Trust activities, do however, involve an element of risk. They must always be carefully spotted and used only with the approval of your immediate supervisor.

Lead-Up Games.   **Lead-up games** are active games that involve the use of two or more of the sport skills, rules, or procedures used in playing the official sport. Lead-up games may be relatively simple or quite complex. In their simplest form they take the form of skill challenge games in which one has an opportunity to test his or her developing skills. Formal games represent the more complex aspects of lead-up games. **Skill challenge games** are those in which the rules are few and simple, and the focus is on "how far?" "how fast?" or "how many?" Playing the game of Horse is a basketball shooting skill challenge game. Circle soccer is a soccer kicking and trapping skill challenge game.

Formal games comprise the more complex aspects of lead-up games. In these activities the rules and strategies of the game have more significance, as well as meaningful use of the skills required. Half-court basketball, or six-a-side soccer are formal lead-up games with a generally accepted set of rules and strategies.

Lead-up games may be viewed as a means to an end or as an end in themselves. As a means to an end, they are preparatory to playing the official sport and are used as a way of further developing one's ability to master the skills, rules, and strategies of the official sport. As an end in themselves, they represent a less complex version of the official sport, which is more suited to one's skill level (intermediate/practice level) and to the available facilities and equipment.

Lead-up games play an important role among upper elementary and junior high school students, and they are frequently more fun to play than the official sport itself. These games allow students to practice and perfect sport skills in a modified environment. Most youngsters are not thrilled with the repetitive practice of skill drills. They are, however, interested when these same skills are used in gamelike situations. Therefore, it is recommended that, after the skill has been reasonably mastered, skill drills be modified to take on game form: give it a name and make it a game. As students gain proficiency, you can make the lead-up games more complex by incorporating a greater number of skill elements and more involved strategies and by requiring a closer approximation of the regulations of the official sport.

Official Sport Games. Official sport games are many and varied. They are most frequently classified as team sports, dual sports, and individual sports. Sometimes, however, they are classified according to the (1) facilities used (court sports, aquatic sports), (2) type of team interaction (contact sports, noncontact sports, combative sports), and (3) equipment used (racket sports, ball sports). An **official sport game** is one governed by a set of rules and regulations that are recognized and interpreted by an official governing body as the standard for performance and play.

Official sports have *no* place in the instructional elementary school physical education program. Official sport games are particularly appropriate for individuals at the advanced/fine tuning level of movement skill learning. Few elementary school students are at this level and need considerable instruction and practice in movement skill learning. They may, however, be engaged in during the intramural program, the interscholastic sports program, or the agency-sponsored youth sport program. The physical education period is a learning laboratory for learning, practicing, and putting new skills to use in a variety of movement situations.

Selecting Appropriate Game Activities

The inclusion of games in the physical education lesson generally begins during the preschool and primary grade years. Games are used by the astute teacher as an educational tool. Every game that is played should be chosen for specific reasons that depend on the nature of the lesson; these may range from practicing specific movement skills and enhancing various components of physical fitness to promoting social learning and academic concept development. If the teacher has clearly defined objectives for the use of a particular game or games in a lesson, then we may be sure that games will serve an educational purpose. If, however, our objective is primarily fun with only remote consideration given to skill, fitness, social, or academic objectives, then we have "missed the boat" entirely and are making little or no contribution to the physical education of children.

When choosing a game for inclusion in the lesson, do not limit selection to the "appropriate" grade level placement so often seen in books and card files of games.

TEACHING TIPS

The following process is recommended for *selecting appropriate game activities* for inclusion in the lesson:

- Determine the specific objectives of your lesson and select games that will help reinforce these objectives.
- Determine the ability level of your students in terms of skill, comprehension, and interest.
- Modify games to fit the specific objectives of the lesson, the ability of the class, and the movement skills used.

Knowing your students' abilities is the easiest way to determine which games should be changed. Rules are not chiseled in granite. It is important that games be modified to suit the ability of your students and not the mythical students addressed in this or any other text.

Children with a sound movement background can easily play and master games graded one or two levels above the one generally expected of their age. The list of active games is almost endless. Books are filled with thousands of different activities. It is not, however, necessary to be familiar with all or even most of these games if the principles of game selection and modification just listed are adhered to. Remember, a game is only a vehicle used to achieve an end. It is not, and should not be, an end in itself in the developmentally based physical education program.

Determining Ability Levels. Once you have clearly determined the objectives of your lesson, you must assess the general ability level of the class. You will also need to know your students' ability to understand and comply with the rules of the game. Finally, you will need a feel for the potential level and duration of students' interest in the activity.

If the skill requirements of the game are beyond the children, they will soon lose interest and quit. If the game is so complex that only a few are able to comply with the

Enabling Ideas for Modifying Ball Type Games

- **Modify Equipment**
  —suitably sized and weighted balls for each child
  —soft and/or textured balls which can be gripped
  —balls with lower bounce speed
  —reachable goals or targets

- **Modify the Rules**
  —time ball may be held before passing
  —opponent may or may not challenge ball holder
  —ball can/cannot be taken from opponent's hands
  —players may run holding the ball or may dribble the ball
     or may not travel with the ball

—players play in zones or may travel anywhere
—only certain people may shoot, or anyone may shoot
—vary type of goals/targets

- **Modify the Number and Grouping of Participants**
  —keep team sizes small but workable
  —sometimes form mixed ability teams
  —sometimes form teams with players of similar ability
  —try to match teams of equal potential

- **Teacher Joins in to Help**
  —work alongside pupils
  —distribute the ball to engage neglected players
  —the teacher does *not* compete

TEACHING TIPS

Games may be *modified* in a variety of ways:

- Change or add to the movement skills used to play the game.
- Alter the rules to more closely suit the objectives of the lesson.
- Modify the equipment used.
- Change the duration of the game.
- Alter the number playing in a group.
- Change the formations or boundaries used.
- Intensify the game by stepping up the pace of the activity.
- Alter the game to encourage problem solving.
- Modify the game to stimulate creativity in making up new games.
- Redesign the game to promote maximum active participation of all students.
- Redistribute teams during the game.
- Modify the game to represent a special holiday or event.

rules, there will be mass confusion and little benefit derived from the activity. If the game involves long waiting for a turn, is an elimination type, or provides little chance for meaningful participation by all, then all but the most highly skilled students will soon lose interest.

Modifying Games.   The game activities that you select for your lesson may be modified to better suit the objectives of the lesson, the ability of your students, and the specific movement skills involved. This may be done simply by carefully reading the description of the game and then modifying it as needed.

Once you know how to modify games, it is possible—even if you have only a limited number of resources—to devise an endless variety of meaningful and educationally sound games. A solid grasp of the lesson objectives, a good imagination, and willingness to experiment will aid greatly in successfully incorporating games into the lesson.

DANCE

Responding to rhythm is one of the strongest and most basic urges of childhood. It is basic to the life process itself, as evidenced by the rhythmical functions of the body, as in breathing, the heartbeat, and the performance

Rhythm is a critical aspect of all coordinated movement.

of any movement in a coordinated manner. **Rhythm,** therefore, is the measured release of energy made up of repeated units of time.

Dance is an extension of rhythmical movement into creative, expressive, interpretative, and joyful activity. It is important that children be exposed to a wide variety of rhythmical experiences. The rhythm and dance offering in the school must be presented in a meaningful and purposeful manner to meet developmental needs of all children.

CONCEPT 10.3
Dance is an important element of the physical education program and should be incorporated throughout the curriculum.

Children begin developing their rhythmical abilities during infancy, as seen in the infant's cooing response to the soft, rhythmical sounds of a lullaby, and by the

infant's repeated attempts to make pleasurable rhythmical sights, sounds, and sensations last. As children develop, they continue to explore their environment. An internalized time structure is established and refined. This ability to respond rhythmically is developed through practice and experience. As a result, rhythmical activities play an important role in the lives of children.

Movement is one important avenue by which rhythmical abilities may be developed and refined. Since rhythm is a basic component of all coordinated movement, the two may be effectively combined to enhance both of these interdependent areas.

Rhythm and Types of Dance

Rhythm is a distinctive and essential quality inherent in all coordinated movement and dance. For motion, sound, or design to be rhythmical, a formed pattern must be present. Rhythm, music, and dance must possess three qualities to be rhythmical. First, there must be a regulated flow of energy that is organized in both duration and intensity. Second, the time succession of events must result in balance and harmony. Third, there must be sufficient repetition of regular groupings.

As children listen to music, they respond to its rhythm in a variety of ways. They kick and laugh, jump and clap. They wiggle and giggle, twirl and skip. Sometimes they listen and relax or simply burst into song and dance. They begin, in their own crude way, to make their own music. They hum, sing, and play a variety of improvised instruments. The formation of a rhythm band using a variety of homemade pieces of rhythmical equipment is an important first opportunity for children to organize their efforts into an expressive whole. All children have music as a part of their being, and it is the teacher's job to help them bring out their interests and explore their potential. Rhythmical music and movement should be a

A close parallel of rhythmics exists between music and movement. Rhythmical structure in music is allied with rhythmical structure in movement and, with rare exceptions, children love both. They enjoy the melodic, rhythmical succession of beats characteristic of music and the opportunity to express this through movement.

vital part of the school program. You may not feel particularly adept at singing or playing a piano, but you can play chords on a guitar or use (1) a tape recorder, (2) records, (3) a small xylophone, (4) a set of simple bells, or (5) a drum.

All coordinated movement involves an element of rhythm. Rhythmical activities may be classified into six general and sometimes overlapping areas: fundamental rhythms, singing rhythms, creative dance, folk dance, social dance, and aerobic dance.

Fundamental Rhythms.

Rhythmic fundamentals are the first and most basic form of understanding and interpreting rhythmical movement. **Rhythmic fundamentals** involve developing an awareness of the various elements of rhythm and being able to express these elements through movement. The following **elements of rhythm** are of concern to the teacher trying to develop fundamental rhythmic abilities.

1. **Underlying beat.** The steady, continuous sound of any rhythmical sequence.
2. **Tempo.** The speed of the movement, music, or accompaniment.
3. **Accent.** The emphasis given to any one beat (usually the first beat of every measure).
4. **Intensity.** The loudness or softness of the movement or music.
5. **Rhythmical pattern.** A group of beats related to the underlying beat.

Each of the elements of rhythm may be expressed through movement that varies in effort, space, and relationships. Hence, an endless variety of movement activities may be devised to develop an increased awareness of both the elements of rhythm and the qualities of movement. A thorough knowledge of the fundamentals of rhythm is prerequisite to adequate performance in any form of rhythmical endeavor such as dance, instrumental music, or vocal music. The child should be able to "feel" the elements of rhythm and be able to express them through coordinated (rhythmical) movement. Remember, participation in stability, locomotor, and manipulative activities that stress the elements of rhythm also helps to improve students' performance in a variety of fundamental movement skills while learning about the elements of rhythm. For example, practice with running, jumping, and skipping to different tempos, intensities, and accents can enhance knowledge of the fundamental elements of rhythm as well as promote increased skill development in the movements themselves.

Singing Rhythms.

Singing rhythms are another form of rhythmical expression that provides children with an opportunity to develop a better understanding of phrasing. Performing the movements required of a particular activity plus singing the words to the rhythm help children to develop a keener sense of rhythmical movement in a variety of gross motor and fine motor activities. **Singing rhythms** include rhymes and poems, finger plays, and singing dances. Each may progress from the very simple to the complex. The activities selected will depend on the ability level, maturity, and interests of your students. Singing rhythms are appealing to children because they (1) tell a story, (2) develop an idea, (3) have a pleasing rhythmical pattern, (4) stimulate use of one's imagination, or (5) have dramatic possibilities.

Singing plays an important role in the life of young children. They love repetition and will sing the songs they know over and over again. Children like to respond to songs through movement. When responding to active songs, they will usually join in the singing. This singing is important because it helps to internalize the rhythm of the song itself. When simple songs are used, children are given a variety of opportunities for repetition of movement and a chance to be creative and express themselves dramatically.

Creative Dance.

Creative dance, a third form of expressing rhythm through movement, is generally considered to be an extension of rhythmic fundamentals and should be included in the elementary school curriculum *after* the children have a basic grasp of the fundamentals of rhythm. Creativity is a major objective of modern education; therefore, creative dance can and should be included in the physical education curriculum. Creative rhythmical movement allows children to express ideas, emotions, feelings, and interpretations and may be expressed in a variety of forms, including exploration, improvisation, rhythmical problem-solving, and simple compositions. We only need to look at the inhibited, stereotypical movements to music of the average fourth or fifth grader to realize that we have not adequately fostered creative expression in many children.

Folk Dance.

Folk dances are a fourth form of expressing rhythm through movement. **Folk dances** are structured dances characteristically performed in many countries throughout the world. In fact, one purpose for including folk dance in the elementary school curriculum is to enhance children's appreciation for other cultures. Furthermore, folk dances encourage social interaction

TEACHING TIPS

Practical suggestions for *teaching creative dance:*

- Begin early. Waiting too long when children are more inhibited will only result in frustration on the part of the teacher.

- Keep activities relatively simple during the early years.

- Stress rhythmical fundamentals first.

- Focus on imitative rhythms at the primary level.

- Emphasize creative rhythmics during the middle grades.

- For older children, use plenty of vigorous activities and work in small groups.

- Be positive and accepting.

- Dance with the children. This will help remove many apprehensions.

- Use more interpretive activities with older children.

- Be sensitive to what children's interests are (e.g., sports, space, contemporary music).

- Develop lesson themes around the children's interests as well as their needs.

- Include plenty of rhythmical problem-solving in the upper grades.

- Permit children to devise simple group compositions.

TEACHING TIPS

Suggestions for *teaching elementary folk, square, and country-western dances:*

- Name the dance, its origin, and other interesting facts.

- Teach new material first.

- Have children listen to the music.

- Demonstrate the dance (or its parts) using a partner or small group of children.

- Permit the entire class to try the whole dance or parts of it (depending on its complexity), first without the music and then with music.

- Unify the parts into the whole dance using the music.

- Select activities that promote skill development prior to emphasizing social development.

- Focus on dances without partners prior to dances with partners.

- Avoid activities that compromise one's gender identification.

- Focus on vigorous activities, particularly during the early stages of learning.

within the peer group and provide opportunities for combining patterns of movement into an integrated whole with the benefit of musical accompaniment.

Country/Western dances are peculiarly North American and reflect the culture of the early settlers. Both line dances and square dances are composed of a wide variety of movements that range from the very simple to the highly complex.

Social Dance.   **Social dance,** a fifth medium through which rhythm may be expressed by movement, is performed with a partner and reflects the mores of the culture at the time of its popularity. The very nature of social dance is constantly changing as our culture changes. For example, a few years ago, break dancing was popular; prior to that it was disco dancing, and before that, the twist and the jitterbug. Often, when preparing to include social dance in the curriculum, we fail to recognize and include these nontraditional forms of social dance. It is frequently assumed that social dance automatically implies waltzes, fox trots, tangos, and other more traditional forms.

Careful consideration should be given to the need for including traditional social dance in the elementary curriculum. For most schools and communities, it is recommended that traditional social dances *not* be included in the curriculum until the children are ready socially. The resistance and immaturity of many fourth, fifth, and sixth graders frequently makes it exceedingly difficult to teach traditional social dances. It is, however, suggested that more modern or nontraditional forms of social dance be considered as a part of the curriculum because children often have an expressed interest in learning these dance forms.

Aerobic Dance.   In recent years aerobic dance activities have become very popular among both adults and children. **Aerobic dance** is simply exercise to music led by an instructor who cues the participants on the proper activity for each phrase of music. Aerobic dance activities have many benefits. First, they add fun to what otherwise are frequently viewed as "boring" exercises. Second, they provide a social environment of group participation that encourages exercise compliance. Third, they reinforce children's ability to listen to and respond rhythmically to a piece of music. Finally, aerobic dance activities are for males and females, young and old, fit and unfit, able and disabled. All can participate in a manner individually suited to them.

With children, it is highly recommended that aerobic dance activities be limited to low impact aerobics. **Low impact aerobics** avoid the wear and tear and constant banging on young bodies and bones. Low impact aerobics help reduce exercise-induced injuries such as stress fractures and growth plate and joint injuries.

Aerobic dance is fun, is fitness enhancing, and contributes markedly to understanding and applying the elements of rhythm discussed earlier. Children love the opportunity to bring in contemporary music, design exercise routines to their music, and try it out with classmates. Aerobic dance has great potential for reaching and teaching children and youth in terms of fitness enhancement and the application of fundamental rhythm concepts.

Selecting Appropriate Rhythmical Activities

The inclusion of rhythmical activities in the physical education program usually begins during the early years with the introduction of fundamental rhythmic activities and a variety of singing rhythms and finger plays. After mastering the fundamentals of rhythm, children generally enjoy expressing their rhythmical abilities through imitative activities, creative rhythmical expression, and simple folk dances. Older children enjoy creative activities that permit interpreting ideas, moods, holidays, and sporting events through movement. They benefit from more complex folk dances and a few simple square dances. They also benefit from creative activities that permit rhythmical problem-solving and forming basic dance compositions. They enjoy more complex square dances and an introduction to aerobic dance activities.

You will need to be keenly aware of the social maturity of the class. These factors greatly influence children's ability and willingness to comply with the requirements of the rhythmical activities you select. Remember to focus on the **skill element** involved in dance prior to the

TEACHING TIPS

Practical pointers for *selecting partners:*

- Have a prearranged system that does not permit random choosing of partners.

- Switch partners often.

- Modify activities that require boys and girls to assume a closed dance position or skater's waltz position. An elbow turn or hand clasp will do.

- Do not require boys to take girls' parts or girls to take boys' parts.

- If the class is all one gender, avoid describing roles as "the girls' part" or "the boys' part." Instead, designate roles by the positions of "lead" and "follow."

Once you have settled on your objectives for including rhythmical activities into the lesson, you must then determine the level of rhythmical abilities of the class. You will need to have a general idea of their level of competence in being able to listen and respond to various forms of musical accompaniment, ranging from the sound of a drum or the clap of your hands to piano music or a recording.

social element. Introducing dances with partners will be of limited success if the children are not yet sufficiently skillful or are socially immature.

SELF-TESTING

Self-testing activities are just what the term implies: movement activities that permit the participant to perform as an individual and to establish personal standards of achievement. This is an especially important part of the physical education program for young children because they often find it difficult to work cooperatively toward group goals. Self-testing activities also benefit

Self-testing activities are frequently classified under the heading **educational gymnastics.** Educational gymnastics is not to be confused with artistic or rhythmical gymnastics but complies with the structure and meaning of the term *self-testing.* Therefore, when you encounter either term you should recognize that their meaning is essentially the same. Self-testing activities (i.e., educational gymnastics activities) may be performed alone or with a group. They do, however, focus on personal goals and individual achievement rather than on group efforts.

Educational gymnastic activities are self-testing in nature.

older children and adults because they permit one to learn new skills and take part in vigorous physical activity without having to rely on a team as a prerequisite for participation. Activities such as jogging, archery, golf, swimming, and cycling are self-testing in nature because they emphasize individual performance and personal standards of achievement.

CONCEPT 10.4

Self-testing activities are an essential aspect of the developmental physical education curriculum because they permit individual levels of practice, participation, and performance.

Types of Self-Testing Activities

Self-testing activities may be classified in a variety of ways, depending on their nature and purpose. In the developmental approach to physical education, self-testing activities are viewed as a tool for enhancing a variety of movement, fitness, and perceptual-motor skills. Therefore, the self-testing content area may be classified into individualized movement challenges, perceptual-motor activities, apparatus activities, and fitness activities.

Individualized Movement Challenges.   Throughout this text we have focused on the importance of fundamental movement and sport-skill development. A **fundamental movement** is an organized series of basic movements, such as running, jumping, throwing, catching, twisting, and turning. A **sport skill** is a fundamental skill that has

been combined with other skills, refined, and applied to a variety of sport-related tasks, such as batting and base running in softball, or the 100-meter dash and high jump in track and field. Both fundamental and sport skills can be further developed and refined through the use of **movement challenges.** Prefacing a challenge with words such as "Who can," "Let's try," or "See if you can" are frequently employed by the teacher who is using individual movement challenges to develop and refine movement skills. The skill theme chapters that focus on fundamental skill development (Chapters 16 through 25) provide an abundance of movement challenge activities.

Perceptual-Motor Activities.   **Perceptual-motor activities** may be gross or fine motor movements that are intended to develop and refine specific perceptual-motor abilities and selected perceptual skills. The perceptual-motor skills most influenced by quality movement programs are body awareness, spatial awareness, directional awareness, and temporal awareness. Likewise, the

TEACHING TIPS

Practical suggestions for *presenting self-testing activities:*

- Stress total participation.
- Stress individual standards of achievement.
- Encourage children to learn from one another.
- View yourself as a facilitator of learning.
- Emphasize the positive aspects of each child's performance.
- Encourage alternate solutions to movement challenges.
- De-emphasize competition and provide a relaxed atmosphere for learning.
- Use informal group organizational techniques (avoid line and circle formations).
- Present activities that offer challenges for all children.

- Practice skills under static conditions prior to dynamic conditions.
- Build skill upon skill.
- Help children understand the "why" of their movement as well as the "how."
- Encourage an awareness of individual capabilities and limitations.
- Emphasize safety at all times.
- Encourage children to attempt progressively more challenging activities.
- Focus on exploration and guided-discovery experiences during the beginning/novice level of skill learning.
- Focus on combining movement skills and skill application at the intermediate/practice level of skill learning.

---

perceptual skills most susceptible to influence through movement activities are visual perception (depth, form, and figure-ground perception), auditory perception (listening skills, auditory discrimination, and auditory memory), and tactile/kinesthetic perception (tactile/kinesthetic discrimination and tactile/kinesthetic memory).

All voluntary movement involves an element of perception. From the standpoint of perception, movement differs only in the type and amount of sensory and motor interpretation required. Therefore, by definition, all voluntary movement is actually perceptual-motor in nature. Hence, from the standpoint of teaching, the difference between a motor activity and a perceptual-motor activity lies in the primary objective of the movement task itself. If the primary objective is skill or fitness enhancement, the activity is not classified as a perceptual-motor experience. If, on the other hand, the primary objective is perceptual enhancement, the activity is classified as perceptual-motor. Remember, however, that these same activities may also serve equally well to improve movement skill and fitness levels.

Apparatus Activities.   Many schools are not equipped with **large apparatus** such as parallel bars, balance beam, indoor climbers, and cargo nets because of expense and storage problems. This is not the case with **small apparatus** such as hoops, wands, beanbags, balls,

balance boards, homemade rackets, and coffee-can stilts. The primary concept behind small-apparatus activities is that there should be sufficient equipment for every child to take part without waiting for a turn. Individualized equipment not only maximizes participation, it also heightens learning and enjoyment. A further benefit tends to be the reduction of boredom and discipline problems.

Fitness Activities.   Activities designed with the objective of enhancing specific components of fitness are frequently considered to be self-testing. Although many games, sports, and rhythmical activities may contribute to one's level of fitness, the primary objective of fitness activities is to improve one's level of fitness. Fitness activities focus on improved aerobic capacity, greater muscular strength and endurance, increased joint flexibility, and improved motor fitness. Therefore, activities such as calisthenics, combatives, weight training, jogging, rope jumping, and distance running are all considered to be fitness development activities.

Selecting Appropriate Self-Testing Activities

The self-testing activities you select for your program will depend on the specific objectives of the lesson and the ability level of your students. Remember that this

The very nature of self-testing activities is self-improvement. Therefore, there should be ample room for individual differences, and the lesson should be personalized to fit the often diverse needs of the group. If the objectives of the lesson center around the use of self-testing activities to promote movement skill learning, it is important to know where the group is in terms of the skills on which you intend to focus. Similarly, if the objectives of the lesson center around perceptual-motor or fitness activities, you will need to assess the students' present level of ability in each of these areas. The key to success with self-testing activities is to challenge each child at whatever his or her present level of ability may be.

content area, like that of games and rhythmics, contains movement activities that may serve a variety of objectives and may be appropriate for varying levels of ability.

SUMMARY

Games are fun, add a dimension of group interaction to the lesson, and may be used to promote movement skill development. However, using games as "filler" for a lesson without clearly stated objectives is educationally indefensible. Competitive games do not teach new skills, they merely reinforce the present skill level of the individual and provide a way to apply newly learned movement skills. Dance activities are also fun and add an exciting dimension to the physical education program. However, rather than lumping the rhythmical experiences for the school year into one three- or four-week unit, it is recommended that rhythmical activities be used throughout the curriculum as a means to many ends or as an end in themselves. Self-testing activities permit children to test and improve their movement abilities without undue concern for group goals or teamwork. By virtue of being self-testing, individualized movement activities permit students to concentrate on the movement task itself.

Teaching by objectives is essential for all sound educational endeavors. The objectives of games, dance, and self-testing activities all center around one or more of the following reasons:

1. Movement Skill Acquisition
   a. To enhance fundamental movement skills (basic stability, locomotor, and manipulative skills).
   b. To enhance sport-skill performance (individual, dual, and team sports).
2. Fitness Enhancement
   a. To promote improved health-related physical fitness (muscular strength and endurance, joint flexibility, cardiovascular endurance, and improved body composition).
   b. To promote improved motor performance (balance, coordination, agility, speed, and power).
3. Affective Development
   a. To promote cooperative group interaction with others (group spirit, fair play, teamwork, and sportsmanship).
   b. To promote positive self-growth (self-concept, self-esteem, and self-confidence).
4. Cognitive Development
   a. To promote learning readiness skills (learning to listen and following directions).
   b. To reinforce academic concepts taught in the classroom (science, mathematics, language arts, and social studies).
   c. To stimulate critical thinking (strategy, knowledge, and application of rules).
   d. To promote perceptual-motor learning (body spatial, directional, and temporal awareness).

The content areas of the physical education program represent the "tools" of your profession. They are not an end in themselves but a means to an end. They are the means by which children become more skillful movers and fit movers. Additionally, they serve as a vehicle for helping children become more effective cognitive and affective learners. Clear delineation of the specific objectives of game playing, dance dancing, and self-testing activity involvement is absolutely essential if physical educators expect to be understood and accepted in the educational community.

COMPLEMENTARY READINGS

Games

Belka, D. E. (1991). Learning to be a games player. *Strategies* 4:8–10.

Belka, D. E. (1994). *Teaching Children Games.* Champaign, IL: Human Kinetics.

Doolittle, S. A., and K. T. Girard. (1991). A dynamic approach to teaching games in elementary PE. *JOPERD* 62:57–62.

Metzler, M. W. (1990). Teaching in competitive games—Not just playin' around. *JOPERD* 61:57–61.

Morris, G. S. D., and J. Stiehl. (1989). *Changing Kids' Games.* Champaign, IL: Human Kinetics.

Petersen, S. C. (1992). The sequence of instruction in games: Implications for developmental appropriateness. *JOPERD* 63:36–39.

Roberts, E. L. (1993). Guidelines for choosing games. *Strategies* 6:12–15.

Werner, P. (1989). Teaching games: A tactical perspective. *JOPERD* 60:97–101.

Werner, P., and L. Almond. (1990). Models for games education. *JOPERD* 61:23–27.

Dance

Joyce, M. (1980). *First Steps in Teaching Creative Dance to Children.* Palo Alto, CA: Mayfield.

Mehrhof, J. H., K. Ermler, and S. Kovar. (1993). Set the stage for dance. *Strategies* 6:5–7.

Pica, R., and R. Gardzina. (1990). *1. Let's Move and Learn; 2. Toddlers Moving and Learning; 3. Preschoolers Moving and Learning; 4. More Music for Moving and Learning.* Champaign, IL: Human Kinetics.

Purcell, T. M. (1994). *Teaching Children Dance.* Champaign, IL: Human Kinetics.

Stinson, S. (1988). *Dance for Young Children: Finding the Magic in Movement (for ages 2–8).* Reston VA: AAHPERD.

Werner, P., et al. (1992). Developmentally appropriate dance for children. *JOPERD* 63:40–43.

Self-Testing

O'Quinn, G. (1989). *Teaching Developmental Gymnastics.* Austin, TX: University of Texas Press.

Rikard, G. L. (1992). Developmentally appropriate gymnastics for children. *JOPERD* 63:44–46.

Sullivan, M. (1982). *Movement Exploration for Young Children.* Washington, DC: National Association for the Education of Young Children.

Werner, P. H. (1994). *Teaching Children Gymnastics.* Champaign, IL: Human Kinetics.

Werner, P., and T. Sweeting. (1991). Gymnastics in schools. *The Physical Educator* 48:86–92.

SUPPLEMENTARY READINGS

Games

Gustafson, M. A., S. K. Wolf, and C. L. King. (1991). *Great Games for Young People.* Champaign, IL: Human Kinetics.

Lichtman, B. (1994). *Innovative Games.* Champaign, IL: Human Kinetics.

Mauldon, E., and H. B. Redfern. (1981). *Games Teaching.* Great Britain: Macdonald and Evans.

Reed, B., and P. Edwards. (1993). *Teaching Children to Play Games: A Resource for Primary Teachers* (A joint publication of the British Council of Physical Education, The National Coaching Foundation, and The Sports Council). White Line Publishing Services, 60 Bradford Road, Stanningley, Leeds, England.

Dance

Benzwie, T. (1991). *A Moving Experience: Dance for Lovers of Children and the Child Within.* Reston, VA: AAHPERD.

Fleming, G. A. (1990). *Children's Dance.* Reston, VA: AAHPERD.

Joyce, M. (1984). *Dance Technique for Children.* Palo Alto, CA: Mayfield.

Stinson, W., ed. (1990). *Moving and Learning for the Young Child.* Reston, VA: AAHPERD.

Weikart, P. S. (1989). *Teaching Movement and Dance.* Ypsilanti, MI: High/Scope Press.

Self-Testing

Fowler, J. S. (1981). *Movement Education.* Philadelphia: W. B. Saunders.

Morrison, R. (1969). *A Movement Approach to Educational Gymnastics.* London: J. M. Dent and Sons Ltd.

Riggs, M. L. (1980). *Jump to Joy.* Englewood Cliffs, NJ: Prentice-Hall.

Williams, J. (1979). *Themes for Educational Gymnastics.* London: Lepus.

VIDEOS

Teaching Children Games Video. Belka, D. E. (1994). Champaign, IL: Human Kinetics. (30 min.).

Teaching Children Dance Video. Purcell, T. (1994). Champaign, IL: Human Kinetics. (30 min.).

Teaching Children Gymnastics Video. Werner, P. (1994). Champaign, IL: Human Kinetics. (30 min.).

Assessing Progress

Key Concept

Individualized Entry Level and Exit Level Assessments of Motor Behaviors and Fitness Levels Are Important Aspects of the Developmental Physical Education Program

Chapter Objectives

The purpose of this chapter is to provide you with the tools to:
• Discuss the importance of entry level and exit level assessment in the developmental skill theme approach.
• Distinguish between process assessment and product assessment.
• List and discuss specific characteristics of several observational assessment devices.
• Describe appropriate techniques for observational assessment.
• Define and give examples of an assessment being valid, reliable, objective, and administratively feasible.
• Distinguish among the following: within-individual assessment, group comparisons, and between-individual assessment.
• Discuss the role and steps in total body observational assessment and segmental analysis.
• Describe what norms are, how they may be used, and their advantages and disadvantages.
• List and then discuss the roles of physical fitness testing in the developmental physical education program.
• Discuss considerations in terms of what to assess and when to assess relative to children's physical fitness.
• List the test items of the most popular field-based fitness tests used in North America today. Describe the merits and limitations of each.
• Describe current software packages available to aid in various aspects of both motor and fitness assessment.

Terms to Remember

Entry Level Assessment
Exit Level Assessment
Self-Referenced Assessment
Process Assessment
Product Assessment
Validity

Reliability
Objectivity
Feasibility
Utility
Between-Individual
    Comparisons

Between-Group
    Comparisons
Within-Individual
    Comparisons
Total Body Assessment
Segmental Assessment

Individualized Assessment
Norms
Fitness Awards
Fitness Education
    Materials

Assessment is an important aspect of any sound physical education program because it helps teachers measure students' current levels of ability, students' progress, and their own teaching effectiveness. Motor and fitness assessment is the collection of relevant information for the purpose of making reliable curricular decisions and discriminations among students.

By assessing the students' current level of performance, you can obtain a baseline or yardstick by which to measure progress. This form of assessment is frequently termed formative or **entry level assessment** and can be done easily and quickly at the very beginning of a unit of instruction. With this information in hand, the teacher can develop an instructional unit based on where students are rather than where they should be. Entry level assessment permits the instructor to fit the program to the needs of the student rather than fitting the student to a predetermined program.

CONCEPT 11.1
Entry level assessment *prior* to instruction in a skill theme is a critical component of the developmental approach to children's physical education.

Assessment is also used to measure pupils' progress over time. Evaluation of progress at the end of a unit of instruction is frequently called summative or **exit level assessment.** If your operational philosophy centers around the goal of individual improvement, then you will want to combine exit level assessment ratings with entry level assessment. For example, you could re-administer a basketball skills test at the end of a unit of instruction to determine if a student has made progress. This method of comparing individual entry and exit levels of achievement is frequently called **self-referenced assessment.** This approach differs from the normative or standards approach, in which students are compared by age against previously established class standards or group norms.

CONCEPT 11.2
Exit level assessment coupled with entry level assessment permits the learner to check on individual progress.

Self-referenced assessment is the preferred method of assessment in the developmentally based physical education program. This type of assessment reinforces the concept of individual differences that is the cornerstone of developmental physical education. Norm-referenced assessment, on the other hand, is based on age-group appropriateness, which is of only secondary importance to developmental physical education.

Teachers can further use assessment to measure their own effectiveness in the classroom. By determining students' level of ability and rate of progress, teachers can estimate their effectiveness in terms of movement skill acquisition and fitness enhancement. If, for example, you are able to show significant progress by your students in their level of basketball skill acquisition, then you can assume that learning has taken place and that you were instrumental in that progress. If, however, little or no progress is evident, then you may question your effectiveness in presenting that unit of instruction.

CONCEPT 11.3
Both motor assessment and fitness assessment must be directly related to the objectives of the program.

With regard to movement skill acquisition and fitness enhancement, self-referenced assessment at both the beginning and the end of a unit of instruction is highly recommended. Part IV, *The Skill Themes,* contains specific information for practical self-referenced entry and exit level assessment.

CONCEPT 11.4
Assessment may take many forms, but it must be administratively feasible, reliable, and yield valid estimates of one's present level of functioning.

MOTOR ASSESSMENT

Master teachers continually assess their students through both informal and formal means. They constantly adjust and revise their lessons to facilitate learning. At the elementary school level, two forms of assessment are appropriate: process assessment and product assessment. Both may be used, depending on the level of student ability, the specific needs of the students and the teacher, and the amount of available time.

Motor assessment is a primary means of assessment in the developmental physical education curriculum. Motor assessment takes two primary forms: process, or observational, assessment, which is subjective in nature, and product, or performance, assessment, which is objective in nature. Both process and product assessments have a place in the developmental curriculum. As new skills are being learned, process assessment is of particular relevance. Once skills have been mastered, product assessment may be of greater value.

Process assessment focuses on the qualitative aspects of movement.

CONCEPT 11.5
Process assessment focuses on the qualitative aspects of movement. Product assessment focuses on its quantitative aspects.

Observational assessment is an effective subjective technique for knowledgeable teachers to use and is an important technique when you consider that your primary goal is to teach movement skills. Concern for the proper mechanics, or the process of movement, must occur before focusing on the product.

Process Assessment

Process assessment is the observational approach to assessment that is concerned with the form, style, or mechanics used to perform a fundamental movement or sport skill. When focusing on the movement process, teachers are little concerned with the product of the act, such as how far the ball travels, how many baskets the child makes, or how fast the child runs the fifty-yard dash. Instead, they are concerned primarily with the body mechanics used to throw the ball, make the basket, or run the dash. The approach used throughout the skill theme chapters advocates that, for children at the fundamental phase of movement skill development, we assess whether they are at the initial, elementary, or mature stage. For those at the specialized movement phase we must determine if they are at the transitional, application, or lifelong utilization sport-skill stage.

It is not enough to assume that all first and second graders will be at one stage, third and fourth graders at another stage, and fifth and sixth graders at yet another stage. Because of the varying opportunities the children have had in terms of practice, encouragement, and previous instruction, a rigidly graded or age-based approach to movement skill acquisition and fitness enhancement is not acceptable as a valid means for curricular planning. Therefore, observational assessment of the process of children's movement becomes basic to effective use of the developmental approach.

Guidelines for Observational Assessment

Because observational assessment is qualitative and subjective, it requires the teacher to know the proper mechanics of a wide variety of movement skills. To this end, verbal and visual descriptions of children performing at the initial, elementary, and mature stages in over twenty fundamental movements is provided in the stability, locomotor, and manipulative skill theme chapters

TEACHING TIPS

When *observing and assessing* the process of children's movement:

- *Be unobtrusive.* This is especially important with young children, who will often alter their pattern of movement if they are aware that they are being observed.

- *Stress maximum effort.* Instructing children to throw as far, run as fast, or jump as high as they can will encourage best performances.

- *Stand where you can clearly view performance.* Stand far enough away that you can observe the entire task.

- *First, observe the total body action.* Try to look at the entire action to get a general impression of individual and group performance levels (i.e., initial, elementary, mature, or sport-skill stage).

- *Second, observe segmentally.* For individuals assessed to be at less than the mature stage, do a segmental analysis of each body part involved in the action. This will help you pinpoint specific problems.

- *Compare.* Occasionally ask another trained individual to observe and assess several children. Compare ratings for objectivity.

- *Be consistent.* Strive for consistency in your observations to maximize the reliability of your process assessments.

(Chapters 16 through 18). Additionally, verbal and visual descriptions of a wide variety of sport skills are contained in the sport-skill theme chapters (Chapters 19 through 25). The purpose of this information is to help you become familiar with the basic body mechanics and techniques used in executing the movement skills that children should learn during the childhood years.

CONCEPT 11.6

Estimates of children's present level of motor performance in fundamental movement skills and specialized sport skills may be obtained through product assessment.

Performance assessment is an effective objective technique to use in skill assessment *after* the mechanics of a task have been mastered. Once students have advanced to the mature stage of a skill, they are ready to begin applying the skill to specific sport-related activities.

Product Assessment

Product assessment is quantitative and is therefore concerned with how far, how fast, how high, or how many. In other words, it is concerned with the end results of one's movement, as measured by elapsed time, as in the 100-yard dash; distance covered, as with the standing long jump or shot put; accuracy, as in basketball goal shooting or target archery; or the number of repetitions, as with chin-ups or push-ups. For example, the mature throwing pattern can now be further developed and applied to throwing a football or pitching a baseball. Remember, a sport skill is often little different from the fundamental movement skill in terms of mechanics. The goal has changed in terms of the speed, accuracy, or distance required for success in the sport activity, but the basic mechanics are essentially the same, adapted only to the specific demands of the task.

Guidelines for Performance Assessment

Form (process) does have some influence on performance (product), but the extent to which performance is related to correct form is largely unknown. The figures located in the "Assessing Progress" section of each sport-skill chapter in Part IV provide examples of performance measures for assessing a variety of sport skills. Each of these performance tests can be modified as needed. The fitness tests discussed in the following section represent four different performance assessments of children's physical fitness.

Motor Assessment Tests

The motor assessment devices discussed here are observational assessment based. The Fundamental Movement Pattern Assessment Instrument originally developed by McClenaghan and Gallahue (1978) and expanded here is an observational assessment instrument for making within-individual comparisons, as is the Developmental

Product assessment focuses on the quantitative aspects of movement.

Sequence of Fundamental Motor Skills Inventory (Seefeldt and Haubenstricker, 1976; Haubenstricker et al., 1981). The Test of Gross Motor Development (Ulrich, 1985) is noteworthy in that it has been standardized and has both observational and performance assessment components. Also, it can be used for between-individual and between-group comparisons, as well as for detecting within-individual changes. Ecological Task Analysis (Davis and Burton, 1991) is an observational assessment tool that is becoming increasingly popular because it takes into account the goal of the task, the environment in which the task is performed, and the nature of the individual learning the task.

CONCEPT 11.7
A variety of observational assessment instruments are available for process assessment of children's fundamental movement abilities.

To maximize the usefulness of performance evaluations, consider the following questions:

- **Validity.** Does the performance measure what it claims to measure?
- **Reliability.** Does the performance measure whatever it is measuring consistently?
- **Objectivity.** Does the performance measure yield highly similar results when administered by others?
- **Feasibility.** Is the performance measure straightforward and easy to set up and administer? Can it be self- or partner-administered, or must it be teacher-administered?
- **Utility.** Can the results be used for valid educational purposes such as self-appraisal, program planning, or reporting progress?

Fundamental Movement Pattern Assessment Instrument (FMPAI). The FMPAI was first published in 1978 (McClenaghan and Gallahue). The expanded version included here has been revised to form the assessment basis for the fundamental movement skill themes that follow. The expanded FMPAI is a carefully developed observational assessment instrument used to classify individuals at the initial, elementary, or mature stage of development in several fundamental movement skills.

The FMPAI has proven to be highly reliable among trained observers. Content validity has been established for most of the fundamental movements. The original version included five fundamental movements (overhand throwing, catching, kicking, running, and horizontal jumping), but it has since been expanded to include several additional items. The developmental sequence for each of the original five movement skills was based on an exhaustive review of the biomechanical literature. The literature was also reviewed (Gallahue and Ozmun, 1995) for the additional items, and developmental sequences were established for walking, vertical jumping, hopping, galloping and sliding, striking, body rolling, dodging, and one-foot balancing. The authors' hypothesized, and therefore nonvalidated, developmental sequences were formulated for jumping from a height, dribbling, ball rolling, volleying, trapping, and beam walking. Sufficient literature is not available at this time to validate the developmental sequences of these fundamental movement skills.

The expanded FMPAI is an efficient, easy-to-use device designed to measure the present status of groups of children or a single child and to assess change in the process of moving over time. The FMPAI does not, however, yield a quantitative score nor can it be used to compare one child or group of children to another child or group (i.e., **between-individual** or **between-group comparisons**). Instead, this instrument is intended to assess developmental changes over time within individuals (**within-individual comparisons**). It uses observational assessment as a valid and reliable way to collect data and compare within individuals.

A set of instructional videos entitled *Assessment of Fundamental Motor Skills* (Ignico, 1994) are available that correspond with use of the FMPAI. These video tapes enable viewers to develop their observational assessment skills and are highly recommended as a means of improving both reliability and objectivity.

Figures 11.1 and 11.2 provide samples of both a total body and segmental group observational assessment charts. Additional charts are located in the Appendixes. Feel free to photocopy additional copies for your personal use. A **total body assessment** chart is best used with groups of children in an informal setting where you are able to observe body mechanics in the performance of any one of the stability, locomotor, or manipulative movements noted in a preceding paragraph. A total body assessment helps you get a general picture of the group's level of ability, and it helps you to identify children who are experiencing difficulty. The **segmental assessment** chart allows you to pinpoint exactly where the problem lies. By segmentally observing the leg, trunk, and arm action you will have a more complete picture of the individual and her or his specific needs. An **individualized assessment** form (Figure 11.3 and Appendixes) is a personalized progress report that you may send home periodically so parents can keep abreast of their children's progress in the developmental physical education program.

The FMPAI is most effectively used with preschool and primary-grade children who are generally at the fundamental movement phase of development. However, it may also be used with older individuals who are delayed in their motor development because of specific limiting conditions, such as early sport specialization, poor or nonexistent physical education programs, or physical or mental disabilities.

For individuals at the specialized movement phase of development a sport skill observational assessment chart is an effective diagnostic tool. The figures located at the end of each of the sport-skill chapters provide examples of observational assessment techniques for children at the specialized movement phase. They follow the same principles as the FMPAI and can be an effective tool in determining whether students are at the beginning, intermediate, or advanced stage in learning a specific sport skill. Additional charts are available in the Appendixes for basketball, softball, soccer, and volleyball skills.

CONCEPT 11.8
Observational assessment of the qualitative aspects of children's movement should incorporate both *total body* and *segmental* analysis techniques.

Developmental Sequence of Fundamental Motor Skills Inventory (DSFMSI).   The DSFMSI was developed by Seefeldt and Haubenstricker (1976) and expanded by Haubenstricker, et al. (1981). The DSFMSI categorizes each of ten fundamental movement skills into four or five stages. The fundamental movements of walking, skipping, hopping, running, striking, kicking, catching, throwing, jumping, and punting have been studied. These developmental sequences are based on data obtained from exhaustive film analyses. Children are observed and matched to both visual and verbal descriptions of each stage and classified along a continuum from stage one (immature) to stage five (mature). Although reliability scores have not been reported, personal communication with the developers has indicated that, with training using specially designed films and a stop-action projector, interrater reliability is quite high.

Test of Gross Motor Development (TGMD).   The TGMD developed by Ulrich (1985) uses principles from both the FMPAI and the DSFMSI, as a means of assessing fundamental movement skills in children from three to ten years of age. Selected locomotor and manipulative skills comprise the twelve-item test. Locomotor skills include running, galloping, hopping, leaping, horizontal jumping, skipping, and sliding. Manipulative skills include striking, ball bouncing, catching, kicking, and overhand throwing.

Administration of the TGMD takes about fifteen minutes per child. A manual with a clear set of test instructions is available. Both test-retest reliability and interrater reliability scores are high. Additionally, the validity of each item has been established. The TGMD is easy to administer and can be used effectively with a minimum amount of special training. It provides both norm-referenced and

FUNDAMENTAL MOVEMENT SKILLS
TOTAL BODY/GROUP OBSERVATION CHART

Class _____ Grade _____ Observer _____

Mark the proper stage (I, E, M, S)* for each skill. Then give an overall rating in the space provided. Name	Stability Skills								Locomotor Skills										Manipulative Skills							
	Static Balance	Dynamic Balance	Body Rolling	Dodging	Springing/Landing	Axial Movements	Inverted Supports	Transitional Supports	Running	Jump for Distance	Jump for Height	Jump from Height	Hopping	Skipping	Sliding	Galloping	Leaping	Climbing	Throwing	Catching	Kicking	Trapping	Dribbling	Volleying	Striking	Ball Rolling

*I–initial stage, E–elementary stage, M–mature stage, S–sport-skill stage

FIGURE 11.1 *Sample total body/group observation assessment chart.*

FUNDAMENTAL LOCOMOTOR SKILLS
SEGMENTAL GROUP OBSERVATION CHART

Class _____ Grade _____ Observer _____

Mark the proper stage (I, E, M, S)* for each body segment. Then give an overall rating in the space provided.

Name

Leg Action	Trunk Action	Arm Action	Overall Rating	Leg Action	Trunk Action	Arm Action	Overall Rating	Leg Action	Trunk Action	Arm Action	Overall Rating	Leg Action	Trunk Action	Arm Action	Overall Rating	Leg Action	Trunk Action	Arm Action	Overall Rating

*I—initial stage, E—elementary stage, M—mature stage, S—sport-skill stage

FIGURE 11.2 *Sample segmental group observational assessment chart for selected fundamental locomotor skills.*

	PHYSICAL EDUCATION PROGRESS REPORT																
Dear Parent: The skills checked have been assessed for this 9-week period. More then one check in a row indicates progress from one stage to another.	Child's Name _____ Grade _____ Class _____																
	1ST 9Wks.				2ND 9Wks.				3RD 9Wks.				4TH 9Wks.				Stage of Development
	Initial Stage	Elementary Stage	Mature Stage	Sport-Skill Stage	Initial Stage	Elementary Stage	Mature Stage	Sport-Skill Stage	Initial Stage	Elementary Stage	Mature Stage	Sport-Skill Stage	Initial Stage	Elementary Stage	Mature Stage	Sport-Skill Stage	Initial stage / Elementary stage / Mature stage / Sport Skill stage
Stability skills: Maintaining balance in static and dynamic situations																	Comments
One-Foot Balance																	
Beam Walk																	
Body Rolling																	
Dodging																	
Landing																	
Locomotor skills: Giving force to the body through space																	Comments
Running																	
Jumping																	
Hopping																	
Skipping																	
Leaping																	
Manipulative skills: Giving force to and receiving force from objects																	Comments
Throwing																	
Catching																	
Kicking																	
Dribbling																	
Striking																	

PARENT COMMENTS

PARENT SIGNATURE _____   DATE _____

PARENT SIGNATURE _____   DATE _____

PARENT SIGNATURE _____   DATE _____

FIGURE 11.3 *Sample progress report for fundamental movement skills.*

criterion-referenced interpretations for each fundamental movement skill and can be used as a device for between-individual and between-group comparisons, as well as for within-individual comparisons.

CONCEPT 11.9
Ecological task analysis incorporates decision making about the goal of the task, environmental conditions, and individual learner characteristics.

Ecological Task Analysis (ETA). Ecological task analysis can be described as examining motor performance with regard for the relationship between the goal of the specific task, environmental factors, and the nature of the performer. Davis and Burton (1991) describe four steps in establishing an ETA. The first step is selecting and presenting the task goal. This involves determining the function(s) of the task or what will be accomplished by the task. The second step is to allow the child or adult who is being tested the opportunity to choose the skill, the movement pattern, and, when the task requires, the implement to complete the task. The third step involves giving the individual guidance by emphasizing the goal of the task and stressing attention to the environmental conditions corresponding to the task. Guidance may also be provided by manipulating certain task dimensions so as to make the task more difficult without altering the task goal. The fourth step involves providing direct instruction regarding the individual's skill selection and movement form. This incorporates more traditional forms of instruction such as giving a demonstration of the proper skill mechanics. These techniques should occur only after the individual has had an opportunity to attempt the task under a variety of conditions. Comparing the movement forms attempted during step 3 to the movement forms demonstrated during step 4 is an important learning component of ETA.

Ulrich (1988) developed an assessment model that addresses many of ETA's considerations. His model uses striking an object as the example task. He provides numerous conditions under which an object may be struck. Aspects that may be manipulated include the striking implement, the movement of the ball, the size of the ball, and the conditions under which the individual is observed (formal test, informal play, or structured play).

Ecological task analysis represents a very promising approach to the assessment of motor behavior characteristics. It increases the opportunity to evaluate an individual's motor performance from a very broad perspective.

FITNESS ASSESSMENT

Fitness testing is common in most schools. The results of fitness tests are used for (1) determining the physical status of children, (2) identifying those who are deficient in certain areas and need special help, (3) classifying students, (4) measuring progress, and (5) aiding in activity selection and program planning. The results of each child's performance on tests of fitness should be placed in the cumulative record and made available to parents. Parents should be encouraged to promote activities for their children that will help overcome deficiencies in fitness levels. Many parents are eager to do whatever they can to help improve their child's physical functioning. Therefore, it is strongly urged that fitness test results and recommendations regarding each child be sent home for parent review and comment.

CONCEPT 11.10
A variety of published instruments are available for assessing children's physical fitness and enhancing their fitness education.

When to Assess

Physical fitness tests can play an important role in the total program if the results of these measures are used to aid the teacher, pupil, and parent in improving children's fitness levels, their attitudes toward the value of fitness, and their knowledge of how to improve their personal level of fitness. Fitness testing can be of real value in determining students' present level of functioning and identifying areas that need special attention. Fitness testing can be an effective motivator and an excellent way to reinforce the value of personal improvement in fitness.

> **W**hen selecting a fitness test for inclusion in the physical education program, be certain that it suits your purposes and meets certain criteria. You will need to consider information concerning reliability, objectivity, validity, norms, utility, and ease of administration in the selection process.

None of this, however, can be achieved if you wait until the end of the school year to assess your students. To be of real value, fitness testing needs to be a systematic and regular part of the program both early in the school year and at the end.

Be careful not to expect too much from children immediately upon returning from summer vacation. Hold off on the initial school fitness testing until four to six weeks after school has begun. By then, children will have had an opportunity to regain conditioning levels they may have lost over the summer.

What to Assess

A great debate has raged in the professional literature and among professional societies and organizations over what should be measured in children's fitness testing. Some claim that only the health-related components of physical fitness should be assessed. Others insist that performance-related components should be included. And still others see the merit of including items from both the health-related and performance-related areas. The decision is yours. Your decision, however, should be based on the curricular goals and fitness objectives of your program. A number of published fitness tests are available, each of which is somewhat different in the items assessed and the support materials available. Careful examination of the contents of each will enable you to select the one that is most compatible with your needs. If none suits the purposes of your program, then it is perfectly appropriate to develop a fitness assessment device personalized to your school, district, or state.

CONCEPT 11.11
Selection of specific physical fitness measures should be based on the goals and objectives of the program.

For each of the published fitness assessment batteries described in the following sections, norms, recognition awards, and educational materials are available. Be certain to review all three in terms of your curricular objectives and the needs of your students.

Norms are standards of performance that have been established so that comparisons may be made within groups of children and between groups of children. Published norms are generally national in scope. However, they may also be established on a school, city, or state basis. Norms permit the teacher to compare pupils'

performance in relation to other students' performances. Norms are helpful only in terms of comparing children against one another, but they rely on age-group appropriateness for their validity. In reality they are of little practical value in the developmental physical education program because of its emphasis on individual appropriateness.

Fitness awards are intended to serve as both extrinsic motivators and as recognition of achieving a predetermined standard of fitness excellence. They generally take the form of patches, pins, or certificates that honor the child for his or her level of achievement in comparison to established norms. Although popular, these awards may convey the wrong message about individual fitness achievement. The very fact that only those with the highest scores receive awards may significantly reduce motivation on the part of the majority of the class because of their inability to achieve in the top percentiles on normed tests of fitness. You may want to consider using fitness awards to recognize positive personal fitness behaviors, behaviors that *everybody* has an opportunity to achieve. The use of fitness awards in this manner can motivate a far greater number of children because they reward positive fitness behaviors (the process) rather than scores on a battery of tests (the product).

CONCEPT 11.12
Children's fitness education is essential for long-term exercise adherence, motivation, and concept learning.

Fitness education materials range from comic books to videotapes and from educational posters and wall charts to lesson plans and entire fitness education curricula. The intent of these materials is not only to motivate children but also to educate them in the essential knowledge and concepts governing fitness attainment, maintenance, and enhancement.

Fitness Assessment Tests

A number of published fitness tests are available for public use, each of which has strengths and limitations. Select the test that best suits your needs. Better yet, devise your own battery of tests and use that as your physical fitness assessment device. Table 11.1 provides an overview of the items for four of the currently most popular fitness assessment tests: The President's Challenge (PCPFS, 1995); AAU Physical Fitness Test (AAU, 1995); YMCA Youth Fitness Test (1989); and Fitnessgram (1994).

TABLE 11.1

Four Popular Tests of Physical Fitness

Fitness Test	Test Items	Fitness Component
The President's Challenge (PCPFS)	Curl-ups	Abdominal Strength/Endurance
	Shuttle Run	Speed
	Mile Run/Walk	Heart/Lung Endurance
	Pull-ups	Upper Body Strength/Endurance
	Flexed-Arm Hang	(Pull-up alternate)
	V-Sit Reach	Flexibility
	Sit and Reach	(Option to V-Sit)
AAU Physical Fitness Test (AAU)	Endurance Run (1/2–1 mile)	Aerobic Endurance
	Sit and Reach	Joint Flexibility
	Sit-ups	Abdominal Strength/Endurance
	Pull-ups (boys)	Upper Body Strength/Endurance
	Flexed-Arm Hang (girls)	Upper Body Strength/Endurance
	Standing Long-Jump	
	Isometric Push-up	
	Modified Push-up	Optional items, choose one to complete test
	Isometric Leg Squat	
	Shuttle Run	
	Sprints (50–100 yd.)	
YMCA Youth Fitness Test (YMCA)	Mile Run	Aerobic Endurance
	Skinfold	Body Composition
	Curl-up	Abdominal Strength/Endurance
	Sit and Reach	Joint Flexibility
	Modified Pull-ups	Upper Body Strength/Endurance
Fitnessgram (CIAR)	Mile Walk/Run	Aerobic Endurance
	Skinfold/BMI	Body Composition
	Back Saver, Sit and Reach	Joint Flexibility
	Curl-ups	Abdominal Strength/Endurance
	Push-ups	Upper Body Strength/Endurance
	Trunk lift	Trunk Extensor Strength and Flexibility

CONCEPT 11.13
Physical fitness tests may be used to supplement and support sound fitness education programs.

The President's Challenge.   President's Challenge Physical Fitness Program is sponsored by the President's Council on Physical Fitness and Sports (PCPFS, 1995). The President's Challenge is by far the most popular fitness test in the United States, being used in approximately 28,000 schools nationwide. The test is designed for children and youth from ages six through seventeen who may strive for the *Presidential Physical Fitness Award* (above the 85th percentile on all five tests), or the *National Physical Fitness Award* (above the 50th percentile on all five tests). A Participation Physical Fitness Award recognizes those who attempt all five tests but score below the 50th percentile on one or more of the items. The State Champion Award recognizes the top three schools in each state, based on enrollment, with the highest percentage of students qualifying for the Presidential Award. Published standards for both the Presidential Award and the less demanding National Award are based on a 1985 fitness survey conducted for the PCPFS by the University of Michigan. A unique feature of the President's Challenge is the inclusion of children with disabilities as potential qualifiers for the National Physical Fitness Award.

The President's Challenge features five events required of both males and females. Curl-ups, a shuttle run, one-mile run/walk, pull-ups (or flexed-arm hang as an alternate for the National Fitness Awards only), and V-sit reach (or optional sit and reach) make up the test battery. Fitness testing is recommended at least twice a year by the PCPFS. In addition, they recommend supplementing the President's Challenge with other health and fitness measures such as body composition, blood pressure, and posture checks.

The AAU Physical Fitness Program.

The AAU Physical Fitness Program is sponsored by the Amateur Athletic Union and administered by Indiana University (1995). The testing program focuses on physical fitness for every "body" and the philosophy that nobody fails a fitness test. In addition to a fitness assessment test, the AAU program offers a comprehensive developmentally based physical fitness curriculum (Benham, 1988), a fitness testing video, computer software package (IBM and Apple compatible), and an awards program.

The AAU Physical Fitness Test is divided into required and optional events. The required events include an endurance run (distances vary with age), bent-knee sit-ups, sit-and-reach test, and pull-ups (outstanding award) and flexed-arm hang (attainment and participation award). The optional events include the standing long jump, isometric push-up, modified push-up (girls only), isometric leg squat, shuttle run, sprint run, and Hoosier endurance shuttle run. Fitness standards for boys and girls from ages six through seventeen have been established. Participation, Attainment, and Outstanding Achievement certificates may be earned based on the results of all four required tests and one optional test item.

YMCA Youth Fitness Test.

The YMCA Youth Fitness Test is sponsored by the YMCA of North America and intended for children and youth six to seventeen years of age. The results of the test are used to provide recognition to participants who exhibit positive fitness behaviors, meet certain fitness standards, and accomplish specific individual fitness goals. Test scores for the five-item battery are classified into three broad categories: *Good, Borderline,* and *Needs Work,* thereby giving the participant a general framework for attainment rather than percentile scores. The test items include a one-mile run, triceps and calf skinfold, curl-up, sit and reach, and modified pull-up. Computer software is not yet available.

Fitnessgram.

The Prudential Fitnessgram is a physical fitness program developed by the Cooper Institute for Aerobics Research (1994) that includes testing, reporting, recognition and educational components. Fitnessgram strives to accurately assess health-related fitness from kindergarten through college. A key feature of Fitnessgram is that participants are not compared to each other but to health fitness standards that have been established for each age and gender. The test consists of a one mile walk/run, triceps skinfold measure, back saver sit and reach (alternative: shoulder stretch), curl-up, push-up (alternatives: pull-up, flexed-arm hang, or modified pull-ups), and trunk lift.

Recognition certificates are available for all who complete the six-item test. The *Get Fit* certificate, ribbon, and patch recognize those who complete a personal fitness log, fulfill an activity contract, and achieve specific activity goals. The *Honor Award* is designed for teachers to use at their discretion for special recognition for those who achieve individualized fitness goals, display special abilities, and strive for healthy active lifestyles despite disabilities. The *I'm Fit* recognition includes stickers, buttons, ribbons, and a patch for those who achieve in the designated "Healthy Fitness Zone" on at least four of the six fitness test items. Recognition is also given to those who demonstrate improvement in fitness performance on at least two test items. The *Fit For Life* certificate and patch is designed to recognize individuals who have displayed commendable exercise behavior. It is self-administered and designed to encourage lifetime fitness activities. There is a small fee for all recognition items for each of the programs.

In addition to the testing, reporting (see next section: Computer Applications for Assessment), and recognition aspects of Fitnessgram, there is an important educational component. Entitled *It's Your Move!,* these activity booklets designed for students in grades K–2 *(Hip Hoppers),*

3–4 *(Movers & Shakers)*, and 5–6 *(Slam Jammers)* provide a variety of motivational activities, including activity ideas, a tracking log, and a daily activity chart. Booklets are sold in sets of 35 for a fee. Through an agreement between the AAHPERD and the Cooper Institute for Aerobic Research, which administers Fitnessgram, an additional educational component is now available (1994). Although the fitness testing aspect of "Physical Best" has ceased to exist, its excellent educational materials promise to make Fitnessgram one of the most comprehensive youth fitness materials available.

COMPUTER APPLICATIONS FOR ASSESSMENT

In recent years computers have become a primary aid to the assessment process. They save valuable time, provide a convenient means for storing information, and are excellent for multi-entry assessments and comparisons. The available software for computer-assisted assessment and instruction is changing rapidly. In fact, by the time this text appears in print the software products mentioned in the following paragraphs will probably be obsolete. It is therefore recommended that you contact one or more of the software vendors listed at the end of this chapter for an up-to-date list of programs suitable for use with your students. If you are serious about motor and fitness assessment but are limited in the time available for testing and overwhelmed by the numbers of students you must evaluate, then you need to seriously consider the purchase and use of one or more of the following software packages.

CONCEPT 11.14
Computer applications for assessment are available, user-friendly, and expanding rapidly in both quality and quantity.

Computerized Motor Assessment

To date, no commercially prepared software packages are available for use with the motor assessment tests discussed earlier. The two that follow, however, may be used in a variety of ways to suit your motor skills assessment needs.

Physical Skills Manager. *Physical Skills Manager* (CompTech Systems Design) is a software program that allows analysis of up to fifteen motor skills of your choice.

Raw scores are converted to a scale of zero to ten and permit the charting of improvement in performance over time.

Physical Education Record Keeper. *The Physical Education Record Keeper* (Richard Hurwitz) is an Apple-compatible software package that enables you to record student progress over time. This software also allows you to record biographic and class data, tests and objectives, target goals for each objective, objectives yet to be met, and an activity prescription to meet program goals.

Computerized Fitness Assessment

A number of computer software packages are available to aid you with the results of your fitness assessment. Programs are available that will assist you with class record keeping, individual reports, tracking individuals over time, and reporting and prescribing personalized fitness profiles. Only three are highlighted here.

President's Challenge Software. The *President's Challenge* now has software packages available to help with record keeping, score tabulation, and generating individualized fitness reports (Harley Software, & Comtech).

AAU Physical Fitness Test Software. *The AAU Physical Fitness Test* has an excellent software package that is both IBM and Apple compatible. The program can facilitate general record keeping, tabulate scores, and generate individualized fitness reports.

Fitnessgram Software. Fitnessgram offers a sophisticated software package that is capable of generating highly personalized printed reports for each participant. This report contains actual test scores, the participant's location in the Healthy Fitness Zone for each item, and exercise recommendations based on test performance. The software package is also capable of generating a statistical overview of class or school results. Fitnessgram report forms are available for a fee, and the software is free.

SUMMARY

This chapter dealt with the important topic of assessment. Both motor and fitness assessment are essential aspects of the developmental physical education program. Assessment may be process-based or product-based. Process (observational) assessment focuses on the body mechanics of fundamental movement skills or sport skills. Product (performance) assessment focuses on the outcome of the movement itself in terms of time elapsed, distance traveled, or number of repetitions accomplished. Both process and product assessments yield useful information in determining a student's present status, measuring progress, and aiding in program planning for movement skill acquisition and fitness enhancement.

Four motor assessment tests were outlined and discussed. Particular attention was given to the Fundamental Movement Pattern Assessment Instrument (FMPAI), which serves as the means of entry level and exit level assessment for program planning in the skill theme chapters in Part IV. Fitness assessment was discussed as an additional important means of determining status, measuring progress, and aiding in program planning. Although many published fitness assessment tests are available, only the four most popular fitness tests were discussed. In addition, they are philosophically sound, scientifically based, and yield valid and reliable results.

Computer-assisted assessment devices were also discussed. The rapid growth of the computer software industry and the continual updating and expanding of existing software make it difficult to provide a critical overview of the most current materials. However, a few of the most popular motor and fitness assessment packages were briefly discussed.

COMPLEMENTARY READINGS

Baumgartner, T. A., and M. A. Horvat. (1988). Problems in measuring the physical and motor performance of the handicapped. *JOPERD* 59:48–52.

Benham, T. B. (1988). *AAU Developmental Physical Fitness Curricular Model.* Bloomington, IN: AAU.

Davis, W. C., and A.W. Burton. (1991). Ecological task analysis: Translating movement behavior theory into practice. *Adapted Physical Activity Quarterly* 8:154–177.

Fox, K. R., and S. J. H. Biddle. (1988). The use of fitness tests: Educational and psychological considerations. *JOPERD* 59:47–53.

Hensley, L. D., et al. (1987). Is evaluation worth the effort? *JOPERD* 58:59–62.

James, R., and J. S. Dufek. (1993). Movement observation: What to watch and why. *Strategies* 7:17–19.

Patterson, P. (1990). Local norms for fitness evaluation. *Strategies* 3:24–27.

Petray, C., et al. (1989). Designing the fitness testing environment. *JOPERD* 60:35–38.

Pinheiro, V. (1994). Diagnosing motor skills—A practical approach. *JOPERD* 63:49–54.

Ulrich, D. A. (1988). Children with special needs: Assessing the quality of movement competence. *JOPERD* 59:43–47.

Wood, T. M., ed. (1990). Measurement and evaluation—Theory to practice. *JOPERD* 61:29–44.

SUPPLEMENTARY READINGS

Franck, D. M. (1994). Assessment: Catalyst learning. *JOPERD* 65: 4–5.

Haubenstricker, J., and V. Seefeldt. (1986). Acquisition of motor skills during childhood. In V. Seefeldt, ed., *Physical Activity and Well-Being,* Reston, VA: AAHPERD.

Morrow, J. R., H. B. Falls, and H. W. Kohl. (1994). *The Prudential Fitnessgram Technical Reference Manual.* Dallas, TX: Cooper Institute for Aerobic Research.

Ostrow, A. C., ed. (1991). *Directory of Psychological Tests in the Sport and Exercise Sciences.* Morgantown, WV: Fitness Information Technology, Inc.

Safrit, M. J. (1995). *Complete Guide to Youth Fitness Testing.* Champaign, IL: Human Kinetics.

Strand, B. N., and R. Wilson. (1993). *Assessing Sport Skills.* Champaign, IL: Human Kinetics.

Motor Assessment Instruments

Gallahue, D. L., and J.C. Ozmun. (1995). *Understanding Motor Development.* Dubuque, IA: Brown & Benchmark Publishers (Chapter 11: Fundamental Movement Abilities).

Halverson, L. E., and M. Roberton. (1984). *Developing Children: Their Changing Movement.* Philadelphia: Lea & Febiger.

McClenaghan, B. A., and D. L. Gallahue. (1978). *Fundamental Movement: A Developmental and Remedial Approach.* Philadelphia: Saunders (original five-item version).

Stott, D. H., F. A. Moyes, and S. E. Henderson. (1984). *Test of Motor Impairment: Henderson Revision.* Brook Educational Publishing Ltd., Box 1171, Guelph, Ontario, Canada N1H 6N3 (519–836–2920).

Ulrich, D. A. (1985). *Test of Gross Motor Development.* PRO-ED, 5341 Industrial Oaks Blvd., Austin, TX 78735 (512–892–3142).

Fitness Assessment Instruments

Amateur Athletic Union. (1995). *The Amateur Athletic Union Physical Fitness Program.* Poplars Research Center, 400 East 7th Street, Bloomington, IN 47405 (1–800–258–5497).

Franks, B. D. (1989). *YMCA Youth Fitness Test Manual.* Champaign, IL: Human Kinetics.

President's Council on Physical Fitness and Sports. (1995). *President's Challenge Physical Fitness Program.* President's

Challenge, Poplars Research Center, 400 East 7th Street, Bloomington, IN 47405 (1–800–258–8146).

The Prudential Fitnessgram. (1994). 12330 Preston Road, Dallas, TX, 75230 (1–800–635–7050).

Computer-Assisted Assessment

AAU Physical Fitness Program Software. Poplars Research Center, 400 East 7th Street, Bloomington, IN 47405 (IBM or Apple compatible).

CompTech Systems Design. *Fit America* and *Physical Skills Manager.* P.O. Box 516, Hastings, MN 55033 (CompTech offers a wide variety of computer software appropriate for children's physical education.).

DinoFit Software System. Burtonville, MD: ARA Human Factors (IBM- or Apple-compatible software for AAHPERD Physical Best test, and other physical education software).

Hurwitz, R. *The Physical Education Record Keeper.* Cleveland State University, Cleveland, OH 44115.

President's Challenge Physical Fitness Test Software. Comtech, 1722 Vermillion, Hastings, MN (IBM or MAC compatible; 1–800–343–2406).

President's Challenge Physical Fitness Test Software. Harley Software, 133 Bridge Street, Dimondale, MI (Apple compatible, 1–800–247–1380).

The Prudential Fitnessgram Software. Fitnessgram, 12330 Preston Road, Dallas, TX 75230 (Apple IIe, Apple IIgs, MAC, IBM software available, 1–800–635–7050).

PART III

The Teacher

12 Effective Teaching

13 Positive Discipline

14 Teaching Styles

15 Safety Considerations and Legal Liability

CHAPTER 12

Effective Teaching

●

Key Concept

Effective Teaching Is a Dynamic, Interactive Process Between Student and Instructor Requiring Communication and Commitment to Individual Learning and Enjoyment of the Content

●

Chapter Objectives

The purpose of this chapter is to provide you with the tools to:
• Identify the many and varied responsibilities of the teacher.
• List and discuss several personal, classroom, and assessment traits of successful teachers.
• Identify the typical stages of concern that teachers encounter in their profession.
• Describe specific techniques for getting and maintaining children's attention.
• Discuss the importance of clarity in communicating with children and list several specific techniques.
• List the various forms of feedback and describe how they may be effectively used.
• Discuss problems associated with changing a well-learned but incorrectly performed movement skill.
• Identify a variety of common nonverbal postures, gestures, and facial expressions used by teachers.
• Speculate on the use of nonverbal communication techniques in effective teaching.
• Demonstrate techniques of conveying enthusiasm.
• Identify the role that physical distance plays in effective communication.
• List and discuss several techniques for analyzing one's teaching effectiveness.
• Analyze the messages received from children's verbal and nonverbal communication.

●

Terms to Remember

Effective Teaching	Feedback	Nonverbal
Verbal Communication	Internal Feedback	Communication
Verbal Clarity	External Feedback	Postures
Checking for	Concurrent Feedback	Gestures
Understanding	Terminal Feedback	Distance Messages
Checking for	KR	Naturalistic Observation
Retention	KP	Self-Study
Set-to-learn	Error Correction	Active Listening

Teachers of physical education may be the regular classroom teacher or the specialized physical educator. In either case, you have the responsibility for helping students to acquire movement skills, to enhance their fitness, and to increase their cognitive and affective learning. Teachers of physical education, like all other educators, need to determine what they are trying to accomplish, how they intend to affect learning, and how they will assess the results of their efforts.

Teachers of physical education must be able to create a highly positive atmosphere between themselves and the children whom they teach. The atmosphere of the gymnasium should be one of informality, active involvement, instructional and behavioral feedback, and, above all, recognition of individual differences within the learning environment. The learning environment should be one of support, encouragement, and success-oriented experiences, skillfully guided by knowledgeable, caring teachers.

This chapter focuses on the many and varied responsibilities of the physical education teacher, the stages of concern that teachers typically go through, and characteristics of effective teachers. Techniques for effective verbal and nonverbal communication and suggestions for improving your communication skills are also discussed. The chapter concludes with important suggestions for actively listening to children.

RESPONSIBILITIES OF THE TEACHER

Physical education teachers assume many responsibilities in carrying out their duties. They must take on the tasks of planning the curriculum, organizing the program, planning and implementing the lesson, and assessing pupil progress. Additionally, teachers accept the seldom-mentioned responsibilities of counseling students, acting as a community representative, and participating in long-term professional growth.

CONCEPT 12.1
Teachers have a variety of important responsibilities that go well beyond classroom instruction.

The ingredients of effective teaching in physical education are not unlike teaching in any other subject area. To do a thorough job you must have specialized training, interest in and enthusiasm for your subject matter, a sound grasp of teaching techniques, the ability to communicate effectively with children, and a continuing desire to understand the developing child.

Planning the Curriculum

The physical education teacher is frequently entirely responsible for developing the overall curriculum, an important task that is crucial to a successful program. Planning the curriculum takes time and requires careful analysis of student needs and interests as well as a survey of available facilities, equipment, and time allotments. Successful curriculum planning requires input from many sources and coordination with fellow teachers and administrators. Refer to Chapter 8 for a complete discussion on the developmental physical education curriculum.

Organizing the Learning Environment

Along with planning the overall curriculum, the teacher is responsible for organizing the learning environment. Physical education teachers are generally responsible for ordering, taking inventory of, and maintaining gymnasium and playground equipment. They assume responsibility for periodic safety checks of gymnasium apparatus and outdoor play equipment. In addition, they are frequently responsible for escorting children to the gymnasium and back to the classroom. As the physical education teacher, you will have to work hard to carry out these obligations and make maximum effective use of your time and the time that you have with your students. Refer to Chapter 9 for a complete discussion on organizing the learning environment.

Planning and Implementing the Lesson

Developing the overall curriculum and organizing the learning environment are important, but they precede the teacher's most vital work: the actual planning and implementation of the lesson. Physical education teachers

Teaching is a dynamic interactive process, not *a spectator sport.*

primarily instruct students how to acquire movement skills, attain and maintain physical fitness, and understand movement. The manner in which a lesson is implemented may take many forms, but the goal is the same: that children become skillful movers, that they develop an understanding of and appreciation for the "why" of physical activity, and that they incorporate it into their daily lives. A variety of teaching approaches and motivational techniques may be used, but your selection and use of these will depend on your philosophy of learning, educational background, personality, and expertise as a teacher. Refer to Chapter 9 for a complete discussion on planning, formatting, and implementing skill themes.

Assessing Pupil Progress

Teachers must serve as evaluators or assessors to determine if the objectives of their instruction have been met. Assessment may be subjective or objective, formal or informal, process-oriented or product-oriented. Assessment of children should stress the positive aspects of their performance, focusing on personal improvement and the discovery of one's individual potential. Child-centered assessment should help promote an "I believe in you; you must believe in you" attitude between teacher and student. Assessment should serve as an important form of feedback to students, parents, and the teacher. Refer to Chapter 11 for a complete discussion on assessing student progress.

Counseling Students

A frequent, although generally unwritten, role of the physical education teacher is that of counselor. For years physical educators and coaches have informally assumed this important but often underappreciated role. Because of the very nature of physical activity and the rapport generated through sensitive, caring instruction, physical education teachers often have numerous opportunities to serve effectively as counselors on a wide range of issues. Routine counseling opportunities may range from helping children adjust to school, home, and peer situations to providing techniques for healthful living and understanding and coping with one's changing body.

Your role as a counselor needs to be recognized and taken seriously. Remember, however, that unless you have special training, your ability and effectiveness in dealing with major problems is limited. Child abuse, drug and alcohol use, sexual activity, gender orientation, homelessness, and coping with the effects of divorce are serious topics that require trained professional assistance. In such cases, it is perfectly appropriate to be supportive, but by all means be certain to seek out professional counseling and advice.

Many experts view today's children as being in a crisis of identity and moral decision making (Hamburg, 1992). The impact that physical education teachers have as counselors is often as great as their impact as instructors. Do not, however, make the mistake of "telling" the child what he or she "must" do. Instead, present all sides of the issue, helping the student find his or her *own* solution. Teachers can guide students in values education and positive moral decision making, but they should not impose their particular value systems on others unless specifically asked to do so. When in doubt about how to respond to a sensitive counseling issue, check first with your immediate supervisor or the building principal. The worst thing you can do is to provide no guidance at all, claiming that it is not part of your job description. Remember, you may be the only one in that particular child's life trusted enough to provide guidance.

Acting as Community Representative

As a professional educator, your views in terms of the education of children will be sought. You will be expected to be knowledgeable about a variety of educational issues and to have formulated rational, intelligent positions. For example, your views on youth sport, weight training for children, diet, and exercise, among others, will be valued. Furthermore, your views will reflect on the school system or agency for which you are a representative.

TEACHING TIPS

Professional journals and newsletters help you keep informed and up-to-date:

- *Adapted Physical Activity Quarterly*
  Human Kinetics Publishers
  Box 5076
  Champaign, IL 61825–5076

- *Athletic Journal*
  1719 Howard Street
  Evanston, IL 60202

- *International Journal of Physical Education*
  c/o Verlag Karl Hofmann
  D-7060 Schorndorf,
  Postfach 1360
  Federal Republic of Germany

- *Journal of Physical Education, Recreation and Dance*
  AAHPERD Circulation Department
  1900 Association Drive
  Reston, VA 22091

- *Journal of Teaching in Physical Education*
  Human Kinetics Publishers
  Box 5076
  Champaign, IL 61825–5076

- *The Physician and Sports Medicine*
  McGraw-Hill Publishers
  4530 W. 77th St.
  Minneapolis, MN 55435

- *The Physical Education Newsletter*
  Physical Education Publications
  Box 8 (20 Cedarwood Dr.)
  Old Saybrook, CT 06475

- *The Physical Educator*
  9030 Log Run Drive North
  Indianapolis, IN 46234

- *Quest*
  Human Kinetics Publishers
  Box 5076
  Champaign, IL 61825–5076

- *The Research Quarterly for Exercise and Sport*
  AAHPERD Circulation Department
  1900 Association Drive
  Reston, VA 22091

- *The Right Moves* (Newsletter)
  NASPE
  Council on Physical Education for Children
  1900 Association Drive
  Reston, VA 22091

- *Scholastic Coach*
  730 Broadway
  New York, NY 10003

- *Spotlight on Youth Sports* (Newsletter)
  Youth Sports Institute
  Intramural Sports Circle
  Michigan State University
  East Lansing, MI 48824

- *Strategies*
  NASPE
  1900 Association Drive
  Reston, VA 22091

- *Teaching Elementary Physical Education* (Newsletter)
  Human Kinetics Publishers
  Box 5076
  Champaign, IL 61825–5076

As an educator you have a tremendous opportunity to serve as an effective community representative. You have training and knowledge about a variety of issues that are important to the public. You can use this knowledge to serve as an effective voice in the community.

Professional Growth

Continued professional growth is an important responsibility of all educators. This may take many forms, but it is generally accomplished through graduate study, continuing education, professional reading, and involvement in professional organizations and societies.

To continually grow as an effective teacher, the professional educator must be committed to advanced education beyond the undergraduate degree. Most states require teachers to pursue a master's degree or some form of continuing education to maintain a valid teaching license. Check with your State Department of Education to be certain of the requirements in the area where you will be employed. Continued professional growth may also be fostered through subscribing to and reading professional journals. Many professional journals and newsletters are especially valuable for elementary physical education teachers and youth sport coaches. If you are serious about continued professional growth, you should subscribe to and read at least one.

Involvement in professional organizations or societies at the local, state, and/or national level is another long-term responsibility of the professional physical educator. This may take the form of attending professional workshops and special meetings, serving on committees and action groups, or even making professional presentations. The American Alliance for Health, Physical Education, Recreation and Dance (AAHPERD) is the professional association to which most physical educators in the United States belong. Local AAHPERD organizations are located in each state and region of the country. The National Association for Sport and Physical Education (NASPE) is an association of AAHPERD with over 25,000 members. NASPE is the primary advocate for physical education in the United States. The Canadian Association for Health, Physical Education and Recreation (CAPHER) has affiliates in each province, and the International Congress for Health, Physical Education and Recreation (ICHPER) is the association to which many physical educators from around the world belong. Professional societies such as Delta Psi Kappa, Phi Delta Phi, and Phi Epsilon Kappa also provide a means for continual professional growth.

> Successful teachers are effective in both communicating with children and listening to children. They are good planners, organizers, and implementers of meaningful learning experiences. Successful teachers consistently demonstrate genuine concern for the welfare of their students.

STAGES IN BECOMING AN EFFECTIVE TEACHER

The process of becoming an effective teacher does not occur overnight. But just what is "effective" teaching? **Effective teaching** is both an art and a science that takes considerable time, effort, and practice. It is a dynamic, interactive process between instructor and student that requires mutual communication and commitment to individual learning and enjoyment of the content. Effective teachers have a genuine concern for their students and manifest this concern in their teaching behavior.

C O N C E P T   1 2 . 2
Teachers typically go through identifiable stages of concern for their personal success, their self-interests, and finally, genuine concern for others on their way to becoming master teachers.

It is interesting to note that on the road to becoming an effective teacher most people go through a series of predictable stages. The following are three stages of concern that you can expect to go through as you strive to become a master teacher.

Concern for Personal Success

No matter how well prepared you are at the completion of your education, or how many practice-teaching experiences you have had, your first concern as a new teacher is most likely to be that of personal success: personal success in the school itself, as well as personal success in the gymnasium and on the playground.

Concern for success in the school at large takes many forms. Adjusting to the policies—both unwritten and written—of your new place of employment is important to success, as is learning the names, roles, and expectations of your fellow teachers and supervisors. Remember, you are "the new kid on the block," and you will have to make adjustments to the structure and roles already in place. Finding your way around the school, locating equipment and supplies, and becoming acquainted with the school custodian and secretary are important to your personal success as a teacher. Often they can help you maintain facilities and equipment and order needed supplies and equipment, and they can often help you adjust to the community mores and the character of the faculty, administration, and students.

Effective teaching requires patience.

Personal success in the gymnasium and on the playground is often a more immediate concern. What happens between you and your students during the early days, weeks, and months will do much to set the stage for their later behavior. All too frequently, new teachers enter a school totally unprepared for gaining and maintaining control of their classes. Too often, their teaching diminishes to a "tug-of-war" of who will be in control. Your success as a teacher depends on your ability to win this battle by commanding the respect of your students, gaining and maintaining their attention, and ensuring class control. See Chapter 13 for a complete discussion of "Positive Discipline." The physical environment of the gymnasium and playground is quite different from that of the classroom. Children often exhibit a different set of behaviors in these environments. Therefore, it is of utmost importance to have a plan of action for ensuring your personal success.

Concern for Self

Once teachers have mastered the basic elements required for success and survival, concern often becomes inwardly focused. Teachers at this stage tend to ask questions such as "What's in it for me?" "How can I make this easier on me?" or "Why me?" At this stage of concern, teachers tend to feel overworked and underpaid. As a result, you are likely to feel misunderstood and unappreciated by your peers as well as your students. Although this stage is self-centered and appears to violate the ideals of "dedicated" teaching, it is a phase that most teachers go through. It does, however, have its benefits. Teachers with an acute concern for self have done much to cause local school boards to reexamine pay scales, workloads, and extracurricular expectations. Therefore, this stage, when viewed in its proper perspective, has contributed much to making the teaching profession a more attractive place to seek employment in the past few years. Teachers frequently demonstrate a healthy concern for self at the beginning of the school year by establishing basic rules and routines that are teacher centered. Rule making, however, should ultimately be a collaborative process between teacher and students. Such a process provides students with input and ownership, two important aspects of individuals at the third stage of becoming effective teachers.

Concern for Students

Genuine concern for learning and the welfare of students is the essence of successful teaching. Teachers at this stage are not encumbered by the anxiety of personal success—they have demonstrated their capability in this arena—nor are they preoccupied with a "What's in it for me?" attitude. They recognize the benefits and liabilities inherent in their profession in general and their own situation in particular, and they have chosen to get on with the business of educating children to the best of their ability.

No teacher progresses through these stages at a set rate. Some teachers are early casualties and never get beyond the quest for personal success stage. Some never advance beyond the concern-for-self stage and continue their careers looking for little beyond a paycheck. Most successful teachers, however, have reached the third stage and demonstrate a genuine, lasting interest in their children, both as students and as individuals. It is hoped that you too will reach this third stage.

Teachers must have personal, classroom, and assessment traits that motivate students toward increased competence.

CHARACTERISTICS OF EFFECTIVE TEACHERS

Effective teachers are those who, through planned instruction, are able to bring about positive changes in the learner. Such changes occur in an environment that is meaningful and nonthreatening, one that aids in developing a thinking and acting individual. The following personal, classroom, and assessment traits contribute to successful teaching.

CONCEPT 12.3
The characteristics of successful teachers are observable, predictable, and obtainable through practice and hard work.

Personal Traits

On entering the classroom or gymnasium, the student sees the teacher. A variety of personal characteristics display the teacher's attitude toward the subject matter, individual students, and the class itself. The following are several of the personal traits possessed by effective teachers.

Interested.   Effective teachers display an interest in students as individuals while refraining from being overly friendly to the point that they cannot act as a disciplinarian if necessary. This interest indicates to students that the teacher cares about them as people as well as students.

Honest.   Effective teachers are honest with themselves and their students. Their lack of condescension and their willingness to admit to a mistake or lack of knowledge shows students that they can be trusted.

Enthusiastic.   Effective teachers are alive with enthusiasm about the subject matter and are eager to share this knowledge. This tends to help students want to learn rather than making them feel that they have to learn.

Human.   Effective teachers smile, have an aura of warmth, and show a sense of humor. Students want to believe that teachers are human; only by acting human can teachers display true concern for the class.

Courteous.   Effective teachers respect students as innately worthwhile human beings and demonstrate their respect by consistently using "magic words" such as "please" and "thank you." Furthermore, they insist on students respecting one another and being courteous also. They encourage students in a positive manner and help them learn to do the same with their peers.

Good Speakers.   Effective teachers have a clear voice and a vocabulary geared to the students' level. They do not talk down to children or at them but talk *to* them in language they can understand. It is a pleasure to listen to teachers who speak well and are easily understood.

Confident.   Effective teachers are confident in their abilities and do not find it necessary to enhance their egos at the students' expense. They are able to be leaders and are sensitive to the needs of the group, which enables students to find comfort in the teacher's leadership without feeling threatened.

Properly Dressed.   Effective teachers recognize that personal appearance does affect how students view them. They dress neatly and appropriately for their age, which creates a positive image of the teacher and enhances the enjoyment of the class.

Knowledgeable.   Effective teachers are in command of their subject matter. They are well read and up-to-date in their knowledge. This helps ensure that the students will receive high quality, current, and correct information.

Traits in the Classroom

As the teacher enters the classroom or gymnasium, the process of rigid scrutiny by students begins. Many factors related to the teacher's actual conduct of the class play an important role in the teacher's success (refer to Chapter 14 for a discussion on selecting and using appropriate teaching styles). Teachers who use up-to-date teaching methods, clearly state their objectives, and strive for clarity and personalized instruction are often viewed as excellent by students. The following are several traits characteristic of effective teachers in the classroom or gymnasium.

Maximize Participation.   Effective teachers are able to maximize participation on the part of all students. They devise strategies for eliminating long lines, sitting, waiting, and watching while others perform. This helps students maximize time on task and learning enjoyment.

Teach by Objectives.   Effective teachers have clearly stated objectives for each lesson that are reflected in the activities selected, teaching styles used, and behavioral outcomes sought. This helps students know what is expected of them and relates the content of the lesson to these expectations.

Prompt.   Effective teachers are early or on time for classes. This illustrates enthusiasm and interest in and respect for the students. It also permits time for questions, comments, or informal conversation.

Prepared.   Effective teachers carefully plan each class period so that all of the time allotted is used wisely. This makes students feel that their time in class is well spent and the content important. Effective teachers do not drag out a class period simply to fill in the time.

Resourceful.   Effective teachers use a variety of outside resources, when applicable, to enhance learning and vary the normal class routine. This broadens the students' scope of knowledge and enhances interest in the class.

Review/Preview.   Effective teachers provide a brief verbal or visual review of the previous lesson and preview of the material to be covered during the current class period. This enables students to link previous information with new information and to follow the day's lesson more closely. A simple means of presenting review/preview information involves use of a chalkboard where the focuses (objectives) of the previous lesson are listed along with those of the current one. The use of colored chalk, trivia questions, and cartoon characters promotes attention and interest in the chalkboard display.

Check for Understanding.   Effective teachers do not assume that students automatically understand what they have been instructed to do. They constantly check for understanding by asking strategic questions. For example, prior to engaging in a skill drill the effective teacher will ask specific questions about key aspects of the drill in order to ensure that all are clear on the procedure.

Practical. Effective teachers recognize the necessity for practical application of ideas and concepts to everyday life. They illustrate the relevancy of the material for students and enable them to more accurately and personally apply the information.

Realistic. Effective teachers are consistent and realistic in their expectations of students. This provides students with clearly stated boundaries of acceptable behavior and standards of performance. Furthermore, they are realistic about what can be learned in the amount of time available to them and their students. They are more concerned about students learning fewer things well than many things at only a mediocre level.

Open. Effective teachers remain open to student questions and comments and create a forum for the exchange of ideas. This encourages thinking and synthesizing of knowledge on the part of students.

Clear. Effective teachers clearly state the objectives of the lesson in language students understand. They do not overload students with verbiage. This helps students focus on what is important.

In Control. Effective teachers are objective, consistent, and constructive in applying disciplinary measures. They recognize the individuality of each student, which assures students that they will be dealt with fairly.

Assessment Traits

All teachers are faced with the responsibility of assessing students, but it is the student who must cope with the variety of techniques employed. Every student is an individual and, as such, prefers certain types of evaluative methods to others. See Chapter 11 for a complete discussion on assessing progress. The following is a list of several characteristics of effective teachers in terms of assessment.

Assess by Objectives. Effective teachers take the time to develop objectives for their students and for themselves. Because students need to know what is expected of them and how they will be evaluated, teachers must identify what goals they want their students to reach and specify how they are going to help them achieve those goals.

Use Valid Instruments. Effective teachers employ valid measures to assess students' mastery of the subject matter. Each assessment should be based on a testing situation relevant to that particular subject matter.

Vary Techniques. Effective teachers do not assess students by totally objective or subjective means. They combine objectivity and subjectivity in testing situations to make the evaluation more meaningful.

Responsive and Timely. Effective teachers give meaningful feedback to their students as quickly as possible. They use assessment of knowledge and performance as a consistent and positive form of feedback. This helps students focus on their strengths and upgrade their weaknesses. The effective teacher will correct assignments and tests and return them as soon as possible with meaningful comments to indicate to students their strong and weak points.

Understanding. Effective teachers understand that people perceive things differently. This indicates that the teacher is interested enough in the students to listen to their interpretations of questions and the reasons for their answers.

Informed. Effective teachers recognize that external factors may affect student performance. They take the time to learn about their students as individuals and to find out what they are involved in.

Fair. Effective teachers steadfastly refuse to let personal prejudice, bias, or preference interfere with fair and honest assessment. This assures students that they will be evaluated on what they know or can do, not on artificial criteria such as hair length, style of dress, or likability.

VERBAL COMMUNICATION

Verbal communication is a crucially important tool for teachers, both in verbal explanations and in verbal presentations of movement challenges. No matter what teaching styles and techniques you use in the lesson, it is vitally important that you be able to get and maintain the students' attention and provide clarity in your instruction.

CONCEPT 12.4
Communication skills must be mastered for effective teaching.

Getting Attention

Getting the attention of a group of children requires a variety of communication skills. First, it is important to stand where you can be seen by all of the class. Standing at the edge of a circle formation or far enough back from a straight-line formation will ensure that all students can see (refer to Chapter 9 for additional information on organizing groups of children). It is much easier to get the attention of the group if you can see and make eye contact with every child. One easy way to ensure that you can maintain eye contact is to have the students seated when you talk to them as a group. In this way, children at the back of the group can be more easily seen and your line of sight will not be blocked by students in the front.

Getting children's attention can most easily be achieved through use of a predetermined signal. You should use the cue you select consistently and only as a signal for the class to stop all activity, face toward you, and listen carefully for the next instructions. Traditionally, a whistle has been used by physical education teachers to get the attention of the class. This is most effective outdoors or when the class is spread out over a large area. However, using a whistle is not always practical, particularly when you are indoors with classrooms located nearby. Instead, some teachers use a drum or tambourine. Others merely clap their hands or silently raise a hand overhead. Still others use a verbal command, such as "Freeze," to stop all activity and get the attention of the class. Whatever technique you select, the key is consistency. Be consistent in using cues and consistent in your expectation that all students are to cease what they are doing and focus their attention on you.

Maintaining Attention

Once you have succeeded in getting the attention of the group, it is important to be able to maintain it with a minimum of distractions. Children, like adults, need to be talked "to," not "at." Therefore, it is important not to be condescending in your approach. The use of a monosyllabic, "singsong" approach is not only condescending to most children but is also offensive. Children can be talked to effectively without resorting to this type of verbal behavior. You may have to modify your vocabulary to suit the level of understanding of the children you are dealing with, but remember, they are not babies and should not be treated as such.

The way you project your voice is important when trying to maintain children's attention in a physical education setting. Because gymnasiums are large structures, often with poor acoustics, and playgrounds are open, it is necessary to project your voice so that all can hear. In no case, however, should you attempt to shout over the din of noise characteristic of children. If you are unable to project your voice so that all can hear you clearly, then use your attention-getting command along with a second cue to rally the group to you.

Vocal intonation is also a concern. Many a teacher has lulled students to sleep with a constant drone. Maintaining a steady pitch in your speech is important, but altering it with inflections where appropriate creates a more interesting speech pattern and is easier to listen to. Avoid a speech pattern that trails off to a whisper. This is very distracting to children and makes it difficult to maintain their attention.

Providing Clarity

Another important factor in effective verbal communication is **verbal clarity.** As teachers, we are generally keenly interested in our subject matter and enthusiastic about conveying our interest to others. Therefore, we may frequently tend to oververbalize and provide too much information. Keep verbal instruction to a minimum. Try to be concise in explanations, taking into account the maturity and skill level of the students. It is often more effective to give only a short explanation of the basic elements of a skill or game, followed by immediate involvement in the activity. In this way, you can easily observe the level of understanding and ability, and you can adjust subsequent explanations to fit individual needs.

When you speak, use good grammar. Classroom teachers are constantly concerned with children's grammar; therefore, it is important for the physical education teacher to set a good example for appropriate use of the English language. Improper use of tenses and terms and failing to use the "ing" at the end of words such as "going," "doing," "something," and "nothing," are unacceptable. Avoid using slang and colloquialisms. It is unnecessary to demonstrate that you are "one of the group." Avoid distracting verbal hitches such as "Okay," "Listen up," and "Ah," as well as overuse of favorite words or phrases. The listener will soon focus on these irregularities of speech and will tend to concentrate on them rather than on the message being conveyed.

To foster clarity, try to summarize using key words or phrases. This helps children understand the information and provides a brief review of the key points of your presentation. The use of key phrases to reinforce instructions or to organize students quickly works well. For example, you may summarize three important classroom management concepts with the words "be quick, quiet, and courteous" rather than rambling on about the virtues of each. Providing frequent opportunities for questions about specific aspects of your verbal instruction is also important. When you explain an activity, stop from time to time to ask if students have specific questions about that portion of the explanation. At all costs, avoid a complete, detailed explanation of an activity or task followed by the general question, "Are there any questions?" This will generally result in a rush of questions that could have been dealt with more easily earlier. Furthermore, when children have a question but must wait until the end for an answer, they tend to shut down all other thought processes and concentrate only on the question. As a result, much of your explanation is not absorbed, often forcing you to repeat yourself a second or even a third time. Much of this may be easily avoided by giving students frequent opportunities to ask questions about specific aspects of your explanation.

Checking for Understanding and Retention

It is essential that you check on children to be sure that they understand what is expected of them, have internalized the concepts that you are trying to convey, or can perform the skills being taught. **Checking for understanding** involves asking recall type questions or asking for brief demonstrations of the material taught. Questioning and demonstrations of competency not only hold students accountable for their learning, they also provide you with both a sequential and an ongoing evaluation of the effectiveness of your teaching. Check for understanding throughout the lesson and especially during the lesson summary (Rauschenbach, 1994). For example, prior to engaging in a skill drill it is appropriate to ask specific questions about key aspects of the drill in order to ensure that all are clear on the procedure. Asking questions about key elements of the lesson during the lesson summary is another effective means of checking for understanding.

You will also find it helpful to check for retention from the previous lesson. **Checking for retention** involves asking questions about the previous lesson and asking for student demonstrations of previously taught content. This can be effectively accomplished during the review portion of the previous lesson prior to the introduction of new information. Checking for understanding promotes children's **set-to-learn,** which involves the students' preparation for, and expectation of, learning to occur. Children frequently associate the open space and informal setting of the gymnasium and playground with free play, recess, and reckless abandon, and not the learning environment of a classroom. The gymnasium and playground are classrooms. They are learning laboratories, and children soon learn this when you hold them accountable for learning.

Providing Feedback

Feedback refers to the information received from the senses during or after a movement. Sometimes known as knowledge of results (KR) and knowledge of performance (KP), feedback is necessary for effective and efficient learning. Teachers and coaches frequently rate their own effectiveness and that of others on their ability to provide the learner with meaningful information during an activity (KP) and after (KR) its completion. Although several factors influence the efficiency of learning a movement skill, the type, quality, duration, and frequency of feedback are among the most critical (Cole, 1991).

Basically, **feedback** is the information that the performer receives as the result of some form of response. This information may be (1) provided through internal or external sources, (2) occur during performance (concurrent feedback) or after it has been completed (terminal feedback), or (3) involve knowledge of performance or knowledge of results (Magill, 1993).

 C O N C E P T   1 2 . 5
Providing the learner with meaningful feedback is at the very heart of effective teaching.

Internal feedback, or intrinsic feedback, as it is sometimes called, is obtained by the learner as a result of the task itself. For example, in preparing to do a forward roll the learner receives internal feedback concerning hand and foot placement and body position throughout the roll. Learners who are at the beginning/novice level of learning a new movement skill are generally ineffective in their use of internal feedback. Those at the intermediate/practice or advanced/fine tuning levels benefit much more.

External feedback, or augmented feedback, as it is often called, takes the form of verbal cues from the instructor or from the use of some mechanical device. The internal feedback of doing the forward roll may be augmented by external feedback through teacher comments about positioning and body alignment. Additional external feedback could be provided by viewing a videotaped replay of one's forward roll.

TEACHING TIPS

Feedback **is one of the most critical elements in effective communication. Because of this it is important to:**

- Identify the type of skill being learned and the level of movement skill learning.

- Determine the cause of the learner's errors.

- Use feedback during and immediately following performance.

- Tell the learner the cause of the error (be precise).

- Tell the learner how to correct the error (be concise).

- Check to see that the learner understands the information given.

- Focus on correcting one error at a time.

- Use positive feedback techniques that encourage the performer.

- Correct errors by beginning with a positive statement, followed by an instructional hint, and finishing with a compliment (the "sandwich approach").

- Be certain to reward approximations with sincere praise and encouragement.

- Use feedback frequently to minimize practice errors, but don't overload the learner with too much information at one time.

- Encourage the performer to improve by continuing to practice outside of class.

- Be certain that the praise you give is genuine, freely given, and rewards individual progress and improvement.

- Provide ample opportunities for knowledge of results.

- Encourage personal skill analysis during the beginning and intermediate levels of learning the skill so the learner can use internal feedback.

- Discourage verbal skill analysis during the advanced level of learning the skill.

- Recognize the individuality of each learner and vary the types and degrees of feedback accordingly.

Feedback that is supplied during the performance of a task is called **concurrent feedback.** Athletes who say that they are in the "groove" or have the "feel" of an activity are using internal cues about their body while performing the task. Feedback provided by the instructor during the activity may focus on the process. For example, one may caution our forward roller to push off with the hands and stay tucked as the performer prepares to roll forward.

Feedback that is provided after performance of a task is called **terminal feedback.** Terminal feedback focuses on the product of one's actions. What occurs as a normal result of the performer's actions is called internal terminal feedback. For example, the forward roller remains tucked and achieves almost enough momentum to complete the roll back to a squat position. The margin of error is then evaluated and corrected for by the tumbler. Instructors can augment terminal feedback through comments to the performer or by using videotaped replays of the activity.

Basically, feedback gives learners information about the correctness of their actions. It serves three basic functions. First, feedback provides the performer with information (**KR,** knowledge of results; or **KP,** knowledge of performance) that leads to error correction and the desired response. Second, feedback reinforces the performer in ways that may be either positive (encouragement) or negative (criticism). Positive reinforcement tends to preserve, augment, or enhance the desired behavior. Negative reinforcement tends to decrease or inhibit the behavior. Corrective feedback should, whenever possible, be positive. Third, feedback motivates the learner. Although it is not completely understood how feedback influences motivation, it is known that feedback of some sort is necessary to heighten the motivational level of the performer.

Changing Well-Learned Techniques

Teachers frequently encounter children who come to them with a well-learned but incorrect technique of performing a fundamental or sport skill. The child may be

TEACHING TIPS

Sequential steps for changing a well-learned but incorrectly performed movement skill:

- Determine if there is sufficient time to make the change (think in terms of weeks and months, not hours or days).
- Determine if the learner really wants to make the change.
- Be certain that the learner understands why the change is being made.
- Be certain that the learner realizes that performance will probably regress before it improves.
- Provide a supportive, encouraging environment.
- Structure practice sessions that will gradually bring the learner from the beginning to the intermediate and finally back to the advanced level of learning the skill.

experiencing some success with the technique, but proper execution of the skill would be more efficient and would lead to even greater success. The teacher is now faced with the dilemma of whether to make an **error correction** in the form of changing the individual's habitual performance peculiarities or to leave the performer alone. A well-learned technique is difficult and often time-consuming to change. Any new learning requires returning a learned behavior to a conscious cognitive level (i.e., bringing it back to the beginning skill level). Under stress and in conditions where rapid decisions are required, the performer is likely to revert to the first or most well-learned response. Only after considerable practice can the performer consistently replace the incorrect response with the correct action.

CONCEPT 12.6
Changing a well-learned but incorrectly performed technique is a process that requires time, effort, and communication between student and teacher.

NONVERBAL COMMUNICATION

Nonverbal communication, or body language, as it is often termed, is the projection of messages through subtle and often unconscious changes in our postures, gestures, and facial expressions. It has been estimated that our verbal vocabulary ranges from about 28,000 to 40,000 words, but our nonverbal "vocabulary" is endless. It is important to learn the subtleties in our nonverbal communication and to recognize the messages that we are transmitting. In fact, we are often more apt to convey these messages in their true form through body expression than through verbal expression. It is important, then, that your body language convey to children that they matter and are valued and that you are pleased to be with them. The following discussion focuses on the use of various postures, gestures, and facial expressions and the messages that they tend to convey.

CONCEPT 12.7
Teachers' nonverbal messages are frequently as meaningful and powerful as their verbal messages.

Postures

The **postures** that you take when standing before a class convey a variety of nonspoken messages. If you stand erect with your weight evenly distributed on both feet, you tend to convey confidence and assuredness. Standing with the body weight on one foot portrays an image of being relaxed, easygoing, and at ease. On the other hand, shifting your body weight from foot to foot is often an indication of uneasiness, nervousness, or boredom.

The use of your arms also conveys messages to students. For example, the arms folded tightly across the chest may convey a variety of messages. When this posture is assumed with an erect body posture with the weight distributed evenly over both feet, the message is one of determination and steadfastness. On the other hand, if the arms are folded and the body weight is shifted from foot to foot, a need for comfort, security, and assurance tends to be conveyed. Placing the hands on the hips or keeping them clasped behind the back are postures frequently assumed by teachers who convey authority or being in control.

Think for a moment of some of your frequent postures, or take time to observe the body postures of one or more of your instructors. What messages are your instructors giving you? It is important to note that one's postures may not provide accurate nonverbal messages. The point, however, is that they do provide a message, and it is this message, accurate or not, to which students react.

Gestures

Most of us use a variety of gestures in our daily communication with others. **Gestures** are movements of the body, head, arms, hands, or face that express an idea, opinion, or emotion. Teachers are often masters of the use of gestures that communicate meaning in very specific terms. In fact, it is often joked that many elementary school teachers would be unable to talk if their hands were tied to their sides. They often use gestures consciously to supplement the spoken word. For example when saying *big, small, high,* or *low,* teachers commonly make corresponding gestures. For young children this is often appropriate and provides visual reinforcement of basic verbal concepts. On the other hand, older children often find these descriptive mannerisms distracting and condescending when overused.

The use of pointing gestures often conveys a clear and undeniable message. Pointing the index finger forcefully at a student tends to be viewed as threatening. It singles the student out from the rest of the group and creates an uncomfortable feeling. Pointing the index finger forcefully downward conveys the message of reinforcing a point, while pointing it upward serves as a message of appeal from a higher authority. Steepling the fingers often conveys the message of "I have the advantage." Rubbing the hands together conveys a sense of expectation, and twiddling the thumbs is often viewed as a sign of boredom. Tapping the fingers or playing with paper clips, rubber bands, or similar objects conveys restlessness or nervousness. Habitual gestures such as persistent tugging on an ear, rubbing your chin, hiking up your pants, or clearing your throat not only convey a feeling of being ill at ease but also distract students from your real message.

Facial Expressions

It is said that a picture is worth a thousand words. Our facial expressions are often just that. Although we verbally say one thing, it is frequently interpreted by others as something else. This may be caused by the multitude of facial expressions that we use when communicating. Raising the eyebrows conveys a message of surprise. Squinting one eye tells others that we are suspicious. Wrinkling the brow provides a message of distaste. Standing with the

Take a few moments to analyze the gestures that you and others characteristically use. What messages are you conveying? What messages are being conveyed to you? Do any of your gestures convey the wrong message, or are any of them distracting mannerisms? If so, try to make a conscious effort to modify or eliminate these habitual forms of nonverbal communication.

mouth open displays awe or surprise, and thrusting the jaw forward gives a message of defiance.

The eyes can be used as a potent nonverbal form of communication. Staring out the window or glancing frequently at your watch convey boredom. Rolling the eyes conveys exasperation or "How could you be so stupid." An eye roll followed by mutual glances to another person convey the same message and indicate a desire for others to share in your nonverbal criticism of the offender. The tendency to focus on and talk to one segment of the class conveys to the others that they don't really count.

These are only a few of the facial expressions frequently used. Each of us has an almost limitless number of expressions that we use every day. It is important to remember and fully understand the messages that you are giving to others with these facial expressions. Often what is "heard" by others directly opposes what was said, because what is said does not match the facial expressions, gestures, and postures. Our actions truly do speak louder than our words.

CONVEYING ENTHUSIASM

One of the most important but frequently overlooked aspects of successful interaction with children is the ability to convey enthusiasm for the subject matter and for the children themselves. Your verbal and nonverbal communication skills may be above reproach, but if you show little genuine enthusiasm in your teaching, you will have little success. Children are remarkably perceptive in their assessment of teachers. If they sense that you have little interest in them or in your subject matter, they will be quick to "turn you off." Let us look briefly at what you can actively do to convey your enthusiasm.

CONCEPT 12.8
Demonstrating real interest in their subject matter and students is an important quality of effective teachers.

Interest in Your Subject Matter

Children are quick to pick up on your interest or lack of interest in various aspects of the curriculum. If they see that you are hesitant to get involved in certain activities, it will negatively affect their attitudes. Trouble will manifest first in a series of groans and moans. It may advance to outright refusal to take part and other forms of belligerent behavior. On the other hand, a display of active, eager involvement by the teacher conveys an attitude of acceptance and eagerness to participate.

Well-planned and executed lessons that move along quickly with a minimum of disruption also convey a sense of enthusiasm. Children do not look for constant effervescent behavior on the part of teachers as a measure of enthusiasm. On the contrary, you may have a quiet and reserved manner and still be viewed by children as enthusiastic. The display of a genuine interest in their learning and your creation of an environment that maximizes their potential for improvement are more important to children than a surface show of energy.

Interest in Your Students

Successful teachers can convey their interest in their students in numerous ways. One basic way is to learn their names. This is often a difficult task, especially for the physical education teacher, who sees several different classes a day. The tendency is to learn only the names of those students who stand out in some way. As a result, you know by name only the students who have persistent behavioral problems or are exceptionally good or poor in physical activities. Unfortunately, the majority of children often go nameless. One way to learn names is to use group cards, with a Polaroid picture of the members of each group. Another is to use name tags (although this may interfere with certain activities) that the children make and decorate themselves during art class. Still another technique is to try to associate the child's name with some outstanding trait, characteristic, or ability. Once you have learned names, try to avoid using only the child's last name. Using the child's given name is much more personal and conveys a message of warmth and interest in the child as a person.

Children judge teachers to be interested in them if they show a genuine interest in their learning and set high but realistic goals for achievement. Teachers show their interest in children by recognizing and respecting the individuality of the learner.

Successful teachers convey their interest in children by establishing acceptable standards for behavior and adhering to these standards consistently. Displaying genuine interest in children and enthusiasm for teaching them is difficult if you are constantly reprimanding, scolding, and disciplining. Whether your boundaries are narrow or broad is not as crucial as your consistent adherence to whatever boundaries you have established and the impartial manner in which you deal with unacceptable behavior.

IMPROVING COMMUNICATION SKILLS

Understanding the various messages conveyed through physical distance, observing children in different settings, and self-study can do much to improve your ability to communicate with children.

CONCEPT 12.9
Communication skills can be improved with practice and should be viewed as a continuing process.

Respect Physical Distance

Distance messages are the messages you give to children and adults based on the physical distance between you and them. How close you stand to those to whom you are talking has a marked effect on what they hear, attend to, and retain. The closer you are to the learner, the greater will be the attention given to you by the learner, up to a point. The greater the distance between you and the learner, the less able you are to attend to each other.

Generally speaking, distances from four to ten feet are the most appropriate for effective teaching and learning. Distances of one to three feet tend to be too close and invade one's "personal space." This space is generally reserved for special people or special occasions. Invasion of this space tends to make the individual feel ill at ease.

Distances greater than ten feet tend to make the learner feel less involved in the learning situation. A distance between teacher and student of up to fifteen feet is

TEACHING TIPS

Physical distances and their nonverbal messages:

Feet	Distance	Message
1 to 3	Intimate	"You are too close and threatening." (This is a personal space reserved for special people and occasions.)
4 to 6	Near Friendly	"I feel more comfortable."
7 to 10	Far Friendly	"We can still communicate, but on less friendly terms."
11 to 15	Formal	"I can move into or out of immediate contact with the situation at will."
16 to 20	Remote	"I am removed from the situation and out of contact."

generally considered to be a formal distance, allowing the individual to psychologically move into or out of the learning environment at will. Distances over fifteen feet are considered to be remote distances in which the individual feels removed from contact with the learning environment. Successful physical education teachers use physical distance as an effective teaching technique, constantly varying their distance from the students to achieve the desired effect.

Observe Children

Another way to improve communication skills with children is through naturalistic observation. **Naturalistic observation** simply involves observation in an unobtrusive manner in a variety of settings. Successful physical education teachers frequently visit the classroom or spend time observing children during recess or at after-school activities. Occasional visits to the classroom serve two important functions. First, they enable you to observe children's behavior and interaction patterns with the classroom teacher, with whom they spend the bulk of the school day. This observation can provide you with valuable information about the child's behavior as well as specific techniques of class management and control. Second, your visit communicates to children that you are interested in them and in what they do when they are not with you.

Sitting in on and taking part in the activities of a reading circle or a science lesson will not only be enlightening but will help establish positive communication between you and the children as well as between you and the classroom teacher. Observing and interacting with children in a variety of settings is a positive step in improving your communication skills. It takes extra time but is well worth the effort.

Self-Study

Effective means of getting feedback on your skills in communicating with children is termed **self-study.** The primary means of self-study are through videotaping, audiotaping, and peer assessment of your lessons. Each of these techniques can offer a great deal of useful information that will help maximize your effectiveness in talking to children.

Taking the time and effort to occasionally have one of your lessons videotaped will provide much useful information about the effectiveness of your nonverbal and verbal communication skills. After viewing themselves, teachers will often respond with comments such as, "Did I really say that?" or "Is that how I look when I do that?" Videotaping enables you to chart the positive and negative aspects of your teaching and clearly document where you have made improvements and where you need continued work.

The audiotape is also an effective tool in assessing communication skills. Although limited to providing feedback about your verbal behavior with children, the audiotape enables you to focus attention entirely on that mode of communication. The audiotape quickly reveals verbal hitches, redundancies of speech, lack of clarity, and problems in getting and maintaining attention.

Peer evaluations are a third technique of providing feedback about your verbal and nonverbal behavior. Peer evaluations are an excellent way to provide information about the organization and implementation of your lessons and whether the objectives of the lesson were achieved. Teachers should look forward to and request regular, systematic assessment of their teaching. The comments and helpful suggestions offered should be taken in a positive manner rather than defensively, as is sometimes the case.

Whether you choose to use videotapes, audiotapes, or peer evaluations of your teaching, it is important to look for objective means by which you can continually analyze yourself as a communicator. Self-study is an ongoing process, which should not be limited to new teachers or nontenured teachers seeking substantiation of their abilities. Self-study is for everyone.

LISTENING TO CHILDREN

An important aspect of effective communication that is sometimes overlooked is actively listening to children. **Active listening** is a process of simply taking the time to stop what you are doing, face directly toward the speaker, provide direct eye contact, and give both nonverbal and verbal feedback, indicating that you are paying attention to the speaker. Active listening skills need to be cultivated by all teachers. Teachers often are so busy with what they have to say and how they are saying it that they forget that the children are also giving messages to them. These messages take many forms and may be classified as verbal messages and nonverbal messages. The manner in which we pick up on and respond to these explicit and implicit messages plays a significant role in our success in effective, two-way communication with children.

CONCEPT 12.10
Taking the time to know children by being an active listener of their nonverbal and verbal messages is essential to effective teaching.

Children's Verbal Messages

Listen carefully to what children are saying to you and how they say it. Try to be alert to the meaning behind their words and the message they are giving you with their speech patterns. Children who speak loudly or tend to mumble may be giving you a message that they have a hearing problem. Boisterous children often speak aggressively, whereas timid children tend to speak with a barely audible voice. Confident children tend to give complete answers or explanations to inquiries and are not hesitant to acknowledge their failure to understand or comprehend. On the other hand, timid children are often slow to speak up if they do not understand or have questions. Furthermore, when forced to respond verbally, they tend to offer shorter replies or explanations and to speak more softly. Children who chatter almost constantly and need to be reminded to be silent are often displaying a need for acceptance or approval. The speech patterns of children can provide meaningful messages and help you to adjust your responses accordingly.

Children's Nonverbal Messages

Alert teachers "listen" to children's nonverbal messages as well as the verbal ones. Often, their nonverbal messages provide clear insights to their many moods. For example, the child who is fidgeting communicates a message of "Let's get moving." Children who do not sit up in an attentive posture indicate that they are not interested in the lesson. Persistent head nodding is often used as approval-seeking behavior.

The manner in which children raise their hands in response to a question is also revealing. Hesitant hand raising tends to communicate that "I think I know the answer, but I'm not quite sure." Wild hand waving communicates "Teacher, teacher, call on me!" Holding the hand high above the head conveys assurance and confidence in knowing the answer. Holding a raised hand in a propped-up position conveys a message of "Please take pity on me and let me answer your question."

Being sensitive to how children use their eyes and the messages they are trying to communicate is important. Avoiding eye contact conveys a message of "I'm not here; don't call on me." Staring out the window or off into space is often a sign of boredom. Rolling the eyes conveys the undeniable message of "Teacher, how could you be so dumb." Doing a double take after making an error or mistake in a game or sports activity (such as dropping a ball) serves as a common means of telling another that "It wasn't really my fault; some outside force caused me to do it."

Knowing the Learner

It is vitally important that you as the teacher know your students and recognize that each comes to you with a different set of motor, cognitive, and affective characteristics. You are confronted with a huge number of individual differences, and you need to consider as many of them as

Children convey nonverbal messages in numerous and unique ways. Remember, these messages may be actual indicators of things as they are or they may be what the child wants you to think they are. In either case, it is important that you "listen" to these messages and respond to them accordingly.

TEACHING TIPS

In terms of individual differences, successful teachers recognize that:

- Children learn at differing rates.
- Children's potential for performance excellence varies.
- Requisite fundamental movement skills must be mastered prior to sport skills.
- Responses to instructional approaches vary among individuals.
- Responses to winning and losing vary among individuals.
- Responses to encouragement, criticism, reward, and punishment vary among individuals.
- The background of related experiences varies from child to child.
- Differences in home life experiences influence children differently.
- Attention span and ability to concentrate vary greatly among individuals.
- The developmental level of children varies, resulting in dissimilar potentials for learning and performance.
- Children will display greater or lesser degrees of movement skill depending on a combination of environmental and hereditary factors.
- The ability to analyze, conceptualize, and problem solve—all important in movement skill learning and sport participation—varies among individuals.

possible when planning the lesson. Some individual differences are easy to detect; others are not and may remain hidden. It will, however, be to your advantage to recognize and adjust to as many factors as possible.

SUMMARY

This chapter first described the many and varied roles of the teacher. But the primary focus of the chapter was the importance of effective teaching. It has been said that there is really no teaching if learning does not occur. If physical education teachers are to be viewed seriously as important contributors to the school curriculum, they must take their responsibility to be effective teachers seriously.

Some of the characteristics of effective teachers include the personal traits of enthusiasm and knowledgeability; the classroom traits of being prepared, realistic, and in control; and the assessment traits of using valid testing measures and being fair. Developing the skills of the master teacher takes time and considerable practice but is within your grasp if you are genuine in your commitment to effective teaching and have a real interest in children.

Techniques for effective verbal and nonverbal communication were discussed as a basic requirement for good teaching. Verbal communication skills are important in getting and maintaining attention, providing clarity and feedback, and helping children relearn incorrectly performed skills. Effective nonverbal communication was discussed as a subtle, but critically important, means of providing children with messages about their performance.

Conveying enthusiasm and improving communication skills were the final topics of this chapter. Both were dealt with in terms of their importance to children. By demonstrating genuine interest in your subject matter and in your students' learning, you can convey the important message of enthusiasm. Skill in communicating with children can be improved through a variety of techniques ranging from observing them and self-study to respecting physical distance and actively listening to what they have to say. The verbal and nonverbal messages that children give are also important clues to knowing the learner. Take time to observe and listen to children. Their messages are generally quite clear and unmistakable.

COMPLEMENTARY READINGS

Ballinger, D. A. (1993). Becoming an effective physical educator. *The Physical Educator* 13–19.

Cole, J. (1991). Feedback: A one-to-one strategy. *Strategies* 4:5–7.

Graham, G. (1992). *Teaching Physical Education: Becoming a Master Teacher.* Champaign, IL: Human Kinetics.

Hellison, D., ed. (1990). Physical education for disadvantaged youth. *JOPERD* 61:36–45 (series of articles).

Rauschenbach, J. (1994). Checking for student understanding: Four techniques. *JOPERD* 65:60–63.

Ritson, R., ed. (1989). Teaching children—Teaming for quality. *JOPERD* 60:47–70 (series of articles).

Siedentop, D., ed. (1989). The effective elementary specialist. *Journal of Teaching in Physical Education,* 8:187–270 (series of articles).

Stein, J. U. (1988). Competition—A developmental process. *JOPERD* 59:30–32.

Wong, H. T., and R. T. Wong. (1994). *The First Days of School: How to Be an Effective Teacher.* Sunnyvale, CA: Harry K. Wong Publications.

SUPPLEMENTARY READINGS

Graham, G. (1992). *Teaching Children Physical Education: Becoming a Master Teacher.* Champaign, IL: Human Kinetics.

Hellison, D., and T. J. Templin. (1991). *A Reflective Approach to Teaching Physical Education.* Champaign, IL: Human Kinetics.

Morrow, J. R., ed. (1991). RQES: Research on teaching in physical education. *Research Quarterly for Exercise and Sport* 62:351–83 (series of articles).

Rink, J. (1993). *Teaching Physical Education for Learning.* St. Louis, MO: Mosby.

Magill, R. A. (1993). *Motor Learning: Concepts and Applications.* Dubuque, IA: Brown & Benchmark Publishers (Chapter 7, Instruction and Augmented Feedback).

VIDEOS

AMPT Pedagogy Course Self-Study Video. Graham, G. (1993). Champaign, IL: Human Kinetics. (60 min.).

AMPT Pedagogy Course Instructor Video. Graham, G. (1993). Champaign, IL: Human Kinetics. (90 min.).

I Choose to CARE. Wong, H. K. (1993). Sunnyvale, CA: Harry K. Wong Publications. (60 min.).

Positive Discipline

●

Key Concept

Positive Discipline Is a Learning Process Effectively Guided by Competent
Teachers, Culminating in the Establishment of Student Self-control

●

Chapter Objectives

The purpose of this chapter is to provide you with the tools to:
• Discuss the concept of discipline from a variety of perspectives.
• List several means of establishing and maintaining teacher control.
• Speculate on the meaning, use, and effects of punishment.
• Provide information on specific techniques for developing children's self-control.
• Describe the importance of consistency in helping children develop self-control.
• Distinguish between an aggressive authority style and an assertive authority style.
• List several techniques for being an effective role model for children.
• Describe several suggestions that might aid in efficient planning.
• Discuss the importance of self-assessment in determining personal strengths and
  weaknesses and in gaining and maintaining class control.

●

Terms to Remember

Discipline   Self-Control
Teacher Control   Thinking Rules
Time-Out   Aggressive Behavior
Punishment   Assertive Behavior
Corporal Punishment   Authority Style

On entering the gymnasium, the first concern of most new teachers is personal survival—being able to take charge and control their students. Without discipline in the gymnasium or classroom, little effective learning can occur. Therefore, one of the first responsibilities of the teacher becomes the creation and nurturing of an atmosphere of positive discipline.

This chapter focuses on what is meant by the word *discipline.* Techniques for imposing teacher control, delivering punishment, and promoting self-control are discussed. The conditions necessary for an environment conducive to positive discipline are also discussed.

DISCIPLINE DEFINED

To some teachers the term **discipline** indicates the level of teacher control existing in one's classroom: "I have effective discipline." To others it signifies a form of punishment: "I had to discipline them." Still other teachers interpret the word to mean a form of self control: "She certainly is disciplined." The fact is that discipline can mean all of these things. Therefore, discipline is a way of enabling students to use their time effectively to meet learning objectives without inhibiting others from attempting to achieve the goals of the lesson.

C O N C E P T   1 3 . 1
The goals of discipline may be interpreted differently, resulting in considerable variation in the techniques used and outcomes achieved.

Teachers with positive discipline are generally viewed as confident, competent adults who are in charge of their classrooms or gymnasia and who are leaders and models for children. They are capable and willing to assume authority in regulating and shaping children's behavior. Teachers with positive discipline do not have to nag or intimidate children to make them behave. On the contrary, teachers who can discipline effectively generally take a series of positive steps to set the boundaries for acceptable behavior and gain the respect and trust of their students.

Positive discipline does not depend solely on externally imposed standards for behavior. It does require self-control and assumption of responsibility for one's actions on the part of students. Positive discipline does not

require that every student be in a rigid line or formation, responding on command. Such a setting does little to promote self-control or ensure long-lasting positive behavior. Overuse of rigidity and structure, when not essential to the lesson, tends to stifle learning and provides little opportunity for children to become self-disciplined. For maximum learning to take place, children must be actively involved in the learning process, and the teacher must serve as a helpful guide and motivator of desirable responses. In the gymnasium and on the playground, learning is often a noisy process with plenty of activity and with children engaged in a variety of related but often different tasks.

C O N C E P T   1 3 . 2
One of the most critical elements of effective teaching is to be able to help children move toward a consistent state of positive self-control.

Discipline has not failed if children overtly express enthusiasm or excitement in exploring the movement potential of their bodies. It has not failed if the gymnasium is humming with task-related conversation or if eight eager youngsters simultaneously burst out with an idea, suggestion, or solution. Discipline, however, has failed if the rights of the class or individuals within the class are infringed upon by one or more disruptive children. It has failed if the specific objectives of the lesson cannot be met effectively because of the climate of the classroom, or if the interest, initiative, or individuality of any person is curbed by one or more disruptive individuals.

TECHNIQUES FOR IMPOSING TEACHER CONTROL

Most techniques of exerting **teacher control** over students fail to solve persistent behavior problems. The best method of handling behavior problems is to have a program designed to prevent them from occurring. However, once problems do occur, several remedial actions can be taken. Remember, though, to apply teacher-imposed discipline with the dignity of the student in mind. It is crucial to respect the innate rights of the individual as a human being and not strip the student of dignity through humiliation or ridicule.

CONCEPT 13.3
Most of the techniques used to impose teacher control over students fail to solve the underlying cause of the discipline problem.

Each of the following techniques has been found to be successful in helping teachers establish and maintain class control through the use of nonverbal, verbal, and time-out responses. It is important, however, to remember that no method of control gets to the heart of the issue—knowing why the problem occurred or how to prevent it from occurring again.

Nonverbal Responses

Teachers can use a number of nonverbal responses to respond to children's misbehavior. Often these quiet forms of control can do much to improve individual behavior and the behavior of the class in general. Your eyes are a valuable tool. Disapproving glances or a fixed gaze on the misbehaving child frequently will stop the misconduct. Stationing yourself close to the area where misbehaving students are located is also helpful. A gentle hand on the shoulder of a child who may be off task is often enough to show that you are displeased with the student's behavior.

Verbal Responses

Your voice can also be a powerful weapon. Use it wisely, because your choice of words, pitch, and tone can convey a very clear message of intent. Remember that to discipline with dignity you must avoid, at all cost, yelling, screaming, being sarcastic, and belittling children for their behavior. Instead, restore order immediately in the least disruptive manner possible. If the infraction is minor, treat it as such. Too often teachers who overreact to small disruptions find themselves exhausted and their children conditioned to their overreaction. As a result, the teacher has little emotion—or voice—to cope with the major problems that are sure to occur. It is more appropriate to give general comments to the class with a brief explanation of acceptable behavior.

Failure to gain control in this manner may require more severe techniques. Singling out those who are misbehaving by name, with a brief comment of what is acceptable behavior, is often effective. For example, "Daniel and Jennifer, it's important for everyone to

Five quick cues to managing inappropriate student behavior:

- *GIVE* the student "the stare."
- *REMIND* student of the correct rule or procedure.
- *ASK* the student to repeat the correct rule or procedure.
- *TELL* the student to stop the rule violation.
- *REMIND* the student, if necessary, to stop the rule violation and attach a consequence.

have their eyes focused up here and listening carefully to the lesson. Do you understand?" Be certain to check for understanding by getting a verbal response to the question at the end of your statement. This helps break the pattern of misbehavior and cause a refocusing of attention.

Time Out

If you are unable to bring disruptive students under control with nonverbal and verbal techniques, it is sometimes appropriate to provide a **time-out** space. This should be a predesignated spot in the gymnasium or on the playground sufficiently removed from the class but in clear view of the teacher at all times.

Removal of a disruptive child from the class for a portion of the lesson gives both the student and the teacher time to regroup and refocus. Be sure, however, not to overuse this technique or to exclude the child for too long a time. Exclusion for longer than five minutes tends to be less effective than shorter periods (French et al., 1990). Also, be certain to talk privately with the child before reentering the class asking: "What did you do to cause me to remove you from class?" "How should you have behaved," or "How can we prevent this from happening again?" and "Are you ready to rejoin the class on your best behavior?" If the problem is between two students, such as in name calling, pushing and shoving, or fighting, and they have been removed for time out, be certain that they talk over the problem and work it out with your help before returning to class.

Steps in maximizing the effectiveness of time out:

- Provide a specific designated spot for the child to go to.
- Place gymnasium thinking rules close by for the child to read.
- Ask the child to reflect on the behaviors that resulted in time out.
- After a brief period of five minutes or less, try the following ideas:
  - Establishing good eye contact, talk quietly to the child out of the hearing range of the rest of the class.
  - Be certain that the child knows why he or she was required to take time out.
  - Briefly explain your expectations in terms of specific positive behaviors.
  - Ask the child if he or she is ready to return.
  - If the answer is "yes," check for understanding by asking the child to reiterate the acceptable behavior required for reentry.
  - If the answer is a simple "no" or is unacceptable, provide additional time for the student to "cool off" and consider the consequences of the poor behavior before you begin the procedure just described again.
- Once the student is back in class, observe for compliance and compliment positive behaviors.

When possible, avoid excluding students from an entire class or sending them to the principal's office. Handling your own discipline problems whenever possible conveys a message to the children of your being in control. Teachers who constantly send disruptive students to the principal's office are actually inviting further difficulties because they are viewed by students and fellow teachers as ineffective leaders, unable to manage their own classrooms. You are less likely to have a behavioral problem solved by a neutral third party. Of course, there are situations in which delegating your authority to another is appropriate and useful, but, as a rule of thumb, avoid it whenever possible.

PUNISHMENT

If it becomes necessary to punish children, punishment should be for the behavior, not the individual. **Punishment** should be explicitly combined with a statement of what would have been the appropriate behavior in the situation, and it should occur immediately after the undesirable behavior to be effective. Physical punishment, unless immediate, will be of little benefit other than to reduce the frustration of the punisher.

CONCEPT 13.4
Punishment frequently has more long-term negative implications than positive benefits.

Using any form of punishment for extended periods tends to reduce its effectiveness. When the punishment or the threat of immediate punishment is removed, the undesirable behavior often returns in extroverted children. On the other hand, introverted children often remain afraid too long and may actually develop phobias or neuroses as a result.

Although the threat of punishment is the most frequently used method of class control, it is often the least effective. Punishment merely represses undesirable behavior; it fails to get at the underlying cause of the problem and often creates harmful anxiety, escape, and avoidance behaviors on the part of children.

Corporal punishment (spanking) provides children with adult models of aggression. As a result of this example, children often view aggression as acceptable. The use of corporal punishment is strongly discouraged and should be avoided even if permitted by the school. Unauthorized or overly aggressive use of corporal punishment may even result in a lawsuit. Other forms of punishment can be used, but they must be immediate to be of real value and also should be accompanied by an explanation of the undesirable behavior so that the child can anticipate the same consequences in the future.

Although punishment can be an effective management tool, it is often difficult to use it effectively in the typical gymnasium or playground setting. Because of large classes and the nature of the physical education lesson itself, the teacher cannot punish a particular behavior each time it occurs. Occasionally a teacher may use inappropriately severe punishment or relish giving punishment; in both cases, normal standards of ethics are violated. Because of these difficulties and the possible negative consequences of punishment, the appropriateness of punishment should be weighed carefully for each situation.

Worry, fear, anxiety, hatred, guilt, shame, and avoidance may be instilled by punishment as a reaction not only to the undesirable behavior but also to the teacher, the class period, or physical education itself. Students who are repeatedly punished or reprimanded may withdraw and try to avoid class or school by being "sick," tardy, or truant. Some students may genuinely fear school because of the emotional and physical pain incurred there. Withdrawal may be accomplished by daydreaming, doodling, or otherwise not paying attention, even though the student is physically present.

The more severe the punishment, the more it increases fear, anxiety, anger, and general emotionality (i.e., out-of-bounds or off-task behavior) in the punished person. Increases in emotion make it more difficult for children to change their behavior and learn new habits and may even increase the likelihood of future misbehavior. Punishment may even lead to aggression, but the amount of punishment necessary to cause aggression differs among individuals, as does the strength or kind of aggression. Almost any punished student is likely to make hostile remarks about the teacher or other punishing adult when out of that adult's immediate range of attention. The student is almost certain to like the teacher less.

Children's behavior and self-esteem are influenced strongly by how they think others perceive them. Punishment increases the chance that the child will come to believe that others have a negative view of him or her, and it increases the chance that the child will develop a negative self-concept. If punishment must be used, the teacher should provide opportunities for the child to experience praise, success, and positive reinforcement.

TECHNIQUES FOR DEVELOPING SELF-CONTROL

The highest form of positive discipline is **self-control.** Children are active, energetic beings in the process of developing self-discipline. The following guidelines have proven helpful to teachers attempting to instill self-control in children.

Though other students may not immediately imitate either the act of punishment or the punished act, it has been found that both of these acts tend to increase in frequency in the absence of the teacher or other punishing adult (Ratliffe et al., 1991). Children who witness shouting, shaking, sarcasm, and so on are more likely to behave in similar ways when other people frustrate them than are children who witness calmer reactions. Much of human behavior is learned from models, and teachers should provide models of fairness and temperance.

A bulletin board can display important messages about the value of positive behavior.

CONCEPT 13.5
Teachers can effectively promote student self-control by consistently applying a variety of developmentally appropriate behavior-shaping techniques.

Establish Routines and Rules

Children are generally more secure when they know what is expected of them and what comes next. A gymnasium with a regular sequence of activities and a limited number of clearly understood classroom and gymnasium thinking rules will do much to provide children with a framework for acceptable behavior. Gymnasium and playground **thinking rules** are written student behavior codes for acceptable behavior. The rules should be clear and concise and should outline the consequences for misbehavior. The rules should be placed on a wall where all can see and be sent home with students so that students, fellow teachers, and parents are all familiar with the requirements for positive discipline in the gymnasium and on the playground.

It is important to remember that you must teach your students what the rules for acceptable behavior are. You cannot expect that they will know or willingly accept these rules unless you help them learn and understand. If children can expect that the routine of the lesson will follow a consistent format, then they will tend to be more at ease and less disruptive. If the rules of the gymnasium have been clearly explained and posted where they can be easily seen by all, then children are less likely to overstep these boundaries. One effective technique in setting rules is to request that students help generate the rules and help determine the consequences for violating them. Such a technique involves students in the decision-making process and promotes self-discipline.

Reduce the "Don'ts"

When establishing guidelines for acceptable behavior, you would be wise to limit the number of "don'ts," because the word reinforces unacceptable behavior. State rules from a positive standpoint rather than a negative one. For example, rather than saying, "Don't run," "Don't talk," or "Don't get out of line," it is generally better to say, "Walk quietly," "Remain silent," or "Stay in line." Emphasizing the positive often has a correspondingly positive influence. You will, of course, need to make exceptions to this if a child's safety is at stake or if you need to protect property. Avoid a long list of "don'ts" if the primary purpose is for your convenience or comfort.

Be Reasonable

Be reasonable; don't invariably demand the desirable or prohibit the undesirable. We have often heard adults complain, "Everything I want to do is either unhealthful, illegal, or fattening." If we, who have had years to reconcile ourselves to society's restraints and curbs on our primitive

Sample Physical Education Behavior Code*

1. During Directions:
   a. Quiet, eyes on teacher, equipment still and silent.
   b. Raise your hand to ask a question.
2. Moving Signals:
   a. Move when you hear the signal.
   b. Stop quickly on signal.
3. Follow Instructions (the first time).
4. Equipment:
   a. Get it out/put it away.
   b. Move equipment quickly, cooperatively, and directly.
5. Positive Behavior:
   a. Cooperate with classmates and teachers.
   b. Follow the school thinking rules.

Consequences for Violating the Code

1. Warning
2. Time out
3. Mini-class
4. Contact home (plus above)
5. Office detention (plus above)

*From a gymnasium wall in Winnipeg, Canada.

drives, still have these feelings, how much more do children resent the restrictions and taboos that are adult-conceived and, at best, only vaguely understood by them?

Follow Through

Immediate follow-up is essential for prompt compliance and avoidance of a "scene." Don't wait until you are provoked, exasperated, or desperate. You cannot give an important instruction while attention is diverted elsewhere. Remember, you are helping to teach children good habits of listening, attending, and promptness—you do not teach these things by scolding or giving punishment. If you follow through, the child will know you mean business, and few warnings will be necessary.

Be Consistent

Perhaps only complete rejection disturbs children's security more than inconsistency. If you expect to get consistency in response to direction, you must provide a

When trying to improve poor compliance to instructions, try this method:

- Start by asking the children to do the things you know they already like to do in order to change their negative behavior toward that direction.
- Ask them to do neutral things that are neither particularly pleasant or unpleasant to them.
- Finally, work up to the tasks or directions that were, in the past, disagreeable.

consistent stimulus and a consistent expectation of performance from day to day. A recent cartoon pinpointed the dilemma in which many children find themselves. The child says, "When you wanna do somethin' scary, you're a little tiny boy, but when they want you to do somethin' scary, you're a great big boy." A reward or punishment that is consistent in frequency of occurrence, in kind, and in application is essential, as is a united front by adults on policy matters. Always let the children know what they can expect from you, and you expect their best of them.

Praise Others

Praise more than you administer discipline. It is important to praise effort as well as performance, because trying hard shows responsibility, even when the results are not perfect. However, be sure that your praise is sincere. Children quickly sense lack of sincerity. Under no circumstances should you ever resort to bribes. They backfire, can cause great harm, and suggest the opposite of good behavior by encouraging deals and the placing of a price tag on being good and responsible. Avoid expecting perfection, and don't be afraid to admit that even you make mistakes.

Be Assertive

It is important to distinguish between the terms *assertive* and *aggressive* as applied to behavioral control. **Aggressive behavior** is displayed by teachers who nag, accuse, argue, speak in anger, get into power struggles, and use harsh punishment. **Assertive behavior,** on the other hand, is apparent in teachers who make clear, direct

Consider the following tips on the value of consistency:

- To survive in society, children must learn to function in their reality. Ignoring their reality or manipulating it does not help them learn how to cope.
- Children must relate to a number of different people during the course of the day (parents, classroom teachers, physical education teacher, coach). Therefore, a single set of expectations makes life easier and increases the probability of acceptable behavior.
- Children respond positively to the security of a consistent routine. It enables them to function more freely and puts them at ease when they know what to expect.
- Consistency in the form of specific statements and direction is much easier for the child to respond to than general comments. This helps reduce ambiguity. For example, it is better to say, "Put the ball in the bag" than "Don't play with the ball."
- Life without limits is unrealistic. Life with inconsistent limits is scary. Clarifying acceptable limits of behavior and consistently applying the consequences of violating these limits promotes security and self-control.
- Self-control develops gradually. The more consistent our treatment of children, the more consistent will be their development of acceptable self-control.
- Children pattern their behavior after significant others. Teachers are significant others; therefore, the role model you provide enables children to act more consistently.

requests; reveal honest feelings; persist; listen to children's points of view; give brief reasons; and carry out reasonable consequences for misbehavior.

When children view you as assertive in your discipline, they will treat you with respect and will attempt to take responsibility for their actions. Teachers who are viewed as aggressive tend to establish control out of fear and do little to help children develop self-control.

Demonstrate Trust

Show children that you have faith in them by the responsibility that you give them. If you believe in them and expect their best, you are more likely to get their best. Don't be afraid of losing their love. Children can understand that it is precisely because you *do* care for them that you provide redirection, restraint, and reprimands when warranted. On the other hand, don't be afraid of "spoiling" children through the generous use of kindness, affection, and consideration. These qualities don't spoil children, but lack of direction, inconsistency, and indecision do.

REQUIREMENTS FOR POSITIVE DISCIPLINE

Teachers with positive discipline exhibit remarkable similarity in their **authority style.** Although there is not a universal formula or set of specific behaviors that will guarantee effective discipline, teachers who are successful in class control tend to develop their authority style by being positive role models, efficient planners, effective communicators, and thorough assessors of behavior.

CONCEPT 13.6
Positive discipline tends to be mastered by teachers who are good role models, effective communicators and accept responsibility for thorough planning and continual self-assessment.

Be a Positive Role Model

Communicating genuine interest in your subject matter, enthusiasm for learning, and a willingness to participate with the class will do much to create a positive atmosphere. Displaying interest in your pupils as people by establishing high but reasonable expectations for them and helping them reach these goals is a key to being a positive role model.

Teachers who are effective role models display confidence and willingness to accept their role of authority, are personable and fair, and react appropriately and consistently when children misbehave. They clearly communicate the boundaries of acceptable behavior and are impartial in using their authority when these boundaries are overstepped.

Techniques for being a positive role model:

- Be assertive.
- Be proactive.
- Act in proportion to the need.
- Be consistent.
- Clearly communicate expectations.
- Convey interest and enthusiasm.
- Set reasonable individual and group goals.

Teachers who set positive examples for children are doing much to provide a role model for self-discipline. Failure to establish a positive role model will inhibit your effectiveness in gaining and maintaining class control.

Plan Efficiently

Teachers with good discipline are generally good planners. They take the time to plan their lessons carefully, are well organized, and make maximum effective use of their time. Thorough planning enables you to be properly prepared. Physical education teachers need to pay particular attention to this because of the size of their teaching environment, the necessity of moving groups of children from place to place, the need for frequent changes in formation, and the nature of the physical activity itself. Teachers with effective class control have taken the time to plan their lessons thoroughly in a manner that is responsive to the needs, interests, and ability levels of their students, and they are organized in their approach to learning.

The lesson and the gymnasium environment itself should be carefully organized to make maximum effective use of your time. Lessons that make the best use of the allotted time are those that provide for a maximum of active involvement by all of the students. Poor lesson planning; failure to organize the class efficiently; and inactivity brought about by lack of equipment, waiting in line, or long, detailed explanations do little to create an atmosphere conducive to positive discipline.

The physical appearance of the gymnasium is also important. An atmosphere that is bright and cheery with a generally pleasant appearance is conducive to positive behavior. Neatly displayed bulletin boards, posters, and

Suggestions for efficient planning:

- Carefully prepare each lesson.
- Overplan for each lesson.
- Develop lessons around individual and group needs.
- Take into consideration the space to be used.
- Plan to minimize formation changes.
- Establish and be consistent in the use of common class management techniques.
- Have ample equipment available, in good repair and quickly obtainable for use.
- Plan for maximum activity and minimum inactivity.
- Create a physical environment that is pleasant and safe.
- Promote an atmosphere of learning enjoyment.

Techniques for effective communication:

- Develop effective verbal and nonverbal communication skills.
- Strive for meaningful interaction with children.
- Work for maximum communication with children.
- Use positive reinforcement techniques.
- Work toward giving *each* child some form of positive reinforcement in each lesson.
- Respond to children's attempts to behave in a positive manner.
- Avoid nagging, teasing, shaming, belittling, and other aggressive forms of communication.
- Be consistent in your meaning and use of verbal and nonverbal forms of communication.

Organization is important to the planning process and is a key element in maintaining good class control in the physical education setting. The consistent use of a variety of class management techniques contributes to class organization. Policies for changing clothes (if appropriate), squad formations, roll-call techniques, and methods of obtaining and securing equipment are all important organizational considerations.

The manner in which you respond to children's behavior is an aspect of communication that is sometimes overlooked. Remember that good behavior is not suddenly or magically achieved by most children. It is a learned process that is shaped over time. This learning process is rooted in the teacher's responses to the students' attempts to improve their behavior. Responses that focus on the positive aspects of behavior rather than on the negative aspects have repeatedly been shown to result in better behavior (Canter and Canter, 1984). In no case should teasing, belittling, or condescending statements be used as a method of responding to students' poor behavior.

---

activity charts that are frequently changed promote interest and give students a sense that you care.

Communicate Effectively

Teachers who can minimize and deal with behavioral problems effectively tend to be good communicators. Those who recognize the power of both the spoken word and the unspoken word and who systematically work at interacting positively with children generally have fewer behavior problems. The use of positive reinforcement techniques rather than negative or criticizing behaviors has been shown to be effective in winning the respect and attention of children. Attempting to give attention to all students (not just the gifted or those who need extra attention) and to reinforce their positive behaviors both verbally and nonverbally are techniques used by teachers with good class control.

Self-Assess

Teachers who periodically assess their own teaching behavior and the learning styles of their students generally have fewer behavior problems with their classes. The process of self-assessment enables teachers to stop for a moment, look the situation over, and chart a new course, if necessary, for a more positive direction. Often minor changes in modeling, planning, or communication techniques will result in dramatically improved behavior on the part of the class. Self-assessment is most effective with the aid of videotaped replays of lessons and peer evaluations of your teaching.

It is a common mistake for physical education teachers to neglect assessing their students' behavior and to assume that they can use identical methods with each class they see during the course of the day. Remember, your job in maintaining class control and promoting self-control is considerably more complex than that of the classroom teacher. First of all, you deal not with one class for the entire day but with many classes for only a portion of the day. Second, the physical environment of the gymnasium or playground itself tends to evoke a different set of behaviors than those found in the classroom. Last, and most important, each class that comes to your program tends to be a direct reflection of the standards for behavior established by the particular classroom teacher. Therefore, you may need to modify your methods for gaining and maintaining control for each class. Constructive feedback from individual teachers and observation in the classroom will help you make any necessary adjustments. Do not assume that because a certain set of techniques worked well the previous year with the third grade (or any other grade), this year's third graders will respond in the same manner. You will be the one who must make the adjustments if you are going to be successful in your discipline.

SUMMARY

This chapter dealt with the important topic of discipline. Successful teaching demands helping children move from teacher-controlled behaviors toward greater self-control. Overreliance on teacher-imposed standards of control and punishment fails to provide children with both opportunities and responsibility for their own behavior.

Techniques of punishment are sometimes valid, but they should not replace greater student responsibility for his or her own self-control. Punishment often fails to get at the underlying cause of the behavioral problem and is merely a short-term attempt to maintain class control.

Several techniques for helping children to develop the long-term goal of increased self-control were discussed. The value of establishing rules and routines, being reasonable and consistent, following through, being assertive, and demonstrating trust in children was discussed. Additionally, the characteristics of teachers with positive authority styles were described in terms of being positive role models, effective communicators, efficient planners, and critical self-assessors of personal teaching behaviors.

TEACHING TIPS

Guidelines for self-assessment:

- Focus on regular, systematic review of your teaching techniques.
- Take stock of the directions your class-control techniques are leading and chart a new direction if warranted.
- Observe children in a variety of settings.
- Observe the classroom teacher's control techniques.
- Modify your techniques as needed to fit the specific children you are dealing with.
- Do not assume that teaching the same way as last year will be appropriate for this year.

COMPLEMENTARY READINGS

Belka, D. E. (1991). Let's manage to have some order. *JOPERD* 62:21–23.

Boyce, B. A., and P. Walker. (1991). Establishing structure in the elementary school. *Strategies* 5:20–23.

French, R., L. Silliman, and H. Henderson. (1990). Too much time out! *Strategies* 3:5–7.

Hill, K. L. (1991). Pay attention. *JOPERD* 62:18–20.

Miller, S., and J. McCormick, eds. (1991). Stress: Teaching children to cope. *JOPERD* 62:53–70.

Ratliffe, T., L. Ratliffe, and B. Bie. (1991). Creating a learning environment: Class management strategies for elementary PE teachers. *JOPERD* 62:24–27.

Spark, W. G. (1993). Promoting self-responsibility and decision making with at-risk students. *JOPERD* 64:74–78.

Vogler, E. W., and P. Bishop. (1990). Management of disruptive behavior in physical education. *The Physical Educator* 47:16–26.

SUPPLEMENTARY READINGS

Canter, L. (1988). Assertive discipline and the search for the perfect classroom. *Young Children* 43:24–26.

Canter, L., and M. Canter. (1984). *Assertive Discipline Elementary Resource Materials Workbook Grades K–6.* Santa Monica, CA: Canter and Associates Inc.

Gartrell, D. (1987). Assertive discipline: Unhealthy for children and other living things. *Young Children,* 42:10–11.

Hitz, R., and A. Driscoll. (1988). Praise or encouragement? New insights into praise: Implications for early childhood teachers. *Young Children* 43:6–13.

Hellison, D. R., and T. J. Templin. (1991). *A Reflective Approach to Teaching Physical Education.* Champaign, IL: Human Kinetics.

CHAPTER 14

Teaching Styles

Key Concept

Effective Teachers Modify Their Teaching Behaviors Based on the Motor
Development and Movement Skill Learning Needs of Their Students

Chapter Objectives

The purpose of this chapter is to provide you with the tools to:
• Identify what is meant by the term *teaching style*.
• Discuss how a child's motor development and level of movement skill learning
  influence the selection and use of various teaching styles.
• Discuss the role of student comprehension and compliance in the selection and
  use of different teaching styles.
• Distinguish between direct and indirect teaching styles, their appropriate use, and
  philosophical base.
• Outline the command, task, reciprocal, small group, exploratory, guided-
  discovery, and limitation methods of teaching.
• Demonstrate how the limitation method draws on elements from a variety of
  teaching styles.
• Speculate about the impact of various teaching styles on the learner.

Terms to Remember

Teaching Style
Student Comprehension
Compliance
Inviting the Learner
Directing the Learner
Manipulating the Learner
Spectrum of Teaching Styles
Direct Teaching Styles
Teacher-Centered Methods
Behavioristic Learning Theory
Command Teaching
Task Teaching

Reciprocal Teaching
Small Group Teaching
Indirect Teaching Styles
Child-Centered Methods
Learning to Learn
Cognitive Learning Theory
Exploratory Teaching
Discovery Teaching
Observation Phase
Movement Challenges
Limitation Method

A variety of teaching styles may be used effectively in the developmental physical education program. In recent years a great deal has been written about various styles of teaching. Probably the best known work, now in its fourth edition, is by Mosston and Ashworth and is entitled *Teaching Physical Education* (1994). This text was one of the first books to present a spectrum of teaching styles ranging from the most direct, or command, style to the most indirect, or exploratory, style.

Selecting an appropriate teaching style to use in a lesson should not be a matter left to chance. Instead, you should carefully examine a variety of factors concerning your students and the environment prior to using a particular style. This chapter focuses on these factors and outlines the structure, advantages, and disadvantages of several teaching styles that have gained popularity in the physical education profession.

FACTORS THAT INFLUENCE SELECTION OF VARIOUS TEACHING STYLES

For years there has been considerable discussion about the relative merits of various teaching styles. In fact, an undeclared "war" was waged between some traditional physical educators, who tended to favor more direct, teacher-centered approaches, and some movement educators, who tended to favor more indirect, child-centered approaches. This disagreement has polarized many professional physical educators and has resulted in their insistence on adopting and using one set of teaching styles to the exclusion of others. This rigid approach is unfortunate because it is the children who lose the benefit of being exposed to a variety of methodologies geared to their developmental level.

Declaring that one style of teaching is superior to another is not sufficient. Teachers who are sensitive to the needs, interests, and developmental level of their students, and who have considered both the environmental conditions and task complexity carefully, select from a variety of teaching styles and refrain from taking sides in the teaching style war.

TEACHING TIPS

The developmental approach to teaching physical education recognizes that:

- All children learn differently.
- Children are learning how to learn.
- Motor development and movement skill learning factors should be primary determiners of the use of specific teaching techniques.
- Student comprehension and compliance factors must be carefully considered before selecting a teaching style.
- Factors within the task, the individual, and environment itself may dramatically influence the selection of one style over another.

CONCEPT 14.1
Use of a particular teaching style is determined, in large measure, by specific student factors of motor development and movement skill learning.

Movement Skill Learning Factors

When children and adults learn a new movement skill, they tend to go through a series of learning levels. The three levels of learning a movement skill discussed earlier in Chapter 3 ("Movement Skill Acquisition") and reiterated here are based on two important developmental

---

A teaching style is a specific set of decisions made by the instructor to achieve the learning objectives of the lesson that result in identifiable behaviors on the part of the teacher.

Recognition of the learner's place in this skill-learning hierarchy is important because it helps to determine both the teaching styles and movement activities selected for use.

concepts: first, that the acquisition of movement skills progresses from the simple to the complex, and second, that people proceed gradually from general to specific as they develop and refine movement skills.

Beginning/Novice Level.   Individuals, be they children or adults, at the beginning/novice level of acquiring a new movement skill first develop an awareness of just what the skill actually entails. They begin to form a mental picture (cognitive map) and then explore the skill itself. Exploration of the skill generally occurs as a single unit; the task is broken down into its simplest elements and practiced rather than being combined with other skills. At this level the learner does not have good control of the skill but gets used to the task and forms a gross general framework idea of the task. During this first level, the learner forms a mental picture of the skill and attempts to bring the skill under conscious control.

As the learner proceeds with exploring the elements of the skill, the process of discovery begins. The learner discovers ways of performing the skill through problem-solving and other indirect means, such as observing others and studying photos, film, or textual information. The learner gradually gains greater control and begins to coordinate the movements involved in executing the skill. During this period, basic performance of the skill tends to be under less conscious control than during the exploratory stage.

Individuals at the beginning level of learning a movement skill benefit from indirect teaching styles that help them develop first an awareness of the skill and foster freedom of movement exploration and guided discovery. These styles permit the learner to explore the movement task in its many forms and to develop a conscious mental image of the task. These same individuals tend to be at the initial and elementary stages within the fundamental movement phase of motor development. They are typically younger children of preschool and primary-grade age but may be older children, adolescents, or adults. Remember that, although development is age-influenced, it is not age-dependent. Therefore, individuals at the early stages of learning a new movement skill—whether they are children *or* adults—will benefit greatly from indirect styles of teaching that help them get a general idea of how to execute the task.

Intermediate/Practice Level.   Once the learner has gotten a general idea of how to perform a skill, it is practiced and combined with other movement skills. At the intermediate/practice level of learning a movement

skill, the individual experiments with movement phrases. Skills are combined, elaborated upon, and practiced in a variety of ways. Teaching styles may be indirect or direct, with emphasis on practice through application of the skill to a variety of game, rhythm, and self-testing situations. The use of indirect teaching styles during the intermediate level is a logical extension of the same indirect teaching styles emphasized during the beginning stage of learning a skill. These experiences differ only in that various movement skills are combined rather than being dealt with in isolation. Individuals at the mature stage within the fundamental movement phase and at the transitional stage within the specialized sport-skill phase of motor development benefit from movement experiences that permit the use of both indirect and direct styles of teaching. Individuals combining numerous movement skills are typically children who have mastered their fundamental stability, locomotor, and manipulative skills. They tend to benefit from movement activities that incorporate combinations of various skills, skill drills, and basic lead-up activities to the characteristic sports and recreational activities of their culture.

Advanced/Fine-Tuning Level.   The advanced/fine-tuning level of learning a movement skill is characterized by a high degree of skill refinement. The combined skills that were selected at the intermediate level are further practiced and refined. The skills are frequently incorporated into competitive and recreational activities. Individuals at the advanced level focus on improved accuracy, precision, and economy of movement. At this level performance appears to be automatic, with little conscious attention given to the elements of the task as it is being performed. Often when a skilled performer reaches the advanced level, unique, personalized modifications begin to appear in the skill. These modifications may be subtle, or they may be blatantly obvious, as in Michael Jordan's basketball acrobatics.

Generally speaking, the teacher in the regularly scheduled elementary school physical education program does not have a great number of children at the advanced level of learning movement skills. Although some children may be at this level in some areas, the majority of children are at the beginning or intermediate level. Appropriate experiences, however, should be provided for children at all levels of ability.

The teaching styles you select and the movement activities you include in the program will be determined by where your students are in their phase and stage of

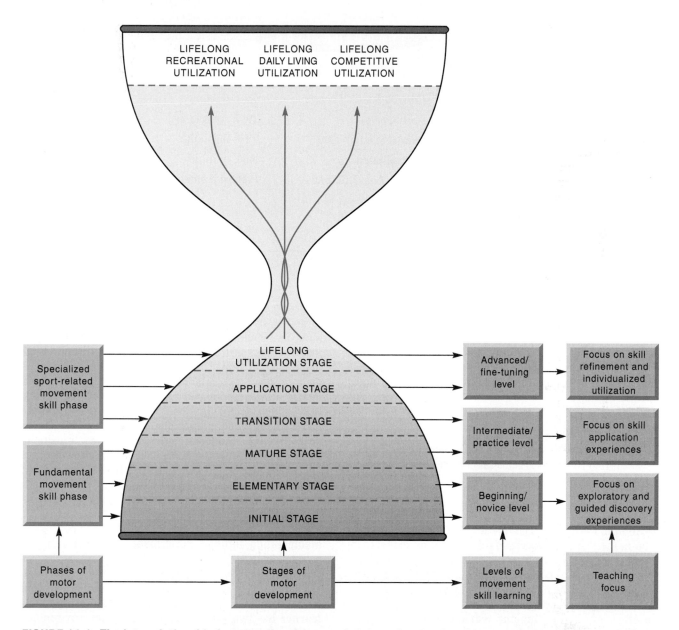

FIGURE 14.1 *The interrelationship between the phases and stages of motor development, levels of movement skill learning, and teaching focus in movement skill acquisition.*

motor development and at what level of movement skill learning they are functioning. Figure 14.1 illustrates the interaction between the phases and stages of motor development, the levels of movement skill learning, and the appropriate teaching focus.

Student Comprehension and Compliance Factors

The level of **student comprehension,** or ability to understand, and the ability and willingness to comply with instructions play an important role in selecting a teaching

TEACHING TIPS

Factors to consider when selecting a teaching style:

Learner Factors	*Environmental Factors*	*Task Factors*	*Teacher Factors*
Stage of motor development	Facilities	Task complexity	Philosophy
Level of movement skill learning	Available equipment	Task difficulty	Personality
Level of cognitive comprehension	Time allotted	Risk of injury	Lesson objectives
Fitness level	Safety considerations	Pattern formation	Ability to adapt
Self-control	Class size		Class control
Interest			Self-confidence

style. **Compliance** deals with the complexity of the movement task, the ability level of the children, and their level of self-control. You must adjust your teaching behavior to the needs of your students and determine whether you "invite" the learner to perform, "direct" the learner to perform, or "manipulate" the learner through the performance.

 CONCEPT 14.2
Student comprehension and compliance play important roles in the selection and use of various teaching styles.

Inviting to Perform.   The first level of teacher intervention in the learning process involves inviting the learner to perform. If the movement tasks that make up the lesson can be easily comprehended, and the children are capable and willing to comply with your instructions, then it is appropriate to extend an invitation to perform. In other words, **inviting the learner** to perform frees you to select indirect teaching styles to satisfy the skill objectives of the lesson. Styles that are child-centered and that incorporate movement exploration and guided discovery approaches are appropriate when inviting performance. These indirect styles of teaching are particularly effective during the early stages of the fundamental movement phase and at the beginning level of learning a new movement skill.

Directing to Perform.   When the individual progresses to higher skill levels or is required to combine two or more movement skills, experienced teachers frequently modify their instructional approach by **directing the learner** to perform. Students' ability to comprehend what the movement task entails or how to actually perform the task is often complicated by the complexity of the task itself. Safety factors involved in performance of the task and available time, equipment, and facilities all have to be considered. Students at the mature and transitional stages of motor development and at the intermediate level in learning a new skill tend to benefit from direct styles of teaching as well as indirect styles. The use of the command, task, reciprocal or small group style is effective for learners at this level.

Manipulating through Performance.   Sometimes, if a movement task is too cognitively complex for the performer, if the requirements are very exacting, or if safety is a major consideration, it becomes advisable to manipulate the learner through the task. **Manipulating the learner** has two aspects: manipulating the environment or physically manipulating the learner. You may, for example, manipulate the environment when teaching the mature overhand throwing pattern by using props or learning devices that help the learner get the idea of stepping forward on the opposite foot or using good hip rotation. On the other hand, when teaching a back handspring, you will, at first, want to physically manipulate the learner through the task several times at reduced speed. Both types of manipulation are used to help give the learner a "feel" for the skill.

Physical manipulation is frequently used with individuals with mental disabilities. Actual patterning through a specific movement task is used to reinforce verbal commands. In this way the learner not only receives auditory and visual cues about the task but also receives tactile and kinesthetic cues. The use of several sensory modalities assists slow learners in grasping the essentials of what is being requested.

Whether you invite, direct, or manipulate children through performance of a movement skill depends on your students. Being sensitive to their individual needs and to the needs of the class as a whole can help you incorporate appropriate teaching techniques at the appropriate time. It is altogether possible that within a single lesson you will do all three. You may invite performance by providing the class with movement challenges and other indirect forms of instruction. You may direct performance by providing specific instructional cues, teacher and student demonstrations, and other direct forms of instruction. You may even manipulate individual children by assisting them through various movement tasks.

STYLES OF TEACHING

A teaching style is a set of identifiable teacher behaviors governed by a pattern of decisions made prior to, during, and after the teaching act itself. It does not refer to one's personal idiosyncrasies of teaching, but to how one actually implements these decisions. A **spectrum of teaching styles,** a term first used by Mosston (1966) and now universally accepted, refers to the framework that contains a variety of teaching styles together (Mosston and Ashworth, 1994).

Skilled teachers are thoroughly versed in a variety of teaching styles that they can apply depending on the needs of their students and the specific objectives of the lesson. Teaching is a learned behavior that is able to be modified and changed. The manner in which we interact with children to help them learn is influenced by many factors. We have already discussed important movement skill learning factors, student comprehension, and compliance factors. Other factors, such as the teacher's personality, expertise, values, and learning goals, also influence the choice of styles. Student factors, such as the level of maturity, behavior, and interest in the lesson must also be considered, as should the available facilities, equipment, time, and safety.

The decisions made before, during and after the teaching act that concern your students, their learning environment, and the specific skills to be learned should lead you to making informed choices concerning the styles of teaching to incorporate into each of your lessons. Table 14.1 outlines the anatomy of any teaching style in terms of the decisions that must be made prior to (preparation), during (evaluation), and after (execution) teaching.

Teaching styles range from those that are direct, or teacher-centered, to those that are indirect, or child-centered. Few master teachers use any one teaching style to the exclusion of all others. Instead, they use a variety of direct and indirect styles based on the factors discussed earlier. Teachers who favor direct styles of teaching tend to use the command and task methods. Those who prefer more indirect styles often use the movement exploration and guided-discovery methods. Teachers who see the merit of both focus on a combination of styles (Figure 14.2).

The following critical considerations should guide you in selecting the teaching style that is appropriate for a particular movement skill theme:
- Phase and stage of motor development.
- Level of movement skill learning.
- Ability to handle the task complexity.
- Comprehension of the task.
- Behavioral ability to comply.
(As you move from lesson to lesson you will need to reassess each of the above factors.)

The act of teaching is governed by decision making—decisions about the learner, the task, and the environment. According to Mosston and Ashworth (1994, p. 3), "The entire structure of the Spectrum stems from the initial premise that teaching behavior is a chain of decision making. Every *deliberate* act of teaching is a result of a previously made decision."

TABLE 14.1   *Key Decisions Made Before, During, and After a Lesson*

Preparation Decisions	Execution Decisions	Evaluation Decisions
• Objectives of the lesson • Location of lesson • Duration of lesson • Pace of the lesson • Equipment to be used • Room organization • Anticipated learning style • Teaching style	• Adherance to preparation decisions • Lesson adjustments	• Forms of learner feedback • Informal student assessment • Formal student assessment • Lesson assessment • Self-assessment

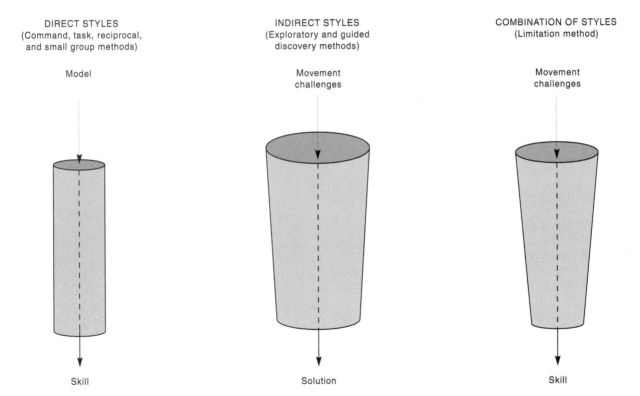

FIGURE 14.2   *Visual representation of three different styles of teaching.*

Direct Styles

Direct teaching styles are the traditional teaching approaches that have been used by many physical educators and classroom teachers for years. These styles are **teacher-centered methods** in that the teacher makes all or most of the decisions concerning what, how, and when the student is to perform. The use of teacher-centered approaches is based on **behavioristic learning theory,** which contends that learning occurs from the outside-in through the correct reproduction of events. Therefore, proponents of the behavioristic viewpoint hold that because we already know how a movement skill should be performed, it is our responsibility as teachers to help children model or learn these "correct" techniques in the most expedient manner possible. Additionally, because time is at a premium and "incorrect" learning will only slow down and interfere with correct learning, direct styles are advocated by those who favor the behavioristic view.

CONCEPT 14.3
Mechanically correct performance of movement skills is a primary objective of teacher-centered styles of teaching.

Direct teaching styles have many advantages. They are efficient and focused, and they leave little chance for misunderstanding or misinterpretation. The structured learning environment of direct styles is conducive to good class control, and direct styles are easy to use with individuals or with large groups of children. They get right to the point: learning the mechanically correct technique for the skillful performance of a movement task. There are some disadvantages in using direct teaching styles of teaching. They often fail to allow for individual differences (developmental appropriateness) and inventiveness of the learner. They are based on the false assumption that children have reached about the same level of learning and progress at the same rate (age-group appropriateness). Direct styles tend to be more concerned with the goal or product of the learning experience than the process of learning involved.

Although direct styles of teaching often have disadvantages, they can be modified in a variety of ways. Both verbal and nonverbal communication techniques may be altered significantly by the teacher. The manner in which the class is conducted need not be like that of a drill sergeant but may rather be one in which duties, responsibilities, and privileges are shared, with the teacher still making the key decisions. The command, task, reciprocal, and small group methods are four of the most popular of the numerous direct styles of teaching.

Command Style.   **Command teaching** is the time-honored method of teaching movement skills. Its primary purpose is to learn the task quickly and accurately, in compliance with the decisions made by the teacher. It is a process of replication, reproduction, and duplication of the "correct performance." Command teaching consists

Task cards can be used effectively with young readers.

of (1) a short explanation and demonstration of the skill to be performed, (2) student practice prior to giving further directions or pointing out specific errors, (3) general comments to the class about their performance, (4) further explanation and demonstration if necessary, (5) student practice with coaching hints to individuals or groups having difficulty, and (6) implementation of the skill in an appropriate activity. The command method makes all of the preperformance and performance decisions for the learner. The teacher controls what is to be practiced, how it is to be done, and when to begin and cease activity. Uniformity, conformity, and replication are emphasized.

Task Style.   **Task teaching,** also known as the practice method (Mosston and Ashworth, 1994), is similar to the command method because the teacher still controls what is to be practiced and how it is to be performed. However, in using the task method, the teacher permits a greater degree of decision making on the part of the children. The learner has more time to practice the skill individually and privately and receives more individual feedback from the teacher. More freedom and flexibility are introduced into the learning environment. Children are given more responsibility for themselves but are not allowed to choose what to do or how to do the assigned task.

When using the task method, the teacher follows a sequence of (1) explanation and demonstration of different levels of the task to be performed (task cards of varying difficulty in written or pictorial form may be used), (2) practice of the designated task by students at their own pace and at their particular level of ability, (3) help for individuals or groups having difficulty and challenges to advanced students to achieve higher levels of performance.

The task method permits children to work at their own level of ability and may be undertaken on an individual, reciprocal, or small group basis. Individuals may work alone at the task provided by the teacher and evaluate themselves, or they may work with partners who assess their performance. Students may work together in groups of three or four on specific tasks, with one performing, a second evaluating, and a third recording the students' performance of the task. The task method provides more freedom for the learner than the command method, is an effective approach to use with large groups, allows for individual standards of achievement, and maximizes active participation with limited resources.

Reciprocal and Small Group Styles.

Reciprocal teaching, sometimes referred to as "peer teaching," permits individual students to work with a partner in learning a new skill. **Small group teaching** is similar except that a third person is involved. With both reciprocal and small group instruction the learner is given immediate feedback from her partner that is based on specific criteria established by the teacher. Reciprocal and small group teaching are excellent means of involving the entire class, focusing on error correction, and promoting positive socialization. In essence, reciprocal teaching establishes one student as the "mini-teacher" and the other as the learner. Care should be taken by the instructor when circulating through the class to reinforce the role of the mini-teacher by giving her information on the learner's performance. Failure to do so, and speaking directly to the learner, will undermine the role and responsibilities of the mini-teacher. Small group instruction is identical to the reciprocal approach but involves a third person who serves as a recorder.

Using archery as an example, one student may serve as the learner, a second as the mini-teacher, and the third as the recorder. The learner performs the specific task of shooting the arrow. The mini-teacher checks for correct notching, stance, arm position, and release, following specific

criteria established by the instructor. The recorder draws a bullseye on a 3 x 5 card and marks where the arrows hit the target. Meanwhile, the instructor circulates among the class speaking directly to the mini-teacher about specific aspects of each learner's archery mechanics, thereby reinforcing her role.

Indirect Styles

Indirect styles of teaching movement skills came into vogue in North America during the early 1960s. Various indirect teaching styles had been advocated prior to that time, but it was not until the work of Rudolph Laban and Liselott Diem found its way to North America that educators began to look seriously at the potential for using indirect teaching styles in movement skill learning. **Indirect teaching styles** focus on the use of **child-centered methods** of teaching, methods that put the child at the heart of the learning process.

CONCEPT 14.4
Learning how to learn is an important objective of indirect styles of teaching.

Indirect styles of teaching were initially rejected by many physical educators steeped in the direct methods of command and task teaching. Soon, however, a distinct division between those who have come to be known as "traditional physical educators" and those called "movement educators" developed. Each group claimed that its

Child-centered teaching methods are based on the philosophy that learning is more than the reproduction and modeling of mechanically "correct" movement behaviors. Teachers using child-centered methods believe that **learning to learn** through experimentation, problem-solving, and self-discovery is essential to any "real" learning. Indirect teaching styles are grounded in **cognitive learning theory,** which holds that learning is an internal process that occurs from the inside-out through incorrect mastery attempts, and that the process of learning is equally as important as the product.

teaching methods were superior; hence, the start of the undeclared war about teaching styles.

The factions who disagree have softened their previously rigid points of view, and many educators, rather than identifying solely with either direct or indirect styles, now recognize the value of both. An important shift in focus from the method to the learner has occurred. In trying to gear their methods of instruction to suit the learner rather than making the learner suit the methods, educators have become more developmentally oriented in their choice of teaching styles. As a result, indirect teaching styles have finally won their place in the spectrum of teaching behaviors used in physical education. Indirect styles of teaching do not automatically ensure optimal learning any more than direct styles do. However, they do provide the learner with greater opportunity for freedom and assumption of responsibility within the educational setting.

Indirect teaching styles allow the student considerable freedom to set goals and determine how these goals are to be accomplished. In other words, children become more involved in the learning process itself by being given opportunities and encouragement to explore and experiment with movement in a variety of ways. Another important advantage of indirect styles of teaching is that they allow for individual differences between learners. All students are able to find a degree of success at their particular level of ability.

The disadvantages of indirect teaching styles are mainly that they are time-consuming and that teachers unfamiliar with them frequently find them difficult to use productively. Indirect styles require practice and patience on the part of the teacher. Plenty of time must be permitted for experimentation, trial and error, and question asking. Because some teachers have not been trained in these techniques, they find indirect styles difficult to use. They often have trouble maintaining class control, structuring challenging movement problems, and providing for continuity both within lessons and between lessons. These disadvantages, however, do not mean that indirect styles are inferior to direct styles of teaching movement. On the contrary, indirect styles play an important role in movement skill learning, particularly at the early levels. Indirect styles of teaching movement generally center on movement exploration and guided-discovery methods.

Exploratory Style.   **Exploratory teaching** for movement skill learning requires the teacher to present broad-based movement challenges or questions without requiring a specific solution. Any reasonable solution of the

task is considered acceptable. The teacher neither demonstrates how to perform the action nor presents a detailed verbal description. The students are given the opportunity to perform the movement task as they see fit. By focusing primarily on the learning process itself rather than on the product of learning, the exploratory method does not emphasize form or precision nor does it require each child to perform the task in the same manner. The teacher is interested, however, in providing meaningful movement tasks in which children are encouraged to explore the movement potential of their bodies, develop mature fundamental movement skills, find success, and express themselves in a creative manner. Movement exploration may be totally free or guided by the teacher.

Guided-Discovery Style.   **Discovery teaching** permits the learner to "discover" a movement or skill concept by responding to a series of questions posed by the teacher. The teacher leads students, by using a set of questions and movement challenges, to a predetermined learning objective. The learner is given plenty of opportunity for expression, creativity, and experimentation but is somewhat restricted in how he may respond to the movement

Three responses to the movement challenge of "How can you balance on three body parts at a low level?"

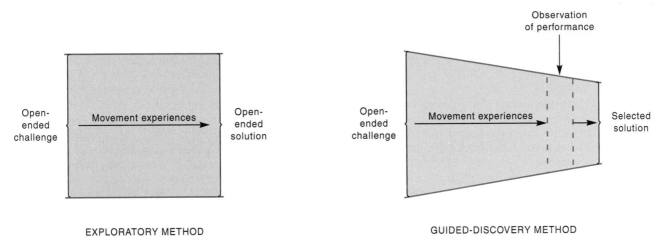

FIGURE 14.3 *Differences between the exploratory and guided-discovery methods, both of which utilize indirect approaches.*

tasks presented by the teacher's structure of the questions. The teacher still encourages a wide variety of responses, but the presentation of the task is modified. For example, the teacher may say, "Can you find three different ways to bounce the ball?" or "Can you move from one end of the balance beam to the other, often changing your direction?" (or level, speed, base of support, and so forth). The children then experiment with several ways of accomplishing the tasks. The teacher continues by asking specific questions and posing movement challenges concerning giving and receiving force to the ball, or about principles of static and dynamic balance. The end goal of the lesson is increased skill and knowledge in ball dribbling or body balancing.

The method that the learner uses to solve the movement challenges posed by the teacher causes movement exploration and guided discovery to be considered separately here. Instead of refraining from establishing a model of performance and accepting all solutions as correct (as with free exploration), the guided-discovery method incorporates an observation phase into the total experience. The **observation phase** takes the form of students observing fellow students, the teacher, or individuals on film or videotape as they solve the movement challenges presented. Only after the students have had an opportunity to solve the problem within the limits of their own understanding and ability is the observation phase used.

Also, instead of movement problems being entirely open-ended, as with the exploratory method, questions are gradually funneled in such a manner that they lead

children to discover for themselves how to perform the particular task. At the end of the process of attempting solutions to the movement problem, the children have an opportunity to evaluate their interpretations in light of the solutions of others (Figure 14.3).

The key to effective use of any indirect teaching style is the thoughtful construction and use of **movement challenges** that allow for a variety of interpretations but still remain within the confines of the stated objectives of the lesson. Although reasonable solutions to movement challenges are considered correct, one should not infer that the lesson will take its own course simply because the instructor poses one or two questions to the class. The teacher must constantly rephrase and restructure questions in an effort to probe and challenge each student. The primary advantages of indirect styles are that they permit greater involvement on the part of the student in the learning process, and they account for individual differences among children by permitting them to solve movement problems presented to them. With no one "best" way to perform, all children work at their own level of ability and experience some degree of success. Indirect styles allow children to develop a movement vocabulary, to express themselves creatively, and to think and develop self-direction in their learning attempts.

Combining Direct and Indirect Styles

The limitation method of teaching movement skills uses both direct and indirect styles of teaching and attempts to include the best aspects of both (Figure 14.4). With the

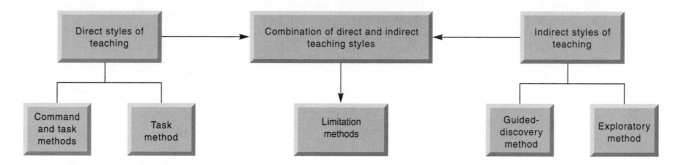

FIGURE 14.4 *The scope of teaching styles and the link between direct and indirect styles.*

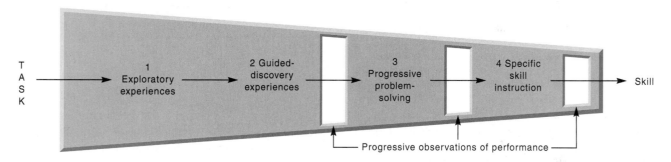

FIGURE 14.5 *Elements of the limitation method, a progressive movement challenge approach teaching movement skills.*

limitation method, children are given indirect movement challenges in the form of questions or movement problem-solving and are permitted the opportunity to explore and discover. In addition, they are also given specific skill instruction by way of direct movement challenges using task or command teaching. This combination of indirect and direct styles can be effectively used at all skill levels. The limitation method is advocated in the refinement of fundamental movement skills and the learning of new sport skills because it recognizes both the individuality of the learner and the necessity for developing a variety of movement skills during the critical elementary school years.

Limitation Method. Briefly, the **limitation method** of teaching involves a combination of indirect and direct teaching styles progressing in order from (1) free exploration to (2) guided discovery, (3) progressive problem-solving, and (4) specific skill instruction (Figure 14.5). The teacher first poses a general task to the students (free exploration). For example, the instructor may say, "Try to get the beanbag from one end of the room to the other any way you wish." Next, a few restrictions are added, and the problem may be modified with, "See how many ways you can get the beanbag across the room while remaining in one spot." Guided-discovery comments such as this are then followed by a series of questions or challenges posed to the student (progressive problem-solving). Each movement problem is stated in a way that limits the learner's response possibilities and leads directly to the desired skill. For example, "Using a throwing motion, see if you can get the beanbag across the room" may be followed by "Can you throw the beanbag overhand (underhand, and so

C O N C E P T   1 4 . 5
Both indirect and direct teaching styles may be effectively combined for effective movement skill learning.

on)?" and concluded with, "How do we stand when we throw?" or "How do we make our bodies move when we want to throw as far as we can?" The teacher continually structures and restructures a variety of questions that are progressively more narrow in scope. Up to this point a specific explanation or demonstration of how to perform the overhand throwing pattern has not been given.

After following the sequence of exploration, guided discovery, and progressive problem-solving, the teacher incorporates specific skill instruction into the lesson as needed. Many students will be able to perform the skill correctly at this point. They may be grouped with those who are experiencing difficulty and instructed to work on the overhand throw using group or peer tutoring (small group and reciprocal teaching). Those still having difficulty may observe other students or the teacher perform the desired skill and then work on it under progressively more direct supervision (task and command teaching).

The limitation method possesses the advantages of both the direct and indirect styles but few of their disadvantages. The major disadvantages are that it is time-consuming and takes practice on the part of the teacher to perfect. These problems may be outweighed, however, by the fact that each child is involved in the process of learning through exploration and guided discovery and is finding success while still working toward the goal of improved skill.

SUMMARY

This chapter focused on selecting and using various teaching styles. Teaching styles should be selected based on a combination of (1) one's philosophy of learning, (2) what we know about the developmental process, and (3) the desired goal or product of learning. If your philosophy of learning subscribes to a cognitive view of learning, then indirect teaching styles are appropriate. Learning how to learn focuses on learning from the inside-out by reconstructing incorrect mastery attempts. This view of learning emphasizes process, not simply product. If, however, your philosophy of learning is based on a behavioristic view of learning, then direct styles of teaching are appropriate. Behaviorism focuses on learning from the outside-in, through the reproduction of correct mastery attempts. The behavioristic view considers learning as primarily a product, with little importance given to the processes involved.

Developmental physical education recognizes that movement skill learning is an individual process that culminates in a product. Children must learn how to learn (the process), but it is equally important for them to become skillful movers (the product). Teachers of developmental physical education thus recognize the potential value of both indirect and direct teaching styles and reject the notion that a single teaching style is universally appropriate. The selection and use of teaching styles should be based on what we know about the learner's phase and stage of motor development, the level of movement skill learning, and the ability to comprehend and comply with the requirements of the task.

Effective teachers are well-versed in a variety of indirect and direct styles of teaching and use a variety of methods to maximize student learning and retention based on the needs of the learner.

COMPLEMENTARY READINGS

Franks, B. D., ed. (1992). The spectrum of teaching styles: A silver anniversary in physical education. *JOPERD* 63: 25–56 (series of articles).

Hopple, C. (1993). Making a change: Three veteran teachers share their experiences. *TEPE* 4, 1–11.

Mosston, M. (1992). Tug-O-War no more: Meeting teaching-learning objectives using the spectrum of teaching styles. *JOPERD* 63:27–31.

Mosston, M., and S. Ashworth. (1994). *Teaching Physical Education.* New York: Macmillan.

Mueller, R., and S. Mueller. (1992). The spectrum of teaching styles and its role in conscious deliberate teaching. *JOPERD* 63:48–53.

Rink, J. (1993). *Teaching Physical Education for Learning.* St. Louis, MO: Mosby.

Siedentop, D. (1991). *Developing Teaching Skills in Physical Education.* Mountain View, CA: Mayfield.

SUPPLEMENTARY READINGS

Darst, P. W., D. B. Zakrajsek, and V. H. Mancini, eds. (1989). *Analyzing Physical Education and Sport Instruction.* Champaign, IL: Human Kinetics (series of chapters).

Hellison, D., and T. Templin. (1991). *A Reflective Approach to Teaching Physical Education.* Champaign, IL: Human Kinetics.

Metzler, M. W. (1990). *Instructional Strategies for Physical Education.* Champaign, IL: Human Kinetics.

Rink, J. (1993). *Teaching Physical Education for Learning.* St. Louis, MO: Mosby.

Siedentop, D. (1991). *Developing Teaching Skills in Physical Education.* Mountain View, CA: Mayfield.

Safety Considerations and Legal Liability

Key Concept

Teachers Must Be Aware of the Conditions for Legal Liability and Understand that They Can Reduce the Possibility of Legal Action by Using Prudent Behavior, Adhering to Written Policies, and Having Risk Management Procedures

Chapter Objectives

The purpose of this chapter is to provide you with the tools to:
- List and discuss the conditions required for proving negligence in a court of law.
- Discuss and give examples of three forms of negligence.
- Describe what is meant by an *attractive nuisance* and provide examples of how this risk may be reduced or eliminated.
- Describe what is meant by the term *malpractice* in an educational setting.
- List and discuss possible defenses against a claim of legal liability.
- Describe common types of lawsuits brought against physical education teachers and list ways to minimize these risks.

Terms to Remember

Legal Liability
Negligence
Established Duty
Breach of Duty
Proximate Cause
Damage
Malfeasance
Misfeasance
Nonfeasance
Attractive Nuisance
Malpractice
Contributory Negligence

Age of Reason
Shared Negligence
Assumption of Risk
Act of Nature
Mandated Legislation
Title IX
PL 94–142
PL 99–457
Individualized Educational Program (IEP)
Risk Management Procedures

The very nature of physical education classes, which take place in the gymnasium, swimming pool, or playground, exposes the teacher to greater liability for accidents and injuries than any other area of the school curriculum. Being aware of this liability is critical.

A clear understanding of what constitutes legal liability, what conditions may lead to legal action, and how such problems may be minimized or avoided will do much to relieve the anxiety and promote a safe and healthful environment in which children can participate with reasonable assurance that proper precautions have been taken. This chapter provides information about some of the legal responsibilities assumed by teachers. Teachers should also become familiar with guidelines and statutes as they apply to local states, provinces, and school districts.

CONDITIONS OF LEGAL LIABILITY

Tort liability, or **legal liability,** as it is generally called, is a term meaning that someone is at fault, that this fault has caused injury or loss to another, and that someone is legally responsible. Legal liability may be incurred by the physical education teacher through three means: negligence, contributing to an attractive nuisance, and malpractice. Each is briefly discussed.

CONCEPT 15.1
Legal liability can be incurred through negligence, contributing to an attractive nuisance, and malpractice.

Negligence

Legally, **negligence** is considered to be failure on the part of an individual to act in a manner judged to be reasonable, careful, and prudent for someone of essentially equal training or status. The physical education teacher who exposes children to unreasonable risks or who fails to supervise activities properly may be considered negligent. Negligence may be claimed but must be proved in a court of law. There are four factors, all of which must be present to establish negligence: established duty, breach of duty, proximate cause, and damage.

Established duty must be determined. It must first be determined that the teacher has a duty to follow certain standards of behavior that protect the student from unreasonable risks. For example, the physical education teacher has the established duty of actively supervising all activities during the regularly scheduled physical education class period.

Breach of duty must be proved. Once an established duty has been determined, it must be proved that the teacher actually failed to conform to these standards of behavior. For example, our teacher decides to make a quick trip to the rest room, leaving the class unsupervised.

Proximate cause must be established. If a breach of duty has been proved, it must then be determined if there is a reasonable relationship between the teacher's breach of duty and the injury received. For example, while unsupervised, a student falls from the top of the climbing ropes. Damage must be determined. If proximate cause is established, damage must be determined.

Damage refers to actual injury or loss. At this point, proved injury or loss entitles the plaintiff to compensation for physical discomfort and financial loss and may place certain legal restraints on the defendant. Our student who fell from the climbing ropes receives injuries, requiring several days of missed school and several thousands of dollars in medical expenses. At this point, if all four of the conditions for negligence are proved, the teacher could be determined to be liable due to negligence for the damages that occurred and thus be required to make restitution.

The best defense against being declared liable for an injury or loss due to negligence is to prove that at least one of the four aspects of negligence is not present. A key to establishing negligence is first determining if one acted in a manner to avoid foreseeable injury or harm. The law is clear in stating that the duty of the physical education teacher is to attempt to anticipate the dangers involved in the program and to guard against negligence. If, in fact, negligence is proved, it will be declared as negligence due to malfeasance, misfeasance, or nonfeasance.

CONCEPT 15.2
Negligence may take three forms: malfeasance, misfeasance, and nonfeasance.

Overcrowded and misused playground equipment can lead to injuries that may result in a lawsuit.

Malfeasance. **Malfeasance** refers to committing an illegal act. For example, failure to comply with and implement the requirements of PL 94–142 (the Education for All Handicapped Children Act of 1975), PL 99–457 (Education of the Handicapped Amendments Act of 1986), or those of Title IX (the Educational Amendments Act of 1972) leaves a teacher liable for negligence due to malfeasance. Similarly, violations of student rights, ranging from students' being denied the due process of law to unauthorized corporal punishment to discriminating against children for hair length and clothing choices, may expose a teacher to the charge of negligence by malfeasance.

Misfeasance. **Misfeasance** is defined as improper performance of a lawful act. In other words, the teacher may operate within the law but not up to the standards deemed to be reasonable. For example, our teacher who left the class unsupervised to use the rest room could be determined negligent through misfeasance. Also, the use of improper first aid techniques in treating an injury that results in permanent disability or death falls under the

category of misfeasance. Misfeasance has occurred if you have been trained to do something but do it incorrectly.

Nonfeasance. **Nonfeasance** is defined as failure to perform a required act deemed appropriate under the circumstances. For example, failure to administer emergency first aid when a student's life is in danger could result in liability due to negligence by nonfeasance. Nonfeasance has occurred if you have been trained to do something but instead do nothing by your failure to act.

Contributing to an Attractive Nuisance

A second manner in which legal liability may be incurred for injury or harm to students is through contributing to an attractive nuisance. An **attractive nuisance** is a place or thing (e.g., a piece of equipment, supplies, or a facility). For example, a swimming pool or weight-training facility may be considered to be an attractive nuisance if left unattended or unsupervised. It is not enough to claim that students were told not to use these facilities or that warning signs were posted. If the facility permits easy, though uninvited or illegal, access, the defendant in a legal suit may be found guilty by reason of contributing to an attractive nuisance. Similarly, gymnastic equipment, boxing gloves, or fencing equipment may all be considered to be attractive nuisances if they are used by students while unsupervised. Take, for example, a situation in which the gymnastics equipment is set up in the gymnasium and the teacher is enjoying a well-deserved planning period or lunch across the hall. A student peeking into the unattended gym, seeing the equipment, and subsequently sustaining an injury may have ample grounds for a lawsuit.

CONCEPT 15.3
In physical education and athletics legal liability is often caused by contributing to an attractive nuisance.

The best way to avoid charges of contributing to an attractive nuisance is to properly store all equipment and supplies under lock and key, to arrange for proper supervision of facilities at all times, or to securely lock all facilities when they are not in use. Remember, children love to explore and experiment with their ever-expanding world. It is perfectly natural for them to be attracted to the physical education facilities and equipment. Your duty as a teacher is to ensure that the facilities and equipment are properly supervised and secured at all times.

Malpractice

Malpractice is a legal concept that has only relatively recently been applied to the teaching profession. Basically, **malpractice** is negligent behavior, improper behavior, or unethical behavior on the part of an individual, resulting in injury or damage to the student. Injury or damage may be mental, social, or emotional, as well as physical. For example, in recent years entire school districts have been sued for malpractice by individuals who were passed on from grade to grade without the basic skills required and who obtained high school diplomas without the minimal competencies expected for graduation. Physical education classes and intramural and athletic programs that use grossly improper teaching techniques (such as unauthorized corporal punishment), inappropriate activities (such as playing "murder ball," using fully inflated volleyballs or soccer balls), faulty or nonexistent spotting procedures (such as requiring

Students have a right to assume that they will receive proper instruction, training, and care. If these rights are violated, they may have grounds for claiming liability on the part of the individual teacher, administrator, or school district. In any such lawsuit, negligence must be proved. The best way to prevent a lawsuit is to exercise reasonable and proper care at all times.

students to climb to the top of the climbing ropes without prior conditioning or mats under the ropes), and archaic training methods (such as failure to provide sufficient water and rest breaks while training in hot or humid conditions) may be liable for charges of malpractice. Also, physical education programs that base grades on nonrelevant criteria may be accused of malpractice. Using criteria for grades such as attitude, hair length, and cleanliness could result in a claim of malpractice.

CONCEPT 15.4
Lawsuits claiming malpractice may be significantly reduced through continuing education and careful adherence to the stated objectives of the school curriculum.

Defenses against Negligence

In the defense of a teacher charged with negligence, several negating factors may need to be considered. These are generally referred to as contributory negligence, assumption of risk, and acts of nature.

Contributory Negligence. **Contributory negligence** refers to the plaintiff's being held partially or wholly at fault for the injury received. Before contributory negligence is determined, the child's age, capabilities (both physical and mental), and prior training are considered. For example, during a supervised class field trip a sixth grader sneaks away from the group, becomes injured, and isn't discovered to be missing for almost one hour. Such a situation may result in a case of contributory negligence if the child is determined to be old enough and capable of complying with the requirement of staying with the class (age of reason), and the supervising teacher is determined to have been negligent in her supervision and inability to locate the missing child sooner. The **age of reason** in most states is generally considered to be age twelve. If the plaintiff shares the fault, then he or she may not be compensated for damages.

In some regions, however, the concept of **shared negligence** has been broadened to include comparative negligence. In these states the plaintiff may be compensated on a proportionally reduced basis that is prorated according to the actual percentage of shared negligence. For example, the wandering student may be found to be 50 percent at fault, thereby limiting the extent of the supervising teacher's liability by one-half of the total dollar amount of the verdict.

CONCEPT 15.5
Legal defenses based on contributory or shared negligence or assumption of risk are frequently difficult to prove with young children because of the concept of age of reason.

Assumption of Risk.   **Assumption of risk** is a legal term indicating that in certain situations one assumes responsibility for his or her own safety. Individuals who participate in nonrequired intramural and athletic activities and are aware of the risks involved are generally considered by the court to have assumed the risk for their own safety and well-being. The same, however, is not so for students in a required physical education class. A claim of negligence due to injury occurring through participation in required physical activities generally will not be considered to fall under the defense of assumption of risk. This is an important concept and has numerous legal implications for the incorporation of stress challenge and risk activities into the required physical education program. The age, experience, and maturity of the students, as well as their awareness of the risks involved and the degree to which they are required to take part in these activities or are given equal opportunity for participation in alternative activities, all need to be carefully considered.

Act of Nature.   An **act of nature** is considered to be something completely unexpected and unforeseen that is *totally* beyond the control of the defendant. If, for example, a tree is struck by lightning on a clear day and the children playing under that tree are injured or killed, this may be considered an act of nature. Acts of nature,

however, are very difficult to prove in a court of law even under the most favorable of legal circumstances.

Proximate Cause.   Proximate cause is a legal defense claiming that an accident and resultant injury was not caused by the negligence of the individual in charge, because it would have occurred regardless of whether or not the teacher was there. Take, for example, a situation in which a child falls and breaks an arm while running down a gently rolling grassy slope on the playground during a regularly scheduled and properly supervised recess period. Running is generally considered to be an appropriate behavior on playgrounds, and running up and down hills is also appropriate, and even encouraged. Furthermore, children do occasionally fall while running, and no amount of teacher supervision could be reasonably expected to prevent such an accident. Therefore, if sued for negligence due to improper supervision, the supervising teacher could mount a defense based on proximate cause.

FREQUENT CONDITIONS LEADING TO LEGAL ACTION

A number of potential danger spots exist that may leave you, the physical education teacher, open to legal action. Being aware of these conditions and taking appropriate preventive measures will greatly reduce exposure to charges of legal liability. Among the most frequent conditions leading to charges of legal liability are ignoring mandated legislation, improper instruction, inadequate supervision, and failure to provide a safe environment.

Ignoring Mandated Legislation

Recent federal and state laws have contained **mandated legislation** concerning certain procedures in the design and implementation of educational programs. Three pieces of mandated legislation that have had the greatest impact on physical education and athletic programs are the Educational Amendments Act of 1972 (Title IX), the Education for All Handicapped Children Act of 1975 (PL 94–142), and Education of the Handicapped Amendments Act of 1986 (PL 99–457).

CONCEPT 15.6
Teachers should be aware of and abide by prevailing federal, state, and local laws as a primary means of minimizing legal liability.

Title IX. **Title IX** makes it illegal to discriminate between students in matters of education based on gender. This law has had vast implications and ramifications within the physical education profession. Considerable progress has been made in implementing Title IX over the last several years, but educators still need to be reminded occasionally of their responsibility. The majority of the accusations of discrimination have charged that female students were not given the same opportunities to participate as their male counterparts. Failure to comply with the requirements of Title IX has resulted in numerous lawsuits. Following the guidelines outlined in the AAHPERD publication will help teachers avoid legal action (Durrant, 1992).

PL 94–142 and PL 99–457. **PL 94–142** and its updated cousin, **PL 99–457,** require that all children with disabilities be provided with a free and appropriate public education. They further mandate that school systems provide means to protect the rights of these children. Most importantly, they provide that students with a limiting condition be mainstreamed (educated in the regular classroom) as much as possible and that an **individualized educational program (IEP)** be prepared and implemented. Furthermore, children with disabilities must now be placed in the least restrictive environment, and their parents must be involved in the educational decisions that affect their child. This sweeping legislation has dramatically changed how children with disabilities are educated in the public schools.

These laws are particularly important to the physical education profession because physical education was the only curricular area targeted as a specific focus of concern within this law. Physical education has been mandated as a direct service that must be provided to all children unless their counterparts without disabilities do not receive physical education. The law does not permit the substitution of services or the use of related services in place of physical education. Failure to implement the provisions of PL 94–142 and PL 99–457 within the school district and within individual schools leaves both administrators and physical education teachers liable for legal action.

Improper Instruction

A frequent cause of legal action against physical education teachers is negligence due to inadequate or improper instruction. The very nature of many physical education

> One of the most frequent types of lawsuits are those claiming that the instruction provided for an activity was inappropriate or nonexistent. It is crucial to have written lesson plans and an approved written curriculum to document the scope and sequence of your instruction.

activities involves an element of risk. Activities in the swimming pool, on the gymnastics apparatus, and on the athletic field all involve risk. The job of the teacher is to reduce this risk through proper instructional techniques and supervision.

Progressive instruction that builds skill upon skill, follows established teaching procedures, emphasizes safety, and provides for the needs of the individual is clear evidence of adequate instruction. On the other hand, failure to follow an established curriculum; nonexistent lesson planning; use of outmoded instructional strategies and questionable activities, such as murder ball, circle dodgeball, and certain combative activities; and failure to follow reasonable safety precautions and spotting techniques all leave the teacher open to legal action.

CONCEPT 15.7
Teachers of physical education are obligated by law, as well as by ethical considerations, at all times to provide adequate supervision and appropriate instructional techniques in a safe and healthful environment.

Inadequate Supervision

Claim of inadequate or improper supervision is another frequent cause of legal action against teachers. As a general rule, the teacher should never leave an individual or class unsupervised, even for a brief period of time. The very nature of most physical education activities and the equipment used makes it imperative that adequate supervision be provided at all times.

Supervision is an active process that may be conducted by the teacher or other approved personnel. Supervision extends to the playground, lunchroom, after-school activities, and school-sponsored events. If an injury does occur while children are being supervised, a number of factors will need to be considered. Among them are the ratio of students to supervisors, whether a written supervisory policy was available and followed, and whether the injury was caused by improper supervision. For example, a teacher who is required to supervise several hundred children alone not only exposes herself to liability but also exposes the school principal and the school district itself.

Proper supervision extends to conduct in the physical education class and on the athletic field. It is the teacher's responsibility to maintain good class control and to ensure that all activities are carefully supervised. Supervision by adult volunteers or other students is not acceptable unless it is expressly permitted by the school district as determined by state law.

Failure to Provide a Safe Environment

Teachers are open to the possibility of legal action when they fail to establish a safe and healthful environment by ensuring the proper condition of supplies, equipment, and facilities. A safe and healthful environment extends further to planning for safe use of locker room and shower facilities.

It is the duty of the physical education teacher to routinely inventory the physical condition of the supplies, equipment, and facilities for which she or he is responsible and to keep an accurate record of the dates and results of these inspections. Any defects or potential safety hazards should be eliminated on the spot when possible or reported immediately in writing to the building principal. Continued use of defective equipment or participation in a hazardous environment is morally indefensible. There is no defensible reason for using defective or broken equipment such as a cracked bat or a brick for second base. All efforts should be made to bring existing facilities and equipment into compliance with acceptable standards of health and safety.

Locker rooms and shower areas are potential danger areas that present unusual hazards. They are frequently small, overcrowded, and slippery, presenting numerous opportunities for injury due to falls, bumps, and burns. A written policy for the use and supervision of locker room and shower facilities should be developed. Traffic patterns, time limits, and a code of acceptable behaviors should be established and enforced.

MINIMIZING LEGAL LIABILITY

An obvious way to avoid exposure to claims of legal liability and negligence is to eliminate the pitfalls already discussed in this chapter. Implementing mandated legislation, requiring proper instruction and supervision, and providing for a safe and healthful environment are all basic to quality education. However, liability may be further reduced through good record-keeping, written and enforced policies for emergency care and extracurricular activities, heeding legitimate excuses, and liability insurance coverage.

CONCEPT 15.8
Record-keeping and risk management procedures reduce both the likelihood of injury and the difficulty of successful lawsuits.

Record-Keeping

An excellent way to both avoid and minimize the effects of a lawsuit is by keeping accurate, up-to-date records. A written record should be kept of all accidents, no matter how minor, and all periodic inventories of the condition of all supplies, equipment, and facilities under your jurisdiction.

Accident Reports.   If an injury does occur, it is essential that an accident report be filled out and filed with the principal's office no later than the close of the school day. Many school districts use a standard accident report form. A sample form is presented in Table 15.1 and may be used if one is not readily available.

Basically, the accident report should contain the name, address, phone number, age, and grade of the injured child. The location where the injury took place, the person responsible for supervision, the time of day, and a brief description of the activity leading up to the accident are essential. This information should be followed by a detailed description of the emergency care given and the personnel involved. A brief description of the nature of the injury, including, if applicable, the name of the physician or school nurse providing treatment is important. How and when the student's parents were contacted should also be included on the accident report form. When the form is completed, it should be signed and dated. The original should be retained in the principal's office, and you should keep a copy for your files. At no

TABLE 15.1 *Sample Accident Report Form*

Student Accident Report

This form should be completed in triplicate and signed by the building principal, school nurse, and supervising teacher. The original will be forwarded to the superintendent's office. The second copy will be kept in the principal's office, and the third copy will be retained by the supervising teacher.

Name of Injured _____

Age _____Grade _____Home Room _____

Home Address _____Phone _____

Date of Accident _____Time of Accident _____

Specific Location of Accident _____

_____

Staff Person(s) Supervising _____

Address _____Phone _____

Description of the Activity Leading to the Accident _____

_____

_____

Nature of the Injury _____

_____

Description of Emergency Care Given _____

_____

_____

Emergency Care Given by _____

Address _____Phone _____

Medical Treatment Recommended_____Yes _____No

Medical Official Providing Treatment_____

Address _____Phone _____

Specify Where Taken After Accident _____

_____First Aid Room _____Home _____Hospital _____Other

Out-of-School Transportation Provided by _____

Address _____Phone _____

Parent/Guardian Name _____

Parent/Guardian Contacted _____Yes_____No _____Time

Additional Comments _____

_____

_____

Name of Person Filing Report _____

Date of Report _____Time of Report _____

Signature of Supervising Teacher _____

Signature of School Nurse _____

Signature of School Principal _____

TABLE 15.2   *Sample Supply/Equipment Report*

Supply/Equipment Condition Report

| | | Condition | | Recommendations | |
Supplies/Equipment	Quantity	Satisfactory	Unsatisfactory	Repair	Destroy

The above supplies and equipment were inventoried by _____ on _____. The items checked "unsatisfactory condition" have been removed from use. The items marked "repair" should be repaired by the earliest possible date or destroyed. I hereby acknowledge receipt of this Supply/Equipment Report:

Signature of report preparer	Date	Principal's signature	Date

time should the teacher discuss the injury with others unless directed to do so by a school official. No attempt should be made to diagnose the injury or to provide treatment beyond emergency first aid until qualified medical personnel can take over. The injured student should not be left alone while the teacher summons help. Help should be obtained, as a matter of written policy, by sending a trusted student to the central office of the school.

Supply/Equipment Reports. Some schools utilize a district-approved form for inventorying the condition and reporting the status of supplies and equipment. If one is not available, the sample form presented in Table 15.2 may be adopted or modified to suit your needs. The form should contain a complete inventory of all the supplies, equipment, and facilities under the teacher's jurisdiction. At the beginning and end of each semester, a complete accounting of all equipment and supplies should be made. The number and condition of all the balls, bats, bases, ropes, hoops, beanbags, and other supplies should be

noted on the form. Defective materials, such as splintered bats, frayed climbing ropes, or broken playground equipment, should be specifically noted and immediately repaired or removed from use. Unsafe conditions should be brought immediately to the attention of the proper building official, in writing. A copy of this correspondence should be retained in your files, along with your complete signed and dated supply/equipment report.

Facility Reports. The physical education teacher frequently has several facilities under his or her jurisdiction. Along with the gymnasium or multipurpose room, the physical education teacher is frequently responsible for supervising and reporting on the condition of the playground and athletic fields. A daily inspection of each of these facilities is recommended. This takes only a few minutes and may identify potential safety hazards such as improperly placed or stored equipment, dirty or unsafe floors, broken glass, potholes, and other unsafe conditions. Many of these potential hazards can be immediately rectified; others may require time. In any case, activity should not continue under unsafe conditions, and the appropriate school official should be notified, in writing, of unsafe conditions.

Written Policies

Written policies that are clearly stated and adhered to will do much to limit the extent of one's exposure to liability. Among the most important written policies are the emergency care policy and the extracurricular activity policy.

Emergency Care Policy.   Along with the accident report form, it is of utmost importance to have a written policy describing what is to be done in the event of an emergency. The emergency care policy should reflect carefully thought-out **risk management procedures** of exactly what will be done in the event of an accident or injury. A copy of this procedure should be made available to all teachers, approved by appropriate school officials, and placed on file with the building principal or superintendent.

Extracurricular Activity Policy.   Participation in extracurricular activities frequently exposes teachers to increased liability. To reduce this exposure, it is important to have a written policy governing the conduct and supervision of these events. Parent permission slips that clearly spell out the nature of the activity are a must, whether the activity is participation in a school-sponsored field trip or an athletic event at another school. Although the parent permission slip does not remove or reduce the limits of liability, it does provide a clear indication that the child's parents are aware and approve of participation. Even with the permission slip on file, you as the physical education teacher still have the same responsibility for proper supervision.

Honoring Excuses.   Children will frequently request to be excused from participating in a physical education class for health reasons or because of religious beliefs. The law is clear in indicating that it is the teacher's duty to honor these requests for nonparticipation or modified participation if they have been written by parents or medical officials. Failure to honor these written requests and insisting that the child take part is an open invitation to a lawsuit.

Even if you suspect that the reasons for the written excuse are not valid and that, based on your judgment, it would be in the best interests of the child to participate, you must honor the written request to be excused. It is perfectly appropriate to question the validity of the

TEACHING TIPS

The following questions will need to be addressed in developing an emergency care policy:

- *Who should administer emergency first aid?* (Ideally, all teachers should be certified in first aid and CPR, but this is rarely the case.)

- *How will help be summoned?* (The on-site teacher should not leave the injured child.)

- *Who will determine if the injured student can be moved?* When in doubt, this decision should be left to a physican or emergency medical technician.

- *Who will determine if the child needs additional medical attention?* If emergency treatment is required, help should be summoned immediately.

- *Who will contact the child's parents, and what information will be given over the phone?* (An updated file with the home and business phone numbers of all parents and their family physicians should be maintained in the central office.)

- *Who will fill out the accident report, and where and when is it to be filed?* (The supervising teacher should be responsible for filling out the accident report, which should be filed by the end of the school day with the principal and other appropriate officials.)

- *Who will take responsibility for follow-up on the injury, and what procedures will be used?* (The principal, school nurse, or other school official should be responsible for follow-up.)

request, but even while you are doing so the child should be excused from participation.

Children are sometimes forbidden to take part in certain activities because of religious beliefs. Often children are asked to be excused from all dancing, coeducational activities, or mass showering. These requests must be honored and carried out in a way that does not bring ridicule or attention to the child.

Requests from parents for their child to be excused from participation due to minor medical reasons should be carefully scrutinized. As a general rule, requests for nonparticipation for over one week should be accompanied by a physician's excuse. If a child needs to be

Important points to consider in formulating an extracurricular activity policy:

- *Who is in charge of supervision?* (This person should be a teacher operating with the permission of the appropriate school official.)

- *Who will be assisting in the supervisory duties?* (Adults, preferably parents of the children involved, should assist with supervision and have specific written responsibilities.)

- *What is the ratio of children to adult supervisors?* (Although no clear legal precedent has been established, it is assumed that the teacher will operate in a reasonable and prudent manner in determining the number of supervisors needed.)

- *Who will arrange for transportation, and how will it be supplied?* (This is a critical point that must be determined in conjunction with the school attorney and insurance officials. It should not be assumed that children can be transported in private automobiles from the school to school-sponsored events without the school incurring additional liability. The law varies from state to state on this issue and should be clarified locally.)

- *How will the nature of the activity and the quality of supervision be assessed?* (To prevent difficulties in the future, it is important to have some means of determining if the supervisory policies enacted are adequate and are being followed.)

Liability insurance coverage may be provided in a variety of ways. First, in some states adequate liability insurance coverage is automatically provided for all teachers. Second, several local school districts carry liability insurance coverage on all their teachers. Third, professional teachers' organizations, including The American Alliance for Health, Physical Education, Recreation and Dance (AAHPERD) and the National Education Association (NEA) offer low-cost liability insurance policies to their members. A fourth source of liability insurance coverage is commercial insurance companies. Many companies offer liability coverage as a rider to home insurance and health insurance policies for little additional cost.

CONCEPT 15.9
Professional liability insurance coverage is available through a variety of sources for a reasonable cost.

Be certain to make yourself aware of the liability coverage available to you and the terms of the coverage. Because of astronomical settlement sums, many teachers are finding it prudent to take out additional liability coverage through their professional education association or through commercial insurance carriers, even though they may already be covered by their state or school district.

The likelihood of being sued and of the plaintiff recovering damages is still small, even though the actual number of lawsuits has been on the rise for several years. The cost of liability insurance is moderate, but the peace of mind provided makes it well worth the investment.

excused from physical education for only a day or two, a written excuse from a parent should be sufficient.

Insurance Coverage

Despite all the precautions advocated and all the professionally responsible efforts made by concerned, caring teachers, accidents and injuries still occasionally occur. Any time an injury occurs, the possibility of some form of legal action exists. Therefore, it is wise to be certain that you have adequate insurance coverage in the unlikely event that you should be found legally liable due to negligence, contributing to an attractive nuisance, or malpractice.

SUMMARY

Although this chapter discussed the conditions required for liability to be proved in a court of law, it is incumbent upon the teacher to use common sense in providing a safe and healthful environment for children. There is no excuse for tolerating preexisting conditions that may lead to an accident or injury resulting in a successful lawsuit. Teachers have a moral obligation to do all in their power to protect children from harm, but at the same time they must recognize that the gymnasium and playground present a special set of circumstances that by the very nature of vigorous physical activity sometimes results in injury.

Legal liability may be minimized through accurate record-keeping, written policies, and emergency procedures that are understood and adhered to. Safety should be the first concern of all teachers, but especially the teacher of physical education.

COMPLEMENTARY READINGS

Adams, S. (1993). Duty to properly instruct. *JOPERD* 64:22–24.

Arnold, D. (1991). Oops! It's broken—Products liability law. *Strategies* 5:516–18.

Barrett, K. R., and L. P. Gaskin. (1990). Running backward in a relay race: Brown v. Burlington City Board of Education. *JOPERD* 61:33–35.

Blucker, J. A., and S. W. Pell. (1986). Legal and ethical issues. *JOPERD* 57:19–21.

Conn, J. H., ed. (1993). The litigation connection: Perspectives of risk control for the 1990's. *JOPERD* 64:15–66 (series of articles).

Cotton, D. (1993). Risk management: A tool for reducing exposure to legal liability. *JOPERD* 64:58–66.

Cotton, D. (1994). Students acting as teachers: Who is liable? *Strategies* 8:23–25.

Durrant, S. M. (1992). Title IX: Its power and its limitations. *JOPERD* 63:60–64.

Figone, A. J. (1989). Seven legal duties of a coach. *JOPERD* 60:71–72.

Gray, G. R. (1995). Safety tips from the expert witness. *JOPERD* 66:18–21.

Hart, J. (1990). Locker room liability. *Strategies* 3:19–20.

Holford, E. (1992). Prayer on the playing field. *JOPERD* 63:29–32.

Kaiser, R. A. (1984). Program liability waivers. *JOPERD* 55:54–56.

Kolander, C. A., J. L. Grayson, and L. K. Miller. (1991). Teachers and coaches at risk: How personal insurance policies help. *JOPERD* 62:76–79.

Merriman, J. (1993). Supervision in sport and physical activity. *JOPERD* 64:20–21.

Pastore, D. L. (1994). A checklist for accident report forms. *Strategies* 7:15–17.

SUPPLEMENTARY READINGS

Clement, A. (1989). *Law in Sport and Physical Activity.* Dubuque, IA: Brown & Benchmark Publishers.

Dougherty, N. J., et al. (1994). *Sport, Physical Activity, and the Law.* Champaign, IL: Human Kinetics.

Dougherty, N. J., ed. (1994). *Principles of Safety in Physical Education and Sport.* Reston, VA: NASPE.

Hurt, J. L., and R. J. Ritson. (1994). *Liability and Safety in Physical Education and Sport.* Reston, VA: NASPE.

Van der Smissen, B. (1991). *Legal Liability and Risk Management for Public and Private Entities.* Cincinnati, OH: Anderson Publishing Company.

Wong, G. (1988). *Essentials of Amateur Sport Law.* Boston, MA: Auburn House Publishing.

VIDEOS

CPR for Everyone. Athletic Institute. (1991). 200 Castlewood Drive, North Palm Beach, FL: The Athletic Institute. (90 min.).

Sports on Trial. Athletic Institute. (1990). 200 Castlewood Drive, North Palm Beach, FL: The Athletic Institute. (60 min.).

Sports Injury Risk Management and the Keys to Safety. Coalition of Americans to Protect Sports (CAPS). 200 Castlewood Drive, North Palm Beach, FL. (videotapes and program manual).

Mini Videos on Legal Topics in Sport and Physical Education. (1992). Reston, VA: AAHPERD. (several videotapes of varying length).

PART IV

The Skill Themes

16   Fundamental Stability Skill Themes

17   Fundamental Locomotor Skill Themes

18   Fundamental Manipulative Skill Themes

19   Stunts and Tumbling Skill Themes

20   Apparatus Skill Themes

21   Disc Sport Skill Themes

22   Basketball Skill Themes

23   Soccer Skill Themes

24   Softball Skill Themes

25   Volleyball Skill Themes

CHAPTER 16

Fundamental Stability Skill Themes

Key Concept

Stability Is the Most Basic of the Three Categories of Movement Because All Locomotor and Manipulative Movements Require an Element of Stability

Chapter Objectives

The purpose of this chapter is to provide you with the tools to:
- Define the word *stability* and discuss how and why it is considered to be a category of movement.
- Demonstrate the stabilizing aspects of a variety of locomotor and manipulative skills at both the fundamental and specialized movement skill phases.
- List and describe the subcategories of stability.
- Demonstrate knowledge of and ability to plan and implement a developmental movement skill theme around one or more stability abilities.
- Identify the initial, elementary, and mature stages for a variety of fundamental stability abilities.
- Be familiar with the essential skill concepts and movement concepts that children should know about their developing stability abilities.
- Describe common developmentally based difficulties that children encounter in mastering fundamental stability abilities and identify appropriate teaching strategies for overcoming these difficulties.
- Demonstrate knowledge of how to incorporate a variety of exploratory and guided-discovery activities into a stability skill theme.
- Provide examples of low-level game activities appropriate for stability skill application.

Terms to Remember

Stability	Static Balance
Axial Movements	Dynamic Balance
Springing Movements	Body Rolling
Upright Supports	Dodging
Inverted Supports	

Stability represents the most basic of the three categories of movement. In fact, there is an element of stability in all locomotor and manipulative movements. Children who are exposed to a variety of movement situations generally have little difficulty in developing fundamental stability abilities. On the other hand, children who do not have a varied background of movement experiences frequently lag behind in the development of basic stability abilities.

Use of the term *stability* goes beyond the notion of non-locomotor movements and static and dynamic balance. **Stability** is the ability to sense a shift in the relationship of the body parts that alter one's balance and the ability to adjust rapidly and accurately for these changes with appropriate compensating movements. Therefore, the concept of stability encompasses axial movements, springing movements, upright supports, and inverted supports, all of which involve static or dynamic balance.

CONCEPT 16.1
Fundamental stability abilities are those that place a premium on gaining and maintaining one's equilibrium in static or dynamic balance situations.

Axial movements are non-locomotor stability movements in which the axis of the body revolves around a fixed point. Movements such as bending, stretching, twisting, turning, reaching, lifting, and falling are generally considered to be axial movements that emphasize maintaining one's balance. **Springing movements** involve forceful projection of the body into space in either an upright or an inverted position. Movement skills such as the straddle jump, headspring, and handspring are considered to be springing movements. Emphasis in these tasks is placed on the sudden loss and regaining of contact with one's base of support.

Upright supports are static or dynamic balance skills in which emphasis is placed on maintaining one's equilibrium when the body is placed in unusual positions. Individual stunts such as the coffee grinder, bear dance, V-seat, and front scale are upright postures. Partner stunts such as the wheelbarrow, swan balance, and shoulder stand are upright postures.

Inverted supports involve supporting the body momentarily or for a sustained period in an inverted position. The tripod, headstand, and handstand are all sustained inverted supports. Momentary inverted supports include forward and backward rolls, cartwheels, and the roundoff. The concept of stability is broad. As used here, the movement category of stability includes any movement in which a premium is placed on gaining or maintaining one's equilibrium. Figure 16.1 provides a partial list of stability skills.

CONCEPT 16.2
The movement category of stability includes axial and springing movements, upright supports, and inverted supports.

The beam walk and the one-foot balance have been selected as representative samples of the many dynamic and static balance skills, along with body rolling and dodging. A verbal and visual description are provided for each, along with teaching tips and concepts children should know. This is followed by a sampling of appropriate skill development activities for body rolling and dodging only. Chapters 19 and 20 ("Stunts and Tumbling Skill Themes," and "Apparatus Skill Themes") are filled with a wide variety of appropriate stability enhancement activities in the form of stunts and tumbling skills and apparatus skills.

STABILITY SKILL SEQUENCING

Because stability is basic to all that we do, fundamental stability abilities begin developing early in life. However, the extent to which these abilities are developed and refined depends largely on environmental factors.

CONCEPT 16.3
When planning a stability skill theme (Table 16.1) it is important to follow a progressive sequence of pre-planning, observing and assessing, specific planning and implementation, and evaluation and revision.

When working on stability skill development, it is important to follow a logical progression of activities from simple to complex, building skill upon skill. Axial movements are a good place to start. Experimenting with how the body can bend, stretch, twist, and turn places

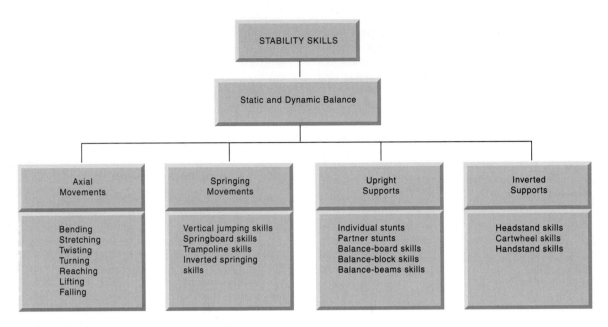

FIGURE 16.1 *Components of the movement category of stability.*

TABLE 16.1   *Developing a Stability Skill Theme*

When planning a developmental movement skill theme around fundamental stability skills you will find it helpful to follow this sequence.

1. Preplan

    a. Determine what fundamental stability skills will be grouped together for each skill theme. The following grouping may be considered:

    —Axial movements and springing movements.

    —Stunts and tumbling skills.

    —Small apparatus skills.

    —Large apparatus skills.

    b. Determine when to include each stability skill theme in your yearly curriculum.

    c. Decide approximately how many total lessons you will spend on fundamental stability skill development in relation to the total curriculum.

2. Observe and Assess

    a. Observe the static and dynamic balance skills of the group to be taught.

    b. Assess whether students are at the initial, elementary, or mature stage in their static and dynamic balance abilities. Study the verbal descriptions and visual descriptions for stability skills on the pages that follow for help.

3. Plan and Implement

    a. Plan appropriate movement activities geared to the needs, interests, and ability level of the group. Study the teaching tips and concepts children should know in the pages that follow for assistance.

    b. Implement a planned program of activities that stress progressive skill development.

4. Evaluate and Revise

    a. Informally evaluate progress in the stability skills being stressed in terms of improved mechanics. The questions found in Table 16.11 at the end of the chapter will be helpful.

    b. Revise subsequent lessons as needed, based on student progress.

children in new and unusual positions. Upright supports are good activities to include next. They provide practice in supporting the body in progressively more difficult ways on the floor, on the mat, or on various pieces of large and small apparatus. Springing activities, in which the body is projected into the air in an upright posture, should be the third level of stability skill sequencing. These activities permit the body to be projected into the air for a short time, and they require progressively more sophisticated coordination as well as dynamic balance abilities. Inverted supports and inverted springing activities should be the last skills incorporated into the skill progression. These skills require considerable coordination and kinesthetic sensitivity to where the body is in space. All stability skill development activities should follow a logical sequence of progression from beginning to intermediate to advanced level activities. Failure to do so will only lead to frustration and failure on the part of students and the development of splinter skills that have little use.

C O N C E P T   1 6 . 4
Proper progression and skill sequencing is especially important in the development and refinement of stability skills.

DYNAMIC AND STATIC BALANCE

Balance is generally defined as the ability to maintain one's equilibrium in relation to the force of gravity, whether in a static posture or when performing a dynamic activity. For a person to be in balance, the line of gravity that passes through the individual's center of gravity must also lie within the base of support. If the line of gravity falls outside the base of support the person cannot remain in balance and will fall unless compensating movements are made. A **static balance** activity may be defined as any stationary posture, upright or inverted, in which the center of gravity remains stationary and the line of gravity falls within the base of support. Standing in place, balancing on a board, or standing on one foot are all examples of static balance from an upright posture. Examples of inverted postures include performing a tripod, tip-up, headstand, or handstand. The essential factor in any static balance activity is that the body is maintained in a stationary position for a specified period of time.

C O N C E P T   1 6 . 5
Individuals progress through a series of developmental stages in acquiring their stability skills, but they must have abundant opportunities for practice, encouragement, and instruction in an ecologically appropriate setting if they are to progress to the mature stage and beyond.

Dynamic balance involves controlled movement while moving through space. In a dynamic balance activity, the center of gravity is constantly shifting. Locomotor and manipulative movements involve an element of dynamic balance. Virtually all movement involves an element of static balance. Therefore, balance is the basis from which all controlled movement emanates. As a result, the balance experiences engaged in by children play an important role in the development of total body control.

This chapter focuses on those activities that clearly place a premium on the gaining and maintaining of one's equilibrium. The beam walk and the one-foot balance have been selected as representative fundamental dynamic and static balance movement patterns, respectively.

Beam Walk

Verbal Description (Table 16.2)

Visual Description (Figure 16.2)

One-Foot Balance

Verbal Description (Table 16.3)

Visual Description (Figure 16.3)

Teaching Tips

- Practice balance activities on the floor prior to using a balance beam or balance board.
- Spot activities carefully, but only as needed.
- Offer your hand for assistance, encouraging the child to grasp it less securely as balance is gained.
- Use a long pole to aid in balancing with the use of both sides of the body.
- Encourage proper focusing of attention by having the child identify numbers that are held up.

TABLE 16.2   *Developmental Sequence for the Beam Walk*

I. Beam Walk

  A. Initial stage

    1. Balances with support

    2. Walks forward while holding on to a spotter for support

    3. Uses follow-step with dominant foot lead

    4. Eyes focus on feet

    5. Body rigid

    6. No compensating movements

  B. Elementary stage

    1. Can walk a 2-inch beam but not a 1-inch beam

    2. Uses a follow-step with dominant foot leading

    3. Eyes focus on beam

    4. May press one arm to trunk while trying to balance with the other

    5. Loses balance easily

    6. Limited compensating movements

    7. Can move forward, backward, and sideways but requires considerable concentration and effort

  C. Mature stage

    1. Can walk a 1-inch beam

    2. Uses alternate stepping action

    3. Eyes focus beyond beam

    4. Both arms used at will to aid balance

    5. Can move forward, backward, and sideways with assurance and ease

    6. Movements are fluid, relaxed, and in control

    7. May lose balance occasionally

II. Developmental Difficulties

  A. Overdependence on spotter

  B. Visually monitors stepping leg

  C. Tying one arm in

  D. Rigid, hesitant movement

  E. Failure to actually negotiate the problem of balance

  F. Inability to perform without holding on to a spotter

  G. Poor rhythmical coordination of both sides of body

  H. Overcompensating for loss of balance

- Work for good body control in different directions and at different levels.
- Have child try to pick up objects while balancing in order to alter the balance problem and to change level.
- Provide plenty of variety and opportunity for experimentation, remembering that the primary objective is to enhance balance and not just to walk a balance beam or balance on a board.
- Provide numerous balance experiences, using various forms of equipment and relationships of the body.
- Begin with low-level activities prior to introducing high-level activities.
- Practice on a low bench and low balance beam prior to using a regulation beam.

INITIAL

ELEMENTARY

MATURE

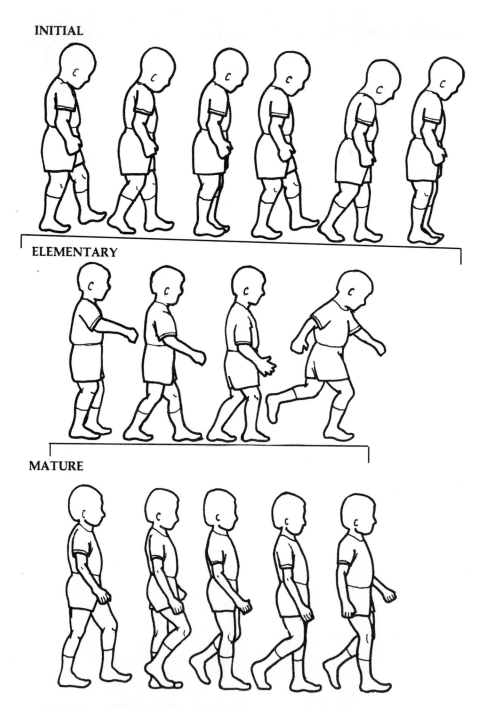

FIGURE 16.2 *Stages of the beam walk.*

TABLE 16.3   *Developmental Sequence for the One-foot Balance*

I. One-foot Balance
   A. Initial Stage
      1. Raises nonsupporting leg several inches so that thigh is nearly parallel with contact surface
      2. Either in or out of balance (no in-between)
      3. Overcompensates ("windmill" arms)
      4. Inconsistent leg preference
      5. Balances with outside support
      6. Only momentary balance without support
      7. Eyes directed at feet
   B. Elementary stage
      1. May lift nonsupporting leg to a tied-in position on support leg
      2. Cannot balance with eyes closed
      3. Uses arms for balance but may tie one arm to side of body
      4. Performs better on dominant leg
   C. Mature stage
      1. Can balance with eyes closed
      2. Uses arms and trunk as needed to maintain balance
      3. Lifts nonsupporting leg
      4. Focuses on external object while balancing
      5. Changes to nondominant leg without loss of balance
II. Developmental Difficulties
   A. Tying one arm to side
   B. No compensating movements
   C. Inappropriate compensation of arms
   D. Inability to use either leg
   E. Inability to vary body position with control
   F. Inability to balance while holding objects
   G. Visually monitoring support leg
   H. Overdependence on outside support

INITIAL

ELEMENTARY

MATURE

FIGURE 16.3   *Stages of the one-foot balance.*

Concepts Children Should Know

Skill Concepts

- Holding your arms out to the side will help you balance.
- Focusing on an object will help you balance.
- When walking on the beam, you should try to use an alternate stepping pattern.
- Be sure to have a spotter at your side.
- Do not rely on your spotter too much.
- The lower your center of gravity, the greater your stability.
- The wider your base of support, the greater your stability.
- Your line of gravity must stay within your base of support in order to balance.
- Balancing on one body part is usually more difficult because of a narrower base of support.

Movement Concepts

- You can balance your body at many different levels.
- You can balance on many different objects.
- You can balance while holding many different objects.
- You can move in different directions while balancing.
- You can balance while moving with others.
- You can widen your base when you balance for greater stability.
- You can lower your body when you balance for greater stability.

CONCEPT 16.6

Children must be able to apply many stability movement concepts and skill concepts in their daily lives if they are to be effective movers.

BODY ROLLING

Body rolling is a fundamental movement that requires the individual's body to move through space around its own axis while momentarily inverted. Rolling may be either forward, sideways, or backward. Children love to roll. The thrill of being upside down, the uncertainty of where they are in space, and the dizziness combine to make rolling an enjoyable activity for most children. Body rolling is a fundamental movement pattern that is integral to the sports of gymnastics and diving. It is found in various forms in the martial arts, wrestling, and acrobatic skiing. The body awareness and spatial awareness demanded of the individual in any activity that involves rotating the body around its own axis is tremendous. Therefore, it is important that children have many and varied opportunities to develop their body-rolling abilities.

Forward Roll

Verbal Description (Table 16.4)

Visual Description (Figure 16.4)

Teaching Tips

- A grassy area or carpet is adequate if mats are not available.
- Provide careful spotting wherever needed.
- It is not necessary to spot every child individually. If individual spotting is desired, show the children how it is done.
- Insist on good spotting when it is used.
- Work crossways on the mats to permit maximum practice.
- Use a block of wood and a tennis ball to demonstrate the difference between a round object (our curled body) and a nonrounded object (our uncurled body) when rolling.
- Set up four or five mat stations (forward-roll mat, backward-roll mat, combination mat, advanced mat, and trouble mat), stationing yourself wherever children need specific instruction.
- Begin with an exploratory approach, but be sure the movement challenges that you present are within the ability level of your children.
- Use a guided-discovery approach to facilitate an understanding of why the body moves as it does and how it moves when rolling.
- Children will often be at diverse levels of ability within a class. Be sure to provide experiences that meet the individual needs of each child. This will require diversity and creativity in teaching.

TABLE 16.4   *Developmental Sequence for Body Rolling*

I. Body Rolling
  A. Initial stage
    1. Head contacts surface
    2. Body curled in loose "C" position
    3. Inability to coordinate use of arms
    4. Cannot get over backward or sideways
    5. Uncurls to "L" position after rolling forward
  B. Elementary stage
    1. After rolling forward, actions appear segmented
    2. Head leads action instead of inhibiting it
    3. Top of head still touches surface
    4. Body curled in tight "C" position at onset of roll
    5. Uncurls at completion of roll to "L" position
    6. Hands and arms aid rolling action somewhat but supply little push-off
    7. Can perform only one roll at a time
  C. Mature stage
    1. Head leads action
    2. Back of head touches surface very lightly
    3. Body remains in tight "C" throughout
    4. Arms aid in force production
    5. Momentum returns child to starting position
    6. Can perform consecutive rolls in control
II. Developmental Difficulties
  A. Head forcefully touching surface
  B. Failure to curl body tightly
  C. Inability to push off with arms
  D. Pushing off with one arm
  E. Failure to remain in tucked position
  F. Inability to perform consecutive rolls
  G. Feeling dizzy
  H. Failure to roll in a straight line
  I. Lack of sufficient momentum to complete one revolution

Concepts Children Should Know

Skill Concepts
- Stay tucked in a small ball throughout your roll.
- Use your hands to support or push off so as little of your head touches the floor as possible.
- Keep your chin against your chest.
- Push off evenly with both hands.
- If you stay tucked during your roll, you can come all the way back to your starting position.
- Focus your eyes on an object in front of or behind you to help you roll in a straight line.
- Rolling is basic to the sports of gymnastics and diving and plays an important part in wrestling and the martial arts.

INITIAL

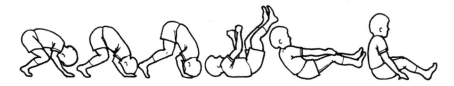

ELEMENTARY

MATURE

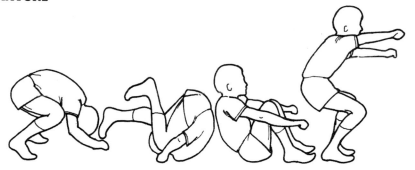

FIGURE 16.4 *Stages of body rolling development.*

Movement Concepts

- You can roll in many directions.
- You can roll from different levels.
- You can roll using a variety of body positions.
- You can roll with objects and with people.
- You can roll at different speeds and with different amounts of force.
- Your roll can be smooth and coordinated, or it can be disjointed and jerky.
- You can combine rolling with a variety of other activities.

Dodging

Dodging is a fundamental movement skill common to the game, sport, and play activities of children and adults. Dodging is similar to sliding, but dodging is often accompanied by running and involves quick, deceptive changes in direction. In the running dodge the knees bend, the center of gravity moves lower, and the body weight is shifted rapidly in a sideways direction. Dodging may occur from a stationary position and may involve a number of axial movements, including bending, twisting, stretching, or falling.

Dodging is an important element in chasing and fleeing games and the dodgeball games of childhood. It is an important element in the sports of wrestling, football, hockey, soccer, baseball, rugby, and lacrosse. Because of the natural combination of running with dodging, you may wish to group these two movement patterns into a common skill theme.

Verbal Description (Table 16.5)

Visual Description (Figure 16.5)

Teaching Tips

- Stress bending at the knees in anticipation of dodging.
- Begin with activities that require changing direction on a cue or verbal command.
- Explore various aspects of dodging in conjunction with effort, space, and relationships.
- Avoid dodgeball activities as a central focus of the lesson.
- Use a limited amount of dodgeball-type activities, but only after the child has reached the mature level. Always use a foam ball or a partially deflated ball.
- Stress the necessity for quickness and deception.
- Work on dodging in all directions. Avoid activities in which only one direction is stressed.
- May be effectively combined as a skill theme with running and leaping or with throwing and catching.

Concepts Children Should Know

Skill Concepts

- Stop your movement suddenly and shift your body weight rapidly to one side.
- Keep your center of gravity low for better balance.
- You keep your center of gravity over your base of support for balance, but you must put your body weight outside your base momentarily to dodge with quickness and deception.
- Use your head, shoulders, eyes, or trunk to face the new direction of your intended movement.
- Dodging is an important element in tagging, dodgeball games, and sports such as football, basketball, lacrosse, soccer, and hockey.

TABLE 16.5   *Developmental Sequence for Dodging*

I. Dodging
- A. Initial stage
  1. Segmented movements
  2. Body appears stiff
  3. Minimal knee bend
  4. Weight is on one foot
  5. Feet generally cross
  6. No deception
- B. Elementary stage
  1. Movements coordinated but with little deception
  2. Performs better to one side than to the other
  3. Too much vertical lift
  4. Feet occasionally cross
  5. Little spring in movement
  6. Sometimes outsmarts self and becomes confused
- C. Mature stage
  1. Knees bent, slight trunk lean forward (ready position)
  2. Fluid directional changes
  3. Performs equally well in all directions
  4. Head and shoulder fake
  5. Good lateral movement

II. Developmental Difficulties
- A. Inability to shift body weight in a fluid manner in direction of dodge
- B. Slow change of direction
- C. Crossing feet
- D. Hesitation
- E. Too much vertical lift
- F. Total body lead
- G. Inability to perform several dodging actions in rapid succession
- H. Monitoring body
- I. Rigid posture

Movement Concepts

- You can alter the effort that you use in your dodging to fit the demands of the situation.
- Your dodge can be altered in the amount of force applied, speed of performance, and flow.
- You can alter your space in which you dodge from place to place.
- You can dodge in different directions and at different levels.

INITIAL

ELEMENTARY

MATURE

FIGURE 16.5 *Stages of the dodging pattern.*

TABLE 16.6   *Exploratory Activity Ideas for Body Rolling*

Effort	Space	Relationships
Force	**Level**	**Objects**
Can You Roll. . . .	*Can You Roll. . . .*	*Can You Roll. . . .*
—as quietly as you can?	—from as low as you can go?	—on the mat?
—as loudly as you can?	—from as high as you can go?	—between the colored panels?
—so I cannot hear you?	—in a medium position?	—through the hoop?
—(rock) back and forth very hard?	**Direction**	—down the mat?
—(rock) very softly?	—forward?	—over the rolled mat?
Time	—sideways?	—on the bench?
—very fast?	—backward?	—while holding on to a ball?
—very slowly?	—in a straight line?	**People**
—in slow motion?	**Range**	—with a partner?
—at your regular speed?	—from a wide base?	—at the same time as your partner?
—(rock) fast?	—from a narrow base?	—together?
—(rock) slowly?	—in your own space?	—and move apart?
Flow	—with your head touching the ground?	—like twins?
—in a tight ball?	—without your head touching the mat?	**Combinations**
—in four separate steps?		After you have provided ample opportunities for students to explore the various elements of rolling, you may want to combine them. For example, "Can you roll forward with a wide base from a high level?"
—in one smooth motion?		
—in a jerky motion?		
—(rock) to my beat?		

SKILL DEVELOPMENT ACTIVITIES

Before you select specific stability activities for the lesson, you will need to determine the typical stage of motor development displayed by the class. This will also provide important cues to their level of movement skill learning. With this information, you will be able to determine whether the lesson should focus on exploratory and guided-discovery activities, skill application activities, or skill refinement activities.

Exploratory Activities

Exploratory activities give students at the initial or elementary stage of developing their stability abilities an opportunity to learn how their bodies can balance alone and in relation to other objects or people. The movement elements of effort, space, and relationships are explored to help children develop a more complete idea of their stability potentials. Tables 16.6 and 16.8 provide a sampling of exploratory ideas for body rolling and for dodging. The same types of exploratory experiences may be used with a wide range of static and dynamic balance skills.

 CONCEPT 16.7
A variety of exploratory and guided-discovery activities can be used effectively in developing the stability abilities of individuals at the initial and elementary stages.

TABLE 16.7   *Guided-Discovery Activity Ideas for Body Rolling*

	1. First explore several of the movement variations and combinations of rolling.
	2. Then begin to place limitations on the response possibilities to the following movement challenges:
General	a. Try rocking back and forth from many different positions. How many ways can you find? Did you notice anything special when you were rocking on your front, or your back, or your side? Did you keep your body straight or did you curve your body? Why?
Trunk	b. Does your head do anything special when you rock? Why do you think you tuck your chin in when you rock on your back or from side to side? Try it with your head up. Does it work as well? Why not?
	c. When we do a forward roll, do we keep our body curved or straight? Can anyone show me how curved you make your body when getting ready for a forward roll?
Head	d. What do you do with your head? Do you keep it up or curve it way down to your chest? Show me how your body and your head look when you do your forward roll. Practice rolling.
Arms	e. What do we do with our hands and arms when we roll forward? Try it, and then tell me. So our hands help us? How? See if you can use your hands more as you roll. Try it.
Feet	f. Can our feet help us when we roll? What can they do? Why does a good push-off help? Show me.
Combination	g. Let's put it all together. Make a tight ball with your body and head, push off with your feet, and use your hands to catch your weight as you come over.
Finish	h. If we want to come right back to our feet, what should we do? Try it. Can you get to your feet without using your hands to push you off?

3. After the mature rolling pattern comes under the child's control, provide numerous opportunities for varying the pattern and combining it with other activities:
   a. Consecutive forward rolls.
   b. Wide-base forward rolls.
   c. One-handed rolls.
   d. No-handed rolls.
   e. Rolls along a bench.
   f. Partner rolls (Eskimo rolls).

You will also find it helpful to introduce the sideways and backward rolls, using many of the same activities used for the forward roll. Variations and combinations of these body-rolling patterns also can be elaborated on once the mature stage has been obtained:
   a. Backward roll to a squat.
   b. Backward roll to a stand.
   c. Backward straddle roll.
   d. Backward roll to a momentary handstand.
   e. Combination forward and backward rolls.

Guided-Discovery Activities

The guided-discovery activities in Tables 16.7 and 16.9 provide you with a variety of problem-solving activities for enhancing rolling and dodging abilities. Guided-discovery activities give children who are at the intermediate level of learning a new stability skill the opportunity to practice the skill, learn more about it, and focus on it in a variety of movement situations. An infinite variety of guided-discovery activity ideas can easily be devised for all types of static and dynamic balance skills.

SKILL APPLICATION ACTIVITIES

Once children have developed basic abilities to balance their bodies in static and dynamic situations, it is appropriate to begin focusing on skill application activities. Static and dynamic balance abilities can be developed through practice in a variety of stunts and tumbling skills, large apparatus skills, and small apparatus skills. Stability skills may be applied to a number of game, rhythm, and self-testing activities. Chapter 19, "Stunts and Tumbling Skill

TABLE 16.8 *Exploratory Activity Ideas for Dodging*

Effort	Space	Relationships
Force	*Level*	*Objects*
Can You Dodge. . . . —with great force? —with no force? —with some force?	*Can You Dodge. . . .* —from a high level? —from a low level? —from a high to a low level? —from a low to a high level? —keeping yourself at a medium level?	*Can You Dodge. . . .* —a fleece ball? —a playground ball? —a tossed ball? —a rolled ball?
Time	*Direction*	*People*
—as fast as you can? —as slow as you can? —alternating fast and slow dodges? —at a medium speed? —with a burst of energy?	—in different directions? —sideways? —to your left? —to your right? —backward? —forward?	—a person chasing you from behind? —a person in front of you? —in the same direction as your partner? —in the opposite direction as your partner?
Flow		*Combinations*
—smoothly? —roughly?	*Range*	After you have provided ample opportunities for students to explore the various elements of dodging, you may want to combine them. For example, "Can you dodge a rolled ball as fast as you can from a low level to a high level?"
	—and concentrate on making different body shapes? —while staying in your own space? —and assess all the space you need? —while on one foot? —without using your arms?	

Themes," and Chapter 20, "Apparatus Skill Themes," contain several stability skill development and application ideas that are appropriate for children.

Stability Games

Although most games of low organization are thought of as locomotor or manipulative games, several activities can help to develop and reinforce fundamental stability abilities. Many of the stability games that follow use locomotor or manipulative tasks, but their primary feature is that they stress one or more aspects of stability (see Table 16.10). Several tag games are included. Tag is a great activity for reinforcing dodging and feinting skills. Most tag games can be adapted to the particular skill and interest level of the group.

Included in this section also are several dodgeball-type activities. Although dodgeball uses throwing and catching skills, the primary focus is on dodging and feinting. Dodgeball is a very popular activity with many children. It should, however, be used only for educational purposes and be taught in a manner that ensures the maximum safety and participation of all students. Therefore, it is strongly recommended that only foam balls or partially deflated balls be used, that elimination games be modified to emphasize maximum continual participation, and that cooperative teamwork be stressed. The primary objectives of the stability game activities that follow are to

1. enhance fundamental stability abilities,
2. improve dynamic and static balance abilities,
3. promote body, spatial, and directional awareness, and
4. foster cooperative behaviors.

TABLE 16.9   *Guided-Discovery Activity Ideas for Dodging*

	1. First have the students explore several variations of dodging.
	2. Then begin to place limitations on the response possibilities to the following movement challenges:
General	a. Can you run forward and change direction quickly? Try it while running backward and sideways. What do you do when you change directions quickly? Do you do the same thing when moving in different directions? Why?
Leg Action	b. Try to tag your partner who is facing you. How does your partner try to avoid your touch? What does she or he do with the feet and legs? Why are the knees bent and the feet apart? Now you try it, but try dodging your partner's touch from a position with your legs straight and starting with your feet together. Which way do you think works better? Try both ways. You're right, but why is it better to dodge from a standing position with your feet apart and your knees bent?
	c. Now try dodging your partner while being chased. How do you avoid being tagged? When you dodge to the right, what do you do with your legs? Why does your right leg step out to one side as you pivot? Show me how you can do it to the opposite side.
	d. Do you find it easier to dodge from a run in one direction than the other? Why? Let's practice dodging to our weak side.
Faking	e. From a position facing your partner, try to avoid his or her tags while using deceptive (feinting) movements of your head, eyes, or trunk. Does it work? What do you do with these body parts when you want to fake out your partner? Look at your starting position. Are your feet apart and your knees slightly bent? Don't forget to use that as your ready position, and then use other body parts to give the impression that you are going one way when you actually are going the other.
	3. When the mature dodging action has been reasonably well mastered, combine dodging with other activities. Often children can dodge satisfactorily in an isolated experience. However, when placed in a situation that requires them to dodge an oncoming object or in a complicated game in which dodging is only one of many elements of the game, children often become confused and unable to dodge with proficiency. Activities such as the ones that follow will help develop more integrated use of dodging.
	a. Dodge one or more persons while running across the playfield.
	b. Dodge oncoming objects. Be sure to use foam balls.
	c. Use dodging maneuvers to advance a ball downfield or downcourt. You can run, dribble, or kick a ball while dodging.

TABLE 16.10

Selected Stability Games Sequenced in Terms of Complexity

Stability Games (page number)	Movement Skills Stressed			
	Dynamic Balance	**Dodging/Feinting**	**Axial Movements**	**Static Balance**
Beanbag Balance Tag (274)	X	X		
Super Beanbag Balance Tag (274)	X	X		
Circle Freeze Tag (274)		X	X	
Mirror Touch Tag (274)	X	X		
Animal Tag (274)		X	X	
Amoeba Tag (274)			X	
Fly Trap (274)			X	
Opposites (275)			X	X
Circle Tug-of-War (275)		X	X	
Silly Simon (275)			X	X
Circle-Point Dodgeball (275)		X		
Team-Point Dodgeball (275)		X		
Engineer and Caboose Dodgeball (275)	X	X		

CONCEPT 16.8
Skill application activities involving low-level games and relays can be used effectively with individuals who have mastered the prerequisite skills.

Beanbag Balance Tag

Movement Skills: Dynamic balance, dodging, and feinting.

Formation: Scatter formation.

Equipment: One beanbag or other suitable object for balancing.

Procedures: One player is "it." This player places the beanbag on top of his head. "It" chases the other players and tries to tag someone. A tagged player then takes the beanbag and becomes "it."

Super Beanbag Balance Tag

Movement Skills: Dynamic balance, dodging, and feinting.

Formation: Scatter formation, each player balancing a beanbag on the head.

Equipment: One beanbag per player.

Procedures: One player is "it" and tries to touch another player. Each player has a beanbag or other suitable object balanced on the head. A player who is tagged becomes "it" and calls out "I'm it." The game continues without interruption or elimination. It is fun to experiment with balancing the object on different body parts: shoulder, elbow, back, hip, thigh, and foot.

Circle Freeze Tag

Movement Skills: Dodging, feinting, and axial movements.

Formation: Single circle facing inward with four to six players on the inside.

Equipment: None.

Procedures: One player is "it." Player tries to tag each of the other players. Players who are tagged must freeze in the position in which they were tagged. Play continues until all players are frozen. Last player tagged becomes "it," and four to six children move to the center of the circle. To make the game more challenging, require "it" to balance a beanbag while tagging.

Mirror Touch Tag

Movement Skills: Dodging, feinting, and balancing.

Formation: Scatter formation.

Equipment: None.

Procedures: One player is "it" and tries to touch another player. Players are "safe" when one or more of the same body parts are touching. You may try using a variety of body parts during the same game of tag. Permit "it" to call out "safe" body parts (hands, hips, backs, knees, elbows, soles of feet, and so forth).

Animal Tag

Movement Skills: Dodging and feinting.

Formation: Scatter.

Equipment: None.

Procedures: One player is "it" and tries to tag another player. After "it" calls out the name of a familiar animal, all players must imitate that creature while trying to avoid being tagged. When a player is tagged, that player immediately becomes "it" and calls out the name of another animal to be imitated. Some good animals to imitate are prancing horses, bears, elephants, rabbits, and crabs.

Amoeba Tag

Movement Skills: Dodging and feinting.

Formation: Scatter formation.

Equipment: None.

Procedures: One player is "it" and tries to tag another player. Players who are tagged link one hand, forming a progressively larger amoeba. Only those players on either end of the amoeba may tag using their free hand.

Fly Trap

Movement Skills: Axial movements.

Formation: Scatter, with half the players seated cross-legged.

Equipment: None.

Procedures: The players that are seated are the "traps." The remaining players are the "flies." The flies run throughout the traps, being sure to stay in the designated playing area. On the teacher's signal to "Freeze," the flies immediately stop. The traps, from their seated position, stretch out and try to touch the flies. If a fly is touched, he changes places with that trap. The game continues.

Opposites

Movement Skills: Axial movements.

Formation: Scatter formation facing a leader.

Equipment: None.

Procedures: The teacher serves as the leader. He moves one limb either up or down, forward or backward, or left or right. The class repeats the action, using the same limb as the teacher and the same direction of movement. This is a more advanced activity than mirroring, requiring transposition of movements.

Circle Tug-of-War

Movement Skills: Dynamic balance and dodging.

Formation: Circle of six to eight players per circle.

Equipment: One Indian club or potato chip can placed one foot in front of each player.

Procedures: Players form a single circle facing inward and lock wrists. On the signal "Go," players push and pull one another, trying to cause a person to knock down his or her own club. When a club is knocked down, one point is scored against that player. Players with the fewest points after a designated time are the winners. Score one point for each when two circle players lose their grip. Do not use as an elimination game. Modify the rules as needed so that everyone continues to play.

Silly Simon

Movement Skills: Axial movements.

Formation: Scatter formation facing a leader.

Equipment: None.

Procedures: Leader begins each movement task with the words "Simon says." Players then do exactly what they were told to do. Sometimes the leader fails to begin a command with the words "Simon says." All players who move are given a letter (*S, I, M, O, N*). Play continues until one or more players spell out the word *Simon.* Then they must do a Silly Simon antic. Play continues. Do not use as an elimination game. Stress a variety of axial movements and static and dynamic balance activities.

Circle-Point Dodgeball

Movement Skills: Dodging and feinting.

Formation: Single circle facing in, with a maximum of eight players inside the circle and eight on the outside.

Equipment: Foam ball.

Procedures: The ball is thrown by the players in the circle in an effort to hit one of the players inside the circle. One point is scored for each hit. The number of hits made in a two-minute time limit is recorded as the score. Teams change position. Do not use as an elimination game. Add a second ball only after sufficient skill has developed. Never use a fully inflated ball; foam balls are safest.

Team-Point Dodgeball

Movement Skills: Dodging, feinting, throwing, and catching.

Formation: Two teams of six to eight players each on either side of a line dividing a thirty-by-thirty-foot area in half.

Equipment: One or more foam balls per game.

Procedures: The balls are thrown back and forth across the line in an effort to hit opposing players on the opposite side. Players have a point scored against their team if any are hit by the ball, or if a player from the opposite team catches a thrown ball. Play continues for a specified time period. Team with the most points is the winner. Do not use as an elimination game; stress inclusion and teamwork. Only use foam balls. Add balls as skill progresses.

Engineer and Caboose Dodgeball

Movement Skills: Dodging, feinting, throwing, catching, and dynamic balance.

Formation: Single circle of eight to ten players facing in, with four more players in the center.

Equipment: One foam ball per circle.

Procedures: Players in the center of the circle hook their arms around the waist of the player in front of them. The first player is the "engineer"; the last, the "caboose." The players in the circle throw the ball, trying to hit the caboose. The engineer calls out directions and tries to maneuver the caboose out of the line of fire. The player hitting the caboose becomes the new engineer, and the caboose moves to the outside

TABLE 16.11   *Self-Question Chart for Fundamental Stability Skill Development*

One-Foot Balance	Yes	No	Comments
1. Can the child balance for thirty seconds on one foot?			
2. Does the child make adjustments with the arms as needed to maintain balance?			
3. Can the child balance for ten seconds with both eyes closed?			
4. Does the child keep the nonsupport leg free?			
5. Does the child focus forward rather than downward?			
6. Can the child balance on either foot?			
7. Is there observable improvement?			

Beam Walk

1. Can the child walk unaided across a ten-foot-long beam that is four inches wide?
2. Does the child use an alternating step?
3. Can the child travel backward and sideways as well as forward?
4. Does the child focus forward rather than downward?
5. Can the child use both arms to compensate for changes in balance?
6. Can the child easily change levels and directions?
7. Can the child walk independent of a spotter?
8. Is there observable improvement?

Body Rolling (forward, backward, and/or sideways)

1. Does the child curve the body adequately?
2. Does the child tuck the head?
3. Does the child push off evenly with both feet?
4. Does the child take the body weight on the hands and arms?
5. Do the head and body stay tucked in throughout the roll?
6. Is the child able to keep the front and top of the head from touching the mat?
7. Can the child come to his or her feet unaided immediately after the roll?
8. Is the child able to travel in a straight line?
9. Can the child perform consecutive rolls?
10. Is there observable improvement?

Dodging

1. Can the child dodge a partner from a facing position?
2. Can the child effectively dodge a partner from a fleeing position?
3. Does the child dodge well in all directions?
4. Is the child able to combine dodging with other game skills?
5. Does the child use deceptive movements when dodging?
6. Is the action quick, fluid, and in control?
7. Is there observable improvement?

circle. Play continues. The engineer is the only player who may use hands to block the ball. Play continues until all have had a chance to be both the engineer and the caboose. It is unsafe to use anything except a foam ball for this game. Players behind the engineer do not have any means of defense other than dodging the ball.

ASSESSING PROGRESS

You can easily evaluate students at the beginning and end of a fundamental stability skill theme. Select and evaluate four or five stability skills that are representative of the particular skill theme. Once you have determined students' entry level of ability, it is an easy matter to determine the types of activities to be included in the lesson. The sample assessment charts located in Chapter 11 ("Assessing Progress") and the Appendixes can be adapted to stability skills. These charts are a practical tool for recording individual and group progress.

C O N C E P T   1 6 . 9
Entry level assessment provides the teacher with important information about students' present levels of skill and serves as the basis for preparing developmentally appropriate lessons..

Fundamental stability abilities may also be informally assessed through a self-question chart similar to the one shown in Table 16.11. You should be able to answer "yes" to each of the questions. If you cannot, you will need to modify subsequent lessons to more closely fit the specific needs of the individual, group, or class being taught.

SUMMARY

Stability is the most basic of the three categories of movement. All locomotor and manipulative movements involve an element of stability. Therefore, it is essential that considerable time and effort be put into planning and implementing stability skill themes. It is critically important that the sequencing of skills should progress from axial movements to upright supports and then from upright springing skills to inverted supports and finally to inverted springing skills.

Children need to learn a variety of movement concepts and skill concepts associated with dynamic and static balance in general and with specific stability skills.

You will need to ensure that fundamental stability abilities are developed and refined in conjunction with fundamental locomotor and manipulative skills and that these concepts and abilities are integrated in a way that encourages motor control and movement coordination.

Exploratory and guided-discovery activities are especially beneficial for children at the initial and elementary stages in the development of their fundamental stability skills. Activities of this nature will permit them to experiment with the movement potential of their bodies and to problem solve for themselves essential concepts of both dynamic and static balance. Children who have mastered the essential aspects of stability will benefit from a variety of skill application activities that permit them to use their stability abilities in a myriad of related low-level games. Remember, however, not to focus on skill application too early in the learning process. It is essential that stability skills and related locomotor and manipulative skills be mastered in terms of body mechanics prior to focusing on other important aspects.

COMPLEMENTARY READINGS

Belka, D. (1993). Educational gymnastics: Recommendations for elementary physical education. *TEPE* 4:1–6.

Hammett Totsky, C. (1992). *Movement Activities for Early Childhood.* Champaign, IL: Human Kinetics.

Pica, R. (1994). *Early Elementary Children Moving and Learning.* Champaign, IL: Human Kinetics.

Pica, R. (1993). *Upper Elementary Children Moving and Learning.* Champaign, IL: Human Kinetics.

Rikard, G. L. (1992). Developmentally appropriate gymnastics for children. *JOPERD* 63:44–46.

Rovengo, I. (1988). The arts of gymnastics: Creating sequences. *JOPERD* 59:66–69.

SUPPLEMENTARY READINGS

Morrison, R. (1969). *A Movement Approach to Educational Gymnastics.* London: J. M. Dent and Sons.

Torbert, M., and L. B. Schneider. (1994). *Follow Me Too: A Handbook of Movement Activities for Three-to-Five Year Olds.* Reading, MA: Addison-Wesley.

Wall, J., and N. Murray. (1990). *Children and Movement.* Dubuque, IA: Wm. C. Brown.

Williams, J. (1979). *Themes for Educational Gymnastics.* London: Lepus.

VIDEOS

Thinking-Moving-Learning. Capon, J. Byron, CA: Front Row Experience. (20 min.).

CHAPTER 17

Fundamental Locomotor Skill Themes

●

Key Concept

Mature Fundamental Locomotor Skills May Be Attained Through a Skill Theme Approach That Uses a Variety of Appropriate Movement Experiences

●

Chapter Objectives

The purpose of this chapter is to provide you with the tools to:
- List and describe the steps in planning and conducting a locomotor movement skill theme.
- Describe essential aspects of several fundamental locomotor movement patterns at the initial, elementary, and mature stages.
- Discuss developmental difficulties and recommended teaching strategies for a variety of fundamental locomotor movements.
- Provide examples of movement concepts and skill concepts for several fundamental locomotor movements.
- Demonstrate ability to incorporate exploratory, guided-discovery, and skill application activities in the teaching of fundamental locomotor movements.
- Devise appropriate ways to observationally assess children's progress in acquiring mature fundamental locomotor movement patterns.

●

Terms to Remember

Phylogenetic	Sliding
Ontogenetic	Differentiation
Skill Sequencing	Integration
Run	Skipping
Leap	Exploratory Activities
Jump	Guided-Discovery Activities
Hop	Skill Application Activities
Gallop	

Locomotor skills are total body movements in which the body is propelled in an upright posture from one point to another in a roughly horizontal or vertical direction. Movements such as walking, running, leaping, jumping, hopping, skipping, galloping, and sliding are generally considered to be fundamental locomotor skills. These movement abilities are necessary for purposeful and controlled movement through our environment and are basic to the numerous skills necessary for sports, dance, and recreational activities.

Locomotor skills do not develop automatically. Although there may be a **phylogenetic** (hereditary) basis for the appearance of the initial and even the elementary stage of several fundamental locomotor movements, attainment of the mature stage depends on **ontogenetic** (environmental) factors. Factors within the environment, such as opportunities for practice, encouragement, and instruction, play a major role in the acquisition of mature patterns of locomotor movement. Failure to develop these mature skills will result in great difficulty in achieving acceptable levels of performance during the specialized movement skill phase of locomotor skill development.

This chapter examines the importance of skill sequencing and the process of developing fundamental locomotor skill themes. Several locomotor skills are examined. Verbal and visual descriptions are provided for each, along with teaching tips and concepts children should know. This is followed by a sampling of appropriate skill development activities that range from movement exploration and guided-discovery experiences to low-level game activities.

CONCEPT 17.1
Preparing and presenting an effective developmental-based movement skill theme requires preplanning, observing and assessing, specific planning and implementation, and evaluation and revision.

LOCOMOTOR SKILL SEQUENCING

Although children are generally considered to have the developmental potential to perform most fundamental locomotor skills at the mature stage by age six or seven, this is often not the case. Because of many factors, elementary school children often exhibit immature fundamental movement patterns. As a general rule, children at the preschool and primary grade level benefit most from a progressive program of fundamental locomotor skill development. Numerous children, however, in the upper grades can also be identified as exhibiting immature stages of development in several locomotor skills.

It is important to know where your students are in terms of their locomotor skill development if you are to plan effectively for all. Remember, **skill sequencing** is a process of building skill upon skill. This requires careful analysis of the complexity of the skills and the activities in which they are to be incorporated.

CONCEPT 17.2
Skill sequencing is critical to a successful movement skill theme.

RUNNING AND LEAPING

The running and leaping patterns begin developing early in childhood. Around the first birthday, the infant achieves an upright gait and begins to walk. Skill in walking develops rapidly until about age six, at which time it resembles the adult pattern in many ways. Care, however, must be taken to monitor the child's walking posture and to provide movement experiences that help him or her focus on the proper walking pattern. By eighteen months, the child is attempting to **run,** but no flight phase in which the child is airborne is apparent. The initial attempts at running resemble a fast walk. A flight phase, marking the onset of true running, generally appears between the second and third birthday. With proper amounts of practice, encouragement, and instruction, the running pattern should continue to improve and be at the mature stage by age seven.

Leaping is a fundamental movement that may be viewed as an extension of the running pattern. The development of mature leaping is dependent somewhat on efficient running. The **leap** is similar to the run except that a longer flight phase is involved and it is generally performed as a single rather than a repeated skill. In other words, when one leaps, the act is either from a stationary position or preceded by a run. The performance of consecutive leaps is possible, but a momentary hesitation from one leap to the next is easily observable in all but the most skilled. Leaping is used in the play and recreational activities of children in hopscotch, hurdling, and crossing a brook; others use it in baseball, basketball, football, and track.

<hr>

TEACHING TIPS

<hr>

Developing a Locomotor Skill Theme

To make the most efficient use of your time, the following sequence is recommended.

1. *Preplan*
   a. Determine what locomotor skills will be grouped together for each skill theme. The following works well:
      (1.) Running and leaping
      (2.) Jumping and hopping
      (3.) Galloping, sliding, and skipping
   b. Determine when to include each locomotor skill theme in the yearly curriculum. You will need to consider whether to space out lessons on each skill over the entire school year (distributed practice) or to group lessons together into concentrated units of instruction (massed practice).
   c. Decide on the approximate total number of lessons that you will spend on locomotor skill development in relation to the entire curriculum.
2. *Observe and Assess*
   a. Observe fundamental locomotor abilities of the children to be taught.

   b. Assess whether they are at an initial, elementary, mature, or sport-skill stage in each of the skills to be included as a skill theme. Study the verbal and visual descriptions for each locomotor skill on the pages that follow for help with this.
3. *Plan and Implement*
   a. Plan appropriate movement activities geared to the needs, interests, and ability levels of the group. Study the teaching tips and concepts children should know on the pages that follow for guidance.
   b. Implement a planned program of activities, stressing progression in skill development.
4. *Evaluate and Revise*
   a. Formally or informally evaluate progress in the locomotor skills being stressed in terms of improved mechanics (process) and performance (product). The questions found in Table 17.26 at the end of this chapter will be helpful, along with the process assessment charts in the Appendixes.
   b. Revise subsequent lessons as needed, based on student progress.

<hr>

Because the movement patterns of leaping and running are basic to our everyday activities, it is essential that they be developed to the mature level. A variety of exploratory and guided-discovery activities can aid in this process. Once the mature pattern has been obtained, these skills may be applied in a variety of games, sports, and dances. Practice in running and leaping will enhance one's performance abilities. Speed and endurance will also continue to improve with practice and will enable the individual to use these abilities in a variety of sport skills.

CONCEPT 17.3
Fundamental locomotor skills may be assessed to be at the initial, elementary, or mature stage of development.

Running

Verbal Description (Table 17.1)

Visual Description (Figure 17.1)

Teaching Tips

- Determine the characteristic stage in running ability.
- Plan activities designed to move the child to the next stage.
- Include plenty of activities involving movement exploration at the beginning level of skill learning.
- Work for good listening skills while running.
- Use the commands "freeze" and "melt" to develop listening skills.
- Stress not bumping into others.

TABLE 17.1 *Developmental Sequence for Running*

I. Running
   A. Initial stage
      1. Short, limited leg swing
      2. Stiff, uneven stride
      3. No observable flight phase
      4. Incomplete extension of support leg
      5. Stiff, short swing with varying degrees of elbow flexion
      6. Arms tend to swing outward horizontally
      7. Swinging leg rotates outward from hip
      8. Swinging foot toes outward
      9. Wide base of support
   B. Elementary stage
      1. Increase in length of stride, arm swing, and speed
      2. Limited but observable flight phase
      3. More complete extension of support leg at takeoff
      4. Arm swing increases
      5. Horizontal arm swing reduced on backswing
      6. Swinging foot crosses midline at height of recovery to rear
   C. Mature stage
      1. Stride length at maximum; stride speed fast
      2. Definite flight phase
      3. Complete extension of support leg
      4. Recovery thigh parallel to ground
      5. Arms swing vertically in opposition to legs
      6. Arms bent at approximate right angles
      7. Minimal rotary action of recovery leg and foot
II. Developmental Difficulties
   A. Inhibited or exaggerated arm swing
   B. Arms crossing the midline of the body
   C. Improper foot placement
   D. Exaggerated forward trunk lean
   E. Arms flopping at the sides or held out for balance
   F. Twisting of the trunk
   G. Poor rhythmical action
   H. Landing flat-footed
   I. Flipping the foot or lower leg in or out

INITIAL

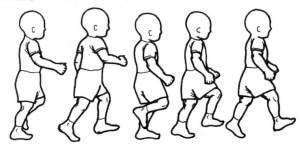

ELEMENTARY

MATURE

FIGURE 17.1 *Stages of the running pattern.*

- Stress stopping without sliding on the knees.
- For tagging games, teach proper tagging techniques.
- Incorporate activities that gradually increase aerobic capacity.
- Provide a wide variety of running activities.

Concepts Children Should Know

Skill Concepts

- Keep your head up when you run.
- Lean into your run slightly.
- Lift your knees.
- Bend your elbows and swing the arms freely.
- Contact the ground with your heels first.
- Push off from the balls of your feet.
- Run lightly.

- Running is basic to the successful playing of numerous games and sports.
- Running is good for your heart and lungs.

Movement Concepts

- You can run at many different speeds and levels.
- You can land heavily or lightly.
- Your run can be smooth or jerky.
- You can run in many different directions and paths.
- Your leg speed is influenced by your arm speed.
- Your stride length is determined by the force of your push-off.

CONCEPT 17.4

A variety of teaching strategies may be used to help students acquire mature fundamental movement skills.

Leaping

Verbal Description (Table 17.2)

Visual Description (Figure 17.2)

Teaching Tips

- Provide definite objects or barriers to leap over.
- Combine leaping with two or three running steps.
- Leap over very low objects followed by higher objects up to mid-thigh level.
- Encourage leading with either foot.
- Young children enjoy imagery when leaping "over deep canyons," across "raging rivers," or simply "over the brook."
- Use Velcro straps or other devices that give way if the child comes in contact with the object that is leaped.

Concepts Children Should Know

Skill Concepts

- Push upward and forward with your rear foot.
- Stretch and reach with your forward foot.
- Keep your head up.

TABLE 17.2   *Developmental Sequence for Leaping*

I. Leaping
  A. Initial stage
    1. Child appears confused in attempts
    2. Inability to push off and gain distance and elevation
    3. Each attempt looks like another running step
    4. Inconsistent use of takeoff leg
    5. Arms ineffective
  B. Elementary stage
    1. Appears to be thinking through the action
    2. Attempt looks like an elongated run
    3. Little elevation above supporting surface
    4. Little forward trunk lean
    5. Stiff appearance in trunk
    6. Incomplete extension of legs during flight
    7. Arms used for balance, not as an aid in force production
  C. Mature stage
    1. Relaxed rhythmical action
    2. Forceful extension of takeoff leg
    3. Good summation of horizontal and vertical forces
    4. Definite forward trunk lean
    5. Definite arm opposition
    6. Full extension of legs during flight
II. Developmental Difficulties
  A. Failure to use arms in opposition to legs
  B. Inability to perform one-foot takeoff and land on opposite foot
  C. Restricted movements of arms or legs
  D. Lack of spring and elevation in push-off
  E. Landing flat-footed
  F. Exaggerated or inhibited body lean
  G. Failure to stretch and reach with legs

- Lean forward at the trunk as you leap.
- Alternate your arm action with your leg action.
- The leaping pattern is used in getting over obstacles and in track and field events.

Movement Concepts

- Your leap can be very forceful or it can be light.
- Your leap can be combined with running.
- Your leap can be high or low or in between.
- Your leap can be only in one direction—forward.

INITIAL

ELEMENTARY

MATURE

FIGURE 17.2 *Stages of the leaping pattern.*

- Your leap can be long or short or in between.
- You can leap over objects or across objects or both.
- You can leap to rhythmical accompaniment.
- Your leap has a longer flight phase than your run and covers a greater distance.
- The distance and height of your leap are determined by the force of your push-off.

JUMPING AND HOPPING

Jumping and hopping are fundamental movement skills that are used in a variety of sport, recreational, and daily living experiences. Jumping and hopping may take many forms,

all of which involve a takeoff, a flight phase, and a landing. A **jump** differs from a hop in that a jump involves taking off on one or both feet and landing on both feet, while a **hop** involves taking off on one foot and landing on the same foot. Jumping may occur in a roughly horizontal plane, in a vertical plane, or from a height. Hopping may occur in place, or it may occur over a roughly horizontal plane.

The fundamental movement patterns of jumping and hopping are basic to numerous sport, dance, and recreational activities. It is essential that the mature stage of each of these patterns is obtained at an early date. Once the mature stage has been achieved, the teacher and the child may begin to focus on improved performance scores and combine hopping and jumping with a variety of other locomotor and manipulative skills.

Horizontal Jumping

Verbal Description (Table 17.3)

Visual Description (Figure 17.3)

Teaching Tips

- Start with exploratory activities and progress to more directed techniques as skill develops.
- Avoid jumping in socks or gym shoes with poor traction.
- Use carpet squares or newspapers as a challenge for children to jump over.
- Emphasize the coordinated use of the arms and legs.
- Children like to measure the length of their jump. This is a good time to reinforce measuring with a yardstick or meter stick.
- See if children can jump a distance equal to their height.
- Try jumping from different surfaces. Discuss differences.

Concepts Children Should Know

Skill Concepts

- Crouch halfway down.
- Swing your arms back and then forward forcefully.
- Explode forward from a coiled position.
- Push off with your toes leaving the ground last.
- Stretch and reach forward.

TABLE 17.3   *Developmental Sequence for Horizontal Jumping*

I. Horizontal Jumping

   A. Initial stage

      1. Limited swing; arms do not initiate jumping action

      2. During flight, arms move sideward-downward or rearward-upward to maintain balance

      3. Trunk moves in vertical direction; little emphasis on length of jump

      4. Preparatory crouch inconsistent in terms of leg flexion

      5. Difficulty in using both feet

      6. Limited extension of the ankles, knees, and hips at takeoff

      7. Body weight falls backward at landing

   B. Elementary stage

      1. Arms initiate jumping action

      2. Arms remain toward front of body during preparatory crouch

      3. Arms move out to side to maintain balance during flight

      4. Preparatory crouch deeper and more consistent

      5. Knee and hip extension more complete at takeoff

      6. Hips flexed during flight; thighs held in flexed position

   C. Mature stage

      1. Arms move high and to rear during preparatory crouch

      2. During takeoff, arms swing forward with force and reach high

      3. Arms held high throughout jumping action

      4. Trunk propelled at approximately 45-degree angle

      5. Major emphasis on horizontal distance

      6. Preparatory crouch deep, consistent

      7. Complete extension of ankles, knees, and hips at takeoff

      8. Thighs held parallel to ground during flight; lower leg hangs vertically

      9. Body weight forward at landing

II. Developmental Difficulties

   A. Improper use of arms (that is, failure to use arms opposite the propelling leg in a down-up-down swing as leg flexes, extends, and flexes again)

   B. Twisting or jerking of body

   C. Inability to perform either a one-foot or a two-foot takeoff

   D. Poor preliminary crouch

   E. Restricted movements of arms or legs

   F. Poor angle of takeoff

   G. Failure to extend fully on takeoff

   H. Failure to extend legs forward on landing

   I. Falling backward on landing

INITIAL

ELEMENTARY

MATURE

FIGURE 17.3   *Stages of the horizontal jumping pattern.*

- Bring your knees to your chest as you prepare to land.
- Your heels contact first upon landing.
- "Give" with your landing and fall forward.

Movement Concepts

- You can land heavily or lightly, but it is best to land lightly.
- If you swing your arms quickly, you will travel farther than if you swing them slowly.
- Your jump can be smooth or jerky, free or bound.
- You can jump in different directions and at different levels.

- You can combine your jump with other movements.
- You can jump in place, for height, for distance, or from a height.
- A jump requires taking off on one or two feet, but the landing must be on both feet.
- Jumping while holding an object will alter your pattern.

C O N C E P T   1 7 . 5
Children need to learn both the movement concepts and skill concepts of how the body can move and how the body should move.

Vertical Jumping

Verbal Description (Table 17.4)

Visual Description (Figure 17.4)

Teaching Tips

- Some children may be "earthbound" and will require special assistance.
- Stress coordinated action of legs and arms.
- Remind children to stretch and reach with the arms and head as they jump.
- Use plenty of exploratory activities at the initial stage, progressing to more directed techniques as needed.
- Try jumping on different surfaces. Inner tubes, mattresses, and trampolines provide exciting experiences.
- Have children chalk their fingers to mark their vertical jumps.
- Have children jump and place a piece of tape to mark their jump.
- Have children jump up and grab an object, keeping eye contact with the object.

Concepts Children Should Know

Skill Concepts

- Crouch about halfway down for your takeoff and landing.
- "Explode" upward.

TABLE 17.4   *Developmental Sequence for Vertical Jumping*

I. Vertical Jumping
  A. Initial stage
    1. Inconsistent preparatory crouch
    2. Difficulty in taking off with both feet
    3. Poor body extension on takeoff
    4. Little or no head lift
    5. Arms not coordinated with the trunk and leg action
    6. Little height achieved
  B. Elementary stage
    1. Knee flexion exceeds 90-degree angle on preparatory crouch
    2. Exaggerated forward lean during crouch
    3. Two-foot takeoff
    4. Entire body does not fully extend during flight phase
    5. Arms attempt to aid in flight (but often unequally) and balance
    6. Noticeable horizontal displacement on landing
  C. Mature stage
    1. Preparatory crouch with knee flexion from 60 to 90 degrees
    2. Forceful extension at hips, knees, and ankles
    3. Simultaneous coordinated upward arm lift
    4. Upward head tilt with eyes focused on target
    5. Full body extension
    6. Elevation of reaching arm by shoulder girdle tilt combined with downward thrust of non-reaching arm at peak of flight
    7. Controlled landing very close to point of takeoff
II. Developmental Difficulties
  A. Failure to get airborne
  B. Failure to take off with both feet simultaneously
  C. Failure to crouch at about a 90-degree angle
  D. Failure to extend body, legs, and arms forcefully
  E. Poor coordination of leg and arm actions
  F. Swinging of arms backward or to the side for balance
  G. Failure to lead with eyes and head
  H. One-foot landing
  I. Inhibited or exaggerated flexion of hips and knees on landing
  J. Marked horizontal displacement on landing

- Forcefully swing and reach upward with your arms.
- Stretch, reach, and look upward.

INITIAL

ELEMENTARY

MATURE

FIGURE 17.4 *Stages of the vertical jumping pattern.*

- Extend at the shoulder of your reaching arm.
- This jumping pattern is used in rebounding and the layup shot in basketball, as well as the block and spike in volleyball.

Movement Concepts

- You must time your jump so that all body parts work together.
- You can jump high or low and with or without use of your arms.
- You jump higher if you use your arms.
- Your movements must be quick and forceful for the highest jumps.
- You can jump while holding objects, but your height will be less.
- You can jump only as high as the force of gravity will let you.
- Vertical jumping requires a two-footed takeoff in an upward direction and a landing on both feet.

CONCEPT 17.6
Children typically encounter a variety of developmental difficulties as they progress from one stage to another in the quest for mature fundamental movement skills.

Jumping from a Height

Verbal Description (Table 17.5)

Visual Description (Figure 17.5)

Teaching Tips

- Start with a low height and gradually work up.
- Observe carefully for children who may be landing stiff-legged. Provide an alternative activity if they are unable to bend appropriately at the knees.
- Place a mat on the floor.
- Spot all jumping carefully.
- Encourage exploration and then gradually focus on the skill element.
- Begin with single-task skills, then combine two or three tasks such as jump, clap your hands, land, and roll forward.
- Stress proper landing techniques.
- Emphasize control while in the air.
- Provide different heights for different ability levels.
- Keep equipment well spaced for safety reasons.

TABLE 17.5   *Developmental Sequence for Jumping from a Height*

I. Jumping from a Height
   A. Initial stage
      1. One foot leads on takeoff
      2. No flight phase
      3. Lead foot contacts lower surface prior to trailing foot leaving upper surface
      4. Exaggerated use of arms for balance
   B. Elementary stage
      1. Two-foot takeoff with one-foot lead
      2. Flight phase, but lacks control
      3. Arms used ineffectively for balance
      4. One-foot landing followed by immediate landing of trailing foot
      5. Inhibited or exaggerated flexion at knees and hip upon landing
   C. Mature stage
      1. Two-foot takeoff
      2. Controlled flight phase
      3. Both arms used efficiently out to sides to control balance as needed
      4. Feet contact lower surface simultaneously with toes touching first
      5. Feet land shoulder-width apart
      6. Flexion at knees and hip congruent with height of jump
II. Developmental Difficulties
   A. Inability to take off with both feet
   B. Twisting body to one side on takeoff
   C. Exaggerated or inhibited body lean
   D. Failure to coordinate use of both arms in the air
   E. Tying one arm to side while using the other
   F. Failure to land simultaneously on both feet
   G. Landing flat-footed
   H. Failure to flex knees sufficiently to absorb impact of landing
   I. Landing out of control

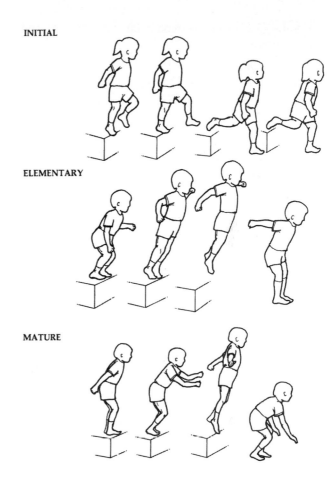

INITIAL

ELEMENTARY

MATURE

FIGURE 17.5   *Stages of the jump from a height.*

- Keep your legs shoulder-width apart to prepare for landing.
- Give at the ankles, knees, and hip joint upon landing.
- Jumping from a height and landing are used in your play activities and in numerous sports.

Movement Concepts
- You can land either heavily or lightly.
- Your jump can be from many different heights.
- The extent of your crouch upon landing is based on the height of your jump.
- You can jump in many different directions, going forward, backward, or to the side.

Concepts Children Should Know

Skill Concepts
- Push off with both feet.
- Your toes are the last thing to leave the ground.
- Lean forward slightly.
- Move your arms forward or sideward in unison for balance.

- Your jump should be smooth, but it can be jerky and awkward.
- Your jump can be far or near, high or low.
- You can jump and land while holding objects, but you must make adjustments for the weight and size of the object.
- Jumping from a height requires taking off and landing on both feet.

C O N C E P T   1 7 . 7
Movement exploration and guided-discovery experiences are especially beneficial to children at the initial and elementary stages of the fundamental movement phase.

Hopping

Verbal Description (Table 17.6)

Visual Description (Figure 17.6)

Teaching Tips

- Provide activities that make use of hopping on the "favorite" foot and on the "other" foot.
- Begin with exploratory activities and progress to more directed experiences as needed.
- Work for rhythmical flow in hopping.
- Stress rhythmical alteration of the feet.
- Do not emphasize hopping for speed or distance too early.
- Work for control and then gradually stress speed and distance.

Concepts Children Should Know

Skill Concepts
- Take off and land on the same foot.
- Lift your arms slightly as you spring up from your hop.
- Push off from your toes and land on the ball of your foot.
- Land softly.
- Hopping is used in combination with jumping in the triple jump and in the ballestra in fencing.

TABLE 17.6   *Developmental Sequence for Hopping*

I. Hopping

  A. Initial stage
1. Non-supporting leg flexed 90 degrees or less
2. Non-supporting thigh roughly parallel to contact surface
3. Body upright
4. Arms flexed at elbows and held slightly to side
5. Little height or distance generated in single hop
6. Balance lost easily
7. Limited to one or two hops

  B. Elementary stage
1. Non-supporting leg flexed
2. Non-supporting thigh at 45-degree angle to contact surface
3. Slight forward lean, with trunk flexed at hip
4. Non-supporting thigh flexed and extended at hip to produce greater force
5. Force absorbed on landing by flexing at hip and by supporting knee
6. Arms move up and down vigorously and bilaterally
7. Balance poorly controlled
8. Generally limited in number of consecutive hops that can be performed

  C. Mature stage
1. Non-supporting leg flexed at 90 degrees or less
2. Non-supporting thigh lifts with vertical thrust of supporting foot
3. Greater body lean
4. Rhythmical action of non-supporting leg (pendulum swing aiding in force production)
5. Arms move together in rhythmical lifting as the supporting foot leaves the contact surface
6. Arms not needed for balance but used for greater force production

II. Developmental Difficulties

  A. Hopping flat-footed

  B. Exaggerated movements of arms

  C. Exaggerated movement of non-supporting leg

  D. Exaggerated forward lean

  E. Inability to maintain balance for five or more consecutive hops

  F. Lack of rhythmical fluidity of movement

  G. Inability to hop effectively on both left foot and right foot

  H. Inability to alternate hopping feet in a smooth, continuous manner

  I. Tying one arm to side of body

INITIAL

ELEMENTARY

MATURE

FIGURE 17.6 *Stages in the hopping pattern.*

- Hopping is used in many dance steps, including the polka, mazurka, and schottische.

Movement Concepts
- You can land heavily or lightly when you hop.
- You can hop in place or move in different directions.
- You can hop at different speeds.
- You can hop at different heights and levels.

- You can hop over objects and in different pathways.
- You can hop smoothly and freely, or the movement can be bound and jerky.
- You can hop with either foot.
- You can alternate hopping feet.
- Hopping requires a takeoff and a landing on one foot.

GALLOPING, SLIDING, AND SKIPPING

Galloping, sliding, and skipping are fundamental movement abilities that begin developing during the preschool years and should be mastered by the first grade. The **gallop** occurs in a forward direction with one foot leading and the other trailing behind. **Sliding** is the same action but is performed in a sideways direction. Children are generally able to gallop and slide prior to being able to skip, which may be partially explained because they are unilateral activities and require less differentiation and integration of neural mechanisms than the neurologically more complex, cross-lateral action of skipping. The term **differentiation** refers to the individual's ability to distinguish among the muscle groups required to perform a movement task. **Integration** refers to the harmonious working together of both motor and sensory systems. It is sometimes referred to simply as eye-foot, eye-hand, or cye-body coordination, depending on the primary muscle groups used.

Galloping and Sliding

Verbal Description (Table 17.7)

Visual Description (Figure 17.7)

Teaching Tips

- Work on sliding in both directions.
- Stress not crossing the feet.
- Begin with exploratory experiences and then progress to skill drills and other activities involving sliding.
- Stress keeping the knees slightly bent and the trunk forward, as well as staying on the balls of the feet ("ready position").
- Rhythmic accompaniment aids sliding.
- Work for ease of movement in both directions.

TABLE 17.7 *Developmental Sequence for Galloping and Sliding*

I. Galloping and Sliding
   A. Initial stage
      1. Arrhythmical at fast pace
      2. Trailing leg often fails to remain behind and often contacts surface in front of lead leg
      3. Forty-five-degree flexion of trailing leg during flight phase
      4. Contact in a heel-toe combination
      5. Arms of little use in balance or force production
   B. Elementary stage
      1. Moderate tempo
      2. Appears choppy and stiff
      3. Trailing leg may lead during flight but lands adjacent to or behind lead leg
      4. Exaggerated vertical lift
      5. Feet contact in a heel-toe, or toe-toe, combination
      6. Arms slightly out to side to aid balance
   C. Mature stage
      1. Moderate tempo
      2. Smooth, rhythmical action
      3. Trailing leg lands adjacent to or behind lead leg
      4. Both legs flexed at 45-degree angles during flight
      5. Low flight pattern
      6. Heel-toe contact combination
      7. Arms not needed for balance; may be used for other purposes
II. Developmental Difficulties
   A. Choppy movements
   B. Keeping legs too straight
   C. Exaggerated forward trunk lean
   D. Overstepping with trailing leg
   E. Too much elevation on hop
   F. Inability to perform both forward and backward
   G. Inability to lead with non-dominant foot
   H. Inability to perform to both left and right
   I. Undue concentration on task

Concepts Children Should Know

Skill Concepts

- Step to the side and draw the other foot up quickly to the first foot.
- Repeat the action, landing with the same foot.
- Use your arms only as needed for balance.

INITIAL

ELEMENTARY

MATURE

FIGURE 17.7 *Stages of the sliding pattern.*

- Move on the balls of your feet.
- Keep your knees bent slightly.
- Lean forward at the waist slightly.
- Sliding is used in a variety of sports such as tennis, baseball, basketball, and fencing. It is also used often in dance.

Movement Concepts

- You can slide to the left or right.
- When you slide forward or backward, the action is called a gallop.

- Your movements can be fast or slow, smooth or jerky, free or bound.
- You can slide at different levels and for different distances.
- You can slide with a partner.
- You can dodge while sliding.
- When sliding sideways, remain on your feet and don't fall to your knees.

The action incorporated in **skipping** requires rhythmically alternating steps followed by a hop on the lead foot. It is recommended that prior to introducing skipping, children be given opportunities to explore the many movement variations of galloping and sliding. Guided-discovery activities should be incorporated with galloping and sliding so that these patterns may be at the mature stage prior to the introduction of a teaching progression for skipping. In other words, if the child is not yet at the mature stage of galloping or sliding (with either foot leading), it is unwise to develop lessons that focus on skipping.

Sliding is similar in many ways to galloping, except that it is conducted in a sideward direction. Once again, it is generally more appropriate to introduce sliding after the child has experienced some success with galloping. The sliding pattern is used extensively in a variety of athletic and dance activities that require rapid lateral movement. Sliding is an integral part of many sport and dance activities. Lateral movements need to be smooth, and the child should be able to make rapid changes in direction. Be sure to point out specific instances where sliding is used in sports and to have students master sliding in relation to its specific use.

Skipping

Verbal Description (Table 17.8)

Visual Description (Figure 17.8)

Teaching Tips

- The child should be able to gallop with either leg leading before learning skipping.
- The child should be able to hop well on either leg before attempting to skip.
- Introduce skipping when child is ready.
- You may need to provide slow-motion demonstrations.
- Once the basic pattern is mastered, encourage exploration of variations of skipping.

TABLE 17.8   *Developmental Sequence for Skipping*

I. Skipping
- A. Initial stage
  1. One-footed skip
  2. Deliberate step-hop action
  3. Double hop or step sometimes occurs
  4. Exaggerated stepping action
  5. Arms of little use
  6. Action appears segmented
- B. Elementary stage
  1. Step and hop coordinated effectively
  2. Rhythmical use of arms to aid momentum
  3. Exaggerated vertical lift on hop
  4. Flat-footed landing
- C. Mature stage
  1. Rhythmical weight transfer throughout
  2. Rhythmical use of arms (reduced during time of weight transfer)
  3. Low vertical lift on hop
  4. Toe-first landing

II. Developmental Difficulties
- A. Segmented stepping and hopping action
- B. Poor rhythmical alteration
- C. Inability to use both sides of body
- D. Exaggerated movements
- E. Landing flat-footed
- F. Exaggerated, inhibited, or unilateral arm movements
- G. Inability to move in a straight line
- H. Inability to skip backward and to side

- Use rhythmical activities that require skipping.
- Work for a rhythmical, flowing motion.

Concepts Children Should Know

Skill Concepts

- Step forward and then hop up on the same foot.
- Do the same with the other foot.
- Lift your knees sharply upward.
- Swing your arms upward in time with your legs.
- The skipping pattern is used in many folk and square dances and is basic to good footwork in numerous sports.

INITIAL

ELEMENTARY

MATURE

FIGURE 17.8 *Stages of the skipping pattern.*

Movement Concepts

- You can skip in different directions, pathways, and floor patterns.
- You can skip at different speeds.
- You can skip in a smooth and free manner, or it can be jerky and bound.
- You can skip at different levels and land heavily or lightly.
- You can skip with a partner and while carrying objects.
- Skipping is a combination of two movements—stepping and hopping.

- Skipping requires you to use both sides of your body in a rhythmic fashion.

SKILL DEVELOPMENT ACTIVITIES

Mastery of fundamental locomotor skills requires environmental conditions that permit practice and provide instruction. Instruction may take many forms. However, when viewing children from a developmental perspective, you must first determine their phase and stage of motor development, which will provide cues to their level of movement skill learning (beginning, intermediate, or advanced). With this information, it is then a simple matter to determine whether the lesson should focus on exploratory activities, guided-discovery activities, skill application activities, or skill refinement activities.

Exploratory Activities

The primary purpose of incorporating **exploratory activities** into the movement lesson is to provide children at either the initial stage or the elementary stage an opportunity to learn how and where their bodies can move when performing locomotor movements. Exploratory activities are intended to help children get in touch with their bodies and to lead them to experiment with the many variations in effort, space, and relationships that they can experience. Combinations of these can be included successfully in the lesson after the gross general framework idea has been established and children are progressing toward the mature stage in the movement skill. Odd-numbered Tables 17.9 through 17.23 provide easy-to-use charts for presenting movement challenges that will permit children to explore their locomotor potential.

Guided-Discovery Activities

The primary purpose of including **guided-discovery activities** in the lesson is to provide children who are at the elementary stage of developing their fundamental locomotor abilities an opportunity to practice the skill. Practice, using a problem-solving technique, permits children to learn more about the skill and how their bodies should move. Emphasis at this level is placed on discovering the proper mechanics and usefulness of various locomotor movements. Even-numbered Tables 17.10 through 17.24 present a sampling of guided-discovery experiences.

TABLE 17.9   *Exploratory Activity Ideas for Running*

Effort	Space	Relationships
Force	***Level***	***Objects***

Can You Run. . . .	*Can You Run. . . .*	*Can You Run. . . .*
—like a pixie?	—very tall?	—on the line?
—like an elephant?	—very small?	—across the line?
—on your tiptoes?	—at a high level?	—under the bars?
—flat-footed?	—at a low level?	—behind the chair?
—as if you were floating?	—at a medium level?	—around the chair?
—as if you weighed a million pounds?	—fast or slow at a high level?	—over the hoop?
—as softly as you can?	—smoothly at a high level?	—through the hoop?
—as hard as you can?	***Direction***	—carrying a ball?
Time		—carrying a suitcase?
	—forward?	—with boots on?
—as fast as you can?	—backward?	***People***
—as slowly as you can?	—to the left or right?	
—starting slowly and showing form?	—diagonally?	—all by yourself?
—alternating fast and slow?	—and change direction once?	—in front of a partner?
Flow	—and change direction three times?	—behind a partner?
	—in a straight line?	—beside a partner?
—as smoothly as you can?	—in a curvy line?	—holding a partner's hand?
—with jerky movements?	—in a zigzag line?	—with the class?
—like a machine?	—in a pattern (show shapes)?	—without touching anyone?
—like a robot?	***Range***	—with two others?
—like a deer?		—in formation?
—like a football player?	—in your own space?	***Combinations***
—without using your arms?	—throughout the room?	
	—as far as you can?	An infinite variety of exploratory experiences can be devised simply by combining various effort, space, and relationship challenges.
	—and not bump anyone?	
	—with your feet wide?	
	—with big steps?	
	—with tiny steps?	

TABLE 17.10   *Guided-Discovery Activity Ideas for Running*

	1. Have the children first explore the numerous variations of running.
	2. Then begin to put limitations on the possible responses to the following movement challenges:
General	a. Run around the gym in a clockwise direction, then in a counterclockwise direction.
Arm Action	b. Run as fast as you can one time around the gym. What do your arms do? Do they move fast or slowly?
	c. When you run slowly, do your arms move fast or slowly? Why?
	d. How do you swing your arms when you run? Do they cross your chest, or do they stop before crossing?
	e. Run with your arms crossing your chest. Now try it without crossing. Which is better? Why?
Leg Action	f. What part of your foot lands first when you are running as fast as you can? What about when you are jogging at a slower pace?
	g. Run uphill. Run downhill. How does your stride change? Why does it change?
Trunk Action	h. Lean forward when you run. Now try to stay very straight. Now try something in between. Which feels the best for you? Why?
Total	i. Show me how you would run a five-mile race. How would you run a mile race, a quarter mile, fifty yards?
	j. Why is your run slightly different for each distance?
	k. Can you run to the rhythm made by the drum?
	l. What happens to your run when the beat speeds up or slows down?
	3. Now combine running with other activities to achieve a more automatic pattern.
	a. Can you tag someone lightly while running?
	b. Can you dodge someone who is trying to tag you?
	c. Run barefooted. Now try it with your street shoes. Now with your gym shoes. How does it feel? Which way is most comfortable? Safest?
	d. Run on different surfaces. How does it affect your running pattern? Why?

TABLE 17.11 *Exploratory Activity Ideas for Leaping*

Effort	Space	Relationships
Force	***Level***	***Objects***
Can You Leap. . . .	*Can You Leap. . . .*	*Can You Leap. . . .*
—and land lightly?	—as high as you can?	—over a rope?
—and land without a sound?	—as low as you can?	—over a hurdle?
—and land forcefully?	—at many different levels?	—over a partner?
—alternating hard and soft landings?	—alternating low and high leaps?	—across two outstretched ropes?
—and swing your arms forcefully?	***Direction***	—over two outstretched ropes?
—and keep your arms at your side?		—from one carpet square to the next?
—holding your arms in different positions?	—forward?	—from one footprint to a corresponding footprint?
Time	—backward?	***People***
	—diagonally?	
—and stay in the air as long as you can?	—with your left foot leading?	—the same distance as your partner?
—and land as quickly as you can?	—with your right foot leading?	—over your partner?
—and swing only one arm?	—alternating left and right foot lead?	—the length of your partner's body?
—in time to the accented beat of the drum?	***Range***	—in unison with your partner?
—in time to the accented beat of the music?		***Combinations***
Flow	—as far as you can?	
	—and keep one leg bent?	After several variations of leaping have been explored singularly, try combining various aspects of effort, space, and relationships. For example, "Can you leap lightly as high as you can over a rope held by two partners?"
—from a three-step approach?	—and bend both legs in the air?	
—from a two-step approach?	—and keep both legs straight?	
—from a one-step approach?	—and twist your trunk in the air?	
—from a stationary position?	—and find different things to do with your arms while in the air?	
	—on different surfaces?	

TABLE 17.12 *Guided-Discovery Activity Ideas for Leaping*

1. First explore the movement variations of leaping.
2. Then begin to place limitations on the response possibilities to the following movement challenges:

Leg Action

   a. Try to leap as far as you can. What do you do when you want to go far? Can you show me? If you don't want to leap far, what do you do? Show me. Try pushing off forcefully with your trailing foot and stretching out with your lead foot. Does it make a difference?

   b. Try leaping and pushing off from different parts of your trailing foot. Try pushing off flat-footed and off the ball of your trailing foot. Which works better? See if there is any difference in the distance leaped trying both ways.

Trunk Action

   c. Try leaping and bending your trunk at different angles. Now try keeping your trunk erect. Which ways feel the most comfortable? Do you bend your trunk differently for different purposes? Watch your partner and see if he or she bends at the waist differently when trying to leap different heights and various distances.

   d. What do we know about bending at the waist? When is it best to bend far forward? When is it best to have very little bend at the waist? Experiment with a partner and then let me know your answer.

Arm Action

   e. Try leaping with your arms in many different positions. How does it feel? Which way helps you leap the farthest or the highest? Experiment and find out.

General

   f. See if you can leap and coordinate the use of your arms, legs, and trunk. What are some important things we should remember when leaping?

   g. Try leaping from a standing position. Now try it from a running approach. Which way helps you go farther? Why?

   h. Try leaping off one foot. Now try the other. Is there a difference? Why? Practice both ways.

3. After a mature leaping pattern has been reasonably well mastered, combine it with other exploratory and guided-discovery activities to reinforce the pattern and make it more automatic.

   a. Listen to the beat of the drum and leap on every hard note.

   b. Beginning at one end of the gym, perform three leaps in combination with running.

   c. Try to leap over the outstretched ropes placed on the floor.

   d. Let's try to run across the gym alternating leaping off our left and right foot.

   e. Can you leap and catch a tossed ball while in the air?

   f. Try leaping across the outstretched ropes and touching the balloon overhead (ringing a suspended bell is a real challenge).

   g. Using carpet squares (on a non-slick surface only) or hoops, practice leaping from spaceship to spaceship, being sure that no other astronaut is in a spaceship that you leap to.

TABLE 17.13   *Exploratory Activity Ideas for Horizontal Jumping*

Effort	Space	Relationships
Force	***Level***	***Objects***
Can You Jump. . . .	*Can You Jump. . . .*	*Can You Jump. . . .*
—as quietly as possible?	—from as small a position as you can?	—over the box?
—as loudly as possible?	—from as big a position as you can?	—across the rope?
—alternating loud and soft jumps?	—and stay under my hand?	—through the hoop?
—like a pixie?	***Direction***	—like a frog or a rabbit?
—like a giant?	—forward or backward?	—while holding this ball?
Time	—sideways?	***People***
—very fast?	—in a straight line?	—with a partner?
—very slowly?	—several times in a zigzag or circular pattern?	—as far as your partner?
—alternating fast and slow jumps?	—making various geometric shapes or letters of the alphabet?	—over your partner?
—as if you were stuck in molasses?	—while staying in the same place?	—at the same time as your partner jumps?
—as if you were on ice?	***Range***	***Combinations***
Flow	—as far as you can?	Numerous combinations of effort, space, and relationships are possible. For example,
—with your arms and legs held stiffly?	—as near as you can?	—for distance and then for height?
—keeping your arms out?	—landing with your feet wide apart?	—as short and as low as possible?
—with your legs out?	—landing with your feet close together?	—as fast and as far as possible?
—in a relaxed manner?		—as quietly and as far as you can?
—like a wooden soldier?		—and toss a ball?
		—and catch a ball?
		—to my rhythm?
		—to the music?

TABLE 17.14   *Guided-Discovery Activity Ideas for Horizontal Jumping*

	1. First explore several of the numerous variations of horizontal jumping.
	2. Now begin to place limitations on the responses to the following movement challenges:
General	a. Try to jump over the unfolded newspaper, outstretched ropes, or tape lines on the floor. Can you get over the short part without touching? How about the long part?
Arm Action	b. What happens when you jump and don't use your hands? Why don't you go as far? What should we do with our arms when we jump? Show me.
	c. Show me how you would use your arms. Several are doing this (demonstrate) with their arms. Why? Oh, I see. It helps you keep your balance.
Landing	d. Can you show me several different ways to land? Try it now just doing different things with your feet. Now try landing with your feet way apart, close together, and in between. Which worked best for you? Why? What happens to your knees when you jump? Why? Should there be any difference if I jumped from a very high height or from a very low height?
Total	e. When you put the entire jump together, what do you do with your head and eyes? Try three different things with your head (look up, down, straight ahead). Which works best? Now try jumping with your eyes closed. Scary, isn't it? Why? What should we remember about the use of our head and eyes when we jump from a height?
	3. When the mature pattern has been reasonably well mastered, combine jumping from a height with other activities to reinforce the pattern and make it more automatic. For example,
	a. Jump and assume different postures in the air.
	b. Jump and perform turns in the air.
	c. Jump, land, and roll.
	d. Jump, turn, land, and roll.

TABLE 17.15   *Exploratory Activity Ideas for Vertical Jumping*

Effort	Space	Relationships
Force	***Level***	***Objects***
Can You Jump Up. . . .	*Can You Jump Up. . . .*	*Can You Jump Up. . . .*
—and land lightly?	—as high as you can?	—and strike the hanging ball?
—and land heavily?	—as low as you can?	—with a weighted object?
—like an elephant?	—alternating high and low jumps?	—with a ball?
—like a robot?	—and touch the same spot five times?	—on a trampoline?
Time	—from a crouched position?	—on a bounding board?
	—from an extended position?	—over a jump rope?
—as fast as you can?	***Direction***	***People***
—as slowly as you can?		
—like a rocket?	—and land in the same spot?	—with a partner?
—like a growing flower?	—and land in a different spot?	—and alternate jumping up with a partner?
Flow	—and land slightly forward, backward, or to the side?	—while holding hands?
	—and turn?	—and touch your partner's spot?
—without using your arms?	***Range***	***Combinations***
—and use only one arm?		
—and keep your head down?	—and land in your own space?	Numerous combinations of effort, space, and relationships are possible. For example,
—and remain stiff?	—and land outside your space?	—and toss a ball?
—as relaxed as you can?	—and land with your feet wide apart?	—and shoot a basket?
	—and land with your feet close together?	—and catch a ball?
		—and hop over a jump rope?
		—and turn?
		—and turn and catch?
		—as lightly, high, and as fast as you can?

TABLE 17.16   *Guided-Discovery Activity Ideas for Vertical Jumping*

	1. First explore several of the numerous variations of vertical jumping.
	2. Now begin to place limitations on the response possibilities to the following movement challenges:
Arm Action	a. What happens when you jump without using your arms? Does one arm help? When you use both arms, which way is best? Try three ways, and then tell me which works best for you. Many of you thought that swinging your arms up as your legs uncoiled was best. Why is that so?
	b. Try bending your knees at three different levels when you jump. Which is best? Why? Measure the height of your jumps from three different leg positions. Why is there a difference with each jump?
Trunk Action	c. Does your trunk stay bent forward when you jump or does it extend? Try both ways. Which is better? Why?
Head Action	d. Jump as high as you can with your head and eyes in three different positions. Which is best for you? Many thought looking up was best. You're right. Think of yourself as a puppet with a string attached to your nose. Every time you jump up, you stretch your entire body out and reach up to the sky with your nose.
Landing	e. Try landing in different ways. Which do you think is best? Why do you bend your knees when you land? How much should you bend them? Why? Did you land in the same spot you took off from? See if you can. Some people are landing in front of their takeoff spot. Do you get more height or less height when that happens? Why?
	3. When the mature pattern has been reasonably well mastered using these and other guided-discovery challenges, combine vertical jumping with other activities to reinforce the pattern and make it more automatic. For example,
	a. Try jumping on different surfaces:
	bounding board
	tires
	trampoline (spot carefully)
	b. Try jumping with other objects:
	hoops (for small children only)
	jump ropes
	high jumping
	stretch ropes
	c. Play jumping games.

TABLE 17.17   *Exploratory Activity Ideas for Jumping from a Height*

Effort	Space	Relationships
Force	***Level***	***Objects***
Can You Jump. . . . —and land as lightly as you can? —and land as forcefully as you can?	*Can You Jump. . . .* —from a crouched position? —from a tucked position? —as high as you can?	*Can You Jump. . . .* —over the wand? —through the hoop? —and catch the ball in the air? —and throw the ball in the air? —and catch a ball you toss while in the air?
Time	***Direction***	***People***
—and land as quickly as possible? —and stay in the air as long as possible? —in slow motion?	—forward? —backward? —sideways? —and make a quarter turn? —and make a half turn? —and make a full turn?	—at the same time as a partner? —and land at the same time as your partner? —and do what your partner does? —and do the opposite of your partner?
Flow	***Range***	***Combinations***
—with different arm actions? —without using your arms? —while holding one arm to your side?	—and land with your feet together? —and land with your feet apart? —and land in this spot? —and make yourself as big as you can?	Numerous combinations of effort, space, and relationship activities involving exploration of jumping from a height are possible and should be used after the child has gained control of singular movements.

TABLE 17.18   *Guided-Discovery Activity Ideas for Jumping from a Height*

	1. First explore several of the variations of jumping from a height.

2. Now begin to place limitations on the response possibilities to the following movement challenges:

Takeoff
   a. How do you take off when you jump? Do you do it with one foot leading or do both feet leave at the same time? Try it both ways. Which way gives you more control or balance? Why? Try turning in the air after you take off, or try a two-footed takeoff.

Flight
   b. What do you do while you are in the air? Try different things with your arms and your legs. To keep your balance best, show me how you use your arms. What happens to your body when it is in the air? Can anyone show me what it looks like? Do you jump straight up? Do you just skim over the floor? Do you do something different?

   c. What happens when you swing your arms forward very hard as you jump? Very softly? What happens when your arms swing all the way up to your head? Try it different ways and see which is best. Is it better to swing hard or soft, all the way up or only partway up when we jump as far as we can? Why? Show me.

Leg Action
   d. When you jump, do you leave the ground with both feet at the same time or with one foot at a time? Try both. Why is it better to use both feet for a standing long jump? Try jumping as far as you can using both feet. Now put a beanbag on one foot and, while trying to keep it there, jump as far as you can. Which works better, one foot or both feet? Why?

Landing
   e. How do you land? Should you land and sit back or fall forward? What happens to your knees when you land? Are they stiff or do you bend them? Why?

Total
   f. Let's put it all together. Jump as far as you can. How does it feel? Can you get your legs and arms to work together? What happens when they do? Should you jump fast (explosively) or is it better to jump more slowly? Try both. Which works best? Why?

3. When the mature pattern has been reasonably mastered, combine it with other activities to reinforce the pattern and make it more automatic.

   a. Play jumping games.

   b. Conduct cooperative jumping contests where partners try to jump the same distance. Two points are scored for jumping the same distance. One point is deducted for jumping different distances.

   c. Jump from different surfaces. What happens to your distance when you jump from a very soft surface? Why?

TABLE 17.19   *Exploratory Activity Ideas for Hopping*

Effort	Space	Relationships
Force	***Level***	***Objects***

Can You Hop. . . . (Effort/Force)
—as quietly as you can?
—as noisily as you can?
—alternating hard and soft landings?
—hard four times on your left, then softly four times on your right?

Time
—as fast as possible?
—as slowly as possible?
—starting slowly and getting slower?
—in time to the music?

Flow
—without using your arms?
—using only the arm opposite your hopping foot?
—alternating feet every eight (four, two) beats?

Can You Hop. . . . (Space/Level)
—in a small ball?
—in a crouched position?
—with little crouched hops?
—as high as you can?
—at a medium height?
—staying lower than my hand?
—staying at the same level as my hand?

Direction
—in place?
—forward?
—backward?
—sideways?
—and turn in the air?
—and make a quarter (half, three-quarter, full) turn?

Range
—in your own space?
—from spot to spot?
—and land on a different carpet square each time?
—and land on the same spot?
—and land in as small a spot as possible?
—and land in as large a spot as possible?

Can You Hop. . . . (Relationships/Objects)
—over the rope?
—in a hoop?
—over the cones?
—around the cones?
—while bouncing a ball?
—while catching a tossed ball?
—while tossing and catching a self-tossed ball?

People
—in rhythm with a partner?
—forward holding hands?
—facing each other and hopping in unison to the wall?
—imitating your partner's arm actions?

Combinations

Numerous combinations of effort, space, and relationships can be explored while hopping after control has been gained in single-problem tasks. For example, "Can you hop as quietly as you can over the rope?"

TABLE 17.20   *Guided-Discovery Activity Ideas for Hopping*

	1.	First explore several of the variations of hopping.
	2.	Now begin to place limitations and questions on the following response possibilities:
General	a.	Hop in place on one foot. Can you do the same on the other foot? Can you hop to the wall on one foot and come back on the other?
Leg Action	b.	Try hopping and putting your free leg in different positions. Which is easiest when you are hopping in place? For distance? Why? Try the same experiment with the other leg. Why do some people hop better on one leg than on the other? Do you have a better leg?
Arm Action	c.	Try hopping as far as you can, using your arms in three different ways to help. Try it without using your arms at all. Which works best for you? Several students seem to lift and swing the arms forward when they hop for distance. Try it. How does that feel?
	d.	Let's try that same arm action while hopping in place. What happened? Why? What do you want to do with your arms when hopping in place? Show me.
	3.	Once the mature hopping pattern has been reasonably well mastered for both the left and the right leg, move on to activities that use hopping in combination with other skills. Incorporation of hopping with other skills will reinforce the pattern and make it more automatic. For example,
	a.	Step-hops.
	b.	Various dance steps (schottische, step-hop, polka).
	c.	Jump rope activities.
	d.	Track and field event activities.

TABLE 17.21   *Exploratory Activity Ideas for Skipping*

Effort	Space	Relationships
Force	***Level***	***Objects***
Can You Skip. . . .	*Can You Skip. . . .*	*Can You Skip. . . .*
—as quietly as you can?	—while making yourself very small?	—without touching any of the lines on the floor?
—as a giant would?	—and gradually get smaller?	—without touching any cracks in the cement?
—as loudly as you can?	—as tall as you can?	—and try to step on each line or crack?
—landing heavily on one foot and lightly on the other?	—with a high knee lift?	—while carrying a heavy object?
—alternating loud/quiet and hard/soft skips?	—barely raising your feet off the ground?	***People***
Time	***Direction***	—with a partner?
—as fast as you can across the room?	—forward or backward?	—going backward while your partner moves forward?
—as slowly as you can?	—sideways (left or right)?	—in unison with a partner?
—as if you were on a sandy beach?	—in a straight line?	—while holding both of your partner's hands?
—downhill?	—in a curved or zigzag pattern?	***Combinations***
—uphill?	—in a circle?	Numerous ingenious combinations of effort, space, and relationships can be explored. For example, "Can you skip as quietly as you can while making yourself very big and without touching any of the lines on the floor?"
—to the beat of the drum?	***Range***	
Flow	—and see how many complete skips it takes to cross the room?	
—without using your arms?	—and measure how much space you cover in one complete skip?	
—swinging your arms outward, inward, or diagonally?	—with your legs wide apart?	
—like a toy soldier?		
—in a relaxed manner?		

TABLE 17.22 *Guided-Discovery Activity Ideas for Skipping*

1. First explore several of the movement variations of skipping.
2. Then help the children discover how their body works when they skip. For example:

Leg Action

    a. Try skipping around the room. Experiment with big steps, little steps, and in-between steps. When would you want to use each?

    b. Be a detective and see if you can find out what two movements with your legs the skip is made up of. Who knows the answer? Good! Show me. Let's all take it apart.

Arm Action

    c. What do you do with your arms when you skip? Try four or five different things. How does it feel when your arms swing as you skip?

    d. Watch your partner. Do his or her arms swing with the same arm and leg leading alternately or with the opposite arm and leg leading alternately?

    e. What other locomotor skills do we do with alternating opposite arms and leg leading? Why do you think we do that? Try leading with the same arm as the leg that is leading. How does it feel? What do your friends look like? So you see it probably is best that we walk, run, and skip with leg and arm alteration because it is more comfortable and helps us move better.

3. When the mature pattern has been reasonably well mastered using these and other guided-discovery challenges, combine skipping with other activities to reinforce the pattern and make it more automatic. For example,

    a. Play skip tag.

    b. Skip to a drum beat.

    c. Skip to selected musical accompaniment.

    d. Modify chasing and fleeing games to incorporate skipping rather than running.

    e. Teach the children folk dances that incorporate skipping.

TABLE 17.23   *Exploratory Activity Ideas for Sliding and Galloping*

Effort	Space	Relationships
Force	***Level***	***Objects***
Can You Slide/Gallop. . . .	*Can You Slide/Gallop. . . .*	*Can You Slide/Gallop. . . .*
—landing flat-footed?	—sideways and get smaller?	—from one line to the other?
—landing on your toes?	—sideways and get bigger?	—from one line to the other and return?
—very quietly?	—somewhere in between big and small?	—from one line to the other as many times as you can in thirty seconds?
—while pretending you are dragging an elephant?	—and change levels as I raise or lower my hand?	—in either direction while bouncing and catching a ball?
—while pretending you are trying to escape a charging elephant?	***Direction***	—in either direction while dribbling a ball?
Time	—sideways?	—in either direction to catch a ball?
—in either direction?	—forward or backward (gallop)?	***People***
—as fast as you can?	—to the left or right?	
—as slowly as you can?	—to the left four steps and then to the right four steps?	—facing a partner and travel in the same direction?
—to the beat of the drum?	—to the left two steps and then to the right two steps?	—facing a partner and travel in an opposite direction?
—in time to the music?	—alternating left and right?	—facing a partner and travel four steps in the opposite direction and then four steps in the same direction?
Flow	—in the direction I point?	***Combinations***
—keeping both legs stiff?	***Range***	
—keeping one leg stiff?		After exploring the many variations of sliding or galloping in isolation, you will want to combine various aspects of effort, space, and relationships. For example, "Can you slide in either direction four steps and touch the line while bouncing and catching a ball?"
—keeping your trunk erect?	—to your right (or left) as far as you can until I say stop?	
—bending forward at your waist?	—taking big steps?	
	—taking small steps?	

TABLE 17.24 *Guided-Discovery Activity Ideas for Galloping and Sliding*

Galloping

1. First explore several of the numerous variations of galloping.
2. Then begin to place limitations on the response possibilities to the following movement challenges:

General
   a. Put one foot forward and gallop around the room. Try it with the other foot leading. Which is easier? Why?

Leg Action
   b. Try galloping with your legs stiff. Then try with them very bent. Now try different amounts of knee bend. What works best for you? Why do you think some knee bend is good?

Foot Action
   c. What happens to your back foot when you gallop forward? Does it come up to meet your front foot, or does it overtake it and move in front? Which do you think is better? Try both. Why is it best not to overtake your front foot with the rear foot.

Arm Action
   d. Gallop across the room. What did you do with your arms? Now gallop back as fast as you can. Did your arms do anything that time?

   e. How can your arms help you when you gallop? Let's time our partner going across the room, first using his or her arms and then without using them. Which was faster? Which was more comfortable? Why?

3. After the mature pattern has been reasonably well mastered, combine it with other activities to reinforce the pattern and make it more automatic.

   a. Experiment with the wide variety of combinations of effort, space, and relationships that are possible.

   b. Conduct a story play or mimetic activities that use imagery with galloping horses.

   c. Practice galloping to the uneven beat of a drum or tambourine.

   d. Gallop to some form of musical accompaniment. Can you gallop to an even beat or an uneven beat?

Sliding

1. First explore the numerous movement variations of sliding.
2. Then begin to place limitations on the response possibilities to the following movement challenges:

Leg and Trunk Action
   a. When you slide sideways, try doing it with your legs stiff. How does it feel? How do you think you could slide better? What happens when your knees are slightly bent and your trunk is bent forward slightly? Which is better—legs straight and back straight, or knees bent slightly and trunk bent slightly? Try both ways.

Foot Action
   b. Do you cross your feet when you slide? Have a partner watch you and check. Now watch my finger and slide in the direction I point, changing direction as fast as you can when I point in the opposite direction.

   c. It's best not to cross your feet, right? Why? When moving to your left, which foot should move first? What about to the right?

3. After the mature pattern has been reasonably well mastered, combine it with other exploratory and guided-discovery activities to reinforce the pattern and make it more automatic.

   a. Watch my hand and slide in the direction I point.

   b. Close your eyes and listen to my call of "left" or "right." Then move in that direction.

   c. Count for your partner and see how many times he or she can slide left and right between these two lines (indicate two parallel lines ten feet apart) in thirty seconds.

   d. Slide left or right to catch the ball thrown to you in that direction. Why don't you cross your feet? What happens when you do?

SKILL APPLICATION ACTIVITIES

After fundamental locomotor skills have been mastered and can be performed at the mature stage with reasonable consistency, it becomes appropriate to focus on skill application activities. **Skill application activities** permit practice and refinement of locomotor skills under dynamic conditions and are applied to a variety of game, rhythmical, and self-testing activities. Greater emphasis is placed on skill development in terms of improved performance

TABLE 17.25   *Selected Locomotor Games Sequenced in Terms of Complexity*

Locomotor Games (page number)	Movement Skills Stressed			
	Walking/Running	Jumping/Hopping	Skipping/Sliding/Galloping	Leaping
Crows and Cranes (310)	X	X	X	
Squirrels in the Trees (310)	X	X	X	
Colors (310)	X	X	X	
Magic Carpet (310)	X	X	X	X
Back-to-Back (310)	X	X	X	X
Hunter (310)	X	X	X	
Spaceship (311)	X		X	
Touch and Follow (311)	X		X	
Where's My Partner? (311)	X	X	X	
Whistle Stop (311)	X		X	X
Frog in the Sea (311)	X	X		
Crossing the Brook (312)		X		X
Jump the Shot (312)		X		
Jack Be Nimble (312)	X			X

abilities, as well as on combining single skills with others in sport, dance, and recreational activities.

Failure to achieve the mature stage in a fundamental locomotor skill prior to attempting to apply it at the sport-related movement phase results in a "proficiency barrier." In other words, inability to perform the fundamental skill at the mature stage makes successful performance of the sport skill version unlikely. Therefore, locomotor skill application activities should be introduced into the program only after the basic elements of these fundamental skills have been mastered.

CONCEPT 17.8
Skill application experiences involving low-level game activities are appropriate for individuals at the mature stage of the fundamental movement phase.

Locomotor Games

Many of the low-level locomotor games presented here have been used for generations and may be found in numerous textbooks. They have been selected for inclusion here because they: (1) provide for maximum activity, (2) promote inclusion rather than exclusion, (3) are easily modified and varied, (4) aid in the development of a variety of locomotor

skills, and (5) are fun for children to play. Although some of the activities that follow have traditionally been played as elimination games, you are encouraged to modify them to ensure that children are *not* eliminated and that all receive maximum activity. A format is used in which each game is first viewed from the perspective of the particular movement skills that it incorporates, then followed by the formation, equipment, and procedures to be employed.

Children enjoy an almost endless variety of locomotor games. The vast majority of locomotor games, however, are designed around running as the primary mode of movement. The alert teacher will feel free to substitute other locomotor movements as they suit the nature of the lesson and the skills being stressed. Each of the games described here may be modified in a variety of ways (see Table 17.25). The primary objectives of locomotor game activities are to

1. enhance fundamental locomotor movement abilities,
2. enhance agility and general body coordination,
3. enhance rhythmical performance of locomotor movements,
4. enhance ability to participate cooperatively in a team effort,
5. develop listening skills, and
6. enhance the ability to follow directions and obey rules.

Crows and Cranes

Movement Skills: Running, dodging, pivoting, starting, and stopping.

Formation: Two lines of children facing each other about ten feet apart.

Equipment: None.

Procedures: The class is divided into two groups. One group is called the crows, the other the cranes. The groups line up at each end of the playing area facing each other. On a signal, they will advance toward one another. The instructor either calls "crows" or "cranes." If crows are called, the crows chase the cranes back to their goal and all persons caught join the crows. If cranes are called, they become the chasers. The instructor calls various names, beginning with *cra ...* before calling crows or cranes (for example, *cra ... ckers, cra ... yfish, cra ... yons*).

Squirrels in the Trees

Movement Skills: Running.

Formation: Groups of three. Two children stand with hands joined; a third child is in between.

Equipment: None.

Procedures: One player is designated as a fox, the others as squirrels. The remaining players scatter in groups of three. Two of the players stand and hold hands above their head (tree); the others squat between them (squirrel). The game begins with the fox chasing the squirrel. To avoid being caught, the squirrel may run under a tree, and the squirrel originally under the tree must flee from the fox. When tagged by the fox, the squirrel becomes the fox and the fox becomes a squirrel.

Colors

Movement Skills: Running.

Formation: Two lines of players facing one another.

Equipment: None.

Procedures: The groups stand on opposite goals with the teacher in the middle. Each group chooses a color and then moves toward the center of the playing area until the two groups are about five to ten feet apart. The teacher calls out a color. When the color selected by either side is called, the players on that side run to their goal and the other group chases them. Those tagged before they reach their goal must join the other side. The teacher may call several colors before he calls one of the colors selected. The side having the most players at the end of the playing time wins the game.

Magic Carpet

Movement Skills: Skipping, running, and walking.

Formation: Scatter formation with lines, circles, and spots drawn on the floor.

Equipment: None.

Procedures: The entire play area is considered to be the "carpet." Spots, circles, and other markings on it represent the "magic spot." The class follows the leader in single file around the play area. When the leader stops, the children run to a magic spot and stand. Those who do not reach a spot are eliminated. The game ends when there are only as many magic spots as there are children. You may designate specific shapes or colors to go to.

Back-to-Back

Movement Skills: Running, skipping, hopping, jumping, and sliding.

Formation: Partners standing back-to-back with one extra child.

Equipment: None.

Procedures: The number of children should be uneven. On signal, each child stands back-to-back with another child. One child will be without a partner. This child can clap his or her hands and call out the next position to be taken, such as face-to-face or side-to-side, and all children change partners, with the extra player seeking a partner. Other commands can be given, such as "Everybody run [hop, skip, jump, slide]" or "Walk like an elephant." When the whistle is blown, they immediately find a partner and stand back-to-back.

Hunter

Movement Skills: Running.

Formation: Scatter.

Equipment: None.

Procedures: One player is the hunter and says to the other children, "Come with me to hunt tigers." The other children fall into line behind the hunter and follow in the hunter's footsteps as he or she leads them away from the goal. The hunter tries to tag as many players as possible before all reach safety. As each child is tagged, the hunter calls out the child's name. The hunter chooses a new hunter from the players who reached the base safely. Since the setting of this game is believed to be the jungle, imitations of animal movements (bearwalk, kangaroo hop, elephant drag) may be used instead of running.

Spaceship

Movement Skills: Running, starting, and stopping.

Formation: Scatter.

Equipment: An object to represent the Earth (beanbag, tree, or the like).

Procedures: Children and teacher decide on an object that will represent the Earth, such as a tree, beanbag, circle, base, and so on. Children are spaceships, and on the countdown "Five, four, three, two, ONE!" the rockets blast the spaceships off the ground; they quickly pick up speed and go into orbit around the earth. After one or more orbits, spaceships return and "splash down." The game may be repeated any number of times, with spaceships flying any number of orbits. To improve endurance, children run longer and faster each time.

Touch and Follow

Movement Skills: Walking, skipping, and galloping.

Formation: Single circle facing in.

Equipment: None.

Procedures: The children stand in a large circle with their hands held out toward the center, palms upward. One child is chosen to be in the center of the circle. That child moves about and then lightly touches the outstretched hand of some child. The child who is touched must follow the first child around the circle, imitating any activity chosen. They may skip, gallop, trot, or perform any other appropriate activity. They go once around the circle and then the follower

becomes the one in the center. The game can also be played so that the entire circle imitates someone rather than involving just one other child.

Where's My Partner?

Movement Skills: Skipping, galloping, walking, running, and hopping.

Formation: Double circle of couples facing each other.

Equipment: None.

Procedures: The children are arranged in a double circle by couples, with partners facing each other. The inside circle has one more player than the outside. When the signal is given, the children in the circles skip to the players' right. When the command "Halt" is given, the children in the circles face each other to find partners. The player left without a partner is in the "mush pot." The game can also be played with music. When the music stops, the players seek partners. The game can also be altered to a gallop, run, walk, or hop, rather than a skip.

Whistle Stop

Movement Skills: Running, stopping, and chasing.

Formation: Scatter formation.

Equipment: Whistle.

Procedures: Children are scattered around the playing area. On the signal "Run!" the children run in any direction. When you blow the whistle, they stop immediately. They start again on the signal "Run!" Children must be able to run and stop on appropriate signals, staying within the boundaries and avoiding other runners. The game may be varied to explore directions, time, and movement.

Frog in the Sea

Movement Skills: Running.

Formation: Circle formation.

Equipment: None.

Procedures: One child is the frog and sits in the center of a circle. Other children dare the frog by running in close to him and saying, "Frog in the sea, can't catch me!" If a child is tagged by the frog, he or she also becomes a frog and sits in the circle beside the first frog. Frogs must tag from a sitting position. The game continues until four players are tagged. Then the first frog chooses a new frog from the players who were not tagged. Jumping like a frog can be performed rather than running.

Crossing the Brook

Movement Skills: Jumping and leaping.

Formation: File.

Equipment: Chalk or tape.

Procedures: Two lines are drawn to represent a brook. The children try to jump over. If they fall in, they must return home and pretend to change shoes and socks. The width of the brook should vary from narrow to wide so that all children will find a degree of success. You may try placing an object in the brook to be jumped on, such as a stepping stone.

Jump the Shot

Movement Skills: Jumping and hopping.

Formation: Single circle facing in.

Equipment: Beanbag on the end of ten-foot line.

Procedures: The teacher squats down in the center of the circle and swings the rope about three to six inches off the ground. The end of the rope should be beyond the outside of the circle. The children jump to avoid being hit. Be sure to warn the children of the dangers of tripping, and do not turn the rope too fast. The children can also gallop, side hop, or perform tricks over the rope.

Jack Be Nimble

Movement Skills: Jumping, leaping.

Formation: Lines of four or more.

Equipment: Indian clubs to represent candles. One for each team.

Procedures: The following rhyme is recited by the children:

Jack (Jane) be nimble,

Jack be quick.

And Jack jump over the candlestick.

As the rhyme is repeated, the first player in each line runs forward and jumps over the candle. The others follow. Anyone knocking down the candle must set it up again. Caution the children to wait for the signal to "jump over the candlestick."

ASSESSING PROGRESS

Assessment is necessary both at the entry level of a locomotor skill theme and at the exit level. Running, leaping, jumping, hopping, galloping, sliding, and skipping abilities should all be assessed. Once the entry level of a skill is known, it is an easy matter to determine what activities should actually be included in the lesson.

CONCEPT 17.9
Comparison of exit level assessments with entry level assessments is essential to diagnostic developmental teaching.

For children at the fundamental phase of developing their movement abilities, observational assessment works quite well. The sample assessment charts in Chapter 11 and the Appendixes are a practical means of charting individual and group progress.

A second way to assess progress in locomotor skill development is to answer a self-question survey similar to the one shown in Table 17.26. If you are unable to answer "yes" to each of the questions, you will need to modify subsequent lessons to more closely fit the specific needs of the individual or group.

SUMMARY

Mature fundamental locomotor movements are basic to the effective functioning of the individual and permit movement through the environment, using efficient and effective means of travel. Locomotor movement skill themes focus on helping children progress from the initial to the elementary and finally to the mature stage in basic skills such as running, leaping, jumping, hopping, galloping, sliding, and skipping. Children frequently encounter common developmentally based problems as they move from one stage to another, and their progress oftentimes is

TABLE 17.26   *Self-Question Chart for Fundamental Locomotor Skill Development*

Running	Yes	No	Comments

1. Are the children able to run from point to point with good postural control?
2. Are they able to make smooth transitions in direction, level, and speed?
3. Can they run about the gym or playyard without bumping into each other?
4. Can they use the running patterns in conjunction with other basic skills?
5. Do they run without undue attention focused on the process?
6. Are their movements relaxed, fluid, and rhythmical?
7. Is there observable improvement?

Leaping

1. Can they leap leading with either foot?
2. Can they make adjustments in height and distance with ease?
3. Is appropriate body lean used for the distance leaped?
4. Are the arms used properly in conjunction with the legs?
5. Is there observable improvement?

Jumping/Hopping

1. Can the children jump or hop with good control of their bodies?
2. Can the children take off simultaneously with both feet and land on both feet at the same time in all three jumping patterns?
3. Can the children take off on one or both feet and land on one foot when hopping?
4. Can they hop equally well on either foot?
5. Are the hopping and jumping actions smooth, fluid, and rhythmical?
6. Is there improved summation of force used to produce a hop or jump?
7. Is there an easy transition from one pattern to another?
8. Is there observable improvement?

Galloping

1. Can they gallop while leading with either the left or right foot?
2. Does the toe-trailing foot remain behind the heel of the leading foot?
3. Is the action smooth and rhythmical?
4. Is there observable improvement?

Sliding

1. Can the children slide equally well in both directions?
2. Do they slide without crossing the feet?
3. Is the action smooth and rhythmical?
4. Is there observable improvement?

Skipping

1. Is the skipping action smooth and rhythmical?
2. Is there rhythmical alteration of both sides of the body?
3. Is there sufficient knee lift?
4. Is the arm action appropriate for the purpose of the skip?

not uniform. When observed segmentally, children are frequently seen to be at one stage in their leg action, another in the arm action, and a third stage in their trunk action. Therefore, entry level assessment of children's present stages of locomotor skill development is essential prior to planning lessons that are both developmentally and age-group appropriate.

Teaching strategies that help children learn the skill concepts and the movement concepts involved in locomotor movements provide them with the tools for knowing how the body should move and how the body can move. The use of exploratory and guided-discovery experiences is particularly appropriate for children who are functioning at less than the mature stage. Low-level locomotor games can be effectively used for children at the mature stage of the locomotor skills being used. Remember, overemphasis on the product of the game or relay activity (i.e., winning) is frequently counterproductive when children have not yet mastered the consistent use of the mature mechanics of a fundamental skill. Be certain to focus first on the process and work toward mastery of the body mechanics, using a variety of individually appropriate techniques, before emphasizing the product of one's movement.

COMPLEMENTARY READINGS

Capon, J. (1981). *Successful Movement Challenges.* Byron, CA: Front Row Experiences.

Morton-Jones, P. (1990). Skill analysis series part 4: The standing long jump. *Strategies* 4:26–27.

Pica, R. (1991). *Early Elementary Children Moving and Learning.* Champaign, IL: Human Kinetics.

Tant, C. (1990). A kick is a kick—or is it? *Strategies* 4: 19–22.

SUPPLEMENTARY READINGS

Gabbard, C. E., S. Leblanc, and S. Lowy. (1987). *Physical Education for Children: Building the Foundation.* Englewood Cliffs, NJ: Prentice-Hall.

Gallahue, D. L., and J. C. Ozmun. (1995). *Understanding Motor Development.* Dubuque, IA: Brown & Benchmark.

Graham, G., S. A. Holt/Hale, and M. Parker. (1993). *Children Moving.* Mountain View, CA: Mayfield.

Wall, J., and N. Murray. (1990). *Children and Movement.* Dubuque, IA: Wm. C. Brown.

Wickstrom, R. L. (1983). *Fundamental Motor Patterns.* Philadelphia: Lea & Febiger.

VIDEOS

Assessment of Fundamental Motor Skills Videotapes: Running; Jumping; Hopping; Sliding; Galloping; Leaping; Skipping. Ignico, A. A. (1994). Dubuque, IA: Brown & Benchmark. (seven-tape set. All locomotor skills correspond with the locomotor movements discussed in this chapter.).

Children and Movement Video Series: Locomotor Skills. Sanders, S. (1993). Durham, NC: Great Activities Publishing Company. (26 min.).

CHAPTER 18

Fundamental Manipulative Skill Themes

Key Concept

Fundamental Manipulative Skills May Be Developed and Refined through a Skill Theme Approach That Uses Movement Experiences That Are Both Individually Appropriate and Age-Group Appropriate

Chapter Objectives

The purpose of this chapter is to provide you with the tools to:
- Describe the steps in developing a fundamental manipulative movement skill theme.
- Illustrate the importance of fundamental manipulative skill sequencing.
- Identify the initial, elementary, and mature stages of a variety of fundamental manipulative skills.
- Describe developmental difficulties that children encounter in their fundamental manipulative skill development and appropriate strategies for overcoming these deficits.
- Discuss the movement concepts and skill concepts that children should know concerning a variety of fundamental manipulative skills.
- Be able to incorporate exploratory and guided-discovery activities into the fundamental manipulative skill theme lesson.
- Discuss the role of low-level games in skill application of fundamental manipulative skills.
- Demonstrate knowledge of how to informally assess progress in a fundamental manipulative skill theme.

Terms to Remember

Throwing	Dribbling
Catching	Ball Rolling
Kicking	Striking
Trapping	Volleying

Manipulative skills, as used here, are gross body movements in which force is imparted to or received from objects. Manipulative movements such as throwing, catching, kicking, trapping, dribbling, ball rolling, striking, and volleying are generally considered to be fundamental manipulative skills. These skills are essential to purposeful and controlled interaction with objects in our environment. In their refined form, they are also necessary for successful playing of many of the sports of our culture.

CONCEPT 18.1
Object manipulation permits the individual to come into meaningful contact with objects in the environment.

Manipulative skills do not develop automatically. Opportunities for practice, encouragement, and instruction are essential for most children to develop mature patterns of manipulative movement. Achievement of the mature stage in many fundamental manipulative skills generally occurs somewhat later than for most locomotor skills because of the many complex visual-motor adjustments that are required for intercepting a moving object, as with catching, trapping, striking, and volleying. Therefore, the instructor should be alert both to children's perceptual abilities and their movement abilities when focusing on manipulative skill development. Modification of the object to be intercepted through the use of balloons, beach balls, or foam balls frequently works well during the initial and elementary stages of the skill.

This chapter focuses on the importance of skill sequencing and on how to develop a manipulative skill theme. Several gross motor manipulative skills are described. Verbal and visual descriptions are provided, along with common developmental difficulties encountered, teaching tips, and concepts children should know. This is followed by a sampling of appropriate skill development activities that focus on exploratory, guided-discovery, and low-level game activities. Suggestions for assessing progress conclude the chapter.

MANIPULATIVE SKILL SEQUENCING

Fundamental manipulative skills begin developing early in children. Young children's interaction with objects and their gross attempts at throwing, catching, and kicking

TEACHING TIPS

Developing a Manipulative Skill Theme

When planning a fundamental manipulative skill theme you will find it helpful to follow this sequence.

1. *Preplan*
   a. Determine which manipulative skills will be grouped together for each skill theme. The following grouping generally works well:
      (1) Throwing and catching.
      (2) Kicking and tapping.
      (3) Striking and volleying.
      (4) Dribbling and ball rolling.
   b. Determine when in the yearly curriculum to include each manipulative skill theme. You will need to decide whether to space out lessons on each skill theme over the entire school year or group lessons into longer units of instruction. Distributed practice tends to work better than massed practice during the beginning level of movement skill learning.
   c. Decide approximately how many lessons you will spend on fundamental manipulative skill development in relation to the total curriculum.
2. *Observe and Assess*
   a. Observe the fundamental manipulative skills of the children to be taught.
   b. Assess whether they are at the initial, elementary, mature, or sport-skill stage in each of the skills to be included as a skill theme. Study the verbal and visual descriptions of each manipulative skill for guidance.
3. *Plan and Implement*
   a. Plan appropriate movement activities geared to the needs, interests, and ability level of the group. Study the teaching tips and concepts children should know in the pages that follow for help.
   b. Implement a planned program of activities, stressing progression in skill development.
4. *Evaluate and Revise*
   a. Informally evaluate progress in the manipulative skills being stressed in terms of improved mechanics and performance. The questions found in Table 18.26 at the end of the chapter will be helpful.
   b. Based on student progress, revise subsequent lessons as needed.

are generally the first forms of gross motor manipulation. Simply by virtue of maturation, most children progress to the elementary stage in their manipulative abilities. Progress to the mature stage largely depends on environmental stimulation. Because of the sophisticated perceptual requirements of most fundamental manipulative skills, children often lag behind in the development of their ability to strike a pitched ball or to volley a ball repeatedly. Therefore, attainment of the mature stage in manipulative skills depends on the combination of maturational readiness, environmental openness, and teacher sensitivity.

CONCEPT 18.2
Preparing for a developmental movement skill theme requires preplanning, observing and assessing, specific planning and implementing, and evaluating and revising.

Although most children have the developmental potential to perform at the mature stage in their fundamental manipulative skills by about seven years of age, many lag behind. In fact, it is not unusual to see numerous older children, and even college students, who are unable to throw, catch, volley, dribble, or strike a ball at the mature stage. It is important to know where your students are in terms of their manipulative skills in order to plan effectively for all.

THROWING AND CATCHING

Throwing and catching are two fundamental movements that fit together especially well in the presentation of a skill theme. **Throwing** involves imparting force to an object through use of the hands. The throw may be performed in many forms: in an overhand, underhand, or sidearm pattern and with either one or both hands, depending on the purpose of the throw. The overhand throwing pattern is dealt with here because it is probably the pattern most frequently used by both children and adults. Throwing abilities begin developing early in life, and it is common to see individuals who have not received any formal instruction and have had only limited opportunity for practice functioning at the elementary level in the overhand throw. Most children progress to the elementary stage more as a function of maturation than

experience. In most cases, however, they will continue to perform at this stage even as adolescents and adults unless they receive sufficient practice and instruction. Throwing for distance will promote the mature pattern. Throwing for accuracy should be stressed only after the mature pattern is well learned.

CONCEPT 18.3
Although most children have the developmental potential to be at the mature stage by age seven, many lag behind because of inadequate instruction, opportunities for practice, and encouragement.

Catching involves receiving force from an object and retaining it in the hands. Practice in catching can be facilitated by using objects of varying sizes, shapes, colors, and firmness. The child at the initial stage, for example, generally experiences greater success with catching a soft, brightly colored beanbag, yarn ball, or beach ball rather than a hard ball of comparable size. The child is able to grip a beanbag more securely than the ball. There is little fear of injury if the child is hit in the face or on a finger by a beanbag, yarn ball, or beach ball. The wise teacher provides opportunities for children to practice catching with a variety of objects. Care is taken to set up experiences that will not result in an avoidance reaction of the head or a closing of the eyes out of fear as the object approaches. During the early stages of learning, you should not require the individual to adapt to the equipment; rather, you should modify the equipment to the developmental needs of the child.

Throwing

Verbal Description (Table 18.1)

Visual Description (Figure 18.1)

Teaching Tips

- Provide numerous opportunities for practice. One or two sessions will not be enough to develop a consistent mature pattern.
- Focus first on throwing for distance, not accuracy.
- Work for speed of movement and good hip rotation.
- Use carpet squares, hoops, or tires as cues for stepping out on the opposite foot.

TABLE 18.1   *Developmental Sequence for Overhand Throwing*

I. Throwing
  A. Initial stage
    1. Action is mainly from elbow
    2. Elbow of throwing arm remains in front of body; action resembles a push
    3. Fingers spread at release
    4. Follow-through is forward and downward
    5. Trunk remains perpendicular to target
    6. Little rotary action during throw
    7. Body weight shifts slightly rearward to maintain balance
    8. Feet remain stationary
    9. There is often purposeless shifting of feet during preparation for throw
  B. Elementary stage
    1. In preparation, arm is swung upward, sideward, and backward to a position of elbow flexion
    2. Ball is held behind head
    3. Arm is swung forward, high over shoulder
    4. Trunk rotates toward throwing side during preparatory action
    5. Shoulders rotate toward throwing side
    6. Trunk flexes forward with forward motion of arm
    7. Definite forward shift of body weight
    8. Steps forward with leg on same side as throwing arm
  C. Mature stage
    1. Arm is swung backward in preparation
    2. Opposite elbow is raised for balance as a preparatory action in the throwing arm
    3. Throwing elbow moves forward horizontally as it extends
    4. Forearm rotates and thumb points downward
    5. Trunk markedly rotates to throwing side during preparatory action
    6. Throwing shoulder drops slightly
    7. Definite rotation through hips, legs, spine, and shoulders during throw
    8. Weight during preparatory movement is on rear foot
    9. As weight is shifted, there is a step with opposite foot
II. Developmental Difficulties
  A. Forward movement of foot on same side as throwing arm
  B. Inhibited backswing
  C. Failure to rotate hips as throwing arm is brought forward
  D. Failure to step out on leg opposite the throwing arm
  E. Poor rhythmical coordination of arm movement with body movement
  F. Inability to release ball at desired trajectory
  G. Loss of balance while throwing
  H. Upward rotation of arm

INITIAL

ELEMENTARY

MATURE

FIGURE 18.1 *Stages of the overhand throwing pattern.*

- Be sure to have an ample supply of balls or beanbags that can be easily gripped.
- Beanbags, newspaper balls, yarn balls, and stocking balls work well and add variety.
- Use beanbags for wall drills to emphasize the throwing action and not catching or retrieving.
- Speed, accuracy, and distance are the performance elements of throwing. Work first for distance, then speed, and finally accuracy.
- Follow a logical teaching progression, using the preceding recommendations as a guide.
- There should be 100 percent participation.

Concepts Children Should Know

Skill Concepts

- Stand with the leg that is on the other side of the throwing arm leading.
- Turn your shoulder toward the target.
- Raise your free arm and point toward the target.
- Raise your throwing arm and hold the ball close to your ear.
- Lead with your elbow on the forward swing.
- Bring your rear foot forward and follow through.
- The overhand throwing pattern is used in the sports of baseball, softball, and on the fast break in basketball. It is also similar to the overhand serves in volleyball and tennis and the smash shot in badminton.

Movement Concepts

- The effort that you give to your throw will influence how fast the ball will travel and the smoothness with which your throwing motion is performed.
- When you throw a ball, it can travel through space in a variety of directions and levels.
- A ball may be thrown using throwing patterns ranging from overhand and underhand to a variety of sidearm patterns.
- You can throw many different types of objects. The size, shape, and weight of the object will affect the distance it travels as well as the pattern you use.
- The coordinated use of your arms, trunk, and legs will affect the speed and distance of your throw.

CONCEPT 18.4

Children can be accurately assessed to be at the initial, elementary, or mature stage in a variety of fundamental manipulative movement skills.

Catching

Verbal Description (Table 18.2)

Visual Description (Figure 18.2)

Teaching Tips

- Use soft objects for initial catching experiences. Yarn balls and beanbags work best.

TABLE 18.2   *Developmental Sequence for Catching*

I. Catching
  A. Initial stage
    1. There is often an avoidance reaction of turning the face away or protecting the face with arms (avoidance reaction is learned and therefore may not be present)
    2. Arms are extended and held in front of body
    3. Body movement is limited until contact
    4. Catch resembles a scooping action
    5. Use of body to trap ball
    6. Palms are held upward
    7. Fingers are extended and held tense
    8. Hands are not utilized in catching action
  B. Elementary stage
    1. Avoidance reaction is limited to eyes closing at contact with ball
    2. Elbows are held at sides with an approximately 90-degree bend
    3. Since initial attempt at contact with child's hands is often unsuccessful, arms trap the ball
    4. Hands are held in opposition to each other; thumbs are held upward
    5. At contact, the hands attempt to squeeze ball in a poorly-timed and uneven motion
  C. Mature stage
    1. No avoidance reaction
    2. Eyes follow ball into hands
    3. Arms are held relaxed at sides, and forearms are held in front of body
    4. Arms give on contact to absorb force of the ball
    5. Arms adjust to flight of ball
    6. Thumbs are held in opposition to each other
    7. Hands grasp ball in a well-timed, simultaneous motion
    8. Fingers grasp more effectively
II. Developmental Difficulties
  A. Failure to maintain control of object
  B. Failure to "give" with the catch
  C. Keeping fingers rigid and straight in the direction of object
  D. Failure to adjust hand position to the height and trajectory of object
  E. Inability to vary the catching pattern for objects of different weight and force
  F. Taking eyes off object
  G. Closing the eyes
  H. Inability to focus on, or track the ball
  I. Improper stance, causing loss of balance when catching a fast-moving object
  J. Closing hands either too early or too late
  K. Failure to keep body in line with the ball

INITIAL

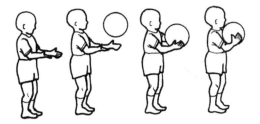

ELEMENTARY

MATURE

FIGURE 18.2 *Stages of the catching pattern.*

- Provide verbal cues such as "Ready? Catch" to avoid surprises.
- Begin with large balls and progress to smaller sizes.
- Use brightly colored balls.
- Be aware of the background against which the ball is to be caught. Avoid figure-ground blending.
- Vary the speed, level, and trajectory of the ball as skill increases.

Concepts Children Should Know

Skill Concepts

- Get directly in the path of the ball.
- Place one foot ahead of the other.

- Adjust your hand position for the height of the ball—thumbs in for balls above the waist, thumbs out for balls below the waist.
- Curve your fingers and keep your eyes on the ball.
- Pull the ball in toward your body.

Movement Concepts

- You can catch an object in many different ways.
- You can catch with different body parts.
- You can catch from a variety of positions.
- The objects you catch may vary in size, shape, color, or texture.
- The objects you catch can come toward you at different levels and with varying degrees of speed.
- You can play a variety of games that involve catching.

CONCEPT 18.5
Children need to learn the skill concepts and movement concepts associated with fundamental movement skill acquisition.

KICKING AND TRAPPING

Kicking and trapping are two fundamental movement patterns that fit nicely together into a common skill theme. Basically, **kicking** involves imparting force to an object with use of the foot and leg. Kicking may take the form of kicking at a pebble, a can, or a ball, or it may be part of a low-level game or part of the sports of soccer and football. In developing a mature pattern of kicking, emphasis should be on kicking for distance. Distance kicking (or kicking as forcefully as possible) will promote the mature pattern. More complete action of the kicking leg on the windup and follow-through, as well as the coordinated action of the trunk and arms, are necessary for a long kick. Kicking for accuracy should not be of concern until after the mature pattern has been mastered.

Trapping is a fundamental movement pattern that requires use of various parts of the body to stop the forward momentum of an oncoming object. With children, trapping a rolled ball should precede trapping a tossed object. The focus of the lessons on trapping should be on gaining control of the ball and being able to make appropriate adjustments relative to the speed of the ball and the level of contact.

TABLE 18.3   *Developmental Sequence for Kicking*

I. Kicking
   A. Initial stage
      1. Movements are restricted during kicking action
      2. Trunk remains erect
      3. Arms are used to maintain balance
      4. Movement of kicking leg is limited in backswing
      5. Forward swing is short: there is little follow-through
      6. Child kicks "at" ball rather than kicking it squarely and following through
      7. A pushing rather than a striking action is predominant
   B. Elementary stage
      1. Preparatory backswing is centered at the knee
      2. Kicking leg tends to remain bent throughout the kick
      3. Follow-through is limited to forward movement of the knee
      4. One or more deliberate steps are taken toward the ball
   C. Mature stage
      1. Arms swing in opposition to each other during kicking action
      2. Trunk bends at waist during follow-through
      3. Movement of kicking leg is initiated at the hip
      4. Support leg bends slightly on contact
      5. Length of leg swing increases
      6. Follow-through is high; support foot rises to toes or leaves surface entirely
      7. Approach to the ball is from either a run or leap
II. Developmental Difficulties
   A. Restricted or absent backswing
   B. Failure to step forward with nonkicking leg
   C. Tendency to lose balance
   D. Inability to kick with either foot
   E. Inability to alter speed of kicked ball
   F. Jabbing at ball without follow-through
   G. Poor opposition of arms and legs
   H. Failure to use a summation of forces by the body to contribute to force of the kick
   I. Failure to contact ball squarely, or missing it completely (eyes not focused on ball)
   J. Failure to get adequate distance (lack of follow-through and force production)

INITIAL

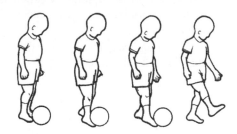

ELEMENTARY

MATURE

FIGURE 18.3   *Stages of the kicking pattern.*

Kicking

Verbal Description (Table 18.3)

Visual Description (Figure 18.3)

Teaching Tips

- Focus on kicking for distance rather than accuracy. Accuracy kicking will not promote use of the mature pattern.
- If possible, have a ball for every other child.

- Begin with a variety of exploratory experiences, but progress to guided-discovery experiences without too much delay.
- Encourage kicking with the non-preferred foot after the mature level has been reached with the preferred foot.
- Work jointly with kicking and trapping, using a peer teaching approach.
- Be sure to work for control of the height of the ball. This will make it necessary to teach the instep and inside-of-the-foot kick as well as the popular toe kick.
- After the mature kicking pattern has been achieved, introduce accuracy kicking activities.
- Incorporate kicking into low-level games and lead-up games after the mature stage has been reached.
- Work for total body control when kicking.
- Practice kicking a stationary ball prior to a moving ball.
- Be sure to use balls about the same size as a standard soccer ball.

Concepts Children Should Know

Skill Concepts

- Stand behind the ball and slightly to one side.
- Step forward on the non-kicking foot.
- Keep your eyes on the ball.
- Swing your kicking leg back and then forcefully forward from the hip.
- The snap down from the knee gives the ball its speed.
- Contact the ball with the top portion of your foot (low ball), with your toe (high ball), or with the inside portion of your foot (ground ball).
- Follow through in the direction that the ball is to go.
- Use your arms for balance and force production.
- The kicking pattern is basic to the sport of soccer and is used in kicking games such as kickball.

Movement Concepts

- You can kick a ball at different levels (high, medium, low) by contacting it with different parts of your feet.

- You can kick either for distance or for accuracy, but the two processes will look different.
- The manner in which you coordinate the use of your entire body will influence the direction, distance, level, and path that the ball takes.
- You can kick the ball at objects and to people. Great precision is needed when kicking at or to something.
- It is important for you to keep your eyes on the ball when it is about to be kicked.
- Your kicks can be long or short, fast or slow, hard or soft and may travel in a variety of directions and at different levels.

CONCEPT 18.6
Children frequently encounter predictable developmentally based difficulties as they move from one stage to another in the acquisition of mature fundamental manipulative skills.

Trapping

Verbal Description (Table 18.4)

Visual Description (Figure 18.4)

Teaching Tips

- Begin with trapping activities involving the feet and legs (foot trap and single- and double-knee trap).
- Teach how to trap a rolled ball prior to an elevated ball.
- Stress eye contact with the ball throughout.
- Introduce trapping a tossed ball only after the concepts involved in trapping a ground ball are mastered.
- Use a foam ball, beach ball, or partially inflated ball in the beginning.
- Foam balls work nicely for the introduction of trapping an elevated object.
- Work for control with the stomach and chest traps by teaching how to deflect the ball downward.
- Emphasize the importance of getting in the path of the ball, "giving" with it, and absorbing its force over as much surface area as possible.
- Do not introduce kicking and trapping drills until both partners are at the mature stage.

TABLE 18.4   *Developmental Sequence for Trapping*

I. Trapping

   A. Initial stage

      1. Trunk remains rigid

      2. No "give" with ball as it makes contact

      3. Inability to absorb force of the ball

      4. Difficulty getting in line with object

   B. Elementary stage

      1. Poor visual tracking

      2. "Gives" with the ball, but movements are poorly timed and sequenced

      3. Can trap a rolled ball with relative ease but cannot trap a tossed ball

      4. Appears uncertain of what body part to use

      5. Movements lack fluidity

   C. Mature stage

      1. Tracks ball throughout

      2. "Gives" with body upon contact

      3. Can trap both rolled and tossed balls

      4. Can trap balls approaching at a moderate velocity

      5. Moves with ease to intercept ball

II. Developmental Difficulties

   A. Failure to position body directly in path of ball

   B. Failure to keep eyes fixed on ball

   C. Failure to "give" as ball contacts body part

   D. Failure to angle an aerial ball downward toward feet

   E. Causing body to meet ball instead of letting ball meet body

   F. Inability to maintain body balance when trapping in unusual or awkward positions

FIGURE 18.4   *Stages of the trapping pattern.*

- During partner practice, prohibit the use of the kick unless foam rubber balls are used. If soccer balls are used, they will travel too high and may hit the partner in the face.
- Work for control and a "feel" for the ball.
- Use a soccer ball only after the principles of trapping are understood and mastered.

Concepts Children Should Know

Skill Concepts

- Get directly in the path of the ball.
- Keep your eyes on the ball.

- "Give" with the ball as it touches the body.
- Deflect an elevated ball downward.
- Let the ball meet your body.
- The trapping pattern is basic to the sport of soccer and any other activity in which the feet, legs, or trunk are used to stop an object.

Movement Concepts

- You can use any part of your body to trap a ball except your hands and arms.
- You can trap a ball at different levels.

- You can trap objects other than balls.
- You and your partner can practice trapping and kicking together.
- Your control of the ball will influence the success of your trapping.

DRIBBLING AND BALL ROLLING

Dribbling is a fundamental movement that involves receiving force from an object and immediately imparting force from that object in a downward (hand dribble) or ground-level, horizontal (foot dribble) direction without the use of an implement. The developmental sequence for hand dribbling appears to be (1) bouncing and catching, (2) bouncing and ineffective slapping at the ball, (3) basic dribbling with the ball in control of the child, (4) basic dribbling with the child in control of the ball, and (5) controlled dribbling with advanced abilities. Dribbling is applied primarily to the sport activities of basketball, soccer, and speedball. It is unique in that it is of only limited direct value to most recreational and daily living skills. Dribbling does, however, provide the individual with important experiences in interrupting an object, and it requires the sophisticated interaction of sensory and motor processes at a precise moment in time. Therefore, when we view dribbling as a fundamental movement, we may also view it as an ideal task for helping the individual learn how to coordinate the use of the eyes with the hands.

The movement pattern of **ball rolling** involves imparting force to an object in such a way that it travels in a forward direction on the ground. Ball rolling has had limited scientific study through controlled experimentation, so little is known about the emergence of ball-rolling abilities. Ball rolling is, however, a fundamental movement pattern that is often applied to the sport and recreational activities of bowling, curling, boccie, and shuffleboard. The basic ball-rolling pattern may be observed in underhand tossing, softball pitching, and lifesaving rope-tossing techniques.

Dribbling

Verbal Description (Table 18.5)

Visual Description (Figure 18.5)

TABLE 18.5 *Developmental Sequence for Dribbling*

I. Dribbling
  A. Initial stage
    1. Ball held with both hands
    2. Hands placed on sides of ball, with palms facing each other
    3. Downward thrusting action with both arms
    4. Ball contacts surface close to body, may contact foot
    5. Great variation in height of bounce
    6. Repeated bounce and catch pattern
  B. Elementary stage
    1. Ball held with both hands, one on top and the other near the bottom
    2. Slight forward lean, with ball brought to chest level to begin the action
    3. Downward thrust with top hand and arm
    4. Force of downward thrust inconsistent
    5. Hand slaps at ball for subsequent bounces
    6. Wrist flexes and extends and palm of hand contacts ball on each bounce
    7. Visually monitors ball
    8. Limited control of ball while dribbling
  C. Mature stage
    1. Feet placed in narrow stride position, with foot opposite dribbling hand forward
    2. Slight forward trunk lean
    3. Ball held waist high
    4. Ball pushed toward ground, with follow-through of arm, wrist, and fingers
    5. Controlled force of downward thrust
    6. Repeated contact and pushing action initiated from fingertips
    7. Visual monitoring unnecessary
    8. Controlled directional dribbling
II. Developmental Difficulties
  A. Slapping at ball instead of pushing it downward
  B. Inconsistent force applied to downward thrust
  C. Failure to focus on and track ball efficiently
  D. Inability to dribble with both hands
  E. Inability to dribble without visually monitoring ball
  F. Insufficient follow-through
  G. Inability to move about under control while dribbling

INITIAL

ELEMENTARY

MATURE

FIGURE 18.5 *Stages of the dribbling pattern.*

Teaching Tips

- Use a playground ball or other ball that does not require as much force in dribbling as a basketball.
- Use different colored or striped balls to avoid blending of figure and ground.
- Work first for controlled bouncing and catching.
- Provide plenty of opportunities for practice in an atmosphere of exploration and experimentation.
- As skill develops, challenge the children with a variety of guided-discovery activities that focus on being more aware of the process.
- Do not introduce low-level games, relays, or lead-up games until the mature stage of dribbling has been reasonably well achieved.
- Master dribbling with the dominant hand prior to practicing with the nondominant hand.

- Stress eye contact at the initial and elementary stage, but work for kinesthetic control in the mature stage.
- Structure experiences that require making modifications in the dribbling pattern congruent with the situation.
- As a last resort, physically manipulate the occasional child who is unable to coordinate the bounce of the ball with the push of the hand. Do this only as long as needed for the child to get a "feel" for the timing of the ball.

Concepts Children Should Know

Skill Concepts

- Push the ball down.
- Your wrist controls the bounce.
- Use your fingertips.
- Follow through.
- Push the ball slightly forward.
- Keep the ball below your waist.

Movement Concepts

- You can bounce the ball at different levels.
- You can bounce the ball with different amounts of force.
- You can control the amount of time between bounces by using different amounts of force and bouncing at different levels.
- The rhythmic flow of the bounced ball is important for controlled dribbling.
- You can bounce many kinds and sizes of balls.
- The density of the ball will influence its bouncing capabilities.

Ball Rolling

Verbal Description (Table 18.6)

Visual Description (Figure 18.6)

Teaching Tips

- Begin practice with a large ball prior to using a small ball.
- Do not stress accuracy during the initial experiences.

TABLE 18.6 *Developmental Sequence for Ball Rolling*

I. Ball Rolling
  A. Initial stage
    1. Straddle stance
    2. Ball is held with hands on the sides, with palms facing each other
    3. Acute bend at waist, with backward pendulum motion of arms
    4. Eyes monitor ball
    5. Forward arm swing and trunk lift with release of ball
  B. Elementary stage
    1. Stride stance
    2. Ball held with one hand on bottom and the other on top
    3. Backward arm swing without weight transfer to the rear
    4. Limited knee bend
    5. Forward swing with limited follow-through
    6. Ball released between knee and waist level
    7. Eyes alternately monitor target and ball
  C. Mature stage
    1. Stride stance
    2. Ball held in hand corresponding to trailing leg
    3. Slight hip rotation and trunk lean forward
    4. Pronounced knee bend
    5. Forward swing with weight transference from rear to forward foot
    6. Release at knee level or below
    7. Eyes are on target throughout
II. Developmental Difficulties
  A. Failure to transfer body weight to rear foot during initial part of action
  B. Failure to place controlling hand directly under ball
  C. Releasing the ball above waist level
  D. Failure to release ball from a virtual pendular motion, causing it to veer to one side
  E. Lack of follow-through, resulting in a weak roll
  F. Swinging the arms too far backward or out from the body
  G. Failure to keep eyes on target
  H. Failure to step forward with foot opposite hand that holds ball
  I. Inability to bring ball to side of the body

- Focus on proper body mechanics. Have the children roll the ball at the wall from greater and greater distances.

INITIAL

ELEMENTARY

MATURE

FIGURE 18.6 *Stages of the ball rolling pattern.*

- After the basic pattern has been mastered, begin working for greater accuracy. Begin with large targets to promote success.
- Gradually increase both distance and accuracy requirements.
- Do not use a bowling ball or other heavy object when working on body mechanics.
- Practice rolling from a stationary position prior to adding an approach.

Concepts Children Should Know

Skill Concepts

- Stand with one foot leading.
- Swing your arm straight back as you rock back on your rear foot.
- Let go of the ball when it is six to twelve inches in front of your leading foot.
- Follow through with your swing in the direction of the target.
- Keep your eyes on the ball.
- The rolling pattern is basic to the sports of bowling, curling, and boccie. It is also used in games such as pin guard and guard the castle.

Movement Concepts

- You can roll a ball at different speeds.
- The force you apply to the ball will control its speed.
- The coordinated use of your muscles as you roll the ball will influence the force of the ball and its speed.
- You can place your body in many different positions when rolling an object.
- You can roll a ball in many different directions and cause it to travel in different pathways.
- You can roll balls of different sizes.
- You can devise many challenging game activities that use ball rolling.

STRIKING AND VOLLEYING

Striking is a fundamental movement pattern that may be performed in several different planes, with or without the use of an implement. Striking may involve contact with a stationary or moving object. However, even though the plane, implement, and nature of the object to be struck may differ in a number of ways, they are all governed by the same mechanical principles of movement. First, the amount of momentum generated depends on the length of the backswing, the number of muscles involved, and the proper sequential use of the muscles. Second, the object to be struck must be contacted at the precise moment that maximum speed of the swing has been reached. Third, the striking implement must follow through toward the intended target. Fourth, the striking implement should

make contact at a right angle to the object. Fifth, the implement should be held out and away from the body to achieve maximum momentum.

The forms that striking takes are many, and its application to sports is varied. The horizontal striking pattern is found in baseball. The vertical striking pattern is found in tennis, golf, volleyball, badminton, handball, and racquetball. Only the horizontal striking pattern with an implement is described here. You should, however, be quick to recognize that the description, teaching tips, and concepts children should know apply equally well to striking an object in other planes or without an implement.

Volleying is a specialized striking-pattern skill that involves receiving force from an object and immediately imparting force to that object in a roughly vertical direction, as with volleyball or with heading and juggling in soccer. Volleying is characterized by the fact that it can be repeated more than once in the same sequence with the same ball. The developmental sequence for effective volleying is much like striking, beginning with ineffective, uncontrolled efforts, followed by gradual control and increased proficiency. Volleying involves the complex interaction of visual and motor processes.

It will be helpful to initiate striking and volleying activities with the use of balloons, beach balls, or other light objects that enable the individual to have a longer visual tracking period. The size and color of the ball may influence volleying and striking activities. Be sensitive to these possible influencing factors, and be ready to make adjustments in ball type, size, or color to maximize the child's success potential.

Horizontal Striking

Verbal Description (Table 18.7)

Visual Description (Figure 18.7)

Teaching Tips

- Follow a sequence of teaching that progresses from striking with the hand and other body parts to using short-handled implements and then long-handled implements.
- Use balloons and beach balls at the initial stages.
- Practice hitting stationary objects prior to moving objects.
- Work with striking large objects and then progress gradually to striking smaller objects.

TABLE 18.7 *Developmental Sequence for Striking*

I. Striking
   A. Initial stage
      1. Motion is from back to front
      2. Feet are stationary
      3. Trunk faces direction of tossed ball
      4. Elbow(s) fully flexed
      5. No trunk rotation
      6. Force comes from extension of flexed joints in a downward plane
   B. Elementary stage
      1. Trunk turned to side in anticipation of tossed ball
      2. Weight shifts to forward foot prior to ball contact
      3. Combined trunk and hip rotation
      4. Elbow(s) flexed at less acute angle
      5. Force comes from extension of flexed joints. Trunk rotation and forward movement are in an oblique plane
   C. Mature stage
      1. Trunk turns to side in anticipation of tossed ball
      2. Weight shifts to back foot
      3. Hips rotate
      4. Transfer of weight is in a contralateral pattern
      5. Weight shift to forward foot occurs while object is still moving backward
      6. Striking occurs in a long, full arc in a horizontal pattern
      7. Weight shifts to forward foot at contact
II. Developmental Difficulties
   A. Failure to focus on and track the ball
   B. Improper grip
   C. Failure to turn side of the body in direction of intended flight
   D. Inability to sequence movements in rapid succession in a coordinated manner
   E. Poor backswing
   F. "Chopping" swing

- Remember that the color of the ball and the background against which it is being struck may influence figure-ground perception.
- Develop an efficient horizontal striking pattern before concentrating on the vertical plane.
- Check frequently to see that the proper grip is maintained and the eyes are on the ball.
- Work for effective weight shifting, summation of forces, and a level swing.

FIGURE 18.7 *Stages of the striking pattern.*

- Stress making a "big swing." Be sure that the ball is contacted with the elbows extended and at the maximum velocity of the swing.
- Stress follow-through in the direction of the target.

Concepts Children Should Know

Skill Concepts

- Be sure that your hands are touching when you grip a baseball bat and that your right hand is on top of your left (right-hand pattern).
- Keep your eyes on the ball at all times.
- Always contact the ball at the point of complete arm extension.
- Shift your weight back and forward as you swing.
- Swing in a level fashion.
- Follow through.
- The striking pattern is used in many sport activities. Some sports use striking with the hand as the implement, such as handball and volleyball. Others, such as baseball, hockey, golf, tennis, and racquetball, use an implement.

Movement Concepts

- You can strike a ball with different amounts of force.
- You can make the ball go fast or slow.
- The sequential and rhythmical use of your muscles will affect the force of your swing and the speed of the ball.
- The ball can be struck at many different levels.
- The ball may be contacted in a horizontal or vertical plane.
- You can hit a ball in many different directions.
- Objects other than balls can be struck.
- You don't always need to use an implement to strike something. You can effectively use your hand, your head, or your feet.
- Striking a moving object is a complex task, requiring precise coordination of your eyes and muscles.
- The success of your striking will be influenced by the size, shape, and color of the ball, as well as the size and shape of the implement and the speed of the object.

Volleying

Verbal Description (Table 18.8)

Visual Description (Figure 18.8)

Teaching Tips

- Work for good positioning under the ball.
- Begin using balloons and progress to beach balls or foam balls prior to using a regulation volleyball.
- When using a volleyball, allow an intermediate bounce prior to contact if necessary.
- Teach the children to make a "window" so that the thumbs and index fingers nearly touch.
- Emphasize looking through the window when contacting the ball.
- Work for good force production by stressing the importance of extending at the ankles, knees, hips, and shoulders upon contact.

TABLE 18.8   *Developmental Sequence for Volleying*

I. Volleying
   A. Initial stage
      1. Inability to accurately judge path of ball or balloon
      2. Inability to get under the ball
      3. Inability to contact ball with both hands simultaneously
      4. Slaps at ball from behind
   B. Elementary stage
      1. Failure to visually track ball
      2. Gets under the ball
      3. Slaps at ball
      4. Action mainly from hands and arms
      5. Little lift or follow-through with legs
      6. Unable to control direction or intended flight of ball
      7. Wrists relax and ball often travels backward
   C. Mature stage
      1. Gets under the ball
      2. Good contact with fingertips
      3. Wrists remain stiff and arms follow through
      4. Good summation of forces and utilization of arms and legs
      5. Able to control direction and intended flight of ball
II. Developmental Difficulties
   A. Failure to keep eyes on ball
   B. Inability to accurately judge flight of ball and to properly time movements of body
   C. Failure to keep fingers and wrists stiff
   D. Failure to extend all of the joints upon contacting ball (lack of follow-through)
   E. Inability to contact ball with both hands simultaneously
   F. Slapping at ball
   G. Poor positioning of body under ball

Concepts Children Should Know

Skill Concepts

- Get into position directly beneath the ball.
- Watch the flight of the ball between the opening formed by your two hands.
- Extend the arms and legs as the ball touches your fingertips.
- Keep the fingers and wrists stiff throughout.
- Follow through in the direction that the ball is to go.

INITIAL

ELEMENTARY

MATURE

FIGURE 18.8 *Stages of the volleying pattern.*

- Keep your eyes on the ball.
- Volleying is a striking pattern that is used in many games and in the sport of volleyball.

Movement Concepts

- You can vary your body position when you control the ball.
- You can alter the level of your body.
- You can make changes in the force that you apply to the ball.

- The coordinated contact of the ball will be influenced by how well all of your body works together.
- You can give direction to the ball.
- You can control the distance that the ball travels.
- You can volley many different objects.
- You can play volleying games with other people.

SKILL DEVELOPMENT ACTIVITIES

Before selecting movement activities to include in the lesson, first determine the typical stage of motor development displayed by the class. Knowing the stage of motor development will provide cues to their level of movement skill learning. With this important information, it is now possible to determine whether the lesson should focus on exploratory, guided-discovery, skill application, or skill refinement activities.

C O N C E P T   1 8 . 7
A wide variety of exploratory, guided-discovery, and skill-application activities can be successfully used to enhance fundamental manipulative abilities.

Exploratory Activities

Exploratory activities provide children at the initial or elementary stage an opportunity to learn how their bodies can move, where they can move, and how they move in relation to other objects. The movement elements of effort, space, and relationships should be explored to develop a more complete idea of one's manipulative movement potential. Odd-numbered Tables 18.9 through 18.23 provide a sampling of exploratory activities that can be used as movement challenges for children at the beginning level of manipulative skill learning. You should present these challenges separately at first. However, they may be combined into an infinite variety of challenges after the basic elements of the skill have been mastered.

Guided-Discovery Activities

The sampling of guided-discovery activities presented in even-numbered Tables 18.10 through 18.24 is intended to provide children with a variety of activities designed to lead them to mature manipulative patterns of movement.

TABLE 18.9   *Exploratory Activity Ideas for Throwing*

Effort	Space	Relationships
Force	***Level***	***Objects***
Can You Throw. . . .	*Can You Throw. . . .*	*Can You Throw. . . .*
—as soft as you can?	—up high?	—a wiffle ball?
—as hard as you can?	—down low?	—a fluff ball?
—so that the ball makes a loud noise when it hits the wall?	—as low as you can?	—a softball?
—alternating hard and soft throws?	—at the wall as high as you can?	—a baseball?
—stepping forward with a loud noise?	—at high-, low-, and medium-height targets?	—a football?
Time	—alternating high and low throws?	—a newspaper ball?
—as slowly as you can?	***Direction***	—a playground ball?
—as fast as you can?	—forward?	—at a target?
—moving your throwing arms as fast as you can?	—backward?	—into the bucket?
—and twist your body (hips) as fast as possible?	—to the side?	—over the rope?
Flow	—at an angle?	—from inside a hoop or inner tube?
—using as little movement as possible?	***Range***	***People***
—using as much of your body as possible?	—as far as you can?	—to a partner?
—like a robot?	—as near as you can?	—as far as your partner?
—like a plastic person?	—with your right hand?	—as hard or soft as your partner?
—without using your legs?	—with your left hand?	—the same way as your partner?
—without using your trunk?	—with both hands?	***Combinations***
—using only one other part of your body besides your throwing arm?	—overhand?	Initial experiences should focus on exploring the various aspects of effort, space, and relationships in isolation prior to structuring experiences involving combinations. For example, "Can you and your partner find three different ways to throw at the target from a far distance?"
—as smoothly as you can?	—underhand?	
	—sidearm?	
	—with your arm going through short and long ranges of motion?	

TABLE 18.10   *Guided-Discovery Activity Ideas for Throwing*

1. First explore the movement variations of throwing.

2. Now begin to place limitations on the response possibilities to the following movement challenges. (You may want to use a beanbag rather than a ball for these activities to promote a minimum of confusion when retrieving the thrown objects.) For example,

General   a. Stand about a body length from the wall and throw your beanbag at it. Now try the same thing from here (fifteen to twenty feet). Try it again from here (thirty to fifty feet). Do you have to do anything different to hit the wall each time? Why?

Leg Action   b. Experiment with different ways of using your legs as you throw. Try throwing with your feet together (initial stage). Now try it by stepping out on the foot on the same side as your throwing arm (elementary). Try it this time by stepping out on the opposite foot (mature). Did you notice any difference in how far the ball went? Which way does a baseball player use? Why?

Trunk Action   c. Try throwing without twisting your trunk. Now try it with twisting. Experiment with different combinations of twisting your trunk and using your legs. Now show me the best combination. Can you stand facing this wall but throw the ball at the wall to your left? Try it first without bringing your hips around. Now try it bringing your hips around to the left (for right-hand throw). Now try it with stepping out on your left foot and turning to your left.

Arm Action   d. Experiment with different ways of using your arms when you throw. Can you find three different arm patterns you can use when throwing? Let's work on the overhand throw. Throw the ball overhand without rotating your hips. Try it while rotating your hips. Which way caused the ball to go the farthest? Throw the ball so that it hits high on the wall. Throw it now so that it hits the wall as hard as possible. Now throw the ball as far as you can. Now throw far but over the outstretched rope (six to eight feet high).

Total   e. Let's see if we can put it all together. Try throwing while stepping forward on the opposite foot and turning your trunk while your arm moves forward. Practice throwing with a partner. Now pretend that it is a hot potato that you must throw back as fast as you can. What happens when you try to get rid of the ball fast? Some of you went back to the elementary stage instead of throwing at the mature stage. Why? Will it help to practice?

3. After the mature throwing pattern has been reasonably well mastered in practice sessions, begin to combine it with other activities. Apply it to numerous situations to make it more automatic.

   a. Introduce basic throwing and catching games that will provide plenty of opportunities for practice.

   b. Throw different objects.

   c. Throw at distances that encourage mature use of the pattern.

   d. Throw at a stationary target.

   e. Throw at a moving target.

   f. Combine distance and accuracy throwing.

TABLE 18.11 *Exploratory Activity Ideas for Catching*

Effort	Space	Relationships
Force	**Level**	**Objects**

Effort	Space	Relationships
Can You Catch. . . .	*Can You Catch. . . .*	*Can You Catch. . . .*
—with your arms in different positions?	—a ball tossed at a low level?	—a playground ball?
—without making a sound with your hands?	—a ball tossed at waist level?	—a small ball?
—as loudly as you can?	—a ball tossed at a high level?	—a large ball?
—keeping your arms straight?	—at many different levels?	—a beanbag?
—keeping your arms bent?	—from a sitting position?	—five different objects?
	—from a lying-down position?	—five different types of balls?
Time	—in many different positions?	**People**
—and go with the ball?	**Direction**	—a ball while holding both hands with a partner?
—without going with the ball?	—a ball tossed from in front of you?	—while holding one hand with a partner?
—the ball as quickly as you can?	—a ball tossed from an angle?	**Combinations**
—after waiting for the ball as long as you can?	—a ball tossed from the side?	Exploratory experiences should begin with these and other activities, first in isolation. Later, combinations of effort, space, and relationships should be added. For example, "Can you catch a self-tossed ball at waist level while jumping in the air?"
	—a ball coming down from above?	
Flow	—a tossed ball coming at you from different directions?	
—a ball as smoothly as you can?	**Range**	
—with varying degrees of smoothness?	—using different body parts?	
	—from different positions?	
	—with one eye closed?	
	—with both eyes closed?	

TABLE 18.12   *Guided-Discovery Activity Ideas for Catching*

	1.	First explore the movement variations of catching.
	2.	Then begin to place limitations on the response possibilities to the following movement challenges. You may find it helpful to experiment with brightly colored balls.
General	a.	Experiment with catching a lightly tossed ball. How many ways can you catch the ball? Try experimenting with different arm positions. Now try catching the ball without it touching your body. Can you catch the ball with your hands only?
Arm Action	b.	What should your arms do when they catch a ball? Do they stay straight? Do they stay bent as if you were making a basket, or are they first straight and then do they bend as you catch the ball? Why do they "give" (bend) when you catch the ball? Try catching a softly thrown ball and a ball thrown hard. Is there any difference in how much your arms give as you catch? Why?
Hand Action	c.	Experiment with different ways of holding your hands when you catch. Is there a difference in how you place them for a high ball and for a low ball? Can you catch a low ball with your little fingers together, side by side? Now try it with your hands facing each other. Are there times when you want to use one ball-catching method and times when you use another? Let's try the same experiment while catching a ball that is above the waist.
Eyes	d.	We all know it's best to catch a ball with our eyes open and looking at the ball, but sometimes we close our eyes or turn our head away. Why do you think some people do that? What are some things we can do to help people look at the ball and not turn away? Let's play catch with a partner and see if we can find some ways to help our partner if he or she has this problem. Should we use a large ball or small ball? Why? Should we tell them we are going to toss the ball or not? Why? Let's try each and see what works better. Find what works better for your partner and practice until he or she feels comfortable. Then begin to try out different size balls, speeds, and heights.
	3.	After the mature catching pattern has been mastered in a structured environment, you will want to provide further practice experiences that permit use of catching in various situations. The attempt now should be to help make the mature pattern more automatic and adaptable to a variety of backgrounds, ball sizes, colors, objects, speeds, and positions in relationship to the body.
	a.	Introduce basic catching and throwing games.
	b.	Stress variations in ball size and hardness.
	c.	Try fielding grounders, fly balls, and balls not directly in line with the body.

TABLE 18.13   *Exploratory Activity Ideas for Kicking*

Effort	Space	Relationships
Force	***Level***	***Objects***

Effort	Space	Relationships
Can You Kick the Ball. . . .	*Can You Kick the Ball. . . .*	*Can You Kick the Ball. . . .*
—as hard as you can?	—high?	—and hit the wall?
—as soft as you can?	—low?	—and hit a big target?
—with a forceful leg swing but a light hit?	—as high as you can?	—and hit a small target?
—with a lazy leg swing but a forceful hit?	—so it stays on the ground?	—over the goal?
—so it goes fast?	—so it doesn't go higher than your waist?	—into the goal?
—so it goes very slowly?	***Direction***	—under the stretched rope?
—from here so it hits the wall in five seconds?		—through the chair legs?
—from here so it hits the wall in two seconds?	—forward?	—around the cones using several controlled kicks?
	—backward?	***People***
—from here and turn around before it hits the wall?	—sideways?	
—and touch the floor before it hits the wall?	—diagonally?	—to a partner?
Flow	—alternating left and right feet (dribbling)?	—to a partner while walking (passing)?
	Range	—at different levels to a partner?
—with a big leg swing?		—in different directions to a partner?
—with no knee bend?	—as far as you can?	—with different amounts of force to a partner?
—without using your arms?	—as near as you can?	—at different speeds to a partner?
—while swinging both arms back?	—with your feet wide apart?	***Combinations***
—while swinging both arms forward?	—with your body in different positions?	
—with no follow-through?	—with your opposite foot?	Numerous exploratory activities that combine elements of effort, space, and relationships can be explored after first trying them in isolation. For example, "Can you find ways to kick the ball with different amounts of force and at different levels with your partner?"
—with no backswing?		

TABLE 18.14   *Guided-Discovery Activity Ideas for Kicking*

	1. First explore the movement variations of kicking.
	2. Then begin to place limitations on the response possibilities to the following movement challenges:
Leg Action	a. Try kicking the ball without bending your leg. Now bend first at your kicking knee. Then kick the ball. Which way caused the ball to go farther? Which felt better? Try kicking the ball as far as you can, using different amounts of knee bend but no follow-through (that is, stopping your leg as soon as you contact the ball). Now try the same thing, but follow all the way through. Which amount of knee bend works best? Does a follow-through on your kick help the ball go farther?
	b. Try different ways of approaching the ball before you kick it, using a full bend at the knee of your kicking leg and extending at the hip. Does the ball go farther after a kick from standing still, or does it help to take a step or two? Why? Let's practice kicking as far as we can, using a step to the ball.
Trunk Action	c. Do you think it will help if you move your trunk backward when you kick the ball? Try it. Now keep your body straight and then try leaning far forward. Do you notice any differences? Let's try to kick the ball as far as we can and practice leaning back a little as we make contact with the ball.
Arm Action	d. What do you do with your arms when you kick the ball? Watch your partner. What does she or he do? Experiment with different arm positions as you kick. Which way works best? Let's practice kicking as hard as we can and swing our arms so the arm opposite our kicking leg is swung forward while the other moves backward.
Total	e. Try kicking the ball as far as you can and as hard as you can. Now try kicking at the target (a suspended hula hoop works fine). Did you notice any changes in how you kick when you kick for accuracy rather than for distance?
	f. Try kicking a rolling ball. Try kicking while on the run. Experiment with kicking the ball, but first tell your partner if it will be a high, medium, low, or ground kick. Can you control the level of your kick? What must you do to control the level? Show me. Try using different parts of your foot when you kick. Use your toe, your instep, the inside of your foot. What differences do you notice in level, in speed, in accuracy, in distance?
	3. After a mature kicking pattern has been reasonably well mastered, it is important to combine it with other activities to reinforce the pattern and make it more automatic.
	a. Make quick kicks.
	b. Kick at a stationary target.
	c. Kick at a moving target.
	d. Kick at a target from a run.
	e. Kick for control in high-, low-, and ground-level kicks.
	f. Kick back and forth to a partner while moving in the same direction (passing).
	g. Maneuver and kick at a target against a defense.
	h. Play kicking relays.
	i. Play kicking games.

TABLE 18.15   *Exploratory Activity Ideas for Trapping*

Effort	Space	Relationships
Force	***Level***	***Objects***
Can You Trap. . . .	*Can You Trap. . . .*	*Can You Trap. . . .*
—a ball that is rolled slowly toward you?	—a ball that is rolling toward you?	—a beanbag?
—a ball that is tossed lightly at you?	—a ball that is rolling off to one side?	—a beach ball?
—a ball that is rolled rapidly toward you?	—a ball at waist level?	—a fleece ball?
—a ball that is tossed forcefully at you (use a fleece ball)?	—a ball at stomach level?	—a playground ball?
—in slow motion?	—a ball at chest level?	—different size balls?
—a fast-moving ball?	***Direction***	—a soccer ball?
—a slow-moving ball?	—a ball moving toward you?	***People***
Flow	—a ball moving away from you?	—a ball and kick it back to your partner?
—a ball and "give" with the ball?	—a ball moving in front of you?	—a ball and have your partner count the number of different ways you can do it?
—a ball without "giving" with the ball?	—a ball moving to one side?	***Combinations***
	Range	Combinations of effort, space, and relationships can be devised and explored after a variety of isolated activities are explored. For example, "Experiment with how much you must 'give' with your body when trapping five different types of balls."
	—a ball with your foot?	
	—a ball with your shin?	
	—a ball with your stomach?	
	—a ball with your chest?	
	—a ball with either foot?	
	—a ball with a large body part?	
	—a ball with a small body part?	

TABLE 18.16   *Guided-Discovery Activity Ideas for Trapping*

1. First explore several of the movement variations of trapping. Remember that a primary purpose of these exploratory activities is to lead the child to a better understanding of the movement concepts of effort, space, and relationships as applied to trapping an object.

2. Then begin to place limitations on the response possibilities to the movement challenges that you present. Remember that your reason for doing this is so that you may lead the individual to the mature pattern of movement through his or her own discovery of the solution to the movement problems that you structure. Trapping, for example, may be performed in a variety of ways. There are the foot trap, knee trap, stomach trap, and chest trap. Although each uses a different part of the body to intercept and stop the oncoming object, all incorporate the same principles of movement, namely (1) absorbing the force of the ball over the greatest surface area possible and (2) absorbing the force of the ball over the greatest distance required for successful trapping. The following are examples of several movement challenges to present that help bring out these movement principles.

General

   a. Try to stop a rolling ball with your feet. What happens to the ball when you let it hit your feet without "giving" when it hits? Why does this happen? How can you cause the ball to stop right after it hits your feet? What do you have to do?

   b. Let's try the same thing with the ball being tossed at your legs (stomach, chest, etc.). What must you do each time to get the ball to drop and stop in front of you? Try different ideas and then show me the one that works best for you. Did you notice how you had to "give" with the ball to get it to stop?

   c. Do you have to "give" with the ball as much if the ball is traveling slowly as when it is traveling fast? Why? Show me how you "give" with the ball when it is coming fast and then when it is coming slowly.

   d. Is it better to try trapping the ball with a small body part or a large body part? Try both ways. Which works better? Why?

   e. If a ball is traveling fast, would you want to "give" with the ball over a longer distance or a shorter distance? How about over a large part of your body or over a small part? Experiment with the different ways of trapping and let me know which is best.

3. After trapping has been reasonably well mastered in controlled guided-discovery lessons, you will find it helpful to structure experiences that demand greater control and rapid decision-making. For example,

   a. Trap a ball kicked by a partner and then kick it back.

   b. Trap a ball coming from different directions and levels and at different speeds.

   c. Play games and take part in relay races involving kicking and trapping.

TABLE 18.17   *Exploratory Activity Ideas for Dribbling*

Effort	Space	Relationships
Force	***Level***	***Objects***
Can You Bounce (or Dribble) the Ball. . . .	*Can You Bounce (or Dribble) the Ball. . . .*	*Can You Bounce (or Dribble) the Ball. . . .*
—as hard as you can?	—at knee level?	—around the chairs?
—as soft as you can?	—at waist level?	—under the outstretched rope?
—changing from hard to soft?	—at leg level?	—over the outstretched rope?
Flow	—higher than your head?	—while walking close to the wall?
	—lower than your knees?	—if it is a basketball?
—and catch it?	—and change levels with each bounce?	—if it is a playground ball?
—repeatedly after catching it repeatedly?	***Direction***	—and notice any difference with different types of balls?
—without catching it? (dribbling)	—in front of you?	***People***
Time:	—to one side?	
	—behind you?	—to your partner?
—as fast as you can?	—in different pathways?	—alternating with a partner?
—as slow as you can?	—in a straight line?	—in time to your partner's bounce?
—alternating fast and slow?	—in a circle?	—and each move away and back together with the same number of bounces?
—and allow as much time as you can between bounces?	—in a curved line?	***Combinations***
—as many times as you can until I say "stop"?	—in a zigzag line?	As the individual gradually gains control of the ball rather than the ball controlling him or her, add various combinations of effort, space, or relationships. For example, "Can you dribble the ball at waist level but to one side of your body as you go around the field?"
	Range	
	—in your space?	
	—hitting the same spot each time?	
	—while moving around the room?	
	—as far away from you as you can?	
	—as close to you as you can?	
	—with other body parts?	
	—with your other hand?	

TABLE 18.18 *Guided-Discovery Activity Ideas for Dribbling*

	1. First explore several of the movement variations of dribbling.
	2. Then begin to place limitations on the response possibilities to the following movement challenges:
General	a. Try dribbling your ball in your own space with your feet together, legs straight, and standing straight. How does it feel? Now try it several different ways. Which way feels best? Why?
Trunk Action	b. When you dribble the ball in place, what do you do with your feet? Your trunk? Is it easier to control the ball in one place standing straight or bent slightly forward at the waist? Try both. Which was better? Why?
Leg Action	c. Experiment with different foot positions when you dribble in place. Are there any differences? Why?
	d. Try moving about the room while dribbling the ball. Is it easier or harder than when you are standing in your space? Why is it harder?
	e. Listen to my commands and move only in the direction I call out. Can you do it? Why is it hard for some people and easier for others? All those who are "experts" try the same thing but use your opposite hand to dribble the ball. Did you "experts" notice any difference in how well you did? Why?
Arm and Hand Action	f. Experiment with using your hand and arm in different ways as you dribble the ball. What do we do with our fingers, our wrist, and our arms when we dribble the ball? Show me. Why do we push the ball down rather than slapping at it? Can you keep your wrist stiff and dribble the ball off your fingertips? Try it.
	g. Try to stay in your own space, dribbling the ball off your fingertips with a stiff wrist and good follow-through. Now try it by slapping at the ball. Which way gives you the most control? Show me. Why?
Eyes	h. Look at the ball as you dribble. Now try the same thing looking up here at me. Try it now with your eyes closed. Which was easier? Which was harder? When you are playing basketball, is it best to look at the ball as you dribble or is it better to be looking where you are going? Let's try to dribble without looking at the ball.
General	i. Let's practice dribbling with the opposite hand. Now let's alternate dribbling first with one hand then the other. Is it harder with one hand than with the other? Why?
	j. See if you can dribble around an object changing hands each time around. Now change hands each time you change direction.
	3. After the mature dribbling pattern has been fairly well mastered, it should be combined with other activities to reinforce the pattern and make it more automatic.
	a. Dribble around obstacles.
	b. Dribble the ball while touching different body parts and changing hands, levels, or directions.
	c. Keep the ball away from an opponent while dribbling.

TABLE 18.19   *Exploratory Activity Ideas for Ball Rolling*

Effort	Space	Relationships
Force	***Level***	***Objects***
Can You Roll the Ball. . . .	*Can You Roll the Ball. . . .*	*Can You Roll the Ball. . . .*
—softly?	—while lying on the floor	—no matter what size it is?
—as hard as you can?	—from your knees?	—on the balance beam?
Time	—from a sitting position?	—on a line?
—as slowly as possible?	***Direction***	—between the boxes?
—as fast as you can?		—into the can?
Flow	—in a straight line?	—through the tube?
—using your arms only?	—so that it curves?	—under a wicket?
—using only one side of your body?	***Range***	—at the pins?
—smoothly?		***People***
—like a robot?	—around yourself?	
—like a champion bowler?	—with your other hand?	—to a partner?
	—as far as you can?	—alternating back and forth?
	—as accurately as you can?	—mirroring your partner?
	—without moving off the line?	—shadowing your partner?
	—with an approach?	***Combinations***
		Numerous combinations of effort, space, and relationships related to rolling are possible as well as combinations with other fundamental movements. For example, "Can you roll the ball with differing amounts of force?" "Can you roll the ball at a low level with a partner?"

TABLE 18.20   *Guided-Discovery Activity Ideas for Ball Rolling*

	1. First explore several of the numerous variations of rolling.
	2. Then begin to place limitations on the responsibilities to the movement challenges you present. Focus on how the body should move and why when rolling an object. For example,
General	a. Let's experiment with different ways of rolling the ball. How many ways can you find? Show me.
	b. What should we do if we want the ball to go as fast as possible? Show me. Why?
	c. What can you do to make the ball go as straight as possible?
	d. If you want the ball to go both fast and straight, how would you roll it? Why?
Arm Action	e. Try rolling the ball from between your legs. Now try placing it by your side and rolling. Which way allows the ball to go the fastest? Which is the most accurate? Why?
	f. What happens when you use a small ball and then a large ball? Which ball will go fastest? Which ball travels more accurately? Try both and then tell me.
Leg Action	g. Why do you think bowlers bowl like this (demonstrate)? Try doing different things with your legs as you roll the ball. Try standing with your feet together and your knees locked. Does it work well? What happened to the ball? Why did it bounce before it began to roll?
	h. See what you can do to prevent the ball from bouncing as it is rolled. Can you do anything with your trunk? Can you do anything with your legs that will help? Show me. Why does it help to bend forward and step out on the leg opposite the ball? Let's all try it and see how straight we can roll our ball.
	3. After a mature ball-rolling pattern has been reasonably well mastered, begin to focus on accuracy and increasing the distance to the target. A variety of low-level games and lead-up activities to bowling can be incorporated at this point. You will also want, however, to combine rolling with a variety of other movements to reinforce the proper pattern and make it more automatic. For example,
	a. Roll different-sized balls.
	b. Roll the balls on different surfaces.
	c. Try to control the direction of a rolled ball.

TABLE 18.21   *Exploratory Activity Ideas for Striking*

Effort	Space	Relationships
Force	*Level*	*Objects*
Can You Strike the Ball (Balloon, Beach Ball). . . .	*Can You Strike the Ball (Balloon, Beach Ball). . . .*	*Can You Strike the Ball (Balloon, Beach Ball). . . .*
—as hard as you can?	—so it travels at different levels?	—off different height cones?
—as softly as you can?	—with your body at different levels?	—off a batting tee?
—so it makes a loud noise?	—from a high level to a low level?	—over the rope?
—like a strong monster?	—from a low level to a high level?	—under the rope?
—squarely?	*Direction*	—through the chairs?
Flow	—in a straight line?	—around the chair?
—limply?	—with a level swing?	—into the bucket?
—with jerky movements?	—up?	—using different-sized objects?
—with smooth movements?	—down?	—using objects with different shapes?
Time	—forward?	—with different implements?
—slowly?	—backward?	*People*
—quickly?	—in different pathways?	—to a partner?
—firmly?	*Range*	—as your partner does?
	—using different body parts?	—tossed by your partner?
	—and keep it in your space?	*Combinations*
	—with your other hand?	After exploring the many variations of striking in isolation, it will be helpful to combine various aspects of effort, space, and relationships. For example, "Can you hit the balloon as hard as you can so that it travels at a low level to a partner?"
	—from the other side?	
	—with a wide base?	
	—with a narrow base?	

TABLE 18.22 *Guided-Discovery Activity Ideas for Striking*

1. First explore several of the numerous variations of striking. Emphasize the idea of striking in terms of effort, space, and the ball's relationship to objects and people.
2. Then begin to place limitations on the response possibilities to the following movement challenges:

Arm Action

  a. Try hitting the ball off the tee using your hand, a paddle, a bat. Which way caused the ball to go the farthest? Why?

  b. Now try using a bat, but keep your arms bent. Then try it with your arms straight when the bat hits the ball. Did you notice a difference? Which works better and why?

  c. See if you can find different ways to swing your bat. Experiment with different ways of holding the bat. Can anyone tell me the best way to hold the bat and the best way to swing it if I want what I'm hitting to go as far as possible?

  d. Now we want to have our right hand on top (right-handed batter) and our left on the bottom, and we want our swing to be level. Let's try it.

Leg Action

  e. Let's try standing in different ways when we strike the ball. Try to find five ways to stand as you hit the ball off the tee. Which helps the ball go the farthest? Show me.

  f. Now let's see what we can do with your feet when we hit the ball. Try standing with your feet together, wide apart, and less apart. Which feels best?

  g. Will it help to step out as we swing at the ball? Try it. Why do you think that it helps?

General

  h. Try hitting the balloon with your hand, a ping-pong paddle, a wiffle ball bat. Which was easiest? Hardest? Why?

  i. Now try to hit the beach ball the same way—first with your hand, then a ping-pong paddle, then a bat. Which was easiest? Hardest? Why?

  j. Let's practice hitting a suspended ball. Can you hit it as it is swung to you? Can you tell me what you need to do with your arms, your trunk, and your legs when you strike the ball? Do we do each separately, or do we try to put them together smoothly? Why?

3. After a mature striking pattern has been reasonably well mastered, you will want to begin practicing hitting a tossed ball. To maximize skill development, you may want to:

  a. Use a large ball, then gradually work down to a small ball.

  b. Use an oversized bat prior to using a regulation bat.

  c. Use a bat that is slightly shorter or have the child "choke up" on the bat.

  d. Toss the ball slowly and then gradually increase its speed.

  e. Experiment with different pitching distances.

  f. Experiment with different ball colors and backgrounds.

  g. Incorporate the striking pattern into a variety of low-level and lead-up games.

TABLE 18.23 *Exploratory Activity Ideas for Volleying*

Effort	Space	Relationships
Force	**Level**	**Objects**
Can You Volley the Ball. . . .	*Can You Volley the Ball. . . .*	*Can You Volley the Ball. . . .*
—very hard?	—when you are in different positions?	—if it is a beach ball?
—very softly?	—from a seated position?	—if it is a balloon?
—high?	—from a kneeling position?	—if it is a large ball?
—low?	—without it going above your head?	—if it is a small ball?
	—with it going as high as possible?	—if it is a volleyball?
Flow		—over the rope?
	Direction	—over the net?
—alternating hard and soft volleys?		—with different body parts?
—but relax your fingers?	—forward?	—with your head (heading)?
—but tense your fingers?	—backward?	—with your knees (juggling)?
—and "give" with the ball?	—to the side?	**People**
—without "giving" with the ball?	—in a circle?	
Time	**Range**	—to a partner?
		—tossed by a partner?
—as many times as you can until I say "stop"?	—and have it drop in your personal space?	—back and forth to a partner?
—as few times as you can in thirty seconds?	—and have it drop outside your space?	**Combinations**
	—from a position directly under it?	Simple exploratory activities with light objects (balloons and beach balls) are essential prior to using volleyballs. Combine activities only after reasonable control has developed. For example, "Can you find ways to volley the ball to your partner so that he or she can volley it back at different levels?"
	—from a position off to one side?	

TABLE 18.24   *Guided-Discovery Activity Ideas for Volleying*

	1. First explore several of the movement variations of volleying, taking care to use an object appropriate to the ability of the individual.
	2. Then begin to place limitations on the response possibilities to the questions you ask. Focus on eliciting the mature volleying pattern, first using a balloon, then a beach ball, and finally a volleyball. To aid children with tracking and accurately interrupting the ball, you may permit an intermediate bounce of the ball before it is actually volleyed in the following activities:
General	a. Can you hit the balloon, beach ball, or other type of ball into the air so that it comes right back to you? Try hitting it several times in a row, staying in your own space. What must you do to be sure that the ball comes back to you? What about your hands? Do you have more control with one or both hands?
Hand and Arm Action	b. Try volleying your balloon with both hands as many times as you can. What must you do to keep it up over your head? Show me. What do you do with your hands and fingers and wrists when you volley the balloon?
	c. Try volleying a beach ball or volleyball. Is it easier or harder than the balloon? Why?
	d. Use your volleyball to volley with, but let it bounce once before you try hitting it again. Is that easier than before? Why?
	e. Let's try volleying different-sized balls. Is there any difference? Can you use two hands as easily with a small ball?
Foot and Leg Action	f. Experiment with different foot positions as you volley. Now try it with your knees locked, with them apart, with them bent slightly. Which works best?
	3. You will need to spend considerable time with discovery activities to help the children focus on control of the object. Intercepting a ball and volleying or striking it are extremely complicated tasks requiring sophisticated interaction of visual and motor processes and exact timing. Be patient in your approach and be sure to use objects and activities that permit the beginner ample opportunity to track the ball visually before intercepting it. Once the volleying pattern has been mastered to a reasonable degree and the individual is exhibiting mature control of the ball, it will be wise to focus on a combination of activities that reinforce the correct pattern and make it more automatic.
	a. Volley the ball to different heights.
	b. Volley from different body levels.
	c. Volley continuously without an intermediate bounce.
	d. Volley against a wall.
	e. Volley with a partner.
	f. Volley with a group.
	g. Volley the ball in a direction different from that in which it came.

This guided approach permits children to learn more about the skill and how their bodies should move. Guided-discovery activities give children an opportunity to practice the skill and to focus on its use in a wide variety of movement situations. Have children practice using different sizes, colors, and textures to promote skill development. Also, it will be helpful to catch nonthreatening objects such as fleece balls, beach balls, or foam balls. Practice with catching different-sized objects is also important.

SKILL APPLICATION ACTIVITIES

Once the mature stage has been attained in a manipulative skill, it is appropriate to focus on skill application activities. The application of manipulative skills to a variety of game, rhythm, and self-testing activities permits practice and refinement of manipulative skills under dynamic conditions in a constantly changing environment. Overlearning of manipulative skills and practice in

TABLE 18.25   *Selected Manipulative Games Sequenced in Terms of Complexity*

Manipulative Games (page number)	Throwing/Catching	Kicking/Trapping	Dribbling/Volleying	Striking/Rolling
		Movement Skills Stressed		
Clean Your Yard (347)	X	X		
Hot Potato (348)	X			
Teacher Ball (348)	X	X	X	
Moon Shot (348)	X			
Spud (348)	X	X		
Keep Away (349)	X	X		
Tunnel Ball (349)				X
Roll It Out (349)				X
Kick-Away (349)		X		
Cross the Line (349)		X		
Balloon Volleying (349)			X	X
Kick the Can (349)		X		
Corner Kickball (350)		X	X	X
Guard the Castle (350)	X	X		X
Target Bombardment (350)	X	X		X

a variety of situations are important to ensure that the mature patterns of movement can be performed consistently. The following pages contain several manipulative skill application ideas that are appropriate for elementary school children.

CONCEPT 18.8
Low-level manipulative games and relays are effective tools for applying newly learned fundamental manipulative skills.

Manipulative Games

Several game activities may be used to reinforce fundamental manipulative abilities. You must keep in mind the desired outcomes of the game and feel free to modify the activity whenever necessary to ensure maximum participation and practice of the skills being stressed. Table 18.25 lists the manipulative games included in this chapter and the movement skills stressed. The basic objectives of manipulative game activities are to

1. enhance fundamental manipulative abilities in throwing, catching, kicking, trapping, bouncing, rolling, striking, and volleying,
2. enhance eye-hand and eye-foot coordination,
3. encourage working together in a group effort,
4. enhance listening abilities, and
5. encourage following directions and obeying rules.

Once again, remember to modify the following games to maximize participation and player safety. Also, avoid eliminating children from games even if the traditional rules call for it. Modify the activity in creative ways so that all students receive maximum benefit from the skill reinforcement potential of the game.

Clean Your Yard (TRASH)

Movement Skills: Throwing or kicking.

Formation: Scatter formation with half the class on each side of the gymnasium. String a rope waist high across the gymnasium.

Equipment: All of the soft objects you can locate (beanbags, yarn balls, beach balls, newspaper balls, etc.) placed in one team's "backyard."

Procedures: On the signal "Go" the team with the trash in its backyard begins to throw objects over the fence (the waist high rope) as fast as they can, while the "neighbors" in the other "yard" return them as fast as they can. Play for a predetermined time (two to three minutes). All objects must be thrown using an overhand pattern as far into the neighbors' backyard as possible (to encourage forceful throws). Count the number of objects left in each team's backyard. Repeat, with the other team trying to get rid of all of its trash.

Variation: Try the same activity, but have children kick the objects under the outstretched rope.

Hot Potato

Movement Skills: Tossing and catching.

Formation: Single circle facing in, with six to ten players per circle.

Equipment: One playground ball.

Procedures: The children sit in the circle an arm's length apart. On the command "Go" the ball is passed around the circle until the signal "Stop" is given. The child left holding the ball drops out of the circle. The game continues until only two players remain. To avoid excluding players from this and many other games, set up a point system. For example, a player who gets caught with the ball twice must sit in the "mush pot" in the center of the circle for one turn or perform a stunt for the class.

Teacher Ball

Movement Skills: Throwing, catching/kicking, trapping/dribbling, and volleying.

Formation: Several circles containing six to eight children each with the "teacher" in the center.

Equipment: One playground ball or foam ball for each group.

Procedures: One child stands in the center of the circle ("teacher") and tosses the ball to each member of the circle. A new "teacher" then goes into the center. This game may be used as a practice drill or be developed into a race between circles as the children's skill level increases. Various sizes and types of balls may be used. Also, various throwing, catching, kicking, trapping, and volleying skills may be developed this way.

Moon Shot

Movement Skills: Throwing and catching.

Formation: Single circle facing in with an outer circle drawn on the floor, one child in the center.

Equipment: Beanbags.

Procedures: Each child stands on the inner circle and in turn tries to "shoot the moon" with the beanbag. The "moon" is a small circle placed inside two larger circles, also drawn on the floor. If the child is successful, he or she moves to the outer circle and shoots from there when a turn comes again. When a child makes a successful throw, that person moves to or remains on the outer circle. When unsuccessful, the player remains on or returns to the inner circle. Each successful throw from the inner circle counts one point, and from the outer circle, two points. The center player is retriever and throws the beanbag to each player in turn, or each player may retrieve his or her own beanbag and pass it to the next player. After the beanbag has gone around the circle once, the retriever (if one is used) chooses a player from the outer circle to be the new retriever and exchanges places with him.

Spud

Movement Skills: Throwing and catching.

Formation: Single circle facing in with the leader in the center.

Equipment: One playground ball for each circle of six to eight players.

Procedures: The leader stands in the center of the circle, tosses the ball into the air, and calls another player's name. The player called runs to the center of the circle and tries to catch the ball. At the same time, the remaining players scatter. "It" catches the ball and says "Stop" as soon as it is caught. The fleeing players freeze. "It" is permitted to take three giant steps in any direction and then can throw the ball at one of the players. If that person, who is not permitted to move, is hit, he or she then becomes "it." If the ball misses, the same player remains "it" and begins the game again with a toss from the center of the circle.

Keep Away

Movement Skills: Throwing, catching/kicking, and trapping.

Formation: Single circle of six to eight participants facing in, one child in center.

Equipment: Playground balls.

Procedures: The children form a circle and one child is placed in the center. The remaining children attempt to pass the ball, keeping it away from the child in the center. If the child in the center catches the ball, the child who threw it takes the place in the center.

Tunnel Ball

Movement Skills: Rolling.

Formation: Single circle of six to eight players facing in, one child in center.

Equipment: Playground balls.

Procedures: Players form a circle with one player in the center. The players in the circle spread their feet apart, and the player in the center tries to roll the ball through their legs or between the players. If successful in the attempt, the player in the center takes the place of the player in the circle. The player in the circle can block the ball with his hands, but he cannot move his feet.

Roll It Out

Movement Skills: Rolling.

Formation: Single circle facing in, either seated or kneeling, with six to eight players per circle.

Equipment: One playground ball per circle.

Procedures: A ball is rolled into the circle. When it comes near a child, the player tries to roll it between two of the circle players by batting it with a hand. The player may stop it first and then roll the ball. If the player succeeds, she or he changes places with the circle player on whose right side the ball goes out.

Kick-Away

Movement Skills: Kicking and trapping.

Formation: Several circles with four to six children per group.

Equipment: One eight-inch playground ball or foam ball per group.

Procedures: One player has the ball on the ground in front of him or her with a foot resting on it. The ball is kicked across the circle, using the inside of the foot to avoid lofting. The child receiving the ball traps it and kicks it quickly away to another child. Children continue to kick the ball until it goes outside the circle. The player who retrieves the ball brings it back to the circle and starts again.

Cross the Line

Movement Skills: Kicking and trapping.

Formation: Four to six players per group facing a kicker.

Equipment: One eight-inch playground ball per group.

Procedures: The "line" is a twenty-five-foot line drawn a distance of twenty to forty feet from the kicking circle. Other players scatter in playing field in front of the wall. The kicker places the ball on the ground inside the kicking circle. The player calls out "Cross the line" and kicks the ball toward the line. Any fielder who can trap the ball before it goes over the line is the new kicker. If the ball crosses the line, the original kicker kicks again. If no one stops the ball after she has kicked three times, she chooses a new kicker.

Balloon Volleying

Movement Skills: Striking and volleying.

Formation: Scatter.

Equipment: Enough round balloons for each child to have one.

Procedures: The player who can keep a balloon up the longest is the winner.

Variation: Practice the activity as a cooperative game with a partner trying to keep the balloon in the air as long as possible.

Kick the Can (or Pinball Soccer)

Movement Skills: Kicking and trapping.

Formation: Two parallel lines thirty feet apart with six to eight players per group.

Equipment: Nerf soccer ball, five large cans, Indian clubs, or cartons.

Procedures: Divide players into two teams, each team standing on its own kicking line. Kicking lines are thirty to sixty feet from center line, depending on the skill of players. Give soccer ball to player on one team, who kicks the ball at a can that has been placed in the center of the playing area from her own kicking line. Opponents trap ball with their feet as it rolls to them and kick from their line. Game continues until all the cans are down. A team makes one point for each can it knocks down. When all cans are down, the team with the higher score is the winner. A player may block the ball with his or her body but may not touch it with the hands unless it goes out of bounds, in which case it is carried to the kicking line and the game is started again. If the ball is touched with the hands, it is a foul, and the opponents win one point.

Corner Kickball

Movement Skills: Kicking and trapping/dribbling.

Formation: Two parallel lines thirty feet apart with six to eight players per group.

Equipment: One soccer-type ball per group.

Procedures: Players divide into two teams, each team standing behind its own restraining line. The ball is placed in circle in center of field. On the signal "Go!" the two end players from each team run to the center and try to kick the ball to a teammate behind them or to the side. (The ball may not be kicked forward on the initial kick.) Teammates try to pass the ball to the center person on their team, who now attempts to kick the ball to the opposing team's goal line. The successful team wins two points. After a score, the kicking players all return to center positions in their own line, and four new ends run out. Line players try to block the ball from going over the goal line and kick or throw it back to their centers. Line players may not cross their own restraining line. Center players may not use hands, but line players may use hands or body to block the ball. Out-of-bounds balls are played in from the point where they went out.

Guard the Castle

Movement Skills: Throwing, kicking, and trapping.

Formation: Circle with an empty milk carton in the center. Six to eight players per group.

Equipment: Utility ball.

Procedures: The circle players throw the ball at the carton, attempting to knock it down. The guard tries to prevent it from being knocked down, stopping the ball in any manner. Whoever knocks the carton down becomes the guard. If the guard accidentally knocks down the carton, the circle player who last threw becomes the new guard. Don't allow circle players to move within the designated area and don't allow the guard to stand over the carton.

Target Bombardment

Movement Skills: Throwing/kicking.

Formation: Two teams of eight to ten spread out on their respective sides of a half-court line.

Equipment: Ten to fifteen empty milk cartons lined up on the two ends of the playing area and two utility balls.

Procedures: Each team tries to knock down the cartons of the other team with thrown balls. The team knocking down all the other team's cartons is the winner. Players may not cross the center line. If a carton is knocked down, it must stay down; this includes cartons knocked down by players on the defending team. Players may not stand over the cartons to guard them.

ASSESSING PROGRESS

It is important to assess children informally at the beginning of a manipulative skill theme and again at the end. Once the children's entry level of ability is known, it is a relatively easy matter to determine the types of activities to include in the lesson. The sample assessment charts located in Chapter 11 (Tables 11.1 and 11.2) and in the Appendixes can be applied to manipulative skills. These charts are a practical means for recording individual and group progress. Fundamental manipulative skills may also be informally assessed through a self-question chart similar to the one depicted in Table 18.26. You should be able to answer "yes" to each of the questions. If you cannot, you will need to modify subsequent lessons to more closely fit the specific needs of the individual, group, or class.

TABLE 18.26   *Self-Question Chart for Fundamental Manipulative Skill Development*

Throwing	Yes	No	Comments
1. Does the child throw consistently with a preferred hand?			
2. Is the child able to control the trajectory of the ball?			
3. Is there noticeable humerus lag of the forearm?			
4. Does the child use arm and leg opposition?			
5. Is there definite hip rotation?			
6. Is there efficient summation of forces in use of the arms, trunk, and legs?			
7. Is there noticeable improvement in throwing ability?			

Catching

1. Does the child maintain eye contact with the ball throughout?
2. Is the child able to adjust easily to a ball thrown at different levels?
3. Is the child able to adjust easily to a ball thrown at different speeds?
4. Are proper adjustments made in the arm and hand action of large and small balls?
5. Is the catching action smooth, coordinated, and in good control?
6. Is there observable improvement in catching abilities?

Kicking

1. Does the child make consistent contact with a stationary ball?
2. Can the child make good contact with the ball from an approach?
3. Can the child control the direction, level, and distance of his or her kick?
4. Is there an acute bend at the knee and backward extension at the hip when the child is kicking for distance?
5. Are the entire trunk and the arms brought into play for a forceful kick?
6. Can the child consistently kick a moving ball?
7. Is there noticeable improvement in the kicking pattern?

Trapping

1. Can the child trap a rolled ball?
2. Can the child trap a tossed ball?
3. Does the child make easy adjustments for trapping balls traveling at different speeds?
4. Does the child make adjustments for the surface area used to trap the ball based on the speed of the ball?
5. Are the movements of the child fluid and in control?
6. Is there observable improvement in trapping abilities?

(continued)

TABLE 18.26   *(continued)*

Dribbling	Yes	No	Comments
1. Is the child in control of the ball?			
2. Is the child able to dribble in her or his own space?			
3. Can the child dribble while moving about the room?			
4. Can the child dribble the ball without stopping to catch it?			
5. Does the child properly use the fingers, wrist, and arms while dribbling?			
6. Is the trunk bent forward slightly while dribbling?			
7. Is the action smooth and rhythmical?			
8. Can the child vary the height and direction of the ball at will?			
9. Can the child dribble with either hand?			
10. Is there observable improvement in the child's ability to dribble with control?			

Ball Rolling

1. Does the child use a rolling pattern to one side of the body?
2. Can the child make adjustments for different-sized balls?
3. Does the child adjust to the distance and accuracy required?
4. Does the child exhibit a good backswing?
5. Is there sufficient follow-through?
6. Can the child control the pathway of the ball?
7. Is there observable improvement?

Striking

1. Can the child strike a balloon with good control (does the child control the balloon or does the balloon control the child)?
2. Can the child strike a ball off a batting tee?
3. Does the child use a level horizontal swing?
4. Does the child grip the implement properly?
5. Is the stance appropriate for the task?
6. Does the child show evidence of proper summation of forces?
7. Is there observable improvement?

Volleying

1. Can the child volley a balloon repeatedly with good control?
2. Can the child volley a beach ball with good control?
3. Can the child volley and remain in his or her own space?
4. Can the child control the direction of the volley?
5. Can the child volley a ball that has been permitted to bounce one time?
6. Does the child exhibit controlled use of the fingers, hands, and arms?
7. Does the child use an efficient summation of forces upon contact?
8. Does the child maintain eye contact throughout?
9. Is there observable improvement?

CONCEPT 18.9
Progress may be assessed in fundamental
manipulative skill acquisition through a process
assessment approach.

SUMMARY

This chapter dealt with fundamental manipulative skill themes. The steps in planning, organizing, implementing, and assessing fundamental manipulative movements were reviewed, along with the importance of developmentally appropriate skill sequencing. Verbal and visual descriptions were provided for several fundamental manipulative skills, along with teaching tips and concepts children should know for each.

Skill development activities in the form of exploratory and guided-discovery experiences were presented to help you begin to use indirect teaching styles. Careful review of these tables along with practice will help the novice use these techniques effectively. A sampling of low-level manipulative games were included as examples of appropriate skill application activities. Many more appropriate games may be found in a variety of resource books. These are intended only to help get you started and to highlight the concept that games activities are used for skill application, not for skill development. Games, particularly where coming in first or winning are the goals, may reinforce one's present level of skill acquisition, but they have little impact on movement skill development in terms of progressing from one stage to the next.

COMPLEMENTARY READINGS

Capon, J. (1975). *Ball, Rope, Hoop Activities.* Belmont, CA: Fearon-Pitman.

Capon, J. (1975). *Bean Bag, Rhythm Stick Activities.* Belmont, CA: Fearon-Pitman.
Hammett, C. T. (1992). *Movement Activities for Early Childhood.* Champaign, IL: Human Kinetics.
Kraft, R. E., and J. A. Smith. (1993). Throwing and catching: How to do it right. *Strategies* 6:24–29.
Morton-Jones, P. (1990). Skill analysis series: Part I, analysis of the place kick. *Strategies* 3:10–12.
Morton-Jones, P. (1990). Skill analysis series: Part II, analysis of the overarm throw. *Strategies* 3:22–23.
Morton-Jones, P. (1991). Skill analysis series: Part VI, catching. *Strategies* 4:23–24.
Worrell, V. (1994). Tennis skills for young students. *Strategies* 7:9–11.

SUPPLEMENTARY READINGS

Gallahue, D. L., and J. C. Ozmun. (1995). *Understanding Motor Development.* Dubuque, IA: Wm. C. Brown & Benchmark.
Roberton, M. A., and L. E. Halverson. (1984). *Developing Children—Their Changing Movement.* Philadelphia: Lea & Febiger.
Wickstrom, R. L. (1983). *Fundamental Motor Patterns.* Philadelphia: Lea & Febiger.

VIDEOS

Assessment of Fundamental Motor Skills: Striking; Throwing; Kicking; Catching; Dribbling. Ignico, A. A. (1994). Dubuque, IA: Wm. C. Brown & Benchmark. (five-tape set. All correspond with the manipulative skills discussed in this chapter.)
Children and Movement Video Series: Throwing/Catching and *Striking Skills.* Sanders, S. (1993). Durham, NC: Great Activities Publishing Company. (23 min. and 19 min.).
Having a Ball. Short, K., Byron, CA: Front Row Experience. (15 min.).

CHAPTER 19

Stunts and Tumbling Skill Themes

Key Concept

The Educational Gymnastic Activities of Stunts and Tumbling Form a Cornerstone for Developing a Wide Variety of Fundamental and Specialized Stability Abilities

Chapter Objectives

The purpose of this chapter is to provide you with the tools to:
- List and describe the steps in planning and implementing a stunts and tumbling skill theme.
- Discuss the importance of safety precautions and proper spotting of stunts and tumbling activities.
- Progressing from simple to complex, list and describe a variety of body-rolling skills involving sideways, forward, and backward rolling.
- Progressing from simple to complex, list and describe a variety of upright and inverted springing skills.
- Progressing from simple to complex, list and describe a variety of individual and partner upright support skills.
- Progressing from simple to complex, list and describe a variety of headstand, transitional support, and handstand skills.

Terms to Remember

Stunts

Tumbling

Spotting

Body Rolling

Springing

Upright Support Skills

Inverted Supports

Aim Chart

Stunts and tumbling skills are performed on the floor or on a mat. **Stunts** are generally considered to be movement activities in which the body maintains a static center of gravity. Skills such as the tip-up, tripod, and headstand are considered to be stunts. **Tumbling** skills, on the other hand, are generally considered to be activities in which the body moves down a mat in ways that cause the center of gravity to constantly shift. A forward roll, headspring, handspring, and walkover are all considered here to be tumbling skills.

Stunts and tumbling skills place considerable emphasis on static and dynamic balancing abilities. The concepts children should know concerning static and dynamic balance (refer to Chapter 16, "Fundamental Stability Skill Themes") can all be learned through a progressive program of stunts and tumbling skill development. This chapter focuses on body-rolling, springing, upright support, and inverted support skills. Each skill is described and sequenced in progression from simple to complex as a beginning, intermediate, or advanced skill.

CONCEPT 19.1
Stunts and tumbling skills are performed on a mat or on the floor and involve a variety of static and dynamic movement skills.

SKILL SEQUENCING

The skills contained in this chapter and the next (Chapter 20, "Apparatus Skill Themes") are sequenced in progression from simple to complex for children at the beginning, intermediate, and advanced levels of learning a skill. Children without previous experience in stunts and tumbling, and apparatus activity, will benefit most from beginning level skills regardless of their grade level. These activities have been carefully selected and sequenced to provide novice gymnasts with success and the necessary background of experiences to progress to intermediate level skills. Most children in the primary grades will be at the beginning level unless they have had previous training.

Intermediate skills are suitable for children who have successfully completed the beginning level. Children in the third or fourth grade are often at the intermediate level if they have completed the beginning level. Fifth and sixth graders are frequently ready for advanced

Developing a Gymnastics Skill Theme

When planning lessons that focus on stability skill development through stunts and tumbling activities or apparatus activities, the following sequence will be helpful:

1. *Preplan*
   Determine when and approximately how many lessons will focus on gymnastic skills. Locate a sufficient number of mats that are clean and in good repair.
2. *Observe and Assess*
   Select a few basic skills, such as the forward roll, star jump, V-seat, and headstand, for observation. Informally assess the group to determine if they are at the beginning, intermediate, or advanced level of gymnastics skill learning.
3. *Plan and Implement*
   Based on your observational assessment, plan a progressive program of activities using the suggested progressions found in Tables 19.1–19.4, and 20.1–20.7.
4. *Evaluate and Revise*
   Informally assess the gymnastic skills of the class by using skill charts similar to the ones found at the end of this chapter.

CONCEPT 19.2
Stunts and tumbling skills should be taught in a logical sequence progressing from simple to complex and from isolated single skills to skill combinations.

level skills if they have been in a progressive program of skill development throughout the earlier grades. The teaching progression charts found in this chapter and the next are listed in increasing order of difficulty within each of the three movement skill learning levels. The progressive presentation of gymnastic type skills is essential for maximizing skill development and learning enjoyment.

CONCEPT 19.3
Children learn much about how the body can move (movement concepts) and how the body should move (skill concepts) through participation in stunts and tumbling skill themes.

SAFETY CONSIDERATIONS

Safety should always be uppermost in your mind, especially when you are conducting a gymnastics skill theme. Gymnastics activities present a special challenge to intelligent supervision, careful spotting, and above all, sequential progression of building skill upon skill. The goal is to minimize safety hazards and to maximize learning enjoyment.

Use several good quality mats for stunts and tumbling activities. Be sure that they are kept clean (use mild soap and water) and neatly stored when not in use. Mats are expensive and cumbersome, but be sure always to carry them from place to place; never drag them.

Stress the importance of a thorough warmup before attempting activities. Stretching and warmup activities are especially important prior to gymnastics. Emphasize individual responsibility for the warmup as well as for skill learning.

TEACHING TIPS

Code of Conduct for Young Gymnasts

- Always warm up.
- Work out with competent supervision.
- Take spotting seriously.
- Follow proper skill progressions.
- Appreciate the risk.
- Know your limitations.
- Be mentally prepared to participate.
- Concentrate and avoid horseplay.
- Double-check all equipment.
- Dress appropriately.

Follow a definite progression of activities geared to the individual learner, building skill upon skill. Never permit a student to attempt tasks beyond his or her ability or a difficult task without a spotter available. Stress the need for mastery of the foundational skills before more advanced skills are attempted.

Avoid backbends, back walkovers, or front walkovers in the regular instructional program. Recent research has revealed that many low-back injuries are caused when these activities are taught too soon. Reserve these and other advanced skills for a special-interest group of gymnasts.

CONCEPT 19.4
Many safety considerations and spotting precautions need to be learned and adhered to when conducting a stunts and tumbling skill theme.

SPOTTING

Spotting is an important aspect of any successful gymnastics program. **Spotting** is a form of assisting the performer through a skill to assure safety or to aid in teaching the skill. Correct spotting is an art. Because protecting the performer is the primary goal of spotting, don't hesitate to act and be alert at all times, never allowing your attention to be diverted. It is crucial that you are in the proper position and are ready to move instantly. Be close enough to the performer to be able to assist as needed, but not so close that you interfere with performance (don't overspot). Be sure that you are thoroughly familiar with the skill and all of the movements the performer must make. Coach the performer through the skill, using key words.

By being confident in your spotting techniques, you will instill confidence in the performer. If you need to catch the performer, it is generally only necessary to check the fall.

Use mature students as spotters after they have been sufficiently trained. Don't assume that a spotter is no longer needed just because no accidents have happened for a long period of time. Use good judgment in selecting skills or individuals who continue to need to be spotted.

BODY-ROLLING SKILLS

Body rolling involves rolling the body over its own axis. Most children enjoy the sensation of rolling, the thrill of turning oneself over, and the sense of vertigo. Be certain,

The following are some important teaching suggestions to consider when teaching stunts and tumbling skills.

- Provide a wide variety of activities.
- Consider the body build, strength, and flexibility of students before presenting new skills.
- Follow a logical progression from simple to complex, thus ensuring success.
- Develop an attitude among the students that practice is important and that instant success is rare.
- Use proper spotting techniques both as a teaching medium and as a safety precaution.
- Provide for individual differences and wide ranges in ability.
- Give students an opportunity to demonstrate their new skills to others.
- Devise simple free-exercise and tumbling routines that combine several skills.
- Give students an opportunity to pursue their further interests in an early morning, noon-hour, or after-school gymnastics program.
- The program should be fun and full of action and should stress learning something new each day.

however, to recognize that some children are totally unfamiliar with this sensation and lack sufficient body and spatial awareness to feel comfortable. Therefore, when working with a group of inexperienced tumblers it is necessary to follow a logical progression of activities, building skill upon skill. Table 19.1 provides such a progression. The objectives of teaching body rolling skills include helping children to

1. enhance dynamic balance by performing a variety of sideways, forward, and backward rolling skills,
2. develop stability abilities in unusual rotational balance situations,
3. enhance the motor fitness components of agility and coordination,
4. enhance the health-related fitness components of muscular strength and joint flexibility, and
5. improve body awareness and spatial awareness abilities.

Sideways Rolling

Sideways rolling is quite easy for most children and involves rolling along the long axis of the body. Emphasize improved body control and directional awareness.

Soldier Log Roll. From an "attention" lying position with the legs straight and the arms held rigid at the sides, roll from one end of the mat to the other.

Rocket Log Roll. From a lying position with the arms extended overhead and the fingers clasped, roll from one end of the mat to the other.

Sideways Roll. From a hands-and-knees kneeling position, drop one shoulder and roll over to the starting position.

Forward Rolling

The forward roll and its many variations can be easily learned if a proper teaching progression is followed. Numerous variations of the forward roll are possible.

Look Back. From a position with the hands on the floor, raise the hips by straightening the legs and look back between the legs.

Tip Over. From a squat position with the hands on the mat and the knees between the arms, raise the hips and look back, placing the back of the head on the mat. Tip over onto the back and finish in a sitting position.

Back Rocker. From a sitting position on the mat with the knees tucked and the hands clasping the shins, sit and rock back onto the back and shoulders. Rock forward and back to a sitting position. Repeat.

Roll-Up. From a sitting position with the legs tucked, the arms outstretched forward, and the chin tucked, rock backward, then forward to a squat position. Be sure to lean the head out over the feet and lift the buttocks when rolling forward.

Forward Roll. From a standing position at the edge of the mat, squat down, placing the hands on the mat close to the feet so that the knees are between the arms. Raise the hips and tip over, being sure to stay in a tucked position. Continue the roll back to a squat position by keeping the head tucked, knees bent, and arms forward (Figure 19.1).

TABLE 19.1   *Teaching Progression for Selected Body-Rolling Skills Sequenced in Terms of Complexity*

Body-Rolling Skills (page number)	Suggested Progression for Children		
	Beginning Level	Intermediate Level	Advanced Level
Sideways Rolling			
Soldier log roll (357)	X		
Rocket log roll (357)	X		
Sideways roll (357)		X	
Forward Rolling			
Look back (357)	X		
Tip over (357)	X		
Back rocker (357)	X		
Roll-up (357)	X		
Forward roll (357)		X	
Consecutive forward rolls (358)		X	
Step-roll (358)		X	
Reach-over roll (358)		X	
Dive roll (358)			X
Partner dive roll (359)			X
Straddle roll (359)			X
Eskimo roll (359)			X
Backward Rolling			
Back rocker (359)	X		
Back tucker (359)	X		
Rabbit ears (359)	X		
Snail balance (359)	X		
Back shoulder roll (359)	X		
Rock-back shoulder roll (359)	X		
Forearm sit and roll (359)		X	
Forearm rock and roll (359)		X	
Backward roll (360)		X	
Consecutive back rolls (360)		X	
Forward-backward roll combination (360)			X
Back straddle roll (360)			X
Back extension roll (360)			X

Consecutive Forward Rolls.   After completing one forward roll back to a squat position, continue down the mat with three or four more rolls.

Step-Roll.   From a standing position one foot from the edge of the mat, step forward and execute a forward roll back to a standing position.

Reach-Over Roll.   From the edge of the mat with a partner or a low object in front (no higher than knee height), bend over the object and do a forward roll.

Dive Roll.   From a standing position two steps from the edge of the mat, take one step forward and a short jump onto both feet on the second step (hurdle step). Spring

FIGURE 19.1 *The forward roll.*

into the air and do a dive roll in which the feet leave the ground before the hands contact the floor.

Partner Dive Roll.   With a partner curled up at the edge of the mat, perform a dive roll over the partner. Be sure to spot carefully from a kneeling position at the far side of the curled partner.

Straddle Roll.   From a standing position with the legs spread wide apart, bend forward at the waist and contact the floor with the hands in the area between the legs. Execute a forward roll, keeping the legs spread. Continue forward, by pushing with the hands, back to a straddle position.

Eskimo Roll.   Lie on your back and grasp the ankles of your partner, who is standing overhead. Raise your legs so that your ankles may be grasped by your partner. Your partner leans forward and places your feet on the floor, while executing a forward roll. Your partner continues forward and back to a stand, while you repeat the same action. The process continues the length of the mat (Figure 19.2).

Backward Rolling

The backward roll is difficult for some children to master. Follow a definite progression from simple to more complex activities and use proper spotting techniques to ensure success.

Back Rocker.   From a sitting position at the edge of the mat with the knees bent and the arms at the side, sit and rock back onto the shoulders, then back to a sitting position. Repeat.

Back Tucker.   From a squatting position at the edge of the mat with the hands grasping the shins, rock back and forth.

FIGURE 19.2 *Eskimo roll.*

Rabbit Ears.   From a squatting position at the edge of the mat with the hands by the ears, facing forward, sit and rock back, keeping the chin tucked, so that the palms of both hands touch the floor and the elbows point toward the ceiling.

Snail Balance.   From the same position as for rabbit ears, rock backward and touch the toes to the mat behind. Explore the area behind with the feet.

Back Shoulder Roll.   From a sitting position, rock backward and execute a shoulder roll by rolling toward the right or left shoulder. Repeat to both sides.

Rock-Back Shoulder Roll.   Do a back shoulder roll from a squat to a squat position.

Forearm Sit and Roll.   From a sitting position with the knees tucked, the fingers clasped behind the head, and the elbows bent, rock back and over to a kneeling position. Be sure to stay tucked and to make the forearms contact the floor.

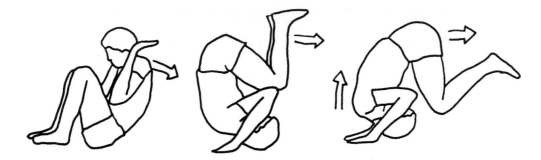

FIGURE 19.3 *The backward roll.*

Forearm Rock and Roll.   This is the same as the forearm sit and roll except from a squat to a squat position. Tuck the chin, use momentum, and curl the toes to get back to a squat position.

Backward Roll.   From a squat position at the edge of the mat, sit back and roll over in a tuck position, pushing off with both hands back to a squat position (Figure 19.3).

Consecutive Back Rolls.   After completing one backward roll, continue down the mat with three or four more rolls.

Forward-Backward Roll Combination.   Beginning at one end of the mat, perform a forward roll, crossing the legs at the end of the roll, turning, and doing a backward roll. Repeat, beginning with a backward roll.

Back Straddle Roll.   From a standing position with the legs spread wide apart, bend forward at the waist and place both hands on the mat between the thighs, while assuming a sitting position. Continue to roll backward, pushing with the hands and keeping the legs straight and spread, back to a straddle position.

Back Extension Roll.   From an inverted backward roll position, extend the legs and push them forcefully upward, while at the same time pushing with the hands. When correctly done, the performer will go through handstand position.

CONCEPT 19.5
Entry level observational assessment is essential prior to making specific plans for a stunts and tumbling skill theme.

SPRINGING SKILLS

Children love to jump and leap. They enjoy the sensation of springing into the air. **Springing** involves momentary loss of contact with the ground and projection of the body into space. It can be done from an upright position or an inverted position. Upright springs can be done off the floor or off a springboard. They should, however, be carefully spotted at all times. Table 19.2 provides a teaching progression chart for springing with a suggested progression of springing activities for children at beginning, intermediate, and advanced skill levels. The objectives of practice in teaching springing skills include helping children to

1. enhance dynamic balance abilities,
2. promote jumping and landing skill development,
3. enhance the health-related fitness components of muscular strength and joint flexibility,
4. improve the performance-related fitness components of movement speed, coordination, and power, and
5. improve body and spatial awareness.

Upright Springing

Upright springing may be performed off the floor or off a springboard. Stress keeping the head up and the eyes focused forward to aid balance.

Rocket Ship.   From a standing position with the arms overhead and the fingers touching, gradually squat down on the count "5, 4, 3, 2, 1." On the command "blast off," jump high into the air.

Knee Lifter.   From a standing position, jump straight up, lifting the knees so that the upper leg is parallel with the floor. Keep the head up and slap the thighs with the hands.

TABLE 19.2   *Teaching Progression for Selected Springing Skills Sequenced in Terms of Complexity*

Springing Skills (page number)	Suggested Progression for Children		
	Beginning Level	Intermediate Level	Advanced Level
Upright Springing			
Rocket ship (360)	x		
Knee lifter (360)	x		
Jump and tuck (360)	x		
Ankle slapper (361)	x		
Butt kicker (361)	x		
Toe toucher (361)		x	
Half-turn (361)		x	
Three-quarter turn (361)		x	
Full turn (361)		x	
Straddle jump (361)		x	
Star jump (362)		x	
Knee straddle (362)		x	
Ankle straddle (362)			x
Toe straddle (362)			x
Inverted Springing			
Low mat roll (362)		x	
Mat headspring (362)		x	
Headspring (362)			x
Neck spring (362)			x
Knee-neck spring (362)			x
Partner handspring (362)			x
Front handspring (362)			x

Jump and Tuck.   From a standing position, jump straight up, lifting both knees toward the chest. Keep the head up and bring the arms momentarily to the shins.

Ankle Slapper.   From a standing position, jump straight up, bringing the feet behind and upward. Slap the ankles at the height of the jump.

Butt Kicker.   From a standing position, jump straight up, bringing the heels to the buttocks at the height of the jump.

Toe Toucher.   From a standing position, jump straight up, pike at the waist. Keep the head up and try to touch the knees. Repeat, trying to touch the ankles and then the toes.

Half-Turn.   From a standing position, jump upward and execute a half-turn to the right or the left.

Three-Quarter Turn.   From a standing position, jump forcefully upward and execute a three-quarter turn to either the right or the left. There should be rapid head, shoulder, and arm rotation.

Full Turn.   Same as the three-quarter turn. There should be a forceful takeoff, rapid rotation, and controlled landing.

Straddle Jump.   From a standing position, jump upward, spreading the legs wide apart and returning them to shoulder-width apart on landing. Try it also from a squat position.

Star Jump. From a squat position, forcefully jump upward, spreading the legs and arms wide apart at the height of the jump. Return to a squat position after each jump.

Knee Straddle. From a standing or a squatting position, jump forcefully upward, and pike at the waist while the legs straddle outward. Touch both knees at the height of the jump.

Ankle Straddle. From a standing or a squatting position, jump forcefully upward. Spread the legs wide apart and pike at the waist. Touch both ankles at the height of the jump.

Toe Straddle. Same as the ankle straddle except that the toes are pointed and touched at the height of the jump.

Inverted Springing

Inverted springs should be done on a mat and under the watchful eye of a competent spotter at all times. Gym helpers and teacher's aids with prior training can be good spotters.

Low Mat Roll. From a standing position two steps away from a rolled mat, take a step forward, placing the hands at the base of the mat and the back of the neck on the rolled mat. Continue to roll forward to a stand.

Mat Headspring. From a standing position one step away from a rolled mat, take a step, placing both hands and the head on the mat. Roll forward, unfolding at the waist, pushing with the hands, and snapping the head forward, to a squat position.

Headspring. From a squat position, place the head close to the mat with the arms in a bent-arm position. Roll forward with the legs straight and the hips leading. Snap (unfold) the hips and legs forward while forcefully pushing with the arms. Finish in a standing position with the arms extended overhead. Be certain to spot carefully, not allowing the head to contact the mat.

Neck Spring. From a squat position, roll back as if doing a backward roll. When the hands contact the mat, forcefully push off while at the same time extending at the waist and snapping the head forward. The return is to a squat position. Spot carefully.

Knee-Neck Spring. Similar to a neck spring except the arms are placed on the knees. The action comes from the forceful pushing on the knees, unfolding at the waist, and the forward head snap.

Partner Handspring. One person lies on his back with the knees bent and the arms outstretched forward. The top person faces the down person and takes one step forward, placing her hands on his knees and her shoulders in his hands. Keeping the head up and kicking through a handstand, the top person continues over to a stand. It is important that the bottom person be strong enough to control the action and that spotters are present.

Front Handspring. From a short run and a one-foot takeoff, the arms are swung forcefully downward and the legs kicked up into handstand position. Momentum carries the body over, and the landing is in an upright position with the hands extended overhead. Spotters are required.

CONCEPT 19.6
Body rolling, springing, upright and inverted support skills comprise the content areas of stunts and tumbling.

UPRIGHT SUPPORT SKILLS

The **upright support skills** found here are subdivided into individual supports and partner supports. Some of them may be performed without a mat. Most, however, should be practiced on a mat to ensure safety. Table 19.3 provides a teaching progression chart for upright support skills. It provides a logical progression of stunts for children at the beginning, intermediate, and advanced levels of stunt skill learning. The primary objectives of upright body support skills are to

1. enhance static and dynamic balance,
2. enhance the health-related fitness components of joint flexibility and muscular strength,
3. enhance the performance-related fitness components of coordination and agility, and
4. improve body awareness and spatial awareness abilities.

TABLE 19.3   *Teaching Progression for Selected Upright Support Skills Sequenced in Terms of Complexity*

Upright Support Skills (page number)	Beginning Level	Intermediate Level	Advanced Level
		Suggested Progression for Children	
Individual Supports			
Rocker (364)	X		
Thread the needle (364)	X		
Coffee grinder (364)	X		
Corkscrew (364)	X		
Turk stand (364)	X		
Egg seat (364)	X		
Egg roll (364)	X		
Seal crawl (364)	X		
Nose dive (364)	X		
Fishhawk dive (365)		X	
Wicket walk (365)		X	
Stump walk (365)		X	
Bear dance (365)		X	
V-seat (365)		X	
Candle stand (365)		X	
Heel click (365)		X	
Greet the toe (365)		X	
Human ball (365)		X	
Inchworm (365)		X	
Knee dip (365)		X	
Knee spring (365)			X
Hitch kick (365)			X
Pirouette (365)			X
Straight fall (365)			X
Shoot through (365)			X
Front scale (365)			X
Side scale (366)			X

(continued)

TABLE 19.3   *(continued)*

Upright Support Skills (page number)	Suggested Progression for Children		
	Beginning Level	Intermediate Level	Advanced Level
Partner Supports			
Butter churn (366)	X		
Partner walk (366)	X		
Two-person rocker (366)	X		
Wheelbarrow (366)	X		
Wring the dishrag (366)	X		
Chinese get-up (366)	X		
Leapfrog (366)	X		
Chest balance (366)		X	
Thigh stand-in (366)		X	
Front swan (366)		X	
Back swan (366)			X
Hand-knee shoulder stand (366)			X
Hand-foot, foot-hand stand (366)			X
Hand-to-foot stand (366)			X
Thigh stand (367)			X
Shoulder stand-out (367)			X

Individual Supports

Children enjoy individual stunts that permit them to balance their bodies in a variety of postures. Stunts that require supporting the body in various upright configurations contribute to improved stability abilities, coordination, strength, and endurance.

Rocker.   Lying on your stomach, arch the back and grasp the ankles with the hands. Rock back and forth, simulating a rocking chair.

Thread the Needle.   Clasp the fingers and form a circle close to the floor in front of the body with the arms. Step through the arms without releasing. Repeat in the opposite direction.

Coffee Grinder.   Lying on your side with the bottom hand contacting the floor and the arm straight, walk around the pivot hand, keeping the legs straight.

Corkscrew.   From a standing position with the feet shoulder width apart, bring the left arm across the back of the legs and touch the right toe. Repeat with the right arm.

Turk Stand.   Cross the legs and the arms, sit down, and return to a stand without uncrossing the feet.

Egg Seat.   Sit with the knees bent. Grasp the toes and extend the legs. Hold a balanced position for 10 seconds.

Egg Roll.   From a squatting position with the arms around the knees and the head tucked, roll around the mat.

Seal Crawl.   From a front support with the legs straight and the toes pointed behind, drag the body forward with the arms and hip action but no leg action.

Nose Dive.   From a kneeling position with the hands behind the back, bend forward to pick up a clean tissue with the teeth.

FIGURE 19.4 *The V-seat.*

FIGURE 19.5 *The inchworm.*

Fishhawk Dive.   This is the same as the nose dive, but done from one knee and using the arms for balance.

Wicket Walk.   Grasp the ankles and walk forward without bending the legs.

Stump Walk.   From a kneeling position on a mat, grasp the toes or ankles with both hands. Walk on the knees. Lean forward slightly to maintain balance.

Bear Dance.   From a squat position with the arms folded, extend one leg forward. Repeat with the opposite leg while bringing the outstretched leg back to position. Repeat in rhythmical alteration.

V-Seat.   From a seat on the floor with the legs straight and both hands on the floor, assume a "V" shape by lifting both legs high (Figure19.4).

Candle Stand.   Lying on the floor with the arms out from the sides, lift the legs straight up over the head and maintain this extended position.

Heel Click.   Hop on the right foot and extend the left leg to the side. Click the heels together. Try for two, then three clicks.

Greet the Toe.   From a standing position, grasp one foot and bring it upward to touch the nose while balancing on one foot. Repeat with the opposite foot.

Human Ball.   From a sitting position with the knees bent and each arm intertwined around the corresponding leg and grasping the toes, roll in a clockwise direction. Repeat in the opposite direction.

Inchworm.   From a front support position on the hands, walk the feet up to the hands without moving the hands. Then walk the hands away from the feet back to a prone support position (Figure 19.5). Repeat.

Knee Dip.   From a standing position with one knee bent and held from behind the back by the opposite hand, squat until the knee touches the mat and return to a stand. Repeat with the opposite leg.

Knee Spring.   From a kneeling position with the toes extended behind, come to a stand by swinging the arms vigorously upward while extending from a bent position at the hips. Try also with the arms folded.

Hitch Kick.   From a stand or a short run and one-foot takeoff, kick both legs high into the air and land on the opposite foot.

Pirouette.   From a standing position, leap into the air, turn the head and shoulders sharply to the left, and pull the right arm across the chest, executing a full turn of the body.

Straight Fall.   Fall toward the mat with one leg elevated. The body is caught and the force absorbed by the arms.

Shoot Through.   From a front support position with the arms straight, the legs extended backward, and the weight on the toes and hands, raise the legs and hips quickly and shoot the legs between the arms, finishing in a sitting position.

Front Scale.   Bend forward at the waist, balancing on one foot with the supporting leg straight. Extend the other leg fully to the rear and raise to shoulder level. The arms are extended out from the side and raised above shoulder level.

Side Scale.   While balancing on the left leg, lean to the left, lifting the right leg. The left arm is extended overhead. The right arm is held alongside the body. The body is parallel to the floor. Repeat to the opposite side.

Partner Supports

Partner support skills should be introduced after children have sufficient strength and body balance to support a person for five seconds or more. Partner supports may be performed in a variety of configurations by two or more people to form a variety of pyramids.

Butter Churn.   Partners stand back to back with elbows hooked. Take turns bending forward and lifting partner's feet off the ground. Do not pull over.

Partner Walk.   Partners face each other, grasping upper arms. One partner stands on the other partner's toes while he walks forward.

Two-Person Rocker.   Partners sit, with knees bent, on each other's feet, with upper arms clasped. They alternate rocking back and forth.

Wheelbarrow.   One person assumes a front support position on the hands with the legs extended behind. Partner stands between the down partner's legs, grasps at the *knees,* and lifts her legs. Partners walk forward a short distance on a mat.

Wring the Dishrag.   Partners face each other, join hands, and raise their arms high. One person turns clockwise and the other counterclockwise, without releasing their grasp, until they are again facing each other. Repeat in the opposite direction.

Chinese Get-Up.   From a position with partners standing back to back with elbows hooked, sit all the way down and come back to a stand without releasing arms.

Leapfrog.   The down partner bends forward at the waist and places his or her hands on knees. The up partner runs up from behind and, from a two-foot takeoff, pushes off from the base of the down partner's shoulders and straddle vaults his or her partner. Alternate.

Chest Balance.   One partner kneels on all fours. The top partner places her arms under the bottom partner's chest and places her chest on the kneeling partner's back. Then

she kicks upward into a chest balance on the partner's back. Spot carefully.

Thigh Stand-In.   The top person is in a half-squat position, facing a partner. The top person places her hands behind the bottom person's neck, while the bottom person places his hands behind the top person's hips. The top person steps onto the bottom person's thighs. When a solid position is reached they join hands and both lean backward. Spot carefully.

Front Swan.   The support partner lies on his back. He grasps the hands of his partner and places his feet on his partner's stomach. The partner being supported rocks forward until she is in a prone position, supported by her partner's feet. Spot carefully.

Back Swan.   The support partner lies on his back and grasps the hands of his partner. He then places his feet on his partner's buttocks and lower back. The partner being supported rocks backward until she is in a back lying position above the floor, supported by her partner's feet. Spot carefully.

Hand-Knee Shoulder Stand.   The support person lies on his back with knees bent, heels close to buttocks, and arms extended in a catch position perpendicular to the floor. The top partner, from a position behind the support partner's head, places her hands on the support partner's knees and her shoulders in his hands. She then kicks up into an inverted support position. Spot carefully.

Hand-Foot and Foot-Hand Stand.   The support partner lies on his back with his legs and arms extended above his body and perpendicular to the floor. The partner on top stands at the head of the support partner and places her hands on the feet of the support partner and her feet in her partner's hands, assuming a support position above the floor. Spot carefully.

Hand-to-Foot Stand.   The support partner lies on his back with his legs extended above the body and perpendicular to the floor. His hands are placed palms-up beside his ears. The partner on top straddles the support's head, places her feet in her partner's hands, and grasps her partner's ankles. On a signal, the person on top jumps into the air, pushing on the ankles of her partner, who in turn pushes her above his head. Once they are balanced, the person on top releases the support person's ankles and stands erect with her arms out to the side for balance. The person supporting locks his elbows and returns his legs to the floor. Spot carefully.

Thigh Stand.   One partner assumes a quarter-squat position with the body weight concentrated on the heels and both arms extended forward at shoulder level. The other partner, standing with her back to her partner, places one foot on his thigh and her hands on his arms. She places the other foot on the thigh and steps upward, leaning forward to a standing position on her partner's thighs. The support partner grasps her thighs and leans backward to offer additional support. Spot carefully (Figure 19.6).

Shoulder Stand-Out.   Partners stand facing one another, grasping right hand to hand and left to left (right hands are on top). The support partner assumes a quarter-squat position. The top partner steps with her left foot to the left thigh of her partner (the heel is placed on the inside of the leg) and steps up and around with her right foot to the right shoulder of her partner. She now steps with her left foot to the left shoulder and releases her hands as she gains her balance. The support partner provides additional support by holding his partner's ankles close to his head. Spot carefully.

C O N C E P T   1 9 . 7
Stunts and tumbling activities may be classified as being beginning, intermediate, or advanced level skills.

INVERTED SUPPORT SKILLS

Inverted supports are classified here as headstand skills, transitional supports, and handstand skills. It is absolutely essential that children be exposed to a progressive program of inverted supports that builds skill upon skill. Neglecting to do so will only lead to failure and frustration on the part of the students. The static and dynamic balance requirements of inverted support skills are too great to be left to chance. The teaching progression chart for inverted supports that follows in Table 19.4 presents a logical teaching progression. The objectives of practice in inverted support skill activities include helping children to

1. improve static balance,
2. enhance dynamic balance (transitional supports),
3. contribute to increased strength development,

FIGURE 19.6 *Thigh stand.*

4. improve coordination, and
5. improve body and spatial awareness.

Headstand Skills

Children enjoy learning how to balance themselves in various inverted positions. However, you must ensure that the muscles of their neck are sufficiently strong before engaging young children in headstand-type activities. Children are generally sufficiently strong in this region of the body by age six.

Head Balance.   From a front kneeling position with all four limbs on the mat, put the head down on the mat so that the top of the forehead touches. Raise hips and straighten the legs for a five-point balance. Now raise the hands off the mat for a three-point balance. Finally, try balancing on only two points, using one foot and the head.

Greet the Elbows.   From a squat position with the hands on the mat outside the knees, place the forehead on the mat, forming a triangle with the head and the hands. Do not move the hands or head. Bring one knee up to touch the elbow and hold in a four-point balance. Return and repeat with the other knee. After good balance is achieved, repeat, but this time balance one knee on the elbow of a support arm while the other leg extends with the toes touching the mat.

Tripod.   The tripod is similar to the preceding skill except both knees are placed on the elbows, forming a three-point balance. See who can balance for three, five, seven, and ten seconds (Figure 19.7).

TABLE 19.4   *Teaching Progression for Selected Inverted Support Skills Sequenced in Terms of Complexity*

Inverted Support Skills (page number)	Suggested Progression for Children		
	Beginning Level	Intermediate Level	Advanced Level
Headstand Skills			
Head balance (367)	X		
Greet the elbows (367)	X		
Tripod (367)	X		
One-knee tripod (368)		X	
Half-headstand (368)		X	
Three-quarter headstand (368)		X	
Headstand (368)		X	
Kick-up headstand (368)		X	
Headstand to a roll (369)		X	
Drag headstand (369)			X
Forearm stand (369)			X
Transitional Supports			
One leg up (369)	X		
Side switch (369)	X		
Half-cartwheel (369)	X		
Cartwheel (369)		X	
Consecutive cartwheels (370)		X	
Olympic cartwheel (370)			X
Heel-click cartwheel (370)			X
One-hand cartwheel (370)			X
Roundoff (370)			X
Running roundoff (370)			X
Handstand Skills			
Swing-up (370)	X		
Mule kick (370)	X		
Wall stand (370)			X
Partner-aided handstand (371)			X
Handstand (371)			X

One-Knee Tripod.   Same as the tripod, except only one knee is balanced on an elbow while the other leg is outstretched and free from support.

Half-Headstand.   From a tripod position, bring the knees together to the chest and hold.

Three-Quarter Headstand.   Same as the half-headstand except that the hips straighten, leaving only the knees bent.

Headstand.   From a tripod position, the knees are brought together at the chest, the hips unfold, and the legs straighten overhead. The body is supported by the hands and the head. The legs are together, with the toes pointed and the back slightly arched. Hold and return in the same manner (Figure 19.8).

Kick-Up Headstand.   From a three-point triangle position with the legs extended behind, walk the feet close to the

FIGURE 19.7 *The tripod.*

FIGURE 19.8 *Headstand.*

head, being certain not to move the hands or head. Raise one leg, straighten overhead, and kick up with the other to a headstand position. Hold and return in the same manner.

Headstand to a Roll.   From a full headstand position, bend at the waist, tuck the head, and roll forward to a squat position.

Drag Headstand.   Lying on the stomach with the toes pointed, hands on the mat at chest level, and forehead on the mat, slowly raise the hips upward and drag the toes, keeping the legs straight, to a headstand position.

Forearm Stand.   From a heads-up kneeling position with the forearms on the mat, the elbows pointed out, and the thumbs and index fingers touching, kick up to an inverted support. The head is raised and the body is supported only by the forearms.

Transitional Supports

Transitional supports include skills such as the cartwheel and the roundoff. These skills require a great deal of dynamic balance and directional awareness. Considerable stress is placed on the coordinated actions of the limbs, sometimes operating in harmony with one another and sometimes in synchronous opposition.

One Leg Up.   From a standing position at the edge of the mat with one foot slightly ahead of the other, bend forward and place both hands on the mat. Keeping the head up, take the body weight on the hands and kick the back leg up behind.

Side Switch.   From a standing position at the edge of the mat with one leg slightly ahead of the other, bend forward, placing the hands down in front of the feet. Lean forward onto the arms, kick the trailing foot into the air, and swing the hips to the preferred side. Both legs will come off the floor, and the forceful turn will bring the body around to the other side of the mat.

Half-Cartwheel.   From a standing position with one leg slightly forward and the hands placed in front of the chest, lean forward and turn slightly to face the leading foot. The hand opposite the lead foot contacts the mat, followed immediately by the other hand. The legs are brought around roughly parallel to the floor.

Cartwheel.   From a standing position with one leg slightly forward, extend the arms overhead and rock back onto the back foot. The arm and shoulder corresponding to the lead foot should be slightly forward. Swing forcefully downward, bending at the hips and kicking the trailing foot into the air. The hands contact the mat (trailing hand first) parallel to each other and shoulder width apart as the legs are brought overhead. The lead leg continues and comes down first opposite the takeoff spot. The trailing leg follows, and the body returns to a standing position facing the direction of takeoff (Figure 19.9).

FIGURE 19.9 *The cartwheel.*

Consecutive Cartwheels.   After the completion of one cartwheel back to a stand, try three or four cartwheels in succession.

Olympic Cartwheel.   From a straddle position with the arms outstretched at the sides, and standing on a line, perform a cartwheel action to the preferred side, trying to land back on the line.

Heel-Click Cartwheel.   Heels are clicked together when the legs are overhead in the cartwheel position.

One-Hand Cartwheel.   The one-hand cartwheel is similar to the cartwheel, except a more forceful downswing is required to increase momentum.

Roundoff.   From a standing position with one leg slightly forward and the arms outstretched overhead, rock back onto the back foot and swing forward at the waist. The hands are brought to the mat simultaneously toward the side that the performer is facing. The legs swing overhead and the hips are rotated so that upon landing, both feet contact the mat at the same time and the performer faces the opposite direction from the takeoff. A forceful snap down of the legs, simultaneous contact, and facing the opposite direction are the key differences between the cartwheel and roundoff. The roundoff is an important preparatory move for numerous backward tumbling activities.

Running Roundoff.   Same as the roundoff but done from a running start, with a one-foot takeoff and more forceful execution of the entire action, resulting in considerable backward momentum in preparation for additional stunts.

FIGURE 19.10 *Partner-aided handstand.*

Handstand Skills

The handstand is an exciting and difficult stunt to master. Because of the inverted posture, high center of gravity, and two-point stance, the handstand usually takes considerable practice to master.

Swing-Up.   From a standing position with one leg slightly forward, bend at the waist and swing both arms down. The hands contact the mat slightly ahead of the lead foot. The trailing leg is kicked first into the air, followed by the lead leg. Practice keeping the arms straight, the head up, and getting the legs and hips up over the head.

Mule Kick.   Same as the swing-up except that from a half-inverted position, both legs are bent and then forcefully extended backward while the hands push off the mat.

Wall Stand.   From a stride position about two feet from the wall, the hands are placed shoulder width apart on the floor with the fingers spread and arms locked. The head is up, and the body weight is over the shoulders. The trailing leg kicks up and is followed by the lead leg. The heels contact the wall. The performer balances herself and lightly pushes away from the wall as the balance position is found.

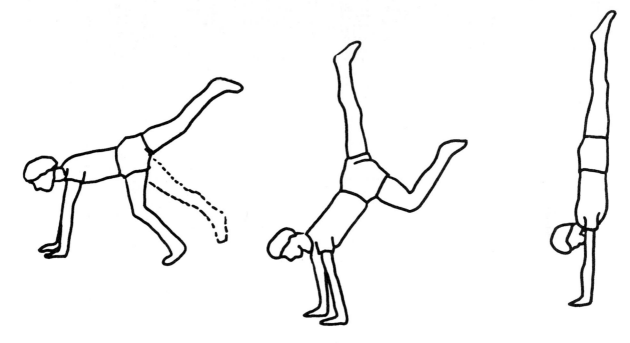

FIGURE 19.11 *The handstand.*

Partner-Aided Handstand.   From a stride-standing position with the arms overhead, rock back onto the rear foot and swing forward, bending at the waist. The hands contact the mat and are shoulder width apart with the fingers spread and facing forward, slightly in front of the lead foot. The trailing leg is brought overhead, followed by the other. The body is balanced in this inverted position with the line of gravity drawn from the center of the base of support. The partner lightly grasps the lead leg at the ankle as needed to help locate the proper balance position (*Note*: never hold both legs) (Figure 19.10).

Handstand.   Same as the partner-aided handstand except without the aid of a spotter (Figure 19.11).

CONCEPT 19.8
Progress can be charted and informally assessed by using both a group and individual stunts and tumbling skills chart.

ASSESSING PROGRESS

Stunts and tumbling skills can be a fun and exciting part of the physical education program if they are properly taught and if they are presented in a logical developmental sequence. Within any class, children will frequently be at the beginning, intermediate, or advanced level of skill learning. Therefore, teaching must be sufficiently personalized to allow for individual differences and various rates of progress. The use of a station approach to teaching stunts and tumbling skills works quite well, especially if accommodations are made for all three developmental levels. You may wish, however, to color-code (red, white, blue) or name-code (rollers, springers, balancers) the three skill levels.

Adapt the sample stunts and tumbling skill chart shown in Figure 19.12 to suit your program of skills, to help motivate students, and to assess your own instruction. **Aim charts** enable children to chart their individual progress and provide an informal means of skill assessment.

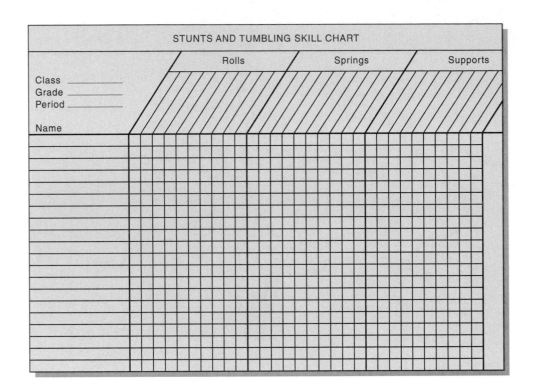

FIGURE 19.12 *Simple skill chart for selected stunts and tumbling skills.*

SUMMARY

Stunts and tumbling activities are enjoyed by most children because of their variety and the opportunity to progress at one's individual rate. Prior to presenting a stunts and tumbling skill theme, it is essential that you conduct an informal observational assessment to determine students' present level of ability. This will enable you to present new skills in their proper progression.

Special care must be taken in a stunts and tumbling skill theme to ensure the safety of all participants. Spotting techniques that assist the performer as needed and help protect against injury are a necessity. A wide variety of body rolling, springing, upright support and inverted support skills may be taught to children at the beginning, intermediate, or advanced level of stunts and tumbling skill learning. The key to success is knowing your students and providing them with movement challenges that are first and foremost individually appropriate.

COMPLEMENTARY READINGS

Belka, D. (1993). Educational gymnastics: Recommendations for elementary physical education. *TEPE* 4:1–6.

Hacker, P., et al. (1993). *Sequential Gymnastics For Grades 3–6*. Indianapolis: USA Gymnastics Publications.

Hammett, C. T. (1992). *Movement Activities for Early Childhood*. Champaign, IL: Human Kinetics.

O'Quinn, G. (1988). *Developmental Gymnastics*. Austin: University of Texas Press.

Ravengo, I. (1988). The art of gymnastics: Creating sequences. *JOPERD* 59:66–69.

SUPPLEMENTARY READINGS

Fodero, J. M., and E. E. Furblur. (1989). *Creating Gymnastics Pyramids and Balances*. Indianapolis, IN: USA Gymnastics Publications.

Gillom, B. C. (1970). *Basic Movement Education for Children*. Reading, MA: Addison-Wesley.

Ryser, O., and J. Brown. (1990). *A Manual for Tumbling and Apparatus Stunts.* Dubuque, IA: Wm. C. Brown.

Turoff, F. (1991). *Artistic Gymnastics.* Dubuque, IA: Wm. C. Brown Publishers.

Werner, P. H. (1994). *Teaching Children Gymnastics.* Champaign, IL: Human Kinetics.

Whitlock, S., ed. (1994). *USA Gymnastics Safety Handbook.* Indianapolis, IN: USA Gymnastics Publications.

VIDEOS

Funtastic Fitness. Athletic Institute. (1991). 200 Castlewood Drive, North Palm Beach, FL: The Athletic Institute. (47-min. developmental gymnastic activities for children to enhance fitness, skill, and self-esteem).

The Foundations of Gymnastic Excellence: I. Pad Drills; II. Beginning Tumbling; and III. Intermediate Tumbling. Mulvihill, D., and L. Mulvihill. (1991). 200 Castlewood Drive, North Palm Beach, FL: The Athletic Institute.

Rolling, Twisting and Turning Your Way to Fitness. Posner, S. (1991). 200 Castlewood Drive, North Palm Beach, FL: The Athletic Institute (55 min.).*Children and Movement Video Series: Basic Gymnastics.* Sanders, S. (1993). Durham, NC: Great Activities Publishing Company. (30 min.).

Children and Movement Video Series: Basic Gymnastics. Sanders, S. (1993). Durham, NC: Activities Publishing Company. (30 min.).

Foundations of Gymnastics Excellence. (1988). New York, NY: Insight Media (four videotapes, 30 min. each).

CHAPTER 20

Large and Small Equipment Skill Themes

Key Concept

Large and Small Equipment Can Be Effectively Used to Develop and Refine Stability, Locomotor, and Manipulative Abilities at Both the Fundamental and Specialized Movement Skill Phases of Development

Chapter Objectives

The purpose of this chapter is to provide you with the tools to:

- Identify several pieces of equipment commonly designated as large equipment and small equipment.
- Demonstrate knowledge of skill progression with a variety of pieces of equipment by classifying activities as beginning, intermediate, or advanced with regard to a specific population of children.
- Discuss the importance of building skill upon skill in the use of both large and small equipment.
- Demonstrate competence in using a movement challenge approach with the use of several pieces of small equipment.
- Illustrate how large and small equipment may be used to develop and refine a variety of fundamental and specialized stability, locomotor, and manipulative movement skills.

Terms to Remember

Large Equipment	Springboards	Balls
Small Equipment	Vaulting Boxes	Beanbags
Low Balance Beam	Turning Bar	Hoops
Climbing Ropes	Parachutes	Jump Ropes
Cargo Nets	Balance Boards	Stretch Ropes
Horizontal Ladder	Coffee-Can Stilts	Wands
Inner Tubes	Round Balloons	

The use of traditional gymnastics equipment is frequently limited at the preschool and elementary school level. The prohibitive cost of commercial equipment, its size, and storage problems often make it difficult to purchase gymnastics apparatus. However, **large equipment** of a nontraditional nature can often be included in the program. The climbing, hanging, and swinging skills developed on horizontal ladders, turning bars, and climbing ropes are especially helpful in developing the muscles of the upper trunk and shoulder girdle. The balancing and springing skills practiced on balance beams, large inner tubes, and vaulting boxes are also important to the development of children. **Small equipment,** or hand apparatus, as it is frequently called, is a must in every children's physical education program. Hand apparatus such as balls, hoops, wands, and beanbags may be commercially purchased or homemade.

CONCEPT 20.1
A wide variety of large equipment activities should be incorporated into the physical education program if problems of equipment storage and placement can be overcome.

This chapter contains a recommended sequence of skill progression for several pieces of large and small equipment frequently available in schools. The equipment listed here includes:

Large Equipment	*Small Equipment*
balance beam	balance boards
climbing ropes and	and stilts
cargo nets	balloons
horizontal ladder	balls
inner tubes and springboard	beanbags
vaulting box	hoops
turning bar	jump ropes
parachute	stretch ropes
	wands

Each has been selected for their potential contributions to fundamental stability, locomotor, and manipulative skill development, their versatility, and their general availability. The objectives for using each piece of equipment are included, along with a recommended progression of movement experiences that range from simple to more complex activities.

A number of important safety factors need to be considered when using large equipment:

- Place mats under the equipment whenever it is being used.
- Know your group, and be sure to spot activities carefully.
- Teach responsible children proper spotting techniques and use them as spotters in nonweight-bearing activities.
- Stress thinking the skill through before attempting it.
- Stress not attempting a skill unless a spotter is present.
- Emphasize building skill upon skill.
- Provide suitable warm-up activities prior to using the equipment.
- Do not tolerate horseplay on the equipment.
- Do not overspot. Permit the performer to get the feel of the skill.
- Caution children to stop and rest when tired.

CONCEPT 20.2
Skill development activities with both large and small equipment may be classified as beginning, intermediate, and advanced in terms of complexity and difficulty.

SKILLS WITH LARGE EQUIPMENT

Large equipment can be used effectively to promote a variety of movement skills. In addition, the use of large equipment in the program provides additional opportunities to help children increase many aspects of their physical fitness, namely, muscular strength and endurance, joint flexibility, and the performance-related components.

The beam walk.

Although frequently cumbersome and difficult to store, large equipment is valuable to the developmental physical education program. Skill themes focusing on specific stability, locomotor, and manipulative skills as well as fitness enhancement can be effectively aided through the use of large apparatus.

Balance-Beam Skills

The **low balance beam** is a useful piece of equipment that is used primarily for improving static and dynamic balance. Balance beams may be purchased commercially, or they may be easily made for a fraction of the price. Stress focusing the eyes forward and performing all movements slowly, in good control. Beam activities should be spotted, being careful not to overspot so that the child gets the full benefit from negotiating the balance problem. Table 20.1 provides a suggested progression chart for balance-beam skills. Movement activities on the balance beam contribute to

1. improved static balance abilities,
2. improved dynamic balance abilities,
3. better coordination and agility,
4. enhanced body and directional awareness, and
5. increased flexibility in the legs.

Beam Stand.   Step up onto the beam and hold a balanced position without falling.

Balance and Touch.   Balancing on the beam, touch body parts called out by the teacher.

Beam Walk.   Walk forward, backward, and sideways the length of the beam. First use a follow step and then an alternating step.

Walk-Turn-Walk.   Walk forward on the beam to the middle, make a half-turn, and finish by walking backward.

Double-Turn Walk.   Walk forward on the beam to the middle, make a half-turn, and walk to the end backward. Return to the middle by walking forward, make a quarter-turn, and finish by walking sideways to the end.

Walk and Touch.   While traveling from one end of the beam to the other, touch three body parts with the hand (one above the waist, one above the knees, and one below the knees).

Toe Walk.   Walk from one end of the beam to the other without the heels touching.

Dip Walk.   Walk the beam using alternate dipping steps.

Crouch Walk.   Walk the beam at a low level.

Cat Walk.   Walk the beam with the hands in contact with the beam, the hips up, and the legs straight.

Knee Touch.   Walk to the middle of the beam, squat down so that one knee touches the beam, and return to a stand.

Full Turn.   Walk to the center of the beam, make a full turn on the toes, and continue to the end.

Step Over.   Step over objects placed on the beam.

Go Through.   Step through two or three hoops held on the beam.

Over and Through.   Alternate stepping over and going through objects on the beam.

TABLE 20.1   *Selected Balance-Beam Skills Sequenced in Terms of Complexity*

Balance Beam Skills (page number)	Suggested Progression for Children		
	Beginning Level	Intermediate Level	Advanced Level
Beam stand (376)	x		
Balance and touch (376)	x		
Beam walk (376)	x		
Walk-turn-walk (376)	x		
Double-turn walk (376)	x		
Walk and touch (376)	x		
Toe walk (376)	x		
Dip walk (376)	x		
Crouch walk (376)	x		
Cat walk (376)		x	
Knee touch (376)		x	
Full turn (376)		x	
Step over (376)		x	
Go through (376)		x	
Over and through (376)		x	
Beanbag pickup (377)		x	
Beanbag balance (377)		x	
Knee scale (377)			x
Front scale (377)			x
V-seat (377)			x
V-seat to knee scale (377)			x
Partner pass (378)			x
Partner scale (378)			x
Toss and catch (378)			x

Beanbag Pickup.   Place several beanbags on the beam. Pick up each bag while walking from one end to the other. The next person puts the beanbags back on the beam while walking from one end to the other.

Beanbag Balance.   With a beanbag or eraser balanced on the head, practice all of the preceding activities.

Knee Scale.   From a single-knee kneeling position, grasp the beam with the hands and raise the nonsupport leg high behind (Figure 20.1).

Front Scale.   From a standing position on one foot at the center of the beam, bend forward at the waist and raise the nonsupport leg high in back.

V-Seat.   From a sitting position, straddle the beam, with the hands grasping the beam from behind, and raise both legs to a V-seat position and hold.

V-Seat to Knee Scale.   From a V-seat, bring the legs down as the body moves forward. Regrasp the beam in front, place one knee on the beam, and execute a knee scale.

FIGURE 20.1 *The knee scale.*

Partner Pass.   With a partner at the opposite end of the beam, walk to the center and pass each other without losing balance.

Partner Scale.   At the center of the beam, clasp hands with a partner and both execute a front scale.

Toss and Catch.   With a partner at the other end of the beam, play catch with a soft ball.

Rope-Climbing and Cargo Net Skills

Many gymnasiums throughout North America are equipped with **climbing ropes** and **cargo nets**. Both pieces of equipment can be fun and challenging if a few basic safety rules are followed. First, spot activities carefully. Second, never require children to attempt any activities beyond their ability level. Third, permit only the most skilled children to climb to the top. Fourth, do not permit sliding down the rope; instead, teach the use of a hand-under-hand grip. Table 20.2 provides a suggested sequence of progression for selected rope-climbing skills. See Figure 20.2 for a visual description of the foot positions for rope climbing.

Practice in activities on climbing ropes will contribute to

1. improved upper-arm and shoulder girdle strength,
2. better climbing abilities,
3. increased leg strength, and
4. improved coordinated use of the hands, arms, and legs.

Head Touch.   From a sitting position, grasp the rope in both hands and lie back until the head touches the mat.

The rope climb.

Back Lift.   From a sitting position, grip the rope, extend at the hips, and arch back so that the body is straight and only the heels touch the mat.

Heel Pivot.   From the back-lift position just described, pivot in a circle around the heels.

Straight Pull.   From a sitting position, grasp the rope and pull to a stand, keeping the legs straight.

Nose Touch.   From a standing position, grasp the rope overhead with both hands, jump up and touch the nose to the hands, and return.

Nose-to-Rope Touch.   From a standing position, grasp the rope with the arms straight overhead, jump up and touch the nose to the rope above the hands, and return.

TABLE 20.2   *Selected Rope-Climbing Skills Sequenced in Terms of Complexity*

Rope-Climbing Skills (page number)	Suggested Progression for Children		
	Beginning Level	*Intermediate Level*	*Advanced Level*
Head touch (378)	x		
Back lift (378)	x		
Heel pivot (378)	x		
Straight pull (378)	x		
Nose touch (378)	x		
Nose-to-rope touch (378)		x	
Jump and grasp (380)		x	
Jump and hold (380)		x	
Swing and hold (380)		x	
Tarzan and Jane (380)		x	
Rope pull-ups (380)		x	
Leg hold (380)			x
Rope climb (380)			x
Bell ringer (380)			x
Double-rope hold (380)			x
Double-rope swing (380)			x
Double-rope candle stand (380)			x
Double-rope pullover (380)			x

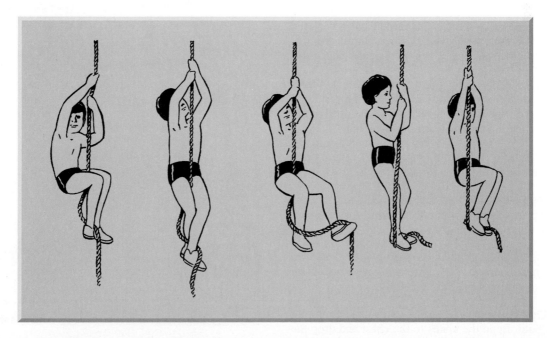

FIGURE 20.2   *Feet positions for rope climbing.*

Jump and Grasp.   From a standing position, grasp the rope overhead, jump up to a mounting support, and wrap the legs around the rope. Hold for three counts and return.

Jump and Hold.   Jump to a hands-and-legs support and hold for up to ten seconds.

Swing and Hold.   Run forward, pull up onto the rope, and hold. Swing forward and drop off at the end of the backswing.

Tarzan and Jane.   From a support position, swing forward and back twice, dropping off at the end of the second backspring.

Rope Pull-Ups.   From a support position, with the hands above the head, pull up and touch the nose to the rope above the hands. Return to a straight-arm hang. Repeat.

Leg Hold.   Jump to a proper arm-and-leg grasp position, release the hands, and hold for three counts with only the legs.

Rope Climb.   The rope is gripped between the shin and the calves, with one foot pressing on the rope. The hips are fully flexed and the arms are extended overhead. As the legs are straightened, the arms pull up and the elbows bend. The bottom hand releases, reaches up over the other hand, and regrasps. The process is repeated halfway up the rope. The process is then reversed when climbing down. Do not slide down the rope. Use a hand-under-hand grip.

Bell Ringer.   Only after individual students have demonstrated sufficient control should they be permitted to climb to the top of the rope. Secure a small bell at the top that can be rung for positive reinforcement.

Double-Rope Hold.   Grasping two ropes, jump up and hold in a bent-arm position with the aid of the legs.

Double-Rope Swing.   Grasping two ropes, run forward and pull up to a bent-arm support, swing forward, and drop off at the end of the backswing.

Double-Rope Candle Stand.   Grasping two ropes in a straight-arm support position, pull up and turn over to an inverted support position. Spot carefully.

Double-Rope Pullover.   Grasping two ropes, jump to a bent-arm hold. Bend the knees to the chest and drop the head back. Pull over to an inverted position and release to a standing position on the mat. Spot carefully.

CONCEPT 20.3
Skill development activities with both large and small equipment follow a logical sequence of progression from simple to more complex within each level of classification.

Horizontal Ladder Skills

Many playgrounds and some gymnasiums are equipped with horizontal ladders. The **horizontal ladder** should be positioned high enough to permit the feet to dangle freely, and mats should be placed underneath for inverted skills. Activities on the ladder should be spotted whenever the body is inverted. Also, emphasize the use of a thumbs-around-the-bar grasp to minimize the chance of losing one's grip. Table 20.3 provides a recommended progression for

The side-rail travel.

TABLE 20.3   *Selected Horizontal Ladder Skills Sequenced in Terms of Complexity*

Horizontal Ladder Skills (page number)	Suggested Progression for Children		
	Beginning Level	Intermediate Level	Advanced Level
Straight hang (381)	x		
Single-knee lift (381)	x		
Double-knee lift (381)	x		
Leg lift (381)	x		
Trunk twister (381)	x		
Bicycle hang (381)	x		
Hang and swing (381)	x		
Half chin (381)		x	
Flexed-arm hang (382)		x	
Chin-ups (382)		x	
Side-rail travel (382)		x	
Single-rail travel (382)		x	
Single-rung travel (382)		x	
Monkey rung travel (382)		x	
Super monkey travel (382)		x	
Inverted push-ups (382)		x	
Inverted hang (382)			x
Inverted swing (382)			x
Pull through (382)			x
Skin the cat (382)			x
Pull to top (382)			x

selected horizontal ladder skills. Practice in activities on the horizontal ladder will contribute to

1. increased strength and endurance in the arms and upper trunk muscles,
2. increased skill in ladder traveling,
3. improved dynamic balance abilities, and
4. increased body and spatial awareness.

Straight Hang.   Grasp a single rung with both hands and hang for up to ten seconds.

Single-Knee Lift.   From a straight hang, raise one leg and then the other.

Double-Knee Lift.   From a straight hang, raise both knees to the chest and return. Repeat.

Leg Lift.   From a straight hang, raise both legs to a position parallel with the floor and hold.

Trunk Twister.   From a straight hang, twist the trunk from side to side.

Bicycle Hang.   From a straight hang, make a continuous bicycle peddling action.

Hang and Swing.   From a straight hang, swing forward and back, dropping off at the end of the backswing. Try dropping at the end of the forward swing also. Discover which is safer.

Half Chin.   From a straight hang, pull to a position in which the arms are flexed at a ninety-degree angle. Hold for three or more seconds.

Flexed-Arm Hang.   Pull to a fully flexed-arm hang with the chin parallel to the bar. Hold.

Chin-ups.   From a straight hang with a palms-facing grip, perform chin-ups or pull-ups.

Side-Rail Travel.   Grasp the outer portion of the side rails with the palms facing in. Travel from one end of the ladder to the other.

Single-Rail Travel.   Grasp one rail and travel sideways from one end to the other.

Single-Rung Travel.   From a straight hang, travel as far as possible with a follow grasp from one rung to the next.

Monkey Rung Travel.   From a straight hang, travel with an alternating grasp with only one hand touching each rung.

Super Monkey Travel.   From a straight hang, travel from one end of the ladder to the other, skipping rungs.

Inverted Push-ups.   From a straight hang, swing the legs upward and hook the knees over the bar. Perform repeated "push-ups" by bringing the nose up to the bar and then returning.

Inverted Hang.   From a straight hang, pull the legs up and hook the knees around one rung. Let go of the hands and hang by the knees. Spot carefully.

Inverted Swing.   From a knee-hanging position, swing back and forth with the arms dangling overhead.

Pull Through.   From a straight hang with the arms slightly more than shoulder width apart, drop the head back as the knees are brought to the chest, turn over backward, and drop to standing position.

Skin the Cat.   From a straight hang with the arms slightly more than shoulder width apart, drop the head back as the knees are brought up to the chest. Turn over backward and hang. Return to a straight hang.

Pull to Top.   From a straight hang, pull the body to a knee-hang position. With aid of the arms, pull the body through a rung and finish sitting on top of the ladder. Spot carefully.

Inner Tube and Springboard Skills

Inner tubes may be obtained from tire-salvage stores. Several large truck tubes may be tied together and placed on tumbling mats. Be certain to secure the valve and stem of each inner tube prior to use and to use proper spotting techniques. Many of the same skills may be performed with the **springboard.** Table 20.4 provides a suggested progression of skills. Inner tube activities help to

1. enhance dynamic balance abilities,
2. improve basic jumping skills,
3. improve body and spatial awareness,
4. develop leg strength, and
5. improve total body coordination.

Sit and Bounce.   From a sitting position on the tube, bounce up and down.

Walk Around.   From a standing position on the tube, walk all the way around without losing balance.

Stand and Bounce.   From a standing position on the tube, bounce up and down. Spot carefully.

Center Jump.   From a standing position on the tube, jump into the center and back up on the other side.

Ins and Outs.   From a standing position on the floor, jump up onto the tube, jump into the center, jump back up on the other side, and jump off.

Half-Turn Bounce.   From a standing position on the tube, bounce and turn halfway around in two bounces. Try one bounce.

Bounce and Touch.   From a standing position on the tube, bounce and touch with your hand body parts named by the instructor.

Bounce and Squat.   From a standing position on the tube, spring upward and land in a squat position on the mat.

Bouncing Bunny.   From a standing position on the tube, facing out, spring upward, landing in a squat position on the mat with the hands also on the mat. Immediately do a bunny hop forward.

Bounce and Roll.   From a standing position on the tube facing out, spring upward, landing in a full squat position on the mat. Immediately do a forward roll.

TABLE 20.4 *Selected Inner Tube and Springboard Skills Sequenced in Terms of Complexity*

Inner Tube and Springboard Skills (page number)	Suggested Progression for Children		
	Beginning Level	Intermediate Level	Advanced Level
Sit and bounce (382)	x		
Walk around (382)	x		
Stand and bounce (382)	x		
Center jump (382)	x		
Ins and outs (382)	x		
Half-turn bounce (382)	x		
Bounce and touch (382)	x		
Bounce and squat (382)	x		
Bouncing bunny (382)	x		
Bounce and roll (382)		x	
Tuck jump (383)		x	
Toe jump (383)		x	
Knee bounce (383)		x	
Full-turn bounce (383)		x	
Partner bounce (384)		x	
Around the world (384)		x	
Feet to seat (384)		x	
Bounce and kick (384)		x	
Jump and half-turn (384)			x
Star bounce (384)			x
Jump and full turn (384)			x
Bounce and knee straddle (384)			x
Bounce and ankle straddle (384)			x
Bounce and jackknife (384)			x
Bounce and toe straddle (384)			x
Double spin (384)			x
Double reverse spin (384)			x
Double spin plus (384)			x

Tuck Jump.   From a standing position on the tube, facing out, bounce and tuck knees to the chest before landing back on your feet.

Toe Jump.   From a standing position on the tube, facing out, jump up and touch the toes prior to landing back on your feet.

Knee Bounce.   From a standing position facing the tube, bounce the knees on the tube and return to a controlled stand. Repeat.

Full-Turn Bounce.   From a standing position on the tube, bounce and do a full turn in three bounces; then try for two.

Partner Bounce. From a standing position on the tube, facing in, partners hold hands and bounce together. Try alternate bouncing also.

Around the World. From a standing position on the tube, facing in with partners holding hands, bounce in a clockwise direction around the tube. Repeat in the opposite direction.

Feet to Seat. From a standing position on the tube, facing in, bounce and land on your seat with feet in the center of the tube.

Bounce and Kick. From a standing position on the tube, bounce up and hit the buttocks with the heels prior to landing on the mat.

Jump and Half-Turn. From a standing position on the tube, facing out, jump and do a half-turn, landing on the mat.

Star Bounce. From a standing position on the tube, facing out, bounce off the tube, spreading both the arms and legs wide apart and landing in a controlled squat position on the mat.

Jump and Full Turn. From a standing position on the tube, facing out, jump and do a full turn, landing on the mat.

Bounce and Knee Straddle. From a standing position on the tube, facing out, bounce and bend the knees backward and touch them prior to landing on the mat in a controlled upright position.

Bounce and Ankle Straddle. From a standing position on the tube, facing out, bounce and do a straddle jump, touching the ankles.

Bounce and Jackknife. From a standing position on the tube, facing out, bounce and lift the legs forward and upward, keeping the feet close together. Touch the ankles or toes with the hands and land on the mat.

Bounce and Toe Straddle. Do a straddle jump, touching pointed toes at the height of the jump. Land in a controlled upright position on the mat.

Double Spin. From a standing position on the tube, facing out, jump and make a full turn in the air, land on the mat, and immediately rebound off the mat with another full turn.

Double Reverse Spin. This is the same as the double spin except that the second full turn is in the opposite direction from the first.

Double Spin Plus. After executing a double spin or a double reverse spin, finish with a forward roll, cartwheel, or roundoff.

Springboard and Vaulting Skills

Springboards and **vaulting boxes** may be purchased commercially or made by a skilled carpenter. Vaulting equipment should be adjusted to the average height of the group. Mats should always be used in the landing area, and proper spotting techniques should be employed at all times. The springboard should be eight to twelve inches from the base of the vaulting box. Springboard vaulting is not recommended for children at the beginning level because of the combination of springing and vaulting skills required. Table 20.5 provides a recommended progression of skills. Springboard vaulting activities help children to

1. improve eye-body coordination,
2. achieve better dynamic balance,

The straddle mount.

TABLE 20.5 *Selected Springboard Vaulting Skills Sequenced in Terms of Complexity*

Springboard Vaulting Skills (page number)	Suggested Progression for Children		
	Beginning Level	*Intermediate Level*	*Advanced Level*
Squat mount (385)		x	
Free mount (385)		x	
Running squat mount (385)		x	
Running free mount (385)		x	
Jump and land (385)		x	
Jump and turn (385)		x	
Upright springs (385)		x	
Jump and roll (385)		x	
Jump, turn, and roll (385)			x
Squat vault (385)			x
Flank vault (385)			x
Straddle mount (385)			x
Straddle vault (386)			x
Shoot squat vault (386)			x

3. increase muscular strength,
4. improve coordination and agility, and
5. improve muscular power.

Squat Mount.   From a standing position on the springboard with both hands on the apparatus, jump up with a two-foot takeoff to a squat position.

Free Mount.   From a standing position on the springboard, jump up to a stand on the box.

Running Squat Mount.   From a run and a two-foot takeoff, place the hands on the box and do a squat mount.

Running Free Mount.   Execute a free mount from a run and a two-foot takeoff.

Jump and Land.   Spring to a position on the box, jump off, and land with good control.

Jump and Turn.   Spring to a position on the box, making a half, three-quarter, or full turn in the air before landing in good control.

Upright Springs.   Spring to a position on the box. Then spring off the box, executing any one of several upright springs.

Jump and Roll.   Spring to a position on the box and then jump off, land, and do a forward roll. Spot carefully.

Jump, Turn, and Roll.   Spring to a partner on the box, jump off, making a half-turn in the air, land, and do a backward roll. Spot carefully.

Squat Vault.   From a run with a two-foot takeoff, place both hands on the box, spring upward, and squat through the arms to a position on the floor on the opposite side.

Flank Vault.   From a run with a two-foot takeoff, place both hands on the box, swing the legs to the side, release the hand to the swinging side, and land on the opposite side of the box. Spot carefully.

Straddle Mount.   From a run with a two-foot takeoff, place both hands on the box and spring upward, raising the hips and keeping the legs straight. Spread the legs wide and mount the box in a straddle position. Spot carefully.

Straddle Vault. Follow the same procedures as the mount, but push forcefully with the hands, landing on the opposite side. Spot carefully.

Shoot Squat Vault.   Perform as a squat vault, but extend the hips as the legs are pulled through, landing in a box-out position. Spot carefully.

Turning Bar Skills

North American children are often weak in the upper arms and shoulder girdle. Activities on the **turning bar** or the low horizontal bar are excellent for developing these muscle groups. Place mats under the bar for all inverted activities. Stress a thumbs-around grip and spot carefully. The following are suggested activities that children may perform on a turning bar, starting with beginning level activities and progressing to advanced activities. Table 20.6 provides a recommended progression of elementary turning bar skills. Spot all carefully.

Turning bar activities help children to

1. increase strength in the muscles of the upper arms and shoulder girdle area,
2. improve inverted balance abilities, and
3. increase body awareness and spatial awareness.

Straight Hang.   Grasp the bar in both hands and hang for up to ten seconds.

Single Toe Point.   From a straight-hang position, point the toes of one foot at designated objects.

Double Toe Point.   From a straight hang, point the toes of both feet at designated objects below waist level.

Double Knee Raise.   From a straight hang, bring both knees up as high as possible and return. Repeat.

Hanging Walk.   From a straight hang, pretend to walk forward with the legs.

Bicycle Hang.   From a straight hang, pretend to peddle a bicycle forward. Repeat, peddling backward.

Hang and Swing.   From a straight hang, swing forward and backward.

Pivot Swing.   From a straight hang, swing the legs forward, sideways, and backward in a circle.

The proper thumbs around safety grip on the bar.

Change Grips.   From a straight hang, change hand grips while performing any of the preceding activities.

L-Seat.   From a straight hang, raise both legs and hold in an "L" position for three counts.

Straight Swing.   Swing forward and backward from the hips, keeping the legs straight.

Toe Toucher.   From a straight hang, bring the toe up to touch the fingers and return. Spot carefully.

Swing and Drop.   Swing forward and drop off at the end of the backswing.

Swing and Clap.   Swing forward and backward, clapping the hands once before landing at the end of the backswing.

Swing and Turn.   Swing forward and backward, dropping off at the end of the backswing with a quarter, half, or full turn.

Bar Travel.   Starting at one end of the bar, travel to the other end using an alternate grip.

Monkey Travel.   Starting at one end with the legs wrapped around the bar and both hands grasping, travel to the opposite end and return. Spot carefully.

Knee Hang.   From a straight hang, bring the knees to the chest and drop the head back. Hook the legs around the bar at the knees and release the hands. Hang by the knees for three counts. Return to a straight hang. Spot carefully.

TABLE 20.6   *Selected Turning Bar Skills Sequenced in Terms of Complexity*

Turning Bar Skills (page number)	Suggested Progression for Children		
	Beginning Level	Intermediate Level	Advanced Level
Straight hang (386)	X		
Single toe point (386)	X		
Double toe point (386)	X		
Double knee raise (386)	X		
Hanging walk (386)	X		
Bicycle hang (386)	X		
Hang and swing (386)		X	
Pivot swing (386)		X	
Change grips (386)		X	
L-seat (386)		X	
Straight swing (386)		X	
Toe toucher (386)		X	
Swing and drop (386)		X	
Swing and clap (386)		X	
Swing and turn (386)		X	
Bar travel(386)		X	
Monkey travel (386)		X	
Knee hang (386)			X
Knee swing (387)			X
Pull through and drop (387)			X
Skin the cat (387)			X
Birds nest (387)			X

Knee Swing.   From a knee-hanging position, swing forward and back with the instructor spotting by using a hand to lightly support the ankles.

Pull Through and Drop.   From a straight hang, lift the knees to the chest and drop the head back. Pull through to an inverted position and then to a reverse straight hang and drop.

Skin the Cat.   This is the same as preceding movement, but has a return to a straight hang.

Bird's Nest.   From a straight hang, lift the knees to the chest and place the backs of the toes on top of the bar. Arch by raising the head up. Spot carefully.

Parachute Skills

The parachute is a piece of equipment enjoyed by both young and older children. **Parachutes** may be commercially purchased from physical education supply companies, or they may be secured through a local air base or Army-Navy surplus store. Parachutes can be used for excellent introductory and organizational activities. Successful parachute activities require group cooperation and teamwork. The following is a compilation of several game-like activities that can be played with the parachute. Parachute activities help children to

1. learn how to cooperate and work together,
2. develop listening skills, and
3. reinforce basic movement skills.

The bird's nest.

Number Chase.   Have students stretch out the parachute and space themselves as evenly as possible. Help students count off by fours (or other appropriate number). Have students raise the parachute to an umbrella position. When the parachute reaches its highest position, the teacher calls out a number (such as two). All (two's) let go of the chute and run in a counterclockwise (or clockwise) direction, trying to tap the person in front of them before they reach their original position around the parachute.

Smash-A-Chute.   Divide class into two teams. Number off so that each person has a different number but matches a number of a player on the opposite team. Give each team a color as a team name. Place two marked foam balls opposite each other with the team and color of ball also opposite, so one team's ball is nearer the other team players. With the class holding the parachute, have them raise the chute to an umbrella position. When the chute reaches its highest position call out a number (such as five). The two number five's run under the parachute and pick up the ball with the same color as their team color and try to hit their opponent below the waist by throwing the ball at him or her before the opponent hits them. The first person to hit the opponent scores one point for their team. If no one is hit before the chute falls, no point is scored for either team.

Parachute Soccer.   Divide players into two teams, lined up opposite each other around the parachute. Use basic soccer skills, already previously practiced. Have the students raise the chute overhead and pass the ball back and forth, trying to get the ball to go between two players on the opposite team. One point is scored for each ball that passes between two players outside the parachute area.

Chute the Bacon.   Place the object to be used as the bacon under the parachute in the middle. Divide the class into two teams. Number off so each person has a different number, one that matches the number of a player on the opposite team. With the students holding the parachute, have them raise the parachute to an umbrella position. Call out a number (such as six). Both sixes release the parachute and run to the middle of the chute. Sixes try to pick up and take a ball back to their team, while a second player tries to tag that player with the bacon. If the "stealer" is successful, that team receives one point. If the tagger is successful in tagging the first player, then a point is scored for that team. If the chute falls before a point is scored, both players return to their original positions with no point scored for either team.

Big Top.   Use the chute as a "circus Big Top" with mats for performing stunts under it.

Pass the Ball.   Players hold the edge of a parachute lowered over one player in the middle, who holds a basketball. On signal, the players lift the chute, and before the other players can bring it down again, the player in the center must pass the ball to a player on the perimeter and exchange places with him before the chute touches either player.

Steal the Ball.   Players hold the edge of chute and each of them is given a number. A basketball is placed on the floor in the center under the chute. At the teacher's command, the chute is lifted overhead and at the same time the teacher calls a number. The player whose number it is must run to the ball, pick it up, dribble once around the circle, place the ball back on the floor in the center, and return to his place on the perimeter before the chute falls and touches the player.

Chute Dribble.   Each player holds the outside edge of the chute with one hand while holding a basketball in the other hand. At the teacher's command, the players begin to walk or run in a circle while continuing to hold the edge of the chute in one hand and dribbling the ball with the other hand.

Simon Says.   Simple parachute routines can be made more exciting by using commands from the game Simon Says. Such activities as raising and lowering the parachute, sitting, kneeling, and standing can be included in these drills. Moving in one direction with the parachute, changing directions, running, stopping, and jumping are also challenging.

Team Popcorn.   With two teams and six light balls (two colors), shake the chute and try to get all of one team's balls off the chute first. The first team to shake off all of the opposing team's balls wins.

Roll Through.   Children hold the chute at waist level. Two balls are put on the chute. As a group, the children try to roll the balls through the center of the chute.

Poison Parachute.   Inflate the chute, take three steps forward, release the chute, and drop to the floor in a front lying position. If the chute falls on any part of children's bodies, those children are "poisoned" and must sit on the sidelines until one or more others are poisoned.

Colors.   Inflate the chute; call out a color. Children wearing that color move to a new position before the parachute comes down. As a variation, have the children do various locomotor activities while changing places.

Mousetrap.   Number off by three's; call a number, and those with that number are the mice. They run in and out under the parachute while it is lifted in the air. On command, the parachute is pulled down, trying to catch the mice.

Huddle.   Number off in three's. Raise the parachute on a signal and then call one of the numbers. Those people form a "huddle" in the middle and see how long they can remain there without getting touched by the chute. They try to get out at the very last moment. Repeat using the other numbers.

Jacks.   The parachute is raised and lowered at an even tempo. While this is being done, one student at a time goes under and collects a number of beanbags. The first person collects one; the next, two; and so on. A person is out if caught under the parachute while trying to collect the beanbags. Then the next student resumes at one beanbag. The student who is out continues to help raise and lower the parachute.

TEACHING TIPS

The following are a number of important teaching suggestions for various pieces of apparatus:

- Build skill upon skill in small increments, recognizing individual differences in muscular strength, coordination, and agility.

- Use pieces of apparatus as a station within a circuit. Place task cards near each piece of equipment for both performers and spotters.

- Begin with low level skills and progress to higher level skills.

- Lines and ropes stretched out on the floor make an excellent medium for practicing balance-beam skills.

- Do not knot the bottom of the climbing ropes; this will prevent children from relying on the knot for support.

- Stress a thumbs-around grasp for all climbing and hanging skills.

- Do not permit sliding down the climbing rope. Use a hand-under-hand method.

- Be certain that the area for swinging activities is clear.

- Turning-bar activities should be done using a low horizontal bar first; progress to a higher bar as skill develops.

- When using the inner tube or springboard, stress keeping the head up and maintaining body control in the air.

Parachute Golf.   With two teams, eight yarn balls (two colors), and the parachute held waist high, use slow movements to try to get the balls through the center hole of the parachute. If the blue balls go through the center hole first, the blue team wins; likewise for the red. Balls falling off the sides do not count.

Heads in the Basket.   Students raise the chute overhead, forming a mushroom. On command, they lie in a prone position on the floor, pulling the chute down and around the back of their necks. Only the heads are inside the parachute. This is a fun culminating activity with the chute.

SKILLS WITH SMALL EQUIPMENT

Children love having an individual piece of equipment to use as they explore the many movement challenges possible with small apparatus. It is important, whenever possible, for each child to have his or her own piece of equipment to use. Such a policy promotes maximum activity on the part of all and will help to reduce behavior problems that frequently erupt while children are waiting for a turn. The hand apparatus challenges in this chapter represent only a sampling of the endless variety possible (see Table 20.7). When selecting activities for inclusion in the lesson, first identify the objectives of the lesson and the ability level of your students. Then it is a relatively simple matter to determine appropriate activities.

CONCEPT 20.4
Work with small equipment is effectively aided if there is ample supply for all, to facilitate maximum participation by all.

Balance Boards and Stilts Activities

Balance boards are easily constructed and offer a variety of challenging activities. A mat should be placed under the balance board to avoid slipping. **Coffee-can stilts** are made easily from metal coffee containers and a length of rope. They offer a new dimension to stability because the center of gravity is raised, thus making balancing more difficult. Practice with balance boards and stilts will help students to

1. improve static balance abilities,
2. enhance dynamic balance abilities,
3. enhance body and spatial awareness, and
4. improve coordination and agility.

While on a balance board, students may try these activities:

- Balance on the board any way possible.
- Balance with the feet apart.
- Balance with the feet together.
- Balance with the arms out from the sides.
- Balance with the arms down at the sides.
- Balance with the eyes closed.
- Squat down and balance.
- Squat halfway down and balance.

- Touch various body parts while balancing.
- Balance with a beanbag or eraser on the head.
- Balance and catch a ball.
- Toss a ball while balancing.
- Throw at a target while balancing.
- Balance on one foot.
- Bounce a ball while balancing.
- Balance with a partner on another board while holding hands.
- Toss and catch a ball while balancing.
- Turn around on the board while balancing.

With a set of coffee-can stilts, students may try these activities:

- Walk in various directions (forward, sideways, and backward).
- Step over a low object.
- Step under objects.
- Walk at various levels (high, low, and medium).
- Walk at various speeds.
- Hop on one foot.
- Jump forward.
- Have races.
- Move a disc forward while walking on the stilts.
- Go through an obstacle course.

Balloon Activities

Round balloons offer an excellent means for children to practice striking and volleying skills. Because of their lightness, balloons are easier to contact than a regulation volleyball or playground ball. They are inexpensive enough for each child to have one and may be used over and over if rubber bands are used to secure inflated balloons instead of a knot. Balloon striking and volleying activities are designed to

1. enhance fundamental striking skills,
2. develop basic volleying abilities,
3. improve eye-hand coordination,
4. promote improved spatial awareness, and
5. promote improved body awareness.

Using a balloon, students may try these activities:

- Toss it to different heights and catch.

TABLE 20.7   *Selected Small Apparatus Activities Sequenced in Terms of Complexity*

Small Apparatus Activities Using: (page number)	Suggested Progression for Children		
	Beginning Level	Intermediate Level	Advanced Level
Balance board (390)	X	X	X
Low stilts (390)	X	X	
Balloons (390)	X	X	
Ball challenges (391)	X	X	X
Beanbag-balancing (392)	X	X	X
Beanbag-tossing (392)	X	X	
Individual hoop (393)	X	X	X
Partner hoops (394)		X	
Hoop-twirling (394)		X	X
Short jump ropes (394)	X	X	X
Long jump ropes (395)	X	X	
Stretch ropes (395)	X	X	
Chinese jump ropes (396)		X	X
Wands (397)	X	X	X

- Toss it from various body positions and catch.
- Toss it up and catch it with different body parts.
- Toss it back and forth to a partner.
- Toss two balloons back and forth with a partner.
- Strike the balloon with the hands.
- Strike the balloon at different levels.
- Strike the balloon with various body parts.
- Keep the balloon in the air as long as possible.
- Stay in one spot while hitting the balloon repeatedly into the air.
- Move to the other side of the room while keeping the balloon in the air.
- Walk in a circle while hitting the balloon.
- Make a full turn each time the balloon is hit.
- Use a table tennis paddle, tennis racquet, or bat to hit the balloon repeatedly.
- Hit the balloon as hard or as softly as possible.
- Hit the balloon using different swinging motions: sidearm, overarm, underhand.
- Volley the balloon with a partner.
- Volley the balloon with a partner, both of you using an implement.

Ball Activities

Balls come in a variety of sizes, shapes, colors, and textures. In the children's physical education program, it is important that each child have a ball when taking part in activities. Playground balls, soccer balls, volleyballs, tennis balls, foam balls, or beach balls can all be used for the activity ideas that follow. These activities represent only a sampling of a progression of challenge activities that can be included in the lesson. Be sure to have children exchange balls frequently so they all get opportunities to try each kind of ball. Practice in ball handling activities helps children to

1. develop the ability to manipulate balls in a variety of ways,
2. be able to control a variety of different types of balls,
3. become familiar with balls in a variety of movement situations,
4. improve eye-hand and eye-foot coordination, and
5. enhance body awareness and directional awareness.

Balls vary greatly in size, color, and texture.

Students might try these individual ball challenges:

- See how many ways you can toss the ball to yourself.
- Find how many directions you can use to throw the ball to yourself.
- Find different ways to throw the ball without using your hands.
- Throw your ball up and catch it. Find different ways to move and still catch the ball.
- Use different levels to toss the ball and catch it.
- Toss the ball up, take three steps, and catch it on the fly.
- Find different ways that you can get the ball from where you are to the wall.
- Make the ball move forward without throwing it.
- Find different ways to make the ball go around you.
- See what you can do with your ball using only one hand.
- Find different levels to bounce the ball.
- See how many different ways you can move while dribbling the ball.
- See how many different parts of your body you can use to bounce the ball.
- Make a full turn after you bounce the ball and then catch it.

- Dribble the ball straight ahead on a line.
- Dribble the ball while moving in different directions.
- Bounce up and down as the ball bounces up and down.
- Dribble the ball as fast as you can.
- Dribble the ball around markers on the floor.
- Dribble the ball focusing straight ahead.
- Dribble the ball so a partner can't take it away.
- Throw at targets on the wall using overhead and underhand throws.
- From a square or circle drawn on the floor, throw the ball up high on the wall and catch it while remaining in the figure.
- With two squares drawn on the floor about ten feet apart and parallel to the wall, throw the ball at the wall from the first square and catch it on the rebound in the second square. Repeat.
- Hit the ball against the wall with a paddle or racket as often as possible.

Beanbag Activities

Beanbags are easy and inexpensive to make and are an excellent implement for practicing throwing, catching, and balancing skills. Whenever possible, each child should have his or her own beanbag. The beanbag activities contained here are intended to

1. enhance the fundamental manipulative skills of throwing and catching,
2. enhance fundamental dynamic and static balance abilities,
3. contribute to improved coordination, and
4. improve body awareness abilities.

In balancing a beanbag, students may try these activities:

- See how many body parts can balance the beanbag.
- Balance the beanbag on parts of the body above the waist.
- Balance it on parts below the waist.
- Balance it on parts of the body that are on the right side.
- Balance it on parts to the left.
- Balance it on parts above the waist and on the right side.

- Balance it on a part below the waist and on the left side.
- Balance it on parts that cannot be seen.
- Move at different levels while balancing on various parts.
- Move in different directions while balancing on various parts.
- Move at different speeds while balancing on various parts.
- Balance it on body parts above the waist and move it to body parts below the waist without using the hands.
- Balance it on body parts below the waist on one side of the body and move to body parts above the waist on the other side without using the hands.
- Without using the hands, balance it on parts that can be seen and transfer it to parts that can't be seen.
- Without using the hands, balance it on parts that can't be seen and transfer it to other parts that can't be seen.
- Repeat all of the preceding activities with a partner.
- Toss it to a partner, who catches the beanbag with designated body parts other than the hands.

In tossing and catching a beanbag, students may try these activities:

- Toss the beanbag up low with both hands and catch it with both hands.
- Toss it up low with both hands and catch it with one.
- Toss it up low with one hand and catch it with the same hand.
- Toss it up low with one hand and catch it with the opposite hand.
- Repeat all of the preceding exercises with higher and higher tosses.
- Toss the beanbag up and catch it with a variety of implements (e.g., scoops, boxes, or towels).
- Throw it in different directions.
- Throw at various speeds.
- Play toss and catch for distance with a partner.
- Throw at a wall target.
- Throw at a suspended tire or hoop.
- Throw through a swinging tire or hoop.
- Play pitch-catcher.

CONCEPT 20.5
With the use of small equipment, a wide variety of movement challenges may be used with an exploratory or guided-discovery format.

Hoop Activities

Hoops are great pieces of small equipment for use with a variety of movement activities. **Hoops** may be purchased, but they can be made easily from surgical tubing or black plastic water pipe. Homemade hoops are generally less expensive and more sturdy than the commercially purchased variety. They can be decorated by using brightly colored tape. Colors can be varied with an equal number of colors for grouping purposes. Hoop activities help children to

1. improve fundamental locomotor skills,
2. improve basic body and object manipulation skills,
3. enhance coordination and agility, and
4. reinforce spatial and body awareness abilities.

When using a hoop by themselves, students may try these activities:

- See how many ways there are to move with the hoop.
- Move around the hoop while keeping it stationary.

Hoop activities are challenging and fun.

- Move around the hoop while it is moving.
- Support the body in and out of the hoop.
- Roll the hoop so it comes back to you.
- Roll the hoop in a straight line.
- Roll the hoop in a circle.
- Roll the hoop using a wand.
- Roll the hoop and then move faster than the hoop.
- Roll the hoop and go through it while it is moving.
- "Jump rope" with the hoop.
- While you are on the floor, roll the hoop on a balance beam.
- While you are on the beam, roll a hoop on the floor.
- Jump through a self-turned hoop while you are on the beam.

When using a hoop with a partner, students may try these activities:

- With a partner holding the hoop, go in and out of the hoop.
- Go under a hoop held by a partner.
- Jump through a hoop held by a partner.
- Without touching them, step over and under a line of hoops that are held by partners.
- While your partner rolls the hoop, you run through it.
- While your partner rolls the hoop, both of you go through it before it stops moving. Then reverse roles.

When twirling a hoop, students may twirl it in these ways:

- Around the wrist.
- Around the forearm.
- Around the waist.
- Around the neck.
- Around the foot.
- Around the foot and jump through with the other foot.
- Around a body part and transfer it, while twirling, to another body part.

When tossing and catching a hoop, students may try these activities:

- Toss the hoop high and catch it.
- Toss the hoop with one hand and catch it with the same hand.

- Toss the hoop with one hand and catch it with the opposite hand.
- Toss the hoop to a partner.
- Toss the hoop to a partner while he or she tosses another to you.
- Toss and catch two hoops at the same time.

Jump Rope Activities

Jump ropes provide a challenging and inexpensive piece of equipment for each child. They can be used effectively in the program for children of all ages and ability levels. Jump Rope For Heart is a popular fund-raising event in many schools, raising millions of dollars for the American Heart Association. The activities that follow progress from simple to complex. Rope jumping activities help children to

1. improve eye-hand and eye-foot coordination,
2. reinforce fundamental jumping, hopping, and skipping skills,

Jump rope skills can be highly developed.

3. increase muscular endurance in the legs, and
4. improve aerobic endurance.

Using a single jump rope, students may try these activities:

- Move the rope back and forth, jumping over it each time.
- Move the rope around the body with one hand. Now try it with the other hand, over the head, to the left side, and to the right side.
- Move the rope under the feet using just one hand.
- Make a circle with the rope and move into the center and out again.
- Turn the rope and jump over it one time. Repeat rhythmically.
- Turn the rope, jump over it, and move around the floor.
- Skip (stand on right foot, hop on right foot, and pass the rope under; stand on the left foot, hop on left foot, and pass the rope under).
- Run (run in place with no hop between steps).
- Single jump (with both feet together, jump the rope without an intervening step).
- Double jump (with both feet together, jump the rope with an intervening step).
- One-leg hop (hold one leg off the floor and hop on the other with an intervening step).
- Distance hop (hold one leg off the floor and hop forward on the other without an intervening step).
- Rocking step (place one foot in front of the other; jump on alternate feet with an intervening step).
- Skip step (place one foot in front of the other; jump and alternate the lead foot).
- Backward skipping, hopping, and jumping (with the rope held in front from a starting position, any of the preceding may be used).
- Stiff-leg kick forward (same as preceding except the raised leg is thrown back on each step).
- Spread eagle (alternate between a closed step with an intervening step and a straddle step with an intervening step).
- Double jump with arms crossed (execute a double jump, cross the arms as the rope is on the downswing, and jump through it; then uncross the arms as the rope nears completion of upswing). This can be done forward and backward.

- Double turn (turn the rope under the feet two times while body is in the air).
- Crossed and uncrossed legs (jump once with the legs uncrossed and then cross the legs and jump again; use an intervening step).
- Toe tap (skip on one foot, touch toe to the floor to the rear with the other foot).

With a long stationary rope, students may try these activities:

- Jump from one foot and land on both.
- Hop from one foot and land on the same foot.
- Jump from one foot and land on the opposite foot.
- Jump from one foot and land on the same foot.
- Jump from both feet and land on both feet.
- Repeat the preceding activities with a pendulum-swinging rope.

Using a long, pendulum-swinging rope, try to follow the same progression as just described.

With a long, turning rope, students may try these activities:

- Run through the rope.
- Run in, take one jump, and run out the same side.
- Run in, take one jump, and run out the opposite side.
- Run in, take one jump with a half-turn, and run out backward.
- Do "front door" (the rope is turned away from the jumper after hitting the floor).
- Do "back door" (the rope is turned toward the jumper after hitting the floor).

Stretch Rope Activities

Stretch ropes are inexpensive to purchase and offer practice in a variety of challenging locomotor activities. **Stretch ropes** may be made easily by purchasing several yards of elastic cord, cutting it to eight-foot lengths, and tying the ends together. Stretch rope activities help children to

1. improve eye-foot coordination,
2. enhance dynamic balance abilities,
3. reinforce fundamental jumping and hopping skills, and
4. improve aerobic endurance.

● TEACHING TIPS ●

Chinese Jump Rope

Tie the rope together at the ends and hook it around the ankles of two partners. A performer is in the middle. A stationary object may be used in place of one person if a third person is not available. The basic routine follows. After each successful completion of a routine, the rope is moved higher. The height progression goes from ankles, lower calf, mid-calf, upper calf, knees, lower thigh, mid-thigh, upper thigh, buttocks, and waist.

Plainies.

- *Big In.* Performer begins with legs straddled outside the rope, takes off with both feet, and lands with feet together inside the rope.
- *Big Out.* Performer straddles the rope again.
- *Side by Side.* Performer straddles rope with one foot in and the other on the outside and repeats to the other side.
- *Ons.* Performer now jumps and lands on the stretch rope.
- *Little In.* Performer jumps and lands with both feet inside the rope.
- *Little Out.* Performer jumps and lands with both feet outside the rope.

Snappies. This is the same routine as the previous one but it is repeated while snapping the fingers in rhythm to the jumps.

Clappies. Repeat the routine, clapping to the rhythm of the routine.

Clickies. Repeat the routine, clicking the heels on each jump.

Twirlies. Repeat the routine with a half-turn on each jump.

Name Game. Facing the rope, hook the rope under one foot and cross over the opposite rope to the opposite side. Put the free foot in between the ropes and push out, forming a diamond shape. The performer now spells his name, making a quarter-turn for each letter. Step to one side with the top rope and jump over the other rope.

Scissors. Begin in a straddle position with both feet outside the ropes. Now slide the feet together and cross them.

- Jump and land with both feet inside the ropes.
- Jump and land with both feet in a straddle position outside the ropes.
- Jump and land with one foot inside and one outside the rope.
- Jump and repeat to the opposite side.
- Jump and land on the ropes.

With a single strand of stretch rope, students may try these activities:

- Walk along the rope.
- Run and step over the rope (vary the level).
- Run and jump over the rope.
- Skip and crawl under the rope.
- Hop over the rope.
- Leap over the rope.
- Go over the rope on four parts of the body.
- Do a balance over the rope. Change balance points.

With a double strand of stretch rope, students may try these activities:

- Step over the first rope and bend under the second rope.
- Jump over the first rope and go under the second rope.
- Go over both ropes (make contact between the ropes).
- Go over the ropes with two body parts.
- Go over the ropes with only one body part.
- Go over the first rope and go under the second rope.
- Jump over both ropes.

- Jump over the first rope and roll under the second rope.
- Jump and roll alternately across the ropes from one end to the other.

Wand Activities

Wands can be made easily from three-fourths-inch dowling cut to three-foot lengths. Plastic golf tubes may also be used. A variety of balance principles may be illustrated with wands. Wand activities can help children to

1. enhance static and dynamic balance skills,
2. improve fine motor control,
3. promote body and spatial awareness, and
4. illustrate critical concepts of dynamic and static balance.

Students may try these activities with wands:

- Balance the wand on the floor horizontally, then vertically. Which is easier or harder? Why?
- Balance a wand vertically, clap hands, and grab it before it falls to the ground.
- Run around the wand while it is balancing and catch it before it falls to the ground.
- Balance the wand horizontally on two fingers.
- Balance the wand horizontally on one finger.
- Balance the wand horizontally on different body parts.
- Find the middle and balance the wand any way possible horizontally.
- Balance the wand horizontally without the balance point being in the middle (use a counterbalance such as a home canning jar lid).
- Balance the wand vertically on a variety of body parts.
- Find out what the eyes do when balancing the wand vertically. Where do they look? Try looking at different parts of the wand while it is balancing vertically.
- Move about the room while balancing the wand vertically.
- Balance the wand vertically while moving from a standing to a sitting position.
- Balance the wand vertically as long as possible.
- Balance the wand vertically and transfer it from one part of the hand to another.

- Balance the wand vertically and transfer it from one finger to the corresponding finger on the opposite hand.
- Change balance points while balancing the wand vertically.
- Lead a partner around the room while balancing the wand horizontally and then vertically.
- Walk around a partner while balancing the wand.
- Go under a partner's outstretched arms while balancing the wand.
- Balance the wand somewhere on a partner's body.
- Pass the wand to a partner, keeping it in balance.
- Find two ways to pass the wand to your partner, keeping it in balance with only one balance point.

ASSESSING PROGRESS

Progress in skill development on large equipment may easily be assessed with the use of a skills chart similar to the one found in the preceding chapter. Charts can be placed on the wall or kept in the teacher's possession. When students are able to perform a new skill, they can check it off themselves or have the instructor record their accomplishments. For self-checked items, you may want to spot-check periodically to be certain that individuals can actually perform the skills that they have checked.

SUMMARY

Both large and small equipment can and should be incorporated into the developmental physical education program. Activities with equipment provide students with an effective way to develop and refine fundamental and specialized movement abilities in a variety of stability, locomotor, and manipulative skills. For example, an entire movement skill theme may be centered around the use of several pieces of large and small equipment that focus on the movement concepts and skill concepts of dynamic and static balance. Balance beams, turning bars, stilts, wands, beanbags, and balance boards can all be used in such a manner that they center on stability skill development. Manipulative skills may be reinforced with balls, hoops, beanbags, and balloons. Horizontal ladders, climbing ropes, and jump ropes can all be used to develop locomotor skills.

The key to the successful use of equipment is maximum participation and minimum waiting time. There is simply no excuse for long lines and inactivity. Large equipment lends itself to a station approach in which several different pieces of equipment are being used at once. Be certain, however, to have trained spotters available at each station. Small equipment lends itself to individual pieces of equipment. Whenever possible try to have ample equipment for all students. Class control problems will be reduced, interest will be heightened, and time on task will increase dramatically.

COMPLEMENTARY READINGS

Capon, J. (1981). *Successful Movement Challenges.* Byron, CA: Front Row Experience.

French, R., and M. Horvat. (1983). *Parachute Movement Activities.* Byron, CA: Front Row Experience.

Hammett, C. T. (1992). *Movement Activities for Early Childhood.* Champaign, IL: Human Kinetics.

Solis, K. M., and B. Budris. (1991). *The Jump Rope Primer.* Champaign, IL: Human Kinetics.

Treanor, L. J. (1993). Making students comfortable with gymnastics. *Strategies* 7, 5–9.

United States Gymnastics Federation. (1994). *I Can Do Gymnastics: Essential Skills for Beginning Gymnasts.* Indianapolis, IN: USA Gymnastics.

SUPPLEMENTARY READINGS

Diem, L. (1991). *The Important Early Years.* Reston, VA: AAHPERD.

Hacker, P., et al. (1994). *Sequential Gymnastics II: The Instructor Guide.* Indianapolis, IN: USA Gymnastics.

Ryser, O. E., and J. R. Brown. (1990). *A Manual for Tumbling and Apparatus Stunts.* Dubuque, IA: Wm. C. Brown.

Stanley, S. (1988). *Physical Education: A Movement Orientation.* Toronto: McGraw-Hill.

VIDEOS

Parachuting on the Ground. Athletic Institute. 200 Castlewood Drive, North Palm Beach, FL: The Athletic Institute. (9 min., teacher's manual included).

The Jump Rope Primer. Solis, K. M., and B. Budris. (1991). Champaign, IL: Human Kinetics. (32 min., accompanies text by the same name).

CHAPTER 21

Disc Sport Skill Themes

Key Concept

Disc Sport Skills Involve Application of a Variety of Fundamental
Manipulative Skills to a Specialized Recreational and Sport Activity

Chapter Objectives

The purpose of this chapter is to provide you with the tools to:
• List and describe the steps in planning and implementing a disc sport skill theme.
• Describe the correct technique for performing a variety of disc tossing and
  catching skills.
• List the movement concepts and skill concepts that children should know in disc
  tossing and disc catching.
• Demonstrate knowledge of common problems that children encounter and
  teaching strategies to help overcome these problems.
• Provide examples of fitness activities and skill drills appropriate to disc sport
  skill learning.
• Modify several disc skill drills, making them into lead-up games.
• Demonstrate knowledge of the rules of the team sport of Ultimate.
• Provide examples of appropriate assessment of disc sport skills among
  elementary school-age children.

Terms to Remember

Backhand Throw   Clap Catch
Forehand Throw   One-Handed Catch
Overhead Throw   Ultimate
Sandwich Catch

Invented in the 1950s, the Frisbee disc was originally marketed in Southern California. Since that time its growth in popularity has been phenomenal. In fact, it is reported that each year more discs are sold than baseballs, basketballs, and footballs combined. Standard discs are excellent for outdoor use, and mini discs and cloth discs work well in more confined areas.

Children and adults can be found tossing discs on the playground, at the beach, or in the backyard. It has developed into a popular recreational pastime for millions and is enjoyed as a sport by many. The game of Ultimate is the team sport version of disc playing. The rules of Ultimate are presented later in the chapter.

CONCEPT 21.1
The steps in planning and conducting a disc sport skill theme are the same as for planning a fundamental movement skill theme, involving preplanning, observation and assessment, specific planning and implementation, evaluation, and revision.

DISC SKILL SEQUENCING

By the second or third grade children should have mastered a variety of fundamental manipulative abilities and be ready to begin learning the basics of disc throwing and catching. The disc skills program should be based on the present level of ability of the class or group as well as being individually appropriate. In terms of disc skill learning, second and third grade children are typically at the beginning level, whereas fourth and fifth graders are often at the intermediate level of skill learning. Children in the sixth grade and beyond are sometimes at the advanced level. Remember, however, that this does not guarantee that all are at the level typical for their age. Some may be ahead, and many others may be behind. It is important to know where *your* students are if you are to be able to plan more effectively for all.

CONCEPT 21.2
Skill sequencing should be based on where children are in their actual level of movement skill development, not on where they should be.

Developing a Disc Sport Skills Theme

Use the following format to help you make the best use of your time and ensure developmentally appropriate planning:

1. *Preplan.*
   Determine approximately how long and when you will include disc skills in the program as a skill theme. Secure a sufficient number of discs so that at least every other child has one.
2. *Observe and Assess.*
   Observe the class or group in terms of their skill levels after studying the following verbal and visual descriptions. Assess ability levels in terms of students' level of movement skill learning, determining if they are at the beginning, intermediate, or advanced level of developing their disc throwing and catching skills.
3. *Plan and Implement.*
   Plan a program of skill development activities. Use the teaching tips and concepts children should know for help. Implement a developmentally appropriate program of sequential skill development activities.
4. *Evaluate and Revise.*
   Evaluate progress through informal observational assessment techniques or through formal skill testing procedures. Revise subsequent lessons based on student progress.

A suggested progression for teaching disc skills and a developmental activities chart are located in Tables 21.1 and 21.2, respectively. These tables will help you to identify appropriate disc sport skills to teach and skill drills to incorporate into your lessons. A brief description of each of these drills is found in the skill development activities section of this chapter, along with a list of several recommended warm-up activities.

DISC THROWING

There are three basic ways to throw the disc: **backhand, forehand,** and **overhand throw.** The backhand toss is generally the easiest to master and is usually taught first. The keys to successful disc throwing are smoothness,

TABLE 21.1   *Selected Disc Skills Sequenced in Terms of Complexity*

Disc Skills (page number)	Suggested Progression for Children		
	Beginning Level	*Intermediate Level*	*Advanced Level*
Throwing			
Backhand throw (401)	Introduce	Refine	
Forehand throw (401)		Introduce	Refine
Overhand throw (403)			Introduce
Catching			
Two-handed Sandwich catch (404)	Introduce	Refine	
Two-handed Clap catch (404)	Introduce	Refine	
One-handed catch (405)		Introduce	Refine
Associated Skills			
Curve	Introduce	Refine	
Hover	Introduce	Refine	
"Trick" catches			Introduce
Tipping			Introduce
Finger delay			Introduce
Skipping			Introduce
Understanding the Game			
Rules (408)		Introduce	Refine
Strategy (408)		Introduce	Refine

control, and good wrist snap. Most children can learn to throw a disc well with a few basic teaching hints. Once this is learned, a whole new world of recreational and competitive play opens to them.

CONCEPT 21.3
A variety of disc-tossing and catching skills can be mastered by elementary school-age children.

Backhand Throw

The cross-body backhand toss is generally the first disc toss learned by children and adults alike.

Verbal Description

- Hold disc lightly with the thumb on top, index finger on the rim, and the remaining fingers spread under the disc.

- Stand with the lead shoulder facing the target and the feet slightly spread.

- The throwing arm is brought back across the body and the trunk twists at the waist.

- The throwing arm moves forward with a straight-arm action, and the body weight is shifted forward.

- The disc is released flat with a snap of the wrist.

- The throwing arm follows through, ending with the index fingers pointing at the target.

Visual Description.   (Figure 21.1)

Forehand Throw

The forehand toss is generally the second disc throw learned by children. It is usually best to teach this skill after the backhand has been reasonably well mastered.

TABLE 21.2   *Developmental Activities Chart for Disc Sport Drills Sequenced in Terms of Complexity*

Disk Sport Skill Drills (page number)	Suggested Progression for Children		
	Throwing Skills	Catching Skills	Associated Skills
Flat throw (407)	x		
Bull's eye (407)	x		
Hoop throw (407)	x		
Throw for distance (407)	x		
Disc bowl (407)	x		
Bird shoot (407)	x		
Distance/accuracy throw (407)	x		
Hover (407)	x		x
Curve (407)	x		x
Throw around (407)	x		
Throw and catch (407)	x	x	
Mobile throw and catch (407)	x	x	
Keep away (407)	x	x	
Gunner (408)	x	x	
Self-throw and catch (408)	x	x	
Self-throw, run, and catch (408)	x	x	
Partner guts (408)	x	x	
Team guts (408)	x	x	
Skip it (408)	x	x	x
Freestyle (408)	x	x	x

FIGURE 21.1 *(a) The proper grip for the backhand throw. (b) Proper body action for the backhand throw.*

FIGURE 21.2 *The forehand throw.*

Verbal Description

- The disc is gripped between the thumb and forefinger with rim at the base of the thumb.
- Thumb firmly grips the top edge.
- Forefinger is extended and grips from the bottom.
- Nonthrowing shoulder leads, facing toward the target.
- Nonthrowing arm points in the intended direction of flight.
- Throwing arm is swung back as trunk twists and weight shifts to the rear foot.
- Arm swings low across the front of the body as weight shifts forward.
- Disc is released flat in a smooth, controlled motion.
- Throwing arm follows through in the direction of flight.

Visual Description.   (Figure 21.2)

Overhand Throw

The overhand toss is more difficult to master than either the backhand or forehand throws. It should be reserved for students at the advanced level of disc throwing.

FIGURE 21.3 *The overhand throw.*

Verbal Description

- Disc is gripped with the same two-finger grip used for the forehand throw.
- Face the target, legs in a slight stride, with the leg opposite the throwing arm leading.
- Disc is brought above and behind the throwing shoulder to a near vertical position as the weight shifts back.
- Arm is brought forcefully forward, the wrist snaps, and the body shifts forward.
- Disc is released and the arm follows through in the intended direction of flight.

Visual Description.   (Figure 21.3)

Teaching Tips

Developmental Difficulties

- Grips the disc improperly.
- Fails to lead with the shoulder.

- Tries too hard, causing too much body rotation and arm action.
- Fails to follow through in the intended direction of flight.
- Unable to keep the disc from wobbling because of poor release technique.
- Fails to snap at the waist, resulting in short and poorly controlled throws.

Recommended Strategies

- Have one disc for every two children.
- Send a note home asking children to bring to school any extra discs that they may have at home.
- Work for smoothness and control before working for distance and speed.
- Work for a good flat spin first.
- Begin with partners about ten meters apart.
- Concentrate on short, flat flights, gradually working back as skill increases.

Concepts Children Should Know

Skill Concepts

- You can move the fingers in close to the rim of the disc for greater power.
- Power comes from your wrist snap.
- Control comes from a smooth delivery.
- Keeping the disc parallel to the ground will result in long, flat throws.
- Raising the front rim of the disc will result in high, arching throws.
- The greater the lift on the front rim, the higher and shorter the throw will be.
- Your disc will spin in different directions in the backhand and forehand throws.

Movement Concepts

- You can throw the disc from many different body positions.
- You can throw the disc at different speeds.
- You can throw the disc in different directions.
- You can throw the disc with varying amounts of force.
- You can throw the disc in different trajectories.

- You can throw the disc over, under, around, and through objects.
- You can throw the disc in a variety of ways to a partner, who can catch it in a variety of ways.

CONCEPT 21.4
Learning disc sport skills depends on mature fundamental movement skills in a variety of stability, locomotor, and manipulative abilities.

DISC CATCHING

Catching a disc is easy to master with a little practice. Because of the tendency of the disc to float in the air, children have more time to get into position and to track the oncoming object. It does, however, take a while to judge where it is best to intercept the disc.

Two-Handed Sandwich Catch

The **sandwich catch** is the most basic pattern used to catch a disc. The two-handed sandwich catch is sometimes called a pancake catch.

Verbal Description

- Feet are in a narrow stride position with either leg forward and both knees bent.
- The eyes track the path of the oncoming disc directly to the hands.
- The arms are held slightly bent in front of the body with one hand facing up and the other down.
- As the disc approaches, the hands are "sandwiched" together, trapping the disc between the palms at its center.

Visual Description.   (Figure 21.4)

Two-Handed Clap Catch

The **clap catch** is two-handed and is usually the second catching pattern learned by children.

Verbal Description

- Stand facing the disc, feet parallel and shoulder width apart, knees slightly bent.
- Track the disc directly to the hands.

FIGURE 21.4 *The two-handed sandwich catch.*

FIGURE 21.5 *The two-handed clap catch.*

- The arms are held slightly bent in front of the body with the fingers spread and elbows out.
- The hands clamp onto opposite sides, with the thumbs on top and the fingers beneath the disc.

Visual Description.   (Figure 21.5)

C O N C E P T   2 1 . 5
Children should know a variety of skill concepts and movement concepts that relate to disc tossing and catching.

One-Handed Catch

The **one-handed catch** is the most popular and most used catching technique. The exact nature of the one-handed catch will be affected by the height of the disc, the speed, and the direction of spin. The one-handed catch is made with the thumb on top for above-the-waist catches and with the thumb on the bottom for below-the-waist catches.

Verbal Description

- Assume the ready position.
- Track the disc to the hand.
- Place the catching arm comfortably in front of the body.
- The hand is open, with the thumb and fingers forming a C shape.
- As the disc approaches, it is clamped between the thumb and the fingers.
- As contact is made, the arm and body give slightly.

Visual Description.   (Figure 21.6)

Teaching Tips

Developmental Difficulties

- Fails to get in the proper ready position.
- Fails to get behind the disc.

FIGURE 21.6 *The one-handed catch.*

- Fails to track the disc to the hands.
- Closes the eyes or looks away as the disc approaches.
- Keeps the catching arm stiff.
- Clamps too late.

Recommended Strategies

- Work with catching skills in conjunction with throwing skills.
- Stress tracking the disc all the way to the hands.
- Use a cloth disc for those who close their eyes or look away.
- Practice catching soft, flat throws directly in front of the body before harder-thrown discs coming from varying trajectories.

Concepts Children Should Know

Skill Concepts

- The direction of spin is different for right- and left-handed players and for forehand and backhand throws, which affects the preparation for your catch.
- Get in the ready position and be prepared to react to unexpected placements of the disc.

- Keep your eyes on the disc all the way to your hands.
- "Give" with the disc as it is caught.

Movement Concepts

- You can catch the disc in various body positions.
- You can catch a disc from different directions.
- You can catch discs traveling at different speeds.
- You can alter your catching in many ways.

CONCEPT 21.6
Children encounter a variety of predictable and developmentally based difficulties in learning to toss and catch a disc successfully. They need to learn many strategies for helping them achieve maximum success.

FITNESS AND SKILL DEVELOPMENT ACTIVITIES

For children to master the skills of Ultimate, they must first practice the skills individually in static drill situations. After the basic elements of a skill have been mastered, it can be practiced under controlled dynamic drill situations in which the conditions of the environment change based on the nature of the drill. Drills that combine the use of two or more skills should then be added, and finally lead-up games should be played. The skill drills presented in this section proceed from simple to complex, in that they range from static to dynamic practice drills and from single-skill to multiple-skill activities. A list of suggested fitness-oriented warm-up activities to be performed prior to engaging in skill drills is also included.

CONCEPT 21.7
Children can take part in a variety of fitness enhancement activities involving disc tossing and catching.

Warm-up Activities

Warm-up activities are essential prior to vigorous play. The activities that follow involve stretching and suppling and may be performed in the gymnasium or on the playing field. A variety of other stretching and suppling exercises may be performed. Variation in the warm-up activities and rapid movement from one exercise to another are keys to a successful warm-up session.

Door Opener.   From a stand with bent arms parallel to the floor and hands at chest height, pull the arms forcefully back and hold for four counts. Repeat.

Arm Circles.   From a stand with the arms extended out from the sides, make small arm circles forward. Repeat in the opposite direction.

Trunk Twister.   From a stand with the feet parallel and shoulder width apart and the arms extended out from the sides, twist left and right from the hips without moving the feet.

Knee Lifter.   From a stand, bring one knee up to the chest, pull tight, and hold for three counts. Repeat with the other leg.

Leg Stretcher.   From a seat with the legs spread, bend forward and grasp one ankle. Pull down and hold. Repeat to the other side.

Wrist Flexer.   From a stand, place palms together with the fingers facing upward. Lower the fingers at the wrist, first forward and away, and then toward you and down. Repeat three to five times.

C O N C E P T   2 1 . 8
Many skill drills and lead-up games can be incorporated into the disc sport skill theme as a means of maximizing learning.

Skill Drills

A wide range of disc skill drills can be successfully practiced by children at all levels of ability. The primary emphasis of disc skill drills should be on improving the skills of throwing and catching under a variety of conditions. A game can be made out of any drill simply by giving it a name, making a few modifications in the procedures, and modifying the objectives. The following is a sampling of disc skill drills appropriate for elementary school children (Table 21.2). Practice in the following skill drills will help children to

1. improve disc-throwing skills (backhand, forehand, and overhand throws);
2. improve disc-catching skills (sandwich, clap, and one-handed catch);

3. enhance aerobic endurance; and
4. improve agility and coordination.

Flat Throw (backhand, forehand throwing).   Practice controlled flat throws at a wall from a distance of ten meters. Gradually increase the distance.

Bull's Eye (throwing).   Practice throwing at a large target taped to the wall from a distance of five meters.

Hoop Throw (throwing).   Practice throwing through a suspended hoop from eight and one-half meters back. Gradually increase distance.

Throw for Distance (throwing).   Practice throwing the disc as far as possible.

Disc Bowl (throwing).   Set up several empty potato chip cans in a group. Players try to knock the cans over.

Bird Shoot (throwing).   Players move around the gym, taking one "shot" at each potato chip can, placed at varying levels. Partner retrieves disc.

Distance/Accuracy Throw (throwing).   Throw the disc as far as possible along a straight line. Total distance is the distance thrown minus the distance off the center line.

Hover (throwing).   Using a backhand throw, release the disc at a forty-five-degree angle, banking the back edge down. Try different angles.

Curve (throwing).   Using a backhand throw, bank the edge down in the intended direction of the curve.

Throw Around (throwing).   Set up an obstacle course with objects to be thrown over, under, around, and through. The disc may be advanced only with successful throws.

Throw and Catch (throwing, catching).   Practice throwing and catching with a partner. Begin five meters apart, gradually increasing the distance.

Mobile Throw and Catch (throwing, catching).   Partners move about the field while passing the disc back and forth.

Keep Away (throwing, catching).   With two partners and a person in the middle, the middle person tries to intercept a passed disc in the air.

Gunner (throwing, catching). Played the same as Keep Away, except the person in the middle is armed with a disc. She may use it to knock down a pass in any way possible.

Self-throw and Catch (throwing, catching). Throw the disc in the air and catch your own throw. Knowledge of trajectory and wind factors is necessary.

Self-throw, Run, and Catch (throwing, catching). Throw the disc as far as possible while still being able to catch it yourself.

Partner Guts (throwing and catching). Player throws the disc as fast as possible to a partner, who tries to catch it. She in turn returns it as forcefully as possible.

Team Guts (throwing, catching). Three players per team, fifteen meters apart. Teams try to throw the disc so that it lands behind the opposing team's goal line. Hard, fast throws and one-handed catches are stressed.

Skip It (throwing, catching, bouncing). Using a backhand throw and a hard surface, throw the disc forcefully so that it hits the floor halfway to a partner. Disc should contact the floor on its edge and rebound upward.

Freestyle (throwing, catching, tipping, "trick" catches, finger delay). With a partner and popular music playing, players are given three to five minutes to throw or catch discs using their own variations.

BASIC RULES FOR ULTIMATE

Ultimate is a team sport that incorporates running, pinpoint passing, and often spectacular catching. It is a fast-paced, noncontact game played on a rectangular field up to one hundred thirty yards long and forty yards wide.

CONCEPT 21.9
The team sport of disc tossing and catching is known as Ultimate.

The game is played with as few as two and as many as seven players per team. The object of the game is to score goals. The disc is moved by passing it to a team member. Once the disc is caught, the player with the disc may not take any forward steps toward the goal. Any time a pass is incomplete, interrupted, knocked down, or contacts an out-of-bounds area, a turnover occurs. A turnover results in an immediate change of possession at the point where the disc is recovered. A goal is scored when a player successfully passes the disc to a teammate in the opposing team's end zone. The game is played in two twenty-four-minute periods. Overtime periods, in case of a tie, are five minutes long. Each team is permitted three time outs per half.

Play is started with a flip of the disc. The team winning the flip may choose the goal they wish to defend, or they may choose to begin the game with the initial throw-off. A throw-off occurs at the beginning of each half and after each goal from anywhere in the players' end zone. The disc may not be touched by an opposing player until after it has first been touched by a teammate of the person making the throw-off. Fouls and violations occur in these cases:

1. More than one defensive player guards a player at a time.
2. There is physical contact between the thrower and the defender.
3. There is contact between opposing players before the disc is caught.
4. A player travels with the disc.
5. A player strips the disc from an opposing player's hands.

A team called for a foul or violation turns the disc over to the opposing team, and play continues in the opposite direction.

ASSESSING PROGRESS

Periodically during a disc sport skill theme you will want to evaluate the progress of individuals and the group. Your assessment can be informal and process-based. It can be conducted during partner practice activities. Table 21.3 gives an example of a simple observational instrument that may be helpful. You should be able to answer "yes" to each of the questions. If you are unable to do so, you will need to modify subsequent lessons to more closely meet the specific needs of students. Assessments may also be product-oriented and include more objective criteria, such as

1. total distances thrown,
2. maximum time aloft,
3. throw, run, and catch for distance, and
4. accuracy throws.

TABLE 21.3   *Self-Question Chart for Disc Throwing and Catching*

Disc Throwing	Yes	No	Comments
1. Does the child use a preferred hand?			
2. Is the child able to control the trajectory of the disc?			
3. Does the child use proper body mechanics?			
4. Is there good wrist snap?			
5. Is there noticeable improvement?			

Disc Catching			
1. Does the child maintain eye contact with the disc throughout?			
2. Does the child adjust easily to a disc throw at different levels?			
3. Does the child adjust easily to a disc throw at different speeds?			
4. Does the child catch the disc successfully on a consistent basis?			
5. Is the catching action smooth, coordinated, and in good control?			
6. Is there observable improvement?			

If you choose to use product measures such as these, assessment is a simple matter of standardizing your assessment items, gathering your information, and interpreting scores. Saving scores over a period of a few years is a good idea if you intend to develop norms.

CONCEPT 21.10
Process, product, and self-referenced assessment techniques may be effectively used with a disc sport skill theme.

Another form of product assessment is the self-referenced method. In this method, the children evaluate their own progress, both at the beginning and at the end of a skill theme. How an individual improves in terms of distance, accuracy, and so forth is noted and becomes the focus of instruction rather than how one compares to the entire group. Examples of self-referenced assessment are given in Chapters 22 through 25. All three forms of assessing progress are acceptable. The methods chosen will depend on your objectives and philosophy of assessment.

SUMMARY

A disc sport skill theme can be easily implemented in most elementary school settings. Discs are inexpensive and easy to store, and they can be used both indoors and outside. Skill in disc sport activities provides children with a valuable recreational and recess play activity as well as the basic skills for modified forms of the team sport of Ultimate.

Elementary school-age children are generally ready to learn a variety of disc tossing and catching skills after they have mastered the fundamental manipulative skills of throwing and catching. Throughout the skill theme strive for maximum participation, providing a disc for every two students. When possible use soft discs for children just beginning to learn how to catch. This will help eliminate the problem of jammed fingers, looking away, or closing the eyes just prior to contact. As skill develops, modify the skill drills contained in this chapter to make them lead-up games. This can easily be done by simply giving the activity a name, making it a game, modifying the rules, and developing scoring procedures.

When children have mastered their basic tossing and catching skills, introduce modified forms of the team sport of Ultimate. Children will love the game, and in terms of rules and strategies it will have carryover value to soccer and flag football. Assessment can be either of a process or a product nature. The choice is yours and depends on your particular situation and your philosophy of assessment.

COMPLEMENTARY READINGS

Kalb, I., and T. Kennedy. (1982). *Ultimate: Fundamentals of the Sport.* Santa Barbara, CA: Revolutionary Publications.

Roddick, D. (1980). *Frisbee Disc Basics.* Englewood Cliffs, NJ: Prentice-Hall.

Roddick, D. (1989). *The Disc Source.* WHAM-O Sports Promotion, 835 E. El Monte Street, San Gabriel, CA 91778–0004.

Tips, C., and D. Roddick. (1979). *Frisbee Sports and Games.* Millbrae, CA: Celestial Arts.

Ultimate Players Association. *The Rules of Ultimate,* P.O. Box 4844, Santa Barbara, CA 93103.

SUPPLEMENTARY READINGS

Donna, M., and D. Poynter. (1978). *Frisbee Player's Handbook.* Santa Barbara, CA: Parachuting Publications.

Tips, C. (1977). *Frisbee by the Masters.* Millbrae, CA: Celestial Arts.

World Flying Disc Federation. (1991). *The Official Rules of Flying Disc Sports.* C/O Dan Roddick, 655 Rim Road, Pasadena, CA 91107.

VIDEOS

The Frisbee Disc Video. Kodak Video Programs. Rochester, NY: Eastman Kodak (30 min.).

CHAPTER 22

Basketball Skill Themes

Key Concept

Basketball Sport Skills Involve Combinations of Mature Fundamental Stability Skills With a Variety of Specialized Manipulative and Locomotor Skills

Chapter Objectives

The purpose of this chapter is to provide you with the tools to:
• Identify the steps in designing a basketball skills theme.
• Describe proper execution of several basketball skills.
• Identify some common developmental difficulties that children encounter as they learn several basketball skills.
• List the skill concepts and movement concepts children should know about basketball passing, catching, dribbling, pivoting, and goal shooting.
• Be familiar with specific means of enhancing basketball skills that are both age-appropriate and individually appropriate.
• List several appropriate warm-up activities for a basketball skills lesson.
• Demonstrate knowledge about the appropriate use of static practice conditions and dynamic practice conditions in basketball skill learning.
• Discuss process and product assessment techniques appropriate for a basketball skills theme.

Terms to Remember

Chest Pass	Stationary Dribbling	Dynamic Practice
Bounce Pass	Moving Dribble	Conditions
One-Handed Overarm	Crossover Dribble	Basketball Process
Pass	Pivoting	Assessment
Two-Handed Overarm	One-Handed Push Shot	Basketball Product
Pass	Jump Shot	Assessment
Two-Handed Underhand	Lay-up Shot	Self-Referenced
Catch	Free Throw Shooting	Assessment
Dribbling	Static Practice Conditions	

Basketball is a very popular game in North American culture and throughout the world. Basketball is truly an American game, invented by Dr. James Naismith in 1892 in Springfield, Massachusetts. Its original intent was to provide a vigorous activity that could be played indoors during the cold New England winters. The original game invented by Dr. Naismith has undergone many changes and has become an international sport enjoyed by both females and males at all levels of ability.

The game of basketball combines and refines numerous fundamental movement skills. Successful basketball sport-skill development depends on attaining mature patterns of fundamental movement. At the elementary school level, basketball instruction should focus on skill development and not on playing the game. This point cannot be overemphasized. Too often teachers skip the skill development phase of the basketball lesson and go directly to playing the game. This may be fine for the more skilled youngsters or for those students who have had previous instruction in the basic skills of the game. However, the less fortunate and less talented are ignored by such an approach. The physical education program that stresses skill development will have little or no time for playing the regulation game of basketball during the regularly scheduled physical education program. Children who desire to play the regulation game should be encouraged to take part in the intramural, interscholastic, or agency-sponsored youth basketball programs found in most communities.

With this in mind, the chapter focuses on the procedures to follow in developing a basketball skills theme or unit and the importance of proper skill sequencing.

CONCEPT 22.1
Basketball skill themes should focus on skill development, not on playing the game.

DEVELOPING A BASKETBALL SKILLS THEME

The primary difficulty encountered in a basketball skills theme with children in the upper elementary grades is the diversity of skill levels. Some children have taken part in youth basketball programs and are relatively proficient in a number of skills. Others have spent hour upon hour shooting baskets or playing playground basketball. And still others have had virtually no experience in any aspect of the game of basketball. The diversity of skill levels in basketball is probably greater than for any other single sport. This presents a unique challenge to the physical educator, namely, to design and implement an instructional unit that will benefit children at all skill levels. To maximize learning and make the best use of your time, it will be helpful to implement the steps of (1) preplanning, (2) observing and assessing, (3) planning and implementing, and (4) evaluating and revising, as discussed in each of the preceding skill theme chapters.

CONCEPT 22.2
Planning and implementing a basketball skills theme involves a four-step process of preplanning, observing and assessing, specific planning and implementation, and evaluation and revision.

BASKETBALL SKILL SEQUENCING

Because of the immense popularity of the game of basketball throughout North America, there will be little difficulty in generating interest among the children. Care, however, must be taken to recognize the wide range of abilities among children in basketball. As a rule of thumb, third and fourth grade students are generally at the beginning level of developing their basketball skills, whereas fifth and sixth graders are typically at the intermediate level.

The suggested teaching progression depicted in Table 22.1 should help you select appropriate basketball skills to focus on as a developmental skill theme. When you have done this, you will need to select appropriate basketball warm-up activities, skill drills, and lead-up games. Basketball warm-up activities are found in the section in this chapter called "Fitness and Skill Development Activities" along with skill drills and lead-up games for basketball. All activities progress from simple to complex and are listed later in the chapter in Tables 22.2 and 22.3. These activities will provide you with a wealth of essential information for implementing a successful basketball skills theme.

CONCEPT 22.3
Elementary school-age children benefit from basketball skill themes stressing skill development in passing, catching, dribbling, pivoting, goal shooting, and a variety of associated skills.

TABLE 22.1   *Selected Basketball Skills Sequenced in Terms of Complexity*

Basketball Skills (page number)	Suggested Progression for Children	
	Beginning Level	Intermediate Level
Passing and Catching		
Chest pass (413)	Introduce	Refine
Bounce pass (414)	Introduce	Refine
One-handed overarm pass (414)		Introduce
Two-handed overarm pass (415)	Introduce	Refine
Catching (415)	Introduce	Refine
Dribbling and pivoting		
Stationary dribble (417)	Introduce	Refine
Moving dribble (417)	Introduce	Refine
Crossover dribble (418)		Introduce
Pivoting (418)	Introduce	Refine
Goal Shooting		
One-handed push shot (420)	Introduce	Refine
Jump shot (420)		Introduce
Lay-up shot (420)		Introduce
Free throw shooting (421)	Introduce	Refine
Associated Skills		
Stopping	Introduce	Refine
Guarding	Introduce	Refine
Rebounding		Introduce
Understanding the Game		
Rules (429)	Introduce	Refine
Strategy (429)		Introduce

PASSING AND CATCHING

Passing and catching are the basic ways in which the ball is transferred from one player to another. There are several types of passes used in basketball. The type of pass used will depend on the distance the ball must travel and the location of opposing players. The manner in which the ball is caught will depend on the location of the passed ball in terms of height and trajectory.

The chest pass, bounce pass, one-handed overarm pass, and two-handed overarm pass are important basketball passing skills to be learned. When they are performing two-handed passes, be sure to remind students to step forward on the same foot as the dominant hand. This will help them achieve maximum force. Teaching tips for passing and catching skills, a list of common developmental difficulties, and recommended teaching strategies follow, along with a list of concepts children should know. Verbal and visual descriptions are also included for study.

Chest Pass

The **chest pass,** the most frequently used form of passing in basketball, is effective for short passes and is used when an opposing player is not in the intended path of the ball.

FIGURE 22.1 *Basketball chest pass.*

Verbal Description

- Ball is held chest-high.
- Hands grip the ball from the side, toward the back.
- Fingers are spread with thumbs close together.
- Elbows are close to the body.
- Step forcefully forward with the dominant foot.
- At the same time, extend arms forcefully.
- Push ball off the fingertips.
- Ball is caught at chest level.

Visual Description.   (Figure 22.1)

Bounce Pass

The **bounce pass** may be executed three different ways. The two-handed bounce pass should be learned first. Only after this has been mastered should the one- and two-handed overhand bounce pass be taught. The bounce pass is an effective passing skill used to cover a short distance when an opposing player prevents use of the chest pass. It is also an effective pass to use to penetrate the defense. Children will need to experiment with the bounce pass at different distances to become familiar with the proper trajectory. The two-handed bounce pass is described here.

Verbal Description

- Ball is held chest-high.
- Hands, arms, and legs are positioned in the same way as for a chest pass.

FIGURE 22.2 *Two-handed bounce pass.*

- Ball is pushed forward and downward.
- Ball contacts floor about three-quarters of the distance from the passer to the catcher.
- Ball rebounds at waist level to catcher.

Visual Description.   (Figure 22.2)

 CONCEPT 22.4
Children encounter predictable developmental difficulties in learning basketball skills that can be overcome through the application of appropriate teaching strategies.

One-Handed Overarm Pass

The **one-handed overarm pass,** or baseball pass, as it is frequently called, is used for long throws. This pass is difficult to control and should be taught only with a smaller than regulation size ball at the elementary school level. When students are performing the one-handed overarm pass, be sure to stress that the lead foot is the same as the throwing arm, thereby aiding in control.

Verbal Description

- Assume stride position.
- Ball is held with fingers spread in throwing hand.

FIGURE 22.3 *One-handed overarm pass.*

FIGURE 22.4 *Two-handed overarm pass.*

- Nonthrowing hand steadies ball as it is brought to shoulder level.
- Body weight shifts to the rear foot and then onto the forward foot.
- As body weight is shifted forward, hips and shoulders forcefully rotate.
- Ball is released with a downward snap of wrist and fingers.
- The arm is extended at the point of aim.

Visual Description.   (Figure 22.3)

Two-Handed Overarm Pass

The **two-handed overarm pass** is used when one player wants to pass to a teammate above the reach of an opponent. It is also effective as an inbound passing technique.

Verbal Description

- Ball is held overhead with arms slightly bent.
- Hands grip the sides of the ball.
- Fingers are spread.
- Step forcefully forward on the dominant foot.
- Weight is transferred to forward foot as ball is brought forward.
- Arms follow through with extension at the elbows.
- Wrists and fingers turn downward and snap forward.

Visual Description.   (Figure 22.4)

Catching

The manner in which the basketball is caught will depend on the height of the ball and the trajectory at which it is intercepted. The chest pass should be caught at chest level, the bounce pass at waist level, and the two overarm passes over the head. The baseball pass is frequently caught using a **two-handed underhand catch** pattern. A description common to all forms of catching a basketball follows.

Verbal Description

- Ball is visually tracked into the hands.
- Both hands contact the ball at the same time.
- Hands make contact on the sides or behind the ball.
- Arms "give" on contact to absorb force.
- Legs are positioned in stride position with knees bent slightly.
- Legs "give" slightly on contact to absorb force.

Visual Description.   (Figure 22.5)

Teaching Tips
Developmental Difficulties

- Has poor control.
- Has insufficient force.
- Lacks accuracy.

FIGURE 22.5 *Basketball catching.*

- Has poor summation of forces.
- Has insufficient follow-through.
- Fails to transfer weight forward.
- Traps a caught ball against the trunk.
- Fails to track a passed ball into the hands.

Recommended Strategies

- Stress control prior to accuracy.
- Stress force after reasonable control is mastered.
- Stress accuracy only after control has been gained and force is sufficient.
- Use a smaller ball to help gain control.
- If possible, have a ball for every other child.
- Stress following through by having the child point at the target after the ball is passed.
- Use floor markings (line, carpet square) as a visual reminder to step forward.

- Practice against a wall before working with a partner.
- Use a Nerf-type ball for children who appear to be afraid of catching the ball.
- Emphasize visual tracking of the ball when catching.
- Attempt to get directly in the path of the ball when catching.

Concepts Children Should Know
Skill Concepts

- Step toward your target as you release the ball.
- Keep your eyes on your target.
- For two-handed passes, keep your elbows in and close to your body.
- For two-handed passes, apply equal amounts of force to each hand.
- Snap your wrists and follow through with your fingers pointing toward the target.
- Lead your teammate with a pass to where she will be when the ball arrives.
- Pass to the opening, not to the player.
- Catch a passed ball before moving toward the basket.
- Passing and catching should first be practiced under static conditions and then in progressively more complex, dynamic game situations.

Movement Concepts

- The speed at which a passed ball travels to a teammate is determined by the summation of forces applied.
- The ball will respond to all of the forces applied to it. Conflicting forces will result in an inaccurate pass.
- The speed of your passes can be and must be adjusted to meet the demands of the situation.
- Your passes will require greater coordinated summation of forces as the distance increases.
- In a dynamic game situation, your passes and your catching will need to be varied as the immediate conditions dictate.
- Catching will occur at unexpected levels and from varying directions during dynamic game situations.
- Balls traveling at different rates of speed require varying amounts of force absorption.

DRIBBLING AND PIVOTING

Dribbling is repeated one-handed bouncing of the ball, the way in which the ball is advanced by a player from one point to another. It is an integral part of the game of basketball and must be reasonably mastered under static practice situations before being used in skill drills and lead-up games, in which the conditions of the environment (an opposing player) are ever changing. Stationary dribbling should be introduced first, followed by the moving dribble, and finally crossover dribbling. While dribbling skills are being mastered, pivoting may be included in the lesson. Pivoting is the primary way in which the player with the ball avoids attempts by an opponent to take the ball away. In the sections that follow you will find teaching tips, concepts children should know that apply to all forms of dribbling and pivoting, and verbal and visual descriptions of each dribbling and pivoting skill.

Stationary Dribble

Stationary dribbling should first be mastered with the preferred hand and then with the nonpreferred hand.

Verbal Description

- Feet assume a narrow stride position.
- Legs are bent slightly.
- Ball is held in hand opposite forward foot.
- Trunk leans forward slightly.
- Ball is pushed downward off the fingertips with follow-through from the arm, wrist, and fingers.
- Downward thrust is controlled.
- Ball returns no higher than waist level and action is repeated.
- Eyes do not monitor the ball.

Visual Description.   (Figure 22.6)

Moving Dribble

Once the stationary dribble has been reasonably mastered, the **moving dribble** should be introduced. The same action is employed, with the addition of the following:

Verbal Description

- Body is held low with bend at the knees and a slight forward lean.

FIGURE 22.6 *Stationary dribbling.*

FIGURE 22.7 *The moving dribble.*

- Ball is pushed slightly forward with each downward thrust.
- Ball is kept to the side of the body as player advances forward.

Visual Description.   (Figure 22.7)

Crossover Dribble

The **crossover dribble** is often difficult for elementary students to master because it requires considerable coordination and use of the nonpreferred hand. All elements are the same as in the stationary dribble, with the addition of the following:

Verbal Description

- Ball is pushed from one side of the body to the other.
- A slight sideward thrust occurs as the ball is projected downward.
- Body is kept low.
- Action is fluid and relaxed.
- Directional changes are made as needed.

Visual Description.   (Figure 22.8)

Pivoting

Pivoting is a basic element of footwork in the game of basketball, and it involves changing direction of movement by rotating around a fixed point. Practice in pivoting should stress movement control with emphasis on maintaining one's declared pivot foot.

Verbal Description

- Feet are parallel and shoulder width apart.
- Knees are slightly bent and weight is evenly distributed.
- Trunk is bent forward slightly.
- Hands are held in front of the body (with or without the ball).
- Eyes focus forward.
- Weight transfers to ball of pivot foot.
- Nonpivot foot pushes off and body makes a one-quarter turn (forward or backward) around the pivot foot.
- Pivot foot remains stationary around a fixed point at all times.

Teaching Tips
Developmental Difficulties

- Visually monitors the ball.
- Slaps at the ball.

FIGURE 22.8 *The crossover dribble.*

- Momentarily palms the ball while dribbling (double dribble).
- Unable to dribble well with either hand.
- Fails to protect the ball from an opponent.
- Has insufficient follow-through.
- Has poor rhythmical coordination of movements.
- Changes pivot feet.
- Drags the pivot foot.
- Fails to crouch properly when pivoting.
- Fails to protect the ball when pivoting.

Recommended Strategies

- Work first for control of the ball.
- Practice stationary dribbling before any other form.
- Practice under static environmental conditions prior to dynamic drill and game situations.
- Stress keeping the ball low and close to the body while dribbling.
- Use wall markings to encourage students not to monitor the ball visually.
- Practice dribbling first with the preferred hand, then, after reasonable mastery, the nonpreferred hand.
- If possible, have a ball for each student in the class.

- Teach pivoting in conjunction with dribbling and catching.
- Use appropriate background music for children having difficulty hearing the rhythm of the movement.

Concepts Children Should Know
Skill Concepts

- Dribble the ball off to the side of the body.
- To be skillful in dribbling, you must not visually monitor the ball.
- Control the downward thrust of the ball with your fingertips.
- Dribble low to minimize the chances of losing the ball.
- Keep your body between the ball and your opponent.
- Once dribbling has been reasonably mastered with the preferred hand, it should be practiced with the other hand.
- Do not get your hand too far under or behind the ball because you will be called for a double dribble.
- Pivot on the ball of the established pivot foot.
- Learn to pivot with both feet or either foot.
- Be in the "ready" position when pivoting, prepared to pass or receive the ball.

Movement Concepts

- You can dribble the ball with varying amounts of force.
- The speed of your dribbling will be determined by the distance the ball must travel.
- The height of your dribble will be determined by the amount of force applied.
- You can dribble at different levels and in different directions.
- Your follow-through will strongly influence return of the ball.
- Dribbling should be rhythmical and controlled.
- The speed of your pivot will be determined by the push-off foot.
- You can pivot forward or backward.
- You can adjust your level while pivoting.

FIGURE 22.9 *The stride stop pivot.*

Visual Description   **(Figure 22.9)**

CONCEPT 22.5
Learning the movement concepts and skill concepts associated with basketball equips children with the essential tools for self-improvement.

GOAL SHOOTING

Basketball goal shooting is an essential skill. Successful shooting demands considerable coordination and sufficient power to be able to get the ball up to the level of the goal. With elementary-age children, it is recommended that the basketball goals be lowered to eight feet and the size of the ball be reduced. If the goals cannot be lowered, two sets of free throw lines can be painted on the floor with tempera paint or taped on the floor, each two feet closer to the goal than the free throw line. These modifications will permit practice with the proper techniques of goal shooting and will promote success. Basketball goal shooting is a very popular recreational activity. Emphasis should be placed, however, on the proper techniques of shooting. At the elementary school level, the one-handed push shot, the jump shot, the lay-up shot, and free throw shooting should be taught. What follows are teaching tips, concepts children should know that are common to all forms of basketball goal shooting, and verbal and visual descriptions of each shot.

One-Handed Push Shot

The **one-handed push shot,** or set shot, as it is frequently called, is generally easier to master and much more frequently used than the two-handed push shot. Therefore, it is recommended that the one-handed shot be taught rather than the two-handed shot. It is generally used when shooting from a fairly long distance without an opposing player directly in the line of the shot.

Verbal Description

- Feet are in a narrow stride position, knees slightly bent.
- Shooting hand corresponds to forward foot.
- Ball is held with both hands opposite the chin and in line with the lead foot.
- Back is straight and the eyes are focused on the rim of the basket.
- Ball is tipped back onto the spread fingers of the shooting hand with the wrist cocked.
- Elbows are kept in.
- Knees and arms extend simultaneously and nonshooting hand releases ball.
- Shooting arm extends forward and upward in a high arc.
- Ball is released from fingertips with a slight snap of the wrist.

Visual Description.   (Figure 22.10)

Jump Shot

The **jump shot** is similar to the one-handed set shot, but it has the addition of the release of the ball at the height of a vertical jump. The jump shot is generally used for shots closer to the basket than the set shot and when an opposing player is in direct line with the shot. It is probably the most difficult shot for children to learn because of the summation of forces required.

Verbal Description

- Same upper body action as the one-handed push shot.
- Jump is from both feet.
- Jump is straight up.
- Ball is released at height of jump.

FIGURE 22.10 *The one-handed push shot (set shot).*

Visual Description.   (Figure 22.11)

Lay-up Shot

The **lay-up shot** involves driving toward the basket by means of dribbling or receiving a pass, leaping into the air, and releasing the ball off one hand. If the basket is approached from the left, the ball will be rolled off the left hand; if from the right, it will be rolled off the right hand. The lay-up shot has the highest scoring percentage in basketball and is frequently easier for children to master than either the one-handed set shot or the jump shot.

Verbal Description

- Approach the basket from either the left or right.
- Takeoff is from the foot opposite shooting arm.
- Execute a one-foot leaping takeoff, moving up toward the basket.
- Ball is brought up as far as possible with both hands.
- The nonshooting hand releases ball.
- The shooting hand is under the ball with fingers spread.
- Ball is pushed with shooting hand gently against backboard.
- Ball contacts backboard slightly above the hoop.

FIGURE 22.11 *The jump shot.*

FIGURE 22.12 *The lay-up shot.*

Verbal Description

- Feet are parallel or in a short stride position with weight evenly distributed.
- Knees are slightly bent and back is straight.
- Both hands are on the sides and slightly under the ball.
- Fingers are spread and ball is gripped by the fingertips.
- Ball is held down and in front of the body with the arms straight.
- Eyes focus on the basket rim.
- The arms swing forward and upward as the legs straighten.
- Ball is released at chest level in a high arc.
- Ball is released simultaneously from fingertips of both hands.
- Back remains straight and arms follow through.

Teaching Tips
Developmental Difficulties

- Elbows jut out from the body.
- Lowers the arms toward the waist when preparing to shoot.
- Places the wrong foot forward.
- Fails to monitor the goal visually throughout the entire shot.
- Lacks follow-through.

Visual Description.   (Figure 22.12)

Free Throw Shooting

The key to successful **free throw shooting** is consistency. Whatever technique is adopted, and there are many, complete concentration, rhythmical execution, and exact repetition of all actions from the moment the player steps to the free throw line to the moment that the ball reaches the basket are a must. The one-handed set shot is the most popular form of free throw shooting. The mechanics are the same as described earlier. The two-handed underhand free throw shot is also often used by elementary-age children and is described here.

- Fails to extend the wrist and fingers.
- Applies unequal force to both hands (for the two-handed set shot and the underhand free throw shot).
- Lacks force to get the ball up to the basket without altering the correct pattern of movement.
- Has limited accuracy.

Recommended Strategies

- Lower the basket.
- Use a smaller ball.
- Emphasize proper mechanics.
- Provide numerous opportunities for practice in a static drill situation prior to dynamic situations.
- Stress visually monitoring the ball until it touches the basket.
- Practice following through on all shots by pointing toward the basket after each shot.
- Modify scoring with less skilled children. (Score one point for hitting the backboard, two points for hitting the rim, and three points for making a basket.)
- Tape a target on the backboard to indicate where ball should strike.
- Focus on the process (mechanics) prior to the product (ball going through the hoop).
- Structure activities for success, particularly at the early stages of skill learning.
- Do not deal in absolutes during the early stages of learning (i.e., reward approximations).
- Remember a smaller ball or a lower basket will reduce many of the problems in mechanics and force production.
- For free throw shooting, stress exact repetition of the entire sequence from the moment you step to the line until the ball arrives at the basket.
- Stress total concentration on all shots.

Concepts Children Should Know

Skill Concepts

- Keep your elbows in close to your body.
- Work for coordinated summation of the forces of the legs, trunk, and arms.
- The angles made by the wrists and elbows form a square prior to extension.

- Look at the basket throughout the shot.
- Follow through with your shots.
- Extend at the wrist and fingers at the end of your shot.
- Work for a high arc on the ball.
- On angle shots, make the ball hit the backboard before it goes through the hoop.
- Remember that the angle of reflection is exactly opposite the angle of incidence.
- With the lay-up shot, you take off on the foot opposite your shooting hand.
- With the one-handed set shot, you assume a narrow stride position with the same foot forward as your shooting hand.
- For the jump shot, release the ball at the height of your jump.
- When shooting free throws, repeat the same process each time.
- Practice, practice, practice.

Movement Concepts

- You can shoot the ball from varying levels.
- You can shoot the ball at varying angles from the basket.
- You can shoot the ball from varying distances from the basket.
- Your field goal percentage will increase as you attempt shots closer to the basket.
- You can cause the ball to travel in varying pathways toward the basket (high arc, low arc, or flat).

FITNESS AND SKILL DEVELOPMENT ACTIVITIES

Mastering basketball skills involves progressing from the simple to the more complex and progressing from practice with single skills to practice with multiple skills. The foundational skills of the game must be mastered before you incorporate them into basketball game activities. The reason for this is simple. **Static practice conditions** (conditions in which the environment remains the same, as in a stationary passing drill or a zigzag dribbling drill) at the beginning level of skill development foster learning. Static practice conditions help the player form a conscious mental picture of the skill and get the idea of how it is to be performed. After this has been accomplished, it is then wise to practice the same skills under **dynamic practice conditions** (conditions in which the environment is constantly changing, as in a two-on-one passing drill or a one-on-one dribbling drill). Players at the intermediate level of movement skill learning benefit from dynamic skill drills. The sampling of warm-up activities, skill drills, and lead-up games presented in this section proceed from simple to complex and may be practiced under static or dynamic conditions.

C O N C E P T   2 2 . 6
Basketball warm-up activities and skill drills serve as an important avenue for fitness enhancement and skill development, respectively.

Warm-up Activities

The warm-up activities that follow should be engaged in for twenty to thirty seconds each, for five to seven minutes. Select several and move quickly from one to the next. Variety and proper execution are important to get maximum enjoyment and benefit from the warm-up session.

Each of the following activities involves the use of a ball. If a basketball is not available for every child, volleyballs, soccer balls, or playground balls will do.

Stand and Stretch.   Holding the ball overhead, stretch forward and hold, sideways and hold, backward and hold, sideways and hold. Repeat in the opposite direction.

Sit and Stretch.   From a sitting position with the legs spread and holding the ball overhead, bend forward and touch the ball to the toes of one foot and hold. Keep the arms straight. Try to touch the floor and hold. Then move to the other foot and hold.

Stretch and Roll.   From a sitting position with the legs together, roll the ball around the body, first in one direction, then in the other. Repeat with the legs spread wide apart.

Push and Catch.   Lying on your back, push the ball up with both hands (four to six feet) and catch it. Repeat with a one-handed push shot.

Stretch and Dribble.   From a sitting position with the legs spread, dribble the ball around the body, first in one direction and then in the other.

Arch.   Lying on your stomach with the ball overhead, raise the ball off the ground as the head and chest lift off. Repeat several times.

Rocker.   This is the same as the preceding exercise, but raise the legs also. Repeat several times.

Half Push-ups.   From a push-up position (use modified push-up position if necessary), lower the body until the nose touches the ball and return. Repeat several times.

Sit-ups.   Lying on your back with the legs straight and arms extended overhead, sit up, bringing the knees to the chest and swinging the arms forward.

Chest Curl.   Lying on your back with the knees bent and ball held at the chest, curl the trunk around the ball until the shoulders and upper back are off the ground. Hold. Repeat several times.

Dribble and Run.   Dribble the ball several times around the perimeter of the gymnasium.

Around the Body.   From a standing position, circle the ball rhythmically around the body several times, starting high and working low and returning to high (head, chest, waist, thighs, knees, and ankles).

Body Weave.   This is the same as the preceding exercise, but weave the ball between the legs while stretching forward.

Human Dribble.   With a partner, one player acts like a ball being dribbled as the other pushes down on her head. Change positions.

Skill Drills

A wide variety of skill drills can be introduced and practiced with elementary school children. (See Table 22.2.) Each of the skill drills that follow can be modified to fit the varying skill levels of the children in a class. By giving the drill a name and introducing an element of competition, you can easily turn it into a game. Be careful, however, not to emphasize the game aspect (product) until the basic mechanics (process) have been reasonably mastered. The primary objectives of the skill drills that follow are to

1. improve passing and catching skills (chest, bounce, one-handed and two-handed passes);

TEACHING TIPS

The following sequence of skill drills and lead-up game activities is recommended to maximize basketball skill learning:

- Introduce single skills under static conditions ("walk-through").
- Practice single skills in a controlled, dynamic environment (drill).
- Introduce multiple-skill drills in a static environment.
- Practice multiple-skill drills in a controlled, dynamic environment.
- Implement multiple skills in simple lead-up game activities.
- Practice multiple skills in increasingly complex lead-up game activities.

2. improve dribbling and pivoting skills (stationary, moving, and crossover dribbles);
3. improve basketball goal-shooting abilities (one-handed push, jump, and lay-up shots);
4. introduce the associated skills of stopping and rebounding;
5. improve endurance levels (aerobic and muscular endurance); and
6. develop group cooperation and teamwork.

Wall Pass (chest pass and catch).   From a position two to three feet from the wall, the player executes a chest pass against the wall and catches it on the rebound. Work for control and then speed. As skill progresses move back from the wall.

Partner Pass (passing and catching).   With a partner, practice passing and catching. Stand about six feet apart and gradually increase distance as skill increases.

Over-Under (chest pass and bounce pass).   One partner performs a chest pass, while the other executes a bounce pass at the same time. This forces each player to react quickly to an oncoming ball and to release the ball quickly.

Keep Away (passing).   With three people, practice chest, bounce, and overhead passes between two players while the third tries to intercept the passed ball.

Overhead Pass (overhead passing).   With a partner, practice overhead passing to a partner ten feet away. As skill develops, increase the distance to twenty feet and play keep-away.

Line Passing (passing and catching).   With six to eight in a line, practice passing in a zigzag manner from one end of the line to the other. Work for control before concentrating on speed.

Star Passing (passing and catching).   With five players in a star formation, each player passes to a second person to the left. Add a second ball as skill increases. Practice passing back and forth. As skill develops, call the player's name to be passed to. Then pivot and pass suddenly without notice. This will help improve reaction time and reinforce the need to be ready to receive a pass at all times.

Stationary Dribble (dribbling).   Players practice dribbling in their own space, first from a double-knee kneeling position, then from a single-knee position, and finally from a standing position. Skilled players may practice crossover dribbles and dribbling between the feet.

Dribble and Look (dribbling).   Players practice dribbling while looking forward at the instructor. The instructor may hold up letters, numbers, or simple math facts to be answered to encourage dribbling without visually monitoring the ball.

Line Dribble (dribbling).   Players each find a line of the floor and dribble while walking forward on the line. Each time a new line intersects, players change direction and follow the new line.

Line-Dribble Pass (dribbling).   This is the same as the preceding exercise, except that each time two players meet coming from opposite directions, they must pass each other while continuing to dribble the ball and remaining on the line.

Wander Dribble (dribbling).   Players dribble informally about the room, taking care not to interfere with each other. This will promote kinesthetic awareness of the player's surroundings and reduce visual monitoring. As skill increases, reduce the area.

TABLE 22.2   *Developmental Activities Chart for Basketball Sequenced in Terms of Complexity*

Drills (page number)	Passing and Catching	Dribble and Pivoting	Goal Shooting	Associated Skills
Wall pass (424)	x			
Partner pass (424)	x			
Over-under (424)	x			
Keep away (424)	x			
Overhead pass (424)	x			
Line passing (424)	x			
Star passing (424)	x			
Stationary dribble (424)		x		
Dribble and look (424)		x		
Line dribble (424)		x		
Line-dribble pass (424)		x		
Wander dribble (424)		x		
Directional dribble (425)		x		
Chair dribble (425)		x		
Dribble and weave (425)		x		
Pivot drill (426)		x		
Pivot wall pass (426)		x	x	
Partner pivot (426)		x	x	
Four-point pivot (426)		x	x	
Pivot keep away (426)		x	x	
Center guard (426)		x	x	x
Spot shot (426)			x	
Two-column free throw shooting (426)			x	
Pass and shoot (426)	x		x	
Dribble and shoot (426)		x	x	
Pass, pivot, and shoot (426)	x	x	x	
Block that shot (426)	x		x	x
Rebound ball (426)	x		x	x

Directional Dribble (dribbling). Players face the instructor and, while dribbling, move in the direction to which instructor points. May be performed with a whistle for less skilled players who visually monitor the ball (one blast = forward, two blasts = backward, three blasts = sideways).

Chair Dribble (dribbling). Players dribble around a chair, being sure to keep their bodies between the ball and the chair.

Dribble and Weave (dribbling). With four to six chairs in a straight line, the player dribbles from one end to another, weaving in and out of the chairs and back. Stress switching hands and keeping the body between the ball and the chair.

Pivot Drill (pivoting). Players face instructor, holding a ball in both hands in the ready position. Instructor points to the left or right, and players pivot in that direction. As skill develops, have the players fake a pass in the direction pivoted. Practice first with quarter-turns and then half-turns.

Pivot Wall Pass (pivoting and passing). From a position three to five feet from the wall, player stands with his back to the wall, pivots, and chest-passes the ball against the wall. Repeat in both directions.

Partner Pivot (pivoting and passing). With a partner, practice pivoting first with the partner standing still, then moving to one side, then moving to the other side.

Four-Point Pivot (pivoting and passing). Player in the center of a square formed by four players pivots and passes from one player to the next. Practice first with small pivots, then larger.

Pivot Keep Away (pivoting, passing, and guarding). One player practices pivoting and passing to a second player, while a third player tries to tie up the ball. Change positions so all have a chance at each position.

Center Guard (pivoting, passing, and guarding). With six to eight players in a circle and two in the center, one player attempts to pivot and pass the ball to the outer circle, while a second attempts to block the pass. When the ball is at the outside of the circle, players attempt to pass to the center player, who is being guarded.

Spot Shot (goal shooting). With six to eight players per basket, players stand in an arc and practice shooting from that spot. When a shot is made from that spot, players move along to another.

Two-Column Free Throw Shooting (goal shooting). With six to eight players per basket, stand in two columns at the free throw line. The first player in column A shoots at the basket and goes to the end of column B. The first player in column B retrieves the ball and passes it to the next player in column A, while going to the back of column A.

Pass and Shoot (goal shooting and passing). One player passes to a partner, who takes a shot at the basket. Practice first from close range, then gradually increase the distance. Practice from several spots on the floor.

Dribble and Shoot (goal shooting and passing). With two columns of six to eight players per column, players in column A dribble forward and attempt a layup shot, while players in column B retrieve the ball and pass to the next person in column A. Players go to end of the opposite column.

Pass, Pivot, and Shoot (passing, pivoting, and goal shooting). One player passes to another who has his or her back to the basket. Player pivots and shoots.

Block That Shot (passing, stopping, goal shooting, and guarding). One player passes to a partner, who stops, sets, and shoots the ball, while a third player attempts to block the shot.

Rebound Ball (shooting, rebounding, and passing). One player shoots at the basket, while a partner rebounds the ball and passes it back. As skill develops, work for rebounding the ball while in the air.

C O N C E P T   2 2 . 7
Lead-up games are an effective and fun means of reinforcing basketball skills in a controlled competitive environment.

Basketball Lead-up Games

Basketball lead-up games are popular with most children. However, be sure to match the game to the skill level of your students. Table 22.3 presents a wide variety of basketball-type games in progression from simple to complex. Modifications can be made in the height of the basket and the size of the ball. The objectives of including basketball lead-up games in the program are to

1. reinforce the basketball skills of passing and catching, dribbling and pivoting, goal shooting, and guarding;
2. introduce the basic rules of basketball through modified game activities;
3. provide opportunities for developing an understanding for, and an appreciation of, basic team strategies;
4. encourage a spirit of cooperation and teamwork toward a common goal; and
5. permit students to play a modified game of basketball with reasonable skill and enjoyment.

Five Passes

Movement Skills: Passing and dribbling.

Formation: Scatter formation with four to six players per team.

Equipment: One basketball for each group.

TABLE 22.3 *Suggested Progression for Introducing Basketball Lead-Up Games Sequenced in Terms of Complexity*

Lead-Up Games (page number)	Passing and Catching	Dribbling and Pivoting	Shooting	Guarding	Team Play
Five passes (426)	x	x		x	
Circle keep away (427)	x			x	
Hands up (427)	x			x	
Dribble-pivot-pass (427)	x	x			
Base basketball (428)	x		x		
Twenty-one (428)			x		
Around the world (428)			x		
Six-Hole basketball (428)			x		
Nine-Court basketball (428)	x	x	x	x	x
Sideline basketball (429)	x	x	x		
Half-Court basketball (429)	x	x	x	x	x
Backline basketball (429)					

Procedures: One team takes the ball and scatters around an area approximately forty feet by forty feet. The other team assumes a guarding position. The object of the game is for the team with the ball to make five complete passes. If the team guarding intercepts a pass, they attempt to complete five passes. A team is given one point each time they complete five passes. Violations occur in several instances: (1) If the ball is passed repeatedly between the same two players, the ball is awarded to the other team. (2) If the team with the ball walks or double dribbles, the ball goes to the other team. (3) If the team with the ball is fouled, it counts as a completed pass. (4) All "jump balls" are awarded to the team previously in possession of the ball.

Suggestions: Use a junior-model basketball for younger children. Use armbands or bandannas to distinguish teams.

Circle Keep Away

Movement Skills: Passing, catching, and guarding.

Formation: Single circle of eight to ten players facing inward, with one player in the center.

Equipment: One basketball per group.

Procedures: The ball is thrown from one player in the circle to another in any sequence. The center player tries to intercept the ball. If successful, that player trades places with the person who touched the ball last and that person becomes the center player.

Suggestions: Vary the passes used. Score one point for each successful pass.

Hands Up

Movement Skills: Passing, catching, and guarding.

Formation: Two teams of six to eight players each. One team forms a circle; the other is scattered within the circle.

Equipment: One basketball per game.

Procedures: One team makes a circle on the outside of the boundaries while the other team gets into a scatter formation on the inside. The outside players try to pass the ball to each other while the players in the center try to stop the ball by keeping their hands up to intercept or knock the pass down. The ball may not be thrown over the heads of the center players. After two minutes, the teams change positions. One point is scored each time the ball is passed successfully below head level through the opposing team.

Dribble-Pivot-Pass

Movement Skills: Dribbling, pivoting, and passing.

Formation: File formation with four to eight players per group.

Equipment: One basketball per team.

Procedures: Players in each group line up one behind the other. The first player on each team quickly dribbles the ball to a line fifteen feet from the starting line, pivots on the right (work on left also), and passes the ball back to the next player in line for one point. The first team to get twenty points (or any number agreed upon) is the winner.

Base Basketball

Movement Skills: Passing, catching, and goal shooting.

Formation: Baseball diamond with thirty-foot bases drawn on the gymnasium floor with home plate under the basket. Six to ten players per team.

Equipment: Basketball and goal.

Procedures: The players are divided into two teams. Each person is given a number so that a player from one team will have the same number as a player on the opposing team. One team is behind home base, while the other team is in the field. Number 1 of the batting team passes the ball to a teammate from the home base using any type basketball pass. The passer then circles the bases without stopping. Meanwhile, the corresponding number sets himself near the basket. His teammates get the ball and must make two or three chest passes, then pass it to him. The person at the basket must make a goal before the runner circles the bases or the runner is safe and scores a point. If the goal is made before the runner circles the bases, an out is made; three outs constitute a change of sides. One point is scored for each run made.

Twenty-One

Movement Skills: Goal shooting.

Formation: Two to six players scattered around a basket.

Equipment: One basketball and a goal.

Procedures: Players alternate taking long and short shots. Long shots (from behind the foul line) are worth two points if made. Short shots (anywhere in front of the foul line) count one point if made. The first player to get twenty-one points is the winner. The player shooting baskets continues alternating long and short shots until he misses or reaches twenty-one; then the next player takes his turn.

Suggestions: Score points for hitting the backboard or rim for beginners.

Around the World

Movement Skills: Goal shooting.

Formation: Group of four to six players in scatter formation around basket.

Equipment: One basketball and a goal.

Procedures: An area around the basket is marked for one-, ten-, and fifteen-foot distances on each side of the basket. Each player attempts to make a basket from each of these areas. A player must first make the basket from the distance closer to the basket before progressing to the next distance. A player shoots until he misses (his effort later resumes where he stopped). The first player to make a basket from each spot wins.

Six-Hole Basketball

Movement Skills: Goal shooting.

Formation: Six three-foot circles marked off around the outside of the free throw shooting area and six to ten players per group.

Equipment: One basketball and one goal for each group.

Procedures: The circles are called holes. Each player in turn tries to make a basket, beginning at circle one. For every basket made, the player advances one hole until he misses. Two holes are marked "safe" (usually two and four). If one player overtakes another and he is not in a hole marked "safe," the first player must return to the first hole and begin again. The first player to get to hole six is the winner.

Nine-Court Basketball

Movement Skills: Passing, pivoting, goal shooting, guarding, and team play.

Formation: Basketball court divided into nine equal areas, with one player from each team assigned to each area.

Equipment: One basketball and two goals.

Procedures: Played like basketball except each player is assigned an area and must stay within that boundary. Players advance the ball toward their goal by passing and may dribble once. Only forwards may shoot at the goal. The ball is put in play by a center jump. An unguarded free shot worth one point is awarded for fouls such as blocking and holding. The ball is taken out of bounds for infractions such as crossing a line or traveling.

Sideline Basketball

Movement Skills: Passing, catching, dribbling, pivoting, and goal shooting.

Formation: Eight to twelve players per team, with half on the sideline and half on the court.

Equipment: One basketball and two goals.

Procedures: Half of the team scatters about the court area and the other half lines up along the sideline. The game begins with a jump ball between any two opponents. The team gaining possession of the ball tries to make a goal (each successful attempt counts two points). The ball is advanced by dribbling and passing. Players on the court may pass the ball to a teammate on the sideline, who in turn may pass the ball to a teammate on the court. After each successful goal attempt, stolen ball, or defensive rebound, the ball must be passed to a player on the sideline. Violations are as follows: (1) For touching, double dribble, and foul violations, the other team is awarded the ball. (2) In jump situations, the team in possession is awarded the ball.

Half-Court Basketball

Movement Skills: All basic basketball skills.

Formation: Scatter formation with five players per team.

Equipment: One basketball and one goal per game.

Procedures: The rules of basketball govern fouls, penalties, and general playing situations. A throw-in is used to start the game and to restart play after each score. The player making the throw-in must be standing with one foot in the center circle. The player taking the throw-in is unguarded. On an out-of-bounds play, two completed passes must occur before a goal may be attempted. Violations include: (1) A player may not try for a goal following a free throw missed by a member of the opposing team until the ball has first been passed to the back court and returned. *Penalty:* The goal, if made, does not score, and the ball is awarded to a member of the opposing team out of bounds at a sideline. (2) A player may not carry or cause the ball to go over the center line. *Penalty:* The ball is awarded to an opponent out of bounds at a sideline of the neutral zone. The scoring is the same as in regulation basketball.

Backline Basketball

Movement Skills: All basic basketball skills.

Formation: Standard scatter formation with five players per team.

Equipment: One basketball and one goal per game.

Procedures: The rules and scoring are the same as in half-court basketball. The one difference is that every time a shot is taken, if it is rebounded by the opposition, it must be taken behind the free throw line before a shot can be taken. If the shot is rebounded by the shooting team, it may be shot again.

BASIC RULES FOR BASKETBALL

Basketball is played on a court up to ninety-four feet long and fifty feet wide. The game is played by two opposing teams of five players each. The object is to gain possession of the ball, advance it into a scoring position by passing or dribbling, and get it through the opponents' basket. The team that does not have the ball tries to stop the other team from scoring by trying to get possession of the ball so they can score at the other end of the court. A field goal counts two points. Free throws, given for an infringement of a playing rule, count one point each.

CONCEPT 22.8
Activity concepts involving basic rules, strategies, formations, and patterns of play should be incorporated into a basketball skills theme.

A team is made up of two forwards, two guards, and a center. A jump ball at the center circle starts the game at the beginning of each half. After a field goal, the ball is put back into play by the team scored upon through a throw-in from out of bounds behind their basket.

Frcc throws from the free throw line are awarded to a player who had a foul committed against her by an opposing team member. For less serious violations of the playing rules, a team loses possession of the ball.

ASSESSING PROGRESS

It will be necessary to assess both the entry and exit level of children's basketball skills. Because of the vast difference in the amount of experience children have had in practicing the skills and playing the game, there will be a wide range of ability levels. Determining ability levels and measuring progress can be done rather quickly and reliably. Although a number of objective basketball skills tests exist, it is recommended that teachers at the elementary school level be concerned with subjective assessment of mechanics or techniques (process assessment) and self-referenced assessment of performance abilities (product assessment).

CONCEPT 22.9
Basketball skills may be assessed using both process and product assessment techniques.

Process Assessment

Basketball process assessment is based on the teacher's judgment of children's level of ability in terms of exhibiting the correct mechanics in the performance of one or more basketball skills. The instructor is concerned primarily that the proper techniques are being used to pass, dribble, and shoot the ball. Children can be informally assessed during a skill drill or lead-up game activity. By charting their abilities at the beginning of an instructional unit and again at the end, you can determine the amount of progress made and what skills need to be emphasized in the future. The rating chart depicted in Figure 22.13 will help you determine where students are in terms of their basketball skills.

Product Assessment

A number of basketball skills tests have been reported in the professional literature. However, their validity for use with elementary school-age children is questionable, along with their administrative feasibility. It is therefore recommended that you consider developing your own **basketball product assessment** of skill attainment.

Teacher-made tests of basketball skills are easy to devise. Simply save your yearly skill test results and develop your own norms from there. Also, it is appropriate at the elementary school level to develop your own **self-referenced assessment** instrument. A self-referenced test of basketball skills is one that is either self-administered or administered with the help of a partner. It simply compares the student's present performance with previous performances. The student compares his or her entry level assessment information with exit level information. This technique works quite well with children, particularly when the operational philosophy of the physical education program is one of individual improvement and the teacher is not pressed into assigning letter grades. The sample self-referenced basketball skills test depicted in Figure 22.14 will help students determine where they are in terms of their basketball abilities. It will also help the teacher objectively measure skill learning and may serve as a useful report to parents of student progress.

SUMMARY

The tremendous popularity of the sport of basketball is undeniable, especially if you live in Indiana. Basketball is a sport enjoyed by boys and girls alike, and the growth of youth basketball programs over the past ten to fifteen years is truly amazing. This, however, frequently results in a problem for the instructional physical education program. Several children in a class may be fairly proficient and at the intermediate level in a variety of basketball skills because of their previous sport experiences, whereas others are complete novices and only at the beginning level of basketball skill learning. When this situation arises, and it surely will, teachers are faced with the dilemma of meeting the needs of two groups with vastly different skill levels and experience.

Care should be taken to structure basketball skill themes so that all students are challenged and all benefit from instruction. Use of a station or circuit approach with two or three different achievement levels for each skill should help motivate all students to achieve. Using more skilled students as helpers is also helpful. At no time, however, is it defensible to bow to the wishes of those vocal students asking you to "just let us play basketball." The entire purpose of a basketball skills theme is to help children at *all* levels improve their basketball skills. Skill drills and lead-up games should be designed so that all will benefit from the unit of instruction.

BASKETBALL SKILLS RATING CHART

Class: _____   Grade: _____

Entry Assessment Date: _____   Exit Assessment Date: _____

Directions	Passing/Catching Skills				Dribbling/Pivoting Skills				Goal-Shooting Skills				Associated Skills		Key
Observe during drill or play situations. Mark entry rating in upper left corner and exit ratings in lower right corner of each square.	Chest Pass	Bounce Pass	Two-handed Pass	Baseball Pass	Stationary Dribble	Moving Dribble	Crossover Dribble	Pivoting	Push Shot	Jump Shot	Lay-up Shot	Free Throw	Guarding	Rebounding	**A: Advanced—** Correct technique plus good control and force production
															I: Intermediate— Correct technique but lacking in control or force production
															B: Beginning— Inconsistent use of correct technique
															Comments:

FIGURE 22.13 *Sample form rating chart for basketball.*

BASKETBALL SKILLS RATING CHART

Student's
Name: _____ Grade: _____ Class: _____ Year: _____

See Reverse for Description		Skills	Entry Rating	Comments	Exit Rating	Comments
Thirty-Second Chest Pass	Thirty-Second Bounce Pass	*Passing*	Date		Date	
B I A <10 10–15 16>	<5 6–10 11>	Chest Pass				
		Bounce Pass				
Down and Back	Zigzag Dribble	*Dribbling*	Date		Date	
B I A 25>sec. 15–25 sec. <15 sec.	30>sec. 20–30 sec. <20 sec.	Moving Dribble				
		Crossover Dribble				
30-Second Layups	10 Free Throws	*Shooting*	Date		Date	
B I A <5 6–10 11>	3 for 10 4–7 for 10 8 for 10	Goal Shooting				
		Free Throw Shooting				

Parent's Signature: _____ Date: _____
Comments:

KEY: B = Beginning Level   **I = Intermediate Level**   **A = Advanced Level**
       of Skill   **of Skill**   **of Skill**

Description of Tests:

30-Second Chest Pass: With a partner, player stands behind a line 3 feet from the wall. On the signal "go" player does chest pass against the wall as many times as possible in 30 seconds. Must stay behind line.

30-Second Bounce Pass: Same as above, but from a line 5 feet from the wall, player executes bounce and catch against wall for 30 seconds.

Down and Back: With a partner timing, player dribbles the ball in a straight line from the starting line to a line 45 feet away and back as fast as possible.

Zigzag Dribble: With a partner timing, player weaves in and out of 4 chairs placed in a line 5 feet apart, beginning 15 feet from the starting line, touches the 45-foot line, and returns.

30-Second Layups: With a partner timing, player shoots the ball at the basket as many times as possible in 30 seconds on the sound of "go." Score number of baskets made in 30 seconds.

10 Free Throws: From behind the free throw line, player takes 10 shots. Score the number of baskets made.

FIGURE 22.14 *Sample self-referenced performance rating card for basketball.*

COMPLEMENTARY READINGS

ACEP. (1991). *Rookie Coaches Basketball Guide.* Champaign, IL: Human Kinetics.

Garchow, K., and A. Dickinson. (1992). *Youth Basketball: A Complete Handbook.* Dubuque, IA: Wm. C. Brown & Benchmark.

Howard, R. (1993). Drills to improve foul shooting. *Strategies* 7:20–23.

Krause, J. (1991). *Basketball Skills and Drills.* Champaign, IL: Human Kinetics.

SUPPLEMENTARY READINGS

Jeffries, S., and R. Levin, eds. (1984). *Y Basketball Coaches Manual.* Champaign, IL: Human Kinetics.

Krause, J. (1990). *Basketball Resource Guide.* Champaign, IL: Human Kinetics.

Levin, R. (1984). *I. Y Basketball Passers Manual; II. Y Basketball Dribblers Manual; III. Y Basketball Shooters Manual.* Champaign, IL: Human Kinetics.

VIDEOS

Basketball Coaches' Corner Teaching Tape. Women's Basketball Coaches Association. Champaign, IL: Human Kinetics. (90 min.).

Becoming a Basketball Player. Champaign, IL: Human Kinetics. (series of five 20 min. videotapes).

Reach for the Skies. Webb, Spud. Charleston, WV: Cambridge Physical Education and Health. (60 min.).

Teaching Kids Basketball. Wooden, J. 200 Castlewood Drive, North Palm Beach, FL: The Athletic Institute. (75 min.).

Youth Basketball: The Team Practice for Boys. Champaign, IL: Human Kinetics. (31 min.).

Youth Basketball: The Team Practice for Girls. Champaign, IL: Human Kinetics. (31 min.).

CHAPTER 23

Soccer Skill Themes

Key Concept

Soccer Skill Themes Focus Primarily on Manipulative Skills with the Feet, But They Also Involve Use of Fundamental Stability and Locomotor Skills

Chapter Objectives

The purpose of this chapter is to provide you with the tools to:
• List and describe the steps in developing a soccer skills theme.
• Design a soccer skills theme that is both age-appropriate and individually appropriate for a given group of elementary school-age children.
• Describe correct execution of a variety of soccer kicking, trapping, dribbling, and volleying and goalkeeping skills.
• Describe common developmental difficulties that children encounter in learning soccer skills.
• Provide evidence of competence in incorporating teaching strategies designed to reduce or eliminate developmental difficulties encountered by children in learning various soccer skills.
• List the skill concepts and the movement concepts that children should know about soccer kicking, trapping, dribbling, and volleying.
• Provide evidence of knowledge of basic soccer rules and strategies.
• Be familiar with a variety of skill drills and lead-up games designed to develop and reinforce soccer skills.
• Incorporate a variety of appropriate warm-up activities into a soccer skills theme.
• Show how both process and product assessment techniques may be effectively used to evaluate children's soccer skills.

Terms to Remember

Instep Kick	Inside-of-Foot Trap	Heading
Push Pass	Inside-of-Thigh Trap	Penalty Kick
Inside-of-Foot Kick	Chest Trap	Free Kick
Punt	Dribbling	Throw-In
Trapping	Inside-of-Foot Dribble	Corner Kick
Shin Trap	Outside-of-Foot Dribble	Goalie Kick
Sole-of-Foot Trap	Juggling	Soccer Fouls

The game of soccer is undoubtedly the most international of all sports. It is played in practically every country and enjoyed by millions worldwide. Historically, the game has been called *football* throughout most of the world. The derivation of this word comes from the London Football Association, which formalized the game and developed the rules in 1863. They called the game *Association Football*. The word *association* was later shortened to *assoc,* which later became *soccer.* Because of the increased popularity of "American football" in North America, the game finally became known as *soccer* in North America, but it remains *football* throughout the rest of the world.

Soccer is a great game for the elementary physical education program because it can be played equally well by boys and girls and it requires no specialized equipment other than a ball. Children of all sizes and skill levels can take part in the game and find enjoyment. Its continuous action and vigorous nature promote many aspects of physical fitness and improved coordination. The rules are simple, the objectives clear, and the variations limitless. For these reasons, soccer has been selected for inclusion in this text rather than the game of football. Although football is an important game in North American culture, it lacks many of the benefits of soccer and may be more appropriately introduced in the physical education programs at the middle school or junior high school level. Furthermore, the popularity of soccer in North America has grown tremendously among children in the last several years and will continue to grow for years to come.

CONCEPT 23.1
A soccer skills theme requires the same sequential progression of preplanning, observation and assessment, specific planning and implementation, and evaluation and revision as any other skill theme.

To make the best use of your time and to maximize learning when focusing on the development of soccer skills, it will be helpful to follow the sequence of (1) preplanning, (2) observing and assessing, (3) planning and implementing, and (4) evaluating and revising.

SOCCER SKILL SEQUENCING

The soccer skills program should be based on the present level of ability of the class or group. In terms of soccer skill learning, third and fourth grade children are typically at the beginning level, while fifth and sixth graders are often at the intermediate level of skill learning. Remember, however, that this does not guarantee that all are at the level typical for their age. Some may be ahead, and others may be behind. It is important, however, for you to know the skill levels of your students if you are to plan more effectively for all. Table 23.1, Selected Soccer Skills, will help you to select appropriate soccer skills to teach. Each of the four basic skill sections contains teaching tips and concepts children should know. Brief descriptions of appropriate warm-up activities, skill drills, and soccer lead-up games are located in the section called "Fitness and Skill Development Activities" at the end of this chapter and are highlighted in Table 23.2.

CONCEPT 23.2
It is essential that skill sequencing for soccer skill development follows both the age-group appropriate and individually appropriate guidelines of developmental physical education.

KICKING SKILLS

Kicking is the primary method of advancing the ball in soccer. Several types of kicks are used. Frequently children unfamiliar with the skills of soccer will want to use a toe kick. This form of kicking is seldom if ever used in soccer because of poor control. The instep kick, push pass, inside-of-foot kick, and punt are all important kicking skills that can be developed with elementary school children.

Instep Kick

The **instep kick** is probably the most frequently used kicking pattern in soccer. The instep is that portion of the foot directly behind the toes, where the laces of your shoes are located. Children will frequently want to kick with the toe, but with practice they can develop skill in using the instep kick. The instep kick is used for passing and goal shooting.

TABLE 23.1 *Selected Soccer Skills Sequenced in Terms of Complexity*

Soccer Skills (page number)	Suggested Progression for Children	
	Beginning Level	*Intermediate Level*
Kicking		
Instep kick (435)	Introduce	Refine
Push pass (438)	Introduce	Refine
Inside-of-foot kick (438)	Introduce	
Punting (439)	Introduce	
Trapping		
Shin trap (441)	Introduce	
Sole-of-foot trap (441)		Introduce
Inside-of-foot trap (442)	Introduce	Refine
Inside-of-thigh trap (442)	Introduce	Refine
Chest trap (443)		Introduce
Dribbling		
Inside-of-foot dribble (444)	Introduce	Refine
Outside-of-foot dribble (444)		Introduce
Volleying		
Juggling (446)		Introduce
Heading (446)		Introduce
Associated Skills		
Basic goalkeeping	Introduce	Refine
Screening/blocking	Introduce	Refine
Tackling		Introduce
Understanding the Game		
Rules (453)	Introduce	Refine
Strategy (453)		Introduce

TABLE 23.2   *Developmental Activities Chart for Soccer Sequenced in Terms of Complexity*

Soccer Drills (page number)	Kicking Skill	Trapping Skills	Dribbling Skills	Volleying Skills	Associated Skills
Wall kick (448)	X	X			
Target kick (448)	X	X			
Partner pass (448)	X	X			
Circle pass (448)	X	X			
Criss-cross passing (448)	X	X			
Distance kick (449)	X				
Accuracy kick (449)	X				
Partner punting (449)		X			
Partner trapping (449)		X			
Toss and trap (449)		X			
Circle trap (449)			X		
Follow the leader (449)			X		
Shadow (449)			X		
One-on-one dribble kick (449)			X		
Dribble shuttle (449)			X		
Obstacle dribble relay (449)			X		
Push-pass relay (449)	X	X	X		
Volley drill (449)				X	
Circle volley (449)				X	
Keep-it-up (449)				X	
Partner keep-it-up (449)				X	
One-on-one (449)	X		X	X	X
Three-on-three (449)	X	X	X	X	X
Three-on-three change (449)	X	X	X	X	X

FIGURE 23.1 *The instep kick.*

Verbal Description

- The ball is approached from behind and slightly to one side.
- The nonkicking foot is in line with the ball, pointing in the direction desired.
- The head and trunk lean forward slightly.
- The eyes focus on the ball.
- The kicking leg is brought backward with an acute bend at the knee and hip.
- The kicking leg is swung forcefully forward and the arms move in opposition.
- Contact is made low on the ball for a high pass and at the center for a low pass.
- The kicking leg follows through in the direction of the intended path of the ball, and the support foot raises to the toes or loses contact with the ground.

Visual Description.   (Figure 23.1)

Push Pass

The **push pass,** or inside-of-foot kick, as it is sometimes called, is an effective kick for short, accurate passes to a teammate and for dribbling. It should be practiced equally with both feet so that it may be performed in either direction. The push pass can be likened to using the inside of the foot as a "daisy-cutter."

Verbal Description

- The head and trunk lean forward slightly to a position directly over the ball.
- The eyes focus on the ball.
- The support foot is placed parallel to the ball, six to twelve inches to the side, with the knee bent slightly.
- The kicking leg is drawn backward from the hip in a straight line.
- The knee is bent, with the inside of the foot cocked and facing the ground.
- The leg is swung forcefully forward with the ankle cocked and stiff.
- Contact is made with the inside of the foot, toward the arch and ankle bone.
- The kicking leg follows through in front of the support leg in the intended direction of the ball.

Visual Description.   (Figure 23.2)

Inside-of-Foot Kick

The **inside-of-foot kick** is a type of push pass used for short passes, when dribbling, and when trying to avoid an opponent. It is not a forceful pass and should be practiced with both feet in order to develop skill in either direction.

FIGURE 23.2 *The push pass.*

FIGURE 23.3 *The inside-of-foot kick.*

Verbal Description

- The head and trunk lean forward slightly to a position directly over the ball.
- The eyes focus on the ball.
- The support leg is parallel to and about the length of one's foot from the ball.
- The kicking foot is lifted with the toes pointed down and rotated inward.
- The ankle joint is locked.
- The leg is swung forward and downward, with contact made on the inside of the foot.
- The leg follows through in the intended path of the ball.

Visual Description.   (Figure 23.3)

CONCEPT 23.3
Children should develop proficiency in a variety of foot manipulative skills involving soccer kicking, trapping, dribbling, and volleying.

Punting

A **punt** is a kick frequently used by the goalkeeper. In fact, the goalkeeper is the only player permitted to punt the ball because it requires contacting the ball with the hands. It is used for lifting the ball high and kicking long distances.

Verbal Description

- The body is in a stride position with the trunk bent slightly forward, and the ball is held waist high with both hands.
- The body weight is transferred to the non-kicking leg, and the eyes focus on the ball.
- The kicking leg is drawn backward with an acute bend at the knee, and the arms are extended forward.
- The leg extends forcefully forward as the ball is dropped.
- Contact is made with the instep, and the leg follows through in the intended path of the ball.
- The closer to the ground that the ball is contacted, the lower the trajectory will be.

Visual Description.   (Figure 23.4)

Teaching Tips
Developmental Difficulties

- Kicks with the toes. The toe kick is rarely used in soccer.
- Fails to get in line behind the ball.
- Takes the eyes off the ball.
- Contacts a moving ball too soon or too late.

FIGURE 23.4 *Punting.*

- Lacks accuracy and control.
- Contacts the ball too low or too high.
- Inappropriate amount of backswing.
- Places the nonkicking foot improperly.
- Fails to use the arms in rhythmic alternation to the legs.
- Has poor summation of the forces of the arms, trunk, and leg.
- Lacks follow-through.
- Fails to lead teammate.

Recommended Strategies

- When indoors, use partially deflated balls, foam balls, or indoor soccer balls.
- Provide a ball for at least every other child.
- Do not teach the toe kick; it will only inhibit learning of other kicking skills.
- Do not permit toe kicks. They lift the ball too high, are difficult to control, and may cause injury.
- Allow children to protect their faces and chests with their arms for high kicked balls.
- Emphasize keeping the ball low and under control.
- Paint or tape a spot on the ball to demonstrate where contact should be made.
- Stress keeping the eyes on the ball.

- Stress the chest being positioned over the ball at the point of contact.
- Emphasize getting behind the ball and following through.
- Practice kicking with both feet.
- Practice first in static and then dynamic drill situations. Then move to increasingly complex lead-up games as skill develops.

Concepts Children Should Know
Skill Concepts

- Get behind the ball.
- Keep your eyes on the ball.
- Step into your kick with the nonkicking leg.
- The placement of your nonkicking foot will determine the direction of flight.
- Use your arms for balance and to aid in force production.
- A toe kick is of little use in soccer.
- It is important to be able to control your kick.
- Follow through.

Movement Concepts

- You can control the speed of the ball by the force of your kick.

- The force of your kick is determined by the coordinated action of your arms, trunk, and leg.
- Snap at the knee.
- You can control the range of your kick through the amount of force applied by the forcefulness of your knee snap.
- You can control the height of the ball by the point of contact.
- You can influence the height of the ball by the portion of your foot that makes contact.
- You can control the direction of your kick by the placement of your nonkicking foot, the portion of your foot that makes contact with the ball, and the angle at which contact is made.
- The greater the surface area contacting the ball, the greater the control you will have.
- You can pass the ball to a partner through controlled kicking.

FIGURE 23.5 *The shin trap.*

CONCEPT 23.4
Soccer skills should be introduced and refined in a progression that is congruent with the individual level of student ability.

TRAPPING SKILLS

Trapping is the method used to stop and control an approaching ball that is rolling on the ground or traveling in the air. The arms and hands are the only portions of the body not permitted to contact the ball when executing a trap. The type of trap used will depend on the height, trajectory, and speed of the ball. Trapping requires precise movements. Several forms of trapping can be mastered by children in the elementary grades. The shin trap, the sole-of-foot trap, the inside-of-foot trap, the inside-of-thigh trap, and the chest trap are discussed in this section.

Shin Trap

The **shin trap** is used for controlling a rolling or low-bouncing ball. It is an excellent skill to learn as an introduction to trapping.

Verbal Description

- The body is brought into position directly behind the ball.
- The eyes track the ball to the point of contact.
- The feet are parallel, about four inches apart.
- As the ball approaches, the knees are flexed and the trunk bends slightly forward.
- The arms move out from the side for balance.
- The ball is wedged downward by the shins as contact is made.

Visual Description.   (Figure 23.5)

Sole-of-Foot Trap

The **sole-of-foot trap** is used for completely stopping a rolling ball. It is often difficult for younger children to master, especially in a game situation, because of the precise eye-foot coordination required.

Verbal Description

- The body is placed directly behind and in line with the ball.

FIGURE 23.6 *The sole-of-foot trap.*

FIGURE 23.7 *The inside-of-foot trap.*

- The eyes track the ball to the point of contact.
- One foot is raised about eight inches off the ground with the ankle cocked, forming a forty-five-degree angle between the ground and the ankle.
- The ball is contacted by the sole of the foot, at the back and toward the top, and squeezed toward the ground.
- The contact leg and foot give slightly upon impact.

Visual Description.   **(Figure 23.6)**

Inside-of-Foot Trap

The **inside-of-foot trap** is used extensively for stopping a rolling, bouncing, or low aerial ball. It is the most frequently used trap in soccer and should be practiced with balls coming from different angles, at different heights, and at various speeds. It should be practiced with both the left and the right foot.

Verbal Description

- The body is placed in as near a direct line with the ball as possible.
- The eyes track the ball to the point of contact.
- The body weight is supported on the nontrapping leg.
- The trapping leg is brought back slightly.
- The ankle is rotated so that the inside of the foot is in direct line with the ball.

- The inside of the foot contacts the back and top portion of the ball.
- The contact foot "gives" slightly as the ball is wedged down toward the ground.

Visual Description.   **(Figure 23.7)**

Inside-of-Thigh Trap

The **inside-of-thigh trap** is used for controlling a ball that approaches at a level above the knees but below the chest. The force of the ball is absorbed by the inner part of the upper thigh. This is not a difficult trap for children to master, but it should be practiced first with a partially deflated or foam ball.

Verbal Description

- The body is placed in line behind the ball.
- The eyes track the ball to the point of contact.
- The arms move out from the side of the body as needed to aid balance.
- The trapping leg is lifted forward and upward, with the knee rotated outward.
- Upon contact midway along the inner thigh, the leg "gives" quickly to absorb the impact.
- The ball is deflected downward to a point just in front of the support foot.

FIGURE 23.8 *The thigh trap.*

FIGURE 23.9 *The chest trap.*

Visual Description.   (Figure 23.8)

Chest Trap

The **chest trap** should be used by elementary-age children only after the other forms of trapping have been mastered. The chest trap takes time to learn and is used for an aerial ball approaching above waist level but below the shoulders. Practice should first be done with a partially inflated or foam ball.

Verbal Description

- The body is brought directly in line with the path of the ball.
- The eyes track the ball to the point of contact.
- The feet are placed in a stride position, with the knees bent and the hips thrust forward.
- The shoulders are behind the hips, with the chest thrust forward.
- The arms are held out from the sides of the body.
- As the ball makes contact with the chest, the knees flex deeper and the chest "gives" with the impact of the ball.
- The ball drops beside the forward foot and is controlled with a sole trap.

Visual Description.   (Figure 23.9)

Teaching Tips
Developmental Difficulties

- Fails to monitor the ball visually.
- Fails to get behind the ball.
- Closes the eyes or turns the head on aerial balls.
- Fails to "give" with the ball upon contact.
- Loses balance.

Recommended Strategies

- Provide a ball for at least every other child.
- Stress keeping the eyes on the ball until it touches the body.
- Emphasize getting in line behind the ball.
- Emphasize "giving" with the ball.
- Practice maintaining a wide base of support while trapping.
- Use foam balls when introducing aerial trapping.
- Strive for control of the ball within six inches of the body.
- Work for control in static drill situations, and then add performing a pass or dribbling immediately after trapping the ball.

Concepts Children Should Know

Skill Concepts

- Get behind the ball.
- Keep your eyes on the ball.
- Maintain a wide base of support.
- "Give" with the ball as it contacts you.

Movement Concepts

- You can trap the ball with different body parts.
- The body part used to trap the ball will depend on the height of the ball.
- The amount of "give" to your trap will be directly proportional to the speed of the ball.
- The trapping surface generally applies downward force to the ball.
- The timing of your trapping action is very important.
- The faster the ball is traveling, the faster your "giving" action must move.
- Trapping is followed by immediate performance of another skill, usually passing or dribbling.

CONCEPT 23.5
The movement concepts and skill concepts learned in a soccer skills theme provide children with the tools for self-practice and independent learning.

DRIBBLING SKILLS

Dribbling is the method by which the ball is moved, under control by the feet, down the field of play. It involves making short pushes of the ball forward or sideways with either foot. Controlled dribbling takes considerable practice, first without an opponent and then with an opponent, who attempts to steal the ball. There are two primary forms of dribbling, the inside-of-foot dribble and the outside-of-foot dribble. Both are presented here.

Inside-of-Foot Dribble

The **inside-of-foot dribble** is the most basic form of foot dribbling. It is the one used most frequently by beginners and skilled players alike.

FIGURE 23.10 *The inside-of-foot dribble.*

Verbal Description

- The body is directly behind the ball in a controlled running action.
- The ball is contacted and pushed diagonally forward with the inside of the forward foot.
- The distance of the push depends on the degree of control desired.
- The ball travels diagonally forward and is contacted by the opposite foot on the next or subsequent forward action of that leg.
- Although visual monitoring is common, effort should be made to look in the direction of travel.

Visual Description.   (Figure 23.10)

Outside-of-Foot Dribble

The **outside-of-foot dribble** is used in conjunction with the inside-of-foot dribble and is especially useful when making sudden changes in direction. It should be introduced after the basic inside-of-foot dribble has been reasonably mastered.

Verbal Description

- Body is aligned with the ball in the same way as with the inside-of-foot dribble.

FIGURE 23.11 *The outside-of-foot dribble.*

- Contact is made with the outside of the foot against the ball.
- The ball is pushed in the same direction as the kicking foot. The exact direction depends on the angle of contact.
- The body realigns itself behind the ball, and forward progress continues with the inside-of-foot dribble.

Visual Description. **(Figure 23.11)**

Teaching Tips
Developmental Difficulties

- Kicks the ball with the toe.
- Kicks the ball too far in front of the body.
- Visually monitors the ball.
- Unable to alter direction.
- Unable to use both feet equally well.

Recommended Strategies

- Use a partially deflated ball or foam ball when learning the skill indoors.
- Stress control prior to speed.
- Stress control while moving forward before making directional changes.

- Practice making short pushing actions, alternating the left and right feet.
- Push the ball diagonally forward and not to the side, unless you are avoiding an opponent.
- Permit visual monitoring only during the early phase of learning.
- After control is gained, work for speed and controlled directional changes.
- Practice static drill situations prior to dynamic game situations.

Concepts Children Should Know
Skill Concepts

- Push the ball; don't kick it.
- Keep the ball under your control.
- Don't use your toes; stay behind the ball.
- Dribble without looking down at the ball.
- Contact the ball as often as possible as you advance it forward.

Movement Concepts

- You can contact the ball with varying amounts of force.
- You can dribble the ball with different amounts of speed.
- You can dribble either forward or sideways.
- You can change direction while dribbling.
- You can dribble with the ball close to you.
- You will not be able to control the ball if you dribble it too far in front of you.
- You can alter the flow of your dribbling.
- Your dribble is a rhythmic step-step-kick action under static conditions, but it alters under dynamic conditions.
- You can use your body to screen an opponent while dribbling.
- You will need to alter the direction of your dribble continually to evade opponents.

CONCEPT 23.6
Children encounter a variety of predictable developmental difficulties as they learn progressively more complex soccer skills.

VOLLEYING SKILLS

Juggling and heading are the two primary ways in which the path of an aerial ball may be altered without first trapping the ball. The ball may be juggled off the instep, knee, or thigh. Heading is a specialized form of volleying in which the direction of the ball is altered by contact with the head. Juggling and heading should be introduced along with the other basic skills of soccer. Heading should generally wait until the other skills have been reasonably mastered. Heading should be introduced only to the most skillful players and generally not before the fifth grade. Controlled heading and juggling require practice first in controlled drill situations with the use of a foam or partially deflated ball. A regulation soccer ball should be introduced only after the basic mechanics have been mastered.

Juggling

Juggling may be done off the inside or outside of the foot, the knee, or the thigh. Repeated juggling of the ball to oneself is an excellent drill for mastering control of the ball.

Verbal Description

- The body part (inside or outside of the foot, thigh) is brought into direct line with the ball.
- The body part selected will be determined by the path of the approaching ball.
- The eyes visually track the ball to the point of contact.
- The body weight is shifted to the support foot and the contact leg is lifted to the desired position.
- The arms are held out to the side to aid balance.
- The body part stiffens upon contact and the leg follows through in the intended new direction of the ball.

Visual Description.   (Figure 23.12)

Heading

Heading, when taught at the elementary school level, should be done from a standing position. Jumping or power heading is too dangerous to be a regular part of the program.

Verbal Description

- The legs are placed in a stride position with the knees slightly bent.
- The hips are thrust forward, and the shoulders are lined up with the rear foot.

FIGURE 23.12 *Juggling.*

- The body weight is on the rear foot.
- The arms are held out from the sides.
- The head and chin are raised, and the eyes follow the path of the ball to the point of contact.
- Contact is made at the hairline.
- The neck is kept stiff.
- As contact is made, the body weight is shifted forward and upward, and the knees straighten.
- Rock into the ball from the hips.

Visual Description.   (Figure 23.13)

Teaching Tips
Developmental Difficulties

- Fails to get directly behind the ball.
- Fails to monitor the ball visually until contact.
- Fails to stiffen the body properly to cause the ball to rebound.
- Relaxes the body part on contact.

Recommended Strategies

- Work first with balloons and foam balls. Then work with a partially deflated ball.
- Color-code the ball and have the student call out the color that is making contact.
- Practice first with lightly tossed balls.
- Stress keeping the eyes on the ball.

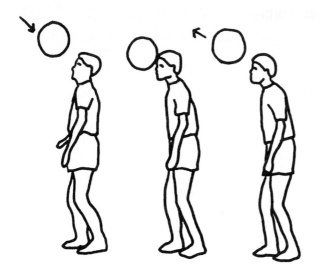

FIGURE 23.13   *Heading.*

- Emphasize following through with the body part in the intended direction of the ball.
- Practice under static drill conditions prior to dynamic game situations.

Concepts Children Should Know
Skill Concepts

- Keep your eyes on the ball.
- Get in direct line with the path of the ball.
- Keep the body part still upon contact.
- Follow through after contact.

Movement Concepts

- You can volley the ball with different body parts.
- Repeated volleying to oneself is called juggling.
- Volleying with the head is called heading.
- The body part used to volley the ball will depend on its height at the point of interruption.
- The trajectory (arc) of the ball will be determined by the point of the ball contacted.
- The distance the ball travels after contact will depend on the amount of force applied.
- The direction the ball travels after impact will depend on the angle at which it was contacted.

FITNESS AND SKILL DEVELOPMENT ACTIVITIES

If children are to master the skills of soccer, it will be necessary for them to first practice the skills individually in static drill situations. After the basic elements of the skill have been mastered, it should be practiced under controlled dynamic drill situations, in which the conditions of the environment change based on the nature of the drill. Drills that combine the use of two or more skills should then be added, and finally lead-up games should be performed in an open environment. The warm-up activities, skill drills, and lead-up games presented in this section proceed from simple to complex, in that they range from static practice drills to dynamic practice activities and from single-skill to multiple-skill activities.

 CONCEPT 23.7
A variety of warm-up activities and soccer skill drills may be used to enhance physical fitness and improve soccer skills.

Warm-up Activities

Warm-up activities are essential prior to vigorous play in the game of soccer. The activities that follow may be performed in the gymnasium or on the playing field. Each child should have a ball. A volleyball or playground ball will do. Each of the activities that follow should last only twenty to thirty seconds, proceeding from simple to complex. Variation in the warm-up drills and rapid movement from one to another are the keys to a successful warm-up session.

Dribble Around.   From a standing position, dribble the ball with the hands around the body, moving clockwise and then counterclockwise.

Roll Around.   From a sitting position with the legs straight, roll the ball with the hands around the legs and body, clockwise and then counterclockwise.

Sit and Stretch.   From a sitting position with the legs straight, lift the ball with both hands back behind the head, stretching back. Then relax forward so the ball touches the toes.

Rocking.   Lying on your stomach with the arms overhead holding the ball, lift the toes and rock.

Jump and Catch.   From a standing position with the ball between the feet, jump up and catch the ball. Work for higher and faster jumps.

Ball Push-ups.   Do push-ups while holding the ball. Spread the legs to aid balance.

Ball Sit-ups.   Do sit-ups, starting with the ball overhead and the legs straight. Sit up, swinging the ball overhead while bending the knees toward the chest.

Prone Dribble.   Lying on your stomach with the arms overhead, bounce the ball with the hands.

Ball Jump.   From a standing position, jump forward, sideways, and backward over the ball.

Body-Ball Roll.   From a sitting position with the legs straight and the ball resting between the legs, roll the ball back and forth from the ankles to the chest without using the hands.

Body-Ball Catch.   From a standing position, toss the ball upward, catching it without using the hands or arms. Repeat several times, using several variations.

Twister.   From a sitting position with the legs straight and the ball between the feet, twist from side to side with the legs elevated.

Twist and Roll.   This is the same as the preceding exercise, but roll over without losing control of the ball.

Jump and Touch.   Jump off the left foot and touch the top of the ball with the right foot. Repeat with opposite feet. Practice in rhythmical cadence.

Sole Dribble.   Dribble the ball with the soles of the feet.

Keep It Up.   Juggle or lead the ball off the instep or thighs.

Aerobic Dribble.   Dribble the ball with the feet from one end of the field to the other, alternating fast and slow dribbles.

Wall Kick.   From five feet away from a wall, kick the ball against the wall as often as possible. Use both feet.

Agility Dribble.   Dribble and trap the ball down the field with direction changes or speed changes every time whistle is blown.

Skill Drills

A wide range of skill drills can be successfully practiced by children at all levels of ability. The primary emphasis of soccer skill drills should be on improving the skills of kicking, trapping, dribbling, and volleying. You can, however, make a game out of any drill simply by giving it a name, making a few modifications in the procedures, and modifying the objectives. The following is a sampling of soccer drills appropriate for elementary school children. The primary objectives of the soccer skill drills that follow are to

1. improve soccer kicking skills (instep kicks, push pass, inside-of-foot kick, and punting);
2. improve trapping skills (shin trap, sole-of-foot trap, inside-of-foot trap, inside-of-thigh trap, and chest trap);
3. enhance dribbling abilities (inside-of-foot dribble and outside-of-foot dribble);
4. develop basic skills in volleying (juggling and heading);
5. introduce basic tackling skills;
6. improve overall fitness (aerobic endurance, coordination, agility, and muscular endurance); and
7. promote group cooperation and teamwork.

Wall Kick (push pass).   From varying distances, practice kicking the inside-of-foot kick against a hard, flat surface. Stress working with both feet. Practice rhythmical alteration of the feet. Practice along with an outside-of-foot kick. First trap the ball on each rebound. Then volley the ball back on each rebound.

Target Kick (instep kick and trapping).   Using an instep kick, practice kicking at a designated target against a hard surface. Stress work with both feet. Trap the ball on each rebound.

Partner Pass (kicking and trapping).   With a partner, practice passing, first from a stationary position and then to a moving partner (be certain to teach players how to lead their partner). Then practice passing from a moving position.

Circle Pass (kicking and trapping).   With six to eight players in a circle, practice passing the ball around the circle. Work for control first, speed later. Then add two or three balls.

Criss-Cross Passing (kicking and trapping).   With six to eight players in a circle, practice passing the ball across the circle. Call out the name of the player being kicked to.

Distance Kick (instep kicking).   Practice the instep kick for distance with a partner at the opposite end of the field.

Accuracy Kick (kicking).   Player stands with legs spread while partner attempts to kick ball between the legs, using an appropriate kick.

Partner Punting (punting).   Practice punting for distance with partner at the opposite end of the field.

Partner Trapping (trapping).   Ball is tossed by a partner at varying heights, angles, and speeds. Player attempts to control the ball, using appropriate trapping actions.

Toss and Trap (chest trap).   Player tosses the ball up and attempts to control it with a chest trap.

Circle Trap (trapping).   With six to eight players in a circle and a leader in the center, the ball is tossed at varying heights without warning to anyone in the circle.

Follow the Leader (dribbling).   Leader dribbles ball in various directions; class follows in the same direction, each with his own ball.

Shadow (dribbling).   One player leads *without* a ball, partner follows, dribbling with a ball. Emphasis is placed on looking ahead.

One-on-One Dribble Kick (dribbling and tackling).   Each partner has a ball. Each dribbles his or her own ball in a defined area while attempting to kick the partner's ball away.

Dribble Shuttle (dribbling).   From a shuttle relay formation with lines forty to sixty feet apart, player A dribbles ball to opposite end. Player B controls ball and returns. Process is repeated. The drill may also be used with players at one end only, passing the ball back to the head of the line.

Obstacle Dribble Relay (dribbling).   Cones or chairs are placed ten to fifteen feet apart. Player A dribbles around the markers and back. Player B controls the ball and repeats the process. The drill may be varied by using shuttle formations with players at each end. Stress control prior to speed.

Push-Pass Relay (push pass and trapping).   Players are in a shuttle relay formation ten to fifteen feet apart. Each player, in turn, passes the ball to the opposite player, who controls the ball and push-passes it back. The drill may be varied by having the player run to the back of the opposite line after passing the ball or run to the opposite line and back to the rear of her own line.

Volley Drill (volleying and heading).   The ball is tossed by a partner at varying heights and is volleyed back to the partner with foot, knee, thigh, or head. Use a partially deflated or foam ball until skill develops.

Circle Volley (volleying and heading).   Players form a circle with a leader in the center. Leader tosses the ball to members of the circle with no warning. Player volleys ball back to leader. Use a partially deflated or foam ball until skill develops.

Keep-It-Up (juggling).   Ball is self-tossed and kept in the air by means of repeated volleying with the foot, knee, thigh, or head. Use a partially deflated or foam ball until skill develops.

Partner Keep-It-Up (juggling).   This is the same as the preceding exercise, but partners alternate control of the ball. This may also be practiced in a circle with four to six players.

One-on-One (dribbling, kicking, and tackling).   Use half of the field only, with two players per side. One player acts as goal, standing astride the goal line. Other player tries to put the ball through the opponents' goal (area between the legs). Positions change after one minute. Stress continuous play and use of dribbling, trapping, and tackling skills.

Three-on-Three (dribbling, passing, trapping, volleying, and tackling).   This is the same as the preceding exercise but with an additional player. Stress passing at least twice before taking a shot. Rotate positions frequently. The objective of this drill is for the players to learn to keep a triangle formation as they move around the field.

Three-on-Three Change (dribbling, passing, trapping, volleying, and tackling).   This is the same as the preceding exercise, but on a given command by the instructor, players rotate positions within their triangle. They attempt to use as much space in the half field as possible and keep a triangle position throughout. Vary the drill by requiring players to change positions by dribbling and passing.

TABLE 23.3   *Suggested Progression for Introducing Soccer Lead-Up Games Sequenced in Terms of Complexity*

Soccer Lead-Ups (page number)	Kicking Skills	Trapping Skills	Dribbling Skills	Volleying Skills	Tackling Skills	Goal Keep	Team Play
Circle soccer (450)	X	X					
Line soccer (450)	X	X	X				
Soccer keep away (451)	X	X					
Sideline soccer (451)	X	X	X	X			
Pin kickball (451)	X	X					
Soccer kickball (451)	X	X	X				
Team keep away (452)	X	X	X	X	X		
Crab soccer (452)	X		X			X	X
Zone soccer (452)	X	X	X	X		X	X
Six-on-a-side soccer (452)	X	X	X	X	X	X	X
Regulation soccer (452)	X	X	X	X	X	X	X

CONCEPT 23.8
Soccer lead-up games serve as an effective means of practicing skills and involving children in controlled, competitive, and fun learning experiences.

Soccer Lead-up Games

The following lead-up games to soccer have been selected because they are easy to organize and fun to play. Each incorporates two or more of the basic skills of soccer. Each activity may be played outdoors or modified for indoor play. A suggested progression for introducing soccer lead-up games is depicted in Table 23.3.

The primary objectives of including soccer lead-up games into the program are to

1. reinforce the various soccer skills of kicking, trapping, dribbling, volleying, and tackling and to apply them to game-like situations;
2. introduce the basic rules of soccer through modified game activities;
3. provide opportunities for understanding and applying basic team strategies;
4. encourage a spirit of cooperation and teamwork toward a common goal; and
5. give students a chance to play a modified game of soccer with reasonable skill and enjoyment.

Circle Soccer

Movement Skills: Kicking and trapping.

Formation: Loose single circle with eight players to each half of the circle.

Equipment: One soccer ball per group.

Procedures: The ball is rolled to one team. Players pass the ball among themselves and then kick to the opposite side of the circle. Opposing players trap or block the ball, trying to prevent it from going outside the circle. A point is scored each time the ball goes out of circle. Three-minute time limit.

Suggestions: Stress passing the ball before kicking. Insist on trapping and controlling the ball before the ball is returned, and do not permit toe kicks. Any ball above the waist may be blocked with the hands or caught without penalty. Do not require players to hold hands. Use a partially deflated or foam ball for beginners.

Line Soccer

Movement Skills: Dribbling, kicking, and trapping.

Formation: Two parallel lines of eight players each, forty to sixty feet apart.

Equipment: One soccer ball per game.

Procedures: Players on each team are given a number. The teacher calls a number and rolls the ball into the center of the playing area. The player who was called attempts to control the ball, dribble it toward the opposing goal line, and score. Goal-line players may trap the ball to prevent a goal. Kicked balls above waist level do not count and may be blocked with the hands or caught. Play continues until a goal is scored. Procedure is repeated.

Suggestions: Emphasize controlling and dribbling the ball prior to kicking. Do not permit toe kicks. As skill increases, call two or three numbers, and stress passing and teamwork. Use a partially deflated or foam ball until skill develops in trapping and kicking. Avoid long waiting for a turn by keeping the size of teams small.

Soccer Keep Away

Movement Skills: Kicking and trapping.

Formation: Single circle of eight to ten players per group, with one player in the center ("it").

Equipment: One Nerf soccer ball per group.

Procedures: Player in the center tries to touch the ball as it is passed from player to player. When "it" touches the ball with his feet, the player who kicked the ball goes to the center.

Suggestions: Stress passing the ball among teammates before kicking across the circle. Do not permit toe kicks. Insist on trapping the ball prior to kicking it back to a teammate.

Sideline Soccer

Movement Skills: Kicking, dribbling, trapping, and volleying.

Formation: Thirty by sixty foot rectangular play area, with eight to twelve players per team.

Equipment: One soccer ball per group; markings to designate teams in the field.

Procedures: Each team is assigned a goal to defend. Half of each team scatters in its half of the playing area; the other half lines up on one sideline. The game begins with a "face-off" between two opposing players. The object of the game is to kick the ball behind the opposing players standing on the sideline. Players in the field may pass to one

another or to teammates on the sideline. Sideline players may pass to players in the field and must use various trapping skills to block the ball. One point is scored for each kick that crosses the opponents' sideline below waist level.

Pin Kickball

Movement Skills: Kicking and trapping.

Formation: Two parallel lines of eight to ten players each.

Equipment: Two soccer balls per group, plus eight pins (bowling pins or milk cartons work well).

Procedures: Each team is given a soccer ball. From behind a restraining line, the object is to kick the ball accurately and knock down the pins. One point is scored for each pin knocked over.

Suggestions: Do not let certain players dominate the game. After a point is scored, require the ball to be passed to another player. Add to the number of pins. Add balls. Increase the distance from the pins as accuracy improves.

Soccer Kickball

Movement Skills: Kicking, trapping, and dribbling.

Formation: Six to eight players per team. Players in the field are informally scattered.

Equipment: One soccer ball per group.

Procedures: The object is to kick the ball from behind the goal and then run to a base about fifty feet away and back before the fielding team can score a goal. Player kicks a stationary ball, runs to the base, and back. Players in the field retrieve the ball without using the hands. They may dribble and pass the ball prior to kicking at the goal area. Players in the field may not stand closer than fifteen feet from the baseline. If the ball is kicked through the goal before the player crosses the baseline, a point is scored for the fielders. If the player crosses the baseline, a point is scored for the kickers. Play continues until all have had a turn at kicking the ball.

Suggestions: As kicking skill develops, lengthen the baselines. As skill in the field increases, narrow the goal. Use a partially deflated or foam ball when indoors. Stress teamwork in the field and using the instep kick when up to "bat." The game may be modified to include punting.

Team Keep Away

Movement Skills: Kicking, dribbling, trapping, tackling, and volleying.

Formation: Team soccer formation with designated boundaries. Six to eight players per team.

Equipment: One soccer ball per group, plus armbands or bandannas to designate team members.

Procedures: The rules are similar to most keep-away games, except that the ball must be kicked or dribbled and not touched with the hands. The object is for a team to maintain control of the ball for as long as possible. Individual players may not control the ball longer than ten seconds before passing. If a foul occurs, the opposing team is awarded the ball.

Suggestions: Use a partially deflated or foam ball when playing indoors. Stress playing one's position. Introduce basic elements of tackling. Emphasize ball control while dribbling and accurate passing.

Crab Soccer

Movement Skills: Kicking, dribbling, goalkeeping, and team play.

Formation: Team soccer formation, with twelve players per team. Indoor playing area at least forty by sixty feet.

Equipment: One large foam ball, beach ball, or cage ball per group.

Procedures: Players assume a crab-walk position in each of the regular positions of soccer. The ball is put into play with a face-off. Players may advance the ball by kicking to a teammate. Hands must remain in contact with the floor. The object is to kick the ball over the opposing team's goal. The goalkeeper may not touch the ball with the hands. Positioning and basic rules of soccer apply.

Suggestions: This is an excellent activity to teach positioning. Stop the game frequently to see that players are in position. Rotate positions after each goal. Remove eyeglasses before playing. Do not permit wild kicking at the ball or mass convergence on the ball.

Zone Soccer

Movement Skills: Kicking, trapping, dribbling, volleying, goalkeeping, and team play.

Formation: Two teams of twelve players each, divided into three zones (divide gym in thirds).

Equipment: One soccer ball per group.

Procedures: Divide each team into three equal groups. The object is to kick the ball over the opposing team's goal line. The ball is put into play with a regulation kickoff. Players must remain in their own zone and may advance the ball by passing to a teammate in another zone. Goal guards are responsible for defending their goal line. Fullbacks are the last line of defense. Halfbacks receive passes from their fullbacks and relay them to the forwards. Forwards attempt to score goals.

Suggestions: Emphasize playing one's position.

Six-on-a-side Soccer

Movement Skills: All soccer skills.

Formation: Outdoor play area forty by eighty yards, with six players per team.

Equipment: One soccer ball per group

Procedures: Assign two forwards (strikers), two halfbacks (midfield players), one fullback (defensive player), and a goalie. Follow the basic rules of soccer, modifying as necessary.

Suggestions: Use a foam ball if played indoors. Stress positioning and team play. Permit players to practice at each position. Introduce more complex strategies as skill improves.

Regulation Soccer

Movement Skills: All soccer skills.

Formation: Regulation soccer field, 300 to 360 feet long, and 180 to 225 feet wide. Eleven players per side.

Equipment: One soccer ball per group and two goals.

Procedures: The procedures and rules for regulation soccer are described in the following section.

Suggestions: Regulation soccer is generally not advised for the elementary physical education class. Various modifications, including six-on-a-side soccer, are more appropriate for teaching skills and developing the basic concept of cooperative team play.

BASIC RULES FOR SOCCER

The regulation game of soccer is played by two teams, each with eleven players that include one goalie, two full-backs, three halfbacks, and five forwards. The ball may not be touched with the hands or arms. It is advanced toward the opponents' goal with the feet, body, or head.

CONCEPT 23.9
Children need to learn the activity concepts of soccer that involve basic rules, strategies, formations, and patterns of play.

At the start of the game, the center forward of the offensive team kicks the ball from the center circle toward a teammate. The ball must travel forward its own full circumference before being touched by an opposing player. The defensive team must remain outside the circle until the ball is touched. Then the players on both teams may cross the center line and play the ball wherever it goes. The object of the game is to move the ball down the field and into the opponents' goal for a score. The ball is moved by dribbling, passing, or volleying to another teammate. A defending player may intercept the ball and reverse the action of play.

When unnecessary roughness takes place, the offending team is penalized by a penalty kick or a free kick. A **penalty kick** is awarded when a foul is committed in the penalty area by the defensive team. The offensive team takes a penalty kick from the penalty mark with all the players except the goalie staying outside the penalty area. A **free kick** is awarded for fouls committed outside the penalty area. The ball is kicked from the spot of the foul. The opponents must be at least ten yards away until the ball is kicked.

If the ball is kicked over the sideline, it is put into play by the opposite team. A halfback usually puts the ball into play from the sideline by a two-handed overhead **throw-in.** When the ball is kicked over the goal line but not through the goal by the offensive team, the goalie of the defensive team punts the ball back into the game. The other team must remain ten yards away until the ball is punted. A **corner kick** is awarded the opposite team when the defensive team causes the ball to go over its own goal line. This kick is taken by a member of the offensive team from the corner of the field closest to the ball when it went out of bounds. One point is awarded for

each goal. After a goal is scored, the team scored against kicks off from the center of the field.

A **goalie kick** is awarded to the defensive team when the ball is kicked by the offensive team over the goal line but not through the goal. The opposing team must be at least ten yards distant. The goalie may pick up the ball with the hands, punt from the goal line, and throw the ball. He may take only two steps with the ball.

Soccer fouls include carrying, handling, and pushing. A carrying foul occurs when the goalie takes more than two steps with the ball in his hands. Handling is touching the ball with the hand or any part of the arm between the wrist and shoulder. Pushing involves moving an opponent away with the hands, arms, or body.

The goalie may pick up the ball with the hands, punt the ball away from the goal line, and throw the ball away from the goal. He may take only four steps with the ball. The other players may dribble, pass, trap, or volley the ball. They may kick the ball to a teammate when trapped by an opponent and stop the ball by blocking with any part of the body except the hands or arms.

ASSESSING PROGRESS

Assessment of soccer skills should include evaluating kicking, trapping, dribbling, and volleying proficiency. Assessment may focus on the process, which includes the techniques employed in performing each skill, or on the product, which is the level of performance, or both. Whatever way is chosen, it is important to assess both entry and exit levels of skill. In this way, the teacher can more effectively plan appropriate movement experiences to maximize the effectiveness of the instructional unit in promoting learning.

CONCEPT 23.10
Assessment of soccer skills may be accomplished through use of a variety of process and product assessment techniques both prior to and after a skills theme.

Process Assessment

The teacher's subjective judgment of the technique used for each skill forms the basis for process assessment. This should be an ongoing procedure, but it is particularly beneficial at the beginning of a skill theme. The instructor is

SOCCER SKILLS RATING CHART

Class: _____   Grade: _____

Entry Assessment Date: _____   Exit Assessment Date: _____

Directions	Kicking Skills				Trapping Skills					Dribbling Skills		Volleying Skills		Associated Skills			Key
	Instep Kick	Push Pass	Inside-of-Foot Kick	Punting	Sole Trap	Shin Trap	Foot Trap	Thigh Trap	Chest Trap	Inside-of-Foot Dribble	Outside-of-Foot Dribble	Juggling	Heading	Goal Keeping	Screening/Blocking	Tackling	
Observe during drill or play situations. Mark entry rating in upper left corner and exit ratings in lower right corner of each square.																	**A: Advanced—** Correct technique plus good control and force production/ absorption
																	I: Intermediate— Correct technique but lacking in control or force production/ absorption
																	B: Beginning— Inconsistent use of correct technique
																	Comments:

FIGURE 23.14 *Sample form rating chart for soccer.*

concerned primarily with the body mechanics used to perform the various skills of soccer. Children may be observed in an appropriate skill drill or lead-up game activity. By charting their abilities at the beginning and again at the end of an instructional unit, you can determine both what needs to be emphasized and how much progress has been made. The sample soccer skills rating chart depicted in Figure 23.14 will help you determine how developed children's soccer skills are.

Product Assessment

Soccer skill tests that assess the performance abilities of children on selected skills can be easily devised. It is a relatively simple matter of selecting the skill tests you wish to use, standardizing their procedures, and collecting and compiling scores from year to year. After a few years, you can establish your own performance norms.

SOCCER SKILLS PROGRESS CHART

Student's
Name: _____   Grade: _____ Class: _____ Year: _____

See Reverse for Description of Tests		Skills	Entry Rating	Comments	Exit Rating	Comments
10 Wall-Goal Kicks	Punt for Distance	*Kicking*	D a t e		D a t e	
B <3	<40'	Instep Kick				
I 4–7	40–90'					
A 8>	90'>	Punting				
10 Traps		*Trapping*	D a t e		D a t e	
B <4						
I 4–7		All Traps				
A 8>						
Figure-8 Dribble		*Dribbling*	D a t e		D a t e	
B 60 sec. >						
I 45–59 sec.		All Dribbling				
A <45 sec.						
Keep It Up		*Volleying*	D a t e		D a t e	
B <4		Heading				
I 4–7						
A 8>		Juggling				

Parent's Signature: _____ Date: _____
Comments:

FIGURE 23.15 *Sample self-referenced performance rating card for soccer.*

Because of the time involved in mass skill testing, it is recommended that self-referenced partner testing be adopted. Self-referenced partner testing encourages children to view improvement on an individual basis and also intermittently involves them in a process that is both fun and educational. The sample soccer skills test presented in Figure 23.15 is an example of a self-referenced assessment tool.

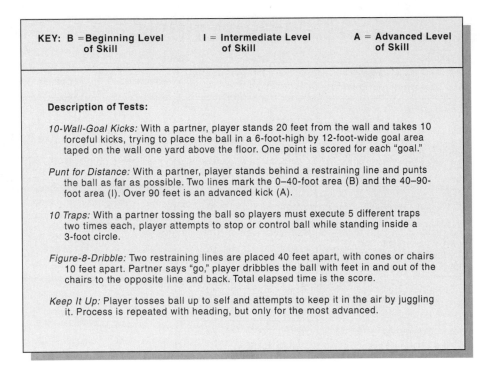

KEY: B = Beginning Level   I = Intermediate Level   A = Advanced Level
of Skill   of Skill   of Skill

Description of Tests:

10-Wall-Goal Kicks: With a partner, player stands 20 feet from the wall and takes 10 forceful kicks, trying to place the ball in a 6-foot-high by 12-foot-wide goal area taped on the wall one yard above the floor. One point is scored for each "goal."

Punt for Distance: With a partner, player stands behind a restraining line and punts the ball as far as possible. Two lines mark the 0–40-foot area (B) and the 40–90-foot area (I). Over 90 feet is an advanced kick (A).

10 Traps: With a partner tossing the ball so players must execute 5 different traps two times each, player attempts to stop or control ball while standing inside a 3-foot circle.

Figure-8-Dribble: Two restraining lines are placed 40 feet apart, with cones or chairs 10 feet apart. Partner says "go," player dribbles the ball with feet in and out of the chairs to the opposite line and back. Total elapsed time is the score.

Keep It Up: Player tosses ball up to self and attempts to keep it in the air by juggling it. Process is repeated with heading, but only for the most advanced.

FIGURE 23.15 *(continued) Reverse side of self-referenced performance rating card for soccer.*

SUMMARY

Soccer is a game enjoyed worldwide by literally millions of children, adolescents, and adults. It is one of a few truly international games, touching almost every country in the world. Soccer enjoys many benefits not possible in other team sports. It requires little in the way of specialized equipment (a ball), facilities (a large flat area), or personal attributes (height and weight). Furthermore, soccer can be enjoyed by all (children and adults, boys and girls), at some level of proficiency (recreational, intramural, youth sport, or interscholastic). Moreover, the game of soccer is outstanding in its contribution to cardiovascular endurance as well as other important fitness components. Popularity of the game of soccer in North America has been on the rise for the past fifteen years. Almost a generation of children have grown up playing the game. Soon it will be a part of the fabric of North American life much the same as football, baseball, basketball, and ice hockey.

COMPLEMENTARY READINGS

ACEP. (1991). *Rookie Coaches Soccer Guide.* Champaign, IL: Human Kinetics.

Athletic Institute. (1991). *Youth League Soccer: Coaching and Playing.* North Palm Beach, FL: Athletic Institute.

Brown, E. W. *Youth Soccer: A Complete Handbook.* Dubuque, IA: Wm. C. Brown & Benchmark.

Celtnieks, V., and B.J. Lenosky. (1993). The soccer circuit: A flexible training program. *Strategies* 6:16–23.

Luxbacher, J. (1987). *Fun Games for Teaching Soccer.* Champaign, IL: Human Kinetics.

Schellscheidt, M. (1991). *Youth League Soccer Skills: Mastering the Ball.* North Palm Beach, FL: The Athletic Institute.

Swedish Soccer Federation. (1988). *Organizing Your Youth Soccer Team.* Champaign, IL: Human Kinetics.

U.S. Soccer Federation. (1990). *Handbook for Youth Soccer.* 350 Fifth Avenue, New York: NY.

SUPPLEMENTARY READINGS

Hopper, C., and M. Davis. (1988). *Coaching Soccer Effectively.* Champaign, IL: Human Kinetics.

Houseworth, S. D. (1985). *I. Y Soccer Coaches Manual; II. Y Jugglers Manual; III. Y Kickers Manual; IV. Y Soccer Strikers Manual.* Champaign, IL: Human Kinetics.

Luxbacher, J. A. (1992). *Teaching Soccer.* Champaign, IL: Human Kinetics.

VIDEOS

New Soccer. LeFevre, D. N., Byron, CA: Front Row Experience. (30 min.).

Soccer. Long, S., Byron, CA: Front Row Experience. (25 min.). *1. Soccer Passing and Support; 2. Soccer Goalkeeping; 3. Soccer Shooting; 4. Soccer Defending.* British Broadcasting System. Dubuque, IA: Wm. C. Brown. (60 min. each).

Soccer for Everyone. Charleston, WV: Cambridge Physical Education and Health. (45 min.).

Soccer Fundamentals. New York, NY: Insight Media. (Three parts, 159 min. total).

Teaching Kids Soccer. Gansler, B., 200 Castlewood Drive, North Palm Beach, FL: The Athletic Institute. (75 min.).

CHAPTER 24

Softball Skill Themes

Key Concept

The Game of Softball Requires Mature Performance of a Variety of Fundamental Stability, Locomotor, and Manipulative Skills and the Application of These Skills in Progressively More Advanced Forms Within the Specialized Sport-Skill Phase

Chapter Objectives

The purpose of this chapter is to provide you with the tools to:
• Identify the essential movement skills associated with the game of softball.
• Describe mechanically correct performance of a variety of softball skills.
• Demonstrate familiarity with common developmentally based problems that children encounter in softball skill acquisition.
• Propose a variety of teaching techniques designed to help children overcome problems in softball skills acquisition.
• Identify the skill concepts and movement concepts that children should know about the skills associated with the games of softball and baseball.
• Develop a warm-up session for preparing children to participate in a softball skills theme.
• Demonstrate knowledge of a variety of skill drills and lead-up activities designed to develop and reinforce selected softball skills.
• Discuss the purpose, advantages, and disadvantages of both process and product assessment of children's softball skills.

Terms to Remember

Overhand Throw	Batting
Sidearm Throw	Bunting
Underhand Throw	Base Runner
Pitching	Pitcher
Fly Ball Fielding	Batter
Catching a Line Drive	Strike
Fielding Grounders	Foul Ball

The game of baseball is deeply embedded in North American culture. Softball is closely related to baseball in that it is played under the same basic rule structure, uses a similar field of play, and involves many of the same skills. Children at the elementary school level have often had at least minimal exposure to the game of baseball through their own participation or through observing others play it. However, the skill level within any grade or class will vary widely. Some children will be quite skilled and may take part in summer league play. Many others will be quite unskilled, with little or no idea how to execute the basic skills or play the game. Therefore, at the elementary school level the primary focus should be on instruction and practice in the skills and rules of the game.

CONCEPT 24.1

Because of the popularity of baseball and softball as youth sport activities, children in the same group or class will frequently be at vastly different levels in their softball skill proficiency.

Slow-pitch softball is generally considered to be better suited than baseball for the instructional program for several reasons. Success can be achieved at lower skill levels because softball skills are somewhat less complex and less demanding than those of baseball. Softball requires less space and equipment and can be learned earlier and played later in life than baseball. Also, both boys and girls play softball, whereas only boys play baseball.

The game of softball combines and refines several fundamental movement skills. Successful development of the skills required to play softball depends on attaining mature fundamental movement patterns. If one is unable to throw, catch, or strike a ball in a mature pattern, then it will not be possible to acquire the sport skills of throwing and pitching, catching and fielding, and batting and bunting that are an integral part of softball. Therefore, at the elementary school level, softball instruction should focus on skill development and not on playing the regulation game. A wide variety of skill drills and lead-up games of increasing complexity should be included in the program and should be used as a means of improving skill and knowledge about the game. However, little time should be spent on actually playing the regulation game of softball during the instructional physical education lesson. Play of the regulation game should be reserved for the intramural, interscholastic, or agency-sponsored youth sport program.

CONCEPT 24.2

The instructional physical education program should focus on skill acquisition and skill enhancement, not on playing the game of softball.

DEVELOPING A SOFTBALL SKILLS THEME

To maximize learning and make the best use of your time when focusing on the development of softball skills, it will be helpful to follow the recommended sequence of (1) preplanning, (2) observing and assessing, (3) planning and implementing, and (4) evaluating and revising. In terms of movement skill learning, determine whether students are at the beginning, intermediate, or advanced level of developing their softball skills. Based on this information and your assessment information, sequentially list the skills that will be stressed in the unit. Then select appropriate drills that are geared to the particular skill levels of the class. Several warm-up activities, skill drills, and softball lead-up games are described at the end of this chapter. After the skill-drill portion of your lesson, you will find it beneficial to incorporate lead-up game activities that focus on implementing the skills.

CONCEPT 24.3

Developing a softball skills theme requires the same step-by-step progression of preplanning, observing and assessing, specific planning and implementing, and evaluating and revising as any other skill theme.

Assess the exit level of softball skills through either informal or formal assessment. You may wish to use the suggestions found in the "Assessing Progress" section at the end of this chapter. Modify subsequent lessons to more closely suit specific individual and group needs.

SOFTBALL SKILL SEQUENCING

Third and fourth graders are typically at the beginning level of softball skill learning. Fifth and sixth graders are often at the intermediate level of softball skill learning.

TABLE 24.1   *Selected Softball Skills Sequenced in Terms of Complexity*

Softball Skills (page number)	Suggested Progression for Children	
	Beginning Level	*Intermediate Level*
Throwing		
Overhand throw (461)	Introduce	Refine
Sidearm throw (462)		Introduce
Underhand throw (462)	Introduce	Refine
Pitching (463)		Introduce
Fielding		
Fly ball (464)	Introduce	Refine
Line drive (465)	Introduce	Refine
Ground ball (465)	Introduce	Refine
Hitting		
Batting (466)	Introduce	Refine
Bunting (467)		Introduce
Associated Skills		
Base running	Introduce	Refine
Base playing	Introduce	Refine
Base stealing		Introduce
Understanding the Game		
Rules (475)	Introduce	Refine
Strategy (475)		Introduce

Some may be at the advanced level. This does not mean however, that all are at the same level. With the popularity of softball/baseball activities in youth sport programs, several children in each class can be expected to be at a relatively high level of skill. Therefore, it is important that you know the current levels of your students' softball skills in order to be able to plan more effectively for all. Table 24.1, "Selected Softball Skills," and Table 24.2 "Developmental Activities Chart for Softball," should help you select appropriate softball skills to teach and skill drills to use. A brief description of each drill is located in the "Fitness and Skill Development Activities" section, along with recommended warm-up activities and softball lead-up games.

CONCEPT 24.4
The progressive sequencing of softball skills should be based on both age-appropriate and individually appropriate criteria.

THROWING

Skilled throwing and pitching are two essential aspects of the game of softball. There are basically three types of throws used in softball: overhand throw, sidearm throw, and underhand throw. The throw used depends on the position in which the ball is fielded, the distance it must

TABLE 24.2   *Developmental Activities Chart for Softball Sequenced in Terms of Complexity*

Softball Skill Drills (page number)	Throwing Skills	Fielding Skills	Base-Running Skills	Batting Skills
Wall toss (469)		X		
Vertical toss and catch (470)		X		
Partner toss and catch (470)	X	X		
Exchange throwing (470)	X	X		
Over/under exchange throwing (470)	X	X		
Alternating over/under (470)	X	X		
Stretch and catch (470)	X	X		
One-bounce drill (470)	X	X		
Fly ball drill (470)	X	X		
Fly ball/pick-off drill (470)	X	X		
Around the horn (470)	X	X		
Throwing/catching shuttle (470)	X	X		
Run, throw, catch (470)	X	X	X	
Fielding grounders (470)		X		
Grounder exchange (470)	X			
Grounder/fly ball exchange (470)		X		
Partner throw-out (470)	X	X		
Strong-side throw-out (470)	X	X		
Weak-side throw-out (470)	X	X		
Grounder shuttle (471)		X	X	
Speed base running (471)			X	
Around the bases (471)			X	
Base-runner pick-off (471)			X	
Base reverse (471)			X	
Suspended-ball batting (471)				X
Swinging-ball batting (471)				X
Tee batting (471)				X
Batting practice (471)			X	X
Pepper (471)			X	X
Pepper pick (471)			X	X
Fungo batting (471)			X	X

travel, and the speed at which it must arrive at its destination. Pitching is a specialized underhand throwing pattern. Included in this chapter are teaching tips for softball throwing and pitching, a list of common developmental difficulties, recommended teaching strategies, and a list of skill concepts and movement concepts children should know. Brief verbal and visual descriptions are also included for study.

Overhand Throw

The **overhand throw** is the basic throwing skill used by all players except the pitcher. The mechanics of the overhand throw in softball are the same as the mature fundamental overhand throwing pattern. The difference lies in the specialized nature of the throw, which requires improved performance in terms of the distance

FIGURE 24.1 *The overhand throw.*

FIGURE 24.2 *The sidearm throw.*

thrown, the accuracy and control of the throw, and the speed at which the ball travels.

Verbal Description

- See Chapter 18 for a description of the mechanics of the mature overhand throwing pattern.
- Grip the ball with the thumb and three or four fingers.
- The fingertips and thumb grip the ball; the palm does not touch the ball.
- Greater speed is imparted to the ball through rapid hip rotation while forcefully bringing the arm around and stepping out on the leg opposite the throwing arm.
- Greater distance is achieved by executing the preceding steps and releasing the ball in a high arc.
- Greater accuracy is achieved by concentrating on the target and by complete follow-through.
- Greater control and consistency are achieved through practice in a variety of drill and game-like situations.

Visual Description.   (Figure 24.1)

Sidearm Throw

The **sidearm throw** is used if the ball is caught when the player is off balance or if the ball is caught to one side of the player's body. It is used frequently by players in the

infield to cover a short distance in a hurry. The same basic mechanics are used for the sidearm throw as are used for the overhand throw except for the following:

Verbal Description

- The throwing arm is extended diagonally from the shoulder.
- The forearm is extended straight from the elbow.
- The arm angle may vary from diagonal to just above the horizontal.
- The arm follows through across the body.

Visual Description.   (Figure 24.2)

Underhand Throw

The **underhand throw** is used in softball to cover a shorter distance than the sidearm throw. It is frequently used when the ball is caught low or scooped up from the ground by an infield player and tossed to another person. The underhand toss is basic to the pattern used in softball pitching.

Verbal Description

- Grip the ball with the thumb and fingertips.
- From a closed stance, transfer the weight to the foot that corresponds to the throwing arm (right arm, right foot).

- At the same time, swing the throwing arm down and backward in a pendular motion.
- Step forward on the foot opposite the throwing arm (right arm, left foot).
- At the same time, swing the throwing arm forward and transfer weight to the forward foot.
- Release the ball off the fingertips in the desired trajectory.
- Follow through in the direction of the target.

Pitching

Pitching is a specialized underhand throwing pattern that should be introduced only after reasonable mastery has been attained in underhand throwing. Accuracy should be stressed prior to speed.

Verbal Description

- Stand with feet parallel in a closed position, facing the batter.
- Both hands hold the ball as it is presented forward to the batter.
- The nonthrowing hand is released as the ball is brought down backward and then forward in a pendular motion.
- The shoulder of the throwing arm rotates slightly down and backward at the height of the backswing, and the body weight is transferred to the rear foot.
- The throwing arm swings forward in a pendular action close to the trunk and leg, and the shoulder rotates forward.
- At the same time, the body weight is transferred to the opposite foot as it steps forcefully forward.
- The ball is released off the fingertips at about waist height.
- Follow-through is made in the direction of the batter.

Visual Description.   (Figure 24.3)

Teaching Tips
Developmental Difficulties

- Fails to grip the ball properly.
- Fails to lead at the elbow for overhand and sidearm throws.

FIGURE 24.3 *Pitching.*

- Insufficient shoulder and hip rotation for forceful throws.
- Poor rhythm of movement.
- Leads with the wrong foot.
- Lacks follow-through.
- Unable to get desired distance.
- Has poor control.

Recommended Strategies

- Practice basic mechanics of throwing to ensure that all are at the mature stage.
- Stress proper mechanics before accuracy or control.
- Practice throwing for distance in both overhand and sidearm patterns.
- Provide infield practice situations for the underhand toss.
- Provide plenty of opportunities for practice with the correct throwing techniques in game-like situations.
- After technique has been mastered, work for accuracy.
- Partner throwing and catching drills will promote control and accuracy.
- Target throwing drills will promote control and accuracy.
- Do not introduce pitching until reasonable control has been mastered with underhand tossing.
- Use smaller and softer balls as needed.
- Stress accuracy in pitching prior to speed.

- Stress gripping the ball with the thumb and fingertips.
- Combine fielding and throwing drills after reasonable skill has been separately attained for each.
- Select skill drills and lead-up games that emphasize increasingly complex skill development.
- Practice moving toward ground balls, picking them up, pivoting, and throwing.
- Stress the importance of the ready position and being alert at all times.

Concepts Children Should Know

Skill Concepts

- Grip the ball with your thumb and fingertips.
- Don't let your palm touch the ball.
- Use plenty of shoulder and hip rotation when you throw the ball.
- Lead with your elbow as you release the ball in the overhand and sidearm throws.
- Step forward on the nonthrowing foot as you release the ball.
- Release the ball at about waist level for the underhand throw.
- Follow through in the direction of your target.

Movement Concepts

- The speed at which the ball travels depends on the proper summation of forces.
- Forceful hip and shoulder rotation will add speed to the ball.
- The distance the ball travels depends on the force applied and the trajectory at which it is released.
- The accuracy with which you can throw a ball overhand depends on the distance to be covered, constant visual monitoring of the target, and complete follow-through.
- In a dynamic game situation, your throwing pattern will vary between overhand, sidearm, and underhand, depending on the immediate conditions.
- You may have to throw from awkward positions dictated by how and where you caught the ball.
- Pitching is a specialized skill requiring considerable practice in order to gain accuracy and control.

CONCEPT 24.5
Children need to know both the skill concepts and movement concepts associated with the many softball skills.

FIELDING

Fielding is an important element of the game of softball. Proficiency in fielding a ball is often difficult for elementary-age children to acquire because of the speed at which the ball approaches, the varying trajectories in which the ball may approach, and the uncertainty of where the ball should be intercepted. The primary catching skills to be learned by elementary school-age children involve fly ball fielding, catching a line drive, and fielding grounders. Teaching tips, including a list of common problems and recommended strategies, follow, along with a list of the skill concepts and movement concepts children should know. Verbal descriptions and visual descriptions of fielding skills are also included for study.

Fly Ball

Catching a high fly ball is exciting to watch and thrilling to perform. The major task in **fly ball fielding** is getting into the proper position. This is a complex skill in itself, requiring sophisticated perceptual judgments from both visual and auditory cues. Based on this information, the fielder moves to the spot where the ball is anticipated to land and prepares to catch the ball.

Verbal Description

- The body is placed in direct line with the path of the ball, in a narrow stride stance.
- The head is raised and eyes track the ball throughout its approach.
- Arms and hands are raised upward, the arms are slightly bent and are in line with the chin.
- Thumbs are close together, with the fingers spread, and the gloved hand is slightly forward.
- Eyes track the ball into the glove.
- As the ball is caught in the pocket, the glove is squeezed together slightly and the nongloved hand covers the ball.
- The knees flex slightly, and the arms bend toward the body to absorb the force of the ball.

Visual Description.   (Figure 24.4)

Line Drive

Catching a line drive, or a low-flying ball, often poses problems to children, especially when the flight of the ball is interrupted just above waist level. Indecision about the proper hand position frequently results in a dropped ball. Any ball intercepted below the waist should be caught with a thumbs-out position.

Verbal Description

- Body is placed in direct line with the ball, the feet are spread, and the knees are slightly bent.
- Hands are brought in line with the ball.
- Fingers are spread, and the hands are close together.
- Ball is contacted out from the body.
- Ball is visually tracked into the glove.
- Nongloved hand covers the ball.
- Arms "give" upon impact.

C O N C E P T   2 4 . 6

Children encounter a number of developmentally based difficulties in learning softball skills. Many effective teaching strategies can help overcome these problems.

Ground Ball

Fielding grounders is an important softball skill that is often made more difficult by rough terrain, which causes the ball to bounce wildly. This and the limited skill level of many children frequently make fielding a grounder in the classic manner difficult to master. The "sure-stop" method of fielding a grounder that follows is generally more appropriate for elementary school children. If the ball is missed by the hands, it will generally be stopped by the body.

Verbal Description

- Body is placed in direct line with the path of the approaching ball.
- The knees bend, with one knee brought near the ground.
- The waist is bent forward, and the hands and arms are extended downward.
- The eyes visually track the ball into the glove.

FIGURE 24.4 *Fielding a high fly ball.*

- The nongloved hand covers the ball as it is brought up to the body in preparation for the throw.
- The hands work together.

Visual Description.   (Figure 24.5)

Teaching Tips
Developmental Difficulties

- Fails to get behind the ball.
- Fails to track the ball visually into the hands.
- Looks away as the ball approaches.
- Fails to reach out to catch the ball.
- Fails to "give" with the ball as it is caught.
- Fails to adjust the hands properly to the height of the ball.
- Fails to catch the ball in the "pocket" of the glove.

Recommended Strategies

- Work for proper mechanics of the basic elements of catching first.
- Stress tracking the ball into the hands.

FIGURE 24.5 *Fielding a grounder.*

- Use yarn balls or beanbags when players are first learning to catch a fly ball or a line drive.
- Use super-soft softballs or white-type balls if gloves are not available.
- Incorporate drills that work on one catching skill at a time in a static manner before introducing more complex activities.
- As skill develops, practice in dynamic, game-like situations that require various forms of catching.
- Gradually increase the speed of ground balls to be fielded.
- Work for control before concentrating on speed in fielding grounders.
- Stress controlling ground balls and keeping them in front of the body.
- Incorporate throwing drills with catching drills.
- Stress getting rid of the ball (throwing to a teammate) immediately after the catch.
- Stress attacking the ball with a quick but balanced release.

Concepts Children Should Know
Skill Concepts

- Get directly in line with the path of the ball.
- Keep your eyes on the ball at all times.
- Adjust your hand position to the height of the ball.
- Intercept the ball away from your body.
- Bring the ball toward your body (give with the ball) as it is caught.

Movement Concepts

- The ball can be caught at different levels.
- The ball can be caught coming from different directions.
- You can catch balls traveling at different speeds.
- You will need to make adjustments in your body position and catching pattern depending on the height and speed of the ball.
- The greater the speed of the ball, the more you will have to give with its force.
- If you intercept the ball away from your body, you will have more distance to absorb the force.
- It is easier to catch and control the ball if you get directly in line with its path.

HITTING

Striking a pitched ball is a very complex task. In fact, it is thought by many to be the single most difficult sports skill in terms of perceptual-motor complexity. Therefore, it is important to proceed slowly in developing children's batting and bunting abilities. Modification frequently must be made for all but the most skilled, especially with younger children.

Batting

Developing skill in **batting** takes time and plenty of practice. Its complexity in terms of the precise skill required frequently makes it difficult for children to learn without initial modification.

Verbal Description

- Stand at the side of the plate with the side of the body facing the pitcher.
- The feet are spread slightly more than shoulder width apart.
- The knees are slightly bent, and the body weight is evenly distributed.
- The bat is gripped with the hands touching each other and the right hand above the left (for a right-handed batter).
- The bat is brought back to a position over the shoulder, pointing up and back.

- Elbows are held away from the body.
- As the ball approaches, the swing begins and the eyes track the ball.
- As the movement progresses, the weight shifts from the back to the front leg.
- The hips rotate toward the pitcher and the forward leg takes a short step forward.
- The bat is brought around parallel to the ground in line with the ball.
- The bat contacts the ball when the arms are fully extended and the weight is transferred to the forward foot. The back foot remains grounded.

Visual Description.   (Figure 24.6)

Bunting

Bunting should be introduced only after reasonable skill has been attained in batting. Bunting is frequently used in softball as a sacrifice move to advance a teammate already on base.

Verbal Description (Right-Handed Batter)

- As the ball is released, the batter turns to face the pitcher.
- The right foot is by the plate; feet are slightly spread, with weight evenly distributed.
- The right hand slides halfway up the bat and holds loosely.
- Be careful of the fingers. Keep the hand that has moved up behind the bat.
- The bat is brought in front of the body, parallel to the ground.
- The ball is contacted along the top half of the bat in a downward motion.
- The ball is directed along the ground toward the first-base or third-base line.

Visual Description.   (Figure 24.7)

Teaching Tips
Developmental Difficulties

- Grasps the bat cross-handed.
- Grasps the bat with the hands apart.
- Grips the bat too high or too low.

FIGURE 24.6 *Batting.*

FIGURE 24.7 *Bunting.*

- Indecisive about where to stand.
- Bends forward at the waist.
- Lays the bat on the shoulder.
- Stands with the legs straight and feet together.
- Fails to assume the proper ready position.
- Pulls the elbows in close to the body.

- Swings down on the ball in a chopping action.
- Swings up on the ball.
- Swings too late.
- Unable to track the ball visually.
- Shies away from the ball as it approaches.
- Has poor summation of forces.
- Lacks follow-through after contact.
- Fails to step toward the ball.

Recommended Strategies

- Practice batting off a tee before hitting pitched balls.
- Use larger balls. A beach ball or utility ball is frequently helpful.
- Vary the color of the ball to promote better tracking.
- Use a large-headed bat to increase success.
- Work just for contact and control.
- Use floor markings to indicate proper foot position.
- Practice striking slowly moving balls before practice on more rapid pitches.
- Provide plenty of opportunities for practice and structure the activity for success.
- As success develops, increase the complexity of the task.

Concepts Children Should Know
Skill Concepts

- Keep your eyes on the ball.
- Grip the bat with your hands together and your right hand on top (right-handed batter).
- Extend at your elbows.
- Keep your swing level.
- Step into your swing.
- Contact the ball at the point of complete extension of your arms.
- Snap the wrists as the ball is contacted.

Movement Concepts

- The distance the ball travels will depend on the amount of force applied.

- The direction the ball travels will depend on the point of contact and the direction of your follow-through.
- Contact with the ball depends on successfully converting what you see (perceptual input) into what you do (motor output).
- Choking up on the bat will give you greater control of your swing.
- Taking a long grip will enable you to impart more force to the ball.
- Moving toward the ball as you swing will increase body balance and force production.

FITNESS AND SKILL DEVELOPMENT ACTIVITIES

If children are to master the skills of softball, they will need to practice them first individually in static drill situations. After they have mastered the basic elements of throwing, pitching, fielding, and batting under these situations, it will be profitable to practice under controlled dynamic drill situations in which the environment changes during the drill. Then it will be helpful to have them add skill requirements to the drill and finally to take part in lead-up games that are performed in a dynamically changing environment.

The skill drills presented in this section proceed from simple to complex, ranging from static skill drills to dynamic skill drills, and from single-skill to multiple-skill activities. A list of suggested warm-up activities to be performed prior to engaging in softball skill drills is also included, along with a sampling of softball lead-up games.

 C O N C E P T   2 4 . 7
A variety of warm-up activities and skill drills can be used to enhance physical fitness and improve children's softball skills.

Warm-up Activities

Warm-up activities are highly recommended prior to engaging in skill drills and lead-up activities. Each of the activities that follow should last twenty to thirty seconds. Keep varying the warm-up drills and move rapidly from one activity to the next to help students maintain interest and obtain maximum benefit. See Chapter 26 for a description of the stretching and strengthening exercises.

Stretching

1. Trunk circles.
2. Static toe toucher.
3. Straddle stretch.
4. Heel stretch.

Suppling

1. Arm circles.
2. Star burst.
3. Giraffe.
4. Chicken hawk.

Strengthening

1. Bent-knee sit-ups.
2. Push-ups/modified push-ups.
3. Rocking horse.
4. Blast off.
5. Heel lifts.

Running

1. Wind sprints.
2. Base running.
3. Shadow.
4. Freeze and melt.
5. Agility running.

Tossing and Catching

1. Repeated vertical tossing and catching from a stand.
2. Repeated vertical tossing and catching from a sitting position.
3. Repeated vertical tossing and catching from a lying position.
4. Tossing and catching at different levels.

Batting

1. Swinging practice.
2. Bat stretching activities.
3. Shadow batting.
4. Fungo hitting.

Skill Drills

Numerous skill drills can be devised to practice the essential elements of softball. The primary emphasis of softball skill drills at the elementary school level should be on improving throwing, fielding, and batting skills. By giving a skill drill a name and introducing an element of competition, you can easily turn what to children may be

TEACHING TIPS

The following sequence of skill drills and lead-up game activities is recommended to maximize skill learning:

- Introduce single skills in a static environment ("walk through").
- Practice single skills in a controlled dynamic environment (drill).
- Introduce multiple-skill drills in a static environment.
- Practice multiple-skill drills in a controlled, dynamic environment.
- Implement multiple skills in simple lead-up game activities.
- Practice increasingly complex lead-up game activities.

a rather dull drill into a lively game. Be careful, however, not to emphasize the game before the children have mastered the mechanics of the movement and practiced under static conditions. Failure to remember this basic point will result in having many children regress in their performance rather than progress. The following is a sampling of softball skill drills appropriate for elementary school children. The primary objectives of the skill drills that follow are to

1. improve throwing skills (overhand, sidearm, and underhand);
2. improve fielding skills (high fly ball, low fly ball, and ground ball);
3. improve striking skills (batting and bunting);
4. introduce the associated skills of base running, base playing, and sliding;
5. improve overall fitness (muscular strength, endurance, coordination, and flexibility); and
6. enhance group cooperation and teamwork.

Wall Toss (catching).   Player tosses ball against a wall from a position five to ten feet from the wall and moves into position to catch it. May be done alternating with a partner's wall tosses and catches.

Vertical Toss and Catch (catching). Player tosses ball vertically into the air and catches it, using high fly ball catching position. Work for height on the throw and proper catching action.

Partner Toss and Catch (throwing and catching). With a partner, practice throwing and catching. Begin ten to fifteen feet apart and gradually increase distance. Stress maximum effort before emphasizing accuracy.

Exchange Throwing (catching and throwing). With a partner, each with a ball, throw to each other at the same time. This forces each player to catch the ball, transfer it to the throwing hand, and release it while getting ready to receive another ball.

Over/Under Exchange Throwing (catching and throwing). This is the same as the preceding exercise, except that one partner throws overhand while the other throws underhand.

Alternating Over/Under (catching and throwing). This is the same as the preceding exercise, but partners alternate in their overhand and underhand throws.

Stretch and Catch (catching and throwing). The player keeps a foot anchored on an imaginary base and stretches as far forward or sideways as possible while catching balls thrown by a partner.

One-Bounce Drill (fielding and distance throwing). One player throws the ball, and a partner retrieves it after one bounce. Work for distance on the throws and for immediate release after the catch.

Fly Ball Drill (high fly ball catching). The player tosses the ball high into the air, while a partner moves under it and makes the catch.

Fly Ball/Pick-Off Drill (high fly ball catching and throwing). This is the same as the preceding exercise, but add an immediate throw to a base to pick off a base runner.

Around the Horn (throwing and catching). Take all infield positions except the pitcher's. The catcher throws to the shortstop, who throws to first, who throws to second, who throws to third, who throws back to the catcher again. Work for control and then speed. Rotate positions so that each player gets to play each position.

Throwing/Catching Shuttle (throwing and catching). Form two columns, twenty to sixty feet apart, of four players per column. The player at the head of column A throws to the player at the head of column B and then runs to the back of the line. The process is repeated over and over. Work first for control, then for speed.

Run, Throw, Catch (throwing, catching, and running). Form two columns, twenty to forty feet apart, with four players per column. The ball rests on the floor between the two groups. The first player in column A runs to retrieve the ball, picks it up, throws (underhand toss for short distance, overhead for longer) to the first player in column B, and goes to the back of that line. The first player in column B catches the ball, returns it to the resting spot, and goes to the rear of column A. Practice at varying distances, first stressing control, then speed, then accuracy.

Fielding Grounders (fielding grounders). One player throws ground balls to a second player. Alternate throwing ground balls between players, gradually adding speed to the throws.

Grounder Exchange (fielding grounders). Two partners, each with a ball, practice throwing grounders to each other at the same time. This will encourage getting the ball away quickly before the other ball arrives.

Grounder/Fly Ball Exchange (fielding fly balls and grounders). This is the same as the preceding exercise, except one player throws grounders and the other throws fly balls.

Partner Throw-out (fielding sidearm throwing). One player throws a grounder, a low fly ball, or a high fly ball. The partner fields the ball and throws immediately back, as if trying to throw the other player out at first base. Practice the sidearm throw with this drill to decrease time.

Strong-Side Throw-Out (fielding and sidearm throwing). This is the same as the preceding exercise, but throw to a third person who is off at an angle to the same side as the throwing arm.

Weak-Side Throw-Out (fielding, sidearm throwing, and pivoting). This is the same as the preceding exercise, but throw to a third person who stands off at an angle on the *opposite* side of the throwing arm. This will force the fielder to pivot prior to throwing.

Grounder Shuttle (fielding grounders and running). Form two columns of four players each, about twenty to forty feet apart. The leadoff player in column A throws a grounder to the lead player in column B, who throws it to the next player in column A. After throwing the ball, the player runs to the end of the opposite column.

Speed Base Running (base running). Players individually practice running the bases, trying to improve their time each trial.

Around the Bases (base running). There are four players per group, each standing on a base. They run the bases and try to overtake the player in front of them. Stress touching each base and running in a slight arc so that they are not at right angles to each other when going from base to base.

Base-Runner Pick-Off (stealing). The class faces the teacher with knees bent, feet shoulder width apart, weight evenly distributed. The teacher points to the right or left; players react either to the left or right, as if trying to steal second base. If the teacher points to their right, they run full out. If the point is to the left, they dive back for the imaginary base.

Base Reverse (base running). This is the same as the preceding activity, but runners reverse directions at the sound of a whistle.

Suspended-Ball Batting (batting). The player practices striking a stationary suspended ball that has been adjusted to the proper height.

Swinging-Ball Batting (batting). This is the same as the preceding activity, but the ball swings through a wide arc prior to contact.

Tee Batting (batting). Using a road cone with a golf tube through the top and a softball balanced on the tube, practice batting. A partner retrieves the ball and rolls it back to the batter.

Batting Practice (batting and fielding). Form groups of six (batter, pitcher, catcher, and three fielders), with four to six balls per group. Players rotate positions after a set number of batted balls. The pitcher throws the ball easily so it can be hit.

Pepper (bunting and fielding grounders). Form groups of six (batter, pitcher, four fielders), with four to six balls per group. Pitcher tosses the ball so it can be easily hit. Batter bunts the ball back. Fielders recover the ball. Rotate after a set number of bunts.

Pepper Pick (controlled bunting and fielding grounders). This is the same as the preceding activity, but the batter calls out the player that is being bunted to.

Fungo Batting* (batting and fielding). Four to five players form a group (one batter, remainder fielders). Batter self-tosses the ball into the air and hits it to the fielders, who throw it back. Rotate after a set number of hits or after a player has made a set number of catches.

CONCEPT 24.8
Softball lead-up games can be an effective tool for practicing new skills and reinforcing old ones.

Softball Lead-up Games

Many softball lead-up games are appropriate for elementary school-age children. The games presented here have been selected because of the skills they contribute to and their ease of organization, and because they are fun to play. They are presented in a progression from simple to complex (see Table 24.3). Many of the games may be modified for indoor play by changing the boundaries and the type of ball used. The primary objectives of the lead-up games that follow are to

1. reinforce the various throwing, fielding, batting, and base-running skills of softball;
2. introduce the basic skills of softball through modified game activities;
3. provide opportunities for developing an understanding of and appreciation for basic team strategies;
4. encourage a spirit of cooperation and effort as a team toward a common goal; and
5. have fun and learn to play the game of softball with a reasonable degree of skill.

---

*A "Fungo" is a self-tossed batted ball.

TABLE 24.3   *Suggested Progression for Introducing Softball Lead-Up Games Sequenced in Terms of Complexity*

Softball Lead-Up Games (page number)	Throwing Skills	Fielding Skills	Batting Skills	Base-Running Skills	Team Play
Team distance throw (472)	X				
Toss-up (472)	X				
Circle overtake (472)	X	X			
Throw softball (473)	X	X			
Around the bases (473)				X	
Base-running overtake (473)				X	
Throw around (473)	X	X		X	
Home-run derby (473)		X	X		
Ground-ball pursuit (474)		X			
Line-ball pepper (474)		X	X		
Softball pop-up (474)		X			
500 (474)		X	X		
Three-pitch softball (474)	X	X	X	X	X
Milk-carton softball (475)	X	X	X	X	X
Tee ball (475)	X	X	X	X	X
Whiffle ball (475)	X	X	X	X	X

Team Distance Throw

Movement Skill: Throwing.

Formation: Columns of four players each in a large outdoor area.

Equipment: One tape measure and one beanbag for each team.

Procedures: After warming up, the first player throws the beanbag as far as possible from behind the restraining line. The entire team advances to the spot where the beanbag lands and lines up behind it. The second player now throws as far as possible. The process is repeated until each child has thrown. The winner is the team with the greatest total distance.

Suggestions: Use a different colored beanbag for each team. Be sure to divide teams evenly. Do not permit long approaches prior to throwing. After the players know how to play the game, work for speed by having them run to the beanbag.

Toss-Up

Movement Skills: Fielding.

Formation: Three players per team in a circular formation.

Equipment: One softball per team (a lighter ball may be used for lower skill levels).

Procedures: Player from one team tosses the ball high into the air within the area of the circle. Anyone from the other team may catch the ball. Teams alternate tossing and catching. If the ball is caught, score one point for the catching team. If it is dropped, score one point for the tossing team.

Suggestions: Number players on each team and call a different number each time the ball is tossed. This will ensure that everyone gets an equal opportunity to toss and catch the ball.

Circle Overtake

Movement Skills: Throwing and fielding.

Formation: Large thirty-foot single circle formed by twelve to sixteen players, with six to eight per team.

Equipment: Two softballs per circle.

Procedures: Number players either "1" or "2." The 1s form one team, the 2s, another. Each team chooses a captain, who stands in the center of the circle. Each captain has a ball. On the signal "Go," the captains throw the ball from opposite sides of the circle to a member of their team. The teammate returns the ball. The captain and teammates continue to throw back and forth in a clockwise direction until one ball overtakes the other.

Suggestions: Use softer balls for less skilled players. Vary the size of the circle and the type of throw used.

Throw Softball

Movement Skills: Throwing and fielding.

Formation: Standard softball formation, with six to ten players per team.

Equipment: One softball and one set of bases per group.

Procedures: The game is played like regulation softball, except that there is no batting. The pitcher throws the ball to the "batter." The batter catches the ball and immediately hits it into the field. The game is then played like regulation softball, except that only one throw per time at bat is permitted, and stealing is not allowed. One point is scored for each run.

Around the Bases

Movement Skills: Base running.

Formation: Six players per team. One team lines up behind first base, the other behind third base.

Equipment: Four bases.

Procedures: The object is for a team to be the first to have everyone run the bases. The teams line up on the inside of the diamond at diagonally opposite bases. The first person makes one complete circuit of the bases and then touches off the second player, who does the same thing. The team finishing first is the winner.

Base-Running Overtake

Movement Skills: Base running, throwing, and fielding.

Formation: Ten players in regulation softball field formation, except one player is designated as the runner.

Equipment: One softball per team.

Procedures: One player is designated as the runner. The others play their position in the field. The runner comes up to home plate and throws the ball into fair territory anywhere in the field. The runner then tries to run around the bases and back to home plate before the ball is fielded and returned to the catcher. Players rotate positions after each try.

Suggestions: Make it a team activity by having one team up to bat and the other in the field.

Throw Around

Movement Skills: Base running, throwing, and fielding.

Formation: Six players, consisting of one base runner and all infield positions except the pitcher.

Equipment: Four bases, one softball.

Procedures: The object of the game is for the base runner, starting at home plate, to get all around the base path before the ball can be thrown around the horn (catcher to shortstop to first to second to third and home again). If the runner beats the ball around, he or she goes again and continues until beaten.

Suggestions: If the infielders are beating the base runner easily, have them throw twice around the horn before the runner is out. Adjust the distance between the bases to the ability of the players.

Home-Run Derby

Movement Skills: Batting and fielding.

Formation: Regular softball formation except for pitcher and catcher, who are placed in the field.

Equipment: Batting tee, bat, softball.

Procedures: A restraining line is drawn from first to third base. The four infielders may not go in front of the line. The three outfielders scatter in the field. The object is to hit the ball off the tee into fair territory beyond the restraining line on the fly. The team in the field tries to field the ball on the fly. If it catches the ball, no points are scored. If it does not, one point is awarded to the team at bat for an infield hit and two points for an outfield hit. Each player gets three swings. Players do not run the bases. Teams trade places after each player has had a turn at bat.

Suggestions: Permit more skillful groups to toss the ball up and hit it (fungo hitting) rather than using a tee stand.

Ground-Ball Pursuit

Movement Skills: Fielding ground balls.

Formation: Three players per team, spread along a goal line.

Equipment: One to three softballs per group.

Procedures: Grounders are thrown by one team to the other. Each grounder must bounce at least once before crossing the midfield line. The fielders receiving the ball try to stop it from crossing their goal line. Whoever fields the ball throws it back at the opposing team. Players stay in their own half of the field. One point is scored for each grounder that crosses an opponent's goal line.

Line-Ball Pepper

Movement Skills: Batting and fielding.

Formation: One player up to bat with four players in the field.

Equipment: One bat and softball per group.

Procedures: Fielders must stay within a lane and not go back past the goal line. Fielders throw the ball to the batter, who bunts it or chops it back. If one of the fielders fumbles the ball or lets the ball cross the goal line through his or her lane, that fielder must step back out of line and act as a backstop for the other fielders as they continue. The remaining fielders move in together so that there is not a vacant lane between them. They carry on in this way until only one fielder is left. This fielder then becomes the batter.

Suggestions: Only the fielder can throw the ball to the batter. If one of the players who has been eliminated and is acting as a backstop gets a ball, it must be given to one of the remaining fielders, who then throws it to the batter.

Softball Pop-Up

Movement Skills: Fielding high fly balls.

Formation: Scatter formation within a fifty-foot circle. Six players per team.

Equipment: One softball per group.

Procedures: Give players on both teams numbers. The object is for the fielding team, scattered informally in the center of a large circle, to catch the fly balls thrown by the throwing team, which forms the circle. Each member of the throwing team, in turn, throws the ball as high into the air as possible. The player in the field who has a corresponding number attempts to catch the ball before it touches the ground in the designated area. When everyone has thrown, the teams exchange roles. One point is scored by the throwing team each time the ball drops in the designated area without being caught.

500

Movement Skills: Batting and fielding.

Formation: One batter, four to five fielders.

Equipment: One bat and one softball per team.

Procedures: Batter hits fungos (i.e., self-tossed batted balls) to the fielders. The first person to reach 500 points becomes the batter. Score 200 points for catching a fly ball, 50 points for fielding a grounder, and 100 points for fielding a grounder on the first bounce.

Suggestions: As skill advances, play as just described, but subtract points if the ball is not played cleanly. If a fly ball is dropped, subtract 100 from the total. If a grounder is missed, subtract 50 points. Subtract 75 points for fumbling a ball on the first hop. Instead of hitting fungos, have someone pitch and then play as just described.

Three-Pitch Softball

Movement Skills: All basic softball skills.

Formation: Two teams with nine players per team. Use a softball diamond and standard player formation.

Equipment: One bat and softball per group; one set of bases.

Procedures: The pitcher is a member of the batting team. The batter is out if he or she cannot get a fairly hit ball in three pitches. When three players are out, the side is retired. Since the pitcher is a member of the batter's team, there should be no bunting or base stealing. The batting team may change pitchers at any time. With the exception of these details, all softball rules apply.

Milk Carton Softball

Movement Skills: All basic softball skills.

Formation: Regulation softball formation.

Equipment: One bat, softball, and set of bases; four half-gallon milk cartons.

Procedures: The object is for the batter, after hitting a fair ball, to circle the bases before the four cartons can be knocked down in order by the fielders. The game is played like softball, but there is a milk carton on each base. On a fair ball, the batter circles the bases and touches home plate. The fielders retrieve the ball and pass it in order to first, second, third, and home. As the baseman receives the ball, she knocks down the pin and throws to the next base. The batter is out (1) on a fly ball, (2) if she knocks down a pin, or (3) if the four pins can be knocked down by the fielders before she gets home. Rotate base positions after each inning. After all players on one side bat, have sides change. One point is scored by the batter if she beats the ball home.

Suggestions: (1) Play by outs; (2) use a batting tee; (3) adjust the number of cartons and base lengths to the ability of players.

Tee Ball

Movement Skills: Batting, fielding, throwing, and base running.

Formation: Standard softball formation.

Equipment: One softball and set of bases per group.

Procedures: This is the same as for regulation softball, except the ball is batted off a tee.

Whiffle Ball

Movement Skills: All softball skills.

Formation: Regulation softball formation with ten players per team.

Equipment: One white ball and bat; one set of bases per group.

Procedures: The game is played by the same rules as regulation softball.

Suggestions: Use a larger ball or a large-headed bat if less skilled children are having difficulty hitting the ball.

BASIC RULES FOR SOFTBALL

The regulation game of slow-pitch softball is played by two teams, each with ten players: a pitcher, catcher, three base persons, a shortstop, and four outfielders. The object of the game is for the team at bat to hit balls delivered underhand by the pitcher into the field in fair territory and score runs. One run is scored for each player who successfully circles the bases and returns to home plate. The team in the field attempts to prevent the batting team from scoring by catching the ball on the fly or by touching the **base runner** with the ball while off base. The base runner must run consecutively from first to second to third base and then home. He may stop at any base after hitting a ball into fair territory, and he may continue to the next and subsequent bases on the next fairly hit ball. After three persons have been put out on the batting team, the teams exchange positions.

CONCEPT 24.9
Learning the activity concepts involving the rules, strategies, formations, and patterns of softball playing equips children with the tools for self-directed play.

The **pitcher** must present the ball to the batter and may take one step forward on the delivery, keeping the rear foot on the pitcher's plate. The ball must be thrown underhand at a moderate speed in an upward arc from six to twelve feet above the ground. The ball should cross home plate between the shoulders and knees of the batter.

The **batter** may swing at a pitched ball or let it go by. It is a **strike** if the batter swings and misses. It is a **foul ball** if the ball does not land in fair territory. A foul ball is counted as a strike unless the batter already has two strikes. The batter is also out in slow-pitch softball if the ball is bunted, hit downward in a chopping motion, or hit foul after the second strike.

After a ball has been hit into fair territory, the batter becomes a base runner. The batter also becomes a base runner if she is hit by the ball on the pitch or if the catcher interferes with the batter. The base runner must touch the bases in regular order. Only one base runner may occupy a base at a time. The base runner is out if he is tagged by the ball while off base, if he runs more than three feet out of the base path, if he passes a preceding runner, if he leaves the base before a fly ball has been caught, or if he leaves the base before a pitched ball reaches home plate.

ASSESSING PROGRESS

Assessment of softball skills is important at both the beginning and the end of an instructional unit. Assessment need not take up large segments of time. Process assessments are subjective and can be informally conducted by the teacher. Product assessments can be self-referenced and student-led. At the elementary school level, little attention needs to be given to comparing children through the use of standardized softball skills tests. The range of skill will vary markedly, depending on the extent of the children's previous experiences. It is more important at this level for you to know how well they can execute basic softball skills and for them to be able to see improvement in their levels of performance.

C O N C E P T   2 4 . 1 0
Softball skills may be evaluated through a variety of process- and product-oriented assessment techniques at both entry and exit levels to a skill theme.

Process Assessment

Process assessment is based on the subjective judgment of the instructor of the demonstrated level of ability in the basic skills of softball. With process ratings, the instructor is primarily concerned with the body mechanics or technique used to perform the various throwing, fielding, and batting skills of softball. The form rating chart depicted in Figure 24.8 is an example of a process assessment instrument that can be used to chart the manner in which these skills are performed quickly and accurately. Charting students at the beginning of an instructional module will help determine where they have improved.

Product Assessment

Students can determine their own level of skill in the various elements of softball by working with a partner and using a self-referenced performance rating card similar to the sample shown in Figure 24.9. Because of the limited amount of time allotted to the physical education period, and the large number of students, it is often impractical for the instructor to administer a softball skills test. Students working in small groups of four to six can easily and accurately determine their own levels of performance with a minimum amount of training. If the primary reason for skill assessment is to chart individual progress and is not the awarding of grades, then there is little danger of children inflating their scores. The softball skills performance rating may be placed on a card, have comments added to it, and be sent home to parents as a progress report.

SUMMARY

The game of baseball is deeply embedded in North American culture. In fact, baseball and softball are generally considered to have a greater number of youth participants than any other youth sport activities. A softball skills theme is an ideal instructional unit for the developmentally based physical education program. Because it requires less space, has simpler rules, has more carryover value, and can be played in a coeducational setting, softball is preferred over a baseball skills theme.

The game of softball is composed of a variety of fundamental stability, locomotor, and manipulative skills that must be refined and adapted to the game in progressively more advanced levels. Children can experience considerable success and enjoyment in slow-pitch instructional softball. Care should be taken to focus on skill development and refinement, not on playing the game. Although playing the game of softball is sometimes appropriate in limited amounts, there is no place for a softball unit that permits day after day playing of the game with little regard for skill instruction.

It is important to instill in children the skill concepts and movement concepts associated with throwing, fielding, batting, and other associated skills. In this way they learn both about how their body *should* move and about how it *can* move in performing skillfully in the game of softball. Additionally, teachers should recognize that children encounter a number of developmentally based problems in softball skills acquisition that can be overcome by

SOFTBALL SKILLS RATING CHART

Class: _____   Grade: _____

Entry Assessment Date: _____   Exit Assessment Date: _____

Directions	Throwing Skills				Fielding Skills			Batting Skills		Associated Skills			Key
	Overhand	Sidearm	Underhand	Pitching	High Fly	Low Fly	Grounder	Batting	Bunting	Base Running	Base Playing	Base Stealing	
Observe during drill or play situations. Mark entry rating in upper left corner and exit rating in lower right corner of each square.													**A: Advanced**—Correct technique plus good control and force production **I: Intermediate**—Correct technique but lacking in control or force production **B: Beginning**—Inconsistent use of correct technique
													Comments:

FIGURE 24.8 *Sample form rating chart for softball.*

SOFTBALL SKILLS PROGRESS CHART

Student's
Name: _____ Grade: _____ Class: _____ Year: _____

See Reverse for Description		Skills	Entry Rating	Comments	Exit Rating	Comments
Distance Throw	Hoop Pitch	*Throwing Skills*	Date		Date	
B 0–30 ft. I 30–90 ft. A 90 ft.>	0–1 for 5 2–3 for 5 4–5 for 5	Distance Throw				
		Accuracy Pitch				
Flies and Grounder Drills		*Fielding Skills*	Date		Date	
B 0–3 for 10 tries I 4–8 for 10 tries A 9–10 for 10 tries		Flies				
		Grounders				
Batting	Bunting	*Batting Skills*	Date		Date	
B 0–1 for 5 I 2–3 for 5 A 4–5 for 5	0–1 for 5 2–3 for 5 4–5 for 5	Batting				
		Bunting				

Parent's Signature: _____ Date: _____
Comments:

FIGURE 24.9 *Self-referenced performance rating card for softball.*

using a variety of recommended teaching strategies. Entry and exit level assessment of either a process or product nature will provide both you and your students with valuable information and a vivid illustration of skill learning through practice.

COMPLEMENTARY READINGS

ACEP. (1992). *Rookie Coaches Softball Guide.* Champaign, IL: Human Kinetics.

Athletic Institute. (1991). *Youth League Baseball: Coaching and Playing Edition.* North Palm Beach, FL: The Athletic Institute.

Elliott, J., and M. Ewing. (1992). *Youth Softball: A Complete Handbook.* Dubuque, IA: Wm. C. Brown & Benchmark.

SUPPLEMENTARY READINGS

Coaching Association of Canada. (1990). *Softball Coaching Manual.* 333 River Road, Vanier, Ontario.

Houseworth, S., and K. Kivkin. (1985). *Coaching Softball Effectively.* Champaign, IL: Human Kinetics.

Pagnoni, M., and G. Robinson. (1990). *Softball: Fast and Slow Pitch.* North Palm Beach, FL: The Athletic Institute.

Stockton, B. (1984). *Coaching Baseball: Skills and Drills.* Champaign, IL: Human Kinetics.

VIDEOS

The Art of Hitting. Pinson, V. Dubuque, IA: Wm. C. Brown. (60 min.).

KEY: B = Beginning Level   I = Intermediate Level   A = Advanced Level
      of Skill   of Skill   of Skill

Description of Tests:

Distance Throw: With a partner, player throws the ball as far as possible from behind
    a restraining line. Field is marked off with three lines. The first line is 30 feet from
    the restraining line (B area), the second is 60 feet (I area), and the third is 90 feet
    (A area). Each player takes 3 throws. Longest throw counts.

Hoop Pitch: With a partner and a hoop suspended at strike-zone height, player
    stands 40 feet away and pitches the ball underhand through the hoop. Each
    player makes 5 pitches.

Flies and Grounders: With a partner 30 feet distant, player alternates throwing 5 high
    balls and 5 grounders. Partner attempts to catch each ball.

Batting: With a partner who pitches the ball so it can be easily hit, player bats the
    ball 5 times as far as possible. Balls that are hit or that roll into the outfield in fair
    territory count one point each.

Bunting: Same as above, but ball must stay in fair territory in the infield.

FIGURE 24.9 *(continued) Reverse side of self-referenced performance rating card for softball.*

Assessment of Softball Skills. Ignico, A. (1995). Dubuque, IA: Wm. C. Brown & Benchmark. (Two 30-min. tapes).

Hitting, Pitching and Fielding for Kids. Charleston, WV: Cambridge Physical Education and Health. (three videos).

Little League's Official How-to-Play Baseball Video. Athletic Institute. 200 Castlewood Drive, North Palm Beach, FL: The Athletic Institute. (70 min. Also available with the *Little League's Official How-to-Play Baseball Book*).

Teaching Kids Baseball. Kindall, J. Dubuque, IA: Wm. C. Brown. (75 min.).

Volleyball Skill Themes

Key Concept

Volleyball Skill Themes Can Be Successful at the Elementary School Level, but the Skills Used and the Level of Student Expectation Frequently Need to Be Modified

Chapter Objectives

The purpose of this chapter is to provide you with the tools to:
• Discuss reasons for and ways of modifying the skill expectations of elementary school-age children in a volleyball skills theme.
• Demonstrate competence in designing a volleyball skills theme for a group of children.
• Be familiar with the mechanically correct way to perform a variety of volleying and serving skills.
• List the skill concepts and movement concepts that children should know concerning volleying and serving skills.
• Be familiar with common problems encountered by children in developing their volleyball skills, and be able to apply effective techniques for overcoming these difficulties.
• Design a warm-up session appropriate for a volleyball skills theme.
• Demonstrate knowledge of a variety of skill drills and lead-up activities designed to develop and reinforce selected volleyball skills.
• Show how process and product assessment techniques may be effectively used at the beginning and at the end of a volleyball skills theme.

Terms to Remember

Overhead Pass	Serve
Bump Pass	Side-Out
Set	Rotate
Dig Pass	Violations
Underhand Serve	Game
Overhead Serve	Match

The game of volleyball was invented by William Morgan, a YMCA physical director in Holyoke, Massachusetts, in 1895. Since then the game has steadily gained in popularity, both as a recreational activity and as a competitive sport. Power volleyball has become very popular throughout North America. It was given a big boost by the extensive coverage of the sport in the Olympic Games and by the superb showing of both the men's and women's teams representing the United States and Canada.

C O N C E P T   2 5 . 1
Altering ball size and texture, lowering the net, and modifying the rules will help promote success in a volleyball skills theme at the elementary school level.

Basic volleyball skills can be developed at the elementary school level only if significant modifications are made. First, the net should be lowered to a height of about six feet for beginning players. Second, the ball should be modified for all but the most skillful players. Beach balls and foam balls work well during the skill development phase. Third, the size of the court should be modified, and a maximum of six players per side should be permitted. Simply dividing the class in half and playing with fifteen to twenty children per side is ridiculous. Such a procedure only promotes inactivity and encourages the more skillful to dominate play. Fourth, children must learn the foundational skills of the game and develop eye-hand coordination before attempting to play regulation volleyball. Care must be taken to adhere to each of these requirements to maximize successful learning.

DEVELOPING A VOLLEYBALL SKILLS THEME

The vast majority of children will have had little or no prior volleyball playing experience, unlike the case of basketball or softball. Therefore, most will be at the beginning level of skill development. This and the complexity of the task of volleying itself make it generally advisable to wait until at least the third grade before beginning to develop children's volleyball skills. When a volleyball skills theme is planned and implemented, it will be helpful to follow the sequence of (1) preplanning, (2) observing and assessing, (3) planning and implementing,

and (4) evaluating and revising. Then select appropriate drills geared to the skill levels of the class. After the skill drill portion of the lesson, you will find it helpful to incorporate volleyball lead-up game activities that focus on further skill refinement. A wide variety of volleyball warm-up activities, skill drills, and lead-up games is located at the end of this chapter.

C O N C E P T   2 5 . 2
Preparing for a volleyball skills theme requires the same four-step procedure of preplanning, observing and assessing, specific planning and implementing, and evaluating and revising as any other movement skill theme.

VOLLEYBALL SKILL SEQUENCING

Children's visual-motor capabilities are sufficiently developed by the third grade for most to benefit from practice in the various modified volleyball skills. Relatively few skills are involved in volleyball in comparison with most other team sports. These skills are, however, quite precise and require sophisticated, coordinated interaction between the visual and motor systems. Third, fourth, and fifth graders are generally at the beginning level of developing their volleyball skills. Therefore, particular attention should be given to modifying the type of ball used, the height of the net, and the number of players involved. By the sixth grade most children have the potential to perform at the intermediate level, given ample opportunities for learning in the previous grades.

C O N C E P T   2 5 . 3
Skill sequencing for a volleyball skills theme depends heavily on children's visual-motor maturity.

The teaching progression for selected volleyball skills depicted in Table 25.1 will help you select appropriate volleyball skills to focus on as a developmental skill theme. Once this is accomplished, it will be necessary to select appropriate skill drills. The "Developmental Activities Chart for Volleyball" (Table 25.2) lists several skill drills that progress from relatively simple single-skill drills to more complex multi-skill drills. A

TABLE 25.1   *Selected Volleyball Skills Sequenced in Terms of Complexity*

Volleyball Skills (page number)	Suggested Progression for Children	
	Beginning Level	Intermediate Level
Volleying		
Overhead pass (483)	Introduce	Refine
Bump (483)		Introduce
Set (484)	Introduce	Refine
Dig (484)		Introduce
Serving		
Underhand serve (486)	Introduce	Refine
Overhead serve (487)		Introduce
Understanding the game		
Rules (494)	Introduce	Refine
Strategy (494)		Introduce

TABLE 25.2   *Developmental Activities Chart for Volleyball Sequenced in Terms of Complexity*

Volleyball Skill Drills (page number)	Volleying Skills	Serving Skills	Associated Skills
Volley and catch (489)	x		
Self-volley (489)	x		
Bump and catch (489)	x		
Bump it up (489)	x		
Over-under (489)	x		
High wall volley (489)	x		
Low wall volley (489)	x		
Partner toss (489)	x		
Partner volley (489)	x		
Spot (489)	x		
Partner set (489)	x		
Three-person set (489)	x		
One-two-three over (489)	x		
Circle volley (489)	x		
Bounce volley (490)	x		
Partner wall volley (490)	x		
Bump and run (490)	x		
Wall serve (490)		x	
Over-net serve (490)		x	
Alley serve (490)		x	
Serve and set (490)	x	x	
Net recovery (490)			x

brief description of each drill and recommended warm-up activities are located in the "Fitness and Skill Development Activities" section. Appropriate lead-up games to volleyball are also included.

VOLLEYING

Volleying, or passing, as it is sometimes called, requires considerable eye-hand coordination for successful performance. The development of volleying skills will require initial modification in the ball used. As skill develops, a regulation volleyball should be introduced. The primary volleying skills used in volleyball are the overhead pass, the bump pass, the set, and the dig pass. This section examines common developmental difficulties encountered by children and recommends strategies for developing volleying skills. The skill concepts and movement concepts that children should know are presented, along with verbal and visual descriptions of each type of volley.

CONCEPT 25.4
Volleying and serving skills take time to master and should be practiced under modified conditions.

Overhead Pass

The **overhead pass** is generally used to pass the ball from the back row to the front row or to clear the ball over the net. It is used for a ball that approaches at chest level or above and is a frequently used pass. The overhead pass is the most critical volleyball skill for elementary school children to learn.

Verbal Description

- Feet are in a stride position, with the knees bent slightly and the back relatively straight.
- Arms are raised upward, with the elbows slightly flexed.
- Fingers are spread, with the thumbs and index fingers closed, forming a "window."
- Eyes track the ball through the "window" as contact is made.
- Fingertips contact ball; wrists are stiff as contact is made, and the arms extend.
- Knees straighten as arms extend.

- Wrists extend as arms follow through in the direction of intended flight.
- Be certain to bend the knees and get under the ball to avoid illegal contact.

Visual Description. (Figure 25.1)

Bump Pass

The **bump pass,** or forearm pass, as it is frequently called, is used when a ball must be contacted below waist level. It is important that the bump pass be learned properly from the very beginning and that contacting the ball with open hands not be permitted. Once an open-hand bump pass is learned, it becomes difficult to change, and it is an illegal pass in the regulation game of volleyball. The bump pass is used to receive the serve and to initiate the set and the spike, or overhead pass, over the net. In addition, as play becomes refined, the bump is used to retrieve a spike.

Verbal Description

- *Method 1.* One hand is placed in the palm of the other with the thumbs together and on top. Be certain that both arms are level.
- *Method 2.* Form a fist with one hand and wrap the other hand around it, making sure not to cross the thumbs.
- *Method 3.* Interlock the fingers and place the thumbs on the index fingers. By pressing downward the wrists and elbows are made to extend, thus allowing a very flat, even surface.
- The arms are straight, with the forearms held close together.
- The body is brought in line behind the ball, with one foot in front of the other.
- The knees are bent deeply, but the back remains erect.
- The eyes track the ball to contact with the flat area formed by the forearms.
- The ball should rebound high off the forearms with little follow-through or leg extension.
- The angle at which the ball is contacted will determine the path of its flight.

Visual Description. (Figures 25.2 & 25.3)

FIGURE 25.1 *The overhead pass.*

 CONCEPT 25.5
Children should understand both the skill concepts and movement concepts associated with volleying and serving.

Set

The **set** is usually the second hit in the series of three permitted. The ball is volleyed high and positioned so the next person can direct it over the net with a spike. Controlled setting takes considerable time and practice to master.

Verbal Description

- Feet are in an exaggerated stride position with plenty of bend at the knees, and the back is straight.
- Arms are raised forward and upward, with the elbows flexed.
- The fingers are spread, with the thumbs and index fingers nearly touching, framing a "window."
- Eyes track the ball through the "window" as contact is made.

- Legs and arms extend as the ball is volleyed off the fingertips.
- Contact is made at the level of the forehead and the arms follow through in an upward direction.

Visual Description. (Figure 25.4)

Dig Pass

The **dig pass** is a one-handed pass used only when a player cannot get directly behind the ball or as a last attempt at contact before the ball touches the floor. The dig should be taught only after all other forms of passing have been mastered. It should never be taught as a standard method of passing a ball.

Verbal Description

- The arm is extended, and a tight fist is made.
- The ball is tracked visually to the point of contact.
- Upon contact, the ball should rebound off the area of the hand and the wrist.
- Little attempt should be made at following through.

FIGURE 25.2 *The bump pass.*

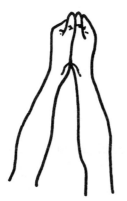

FIGURE 25.3 *Hand position for the forearm pass.*

FIGURE 25.4 *The set.*

Teaching Tips
Developmental Difficulties

- Fails to get under or behind the ball.
- Insufficient use of the legs in conjunction with the arm action.
- Fails to track the ball visually.
- Relaxes the wrists, causing the ball to travel backward with the overhead pass or set.
- Contacts the ball with the palms of the hand.
- Slaps at the ball.

- Fails to assume ready position.
- Has poor summation of forces.
- Excessive arm swing (bump).
- Ball contacts the upper portion of the arm rather than the forearms (bump).
- Contact is made with only one arm, rather than simultaneous contact with both arms (bump).

Recommended Strategies

- Stress control of the ball.
- Use balloons, beach balls, foam balls, and volleyballs in a progressive sequence.
- Practice volleying a tossed ball first, then a self-tossed ball, and finally wall volleys.
- Practice volleying to oneself.
- Practice volleying with a partner, and finally in a small group of four to six.
- Emphasize getting under the ball or behind the ball.
- Practice under static drill conditions, using modified balls, prior to introducing dynamic game situations, using regulation balls.
- Stress keeping the eyes on the ball.
- Work with the overhead pass before trying other passing skills.
- Introduce the bump pass and set only after children have reasonably mastered the overhead pass.

Concepts Children Should Know

Skill Concepts

- Get directly in line with the path of the ball.
- Keep your eyes on the ball.
- For overhead volleying, make a "window" with your hands (thumbs and index fingers nearly touch); look through the window as you contact the ball.
- Bend your knees before contacting the ball.
- Straighten your legs and your arms as you make contact with the ball.
- Don't slap at the ball.
- Don't contact the ball with your palms.
- A ball will rebound off a flat surface in a more predictable direction than off an angular surface.
- Keep your wrists stiff throughout.
- Follow through in the desired path of the ball.

Movement Concepts

- You can contact the ball at many different heights.
- You can contact the ball from many different levels.
- You can contact the ball with varying amounts of force.
- You may not contact the ball more than once in succession (unless contact is made off a block).

- You can control the direction of the ball.
- You can make contact from underneath the ball, from behind the ball, or from the side of the ball.
- You can volley many different types of balls.
- Light balls are easier to volley than heavy balls.

SERVING

Serving is a basic element of the game of volleyball. With practice, children can develop a reasonable degree of proficiency in serving. The underhand serve should be taught prior to the overhead serve. This section focuses on common problems in learning how to serve and recommended strategies for teaching serving skills. The skill concepts and movement concepts children should know are presented, along with verbal and visual descriptions of both the underhand and overhead serves.

Underhand Serve

The **underhand serve** is generally the first serve learned by children in elementary grades. With practice, it can be mastered by most children in the intermediate grades with a regulation volleyball.

Verbal Description (Right-Handed Server)

- Feet are in a narrow stride position, with the left foot slightly ahead of the right.
- Knees are bent slightly.
- Ball is held in the palm of the left hand just below waist level.
- Eyes focus on the ball until contact is made.
- The right arm is swinging downward and backward in a pendular motion, and weight is transferred to the rear foot.
- The right arm swings forward in a pendular action, and the weight is transferred to the front foot as contact is made and the knees straighten.
- Contact is made with the heel of the hand from a half-fist position.
- The wrist remains stiff throughout, and the arm follows through in the intended direction of the ball.

Visual Description. (Figure 25.5)

FIGURE 25.5 *The underhand serve.*

CONCEPT 25.6
Children frequently encounter many developmentally based problems in volleying and serving that may be overcome through a variety of teaching strategies.

Overhead Serve

The **overhead serve** is somewhat more difficult to master than the underhand serve. However, it should be introduced when the skill level of individuals or the class permits, because it is virtually the only serve used in the regulation game of power volleyball. The overhead serve may eventually be developed into a "floater" or a top-spin serve, both of which are more difficult to return than the underhand serve.

Verbal Description (Right-Handed Server)

- Feet are in a stride position with the left foot forward, pointing toward the opposite court.
- The body rotates partially to the right as the right arm begins its backswing.
- The ball is raised up in the left hand and tossed lightly upward to a position slightly in front of the head and over the right shoulder.
- The weight shifts to the rear foot as the toss is made.
- As the ball descends, the weight is shifted forward as contact is made with the right hand.
- The right arm is straight and makes contact with the ball at the peak of its arc.

- Contact is made with stiff heel of the hand, or with a fist, at midcenter of the ball and slightly forward of the head and right shoulder.
- The hips and shoulders rotate to face forward, and the legs straighten as the arm follows through.

Visual Description. (Figure 25.6)

Teaching Tips
Developmental Difficulties

- Takes the eyes off the ball.
- Holds the ball too high or too low.
- In the underhand serve, tosses the ball in the air before hitting it.
- Holds the ball too far to one side of the body.
- Makes contact with the palm of the hand rather than with the heel of the hand.
- Makes contact with the elbow bent.
- Has insufficient backswing.
- Has poor summation of forces, which causes the ball to fall short of the net.
- Lacks follow-through.

Recommended Strategies

- Practice first with lighter balls.
- Practice without a net before using a net.
- Practice at a shorter distance from the net before practicing at full-court distance.

FIGURE 25.6 *The overhead serve.*

- Measure where the ball should be held by swinging the contact arm back and forth one time.
- Stress proper positioning.
- Emphasize maintaining visual contact with the ball.
- Use a carpet square to stress weight transference to the front foot as the ball is hit.
- Let students experiment with various hand positions.
- Practice the preferred technique repeatedly.
- Master the underhand serve before teaching the overhead serve.
- Practice throwing the ball across the net using the underhand and overhead throwing patterns before practicing the actual serve. This allows students to warm up and to get the feel of the action.

Concepts Children Should Know
Skill Concepts

- Keep your eyes on the ball.
- Make contact with the heel of your hand or with your fist, not with your knuckles.
- Keep your wrist stiff.
- Follow through in the direction you want the ball to go.

Movement Concepts

- You can contact the ball with varying amounts of force.
- You can make the ball travel faster by putting greater force behind the ball.
- Good summation of forces will put more force behind the ball.
- You can make contact with the ball at different heights.
- The level of your body can be varied when you serve the ball.
- You can make contact on different parts of the ball.
- You can cause the ball to travel in different areas based on your follow-through.
- You control the direction of the ball through your point of contact.

FITNESS AND SKILL DEVELOPMENT ACTIVITIES

Mastery of volleyball skills involves careful sequencing and progression of activities from simple to complex. Simply by changing the ball from a balloon to a beach ball, and then to a foam ball, and finally to a volleyball will dramatically affect the success of any skill-drill activity. Each of the activities that follow can be significantly altered in terms of difficulty merely by altering the object to be volleyed or served.

Warm-up Activities

The warm-up activities suggested for basketball, soccer, and softball are all appropriate for volleyball. Warm-up activities should emphasize the muscles of the upper trunk as well as the leg muscles.

Skill Drills

Each of the skill drills that follows may be practiced with different types of balls. Many of them may be practiced alone; others may be practiced with a partner or in a small group. It is of critical importance that the ball used by any child be geared to his or her present level of ability. As skill develops, heavier balls should be used, progressing to a regulation leather volleyball only after skills have been developed using balloons, beach balls, and foam balls.

The primary objectives of the skill drills found here are to

1. improve volleying skills (overhand, set, bump, and dig passes);
2. improve serving skills (underhand and overhead serves);
3. improve various aspects of motor fitness (eye-hand coordination, eye-body coordination, and agility); and
4. introduce the associated skills of blocking and spiking.

Volley and Catch (overhead volley set).   Player tosses the ball into the air, volleys it upward, and catches it as it comes back down. Process is repeated several times, with player trying to remain in the same spot. As skill develops, vary the height of the toss and the height of the volley.

Self-Volley (overhead volley).   Player tosses the ball overhead and tries to keep it in the air with repeated overhead volleys. Progress from two to three to four or more volleys. Work for height and control.

Bump and Catch (bump pass).   Player tosses the ball upward and contacts it below the waist with a bump pass. Bump it up and catch it. Work for greater control and height.

Bump It Up (bump pass).   This is the same as the preceding activity, but work for two, three, four, or more consecutive bump volleys.

Over-Under (overhead volley and bump pass).   A player tosses the ball overhead and tries to keep it in the air by alternating overhand and bump passes.

High Wall Volley (overhead volley).   A player stands three to five feet from the wall and volleys the ball upward repeatedly against the wall. Work for clean, crisp volleys and for increasing the height of each volley.

Low Wall Volley (bump pass).   This is the same as the preceding exercise, but the ball is contacted below the waist. Work for high bump passes and good control.

Partner Toss (overhead volley).   A player tosses the ball up and returns it with an overhead volley. A partner catches the ball and repeats. Partners work for height and control.

Partner Volley (overhead volley).   Partners volley repeatedly back and forth, working for control and height on each volley.

Spot (set).   Player tosses ball up and volleys it high, so that it lands within a designated spot. Start with the free-throw circle and work down to setting into a hoop or box lying on the floor.

Partner Set (set pass).   Player tosses the ball upward and sets it up to a partner, who sets under the ball but catches it.

Three-Person Set (set).   One player executes a self-tossed overhead pass to a second player, who in turn executes a set-up to a third player. Third player catches the ball.

One-Two-Three Over (overhead pass and set-up).   Same as preceding exercise, except that on the third hit, the ball is volleyed over the net.

Circle Volley (set).   With six to eight players per circle, the teacher (or a child) tosses the ball to a player, who sets the ball back to the teacher. As skill develops, toss the ball high or low or off to one side. The teacher (child) may also set the ball back.

Bounce Volley (overhead volley and bump pass).   Player volleys the ball high into the air with an overhead pass, lets it bounce, then volleys it again with a bump pass. Repeat.

Partner Wall Volley (overhead volley or bump pass). With a partner, and with both players standing five to ten feet from the wall, one player throws the ball high against the wall, while the partner moves to intercept, sets, and volleys the ball upward. Partners change positions.

Bump and Run (bump pass).   With partner about ten feet away, the first player tosses ball to either side. The partner runs to that spot and attempts to bump pass the ball upward before it hits the ground. For beginners, point to where the ball will be tossed. Later toss it to either side without warning.

Wall Serve (serving).   Player stands thirty feet from the wall and serves the ball underhand to a spot six to eight feet up on the wall. As skill develops, introduce the overhead serve.

Over-Net Serve (serving).   With partners at opposite ends of the gymnasium, practice serving back and forth. Work for distance and then control. As both develop, introduce the overhead serve. Start at a shorter distance (spiking line) and gradually move back.

Alley Serve (serving).   With four players per group, one player serves the ball three times, trying to get it to drop into one of three alleys that have been drawn on the floor on the opposite side of the net.

Serve and Set (serving and setting).   The player stands twenty feet from the wall, serves the ball against the wall, moves to position on its rebound, and sets it back against the wall.

Net Recovery (dig and bump pass).   One player throws the ball forcefully into the net; a partner uses a dig to pass the ball upward.

C O N C E P T   2 5 . 7
Skill drills and lead-up games are effective in developing, refining, and reinforcing children's volleyball skills.

Volleyball Lead-up Games

The sport of volleyball requires considerable eye-hand coordination and is difficult for many elementary school-age children to master. To minimize frustration and to maximize skill learning and enjoyment, it is recommended that you modify the type of ball used for the lead-up activities that follow. Progress from using balloons to beach balls, to foam balls, and then to volleyballs. The lead-up games selected for inclusion here are easy to organize and are challenging and fun. They are presented in a progression from simple to complex in Table 25.3. The primary objectives for including volleyball lead-up games into the lesson are to

1. reinforce the various skills of volleyball,
2. introduce the basic rules of volleyball through modified game activities,
3. provide opportunities for developing an understanding of and appreciation for basic team strategies,
4. encourage a spirit of cooperation and teamwork, and
5. have fun and learn to play modified volleyball with a reasonable degree of skill.

Ten Volleys

Movement Skills: Volleying and setting.

Formation: Circles with four to eight players per circle.

Equipment: One volleyball per circle.

Procedures: At the signal "Go," first player volleys the ball upward and calls out "One." Second player calls out "Two" as she volleys the ball, and so on to "Ten." Players may not contact the ball twice in succession, nor may they lift the ball. If the ball contacts the floor, start over. First team to reach ten wins.

Suggestions: Use large plastic balls, beach balls, or foam balls for less skilled groups.

Block Volley

Movement Skills: Volleying and setting.

Formation: Circle with four to six players.

Equipment: One volleyball per group.

TABLE 25.3

Suggested Progression for Introducing Volleyball Lead-Up Games Sequenced in Terms of Complexity

Volleyball Lead-up Games (page number)	Passing Skills	Setting Skills	Bump Skills	Serve Skills	Rotating Skills	Team Play
Ten volleys (490)	X	X				
Block volley (490)	X	X				
Balloon volleyball (491)	X	X				
One bounce (491)					X	X
One-line volleyball (492)	X			X		
High ball (492)		X	X		X	X
Deck tennis (492)					X	X
Newcomb (492)					X	X
Shower service ball (492)				X		
Serve, pass, and catch (493)	X			X		
Bump game (493)			X			
Modified vball (493)	X	X	X	X	X	X
Volleyball (493)	X	X	X	X	X	X

Procedures: Arrange players in a circle, ten feet apart. One player, "it," is at the center of the circle. The players in the circle volley the ball back and forth to each other across the circle while "it" tries to block the ball from crossing to other players. A player in the circle becomes "it" if his batted ball is blocked, and the first "it" takes his place in the circle. The object of the game is to try to volley the ball up so that "it" will not be able to block. Team scoring is based on the number of the times the ball is volleyed before it is blocked.

Suggestions: Use balloons, beach balls, or foam balls for less skilled players.

Balloon Volleyball

Movement Skills: Volleying and setting.

Formation: Two teams on either side of a rope stretched six feet off the ground. Three to four players per side in a fifteen- by fifteen-foot court.

Equipment: One balloon per group.

Procedures: Players get two attempts to serve the balloon. A serve may be relayed once before going over. The balloon may be hit five times before going over the net. Points are scored the same as in volleyball.

Suggestions: As skill develops, progress to using a beach ball, foam ball, and finally a volleyball.

One Bounce

Movement Skills: Team play.

Formation: Two teams of six players, one team on each side of a net three to six feet high.

Equipment: One volleyball and one net per game.

Procedures: Play is begun by throwing the ball over the net. The receiving team must catch the ball on the fly or after one bounce. The ball is then thrown back over to the other side. If the ball hits the floor more than once, the opposite team scores. The first team to reach fifteen points wins. Players rotate as in regulation volleyball.

Suggestions: As skill develops, raise the net from three feet to six feet. If skill level is low, allow two bounces.

One-Line Volleyball

Movement Skills: Passing and serving.

Formation: Regulation volleyball formation with six players per team, or a modified formation with nine players per team.

Equipment: One volleyball and one net per game.

Procedures: The ball is served by a player from the right-hand corner position. The ball is volleyed back and forth until it goes out of bounds or fails to be returned, or until a foul (touching net or stepping over line) occurs. The ball may be hit any number of times on a side before it is returned, but not twice in succession by the same player. Players rotate when their team wins the serve. Teams may serve for a specified number of points and then change service.

Suggestions: Teacher may limit the number of times the ball may be hit on each side of the net. The size of the court may be made smaller to take into account the type of ball being used and the skill level of the players.

High Ball

Movement Skills: Set and bump.

Formation: Teams of six to eight players, arranged in a circle with one player in the center.

Equipment: One volleyball per group.

Procedures: The object is to keep the ball in the air by using a set-up or bump pass. The player in the center of the circle volleys to a player in the circle, who volleys it back. Play continues around the circle until one of the balls is missed or handled twice in succession by the same player. Illegal hitting and digging are not allowed. When an error is made, the next player of the group puts the ball into play as rapidly as possible. Each time the ball is successfully volleyed from player to player, one point is made. When an error is made, that score is terminated. A new score begins with each renewal of play.

Suggestions: A continuous match may be played by keeping the highest daily score of each group and totaling these scores each week. Use a lighter ball for less skilled groups.

Deck Tennis

Movement Skills: Rotating skills and team play.

Formation: Two teams of six players on each side of a net three to five feet high.

Equipment: One rubber deck-tennis ring and one net or suspended rope per game.

Procedures: One team begins the game by throwing the deck-tennis ring over the net. If the opposing team fails to catch the ring, a point is scored for the throwing team. If the thrower fails to get the ring over the net, a point is scored for the other team. A throw that goes outside the boundary lines is a point for the opposite team. A player may not move once he catches the ring. After the ring strikes the floor, the closest player picks it up and starts a new volley for a point by throwing it over the net.

Suggestions: Require the server to call out the score prior to each serve. Use a standard volleyball rotation system. If a deck-tennis ring is not available, try a Frisbee disc.

Newcomb

Movement Skills: Team play and rotating skills.

Formation: Two teams of six players each, one team on each side of a net three to seven feet high.

Equipment: One volleyball and one net per game.

Procedures: The ball is served by throwing it from the back right corner. Players on the opposite side try to catch the ball before it touches the ground. If the ball is caught, it may be thrown back over the net or passed to a teammate (two passes are allowed) before it is thrown over the net. Play continues until the ball hits the floor. A player may not change positions after catching a ball. The object is to score fifteen points or as many points possible in a set time limit.

Suggestions: Insist on players playing their positions and not others. Use a lower net or different ball for less skilled players.

Shower Service Ball

Movement Skills: Serving.

Formation: Two teams of six to nine players on either side of a suspended net.

Equipment: Several volleyballs and one suspended net for each game.

Procedures: To start the game, the volleyballs are divided between the teams and are handled by players in the serving area. The serving area is between the baseline and the line drawn through the middle of each court. Balls may be served at any time, just so long as the server is in the serving area of his or her court. Any ball that is served across the net is to be caught by any player near the ball. The person catching or retrieving a ball from the floor moves quickly to his or her serving area and serves. A point is scored for a team whenever a served ball hits the floor in the other court or is dropped by a receiver. Two scorers are needed, one for each side.

Suggestions: As skill develops, add several balls to the game.

Serve, Pass, and Catch

Movement Skills: Serving and passing.

Formation: Two teams of six players on each side of a six- to seven-foot net.

Equipment: One volleyball and one suspended net per game.

Procedures: Players line up as if they were playing an actual game. When the ball is served, the receiver makes one bump pass to another team member, who catches the ball. A point is scored if the ball is not properly passed or is not caught. Side-out is called if the ball is passed correctly and caught. Fifteen points constitute a game.

Suggestions: Limit play to five minutes per game.

Bump Game

Movement Skills: Bump pass.

Formation: Two lines of six players each, perpendicular to the net.

Equipment: One volleyball per team.

Procedures: Divide the class into groups. Team members are lined up behind each other on each side of the net. The first player in line runs out to bump a ball that has been tossed out. The ball is bumped over the net, with the first player in the opposite line running out to midcourt to bump it back. Once that player has bumped, the next person

in the same line comes out and is ready to bump the next ball that comes over the net. Score is kept. If the ball touches the floor, or if anything other than a bump pass is used, a point is scored by the opposite team.

Suggestions: Do not require the ball to go over the net. Work for successful forearm passes.

Modified Volleyball

Movement Skills: Serving and volleying.

Formation: Two teams of six players each, one on each side of a six- to seven-foot net.

Equipment: One volleyball and net per game.

Procedures: A regulation volleyball game is played, with one or more of the following modifications: (1) The server may serve from a position in the center of the court. (2) Two or more service trials may be allowed. An assisted serve is permissible; that is, a teammate may relay a ball that has been served in an effort to send it over the net. (3) During the volley, an unlimited number of players may bat the ball before it goes over the net. (4) Although position play should be encouraged, it is not a requirement. (5) The ball may not be hit more than three times in succession by the same player. (6) The ball may be played from a bounce or from the air.

Volleyball

Movement Skills: Set-up, bump, dig, spike, block, net recovery, and serve.

Formation: Two teams of six players each. (May be modified to accommodate nine players on a thirty-by sixty-foot court.)

Equipment: One volleyball and one net suspended seven and one-half feet above the floor.

Procedures: The ball is served from the back right corner of the court. The server must stay behind the endline while serving. After the serve, he should move to his position on the court. The serving team scores when the receiving team fails to return the ball to the opponents' court. Only the serving team may score. The receiving team gains the serve when an opponent fails to return the ball over the net. The players may not reach over or touch the net. A player may not play the ball twice in succession. A ball may be played a maximum of three times by any one team before going over the net. A ball touching a boundary line is considered inbounds. A team wins when it scores fifteen points and has a two-point advantage. Play continues until the two-point advantage is obtained. Teams exchange courts at the end of each game. The losing team begins a new game. The best three out of five games wins the match.

Suggestions: Modify the regulation game by using a lighter ball. Permit a maximum of nine players per team. Do not divide the class in half for mass volleyball of ten or more per side.

BASIC RULES FOR VOLLEYBALL

The regulation game of volleyball is played with six players per team, which includes three forward players and three back players. The object of the game is to keep the ball in the air on your side and cause it to contact the floor on the opposing team's side.

CONCEPT 25.8
Activity concepts involving basic rules, strategies, formations, and patterns of play should be learned as part of a volleyball skills theme.

The ball is put into play with a **serve** from behind the rear line within ten feet of either sideline. The player in the right back position must serve the ball. The ball may be hit in any manner with the hand. Only one attempt is permitted. The ball must go over the net in the opponents' court for it to be played.

If the ball lands out of bounds or touches the net, it is a **side-out;** otherwise, the ball is played by the opposing team. A side-out is also called if one team fails to get the ball over the net into the opponents' court after a maximum of three hits. After a side-out, the nonserving team **rotates** so that the right back from that team serves the ball and play continues. Teams rotate by moving one player to the right in a clockwise direction.

If a violation is committed by the nonserving team, the serving team is awarded a point. If a foul is committed by the serving team, it is side-out and the opposing team is given the ball to serve. **Violations** are committed

when a player touches the net or steps over the center line, a player lifts or throws the ball (hand ball) rather than making a distinct hit of the ball, a player touches the ball more than once in succession (unless off a block), four or more hits are made before the ball goes over the net, a back-court player blocks or spikes in front of the ten-foot spiking line.

Fifteen points constitute a **game.** Teams must win by at least two points. The best three out of five games constitute a **match.** Teams change courts after each game. Balls landing on a boundary line are in bounds.

ASSESSING PROGRESS

Throughout the volleyball unit, you will want to check periodically on the progress of individuals and the group. Assessment can be quick, informal, and instructive. It need not take up large segments of time and should be focused on the operational goal of individual improvement. Both process and product assessments can be made at the beginning of the unit and again at the end.

CONCEPT 25.9
Volleyball skills may be evaluated through a variety of process- and product-oriented assessment techniques, each of which provides useful measures of status and progress.

Process Assessment

Process assessments are based on the instructor's subjective judgment of the student's level of ability in each of the basic skills of volleyball. The instructor is primarily concerned with the body mechanics or techniques used to execute the various volleying and serving skills of volleyball. Developing and using a rating chart like the one shown in Figure 25.7 will help determine the level of students' volleyball skills and where to focus instruction. It will also help to determine the extent of progress that has been made at the end of the volleyball unit.

Product Assessment

Numerous tests of volleyball skills have been reported in the literature. Their validity, however, for use with elementary school children is questionable. Also, the feasibility of

VOLLEYBALL SKILLS RATING CHART

Class: _____   Grade: _____

Entry Assessment Date: _____   Exit Assessment Date: _____

Directions	Volleying Skills				Serving Skills		Associated Skills		Key
	Overhead	Set-up	Bump	Dig	Underhand	Overhead	Blocking	Spiking	
Observe during drill or play situations. Mark rating in upper left corner for entry assessments and lower right corner for exit assessments.									**A: Advanced**—Correct technique plus good control and force production **I: Intermediate**—Correct technique but lacking in control or force production **B: Beginning**—Inconsistent use of correct technique
									Comments:

FIGURE 25.7   *Sample form rating chart for volleyball.*

administering these tests as part of the instructional program is questionable. Therefore, it is recommended that you devise your own test, collect information over several years, and establish your own norms. You may also wish to develop your own self-referenced assessment of volleyball skills in which the children themselves determine their level of proficiency. A self-administered volleyball performance test is shown in Figure 25.8. The performance rating card can be filled out by students, and comments can be added by the teacher. If desired, it may be sent home to parents as a progress report.

VOLLEYBALL SKILLS PROGRESS REPORT

Student's
Name: _____ Grade: _____ Class: _____ Year: _____

See Reverse for Description		Skills	Entry Rating	Comments	Exit Rating	Comments
Self-Volley Drill		*Volleying Skills*	Date		Date	
B I A	0–3 times 4–7 times 8–10 times	Overhead				
		Bump				
Over-Net Serving Drill		*Serving Skills*	Date		Date	
B I A	0–2 for 5 tries 3–4 for 5 tries 5 for 5 tries	Underhand				
		Overhead				
Blocking/Spiking Drill		*Associated Skills*	Date		Date	
B I A	2 for 5 tries 2 for 5 tries 3 for 5 tries	Blocking				
		Spiking				

Parent's Signature: _____ Date: _____
Comments:

KEY: B = Beginning Level of Skill   I = Intermediate Level of Skill   A = Advanced Level of Skill

Description of Tests:

Self-Volley: Player tosses the ball overhead and attempts to volley it repeatedly upward for up to 10 times (overhead and bump volley are done separately).

Over-Net Serve: With a partner at the opposite end of the court, player serves the ball five times from behind the serving line (underhand and overhead are done separately).

Blocking/Spiking Drills: With a partner, player attempts to block or spike a ball set in position up to 5 times each. The net is 6' high.

FIGURE 25.8 *Sample self-referenced performance rating card for volleyball.*

SUMMARY

A volleyball skills theme is appropriate for elementary school-age children if certain modifications are made in the skill requirements of the game. Because of the complex visual-motor requirements of both volleying and serving skills, you must be sure to present activities that are developmentally appropriate. To ensure success and promote continued interest, you might lower the net; use light balls such as balloons, beach balls, and foam balls before using a regulation volleyball; and alter the rules of the game.

Volleying and serving skills should be practiced in a manner that permits maximum participation by all. There is no defensible reason for mass volleyball activities with large groups on each side. Children need to learn the skill concepts and movement concepts associated with volleyball skill acquisition. Likewise, teachers need to be familiar with common developmentally based problems that children encounter, and be able to intervene with appropriate teaching strategies. Warm-up activities should be incorporated into the volleyball skills theme, followed by skill drills and lead-up activities designed to develop and reinforce specific skills. Assessment of children's volleyball skills is appropriate at the beginning and end of the skills theme, using both process and product techniques.

COMPLEMENTARY READINGS

American Coaching Effectiveness Program (ACEP). (1993). *Rookie Coaches Volleyball Guide*. Champaign, IL: Human Kinetics.

Ellery, P. (1993). Cutting volleyball down to size. *Strategies* 6:8–11.

Viera, B. L., and B. J. Ferguson. (1989). *Teaching Volleyball: Steps to Success*. Champaign, IL: Human Kinetics.

SUPPLEMENTARY READINGS

Bertucci, B. Ed. (1987). *The AVCA Volleyball Handbook*. Indianapolis: Morsters Press.

Scates, A. E. (1989). *Winning Volleyball Drills*. Dubuque, IA: Wm. C. Brown.

VIDEOS

Beginning Girls Volleyball: 1. Individual Skills; 2. Team Tactics; 3. Individual and Team Drills. Charleston, WV: Cambridge Physical Education and Health. (three 90-minute tapes).

Coaching Boy's Volleyball. Charleston, WV: Cambridge Physical Education and Health. (six 60- to 90-minute tapes).

Do It Better Volleyball. 200 Castlewood Drive, North Palm Beach, FL: The Athletic Institute. (30 min.).

The World of Volleyball. Champaign, IL: Human Kinetics. (30 min.).

Assessment of Volleyball Skills. Ignico, A. (1995). Dubuque, IA: Brown & Benchmark. (two 30-min. tapes).

PART V

The Program Strands

26   The Vigorous Activity Strand for Fit Movers

27   The Perceptual-Motor Strand for Multisensory Learners

28   The Creative Dance Strand for Expressive Movers

29   The Folk Dance Strand for Cooperative Social Learners

CHAPTER 26

The Vigorous Activity Strand for Fit Movers

Key Concept

Health-Related Fitness May Be Improved by Following the Principles of Exercise Frequency, Intensity, and Time through a Program That Emphasizes Exercise Enjoyment and Variety

Chapter Objectives

The purpose of this chapter is to provide you with the tools to:

• List and discuss several techniques for motivating children to engage in positive fitness behaviors.
• List and describe essential fitness principles that children should know and provide examples of how each may be taught.
• Provide examples of developmentally appropriate aerobic endurance activities for children.
• Provide examples of developmentally appropriate muscular strength and endurance activities for children.
• Provide examples of developmentally appropriate joint flexibility activities for children.
• Discuss what is meant by a "fitness strand" and why it is critical for this strand to be a planned part of each instructional lesson.

Terms to Remember

Aerobic Endurance	Variety
Intensity	Conditioning Exercises
Duration	Combatives
Frequency	Flexibility
	Static Stretching

Fitness activities are included in the physical education program for the specific purpose of contributing to the health-related aspects of physical development. Cardiovascular endurance, muscular endurance, muscular strength, and joint flexibility are the primary components of health-related physical fitness. Virtually all of the activities presented in the preceding chapters contribute in some measure to the development or maintenance of one or more aspects of physical fitness. These activities, however, focused on movement skill acquisition as their primary objective, with the fitness benefits being a worthy by-product. The low level of physical fitness that has been repeatedly demonstrated among many children and youth makes it vitally important that physical fitness activities be included in the instructional program for their own sake.

A portion of the physical education lesson should be devoted to instruction in fitness as well as skill development. Ideally, an in-school, home, or community-based daily fitness program should be available to every child. Unfortunately, this is not always the reality. Therefore, the physical education program has the responsibility to

1. increase children's knowledge base and develop positive attitudes toward the importance of fitness,
2. motivate children to take part in regular vigorous physical activity,
3. teach children how to exercise and what to do to improve their personal levels of fitness, and
4. provide opportunities for children to enhance their physical fitness.

CONCEPT 26.1
Because of the transient nature of health-related fitness, it needs to be included as a *primary* strand throughout the developmental physical education program.

Physical education is *not* physical fitness. Fitness activities should be a *primary* strand running through the entire physical education curriculum. Rather than focusing on fitness as a theme for a single unit of instruction, it is highly recommended that fitness instruction be included as a part of *each* lesson throughout the entire school year. Fitness is not an isolated part of the physical education program; it should be fostered continually through a vigorous program of movement skill acquisition and fitness enhancement for its own sake.

Properly presented, running for aerobic activity can be fun and sustained sufficiently for a training effect.

This chapter contains several practical suggestions for motivating children toward fitness. A variety of aerobic endurance, muscular strength and endurance, and flexibility activities are included. The activities are listed in progression from simple to more complex in terms of the requirements placed on the child to perform them and the complexity of the activities themselves. A personal fitness profile suitable for use with children may be found in Figure 26.1. You may find it helpful to refer back to Chapter 4, "Fitness Enhancement," and each of the skill theme chapters (Chapters 16 through 25) for additional information and specific fitness activity ideas.

AEROBIC ACTIVITIES

Aerobic endurance is the ability of the heart, lungs, and vascular systems to function efficiently during the stress of exercise. Experts consider aerobic endurance to be the most important component of total fitness. Any activity resulting in a sustained elevated heart rate is considered to be aerobic in nature. The keys to

PERSONAL FITNESS PROFILE

NAME: _____ GRADE: _____

Body Build Profile

	Trial 1	Trial 2	Trial 3	Trial 4
Date				
Age				
Height				
Weight				
Frame size				

Aerobic Fitness Profile

	Trial 1	Trial 2	Trial 3	Trial 4
Distance run				
Resting heart rate				
Exercise heart rate				
1-minute recovery rate				
5-minute recovery rate				

Physical and Motor Fitness Profile

	Trial 1	Trial 2	Trial 3	Trial 4
Arm endurance: push-ups				
Abdominal endurance: sit-ups				
Leg power: standing long jump				
Arm power: softball throw				
Flexibility: sit and reach				
Speed: 50-yard dash				
Agility: shuttle run				
Coordination: cable jump				
Balance: one-foot stand				

Summary:

I am: ___overweight, ___about right, ___underweight
I have: ___too much fat, ___about right, ___too little fat
My aerobic
   condition is: ___excellent, ___good, ___fair, ___poor
My general
   fitness is: ___excellent, ___good, ___fair, ___poor

My goals are:

1. _____
2. _____
3. _____

FIGURE 26.1 *Sample personalized fitness profile.*

TEACHING TIPS

Motivational ideas for encouraging children to be eager movers include the following:

- Work out with a partner.
- Work out to music.
- Chart laps and repetitions.
- Vary distances, number of repetitions, or time.
- Develop fitness bulletin boards.
- Publish information on fitness in the school newspaper.
- Develop graphs and charts of individual performance scores.
- Incorporate obstacle courses into the program.
- Use timed circuits, varying the circuit regularly.
- Try treasure hunts and orienteering skills.
- Develop a run-a-thon, or join the Jump Rope For Heart program sponsored by the American Heart Association and AAHPERD.
- Hold a cross-country meet.
- Develop a jump-rope, cross-country, aerobics, or fitness club.
- Provide small awards such as buttons, pins, ribbons, or certificates for individual improvement.
- Exercise with the children.

developing increased aerobic capacity are exercise frequency, intensity, duration, and variety.

CONCEPT 26.2
Children frequently need to be motivated to engage in positive fitness behaviors. By giving "it" a name and making it a game, you can ensure that the children will usually be eager to take part in vigorous fitness activities.

TABLE 26.1   *Selected Aerobic Activities Sequenced in Terms of Aerobic Requirements*

Aerobic Activities (page number)	Suggested Progression for Children		
	Beginning Level	Intermediate Level	Advanced Level
Partner tag (504)	X		
Monster tag (504)	X		
Shadow (504)	X		
Shipwreck (504)	X		
Rabbit and turtle (504)	X		
Freeze and melt (504)	X		
Red, white, blue (504)	X		
Circle chase (504)		X	
Circle change (504)		X	
Beanbag drop (504)		X	
Line touch (504)		X	
Rhythmical running (504)		X	
Rhythmical rope jumping (504)		X	
Aerobic rhythm exercise (504)		X	
Hit the deck (504)			X
Capture the flag (505)			X
Take the point (505)			X
Run for distance (505)			X
Run for time (505)			X

For children to receive the most benefits from vigorous exercise, it must be of sufficient **intensity** to elevate the heart rate to about 150 beats per minute or more. The average daily routine of most North American children provides few occasions for the heart rate to reach such levels.

The **duration** that the heart rate is elevated is the second key to aerobic endurance in children. Experts agree that it isn't enough to simply achieve an elevated heart rate, but that it must be sustained for ten minutes or longer to achieve a positive training effect. Again, the normal daily routine of many children does not provide for situations in which high heart rates are sustained for a sufficient duration to achieve an aerobic benefit.

Frequency is the third key to increased aerobic capacity. In addition to elevating one's heart rate for a sustained period of time, aerobic exercise must be engaged in no less than three times per week for a positive training effect. In fact, most experts recommend

five times per week as the ideal. A daily fitness program in the schools is the only place where we can guarantee that every child will have the frequency of exercise needed.

CONCEPT 26.3
The principles of fitness training must be followed for children to realize benefits from fitness training activities.

The fourth, and probably most important, key to increasing aerobic endurance is exercise **variety.** Children respond favorably if there is variety in the aerobics training program. For children, the activity must be fun. If it isn't, many will soon tire of the activity and quit. Aerobic activities are presented here with the concepts of variety and progression in mind (see Table 26.1).

The primary objectives of the aerobic endurance activities that follow are to

1. improve one's level of aerobic endurance;
2. understand the four keys to improved aerobic endurance: intensity, duration, frequency, and variety;
3. identify vigorous physical activities that contribute to aerobic endurance; and
4. select one or more aerobic activities and take part in it on a regular basis.

Partner Tag.   One player chases another until tagged; then they reverse.

Monster Tag.   The entire group runs to try to escape the "monster." The monster tries to tag someone. When tagged, that person immediately becomes the monster. Keep groups small, and do not permit "tag backs."

Shadow.   One player attempts to get away from another by running, dodging, and feinting. The partner attempts to be a "shadow" by staying directly behind.

Shipwreck.   The play area is marked off as the bow, stern, port, and starboard of a ship. The leader calls out a part of the ship, and the children run to that area. If desired, score may be kept by awarding a point to the first one there.

Rabbit and Turtle.   The leader tells a story about the rabbit and the turtle. Every time the word *rabbit* is mentioned, the players run in place as fast as they can. Every time *turtle* is mentioned, they run slowly in place.

Freeze and Melt.   Players run around the perimeter of the gymnasium or the play area. Each time the leader says "Freeze," they stop in their tracks and hold a motionless position until they hear the leader say "Melt."

Red, White, Blue.   From a large circle formation, children are counted off into the colors red, white, and blue. All sit down except one color. All the children who are this color take two giant steps back and face in one direction. On the signal "Go," runners try to get around the circle as many times as they can in a designated time. Repeat with each color.

Circle Chase.   From a large circle formation, count off by three's. All groups sit except one. The group left standing runs around the circle, trying to tag the person in front of them. If they get tagged, they keep running, trying to tag the next person in front. Repeat with all members.

Circle Change.   From a large circle formation, count off by three's. All groups are seated except one. The standing group runs around the circle as fast as they can, changing direction each time the leader says "Change." Allow one to two minutes for each group.

Beanbag Drop.   Hoops are arranged in a large circle around the gym or play area. One partner sits in the hoop; the other serves as the runner. Runners run around the area as fast as possible, picking up a beanbag (or other suitable object) from a central location. They continue around the circle, and each drops the object in his hoop. Leader calls "Halt" after one to two minutes or when all the beanbags have been taken. The pair with the most beanbags in their hoop is the winner. The activity is repeated in the opposite manner with the second person returning beanbags to the central location.

Line Touch.   Five or more parallel lines are drawn five meters apart, with the players lined up on the first line. On the signal "Go," they run and touch line two and return to line one, then up to line three, back to line one, then up to line four and back to line one, and so forth. Repeat the opposite way.

Rhythmical Running.   Players run around the gymnasium or play area. The leader calls out "Fast," "Medium," or "Slow." Runners change speeds on each command.

Rhythmical Rope Jumping.   Each child has an individual jump rope. Players jump rope for increasing lengths of time. Musical accompaniment serves as a great motivator. Develop jump rope routines. Jump with a partner. Vary the routines.

Aerobic Rhythm Exercise.   Perform a variety of stretching and in-place running activities to music. Gradually increase the tempo of the music and the length of the exercise session.

Hit the Deck.   Players face the leader, running in place. Leader calls out the following commands and the players perform: (1) "Run in slow motion" (in place), (2) "Double time," (3) "Hit the deck" (down on the floor on the stomach), (4) "On your back," (5) "Back to your feet," (6) "Slap your thighs" (high-knee running with hands slapping the thighs). Repeat several times.

Capture the Flag.   The class is divided into two teams. Each child has a flag tucked loosely into his belt or waist. Flags may be made from strips of cloth. The object of the game is to steal flags from the opposing team. When a flag is stolen, it is placed at one end of the gymnasium and the person losing it becomes a prisoner. To get the flag back, the player must do a specified activity (such as twenty jumping jacks or a seal crawl the length of the room). Once the flag is retrieved, the person can try again to capture other flags.

Take the Point.   Children are in a group of four to six, jogging single file around the gymnasium or play area. On the teacher's signal, the end runner must overtake the lead runner and become the "point" person. Jogging continues until each has had a chance to run the point position.

Run for Distance.   Using a running course set up in the gymnasium or on the playing field, children run around the course as often as possible in a specified time. Gradually increase the time as endurance increases.

Run for Time.   The children run a specified distance in as short a time as possible. Gradually increase the distance as endurance increases.

CONCEPT 26.4
Fitness training must be geared to the present capabilities of the participants and may be classified as beginning, intermediate, or advanced level activities.

MUSCULAR STRENGTH AND ENDURANCE ACTIVITIES

Muscular strength is the maximum force that a muscle can exert in one effort. Muscular endurance refers to the ability to sustain effort over time against a submaximal load. Both muscular strength and muscular endurance are important aspects of the fitness training program. They are closely related and are improved in children primarily through conditioning exercises and combative activities.

Conditioning exercises are familiar to most people. They are repetitive exercises such as sit-ups, push-ups, and jumping jacks. They can be performed without equipment and either alone or with a group. Mass conditioning has received renewed interest among many with

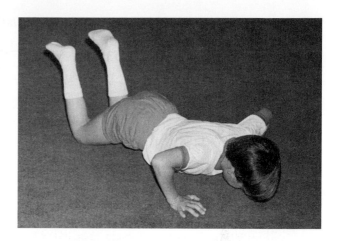

Modified push-ups.

the surge of popularity in exercising to music. This concept should be kept in mind when using conditioning exercises with children. Introduction of a rhythmic component plus the fast-paced change from exercise to exercise tends to heighten interest and encourage participation. Also, the use of a timed-circuit or station approach to conditioning exercises is recommended. Movement from station to station and achievement of specific individual goals for each exercise frequently heighten interest in conditioning activities. Table 26.2 provides several exercises that can be engaged in by children at the beginning, intermediate, and advanced levels of developing their muscular strength and endurance.

CONCEPT 26.5
Conditioning activities are especially effective when they are individualized or performed to music.

Combatives are a second form of muscular strength and endurance training enjoyed by elementary school children. They pit one child against another of similar size and ability in a contest of strength or endurance. Combative contests may be used at the beginning or at the end of a class period and need not occupy more than five to ten minutes. Figure about one contest for every two minutes. A single contest may be used throughout the combative session with frequent partner changes, or several contests may be performed. The key to success in

TABLE 26.2   *Selected Conditioning Activities for Muscular Strength and Endurance Sequenced in Terms of Strength Requirements*

Strength/Endurance Activities (page number)	Suggested Progression for Children		
	Beginning Level	*Intermediate Level*	*Advanced Level*
Arm and Shoulder			
Seal crawl (507)	X		
Coffee grinder (507)	X		
Spread-eagle walk (507)	X		
Modified pull-ups (507)		X	
Bent-knee push-ups (507)		X	*
Push-ups (507)		X	*
Abdominal			
Shoulder curl (507)	X		
Half-curl (508)	X		
Half-V-sits (508)	X		
Bent-knee sit-ups (508)		X	*
Alternate-knee-touch sit-ups (508)		X	*
V-Sits (508)		X	*
Lower Back			
Alternate leg lifts (508)	X		
Double leg lifts (508)		X	*
Back arch (508)		X	*
Rocking horse (508)		X	*
Leg			
Rabbit hop (508)	X		
Blast off (508)	X		
Sprinter (508)	X		
Heel lifts (508)	X		
Heel drops (508)		X	*
Pogo jumps (508)		X	*
Squat thrusts (508)		X	*

*These exercises may be upgraded to the advanced level by increasing repetitions or resistance.

combative contests is action. Keep the contests going with as little wasted time as possible. Stress participation and giving your best effort. Do not overemphasize winning or determine a class champion. Table 26.3 lists several combative activities appropriate for children.

The primary objectives of the conditioning exercises and combative activities that follow are to

1. enhance muscular endurance and muscular strength,
2. become knowledgeable about the differences between strength and endurance and how each is developed,
3. know the major muscle groups of the body and how to exercise each,

TABLE 26.3   *Selected Combative Activities for Muscular Strength and Endurance Sequenced in Terms of Strength Requirements*

Combative Activities (page number)	Suggested Progression for Children		
	Beginning Level	Intermediate Level	Advanced Level
One-person pull (508)		X	
One-person push (508)		X	
Rooster fight (509)		X	
Hand push (509)		X	
Hand wrestle (509)		X	
Back-to-back tug (509)		X	
Knee slap (509)		X	
Club knock (509)		X	
Leg wrestle (509)			X
Breaking arms (509)			X
Drake fight (509)			X
Elbow struggle (509)			X
Back-to-back lift (509)			X
Back-to-back push (509)			X
Stepping on toes (509)			X
All-fours ankle drag (510)			X
Ball wrestle (510)			X
American wrestle (510)			X

4. determine one's own level of strength and endurance and make individual improvement, and

5. develop an appreciation for and desire to be involved in vigorous physical activity.

Arm and Shoulder Activities

Seal Crawl (arms and shoulders).   From a push-up position with the arms extended and toes pointed, drag the body forward, using only the arms.

Coffee Grinder (arms and shoulders).   From a side-support lying position with the support arm extended, walk around the support arm several times. Repeat with the opposite arm.

Spread-Eagle Walk (arms and shoulders).   From a push-up position with the arms extended and wide apart and the legs wide apart, walk forward, then back.

Modified Pull-Ups (arms and shoulders).   From a back-leaning position with the feet on the floor and the hands gripping a low horizontal bar, perform pull-ups bringing the nose to the bar.

Bent-Knee Push-Ups (arms and shoulders).   From a push-up position with the knees bent and the arms extended, do push-ups, bringing the nose to the surface in front of the hands.

Push-Ups (arms and shoulders).   From a push-up position, do repeated push-ups, keeping the back flat and touching the chest back to the floor.

Abdominal Activities

Shoulder Curl (abdominals).   From a bent-knee sit-up position with the arms folded across the chest, raise the head and shoulders off the surface and hold for three counts. Return and repeat several times.

Half-Curl (abdominals).   This is the same as the shoulder curl except the upper back is raised entirely off the surface. Be certain that the lower back remains in solid contact with the surface. Repeat several times.

Half-V-Sits (abdominals).   From a sitting position on the floor with the legs straight and together and the hands supporting the hips, raise one leg and hold for three counts and return. Repeat with the opposite leg. Repeat several times.

Bent-Knee Sit-Ups (abdominals).   From a bent-knee back-lying position with the feet flat on the surface and the arms crossed in front of the chest or behind the head (more difficult), perform repeated sit-ups.

Alternate-Knee-Touch Sit-Ups (abdominals).   From a back-lying bent-knee sit-up position with the hands behind the head, sit up and twist to one side, touching the elbow to the opposite knee.

V-Sits (abdominals).   This is the same as the half-V, except that both legs are raised at the same time. Repeat.

Lower Back Activities

Alternate Leg Lifts (lower back).   From a back-lying position with the legs straight and the hands at the side, raise one leg at a time to a vertical position and return. Repeat several times.

Double Leg Lifts (lower back).   From a back-lying position, bend both knees up to the chest. Straighten overhead and slowly lower. Stress keeping the lower back flat on the floor. Repeat.

Back Arch (lower back).   From a front-lying position with the arms extended overhead, raise the head and legs off the ground, hold, and return. Repeat.

Rocking Horse (lower back).   This is the same as the back arch, except the body is rocked back and forth from the arched position.

Leg Activities

Rabbit Hop (legs).   From a squat position, reach forward with the hands. Kick the heels up and forward to reach the hands. Repeat the action several times.

Blast Off (legs).   From a stand with the arms extended overhead and touching, count down "5, 4, 3, 2, 1," as the children gradually assume a half-squat position. On the signal "Blast off," they spring high into the air. Repeat several times.

Sprinter (legs).   From a squat position with one leg extended back and the hands placed on the surface outside the knees, alternate bringing one leg forward and then the other. Repeat rhythmically several times.

Heel Lifts (legs).   From a stand, raise up on the toes as high as possible and return. Repeat several times.

Heel Drops (legs).   From a standing position on the edge of a stair, block of wood, or book, drop the heels as low as possible, hold, and then slowly push up onto the toes. Repeat several times.

Pogo Jumps (legs).   From a stand with the hands laced behind the head, alternate jumping with a half-squat, placing one foot forward and then the other.

Squat Thrusts (legs).   From a standing position, squat down with the weight placed on the hands, extend the legs straight back, return to a squat, and stand. Repeat rapidly several times.

CONCEPT 26.6
Combative activities are a challenging and fun way to build muscular strength and endurance.

Combative Activities

One-Person Pull (arms and shoulders).   Two contestants face each other at a distance of three feet. Establish a line ten feet in back of each contestant—that is the contestant's baseline. Each contestant grasps the opponent's wrists. At the signal, each attempts to pull the opponent back across his baseline.

One-Person Push (arms and shoulders).   Two contestants face each other at a distance of three feet. Establish a line ten feet in back of each contestant as his baseline. Each contestant places his hands on the shoulder of the opponent. At the signal, each contestant attempts to push his opponent back across the baseline. Only straight pushing is permitted.

Rooster Fight (legs).   Two contestants stand facing each other at a distance of five feet. Each stands on the right foot, clasps the left foot with the left hand, and places the right arm across the front of the body, clasping the left arm. At the signal, each contestant hops forward and attempts, by bucking or sidestepping, to overthrow the opponent or cause him to release his grasp on foot.

Hand Push (arms).   Two contestants stand toe to toe, facing each other with feet spread. They raise both hands and place them against the opponent's palms at shoulder level. At the signal, each contestant pushes against the hands of the opponent, attempting to make her step back.

Hand Wrestle (arms and legs).   Two contestants stand with their feet firmly spread in a stride position; each contestant has the right foot forward and touching the outside of the opponent's foot. Contestants grasp right hands at the signal, and each attempts, by pulling, pushing, turning, and twisting of hands, to overturn the opponent or cause her to move either foot from its original position. Repeat with the left hand.

Back-to-Back Tug (legs and back).   Two contestants stand back to back with both arms linked at the elbows. Establish a line ten feet in front of each opponent. At a signal, each contestant attempts to drag the opponent over her baseline. Lifting and carrying of the opponent are permitted. Contestants must maintain their original position with arms linked. The contestant pulled across the opponent's baseline loses.

Knee Slap (arms and legs).   Place two contestants in an upright "referee's position," as in wrestling. At the signal, each attempts to slap one of the opponent's knees with the right hand. The left hand remains behind the opponent's head. Keeping legs back and bending forward at the hips are the important points.

Club Knock (legs and arms).   Set an Indian club or potato chip can on end. Two contestants face each other on opposite sides of the club, each holding the other by both shoulders. At the signal, each tries to force the other to knock over the club. Pulling, pushing, twisting, and turning may be used. Hands must remain on the opponent's shoulders at all times.

Leg Wrestle (legs).   Two contestants lie side by side on their backs with their heads in opposite directions (each contestant's head is resting at a point just opposite the

opponent's buttocks). Contestants place inside arms straight down by their side on the opponent's shoulder. Opponents place outside hands on their hips. At the count of three, each contestant lifts the inside leg, with the leg stiff, to a point just above the vertical, hooks ankles with the opponent, and attempts to roll the opponent over backward. Repeat with the other leg.

Breaking Arms (arms and shoulders).   Two contestants face each other on their knees on a mat at a distance of three feet. Each contestant makes a circle with her arms, each clasping her own hands within the circle created by the opponent (the arms link together like the links of a chain). At a signal, each attempts to "break" the opponent's linked arms. Twisting, jerking, pulling, turning, and other tactics that do not involve bodily harm are permissible.

Drake Fight (legs).   Two contestants face each other at a distance of four feet. Each leans forward and grasps one of his own ankles with both hands. At a signal, each moves forward and, by butting, shouldering, and sidestepping, attempts to cause the other person to release one or both hands.

Elbow Struggle (arms).   Two contestants lie on their stomachs, facing each other. They place right elbows on the mat surface so that the points of the elbow touch. They clasp hands. On a signal, each contestant attempts to force his opponent's hand to the side. The elbow must keep contact with the surface in their original position throughout the contest. The person forced to touch the back of her hand on the floor loses. Repeat with opposite arms.

Back-to-Back Lift (lower back).   Place two contestants standing back to back with elbows linked. At a signal, each one, by pulling and bending forward, attempts to lift the other off the floor. The contestant lifted off the floor loses the bout. Do not permit students to pull each other over their shoulders.

Back-to-Back Push (legs and back).   Two contestants stand back to back with elbows linked. Establish a line ten feet in front of each contestant. At a signal, each pushes backward and attempts to push the other over the line.

Stepping on Toes (legs).   Two contestants face each other at a distance of four feet. At the signal, each attempts, through quick stepping and jumping, to step on the toes of the opponent's feet. The hands are not used and should be clasped behind the back throughout the contest.

All-Fours Ankle Drag (arms, abdominals, and legs).
Two contestants face in opposite directions in a hands-and-knees position on a mat. Their bodies should be side by side with the right sides touching. Each grasps the right ankle of the opponent. At the signal, each contestant attempts to drag the opponent over the line ten feet in front. Contestants must remain on all fours throughout the contest.

Ball Wrestle (arms and abdominals).
Two contestants face each other at a distance of three feet in a kneeling position on a mat. They wrap both arms around a playground ball. At the signal, each attempts to take the ball away from the other. In attempting to secure the ball, no part of the body other than the arms may touch the ball.

American Wrestle (legs and arms).
Contestants stand facing each other on a mat with their chests touching. Each places his left arm over the opponent's shoulder and his right arm about the opponent's waist, clasping his two hands behind the opponent's back. At a signal, the contestants attempt to get in back of their opponent with the arms encircling the opponent's waist. After the signal has been given, the original hold may be broken. The contestant who secures the opponent around the waist from behind, whether standing, sitting, lying, or kneeling, wins.

JOINT FLEXIBILITY ACTIVITIES

Flexibility refers to the range of motion of a joint. Although children are generally thought to be flexible, research clearly indicates that flexibility is related to the type and amount of physical activity engaged in by the individual. Joint flexibility diminishes without sufficient stretching and suppling activities. The activities that follow are designed to maintain and improve flexibility in the back and trunk, the upper arms and shoulders, and the lower limbs. These activities should be performed in a **static stretching** manner; that is, passive stretch should be placed on the muscles rather than the ballistic action of dynamic stretching. Table 26.4 lists a recommended progression of stretching experiences for children at the beginning, intermediate, and advanced levels of joint

The sit-and-reach.

flexibility. Each activity will contribute to improved flexibility if properly and regularly performed.

CONCEPT 26.7
Static stretching activities are a key to maintaining and improving joint flexibility.

The primary objectives of the activities that follow are to

1. improve flexibility in the back and trunk, upper arms and shoulders, and upper and lower leg;
2. become knowledgeable about the importance of flexibility;
3. know how to maintain and improve flexibility at a joint; and
4. take part in a variety of static stretching activities.

Back and Trunk Stretching Activities
Side Stretch (back and trunk). Standing with the feet spread, bend at the waist slowly to one side and hold. Repeat to the opposite side. Holding a hoop, rope, or wand overhead aids in performance. Repeat.

TABLE 26.4   *Selected Activities for Improving Flexibility Sequenced in Terms of Flexibility Requirements*

Flexibility Activities (page number)	Suggested Progression for Children		
	Beginning Level	Intermediate Level	Advanced Level
Back and Trunk Stretching			
Side stretch (510)	X		
Windshield wiper (511)	X		
Trunk circles (511)	X		
Simon says (511)	X		
Knee lifts (511)		X	
Ankle pull (512)		X	
Bicycle (512)		X	
Knee arch (512)			X
Drawbridge (512)			X
Willow bend (512)			X
Arm and Shoulder Stretching			
Arm circles (512)	X		
Star burst (512)	X		
Giraffe (512)		X	
Chicken hawk (512)		X	
Greet yourself (512)			X
Towel stretch (512)			X
Towel dislocate (512)			X
Leg Stretching (513)			
Toe-toucher (513)	X		
Straddle stretch (513)		X	
Center stretch (513)			X
Fencer's lunge (513)		X	
Heel drop (513)			X
Heel stretch (513)		X	
Ankle circles (513)			X

Windshield Wiper (back and trunk).   From a standing position with the feet spread and arms out from the side, twist first in one direction slowly as far as possible without moving the feet, then twist in the opposite direction. Repeat (Figure 26.2).

Trunk Circles (back and trunk).   From a stand with hands on the hips, bend forward, sideways, and backward at the waist in a circular motion.

Simon Says (back and trunk).   Modify this traditional game to emphasize bending and stretching in a wide variety of ways.

Knee Lifts (back and trunk).   From a stand, bring one knee up and pull to the chest with both arms; stretch and hold. Repeat with the other leg.

FIGURE 26.2 *The "windshield wiper."*

FIGURE 26.3 *Arm circles.*

Ankle Pull (back and trunk). From a stand with the feet together, bend forward at the waist as far as possible while keeping the legs straight and grasping the ankles. Hold for four counts and return slowly to an upright position. Repeat several times.

Bicycle (back and trunk). From a back-lying position, extend the hips upward and pretend to peddle a bicycle with the legs.

Knee Arch (back and trunk). From a kneeling position on a mat, extend and lift one leg. Hold for three counts. Repeat with opposite leg.

Drawbridge (back and trunk). From a kneeling position on a mat, arch back upward and hold for three counts. Repeat.

Willow Bend (back and trunk). From a kneeling position on one knee with the other extended to the side, bend to the extended side at the waist and hold. Repeat to the other side.

Arm and Shoulder Stretching Activities

Arm Circles (arms and shoulders). From a standing position with the arms out from the sides, make small circular motions first in one direction, then in the other. For variety and challenge, try one arm in one direction and the other in the opposite direction (Figure 26.3).

Star Burst (arms and shoulders). From a stand with the hands clasped, keep the arms and body straight and raise the arms. Slowly release and push them back past the head.

Giraffe (arms and shoulders). From a stand with the hands clasped behind the back, bend forward at the waist while raising the arms to a vertical position and hold.

Chicken Hawk (arms and shoulders). From a stand or seat with the hands clasped behind the neck, press the elbows back and hold. Repeat.

Greet Yourself (arms and shoulders). From a stand, try to clasp hands behind the back by putting one arm over the shoulder and bending the opposite behind the back (Figure 26.4). Stretch and hold.

Towel Stretch (arms and shoulders). From a stand with the arms grasping a towel or rope overhead about shoulder width apart, pull outward on the towel and stretch the arms back. Hold and repeat.

Towel Dislocate (arms and shoulders). From a stand with the arms greater than shoulder width apart, grasp a towel or rope overhead. Try to bring the towel down behind you without bending the elbows. The wider the grip, the easier the exercise. Repeat.

FIGURE 26.5 *Half-straddle stretch.*

FIGURE 26.4 *The shoulder stretch, a variation of "greet yourself."*

FIGURE 26.6 *Straddle stretch.*

Leg Stretching Activities

Toe-Toucher (upper leg).   From a stand with the feet crossed, bend forward slowly at the waist and try to touch the toes. Bend as low as possible without bending at the knees. Hold.

Straddle Stretch (upper leg).   From a sitting position with the legs spread and the toes facing skyward, bend forward at the waist, grasp one leg, and try to pull the chin to one knee. Hold for several seconds. Repeat to the other leg (Figures 26.5 and 26.6).

Center Stretch (upper leg).   Same position as the straddle stretch except that the pull is toward the center while grasping both ankles at the same time. Bend, stretch, and hold.

Fencer's Lunge (upper leg).   From a fencer's on-guard position, lunge forward, stretch, and hold. Repeat in the opposite direction.

Heel Drop (lower leg).   Stand on the edge of a step or object four to six inches high. Drop the heels over the edge and hold.

Heel Stretch (lower leg).   From a feet-together standing position about three feet from a wall, lean forward to a bent-arm position against the wall, stretching the lower calf and ankles.

Ankle Circles (lower leg).   From a sitting position, grasp one ankle and slowly rotate it, first in one direction and then in the other.

SUMMARY

The generally poor fitness level of today's children should concern us all. Recent research clearly indicates that children are less fit and more fat than their counterparts of just twenty years ago. This alarming statistic is compounded when you recognize that American children of a generation ago were already considered by most experts to be unfit and overfat. Clearly it is in the best interest of all that this deplorable situation end. Quality physical education, with a portion of each instructional period spent in the quest for physical fitness, is the only reasonable answer. By helping children become fit movers, informed movers, and eager movers, teachers do much to provide the means for healthful living and an active way of life.

The health-related components of physical fitness are transient and highly susceptible to change. Children need to learn and apply the essential fitness principles of exercise frequency, intensity, duration, and variety. Adherence to these principles in the quest for cardiovascular endurance, muscular strength and endurance, and joint flexibility will provide children with the knowledge and skills required for a lifetime of physical activity and positive fitness behaviors. The fitness strand in the developmental physical education program is necessary and critically important if we are serious about the need and potential for fitness literacy among the children and youth of North America.

COMPLEMENTARY READINGS

Allsbrook, L. (1992). Fitness should fit children. *JOPERD* 63:47–49.

Blakemore, C., N. R. Hawkes, and H. G. Hilton. (1992). Making fitness work for students. *Strategies* 5:26–29.

Darby, L. A., and R. L. Pohlman. (1993). Heart rates help personalize fitness. *Strategies* 7:9–15.

Gabbard, C. (1990). Health-related fitness in elementary physical education. *Strategies* 3:14–18.

Hester, D., and D. Dunaway. (1990). Beyond calisthenics: Fitness and fun in elementary physical education. *Strategies* 3:25–28.

Hinson, C. (1995). *Fitness for Children.* Champaign, IL: Human Kinetics.

Kirkpatrick, B., and M. M. Buck. (1995). Heart adventures challenge course: A lifestyle education activity. *JOPERD* 66:17–24.

Kuntzelman, C., et al. (1991). *Aerobics With Fun.* Reston, VA: AAHPERD.

Levitt, S. (1993). Motivate your students: Participate. *Strategies* 6:10–11.

Solis, K. M., and B. Budris. (1991). *The Jump Rope Primer.* Champaign, IL: Human Kinetics.

Tenoschok, M. (1993). Jog around the world. *Strategies* 6:18–20.

SUPPLEMENTARY READINGS

Alter, M. J. (1988). *Science of Stretching.* Champaign, IL: Human Kinetics.

American Heart Association. *About Your Heart and Blood Pressure; About Your Heart and Diet; About Your Heart and Exercise.* National Center, 7320 Greenville Ave, Dallas, TX 75231.

Corbin, C. B., and R. Lindsey. (1994). *Fitness for Life.* Glenview, IL: Scott, Foresman.

Kusinitz, I., and M. Fine. (1991). *Your Guide to Getting Fit.* Dubuque, IA: Wm. C. Brown.

Safrit, J. (1995). *Fitness Testing in Children.* Champaign, IL: Human Kinetics.

VIDEOS

Slim Goodbody Presents All Fit. Burstein, J., and D. Gabor. Champaign, IL: Human Kinetics. (teacher's guide and three videotapes; 225 min.).

Slim Goodbody Presents Step by Step for Kids. Burstein, J., and D. Gabor. Champaign, IL: Human Kinetics. (40 min.).

Fitness Fanfare. AAU Physical Fitness Program. Poplars Building, Bloomington, IN. (28 min. motivational; 11 min. instructional).

Footbag Basics. Charleston, WV: Cambridge Physical Education and Health. (30 min.).

Get Moving, Get Eating, Get Fit. Rosemont, IL: National Dairy Council. (7:30 min.).

Herschel Walker's Fitness Challenge for Kids of All Ages. 200 Castlewood Drive, North Palm Beach, FL: The Athletic Institute. (30 min.).

Junk Food: Nothing to Snickers About. Charleston, WV: Cambridge Physical Education and Health. (30 min.).

Rope Skipping: Beginning and Advanced Skip It, and Double Dutch. 200 Castlewood Drive, North Palm Beach, FL: The Athletic Institute. (20 min. each).

Ropics. Charleston, WV: Cambridge Physical Education and Health. (55 min.).

RECORDINGS

Chariots of Fire. Polydor XR-1-6335 (cassette).

Mousercise. Disneyland Records 65216.

COMPREHENSIVE FITNESS EDUCATION PROGRAMS

Fitnessgram. The Institute for Aerobics Research, 12330 Preston Road, Dallas, TX 75230.

Sunflower Project. Shawnee Mission Instructional Program Center, 6649 Lamar, Shawnee Mission, KS 66202.

The A.A.U. Developmental Physical Fitness Curriculum, Grades 5–8. Poplars Building, Bloomington, IN 47405.

The Heart Smart Program. National Research and Demonstration Center, L.S.U. Medical Center, 1542 Tulane Avenue, New Orleans, LA 70112–2822.

The Heart Treasure Chest, American Heart Association. National Center, 7320 Greenville Ave., Dallas, TX 75231.

Thomas, K. T., A. M. Lee, and J. R. Thomas. (1990). *YMCA Youth Fitness Program.* Champaign, IL: Human Kinetics.

The Perceptual-Motor Strand for Multisensory Learners

Key Concept

Practice in Perceptual-Motor Activities May Enhance Perceptual-Motor Abilities

---

Chapter Objectives

The purpose of this chapter is to provide you with the tools to:

- Discuss the concept of children being multisensory learners.
- Define the term *perceptual-motor learning,* and speculate on its impact on learning readiness in young children.
- List the perceptual-motor components and provide examples of activities to enhance each.
- Discuss what is meant by the term *temporal awareness* and give several examples of movement activities that contribute to each element of the child's developing temporal world.
- Illustrate how movement may contribute to improved visual, auditory, and tactile/kinesthetic perception.
- Provide several examples of movement contributing to both perceptual and motor development in children.

Terms to Remember

Perception	Objective Localization	Sequence	Auditory Perception
Perceptual-Motor Learning	Directional Awareness	Eye-Hand Coordination	Auditory Discrimination
Readiness	Laterality	Eye-Foot Coordination	Auditory Memory
Body Awareness	Directionality	Visual Perception	Tactile Perception
Spatial Awareness	Temporal Awareness	Depth Perception	Tactile Discrimination
Subjective Localization	Synchrony	Form Perception	Tactile/Kinesthetic Memory
	Rhythm	Figure-Ground Perception	

We are all constantly being bombarded with stimuli from our environment. The ability to recognize these stimuli, absorb them into the flow of mental processes, and store them for future use is called **perception.** Being able to absorb, assimilate, and react to the incoming multisensory information through movement is frequently called **perceptual-motor learning.** Because the very essence of physical education is movement, perceptual-motor activities can be easily introduced, practiced, and refined in a developmentally based physical education program that is sensitive to the needs of children. Indeed, the physical education program is not the sole place where this type of learning occurs. Programs of this type can and should be carried out by the classroom teacher as well. Perceptual-motor learning is important, and it should be viewed as an essential part of the curriculum of every young child.

CONCEPT 27.1
All voluntary movement involves an element of perception.

The physical education curriculum affords a natural teaching base for perceptual-motor skills, because in reality all voluntary movement and all interaction with our environment are perceptual as well as motor processes. Voluntary motor processes depend on perceptual information. Conversely, the perceptual stimuli received by the organism rely on the development of one's voluntary movement abilities.

What we have, then, is a process of stimulation and reaction that is essential to human life. The best time for this perceptual-motor learning to occur is when children are young and are open to a wide variety of new and different situations that can enhance their perceptual-motor abilities.

Perceptual-motor activities help children achieve a general stage of **readiness** that in turn helps prepare them for the academic work of the classroom. These activities provide a foundation for future perceptually based learnings. Through a program of perceptual-motor skill development, children can develop and refine both their movement abilities and their perceptual-motor abilities. Programs that stress the development of fundamental stability, locomotor, and manipulative skills directly enhance the perceptual-motor components of (1) body awareness, (2) spatial awareness, (3) directional awareness, and

(4) temporal awareness. Please refer to Chapter 5, "Cognitive Learning," for a complete discussion of each of these components.

CONCEPT 27.2
Perceptual-motor activities may contribute to learning readiness in young children.

BODY AWARENESS ACTIVITIES

Children are continually exploring the movement potential of their bodies. They are in the process of gaining increased information about **body awareness**—what the body parts can do and how to make them do it. Teachers can assist in this exploratory process by structuring informal learning experiences that maximize children's opportunities for using a variety of body parts in a multitude of activities. The following is a compilation of some activities that will be helpful in enhancing body awareness. Table 27.1 provides a suggested progression of body awareness activities for children at the beginning and intermediate levels of perceptual-motor skill learning.

Body rolling promotes improved body awareness.

TABLE 27.1   *Selected Body Awareness Activities Sequenced in Terms of Complexity*

Body Awareness Activities (pg. no.)	Suggested Progression for Children	
	Beginning Level	Intermediate Level
Locating the large body parts (517)	X	
Locating the small body parts (517)	X	
Move and listen (517)	X	
Partner practice (518)	X	
Body-part differentiation (518)	X	
Where can you bend? (519)	X	
Paired parts (519)	X	
Put-together people (519)		X
Mirror activities (519)		X

By participating in body awareness activities, children will learn

1. the location of the various parts of the body,
2. the names of these parts,
3. the relationship of one body part to another,
4. the importance of a single body part in leading movement,
5. how to move the body more efficiently,
6. to be aware of the body and its parts at all times, and
7. to be able to contract and relax specific muscles.

Locating the Large Body Parts

- Have the children find the location of their large body parts. Have them see how quickly and accurately they can touch each part as you name it. See how quickly they can touch their:

head	stomach	shoulders
neck	hips	back
chest	legs	spine
waist	elbows	front

- Repeat the activity, this time reversing the procedure. That is, point to the body parts and have the children name them. The body parts may be as general or as specific as you wish, depending on the children's abilities.
- Have the children find out how large their body parts are. For example:

    Move your hand down the length of your arm. Where does it start and where does it stop? Place two hands around your waist. How big is it? How can you move at the waist? Try bending forward, backward, and sideways. Can you twist at the waist?

- Help the children discover all about the sides of their bodies. For example, you may request that they
    Move one hand down the sides of their bodies. Find the side of the head, shoulder, chest, waist, hip, knee, ankle, and foot.
    Repeat the same procedure on the opposite side of the body.

Locating the Small Body Parts

- While the children are standing, the teacher may have the children do these activities:

Put their elbows together.	Touch their toes with their arms crossed.
Put their feet apart.	Touch one knee and one foot.
Touch one elbow.	
Put their knees together.	Place their palms together.
Touch their noses.	Touch their heels.
	Touch their eyelashes and eyebrows.

- Use other body parts in place of or in addition to those just mentioned.

Move and Listen

- Have the children perform a locomotor task, but have them stop and position themselves on your command. For example, you may have them moving about the room and tell them to stop on

one foot	head, hands, and feet
both feet	hands and knees
one hand	back
seat and both feet	one foot and one hand
feet and fingers	one foot, two hands, and head

- Permit the children to choose their own way of stopping and positioning themselves on your command of "Freeze."

Partner Practice

- Have the children move around the floor to a different person each time and touch the following body parts on that person, as directed by the teacher:

spine	arms	toes	back
ears	elbows	hands	knees
neck	legs	fingers	hips
chin	ankles	chest	feet
shoulders	wrists	stomach	heels

- Repeat the first activity with the children using the body parts you named, instead of the hands, to touch the corresponding body part of another child.

CONCEPT 27.3
Body awareness activities help young children learn more about their bodies and what they can do in space.

Body-Part Differentiation

- To show hip movement with bending at the knee, have the children do the following activities:

Draw the knees up to the chest, then thrust them out straight while on the back.
Do the same thing but make continuous circular thrusting movements.
While lying on the back, draw both knees up under the stomach and then extend them both outward.
While on the stomach, bend one knee and draw it up alongside the body, on the floor, until it is in line with the hip.

- While they are lying on their backs, have the children do the following activities:

Lift one leg and lower it.
Move the leg out to the side along the floor.
Then return it to the midposition beside the other leg.
Swing the leg out to the side and back.

Rotate the leg back and forth on the heel.
Lift one leg and cross it over the other leg, touching the floor if possible.
Swing one leg over the other.
Lift the leg and rotate it at the hip, making circles in the air with the foot.
Hold tightly an object placed between his knees.

- Repeat the preceding activities while on the stomach.
- While they are standing, have the children perform the following shoulder movements:

Move a hand up alongside the body, extend it over the head, and lower it in the same way.
Extend an arm out at the side and then lower it.
Extend an arm over the head and then lower it.
Extend an arm out in front and then lower it.
Extend an arm out in front. Then move it from the center out to the side and back again.
Hunch the shoulders up and down with the arms at the sides. Then swing them forward and backward.
Swing the arms in a circle in front of the body.
Swing the arms in a full circle at the side.
Extend the arms out at the sides and swing them in circles of various sizes.
Move just the shoulders forward and backward.
Move the shoulders in a circle.

- While they are seated, have the children perform the following hand and finger movements:

Make a fist.
Spread the fingers apart. Then move them back together.
Bring the tip of the thumb and all of the fingers together.
Bring the tip of the thumb and the "pointer" finger (forefinger) together.
Extend the fingers and thumb to maximum and then relax.
Move the thumb across the four fingers and back.
Touch each fingertip with the tip of the thumb. Begin with the "pointer" finger and move to the little finger and then back.
Grasp a ball in one hand, then lift one finger at a time.
Close the hand to a fist, and then release one finger at a time.
Extend the hands, then lower one finger at a time to form a fist.

Where Can You Bend?

- Permit the children to experiment with a still dowel and with a jointed Barbie doll to see where the body parts bend. If possible, a paper skeleton or a real one and a dentist's jaw could be used to graphically portray the body parts that bend.
- Encourage the children to move the following joints in as many ways as possible:

jaw	wrist	knee
neck	fingers	ankle
shoulders	waist	toes
elbow	hip	

- Experiment with what movement is like without one of the preceding joints, one at a time.

Paired Parts

- Have the children touch one body part to another. The following is a list of examples:

Touch your ear to a shoulder.
Touch your shoulder to a knee.
Touch your nose to a knee.
Touch your elbow to a thigh.
Touch your thigh to a knee.
Touch your knee to an ankle.
Touch your toe to a knee.
Touch your toe to the chin.

- There are numerous other possibilities for touching paired parts. Have the children explore them.

Put-Together People

- Have the children make a life-sized figure by crushing single pieces of newspaper and stuffing them into long underwear. After the underwear is completely stuffed, dress the figure and have the children each draw a head and features on a paper bag. The hands and feet may be made with gloves and an old pair of shoes. The stuffed figure may represent a particular time of the year or theme.
- Cut out the body parts of a "person" using construction paper or poster board. Have the children assemble the legs, arms, head, and torso of the figures. Hook the pieces together with brads, or tape the pieces together to complete the figure.
- Cut out the body parts of two or more "people." Give each child in the group one body part. See if they can assemble the figure. The same activity may be repeated as a relay.
- Using a doll with movable joints, have the children bend it into various positions and then see if they can reproduce these positions with their bodies.
- *Giants:* The children sit in a circle around two giant paper cutout parts of two bodies, one a boy, the other a girl. Two children are chosen to compete in putting the parts together; the one completing the giant figure first is the winner.

Mirror Activities

- One child stands in front of a full-length mirror. The other children give directions to locate his body parts. The child can only look at his reflection in the mirror when touching the designated part. If he makes a mistake, the child giving the last instruction takes the mirror position.
- Repeat the preceding activity, but have the mirror child use both hands to touch his body.
- Repeat the preceding activities, but indicate the right or left parts of the body in the mirror reflection.
- The teacher serves as the mirror. The children imitate the movements of the "mirror."

SPATIAL AWARENESS ACTIVITIES

Spatial awareness involves two primary factors: subjective localization and objective localization. **Subjective localization** involves development of a space structure in which objects in the environment are located by the child relative to his or her own position in space. **Objective localization** is more advanced and involves development of a space structure in which objects are located independent of one's own position in space. See Table 27.2 for a suggested progression for spatial awareness activities.

Through practice in spatial awareness activities children will

1. learn how much space their bodies occupy,
2. be able to project their bodies into external space,
3. be able to locate objects in space from a personal frame of reference (subjective localization),
4. be able to locate objects in space independent of one another (objective localization),
5. improve fundamental movement skills, and
6. enhance their efficiency of movement.

TABLE 27.2 *Suggested Spatial Awareness Activities Sequenced in Terms of Complexity*

Spatial Awareness Activities (pg. no.)	Suggested Progression for Children	
	Beginning Level	Intermediate Level
Big and small (520)	X	
Maze walk (520)	X	
Rope walking (520)	X	
Back space (520)	X	
Obstacle course (521)	X	
Body space (521)		X
Other space (521)		X
Near and far (521)		X
Map activities (521)		X
Miscellaneous activities (521)	X	X

Crawling through an improvised tunnel is an excellent spatial awareness activity.

Big and Small

- Have the children find a place where they are free from contact with others. Ask them to make themselves as small as possible. Point out that as small "balls," each child takes up very little room and so does not bother other children.

- Now have the children make themselves as big as possible. Point out that as they get bigger, so do their neighbors. This means that each needs more room to keep from bumping someone else. The children become familiar with their spatial relationships to others.

- Ask the children to assume different shapes such as a tree, rock, or telephone pole. Have them assume the new positions at varying rates of speed. Assuming the shapes of letters and numbers may also be performed.

Maze Walk

- Children walk through a maze of chairs and tables without touching.

  Walk between objects.
  Step over objects.
  Crawl under objects.
  Walk around objects.
  Step on objects.

- Perform the maze activities using a variety of locomotor activities.

  jumping
  hopping
  skipping
  crawling

Rope Walking

- Place ropes in various patterns and geometric shapes on the floor. Have the children walk the rope forward in these shapes:

  wavy lines
  circle
  square
  triangle

- Then have them step over and through objects.

- Repeat the activities, but do them while blindfolded. Have children tell you about the shape of the line they are walking on.

Back Space

- Walk backward on a rope placed on the floor. Place the rope in various patterns.

- Throw objects backward to a visualized goal.

- Sit down on an object without visually monitoring it.

  chair
  beanbag chair
  inner tube

- Walk backward through a simple obstacle course that the child has had an opportunity to memorize visually.

- Count the number of steps to a point on the floor while walking forward. Repeat while walking backward and see how close the children come to the predetermined point.

CONCEPT 27.4

Progressing from a subjective space structure to an objective space structure is facilitated through activities that promote improved spatial awareness.

Obstacle Course

- Use tasks such as

  "footsteps" placed on the floor
  carpet squares on the floor
  climbing and sliding ropes
  crawling over and under and through objects
  stepping into shoe boxes

- Use a "map" task: Follow a yarn line through the obstacle course.

Body Space

- Outline the children's bodies on a sheet of newsprint while they are lying on their backs. Have the children

  cut out their bodies
  color their bodies
  dress their bodies
  hang up their bodies
  compare sizes

- Have the children try gross motor activities:

  Have them roll over and see how much space they occupied.
  Have them spread out and see how much space they can occupy.

Have them see how little space they can occupy.
Have them crawl under a table and other objects of different heights and see how well they fit without touching.
Count steps, jumps, and so on taken to go from one point to another.

Other Space

- Use empty milk cartons to have children try these activities:

  Compare different-sized milk cartons (half-pint to gallon containers).
  Compare the water-holding capacity of the containers. Compare size by pouring from carton to carton.
  Fill different-sized containers with sand. Compare the weights of the containers.
  Compare the volumes of sand held by each container.

Near and Far

- To illustrate subjective localization, have children estimate the distance from where they are standing to a specific point by the number of steps that it will take to get there. Also measure the distance in steps. Compare estimates.

- To illustrate objective localization, have children estimate the distance between two independent points, for example, the doll house and the carpentry bench. Step off the distance and compare.

Map Activities

- Place a large map of the classroom, school, community, or state on the floor. Give children a route to follow, indicating specific points that they must visit before proceeding to the next point.

- Give each child a map with clues to the "treasure." Indicate in precise terms where they should go and the procedures to be followed.

Miscellaneous Spatial Awareness Activities

- Locomotor movements include

  creeping
  leaping
  jumping

- Axial movements include

  bending
  rising
  stretching
  reaching
  twisting
  falling

- Have children follow objects such as colors, arrows, and words. You might also have them crawl in a tunnel.

- Have children explore space:

  self-space
  common space
  moving at different levels
  moving in different floor patterns

DIRECTIONAL AWARENESS ACTIVITIES

Directional awareness is of considerable concern to the classroom teacher and to children who are beginning formal instruction in reading. **Directional awareness** involves both an internal and external sensitivity for sidedness. See Table 27.3 for a recommended progression of directional awareness activities.

Practice in movement activities that emphasize the directional aspect of the task

1. contribute to the development of **laterality** (internal awareness of direction),
2. contribute to the development of **directionality** (external projection of laterality),
3. contribute to the development of fundamental movement abilities, and
4. enhance one's ability to move efficiently through space.

Clock Games

- Make a clock on a chalkboard about eighteen inches in diameter. Instruct a child to place his right hand on one of the numbers and his left hand on a second number, holding a piece of chalk in each hand. Ask him to move his left hand to a different number and his right hand to a different number on your command. Both hands should move at the same time and arrive at their goals at the same time. Variations include these:

TABLE 27.3   *Selected Directional Awareness Activities Sequenced in Terms of Complexity*

Directional Awareness Activities (page number)	Suggested Progression for Children	
	Beginning Level	Intermediate Level
Clock games (522)	X	
Swinging-ball activities (522)	X	
Directional commands (523)	X	
Over, under, and around (523)	X	
Walking-board activities (523)	X	
Unilateral, bilateral, and cross-lateral activities (523)	X	X
Throwing activities (524)	X	
Chalkboard activities (524)		X
Ladder activities (524)		X
Twist-board activities (524)		X
Creeping and walking activities (524)		X
Ball activities (524)		X

Toward the center: Place hands on the circumference of circle and bring both to center (*0*). Place hands on the numbers *1* and *5* and bring to *0*, then *6* and *2* to *0*.
Away from the center: Begin with both hands on *0* and move out to specified numbers.
Parallel movements: Put the left hand on the number *7* and right hand on *0*, then move the left hand to *0* and right hand to *3*. Change directions.
Crossed midline movements: Place the left hand on the number *7* and right hand on *1*, then move both hands to *0*. Change directions.

Swinging-Ball Activities

- Attach a ball to a string. Move it in different directions and in different orientations to the child.

  Tap it and then catch it.
  Swing it with one hand, then the other, and then with both.

- *Swinging activities:*

  Swing ball to the left and to the right.
  Swing ball forward and backward.
  Swing ball in circles around the child.
  Swing ball in circles in front of the child.
  Swing ball in different planes above the child as he
      lies on his back.
  While he is on his back, swing ball from left to right
      and then from head to toe.

- *Striking activities:* Repeat the preceding activities
  but use striking motions.

Directional Commands

The following are some examples of patterns in which
children may move to enhance directional awareness.
The number of possibilities is limitless. Use your imagination.

- Run forward ten steps and walk backward five
  steps.
- Put your feet together and jump to one side. Hop
  forward three times on one foot, then backward
  three times on the other foot.
- Move sideways across the room.
- Have the child move close to you and then move far
  away.
- Move from the front of room to the rear of room,
  going over one object and under another object.
- Stand near the desk.
- Stand far away from the pencil sharpener.
- Point to the wall nearest you and walk to that wall.
- Place the closest chair between the desk and the
  wall.
- One child sits and another stands. Have the standing
  child move in front of (or to the side of, etc.) the
  sitting child.

Over, Under, and Around

- Using a long jump rope, have two people hold the rope
  and place it on the floor. The child runs and jumps
  over it. The rope is raised slightly for each succeeding
  jump. Game ends when the child hits the rope. Go
  under a high rope, which is then lowered slightly each
  try. Walk over instead of running and jumping.

- Place several objects around the gym, such as jump
  ropes, walking boards, mats, chairs, tires, ladder, or
  any large equipment. Children follow the leader and
  imitate as he moves around the obstacles.

- This could be played in the classroom as leader
  moves around room. Place objects on the floor and
  permit each child to go around the objects in his or
  her own direction and name the direction in which
  he went. Give verbal commands for the direction of
  each obstacle.

- Blindfold the children. Have them work with a
  "seeing" partner who gives directional commands
  (no tactile clues) on how to get to the object.

CONCEPT 27.5
Movement activities that focus on internalizing
children's concepts of direction in both three-
dimensional and two-dimensional space facilitate
readiness for learning.

Walking-Board Activities

- Walk forward.
- Walk backward—discourage looking back.
- Walk sideways—slide one foot over and then bring
  the other one to meet it.
- Turn on the board:

  Walk forward, turn, and walk sideways. Walk
      forward, turn, and return, walking forward.
  Walk backward, turn, and return, walking
      backward. Vary combinations.

- Step over and under objects placed on the board.
- Walk across the board carrying heavy objects.

Unilateral, Bilateral, and Cross-Lateral Activities

- *Unilateral and cross-lateral movements:* Lie flat on
  the floor on your back with your arms at your sides
  and your feet together.

  Move the right leg only to an extended position and
      return it.
  Repeat, with the left leg only, right arm only, and
      left arm only.
  Move the right leg and right arm together.
  Move the left arm and leg together.

Move the right and the left arms together.
Move the left arm and the right leg.

- *Bilateral movements:* Lie flat on the floor on your back with your arms at your sides and your feet together.

    Move your feet apart as far as you can, keeping the knees stiff.
    Move the arms along the floor until the hands come together above the head, keeping elbows stiff.
    Move the arms and legs at the same time.

Throwing Activities

- Use a beanbag and a wastebasket for this activity. Set a basket in front of the child and have him throw at it. Vary the basket's orientation to the right or left and have the child throw at it.
- Use a ball to roll at a bowling pin for this activity. Vary the location of the bowling pin or the child, or vary the distance of the roll.
- From a prone position or a supine position, have the child throw a beanbag upward, forward, backward, or to each side.

Chalkboard Activities

- The teacher makes two dots. The child connects the two. The teacher makes a third dot and child connects, and so on. (Do not cross child's midline here.)
- Have the child connect dot-to-dot, but do cross child's midline.
- Draw double circles and change directions after completion or in the middle of drawing.
- Draw "lazy-eight" figures with one hand and then the other. Try it in one direction and then reverse.
- Draw vertical lines, up–down and down–up.
- Draw horizontal lines, left–right and right–left.
- Draw horizontal lines and vertical lines simultaneously.
- Draw a square, then alter the size, direction, and starting point.

Ladder Activities

- *Walking:* Looking straight ahead, the child walks the length of the ladder. Walk the rungs (forward, backward, sideways).

Walk forward in the spaces.
Walk backward in the spaces.
Walk sideways in the spaces. Walking sideways may be done by leading with the left foot, leading with the right foot, continually crossing the lead foot in front, or continually crossing the lead foot in back.

- *Creeping:* The ladder is turned on its side. To secure it, the teacher sits on the top side. The children crawl in and out of the spaces. They can crawl forward, backward, and, if possible, may not touch the rungs.

Twist-Board Activities

- Place the feet about shoulder width apart on the board and bend the knees slightly. Twisting occurs by

    moving both arms to one side and then to the other side; and swinging one arm forward and up while swinging the other arm backward and down.

- Put the left arm behind the back and use the right arm to simulate a one-arm breast stroke. This will cause the child to turn completely around.
- Repeat, changing arm positions (right arm behind back, left arm moving).
- While twisting, the child

    crosses arms in front of the chest and
    extends arms (hands clasped) in front of the body, behind the body, and over the head.

Creeping and Walking Activities

- *Creeping:*

    Creep in a homolateral pattern (left hand with left knee, right hand with right knee) while looking at a target placed at eye level.
    Creep in a cross-lateral pattern (left hand with right knee, right hand with left knee) looking first at an eye-level target and then at the forward hand.
    Creep in a homolateral pattern while looking at the hand that goes out in front.
    Creep forward, backward, and to the side using the preceding patterns.

- *Walking:*

    Walk in a homolateral pattern (left hand points to left toes while right arm is stretched behind the child; then right hand points to right toes).
    Walk in a cross-lateral pattern.

- *Midair change:* Begin with the left arm forward and the left foot forward, with the weight evenly distributed on both feet. Right arm should be straight out in back. On command "Change," each child jumps up in the air, reversing the position of arms and legs. The eyes should fixate on a target at all times and the child should land on the takeoff spot.
- *Midair change:* Use a cross-lateral movement (left arm and right leg forward) to do the preceding activity.

Ball Activities

- Use one hand and then repeat the following skills with the other hand:

  Tap a swinging ball.
  Bounce and catch a ball with one hand.
  Dribble a ball with one hand.
  Bounce and catch with alternating hands.
  Throw in various directions.
  Catch from different directions.

- Use one foot and then repeat the following skills with the other foot:

  Kick a ball with alternate feet, using the toe.
  Kick a ball with alternate feet, using the instep.
  Trap a ball with one foot and then the other.
  Trap a ball with one knee and then the other.

TEMPORAL AWARENESS ACTIVITIES

Temporal awareness involves the development of a sense of timing within the body. Eye-hand coordination and eye-foot coordination refer to the child's ability to coordinate movements and are the result of a fully established internal time structure. This "clock mechanism" helps children to better coordinate the movements of their bodies with the various sensory systems. Refer to Table 27.4 for a recommended progression of activities.

Through temporal awareness movement activities, children will learn:

1. **Synchrony,** which is the ability to get the body parts to work together smoothly,
2. **Rhythm,** which is the process of performing many synchronous acts in a harmonious pattern or succession,

The bounce pass requires synchrony, rhythm, and proper sequencing of movements if it is to be effectively used in the game of basketball.

TABLE 27.4 *Selected Temporal Awareness Activities Sequenced in Terms of Complexity*

	Suggested Progression for Children	
Temporal Awareness Activities (pg. no.)	*Beginning Level*	*Intermediate Level*
Ball activities (526)	X	
Rhythmic movement (526)	X	
My beat (526)	X	
Free flow (526)	X	
Moving-target toss (526)	X	X
Balloon-volleying activities (526)	X	X
Miscellaneous large-motor temporal activities (526)	X	X
Miscellaneous fine-motor temporal activities (527)	X	X

3. **Sequence,** which is the proper order of actions required to perform a skill, and
4. **Eye-hand coordination** and **eye-foot coordination,** which are the results of synchrony, rhythm, and sequence being efficiently integrated.

Ball Activities

- *Stationary ball:* Contact it with an open hand, an implement, or various body parts. Kick at it.
- *Swinging ball:*

  Contact it with an open hand as a fist. Then alternate left and right hands.

  Contact it first with various body parts and then with various implements, moving from shorter to longer levers (spoon, table tennis paddle, tennis racket, squash racket, baseball bat).

  Catch the swinging ball with both hands and then with only one hand.

  Visually track the ball as it swings, without moving the head.

  Visually track the ball and point at it as it swings.

Rhythmic Movement

- On the signal, have children find their own "personal space." Have them make a low, balanced shape, keeping one hand free to tap on the floor along with the beat of the drum. When the drum changes beat and pattern, the children must do the same.
- Have the children, remaining balanced, tap with a foot, an elbow, and a heel. Have a body part move in the air, following the drum. Use different tempos in each position. Keep the tempo even. Don't accelerate or decelerate.

My Beat

This activity enables the children to make and follow their own tempos and sequences.

- Each child makes his or her own accompaniment and sets his or her own beat. They can make noises with their mouths or slap a hand against their bodies. Once they have established even beats, have them explore their personal space (the area around them) while moving to the beat.
- Have each child explore around the room while moving to the beat. Let them move to a different tempo.

Free Flow

- Ask the children to perform a relaxed, smooth, swinging motion with their bodies. The motion can take them anywhere around the play area. (Stress spatial awareness to avoid collisions.) Have them perform a controlled swing so that it can be stopped on command. Make sure that when they stop a movement, they are in complete balance and control.
- Introduce physical obstacles that the children must successfully negotiate in order to improve body control and movement.

C O N C E P T   2 7 . 6
All movement occurs in both time and space, thereby serving as a vehicle for internalizing important concepts dealing with the synchronization of movement, the rhythm of coordinated movement, and the sequence of movement in pattern formation.

Moving-Target Toss

- Have the children line up facing the target. Use an inflatable toy punching clown that will right itself after being pushed down. Use a barrel, wastebasket, or pot and attempt to toss such an object at the clown while it is moving from a reclining position to its normal upright position.
- Suspend a hoop from a rope. Start it swinging in a pendular motion. Have children throw beanbags through the swinging hoop.
- Roll a hoop or tire along the floor. Toss objects through it.

Balloon-Volleying Activities

Keep a balloon up in the air by using a volleying motion, hitting it underhand, hitting it above the head, hitting it below the waist, using various body parts to hit it, and weighting the balloon slightly and repeating the preceding activities.

Miscellaneous Large-Motor Temporal Activities

- Move in different ways to a beat.
- Jump rope to a beat.
- Bounce a ball to a beat.
- Pass a ball rhythmically.

- Partners make their own beat and move to it.
- Perform movements in sequence.
- Accelerate and decelerate movement.
- Create and absorb force.
- Perform tossing and catching activities.
- Perform kicking and trapping activities.
- Perform dodging activities.

Miscellaneous Fine-Motor Temporal Activities

- Bead stringing.
- Playing jacks.
- Playing pick-up sticks.
- Lacing and sewing cards.
- Clay modeling.
- Cutting.
- Coloring and pasting.
- Finger painting.
- Playing with nuts and bolts.
- Sewing.
- Weaving.
- Zipping, snapping, and buttoning.
- Carpentry activities.
- Puppetry.
- Chalkboard activities.
- Tracing.
- Pouring skills.

VISUAL PERCEPTION ACTIVITIES

The visual apparatus is complete and functional at birth. Visual abilities develop rapidly during the early years of life and are crucial to effective functioning in a world that is visually oriented. The processes of maturation and gaining experience both contribute to the development of highly sophisticated **visual perception** abilities. It has been estimated that up to 80 percent of all information we take in and use comes from vision. As a result, it becomes abundantly clear that developing and refining accurate visual perception are extremely important. The following pages contain a variety of movement experiences that have been found helpful in developing three aspects of visual perception crucial to effective functioning in school and the world, namely depth perception, form perception, and figure-ground perception. Refer to Table 27.5 for a recommended progression of activities for children at the beginning and intermediate levels of skill in visual perception development.

Depth Perception

Depth perception is the ability to judge relative distances in three-dimensional space. Teachers working with depth-perception activities need to consciously plan many and varied spatial and dimensional cues to serve as reference points for judgment of distance.

Depth-perception enhancement activities are designed to

1. enhance the ability to accurately judge distances and depth,
2. increase the ability to use external clues to determine depth, distance, and size,
3. enhance the ability to move efficiently in three-dimensional space, and
4. enhance fundamental movement abilities.

Bowling.   When rolling a ball toward an object, line the lane moving toward the target with Indian clubs or markers of some type. As skill develops narrow the width of the lane.

Targets.   Use a box within which balls land in various lengths and depths. It can be used as a target for throwing, striking, and kicking a light ball. Target throwing with all types of objects and at various distances is helpful. Remember, however, target throwing will elicit only a partial throwing or kicking pattern. Forceful throwing and kicking for distance will elicit the child's best (most mature) pattern.

Hoops.   Crawling through hula hoops arranged in three-dimensional formations, plywood boxes with shapes cut out of the sides, pipes, and logs is good for tactile realization of depth.

Jumping.   Jumping from heights, over objects, and from one object to another develops perception of depth and distance. You may also use jumping from various heights on an angled balance beam or steps to the floor.

Balance Beam.   Place a balance beam diagonally toward the wall. Have the children find the point where they can reach and touch the wall while walking on the beam. Tape several points onto the balance beam. Show

TABLE 27.5 *Selected Visual Perception Activities Sequenced in Terms of Complexity*

Visual Perception Activities (pg. no.)	Beginning Level	Intermediate Level
Depth-Perception Activities		
Bowling (527)	X	
Targets (527)	X	
Hoops (527)	X	
Jumping (527)		X
Balance beam (527)		X
Boxes (528)		X
Form-Perception Activities		
Shape walking (528)	X	
Tracing (529)	X	
Making things (529)	X	
Body shapes (529)	X	
Shape tag (529)	X	
Stepping shapes (529)	X	
Matching shapes (529)	X	
Beanbag toss (529)		X
Shadow pantomime (529)		X
Figure-Ground Perception Activities		
Discrimination (529)	X	
Sorting (529)	X	
Attention (530)	X	
Ladder maze (530)	X	
Target toss (530)	X	
Eggshell walk (530)	X	
Rope walk (530)	X	
Paddle balance (530)		X
Rope maze (530)		X
Candyland (530)		X
Hidden objects (530)		X
Finger fixation (530)		X
Pencil-wall fixation (530)		X
Paper-punch pictures (530)		X

the children one piece of tape; remove it and have the children walk and stop where they think the tape was.

Boxes. Place boxes of various heights in the center of a room. Attach objects at various heights to the wall. Instruct the children to select the box that will best assist them in retrieving the object they want.

CONCEPT 27.7
Visual perceptual abilities influence, and are influenced by, movement activities that place a premium on combining visual information with motor processes that result in coordinated movement.

Form Perception

Form perception, or the ability to recognize shapes, forms, and symbols, is necessary for academic success. Children may be able to identify shapes correctly but, because of distortions of their visual memory, are often unable to reproduce them. Perception of shape constancy becomes crucial to children's ability to recognize shapes. They must learn that two- and three-dimensional forms belong to certain categories of shapes, regardless of size, color, texture, mode of representation, or the angle seen by the perceiver. Recognition of similarities and differences is the first step in identifying shapes and forms. Object discrimination is the second.

Three- and four-year-olds tend to rely on shape or form rather than color to identify objects. At five years of age, color is generally a more important tool than form for identifying an object. By ages six or seven, color and form are generally both important.

Form perception activities are used to help children

1. recognize and reproduce basic shapes,
2. perceive differences in shapes and pieces of a puzzle,
3. match similar symbols,
4. recognize and reproduce basic forms and use them in generalized situations (e.g., to be able to see that a square and a triangle can form a house), and
5. draw forms that exist in the environment and that can be seen in isolation of one another.

Shape Walking. Walk simple geometric shapes placed on the floor.

- Have the children walk a rope that is placed in various geometric shapes. Walking barefoot will enhance the tactile clues.
- Walk a masking-tape line and "feel" the shape with your toes.
- Present a simple geometric shape to the children. Permit them to monitor it visually while they attempt to walk out the shape on the floor. They should strive to arrive back at the starting point when they complete the shape.
- Repeat the preceding activity, but do not permit visual monitoring of the displayed form.
- Name a shape and have the children walk it out, returning to their starting points when they have completed the shapes.

Tracing.   Trace around geometric shapes with the fingers.

- Use three-dimensional shapes.
- Use templates.
- Trace shapes drawn on a sheet of paper.
- Reproduce the shapes by tracing over them.
- Have the children complete incomplete geometric shapes drawn for them.

Making Things.   Make a variety of things using various shapes.

- Make a collage of geometric shapes.
- Use various-shaped blocks to build a familiar object.
- Draw a picture of a person composed entirely of different geometric shapes.
- Make shapes using toothpicks, straws, or tongue depressors.

Body Shapes.   Have the children use their bodies to make a variety of shapes.

- Have the children form various shapes, letters, and numerals with their bodies.
- Have the children form part of a shape with their bodies. Ask one to help complete the shape that he or she thinks the others are forming.

Shape Tag.   Play tag using selected shapes as free places.

Stepping Shapes.   Spread various shapes on the floor around the room. Have the children step only on certain shapes. Make and play a game of twister, using shapes as the focal point.

Matching Shapes.   Play matching games using various shapes and sizes. Sort objects according to shape.

Beanbag Toss.   Throw beanbags at targets with different-shaped holes cut out. Points are scored for throwing through the various shapes. Be sure that the holes are large enough to promote success and maintain motivation.

Shadow Pantomime.   Hang a sheet with a light in front of it in a closet with the door open. Have a child imitate physical activities while the others guess what they think is being done.

Figure-Ground Perception

Figure-ground perception is the ability to select a limited number of stimuli from a mass. These particular stimuli (auditory, tactile, olfactory, kinesthetic, visual, or gustatory) form the figure. The others form a dim field. This figure is the center of attention. When attention shifts, the former figure fades into the background. We can only perceive something in its relation to its field.

In teaching children who have not fully developed their visual figure-ground perception, attempt to limit the number of stimuli in the background and progress by adding gradually. For example, practice dribbling the "red" ball, not on the red-and-black tiled floor, but on a posterboard (white or light solid color) or sheet to simplify contrasting the figure of attention and the background. Do not place the children in a milieu of posters, streamers, and other attention-grabbers.

Visual figure-ground activities help children

1. focus attention on the object of regard,
2. move efficiently through the visual field,
3. locate objects located in the field of vision, and
4. improve eye-hand and eye-foot coordination.

Discrimination.   Discriminate between various objects in a room.

Find objects that are difficult to locate.

Sorting.   Sort according to size, shape, color, texture, number, thickness, and length.

Attention. Practice shifting attention by selecting designated objects from a box or bag.

Ladder Maze. Place a ladder on a floor of a solid design, on one with a diagonal design, and on one with various other designs. Have the children step between the rungs without touching them.

Target Toss. Use targets to focus attention. Throw beanbags at selected parts of the target. For example, you may use a large human picture and throw at various body parts.

Eggshell Walk. Place a path of eggshell halves on the floor. Cross that path with other paths of various materials, such as rope, tape, and paper. Have the children step on anything except the eggshells.

Rope Walk. Walk on a rope winding through a myriad of objects.

Paddle Balance. Have the children balance a ball on a paddle or board.

Rope Maze. Form a maze of rope paths on the floor. Have identical clues at each end of the same rope. Send the children to find the match of the clue they are given.

Candyland. Play a life-sized version of "Candyland" (by Parker Brothers), in which the children spin for colors and take their places on the appropriate color on the "board."

Hidden Objects. Use *Highlights* magazine for pictures with concealed objects that the children can find.

Finger Fixation. Have the children hold their right and left forefingers about a foot apart and a foot from their eyes. Then have them look quickly from one finger to the other. They must be sure to "land" each time. If they have difficulty, they can be helped by having another person move her own finger in the same way the eyes are to move.

Pencil-Wall Fixation. Each child holds a pencil erect about ten to twelve inches in front of his nose. He then looks from pencil to numbers on a calendar (or picture on the wall) and back again for several "round trips." The children must move their eyes quickly and fixate on each object.

Paper-Punch Pictures. Punch holes in a picture until the children are no longer able to obtain meaning from

Listening and responding to auditory cues promotes improved auditory perception.

the pictures. Pictures of many objects are harder to perceive than pictures of only one subject.

AUDITORY PERCEPTION ACTIVITIES

The development of **auditory perception** has not received the attention by authors and practitioners that the visual modality has. Auditory perception is important, however, particularly with young children. Their inability to read makes their formal education primarily one of (1) listening to auditory clues, (2) discriminating between sounds, and (3) applying meaning to them.

Auditory perception is enhanced when children attend to verbal directions, translate music into movement, and interpret the "feel" of various sounds through movement. The use of musical instruments aids in developing the auditory abilities. The following pages contain numerous activities for developing and reinforcing listening skills, auditory discrimination, and auditory memory abilities. Refer to Table 27.6 for a recommended progression of activities.

Listening Skills

It is important for children to hear and remember what is said, but it is also crucial that they have the listening skills to hear and respond to what is being said. Learning to listen is basic to auditory perception. Many children have been conditioned to "tune out" certain auditory clues. Take, for example, the child engrossed in a television program who somehow manages not to hear the pleas of mother or father to come to dinner. We are all familiar with children who "never listen." Learning to listen to auditory clues can be developed through a variety of activities. Games that involve an awareness and identification of sound sources enhance listening abilities. Activities that require following simple directions are also helpful, as well as activities that require a motoric response to a verbal command.

Auditory perception activities help children's ability to

1. develop an awareness of sound sources,
2. identify various familiar sounds,
3. listen to auditory clues in the immediate environment,
4. respond appropriately to auditory commands,
5. respond efficiently, through movement, to auditory clues, and
6. discriminate between various auditory clues.

Traditional Games. Many traditional games that children have played down through the years involve a considerable amount of listening skills. Some of these games include Simon Says, Mother May I?, Red Rover, and Red Light.

Hot and Cold. Hide an object somewhere in the room while "it" is not looking. "It" attempts to find the object by moving around the room and listening to the loudness or softness of the class's clapping. As he or she approaches the object, the clapping becomes louder. As he or she moves away from it, the clapping becomes softer.

Clap Clap. The class is spread out around the room. One child is told to clap her hands twice when "it" says "Clap clap." "It" points to the person who she thought did the clapping.

Poems. Read a poem to the class, requesting them to fill in the rhyming words.

TABLE 27.6 *Selected Auditory Perception Activities Sequenced in Terms of Complexity*

Auditory Perception Activities (pg. no.)	Suggested Progression for Children	
	Beginning Level	Intermediate Level
Listening Skills		
Traditional games (531)	x	
Hot and cold (531)	x	
Clap clap (531)	x	
Poems (531)	x	
Music (532)	x	
Bounce bounce (532)	x	
Active animals (532)	x	
Hands (532)	x	
Echo (532)	x	
Listening walk (532)	x	
It is I (532)		x
Tape recorder sounds (532)	x	
Voice recording (532)		x
Freeze and melt (532)		x
Marching (532)		x
Auditory Discrimination		
Close your eyes (533)	x	
Musical instruments (533)	x	
What does it sound like? (533)	x	
What is it? (533)	x	
Where is the bell? (533)	x	
Keep off (533)		x
Sound targets (533)		x
Bounce off (533)		x
Match the cans (533)		x
Auditory Memory		
A trip to the zoo (534)	x	
Story telling (534)	x	
Action rhymes (534)	x	
Instrument Playing (534)	x	
Silly hat (534)		x
Horse race (534)		x
The winner is. . . . (534)		x
Lost and found (534)		x

Music.   Listen to music that has a variety of fast and slow sections. Request that the children move about the room in time to the music. If space does not permit active movement, simply have the children raise their hands when they hear the fast part or the slow part.

Bounce Bounce.   Have a small group of children sit down with their backs toward you. Drop a utility ball from waist height and let it bounce. Children should count the number of bounces that the ball makes.

Active Animals.   Use a variety of rhythm instruments to depict the sounds of moving animals while telling a story containing the names of several animals. Whenever the animal's name is mentioned, the child with the corresponding instrument makes its sound. For example:

- Drum for a lumbering elephant.
- Sandpaper blocks for a slithering snake.
- Triangle for birds.
- Xylophone for caterpillar.
- Rhythmic sticks for galloping horses.

Hands.   One child is blindfolded and must guess what another child is doing with her hands. She may, for example, be clapping, snapping, rubbing, scratching the desk, or tapping the chalkboard.

Echo.   The teacher claps out a simple rhythmic pattern, using slow or fast beats, even or uneven beats, and the children respond by moving around the room to the appropriate beat.

Listening Walk.   The children and teacher take a walk around the playground for the purpose of listening to and identifying different sounds. Sounds may be categorized as human sounds (walking and talking), animal sounds (running and cries of cats, dogs, or birds), machinery sounds (noise of cars, buses, power mowers, or trucks), and nature sounds (wind, rustling of trees or leaves).

It Is I.   Play this game when the children know one another fairly well. One child sits in a chair with his back to the class. Another child comes up behind the seated child and knocks three times on the back of the chair. The seated child asks, "Who is knocking at my door?" and the other child replies, "It is I." The seated child tries to guess who is knocking by identifying the child's voice. The teacher sets the number of guesses permitted.

Tape Recorder Sounds.   Use a tape recorder to record many familiar and easily distinguished sounds, such as a car horn, paper tearing, breathing, crying, clock ticking, sneezing, and so forth. Make a list of the sounds in their proper order so that you know what they are. Have the children try to identify the sounds.

Voice Recording.   Record several children's voices on the tape recorder and have them attempt to identify their classmates' voices and their own.

Freeze and Melt.   The teacher or a student says "Freeze" while the class is moving about the room. They immediately stop what they are doing and cease all movement (of the body and the mouth). When "Melt" is called out, they resume moving around the room. This is an effective activity for the teacher to introduce as a game and to incorporate later into the classroom routine as a way to get the immediate attention of the class.

Marching.   Performing a variety of marching activities, in which the children must respond to verbal commands, is excellent for helping older children learn to listen. Marching is also helpful in developing directional awareness.

CONCEPT 27.8
Children's listening skills, as well as auditory discrimination and memory skills, may be promoted through a variety of developmentally appropriate movement activities.

Auditory Discrimination

Auditory discrimination is similar to visual figure-ground perception. It is the ability to detect one specific tonal quality and frequency within a whole complexity of sound stimuli. Individuals tend to initiate movement toward the direction from which the sound cue emerges (directional awareness). Auditory rhythm is an aspect of discrimination and is the ability to identify a regulated series of sounds interspersed by regulated moments of silence in repeated patterns.

Auditory discrimination activities enable children to

1. respond to sounds or verbal commands,
2. react independently to verbal commands without visually monitoring others,
3. listen to a command and then carry it out without verbal repetition,

4. enhance fundamental rhythmic abilities,
5. distinguish between similar sounds, and
6. distinguish between dissimilar sounds.

Close Your Eyes.   Ask the children to close their eyes as you clap your hands several times. Ask the children to "clap just as I did." Vary this procedure by clapping in different rhythms.

- You may also use two drums, having children imitate drum beats.
- Repeat the activity with stamping, clapping, and snapping fingers.
- Begin with even beats and progress to a syncopated rhythm.

Musical Instruments.   Select several rhythm-producing instruments, such as a drum, a triangle, a sand block, or a wooden block. Children watch as you make a sound on each. Ask the children to close their eyes and listen carefully. Strike a sound on one of the instruments and have the children open their eyes and tell you which instrument you played. Next have the children close their eyes as the teacher plays two instruments. Have the children tell you which instrument was played first, and which one was played last.

What Does It Sound Like?   Using familiar noises, have the children differentiate between loud and soft, fast and slow, first and last, high and low.

What Is It?   Place a number of objects on a table. Tap these objects to familiarize the children with the sound produced. Have the children put their heads down. Tap an object and ask, "What is it?" After the children have become familiar with the objects, tap several of them and ask which you tapped first, second, and so on.

Where Is the Bell?   Seat the children in a circle. Have one child leave the room. Give one of the children in the room a bell small enough to hide in his hand. Ask the child who left the room to come back in. When the child has returned, have all of the children stand and shake their fists above their heads. You may use more than one bell when the children become accustomed to the game.

Keep Off.   A stretched canvas piece is strung taut in a rectangular frame, about three and one-half feet off the floor. The child is beneath. The teacher tosses a beanbag onto the canvas. By the sound of its landing, the child can hear where to bump it to hit it off the canvas.

TEACHING TIPS

General teaching hints for children experiencing difficulty in *auditory discrimination*.

- Speak slowly, distinctly, and on the child's level.
- Speak in natural volume. Extra volume can confuse the child's ability to discriminate what you say.
- Speak so that the child can see your lips (for severe disabilities).
- Maintain eye-to-eye contact.
- Deliver brief, simple directions.
- Control the environment.
- Use situations with verbal responses, physical responses, and both responses.
- Avoid repeating directions whenever possible.
- Use a blindfold for emphasis on developing auditory sensations.

Sound Targets.   Throwing blindfolded, the children listen to hear their beanbag hit a target made out of resounding material.

Bounce Off.   Various textures and materials are situated as targets around the gym. They are used as rebound targets for the children throwing balls to hear the difference in sounds the bounces make.

Match the Cans.   Take ten cans. Fill five with five different materials and duplicate these with the last five cans. Mix up the order and ask the child to match the cans by sound.

Auditory Memory

Auditory memory is the ability to retain auditory clues. Since much of the child's world involves the auditory modality, a great deal of information must be stored and retained. The following activities are designed to encourage retention of auditory clues.

Auditory memory activities are designed to

1. enhance the ability to remember auditory clues,
2. enhance the ability to readily remember directions,
3. develop listening skills,

4. enhance comprehension of what is heard, and
5. increase the ability to move efficiently to a series of auditory clues.

A Trip to the Zoo.   Begin a story about a trip to the zoo and all the animals that you will see. Give each child the name of an animal to imitate. When you name that animal in the story, the child with the name of that animal acts out his or her interpretation. Perform the same activity, having the children repeat the actions of the animal mentioned along with those that preceded it.

Story Telling.   Tell a familiar story (such as "Green Eggs and Ham," "Cat in the Hat," or "Jack and the Beanstalk"), having the children supply the repetitive phrases at the proper place in the story.

Action Rhymes.   Sing a familiar "action" rhyme such as "Head, Shoulders, Knees, and Toes." Omit a word from the song, such as head, and have the children touch that body part instead of naming it.

Instrument Playing.   Using the same idea as in previous exercise, play a simple pattern of notes on a xylophone several times. After the pattern is well known, omit a note and have the children fill it in.

Silly Hat.   Using an old hat (a beanbag will do), give the children a series of silly things to do. Start with two directions and gradually increase the number and complexity of the instructions.

Horse Race.   Using children as the "horses," conduct a horse race. Put a number on each child. Begin the race using only two or three "horses." Have them race (gallop) to a designated point and declare a winner, indicating the number of the "horse" and its place (i.e., "number three came in first, and number eight came in second"). Have the remainder of the group tell you the order of the finish using the horse numbers only. Increase the number of horses to four or more after practice with having the children recall the first three, four, or five "horses" to cross the finish line.

The Winner Is. . . .   Repeat the preceding activity, but declare the ribbon winners. For example, "The horse that came in first wins the blue ribbon. Which number was it? The horse that came in second wins the red ribbon. Which number was it?" and so forth. You may then want to continue with "What color ribbon did number four win?" and so forth.

Lost and Found.   Pretend that several children in class each lost an article of clothing. Have the children recall the names of those missing something.

TACTILE/KINESTHETIC PERCEPTION ACTIVITIES

The development of the sense of touch helps to enhance children's knowledge of the world about them. It is the modality by which they come into actual physical contact with their world. As with the visual and auditory channels, the tactile modality is developed through experience with objects in the environment. Tactile discrimination is the first and most basic aspect of **tactile perception** and involves the development of an awareness of the "feel" of things. Tactile memory involves the ability to associate tactile impressions with known objects.

The tactile modality is often neglected in the education of young children and is assumed to develop "naturally." It has been the experience of the author, however, that touch plays an important role in developing a more accurate sense of body awareness. Children should learn to direct their tactile movements in such activities as climbing a ladder, crawling through a tunnel, tracing a maze blindfolded, or walking on a slippery surface. See Table 27.7 for a suggested teaching progression for tactile perception.

CONCEPT 27.9
Children's tactile/kinesthetic abilities may be enhanced through a variety of fine-motor activities that are both fun and developmentally appropriate.

Tactile Discrimination and Matching

Tactile discrimination is the earliest form of tactile development and involves developing an awareness of things through touch. Young children developing their tactile discrimination abilities are also in the process of developing a corresponding vocabulary of words such as *hard, soft, spongy, rough, smooth, bumpy, coarse, slick,* and *sticky.* The ability to distinguish form through tactile clues also begins to develop. Differentiating between

TABLE 27.7   *Suggested Tactile Perception Activities Sequenced in Terms of Complexity*

Tactile/Kinesthetic Perception Activities (page number)	Suggested Progression for Children	
	Beginning Level	Intermediate Level
Tactile Discrimination and Matching		
Collections (535)	x	
Textured paintings (535)	x	
Collages (535)	x	
Creative movement (535)	x	
Mystery bag (535)	x	
Tag an object (535)	x	
Geometric shapes (536)	x	
Shape trace (536)		x
Heavy and light (536)		x
Sandpaper sort (536)		x
Touch tag (536)		x
Search (536)	x	
Tactile/Kinesthetic Memory		
Where is it? (536)	x	
Guess who? (536)	x	
Put in order (536)	x	
Memory ball (536)		x
Sandpaper numbers and letters (536)		x

- Cloth (nylon, cotton, velvet, fur, burlap, dotted swiss, leather, wool, corduroy, etc.).
- Balls (ping-pong, rubber, cork, styrofoam, steel, fringe balls, beach balls, golf balls, bowling balls, etc.).
- Seeds (from pine cones, black walnuts, chestnuts, buckeyes, acorns, coconuts, sumas, beans, pods, etc.).
- Minerals (shale, sandstone, gypsum, granite, marble, limestone, etc.).
- Sandpaper (assorted grades of sandpaper, ranging from coarse to very fine).
- Food wrap (aluminum foil, waxed paper, plastic wrap, butcher paper, cellophane, brown paper bags, etc.).
- Household staples (salt, sugar, flour, peppercorns, rice, macaroni, etc.).
- Kitchen items (blunt scissors, butter spreader, various-sized spoons, fork, spatula, rubber scraper, cookie cutter, etc.).
- Miscellaneous (plastic, metal, aluminum, steel, glass, tin, etc.).

Textured Paintings.   Make textured paintings, using glue to secure such things as rice, sawdust, tissue paper, small stones, seeds and pods, popcorn, and sand.

Collages.   Make collages using a wide variety of textures.

Creative Movement.   Discriminate between various textures through movement. Have the children feel a texture such as silk and interpret it by moving the way it feels. Use a variety of textures that exhibit characteristics, such as bumpy, smooth, coarse, and prickly.

Mystery Bag.   Place familiar but similar objects in a sack, such as a toy car, boats, and trucks. Have a child reach in the bag, without looking, and describe to the class how one object feels. Children guess what object is being held. Repeat the preceding activity, but have the child who is reaching in guess what the object is after describing it to the class.

Tag an Object.   Place several different objects on the floor (use as many different objects as there are children). Blindfold each child (four to eight at a time works well) and whisper the name of the object they are to locate. On the signal "Go," send them around the area trying to locate their object. They may remove their blindfolds when they think they have located the proper object. Repeat the same activity using several geometric shapes.

circles, squares, and triangles as well as large and small objects develops, along with the ability to sort and match objects by tactile means (see Table 27.7).

Tactile perception activities are designed to

1. develop an awareness of tactile sensations,
2. aid in discriminating between tactile clues,
3. develop the ability to sort objects according to tactile characteristics, and
4. develop the ability to match objects according to feel.

Collections.   Make collections of several types of objects and describe how they feel.

Geometric Shapes.   Blindfold a child. Hand the child one geometric shape at a time. Have him tell all about it and name the shape.

Shape Trace.   Using your finger, trace a geometric shape on the child's back. The child then tells about the shape and names it if possible.

Heavy and Light.   Sort a variety of objects into two categories of heavy and light. The same may be done with rough and smooth or soft and hard.

Sandpaper Sort.   Using different grades of sandpaper, sort them blindfolded according to texture. Repeat the same activity, but sort according to size, shape, and texture. Perform first while visually monitoring and then with a blindfold.

Touch Tag.   Play a game of tag in which you tell the children to touch something soft, hard, smooth, wide, sharp, and so forth. The last child touching that type of object sits in the "mush pot" for one turn (avoid excluding children in games of this nature).

Search.   Place several different objects in a large cloth bag. Have the children reach in without looking and find, by touch, the correct object described, such as, "find something you eat with," "find something you wear," or "find something you write with."

Tactile/Kinesthetic Memory

Tactile/kinesthetic memory activities are similar to discrimination activities, but they involve a greater degree of sophistication. Memory activities require the child to discriminate nonvisually between familiar and unfamiliar objects and to apply verbal labels to these tactile clues. Tactile memory activities help children to

1. remember what objects feel like,
2. identify unfamiliar objects by touch, and
3. identify familiar objects by touch.

Where Is It?   Using a textured drawing of a familiar figure (e.g., kitten, donkey, Santa Claus), have the children locate its various body parts while blindfolded.

Guess Who?   Have the children form a circle. "It" is blindfolded, turned around twice, and placed in the center of the circle. He then steps forward until he touches another child and attempts to determine who it is. He feels the child's clothing, hair, face, and so forth. Three guesses are permitted; then a new child is "it."

Put in Order.   Scatter several objects on the floor. Blindfold the children and tell them the type of object they must locate. Begin with three types. Have them locate the objects and place them in order. For example, tell them to find something round, then something hard, then something smooth.

Memory Ball.   Use several different types of balls from the gymnasium (football, basketball, baseball, softball, soccer ball, volleyball, kick ball, tennis ball, and white ball). Place the balls on the floor and have the children, blindfolded, locate and name the various balls and tell what they are used for.

Sandpaper Numbers and Letters.   Blindfold the children and have them distinguish between various numbers and letters by touch. Older children can solve simple addition or subtraction problems using the numbers, or they can spell words using the letters.

SUMMARY

This chapter dealt with children as multisensory learners, learners who during the preschool and early elementary school years are developing their perceptual-motor abilities. Perceptual-motor activities provide children with a wealth of important information that has the potential to enhance their learning readiness. The spatial world of young children is enhanced through a variety of body awareness, spatial awareness, and directional awareness activities. So too, is their temporal world enhanced through movement activities that focus on the proper synchrony, rhythm, and sequence of movement. Activities for enhancing both spatial and temporal components of children's developing perceptual world were presented for those at the beginning and intermediate levels of development. The research evidence is clear: practice in perceptual-motor activities can enhance perceptual-motor abilities. Perceptual-motor abilities play a role in the learning readiness of young children.

The developmental physical education program also incorporates a variety of movement experiences that enhance children's visual, auditory, and tactile/kinesthetic perception. Virtually all of the movement activities contained in this text contribute to perceptual and perceptual-motor skill development, because all voluntary movement involves an element of perception. However, the activities presented in this chapter focus on children as multisensory learners. As such, the perceptual elements of the tasks are highlighted rather than the motor aspects.

COMPLEMENTARY READINGS

Bossenmeyer, M. (1989). *Perceptual-Motor Development Guide.* Byron, CA: Front Row Experience.

Capon, J. (1975). *Perceptual-Motor Development Series: 1. Basic Movement Activities; 2. Ball, Rope, Hoop Activities; 3. Balance Activities; 4. Beanbag, Rhythm Stick Activities; 5. Tire, Parachute Activities.* Byron, CA: Front Row Experience.

Capon, J. (1981). *Successful Movement Challenges.* Byron, CA: Front Row Experience.

Smith, G. L. (1993). *Hoop Fun For Everyone.* Byron, CA: Front Row Experience.

Zukowski, G., and A. Dickson. (1991). *On the Move.* Carbondale, IL: Southern Illinois University Press.

SUPPLEMENTARY READINGS

Pila, R. (1995). *Experiences in Movement with Music, Activities, and Theory.* Albany, NY: Delmar Publishers.

Sherrill, C. (1993). *Adapted Physical Activity, Recreation and Sport.* Dubuque, IA: Brown & Benchmark.

Williams, H. (1983). *Perceptual and Motor Development.* Englewood Cliffs, NJ: Prentice-Hall.

RECORDINGS

Body/Spatial/Directional/Temporal Awareness

Brazelton, A. *Clap, Snap, and Tap.* Kimbo Records, Box 246, Deal, NJ 07723 (EA48).

Capon, J., and R. Hallum. *Perceptual—Motor Rhythm Games,* Educational Activities, Inc., Box 392, Freeport, NY 11520 (AR50, AC50).

Cratty, B. J. *Physical Development for Children.* Kimbo Records, Box 246, Deal, NJ 07723 (EA-PD).

Glass, H. "Buzz." *Learning by Doing, Dancing, and Discovering.* Educational Activities, Inc., Box 392, Freeport, NY 11520 (AR76).

Hallum, R., and H. "Buzz" Glass. *Individualization in Movement and Music.* Educational Activities, Inc., Box 392, Freeport, NY 11520 (AR49, AC49).

Hassam, H. *Coordination Skills.* Educational Activities, Inc., and Kimbo Educational Records, P.O. Box 392, Freeport, NY 11520 (KEA 6050).

Lee, K. *Music for Movement Exploration.* Educational Activities, Inc., Box 392, Freeport, NY 11520 (KEA 5090).

Lewandowski, D., et al. *Limb Learning.* Educational Activities, Inc., Box 392, Freeport, NY 11520 (KEA 1145).

Palmer, H. *Creative Movement and Rhythmic Exploration.* Educational Activities, Inc., Box 392, Freeport, NY 11520 (AR/AC 533).

Palmer, H. *Easy Does It.* Educational Activities, Inc., Box 392, Freeport, NY 11520 (AR/AC 581).

Palmer, H. *Getting to Know Myself.* Educational Activities, Inc., Box 392, Freeport, NY 11520.

Palmer, H. *Homemade Band.* Educational Activities, Inc., Box 392, Freeport, NY 11520 (AR/AC 545).

Palmer, H. *Mod Marches.* Educational Activities, Inc., Box 392, Freeport, NY 11520 (AR/AC 527).

Riccione, G. *Developmental Motor Skills for Self-Awareness.* Kimbo Records, Box 246, Deal, NJ 07723.

Visual/Auditory/Tactile Perception

Berman, M., P. Zeitlin, and A. Barlin. *Body Jive.* Educational Activities, Inc., Box 392, Freeport, NY 11520 (AR 96, AC 96).

Berman, M., P. Zeitlin, and A. Barlin. *Clap, Snap, and Tap.* Educational Activities, Inc., Box 392, Freeport, NY 11520 (AR 48).

Berman, M., P. Zeitlin, and A. Barlin. *Get Fit While You Sit.* Educational Activities, Inc., Box 392, Freeport, NY 11520 (AR 516).

Berman, M., P. Zeitlin, and A. Barlin. *Only Just Begun.* Educational Activities, Inc., Box 392, Freeport, NY 11520 (KEA 5025).

Berman, M., P. Zeitlin, and A. Barlin. *Rainy Day Dances, Rainy Day Songs.* Educational Activities, Inc., Box 392, Freeport, NY 11520 (AR 570).

Finger Games. Bridges, 310 W. Jefferson, Dallas, TX 75208 (HYP506).

Gallina, J., and M. Gallina. *Hand Jivin'.* Educational Activities, Inc., Box 392, Freeport, NY 11520 (AR 95, AC 95).

Glass, H. "Buzz." *It's Action Time—Let's Move!* Educational Activities, Inc., Box 392, Freeport, NY 11520 (AR 79).

Glass, H. "Buzz," and R. Hallum. *Rhythm Stick Activities.* Educational Activities, Inc., Box 392, Freeport, NY 11520 (AR 55).

Hallum, R. *Fingerplay Fun.* Educational Activities, Inc., Box 392, Freeport, NY 11520 (AR 529).

Johnson, L. *Simplified Lummi Stick Activities.* Educational Activities, Inc., Box 392, Freeport, NY 11520 (K 2015).

Kaplin, D. *Perceptual Development Through Paper Folding.* Bridges, 310 W. Jefferson, Dallas, TX 75208 (LP9010).

Lummi Stick Fun. Kimbo Records, Box 246, Deal, NJ 07723 (KIM2000).

Riccione, G. *Fun Activities for Fine Motor Skills.* Kimbo Records, Box 246, Deal, NJ 07723 (KIM9076).

Smith, L., and G. DeSantis. *Roomnastics.* Educational Activities, Inc., Box 392, Freeport, NY 11520 (KEA 1131).

Williams, L., and D. Wemple. *Sensorimotor Training in the Classroom,* Volume I. Educational Activities, Inc., Box 392, Freeport, NY 11520 (AR 532).

Williams, L., and D. Wemple. *Sensorimotor Training in the Classroom,* Volume II. Educational Activities, Inc., Box 392, Freeport, NY 11520 (AR 566).

CHAPTER 28

The Creative Dance Strand for Expressive Movers

Key Concept

Creative Rhythmic Movement Is an Excellent Means for Children to Become More Expressive Movers

Chapter Objectives

The purpose of this chapter is to provide you with the tools to:
• Discuss the role of rhythmic movement in helping children be expressive movers.
• Define each of the elements of rhythm and give several examples of how they may be taught to children.
• Demonstrate competency in activities designed to help children with discovering rhythm and applying rhythm.
• Discuss the role of singing rhythms in creative rhythmic expression.
• Speculate as to why children enjoy rhymes and poems, finger plays, and singing dances. Discuss the values of each.
• Discuss what is meant by the term *creativity* and how rhythmic movement can be used to foster creative rhythmic expression.
• Provide several examples of how ideas, songs, words, and music may be used to encourage creative rhythmic expression.
• Describe what is meant by the terms *imitative dance* and *interpretative dance*. Give several examples of each.
• Discuss the ways and means of dance making with children.

Terms to Remember

Rhythmic Fundamentals	Singing Rhythms	Creative Rhythmic
Underlying Beat	Finger Plays	Expression
Rhythmic Pattern	Rhymes and Poems	Imitative Dance
Tempo	Singing Dance	Interpretative Dance
Accent	Creativity	Dance Making
Intensity	Creative Dance	

Moving to rhythm is FUNdamental and is an essential element of all coordinated movement. Children love the rhythmical element of recordings, rhythm bands, singing, and dance making. They enjoy putting movement to music and being expressive movers through dance. Dance is an important vehicle for helping children express themselves creatively through movement. This chapter centers on three forms of children's dance as a means for children becoming more expressive movers: fundamental rhythms, singing rhythms, and creative dance. Expressive movers move with joy and efficiency, coordination and control. The suggestions in this chapter will provide you with many activity ideas for involving children in creative rhythmic movement.

CONCEPT 28.1
Creative rhythmic movement is FUNdamental to children's ability to move with joy and efficiency.

RHYTHMIC FUNDAMENTALS

Rhythmic fundamentals involve developing an understanding and feel for the elements of rhythm, namely underlying beat, tempo, accent, intensity, and rhythmic pattern. Each of these may be achieved effectively through movement. When teaching children about the elements of rhythm, you may use a drum, tambourine, two sticks, record player, or piano to supply the musical phrasing. In fact, the children may provide the musical accompaniment themselves through sounds, body percussion, or homemade rhythm instruments.

Using movement as a way to develop the elements of rhythm reinforces fundamental movement skill development and fosters an understanding and feel for rhythm. This is an important point because all coordinated, purposeful movement requires an element of rhythm, and practice in rhythmic fundamentals and singing rhythms reinforces the development of coordinated movement. Through practice with certain fundamental movements, children begin to understand the structural elements of rhythm and are able to express this understanding through coordinated, purposeful movement.

CONCEPT 28.2
Rhythmic fundamentals are an important means for children to learn about and respond to the elements of rhythm.

Understanding the Elements of Rhythm

When teaching the elements of rhythm, you might use a drum, two sticks, or any percussive instrument while the children perform. The children may even provide the rhythmic accompaniment themselves, or a record may be used. Jumping rope to music or bouncing balls to the beat of the music often aids in developing an understanding of the elements of rhythm.

Underlying Beat.   **Underlying beat** is the steady, continuous sound in any rhythmical sequence. Listening and responding to the underlying beat can be promoted by (1) children responding to the beat of a drum or tambourine with appropriate locomotor or axial movements; (2) children providing their own beat and moving to it; (3) marching to recordings by John Philip Sousa, the Marine Band, and other march recordings; (4) jumping rope to the beat of the music; (5) bouncing balls to the beat of the music; or (6) keeping time with the beat of the music with a homemade rhythm instrument.

Rhythmic Pattern.   **Rhythmic pattern** is a group of beats related to the underlying beat. The underlying beat may be even or uneven. Children may develop and express an understanding of rhythmic pattern by (1) walking, running, hopping, and jumping to an even beat; (2) skipping, sliding, or galloping to an uneven beat; (3) clapping rhymes; (4) playing "echo" (see page 542); (5) playing "names in rhythm" (see page 542); (6) using wooden sticks; or (7) tinikling (see page 571).

Tempo.   **Tempo** refers to the speed of the movement, music, or rhythmic accompaniment. Children may increase their understanding of tempo by (1) responding to speed changes in the beat of a drum with various locomotor and stability movements, (2) performing animal walks at various speeds, (3) bouncing a ball at various speeds, or (4) jumping rope to different tempos.

Accent.   **Accent** is the emphasis that is given to any one beat. The accented note is usually the first beat of every measure. Children may develop a keener awareness of accent by (1) listening to the music and clapping on the accented beat; (2) moving about the room with the appropriate rhythmic pattern and changing direction or level on each accented beat; (3) clapping on every beat except the accented one; (4) varying the response to the accented beat with a specific locomotor, stability, or manipulative movement.

Intensity.   **Intensity** is the quality of the music in terms of its loudness or softness. Children can develop an understanding of intensity by (1) altering their movements for various intensities, (2) changing their level for different intensities, (3) changing the amount of force they use to move for different intensities, (4) bouncing a ball with appropriate amounts of force, (5) dribbling a ball as softly as possible and then as loudly as possible.

CONCEPT 28.3
The elements of rhythm are found in all forms of coordinated movement.

Discovering Rhythm

The following compilation of fundamental rhythmic activities is designed to aid children in discovering rhythm. Most of the activities may be used from grades one through grade six, depending on the rhythmic sophistication of the group. Practice in activities that permit children to discover rhythm will help them to

1. develop an understanding of the elements of rhythm,
2. express the elements of rhythm through movement,
3. "feel" the beat of a musical composition, and
4. translate the beat of a musical composition into action.

In Beat

Formation: Any number of children seated in a semicircle, facing the teacher.

Equipment: A record player and a well-known song such as "Clap, Clap, Clap Your Hands" (primary) or "He's Got the Whole World in His Hands" (upper level). If a record is not available, the class may sing the song. A chalkboard or large piece of writing paper and either chalk or magic marker.

Procedures: Lead in with a discussion of rhythm around us and what has a steady beat (heartbeat, a clock, and so on). Then sing or listen to the song, following up by asking the children to keep the steady beat of the song by slapping their thighs. Discover the length of the song by putting a chalk mark on the board for each time the beat occurs in the song. Use a different body instrument every time the song is sung (clap, slap stomach, tap feet). Discover new body sounds (elbow, jaw). Combine

these body percussion instruments into a particular sequence such as

Feet – Thighs – Clap – Snap (repeat)
  1   2   3   4

Suggestions: Use a currently popular song and let the children make up their own patterns of body percussion as well as varying the old patterns. Younger children may start with only clapping and thigh slapping until they can add the others without difficulty.

Body Talk

Formation: Group seated in a semicircle, facing the teacher.

Equipment: A list of several easy poems or nursery rhymes, written either on a chalkboard or on a large piece of paper.

Procedures: Have children listen to the poem, song, or nursery rhyme to feel the rhythm of the composition. Decide on appropriate body instruments to be used and what pattern or sequence they should follow. Say the poem or rhyme, letting the children put their body instruments to work.

Suggestions: The children could make up their own short compositions and create new patterns or sequences of body percussion. Simple melodies could be used to enhance the composition. Some appropriate rhymes or sayings:

- "April Showers Bring May Flowers."
- "Birds of a Feather Flock Together."
- "A Bird in the Hand Is Worth Two in the Bush."
- All Is Not Gold That Glitters."
- "The Early Bird Catches the Worm."
- "An Apple a Day Keeps the Doctor Away."
- "Rain, Rain Go Away, Little Johnny Wants to Play."
- "A Stitch in Time Saves Nine."
- "Early to Bed, Early to Rise, Makes One Healthy, Wealthy, and Wise."
- "If at First You Don't Succeed, Try, Try Again."

Copycat

Formation: Group seated in a circle, square, or arc formation.

Equipment: A good recording suitable for the age of the children involved. Older children might enjoy a currently popular record with a lot of percussion sound; younger children might enjoy more descriptive or program music, such as a selection from Mussorgsky's *Pictures at an Exhibition.*

Procedures: One child is chosen to stand in the center and do an assortment of axial movements called for by the music. The other children "copycat," doing exactly what the leader does.

Suggestions: Older children can be encouraged to give the movement separate form or pattern, such as a basic round form (A, B, A, C, A, D, A . . . with A for bending, B for stretching, A for bending, C for twisting, and so on).

The Accent

Formation: Class seated in a semicircle.

Equipment: A chalkboard or large piece of paper on which to write several series of numbers.

Procedures: Put the following number pattern on the board:

1	2	3	4	5	6	7	8
1	2	3	4	5	6	7	8
1	2	3	4	5	6	7	8
1	2	3	4	5	6	7	8
1	2	3	4	5	6	7	8
1	2	3	4	5	6	7	8

Clap only on the underlined numbers. Clap as a round in two parts, three parts, up to six parts. Use rhythm instruments (tambourine, cymbals, shakers, and so on) instead of clapping.

Suggestions: Let the children make up their own patterns. Use different body parts for each different section. Change the meter from fours to sixes.

Echo

Formation: Groups seated in semicircles.

Equipment: A set of rhythm instruments for each group of six to eight.

Procedures: The teacher beats out a certain rhythmic pattern, such as:

| - = slow   a. | | - | | |
|

                         1   2   3   4

| = quick   b. | - | | - | | | | | - | | - | | |
                         1   2   3   4   5   6   7   8

The children try to duplicate the pattern by clapping their hands or using other body instruments. The teacher sings a pattern. The children respond, either with their voices or a body instrument. Rhythm instruments may be substituted.

Suggestions: Let each child have a turn to be "teacher." The silent beat could be discovered by conducting the preceding activity with imaginary beats instead of audible ones.

Names in Rhythm

Formation: Groups seated in semicircles.

Procedures: Each child is led to discover the rhythm of his or her name by saying it and clapping it aloud. They can learn to notate this by clapping | - | for long vowel sounds and | for short vowel sounds. Thus, *Suzie Smith* would look like this: | - | | - | | and *Bobby Taylor* would look like this: | | - | |.

Suggestions: A song could be used to enhance the name patterns. The class could sing "What Is Your Name?" and the children would have to sing back their answer by using the same tune. Several of the names can be put together and organized into a chant or a song.

Conversations

Formation: Small groups in circles.

Procedures: One person begins with a rhythmic pattern and tells it to the next person by using body language. The next person repeats what the first person did and adds his or her own rhythmic phrase. This can continue until each child has had a turn.

Suggestions: This is a good activity for memory, but it probably should be saved for the upper grades.

CONCEPT 28.4
Children internalize the elements of rhythm through activities that permit them to discover and apply rhythms.

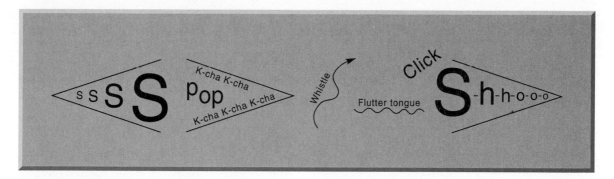

FIGURE 28.1 *A sound montage.*

Applying Rhythm

The following rhythmic activities are designed to help children apply their knowledge of rhythmic fundamentals to a variety of fun and challenging activities. Each of these activities is appropriate throughout the elementary grades, depending more on the rhythmic sophistication of the children than on their movement abilities. Practice in applying rhythms will help children to develop

1. an understanding of the elements of rhythm,
2. the ability to express rhythm through controlled, measured movement,
3. listening skills, and
4. fine motor control.

Sound Compositions

Formation: Groups of six to eight in a scatter formation.

Equipment: Rhythm instruments such as wood block, cymbal with mallet, drum, rachet, and xylophone.

Procedures: Have the children decide on the movements to use and the rhythm instruments to play for each movement, such as:

- neutral position . . . drum
- lift arms . . . xylophone (ascending)
- lower arms . . . xylophone (descending)
- twisting . . . cymbal with mallet
- nodding head . . . wood block

Choose children to play the various instruments and give them time to decide in what order they will play. Have the children play their instruments one at a time, and allow the class to respond in the decided fashion. Now try the activity without looking at the instrument players.

Suggestions: When the activity has been mastered, have the children write their composition so it can be saved and used later. Read the symbols and perform the movements without the instruments. Create sound montages and have the children perform them. Make the sounds indicated in Figure 28.1.

Tampering with the Elements

Formation: Class in a scatter formation.

Equipment: A large sheet of paper or chalkboard containing the words of the army wake-up song "Reveille" and an accompaniment instrument (drum, piano, and so on).

Song:

I can't get 'em up, I can't get 'em up,
I can't get 'em up in the morning (repeat).
The corporal's worse than privates;
The sergeant's worse than corporals;
Lieutenant's worse than sergeants;
And the captain's worst of all!

Procedures: Chant the words in rhythm. Then sing the words with accompaniment. Once the words are learned, begin experimenting with the expressive qualities. Remember, though, to keep the beat steady.

- Go from quiet to loud and back to quiet again.
- Go from loud to quiet to loud again.

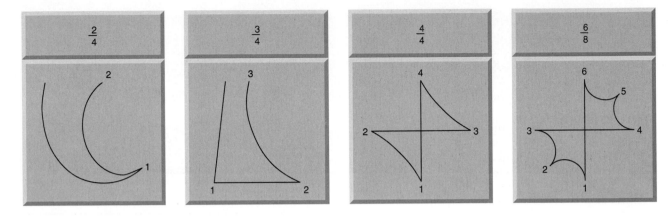

FIGURE 28.2 *Diagram of conductor's beat pattern.*

- Begin slowly and accelerate to the end.
- Begin fast and get slower.
- For color and mood, sing in the major key (the normal way); then sing it in the minor key (variation).

  Suggestions: So the children can visualize what is actually taking place, have them move their bodies to their expressions.

- Extend arms very far apart and bring them together when the music becomes softer.
- Place the hands together and then extend them to show a crescendo (increasing loudness).
- Bend down in a crouching position as the song gets louder, extending upward to a standing position. Reverse the procedure when the music gets softer.

Conducting the Beats

Formation: Six to eight per group, seated in a semicircle.

Equipment: A conductor's baton if available, or a pencil will be fine for substitution. Record player and recording with a selection of strong, steady beat patterns (such as "Stars and Stripes Forever" (2/4) and "Dixie" (4/4). Chalkboard with chalk or a large piece of paper and a magic marker.

Procedures: Discover the meter (how the song is counted), whether it is in groups of twos, threes, fours, or sixes. Don't use unusual groups such as

fives, sevens, or elevens at first. Diagram on a chalkboard or piece of paper the conductor's beat patterns (Figure 28.2). Let the children take their preferred hand and trace the patterns in the air. Then use the nonpreferred hand to do the same. After both hands have traced the patterns, do the same exercise with a conductor's baton. Play a recording and let the children conduct with the recording.

Suggestions: Let the children conduct each other in singing and let them see the importance of keeping the beat constant. Use a variety of meters as well as a variety of songs.

Percussion Instrument Stories

Formation: Eight to ten per group in a circle formation.

Equipment: The following story, either written on a chalkboard or on a large piece of paper where the children can easily read it, or have the story duplicated on individual sheets so each child may have a copy; rhythm instruments.

Story:
One day I went for a walk. As I walked along on the sidewalk, I could hear my footsteps going . . . walk, walk, walk. Some other people came by there and their footsteps went . . . walk, walk, walk, walk. I passed a new house. The men were fixing the roof. I could hear their hammers going . . . tap, tap, tap, tap. I heard a train coming, so I ran

to the corner to watch it. My feet went . . . run, run, run. Oh, it was a big, long train. The wheels were going 'round and 'round, 'round and 'round while they went . . . clickety-clack, clickety-clack. Then I heard some bells . . . tinkle, tinkle, tinkle. Where were they coming from? I turned around, and there, coming down the street, was an ice-cream man. He was ringing the bells . . . tinkle, tinkle, tinkle. He didn't have a truck. He was riding in a wagon being pulled by a horse. The horse's hoofs went . . . clip-clop, clip-clop. The bell and the horse and the train all together sure made a lot of noise . . . clip-clop, tinkle, tinkle, and clickety-clack. It was getting very late. My watch said . . . tick, tick, tick. It was very late for my dinner. I ran all the way home. My feet went . . . run, run, run. I came to my house and knocked on the door . . . knock, knock, knock. My mother opened the door and slammed it shut . . . slam. I washed my hands and sat down to eat. Everyone was talking . . . yak, yak, yak, yak. It sounded like a broken television . . . noise!"

Procedures: Let the children choose instruments (rhythm and body) to imitate the sounds mentioned in the story (such as a triangle for the tinkling sound of the ice-cream man's wagon). Let them have fun exploring with the different sounds. They might even want to bring some sound instruments from home. Have someone read or tell the story. As a particular sound is mentioned, let that sound be heard the number of times indicated. At the end, all the instruments can make the noise.

Suggestions: Have the children make up their own story. Older children particularly enjoy this. Let some of the children go through the motions of what is being sounded.

Orchestration

Formation: Entire class seated in a circle formation. Later break into smaller groups.

Equipment: Rhythm instruments, a recording of a song.

Procedures: Sing the selected simple song for the children, or have everybody listen to a song on a recording. Let them sing or chant along and learn the words and the tune. Practice all rhythms to be played before passing out the instruments. Use body instruments first and then transfer to others.

- Drum.
- Maracas (rattlers).
- Balls.
- Sand blocks.

Pass out instruments to only a few children who seem to have the idea. Let these children have "understudies" who will concentrate only on that part and will eventually get to have a turn when they catch on. Let the drum begin as an introduction. When the child has established the proper beat, gradually add the other instruments. After the instrument players are settled in their parts, add the singers. End the composition in reverse order: singers, the last instrument to the first, and finally the drum. Let the drumbeat fade out gradually.

Suggestions: Have singers work out a body percussion ensemble to join in with the rhythm instrument ensemble. Vary the rhythm patterns as well as the instruments. Make up a dance to go along with the chant or song.

SINGING RHYTHMS

Children need and enjoy singing rhythms. **Singing rhythms** are made up of actions that the children do as they sing or chant a particular song or repeat a particular rhyme. The amount of variation in the action patterns used in singing rhythms will depend on how the children follow and interpret the actions suggested by the auditory cues, their willingness to express themselves freely, and the teaching cues used.

The incorporation of action patterns with various singing rhythms will do much to enhance auditory rhythmic abilities. Developing and reinforcing an internal sensitivity to tempo, accent, intensity, and rhythmic pattern will be by-products of successful participation in singing rhythmic activities requiring a movement response.

The importance of developing the ability to express internally perceived rhythm motorically cannot be overemphasized. By developing a temporal awareness children can establish a meaningful and effective time structure. To see why the ability to interpret auditory rhythmic patterns is important, we need only look at how children first learn the alphabet or a new song. The singsong rhythmic cadence used to recite the alphabet or song seems to make it easier to recall and retain. As adults, we find it much easier to recall the words to an old, long-forgotten song than those uttered by your instructor just yesterday. For example, listening to the melody of an old Beatles tune ("She Loves You," "I Want to Hold Your Hand") will often trigger recollection of the words that accompany the tune. This would be considerably more difficult if our auditory rhythmic abilities were not adequately developed and refined. Hence, children's practice of and participation in auditory rhythmic activities are important. Incorporation of movement makes these experiences more enjoyable and increases the number of sensory modalities involved.

The following pages present numerous examples of finger plays, rhymes and poems, and singing dances that may be effectively used with children. Finger plays and most nursery rhymes are generally most appropriate for preschool and primary-grade children. Singing dances are generally effective from kindergarten through the second grade.

CONCEPT 28.5
Singing rhythms involving finger plays, rhymes and poems, and singing dances are especially appropriate for young children as a first step toward creative rhythmic expression.

Finger Plays

Finger plays are generally the first verses that children commit to memory. They are usually short and easy to learn. Many of them have been handed down from generation to generation. The small muscles of the hands and fingers are less well developed in children than their other muscles, so practice in finger plays does much to aid in increasing finger dexterity. They also provide children with an opportunity to begin using movement to interpret specified rhythmical verses. Table 28.1 lists the finger plays contained in this chapter in a recommended progression from simple to more complex. Practice in finger rhythms will help to develop children's

1. auditory rhythmic abilities,
2. fine motor dexterity,
3. auditory memory abilities,
4. ability to combine rhythmical, auditory, and movement sequences into a coordinated whole, and
5. ability to use movement to interpret specified rhythmical sequences.

TABLE 28.1 *Selected Finger Plays Sequenced in Terms of Complexity*

Finger Plays (page number)	Recommended Progression for Children
	Beginning Level
Here Is the Beehive (546)	x
This Little Clown (546)	x
I'm a Little Teapot (547)	x
Over the Hills (547)	x
Row, Row, Row (547)	x
Dig a Little Hole (547)	x
Ten Fingers (547)	x
Little Fish (548)	x
Bunny (548)	x
If I Were a Bird—1 (548)	x
If I Were a Bird—2 (548)	x
Two Little (548)	x
Flowers (548)	x
Left and Right (548)	x

Here Is the Beehive

Here is the beehive.

(Fold hands.)*

But where are the bees?

(Puzzled look.)

Hiding inside, where nobody sees.

(Peek inside.)

They're coming out now. They're all alive.

(Show surprise.)

One, two, three, four, five.

(Raise fingers one at a time.)

Bzzzzzzzzzzzzzzzzzzz.

This Little Clown

This little clown is fat and gay.

*Words in parentheses indicate the suggested action pattern.

(Hold up thumb.)

This little clown does tricks all day.

(Hold up forefinger.)

This little clown is tall and strong.

(Hold up middle finger.)

This little clown sings a funny song.

(Hold up ring finger.)

This little clown is wee and small.

(Hold up little finger.)

But he can do anything at all.

I'm a Little Teapot

I'm a little teapot, short and stout.
Here is my handle.

(Place hand on waist, forming handle.)

Here is my spout.

(Form spout with the other arm.)

When I get all steamed up, then I shout:

(Hiss.)

Tip me over and pour me out.

(Pour the "tea" out the "spout.")

Over the Hills

Over the hills and far away

(Pounding motion of hands.)

We skip and run and laugh and play.

(Clap hands.)

Smell the flowers and fish the streams,

(Sniff a flower; cast a line.)

Lie in the sunshine and dream sweet dreams.

(Sleep with cheek on hand.)

Row, Row, Row

Row, row, row your boat

(Rowing motion with both hands.)

Gently down the stream.

(Forward waving motion, one hand.)

Merrily, merrily, merrily, merrily,

(Clap hands in rhythm.)

Life is but a dream.

(Sleep.)

Dig a Little Hole

Dig a little hole,

(Dig.)

Plant a little seed,

(Drop seed.)

Pour a little water,

(Pour.)

Pull a little weed.

(Pull up and throw away.)

Chase a little bug,

(Chasing motion with hands.)

Heigh-ho, there he goes!

(Shade eyes.)

Give a little sunshine,

(Cup hands, lift to the sun.)

Grow a little rose.

(Smell flower, eyes closed, smiling.)

Ten Fingers

I have ten little fingers;

(Extend the ten fingers.)

They all belong to me.
I can make them do things;
Would you like to see?
I can open them up wide,

(Spread fingers apart.)

Shut them up tight,

(Clench fists.)

Put them out of sight,

(Place hands behind back.)

Jump them up high,

(Raise hands.)

Jump them down low,

(Lower hands.)

Fold them quietly, and sit

(Fold them in lap.)

Just so!

Little Fish

I hold my fingers like a fish,

(Hold hands back-to-back with fingers spread; wave hands to the side as in swimming; continue to and fro.)

and wave them as I go,
Through the water with a swish,
So gaily to and fro.

Bunny

Hippity, hoppety, hop, hop, hop,

(Raise hands to side of head.)

Here comes a little bunny,

(Children hop on both feet.)

One ear is down, one ear is up,

(Press fingers of one hand against head.)

Oh, doesn't he look funny?

If I Were a Bird—1

If I were a bird, I'd sing a song

(Entwine the two thumbs so that palms of the hands are facing inward.)

And fly about the whole day long,

(Flutter the hands.)

And when the night came, go to rest

(Fold hands and go to sleep.)

Up in my cozy little nest.

If I Were a Bird—2

If I were a bird, I'd sing a song,

(Raise both arms, waving them as a bird flying.)

And fly about the whole day long.
And when the night came, go to rest,

(Place both hands together on one side of face, like sleeping.)

Up in my cozy little nest.
Oh, look and see out—airplanes

(Raise both arms in horizontal positions, as an airplane.)

Away up in the sky.
Watch us gliding through the air,

(Fly about, as an airplane.)

This is how we fly.

Two Little

Two little eyes that open and close,

(Children point to parts of the body indicated by the verses.)

Two little ears and one little nose,
Two little lips and one little chin,
Two little cheeks with the rose shut in,
Two little elbows so dimpled and sweet,
Two little shoes on two little feet.
Two little shoulders so chubby and strong,
Two little legs, running all day long.

Flowers

See the blue and yellow blossoms,

(Hold both hands above the head with fingers touching.)

In the flower bed.
The daisy spreads its petals wide,

(Spread hands apart.)

The tulip bows its head.

(Drop one hand.)

Left and Right

This is my right hand, raise it up high,

(Raise right hand high.)

This is my left hand, I'll touch the sky.

(Raise left hand high.)

Right hand, left hand, whirl them 'round.

(Whirl hands before you.)

Left hand, right hand, pound, pound, pound.

(Pound left fist with right.)

This is my right foot, tap, tap, tap.

(Tap right foot three times.)

This is my left foot, pat, pat, pat,

(Tap left foot three times.)

Right foot, left foot, run, run, run,

(Run in place.)

Right foot, left foot, jump for fun.

(Lift right foot, and down; lift left foot, and down; jump up and down.)

Rhymes and Poems

Many **rhymes and poems** have been passed from generation to generation, and we are all familiar with them. The following rhymes and poems may be less familiar, but they are equally suitable for adding action sequences. Rhymes are particularly enjoyed by preschool and primary-grade children. Table 28.2 lists a suggested progression of activities from simple to more complex. Practice in rhymes and poems that incorporate action sequences will help children to develop

1. auditory rhythmic abilities,
2. listening skills,
3. auditory memory abilities,
4. an ability to combine rhythmical auditory sequences effectively with coordinated action patterns, and an
5. ability to use movement to interpret specific rhythmical sequence.

My Hands

I raise my hands up high,
Now on the floor they lie.
Now high, now low,
Now reach up to the sky.
I spread my hands out wide,
Now behind my back they hide.
Now wide, now hide,
Now I put them at my side.
I give my head a shake, shake, shake,
Now not a move I make.
Now shake, shake, shake,
Not a move I make.
Now my whole self I shake.

The Noble Duke of York

The noble Duke of York,
He had ten thousand men.
He marched them up a hill,
And marched them down again.
So when you're up, you're up,
And when you're down, you're down.
And when you're only halfway up,
You're neither up nor down.

(Children stand and sit in response to the words up *and* down.)

TABLE 28.2 *Selected Rhymes and Poems Sequenced in Terms of Complexity*

Rhymes or Poems (page number)	Recommended Progression for Children	
	Beginning Level	Intermediate Level
My Hands (549)	x	
The Noble Duke of York (549)	x	
Choo-Choo (549)	x	
Windy Weather (549)	x	
Funny Clown (549)	x	
My Little Puppy (550)	x	
How Creatures Move (550)	x	
Jack-in-the-Box (550)	x	
Stormy Days (550)	x	
Follow-the-Leader Rhymes (550)		x
Drawing Numerals in Space (550)		x
Head, Shoulders, Baby (550)		x

Choo-Choo

"Choo-choo" we hear the train.
"Choo-choo" it goes again.
It pulls a heavy load all day.

(Pull self while sliding; use arm and foot movements.)

Windy Weather

Like a leaf or a feather
In the windy, windy weather,
We will whirl around
And twirl around
And all sink down together.

Funny Clown

I am a funny clown.
I move like a funny clown.
I jump, I skip and run.
I stop and have a lot of fun.

My Little Puppy

My little puppy's name is Rags,
He eats so much that his tummy sags.
His ears flip-flop, his tail wig-wags,
And when he walks, he zigs and zags.

How Creatures Move

The lion walks on padded paws,
The squirrel leaps from limb to limb,
While flies can crawl straight up a wall,
And seals can dive and swim.
The worm, he wiggles all around,
The monkey swings by his tail,
And birds may hop upon the ground
Or spread their wings and sail.
But boys and girls have much more fun;
They leap and dance and walk and run.

Jack-in-the-Box

Jack-in-the-box,
All shut up tight,
Not a breath of air,
Not a peep of light.
How tired he must be,
All in a heap.
I'll open the box
And up he'll leap.

Stormy Days

On stormy days
When the wind is high
Tall trees are brooms
Sweeping the sky.
They swish their branches
In buckets of rain
And swish and sweep it
Blue again.

Follow-the-Leader Rhymes

Who feels happy? Who feels gay?
All who do clap your hands this way.
Who feels happy? Who feels gay?
All who do tap your feet this way.
Who feels happy? Who feels gay?
All who do skip around this way.

(Add other activities as desired.)

I'll touch my hair, my eyes,
I'll sit up straight, then I'll rise,

I'll touch my ears, my nose, my chin,
Then quietly I'll sit down again.
The elephant walks just so,
Swaying to and fro—
He lifts up his trunk to the trees,
Then slowly gets down on his knees
Tip-toe, tip-toe, little feet,
Tip-toe, tip-toe, little feet,
Now fast, now slow,
Now very softly—
Tip-toe, tip-toe, little feet.
Tip-toe, tip-toe, little feet.

(Add other activities as desired.)

Shall we go for a walk today?

A walk today, a walk today?

(Repeat, using "pick flowers, smell flowers" i.e. Shall we pick flowers today, etc., Shall we smell flowers today, etc. Use any other ideas to incorporate bending, jumping, and other movements into the above verses.)

Drawing Numerals in Space

A line straight down and that is all

  (Repeat twice.)

To make the numeral 1.
Around and down and to the right

  (Repeat twice.)

To make the numeral 2.
Curve around and curve again. (3)
Down, across, then all the way down. (4)
Down, curve around, a line at the top. (5)
Curve down and all the way around. (6)
A line across and then slant down. (7)
Curve around and then back up. (8)
Curve around and then straight down. (9)
A straight line down and circle around. (10)

(Have the children sit or stand and perform the actions of the words as they are sung.)

Head, Shoulders, Baby

Head, shoulders, baby, 1, 2, 3.

  (Repeat.)

Head, shoulders, head, shoulders, head, shoulders, baby,
1, 2, 3.
Chest, stomach, baby, 1, 2, 3.

(Repeat.)

Chest, stomach, chest, stomach, chest, stomach, baby, 1, 2, 3.

(Repeat, using Knees, ankles. Ankles, knees. Stomach, chest. Shoulders, head.)

Singing Dances

A **singing dance** is one in which children sing verses to a song that provides them cues on how to move. The children will first need to learn the words to the song. If musical accompaniment is used, they should listen to it until they have a general grasp of the words. The action phase of the activity should be added last. Table 28.3 lists a suggested progression of activities from simple to more complex. Practice in singing dance activities will help children develop

1. auditory memory skills,
2. listening skills,
3. auditory rhythmic abilities, and
4. fundamental movement abilities.

Mulberry Bush

Formation: Single circle facing in with one child at the center of the circle. Any number may participate.

Song:

Here we go round the mulberry bush, the mulberry bush, the mulberry bush,
Here we go round the mulberry bush so early in the morning.
This is the way we wash our clothes, we wash our clothes, we wash our clothes,
This is the way we wash our clothes, so early in the morning.

(Continue with:)

This is the way we hang our clothes.
This is the way we iron our clothes.
This is the way we fold our clothes.
This is the way we rake the leaves.
This is the way we sweep the floor.

Procedures: Children may form a circle; one child, designated as the mulberry bush, stands in the center. Let them skip around the circle holding hands as they sing the chorus and stopping to perform the action of the verses.

Suggestions: Make up other words to the songs. (For example, if you are doing a circus unit, the words might be "This is the way the elephant walks," "This is the way the seals clap," and so on.)

TABLE 28.3   *Selected Singing Dances Sequenced in Terms of Complexity*

Singing Dances (page number)	Recommended Progression for Children
	Beginning Level
Mulberry Bush (551)	x
Ten Little Jingle Bells (551)	x
Lobby Loo (552)	x
Blue Bird (552)	x
Farmer in the Dell (552)	x
How Do You Do, My Partner? (552)	x
Round and Round the Village (553)	x
I See You (553)	x
A-Hunting We Will Go (554)	x
Did You Ever See a Lassie? (554)	x
Jolly Is the Miller (554)	x

Ten Little Jingle Bells

Formation: Double row of ten children each row behind the leader (*horse*).

Song:

Ten little jingle bells hung in a row,
Ten little jingle bells helped the horse go.
Merrily, merrily over the snow,
Merrily, merrily sleighing we go.
One little jingle bell fell in the snow
Nine little jingle bells helped the horse go.
Merrily, merrily over the snow,
Merrily, merrily sleighing we go.

(Continue subtracting bells until one is left.)

One little jingle bell fell in the snow.

(Sing slowly.)

No little jingle bells help the horse go.
Slowly, so slowly the bells are all gone.
We'll get some new ones and put them right on.

Procedures: One child may be the horse and ten children the jingle bells in a double row behind the horse. One jingle bell drops off during each verse until only the horse is left. The children should carry sleigh or jingle bells and ring them as they move to the rhythm.

Suggestions: Have two or three teams of horses so that full participation of all class members is going on.

Lobby Loo

Formation: Single circle, all facing center with hands joined. Any number may participate.

Song:

Here we dance lobby loo,
Here we dance lobby light,
Here we dance lobby loo,
All on a Saturday night.
I put my right hand in,
I take my right hand out,
I give my right hand a shake, shake, shake,
And turn myself about.

(Continue with:)

I put my left hand in, etc. . . .
I put my right foot in, etc. . . .
I put my left foot in, etc. . . .
I put my head way in, etc. . . .
I put my whole self in, etc. . . .

Procedures: On the verse part of the dance, the children stand still, facing the center, and follow the directions of the words. On the words "and turn myself about," they make a complete turn in place and get ready to skip around the circle. On the last verse, the children jump forward and then backward, shaking themselves vigorously, and then turning about.

Suggestions: This is an excellent activity to help children with left-right concepts. Be sure to use it as such.

Blue Bird

Formation: Single circle facing inward, with eight to ten children per circle.

Song:

Blue bird, blue bird, in and out my windows,
Blue bird, blue bird, in and out my windows,

Oh! Johnny, I am tired.
Take a boy (girl) and tap him (her) on the shoulders.

(Repeat two more times.)

Procedures: The boys and girls form a circle facing inward, with hands joined and raised to form arches. One child (the bluebird) stands outside the circle. Sing the words of the song as the bird goes in and out of the arches. The child who has been tapped becomes the new bluebird, while the former one takes the vacant place in the circle. Repeat until everyone has been the blue bird.

(You may need more than one circle.)

Suggestions: Let the children form a chain of blue birds until all of the children become birds and there are no windows left.

Ten Little Indians

Formation: Single circle facing inward, with eight to ten children per group.

Song:

First verse:
1 little, 2 little, 3 little Indians,
4 little, 5 little, 6 little Indians,
7 little, 8 little, 9 little Indians,
10 little Indian boys (girls).
Second verse:
10 little, 9 little, 8 little Indians,
7 little, 6 little, 5 little Indians,
4 little, 3 little, 2 little Indians,
1 little Indian boy (girl).

Procedures: The children stand in a circle facing the center. Each child is given a number from one to ten. As the first verse is sung, the children squat when their number is called. During the second verse, they stand when their number is called. The song is repeated with the children hopping and skipping counterclockwise during the first verse and clockwise during the second verse.

Farmer in the Dell

Formation: Single circle facing inward, with eight children per circle.

Song:

First verse:
The farmer in the dell,
The farmer in the dell,
Heigh-ho the dairy, oh,

The farmer in the dell.
Second verse:
The farmer takes a wife—

(*Repeat first verse except for* The farmer in the dell.)

Third verse:
The wife takes a child—
Fourth verse: The child takes a nurse—
Fifth verse: The nurse takes a cat—
Sixth verse: The cat takes a mouse—
Seventh verse: The mouse takes the cheese—
Eighth verse: The cheese stands alone—

Procedures: The children form a circle holding hands, with one child (the farmer) in the center of the circle. The children walk or skip counterclockwise as they sing the song. As they sing the second verse, the farmer chooses somebody to be his wife, and during the singing of the third verse, the wife chooses somebody to be her child. Each time a new verse is sung, a child is chosen to play the role of the character about whom they are singing. The last child selected always chooses the next child. When the children finish the last verse, the "cheese" chases the children about the room. The child tagged becomes the farmer for the next time the dance is performed.

How Do You Do, My Partner?

Formation: Single circle facing inward. Any number may participate.

Song:
How do you do, my partner?
How do you do today?
Will you dance in a circle?
I will show you the way.
Chorus: Tra-la-la-la-la-la.

Record: Educational Record Sales (ERS), "Folk Dance Fundamentals." (See "Audio Resources," for address.)

Procedures: One child is stationed in the middle of the circle. He faces a member of the circle and shakes hands while the children sing the song. As the song ends, the two skip around the circle as everyone sings, "Tra-la-la-la-la-la." When the chorus ends, the two face new partners and the song begins again. Continue this procedure until all children are dancing.

Round and Round the Village

Formation: Single circle facing inward with one child on the outside. Ten children per circle.

Song:
Chorus:
Go round and round the village,
Go round and round the village,
Go round and round the village,
As we have done before.
First verse: Go in and out the windows—
Second verse: Now stand and face your partner—
Third verse: Now follow me to London—

Record: ERS, "Folk Dance Fundamentals." (See "Audio Resources" for address.)

Procedures: The children stand in a circle with hands joined, and one child stands outside the circle. The children walk counterclockwise, singing the chorus (the child outside the circle skips clockwise). After the chorus, the children stop and raise their arms to make "windows" while singing the first verse. The child on the outside of the circle goes in and out of the windows. As the circle sings the second verse, the child selects a partner. The partners skip around on the outside of the circle while the other children sing the third verse. Repeat this procedure until all children have a partner.

I See You

Formation: Double circles facing inward, one behind the other. Any number may participate.

Song:
First verse:
I see you, I see you,
Tra-la, la-la, la.
I see you, I see you,
Tra-la, la-la, la.
Second verse:
You see me and I'll see you,
You swing me and I'll swing you,
You see me and I'll see you,
You swing me and I'll swing you.

Record: ERS, "Folk Dance Fundamentals." (See "Audio Resources" for address.)

Procedures: The children form a circle with the girls standing behind the boys with their hands on the boys' shoulders. They then proceed to play "peek-a-boo" over the boys' shoulders on the first verse in tempo with the verse on each "see" and each "tra-la," "la-la," and "la." On the second verse, the boys face their partners, hook elbows, and skip around in a circle. The boys then change places with their partners and play "peek-a-boo" as the song begins again.

A-Hunting We Will Go

Formation: Two parallel lines facing one another. Six to eight children per line.

Song:

A-hunting we will go,
A-hunting we will go,
We'll catch a fox and put him in a box
And then we'll let him go.

Procedures: The head couple holds hands and slides down the line with eight fast steps and back again as the song is sung the first time. As the song is repeated, they lead a "parade" of all of the couples skipping in a circular pattern to the foot of the set. The head couple then forms an arch while the other children take the hand of the person across from them and walk through the arch and back to their places. The entire verse is sung while doing this. The dance is repeated until all have had an opportunity to be the head couple.

Did You Ever See a Lassie?

Formation: Single circle facing inward, with eight to ten children per circle.

Song:

Chorus:
Did you ever see a Lassie, a Lassie, a Lassie,
Did you ever see a Lassie go this way and that?
Go this way and that way, go this way and that way;
Did you ever see a Lassie go this way and that?

Procedures: The children join hands and form a circle. One child is placed in the center of the circle and is designated to be a Lassie (or Laddie). The other children are also given character names such as farmer, soldier, fireman, cowboy, and so on. When the verse is sung, the child in the center

---

TEACHING TIPS

To foster *creativity* in young children:

- Encourage curiosity.
- Ask questions that require thought.
- Allow for an incubation period of thoughtful reflection.
- Encourage divergent thinking.
- Accept all sincere creative efforts.
- Recognize original creative behaviors.
- Respect questions and unusual ideas (show children that their ideas have value).
- Provide opportunities for learning in new and unusual ways.
- Show a genuine interest in each child's efforts.

---

performs various movements to the rhythm of the song and the children in the circle try to imitate these movements. Each time the verse is sung, another name is substituted for Lassie and the procedure is repeated.

Jolly Is the Miller

Formation: Double circle facing counterclockwise. Any number may participate.

Song:

Oh, jolly is the miller who lives by the mill.
The wheel turns round with a right good will.
One hand in the hopper and the other in the sack,
The girl steps forward and the boy steps back.

Procedures: The children form a double circle facing counterclockwise, and each holds a partner's hand. One child is placed in the center of the inner circle (the miller). The children move counterclockwise as they sing the song. They change partners on the words the "girl steps forward." At this time the "miller" attempts to get a partner and the child left without a partner becomes the "miller."

CREATIVE DANCE

Creativity is often talked about, but what is it? When one creates something external, symbols or objects are manipulated to produce unusual events uncommon to the individual or environment. To create means to bring into existence, to make something out of a word or an idea for the first time, or to produce along new or unconventional lines. Generally speaking, we have not been trained to use our imaginations to apply knowledge we already have and to extend it into creative behavior. Creativity hinges on the need for freedom to explore and experiment. It relies on a flexible schedule that permits time to explore, stand back and evaluate the results, and then continue with the idea or project. Rhythm and dance constitute one avenue for enhancing creative expression. **Creative dance** activities require flexibility on the part of the teacher and classroom techniques oriented toward creativity. The teacher must not leave creativity to chance.

As humans, we have the unique capacity to think and act creatively—an ability that makes it possible to reach out for the unknown. All persons have the potential capacity to create, although some seem to have more innate ability than others. Highly creative individuals tend to possess characteristics such as openness to new experiences, aesthetic sensitivity, and imagination. However, all children should be encouraged to develop their creative abilities to the fullest. In order to develop, they must have opportunities to be creative and thus expand their insight, skill, and confidence.

Dance as an art form is concerned with creativity. Even the beginners should be encouraged to make imaginative responses and to self-direct their activities. Creative responses can be attained through the process of exploration and improvisation, as well as through dance-making opportunities that encourage children to think, feel, imagine, and create. Creative growth depends on experience and needs time to develop. Children must have the opportunity to progress from the simple to the complex, and the demands of each creative rhythmic endeavor must be related to the developmental levels of the individuals.

Children are born with a natural drive for movement. They gradually expand their horizons by cultivating their inner impulses and urges for movement. They learn to think, act, and create as they move. Creative dance is one avenue through which these desirable abilities can be developed and expanded in children. Music and movement ideas that are used in creative rhythms must relate to the child's world if they are to initiate spontaneity. As the teacher, you are an essential catalyst in helping children develop and expand their powers of creativity and self-expression. You will need to take the time to carefully plan and execute lessons that foster creativity.

CONCEPT 28.6
Creative dance activities involving imitative rhythms, interpretative rhythms, and dance making are a primary means for helping children realize their potential as expressive movers.

Creative Rhythmic Expression

Creative rhythmic expression is a form of movement that permits one to express ideas, feelings, and moods through some form of accompaniment. It is a creative extension of rhythmic fundamentals into new and individually unique ways of expressing oneself rhythmically. Dances may be created from ideas, songs, words, and music. With children in the regular physical education program, creative rhythmics generally take three forms: dance making; imitative rhythms, in which various animate and inanimate objects are imitated; or interpretative rhythms that permit acting out of an idea or an event. Table 28.4 provides a list of all three types and a recommended progression of activities.

Ideas and Creative Dance. Children in the primary grades enjoy making up dances "about" something. They project themselves into both animate and inanimate things with little difficulty. They respond readily to "Let's pretend," or "Let's be . . ." or "Let's move like . . ."

In selecting simple ideas, you may have the children move like "a new toy," "the snow that fell this morning," and so on. The children will have many ideas. It is important to challenge their imaginations. You may point out contrasts in movement, high and low, big and little, forward and backward.

Children in the upper elementary grades, unlike those in the primary grades, who may pretend to be the objects themselves, relate to objects in one way or another. For example, younger children are the balls that bounce; older children manipulate the balls.

Accompaniment for dances may be improvised and may be music or words. The piano used as a percussion instrument or homemade rhythmic instruments are also suitable.

TABLE 28.4   *Selected Creative Rhythmic Activities Sequenced in Terms of Complexity*

Creative Rhythmic Activity (page number)	Suggested Progression for Children		
	Beginning Level	*Intermediate Level*	*Advanced Level*
Imitative Dances			
Imitating Living Creatures (557)	X		
Imitating Things in Nature (557)	X		
Imitating Objects (557)	X		
Imitating Events (558)	X		
Interpretative Dances			
Interpreting Action Words (558)		X	
Interpreting Feelings and Moods (558)		X	
Interpreting Art (558)		X	
Interpreting Action Sequences (559)		X	
Interpreting Pendular Movements (559)		X	
Interpreting Special Holidays (559)		X	
Dance Making			
Name Dances (560)			X
Rhyme Dances (560)			X
Slogan Dances (560)			X
Menu Dances (560)			X

Songs and Creative Dance.   Dances made from songs are probably the easiest. "Movement" songs, those in which one or two movements express an idea, are suitable for primary children, whereas some songs for primary children can be interpreted in more than one way. Older children enjoy using folk songs, rounds, and currently popular songs for creative rhythmic dance making.

Words, Music, and Creative Dance.   Children like to make up dances using nursery rhymes, nonsense words, chants, and poems. When poetry is used, it is generally best to begin with narrative poetry and then progress to lyric poetry, in which feelings are expressed. Children like to use names of classmates for simple dance making, clapping out the rhythm and then fitting appropriate movement to the rhythmic pattern. The procedure used for including music involves selecting the piece of music; listening carefully to determine the quality of movement, tempo, and accent; improvising and experimenting with movement; and listening to the music more critically for its structure. Creative rhythmic expression to words and

to music is fun and should be made progressively more challenging as the children become more skilled.

Children like to make dances by combining locomotor and nonlocomotor movements until a pleasing form is obtained. For younger children, this exploration usually results in "being" something. The child dances what the music "tells" him to dance. Older children enjoy movement experimentation. They respond wholeheartedly to a problem in movement in which they can invent movements or manipulative objects to achieve a goal.

Imitative Dances

Through **imitative dance** children express themselves by trying to "be something." The teacher should, however, be careful to ensure that the children realize the movement potential of their own bodies before they are introduced to imagery as a part of the lesson. In their own minds the children take on the identity of what they are imitating and act out this identity with expressive movements. They are encouraged to explore and express themselves in various original movements. There are three general approaches to imitative rhythms. In the first, the teacher begins with a rhythm and lets each child decide what to imitate based on the characteristics of the rhythm. This approach is one of "What does this rhythm make you think of?"

In the second method, the teacher selects a piece of music and has the class choose what to imitate. All of the children imitate the same thing. Each child creates the selection as he or she wishes. If the choice were a giant, each child would interpret her own individual concept of a giant.

The third approach begins with a selection for imitation and then choosing an appropriate rhythm for movement. Listening to the musical accompaniment is important in all three approaches, because the children must "feel" the character of the music. The music (ranging from clapping or a drumbeat to piano music or a recording) must be appropriate for the identity to be assumed in order to be effective; otherwise, the movement becomes artificial. The movements of the children should be in time with the music and should reflect a basic understanding of the elements of rhythm. Practice in creative imitative rhythmic activities with children will contribute to their ability to

1. think of and act out creative movement sequences in response to rhythmic accompaniment,
2. imitate the function of animate and inanimate objects through creative rhythmic movement,
3. move efficiently through space in a controlled, rhythmic manner, and
4. think and act creatively.

Imitating Living Creatures   Children enjoy imitating many different living creatures. These imitations may be done to the beat of a drum, piano, record, or without any form of accompaniment.

Animals

Elephant	Snake	Fish
Giraffe	Rabbit	Bird
Bear	Kangaroo	Kitten
Lion	Puppy	Pony
Seal	Duck	

People

Fire fighter	Soldier	Ballet dancer
Letter carrier	Airplane pilot	Cowpoke
Doctor	Mountain	Carpenter
Sailor	climber	

Imaginary People and Animals

Martian	Giant	Troll
Goblin	Ninja Turtle	Monster
Elf	Incredible Hulk	Dragon
Terminator	R2 D2	

Imitating Things in Nature.   Young children are rapidly expanding their knowledge and understanding of the world of nature. They will enjoy imitating many things in nature. Through these experiences, they will increase their knowledge and nature vocabulary.

Weather Conditions

Wind	Sleet	Tornado	Sun
Rain	Hail	Clouds	Rainbow
Snow	Hurricane	Storm	

Climatic Conditions

Hot	Cool	Autumn
Cold	Sunny	Winter
Warm	Summer	Spring

Miscellaneous

Smoke	Sun	Mineral	Wave	Star
Fire	Moon	Soil	Water	Flower

Imitating Objects   Children also enjoy imitating several play objects and machines.

Play Objects

Swing	Merry-go-	Pull toy	"Slinky"
Slide	round	Yo-yo	Silly putty
Seesaw	Ball	Frisbee	

Modes of Transportation

Rowboat	Car	Bicycle
Snowmobile	Canoe	Motorcycle
Truck	Rocket	Train

Machines

Elevator	Cement	Pneumatic	Coffee
Tractor	mixer	drill	grinder
Bulldozer	Record	Lawn	Tape player
Crane	player	mower	Computer
			Blender

Imitating Events   As children's worlds expand, so does their exposure to special events outside the home. The following is a list of suggested activities and events that may be imitated at strategic times during the year.

The Circus

Clown	Trapeze artist	Trained animal
Acrobat	Lion tamer	Marching band
Juggler	Barker	member
High-wire walker	Ringmaster	

Sporting Events (In slow motion, imitate movements found in the following athletic events)

Soccer	Volleyball	Tennis
Football	Track and field	Bowling
Baseball	Swimming	Ice hockey
Basketball	Fencing	Diving

Interpretative Dances

Interpretative rhythms are a second form of creative dance. In **interpretative dance,** the children act out an idea, a familiar event, or an ordinary procedure. They may also express feelings, emotions, and moods through movement. The quality and direction of the interpretative movements depend on the mood, intelligence, and personal feelings of the children. In interpretative movement, the teacher creates the atmosphere for the children to express themselves. There are three general approaches.

In the first approach, the teacher begins with an idea or a story. As the story progresses, suitable rhythmic background is used. A recording, piano selection, percussion instrument, or even a rhythm band can be used. The teacher often provides the verbal background and directions for the drama, but the story can unfold without this.

The second approach begins with a piece of music, generally a recording, and develops an idea to fit the music. The piece of music selected should have sufficient changes in tempo and pattern to provide different kinds and qualities of background. A general idea or plan of action can be selected and fitted to the music. An idea such as "going to the fair" may be selected and an adaptable recording chosen.

In the third approach, the children express moods or feelings. A piece of music may be played, and the children may act out how the music makes them feel. An alternative method is simply to give cue words that denote specific moods (*happy, sad,* and so on) and have

the children express these words through movement. Practice in creative interpretative rhythmic activities with children will contribute to their ability to

1. think through and act out creative movement sequences in response to rhythmic accompaniment,
2. interpret moods, feelings, and ideas and express them through creative, rhythmic moves,
3. solve rhythmic problems creatively through expressive movement,
4. move efficiently through space in a coordinated rhythm,
5. think and act creatively, and
6. "feel" auditory and visual symbols and be able to express these feelings through movement.

Interpreting Action Words.   Numerous verbs provide opportunities for creative movement. Try several during the first few minutes of the lesson. The following represent only a few of the numerous possibilities:

Bang	Twinkle	Bump	Punch	Bop
Crack	Glow	Tingle	Float	Zip
Spin	Bubble	Grab	Dart	Boom
Pop	Blow	Grumble	Zoom	Pluck

Interpreting Feelings and Moods.   Children experience many feelings and moods during the course of their day, and they will enjoy openly expressing them through movement. Musical accompaniment may be used to enhance the experience.

Happiness	Gladness	Hurt	Laughter
Sadness	Love	Surprise	Tears
Confusion	Hate	Bravery	Gaiety
Pride	Friendship	Shyness	
Disappoint-	Jealousy	Boredom	
ment	Fear	Interest	

Interpreting Art.   Art is an experience that may, through guided discovery, be successfully interpreted in movement. Various lines, forms, colors, and textures may be expressed this way. Remember that the children should be encouraged to express how these things make them feel. Guessing games may be played, with one group trying to guess what the other is imitating. Discuss the various art forms with the children before they show you their interpretation.

Line: straight, curved, zigzag, dotted, dashed, or broken.

Form: circle, square, triangle, rectangle, and hexagon.

Color: red, white, green, blue, yellow, black, purple, pink, brown, and orange.

Texture: smooth, slippery, bumpy, rough, hard, soft, furry, silky, scratchy, and slick.

Interpreting Action Sequences.   Children enjoy interpreting an unlimited number of action sequences. The following is a list of only a few of the possibilities that may be explored.

Move through molasses
Shoo the flies away
Float in water
Hit the punching bag
Grow like a flower
Sway like a tree in the breeze
Build a house
Fight a fire
Rocket to the moon
Ride a bumpy road

Interpreting Pendular Movements.   Have the children think of objects that swing (clock, golf club, baseball bat, swing, and so on). Let them move like each one. Use an object that has a pendular motion so they can keep time. Encourage them to swing with their eyes closed and then open to see if they are still in time with the beat. Encourage the children also to swing individual parts of their body one at a time.

Interpreting Special Holidays.   Discuss the meaning of various special holidays with the children, encouraging them to share their experiences with the class.

Christmas/Hanukkah
Passover
Halloween
Easter
Valentine's Day
Ramadan
Flag Day
Thanksgiving
Independence Day
Summer vacation
Snow days
Ground Hog Day

TEACHING TIPS

The following sequence is suggested for successful experiences in *dance making:*

- Divide the class into small groups of four to six per group. Permit each group to decide on what is to be danced (an idea, words, a song, music).

- Discuss the selection. What does it feel like? What are its characteristics? How can you move to it?

- Encourage the children to experiment with movements based on their discussion.

- Encourage further discussion and experimentation.

- Plan the sequence of the dance, adding the parts best suited to it and discarding others.

- Decide what accompaniment is to be used. Body instruments or rhythm are appropriate if children are dancing to words or an idea.

- Try out the entire sequence with the accompaniment. Make modifications as necessary, adding elements or deleting elements from the dance.

- Practice the dance two or three times.

- Perform the dance for anther group or for the entire class.

Dance Making

Older children and children with a firm grasp of rhythmic fundamentals enjoy the challenging experience of making their own dances. **Dance making** involves goal-directed creative rhythmic expression and permits children the freedom to make their own forms of expression and communication. Children need an opportunity to tell the world who they are, what they feel, and what their world means to them. Dance making permits this and encourages children to work together cooperatively toward a common goal. It permits them to attach meaning and dimension to music through the use of their bodies in an expressive form of movement.

The role of the teacher in the process of dance making is to establish an environment conducive to expression—one that is accepting of the children's creative efforts. The teacher's job is to set the stage and act as a catalyst to guide the creative process. Attempts at creative dance making are likely to meet with only limited success if the children do not have a background in rhythmic fundamentals or if they feel inhibited in expressing themselves through movement. Therefore, it is recommended that, prior to introducing children to dance making, fundamental rhythmic activities, such as those presented earlier, be introduced, followed by the imitative and interpretative rhythms just presented.

Dances are based on the elements of movement (effort, space, relationships). Dances may be made up from songs, instrumental music, words, or ideas. With older children, dance making from songs that they are familiar with is the easiest and most popular technique. There are, however, a few things to guard against. First, avoid songs that are too abstract or overly sentimental. Second, avoid too literal an interpretation of the words. Choose songs that children can understand and that involve something concrete. Permit the children to listen to the song and to become familiar with the words or instrumentation. After they have learned the words, encourage each group to discuss their meaning and how they can best be danced.

When making dances from an instrumental music selection, children will respond best to music that is familiar and popular. The dance should reproduce the music in terms of accent, tempo, intensity, and rhythmic pattern. Movement phrases should parallel changes in the melody and the quality of the music and variations in the accompaniment. The children should be permitted to listen to the structure of the music to determine which phrases are repeated. The teacher should help the children become sensitive to the quality of the sound by encouraging them to describe what they hear, such as high-low, fast-slow, light-heavy, soft-loud. Experimentation with movements to interpret the structure of the music is the next step, followed by practice and presentation to the class or another group.

Using words and ideas as the stimulus for dance making is somewhat more abstract and should be practiced by children only after they have had experiences with making dances based on songs and music. Most age-appropriate rhymes, poems, and brief stories may be used as a basis for a dance. Children should first listen to the rhythm of the words and then to the idea conveyed. Dances may be devised that express either. First-time experiences with dance making to words or ideas will need to be relatively simple and in tune with the children's interests. As skill develops in dance making to words and ideas, the words or ideas may become increasingly more abstract. Practice in dance making fosters

1. creativity,
2. freedom of expression,
3. an understanding of the meaning and dimension of music through movement, and
4. cooperative group problem solving.

Name Dances.   Working in small groups, select one of the children's names. Clap out the rhythm of the name, then add expressive movements. As skill progresses, add combinations of first and last names in the group to form a complete phrase.

Rhyme Dances.   Working in small groups, select an appropriate rhyme or short poem (geared to the maturity level of the group) and develop a dance based on it.

Slogan Dances.   The teacher selects and combines popular sayings or slogans into a musical phrase. Small groups develop a dance based on the words and the idea conveyed. For example, try:

"Just do it"

"Give a hoot, don't pollute"

"When it's sugar and spice, everything's nice."

"Only you can prevent forest fires."

"With a stitch in time that saves nine."

Menu Dances.   Working in small groups, each group selects a menu for either breakfast, lunch, dinner, or a snack. Combine the sounds, movements, and rhythms of the foods chosen. For example, try:

Breakfast

Boiled eggs (roll like a ball)	Pancakes (flip over)	Toast (pops out of the toaster)
Bacon (sizzle and shrink)	Syrup (act sticky and runny)	

Dinner

Spaghetti (be real stiff, then limp)	Salad (mix and toss)	Bread (long, loaf)

Snack

Ice cream (melt)	Popcorn (snap and pop)	Pretzels (twist)

SUMMARY

This chapter dealt with three important means of helping children be expressive movers through dance: rhythmic fundamentals, singing rhythms, and creative dance. Rhythmic fundamentals are a necessary first step in dance. Children must learn about and be able to respond to the elements of rhythm. The elements of underlying beat, accent, tempo, intensity, and rhythmic pattern provide them with the essential tools for rhythmic movement. Children also need to discover rhythm both internally and externally and be able to apply rhythm to their movement.

Singing rhythmic activities were discussed as a second means of helping children become more effective expressive movers. Singing rhythms are especially enjoyed by young children and involve finger plays, rhymes, poems, and singing dances. They enable children to combine words and music with body actions. This helps establish the child's internal rhythm and brings coordination and control to movement.

Creative dance is a third means of fostering expressive movement among children. Creative dances may be devised from ideas, songs, words, or music. The key to successful experiences with creative rhythmic expression is to permit children to experiment and explore in an environment that is both encouraging of their efforts and accepting of the results. Children should progress from imitative dances, to interpretative dances, and finally to dance making as they become more liberated in their abilities as expressive movers.

COMPLEMENTARY READINGS

Benzwie, T. (1991). *A Moving Experience: Dance for Lovers of Children and the Child Within.* Reston, VA: AAHPERD.

Fleming, G. A. (1990). *Children's Dance.* Reston, VA: AAHPERD.

Hankin, T. (1992). Presenting creative dance activities to children: Guidelines for the nondancer. *JOPERD* 63:22–24.

Joyce, M. (1994). *Dance Technique for Children.* Mountain View, CA: Mayfield.

Shuker, V., and P. Brightman. eds. (1992). Dance dynamics: Dance education k–12—Theory into practice. *JOPERD* 63:37–57 (series of articles).

Werner, P., E.T.A. (1992). Developmentally appropriate dance for children. *JOPERD* 63:40–43.

SUPPLEMENTARY READINGS

Gilbert Green, A. (1992). *Creative Dance for All Ages.* Reston, VA: AAHPERD.

Stinson, S. (1988). *Dance for Young Children: Finding the Magic in Movement.* Reston, VA: AAHPERD.

Weikart, P. S. (1987). *Rhythmically Moving I-9.* Ypsilanti, MI: High Scope Press.

VIDEOS

Children and Movement Video Series: Rhythmic Activities. Sanders, S. Durham, NC: Great Activities Publishing Company. (25 min.).

AUDIO RESOURCES

Fundamental Rhythms

Classroom Rhythms. Educational Record Sales, 157 Chambers Street, New York, NY 10007 (B1037).

Exploring the Rhythm Instruments. Educational Record Sales, 157 Chambers Street, New York, NY 10007 (B1032).

Interpretive Rhythms. Educational Record Sales, 157 Chambers Street, New York, NY 10007 (B1050).

Introducing the Rhythm Instruments. Educational Record Sales, 157 Chambers Street, New York, NY 10007 (B1020).

Kindergarten Sing-A-Long. Educational Record Sales, 157 Chambers Street, New York, NY 10007 (B1146).

Marches. Educational Activities, Inc., Box 392, Freeport, NY 11520 (Hyp-B11).

Our First Rhythm Band, vols. 1 and 2. Educational Record Sales, 157 Chambers Street, New York, NY 10007 (B1066, B1075).

Rhythm from the Land of Make-Believe. Educational Record Sales, 157 Chambers Street, New York, NY 10007 (B1055).

Singing Rhythms

Action Songs and Sounds. Bridges, 310 W. Jefferson, Dallas, TX 75208 (HYP508).

Finger Play. Educational Record Sales, 157 Chambers Street, New York, NY 10007 (B1043, B1046).

Fun Dances for Children. Kimbo Records, Box 477, Long Branch, NJ 07740 (KEA1134).

Holiday Songs and Rhythms. Educational Activities, Inc., Box 392, Freeport, NY 11520 (AR538).

Let's Sing and Act Together. Educational Record Sales, 157 Chambers Street, New York, NY 10007 (B1057).

Nursery Rhymes for Dramatic Play. Educational Record Sales, 157 Chambers Street, New York, NY 10007 (B1051).

Primary Musical Games. Educational Activities, Inc., Box 392, Freeport, NY 11520.

Rhythmic Activity Songs for Primary Grades. Bridges, 310 W. Jefferson, Dallas, TX 75208 (LP1055, LP1066, LP1077, LP1088).

Simplified Folk Songs. Educational Activities, Inc., Box 392, Freeport, NY 11520 (AR518).

Singing Action Games. Bridges, 310 W. Jefferson, Dallas, TX 75208 (HYP507).

Singing Games Through Folk Dancing. Educational Record Sales, 157 Chambers Street, New York, NY 10007.

We Move to Poetry. Bridges, 310 W. Jefferson, Dallas, TX 75208.

Won't You Be My Friend. Bridges, 310 W. Jefferson, Dallas, TX 75208 (AR544).

Creative Dance

And the Beat Goes on for Physical Education. Folk Rock. Kimbo Educational Record Company, Box 477, Long Branch, NJ 07740 (KEA 5020-C).

Balloons. Educational Department, RCA Victor Records, 155 E. 24th Street, New York, NY 10010.

Clap, Snap, and Tap. Kimbo Educational Record Company, Box 477, Long Branch, NJ 07740 (EA48-C).

Creative Rhythm Album. (A visit to a farm, park, and circus). 622 Rooter Drive, Glendale, CA 91201.

Creative Rhythms for Children. Phoebe James Products, Box 134, Pacific Palisades, CA 90272.

Dance Me a Story. Educational Department, RCA Victor Records, 155 E. 24th Street, New York, NY 10010.

Dances Without Partners. Educational Activities, Inc., Box 392, Freeport, NY 11520.

Flappy and Floppy. Educational Department, RCA Victor Records, 155 E. 24th Street, New York, NY 10010.

Keep on Steppin. Educational Activities, Inc., Box 392, Freeport, NY 11520.

Little Duck. Educational Department, RCA Victor Records, 155 E. 24th Street, New York, NY 10010.

Living with Rhythms Series. Basic Rhythms for Primary Grades; Animal Rhythms; Rhythms and Meter Appreciation. David McKay Company, 119 W. 40th Street, New York, NY 10010.

Machine Rhythm. Educational Record Sales, 157 Chambers Street, New York, NY 10007 (B1077).

The Magic Mountain. Educational Department, RCA Victor Records, 155 E. 24th Street, New York, NY 10010.

Make Believe in Movement. Kimbo Educational Record Company, Box 477, Long Branch, NJ 07740 (KIM0500-C).

Modern Jazz Movements. Kimbo Educational Record Company, Box 477, Long Branch, NJ 07740 (KIM3030-C).

Move Along Alphabet. Kimbo Educational Record Company, Box 477, Long Branch, NJ 07740 (KIM0510-C).

Music for Creative Movement. Bridges, 310 W. Jefferson, Dallas, TX 75208.

Music for Modern Dance. Kimbo Educational Record Company, Box 477, Long Branch, NJ 07740 (KIM6090-C).

Noah's Ark. Educational Department, RCA Victor Records, 155 E. 24th Street, New York, NY 10010.

Rhythms for the World, Birds, Beasts, Bugs, and Little Fishes. Folkways, 117 W. 46th Street, New York, NY 10010.

To Move Is to Be. Educational Activities, Inc., Box 392, Freeport, NY 11520.

CHAPTER 29

The Folk Dance Strand for Cooperative Social Learners

●

Key Concept

Folk Dances Are an Excellent Means for Helping Children Become More Cooperative Social Learners, as Well as Skillful Movers and Expressive Movers

●

Chapter Objectives

The purpose of this chapter is to provide you with the tools to:
• Discuss the dual role of structured dance in helping children become more skillful movers and social learners.
• Discuss how to get ready to teach a new dance activity.
• List the steps in teaching a new dance activity.
• Describe several steps common to folk, line, and square dances.
• Demonstrate knowledge of basic folk dance terms.
• Diagram several formations commonly used for structured dances.
• Select among structured dances for beginning, intermediate, or advanced activities for selected groups of elementary school-age children.

●

Terms to Remember

Bleking Step	Waltz Run Step	Honor Your Partner or
Buzz Step	Allemande Left	Corner
Grapevine Step	Circle Eight Hands Around	Ladies Chain
Polka Step	Corner	Partner
Schottische Step	Do-Si-Do	Promenade
Step-Close	Elbow Swing	Right-Hand Star
Slip Step	Forward and Back	Right and Left Through
Step-Hop	Grand Right and Left	Sets
Two-Step		

Folk dances are the oldest form of structured dance, having been used for hundreds of years in ceremonies, rituals, and as an expression of everyday experiences. Folk dance is deeply embedded in the culture of most countries. The specific dances of the culture have been passed from generation to generation and are enjoyed by both children and adults today.

Line dance is a form of folk dance that is enjoying renewed popularity throughout North America. Most line dances, sometimes called country and western dances, are performed without a partner and can be enjoyed by both children and adults. Line dances are especially effective with children because they avoid the often difficult problem of dancing with a partner. Children who are not socially mature enough to dance with a partner of the opposite sex will find line dances nonthreatening, challenging, and fun.

CONCEPT 29.1
Folk dances represent the many cultures of the world and can be effectively integrated with classroom social studies.

Square dance is uniquely North American. A square dance is a form of folk dance, but it generally uses a square formation rather than the traditional circle and line formations of folk dance. The terminology used in square dancing is also different from that used in folk dance. Both folk and square dancing are concerned primarily with the use of locomotor movements to music. Because folk dances are closely related to fundamental locomotor movements, they are excellent ways to practice and reinforce these skills. They offer a relaxed environment for developing basic cooperative social skills and improving one's confidence when placed in a social setting with members of the opposite gender.

All forms of folk dance are enjoyable and easy to incorporate into the curriculum. Emphasis, however, on the social element at the expense of the skill element is not recommended. This chapter focuses on preparing to teach a variety of ethnic folk dances, basic steps, terms, and formations used. Several dances are then presented. Each describes the movement skills and desired outcomes of the activity as well as how the dance is performed. A record resource is given for each dance. Complete addresses for obtaining these records are provided at the end of the chapter. A listing of other recommended folk dance recordings is also given.

PREPARING TO TEACH A DANCE

Preparation is the key to success in teaching folk dances. It is of utmost importance that you know your students and their capabilities prior to selecting a dance. The dances found here are presented in a progressive order of difficulty, according to the skill requirements and the complexity of the dance pattern. Selecting a dance that is beyond the present level of ability of your students will only result in frustration and failure. Conversely, selection of an activity that is below the level of social maturity of your students will lead to unnecessary and unwanted difficulties. Therefore, the first requirement in getting ready to teach a dance is to select one that is appropriate in terms of both the skill and the social requirements.

CONCEPT 29.2
The social element inherent in folk dance must be matched with the social maturity of the children being taught.

Once you have selected the dances to be taught, it is important to review the music and the steps involved. When purchasing folk dance compact discs or tapes, be sure that an instruction sheet accompanies the music. In fact, it is a good idea to make a duplicate of the instruction sheet and store it in a safe place.

When reviewing the music, listen for the introduction and for the point when the dance begins. Be sure to know the phrases of the music and how they fit the steps or figures of the dance. Be certain to note rhythmic changes in the music and where transitions occur.

After you are familiar with the music, practice the steps yourself, first without the music and then with the music. Become comfortable with putting the steps to the music by practicing several times. Talk through the dance while practicing in the same manner in which you will talk to your students. Be certain to count out the beats in each measure and to use the correct name for each step. Practice cueing the start and finish of steps and figures.

BASICS OF FOLK DANCE

Folk dances use a variety of steps, terms, and formations. Children should be familiar with them in order to understand and be able to perform the dances. The following is

Helpful hints for teaching a structured dance:

- Progress from simple to complex when teaching a dance. The progression you use will be an important factor in the ease with which the dance is learned.

- Move from a slower tempo to the normal tempo.

- Move from familiar steps to unfamiliar ones.

- Get the basic idea of the dance across. Don't be overly concerned with form.

- Set reasonable standards for achievement for the children. Standards that are too high will limit enjoyment.

- Break the dance down into parts and progressively teach each one, building skill upon skill.

- Be certain to have the children in the formation required by the dance when they are listening to the music and you are teaching the steps. This will help the children visualize the activity.

- Be liberal in your use of praise and positive encouragement.

- Modify dance positions that require partners if children are not ready for close contact with members of the opposite gender. For example, an elbow turn will work just as well as a more advanced waltz turn.

- Do not ororverbalize. Demonstration and the use of key words works best.

- Keep the lesson informal and stress a wholesome social environment. Folk and square dances are fun, and the children should be encouraged to feel the energy and excitement that they generate.

Recommended steps in presenting a structured dance:

- Tell the class the name of the dance, its origin, and a little about the country that it comes from.

- When possible, try to relate the dance to other experiences children might be familiar with.

- Let the children listen to the music. Then briefly discuss the rhythm, tempo, and other qualities of the music.

- Teach the basic steps of the dance.

- Teach difficult steps and figures separately.

- Use a walk-through, talk-through approach without the music, beginning slowly and gradually working up to actual speed.

- Practice with the music. If the speed of the music can be slowed, do so at first.

- For dances that have several different figures, teach one figure at a time, first without the music.

- Progressively combine the figures of the dance and work up to the normal tempo.

- Repeat the dance two or three times so that the students learn it well and have an opportunity to enjoy the activity.

a brief description of steps, terms, and formations commonly used in folk and square dance.

Steps

The following is a list of ten steps common to most folk dances.

Bleking Step. The **bleking step** is done to an even rhythm. Hop left; at the same time, place the right heel forward with the right leg straight. Jump up and reverse position with the left heel forward and the left leg straight. The action is rhythmically repeated springing from one foot to another.

Buzz Step. The **buzz step** is used for turning a partner. The partners are in a waltz position. The right foot of the person in the lead is forward, with the weight on the front of the feet. The right foot remains stationary while the left foot pushes off, turning in a clockwise direction.

Grapevine Step. The **grapevine step** is done by stepping right, crossing the left foot in front, then stepping right again and crossing the left foot behind. The process is rhythmically repeated, alternating crossing in front and behind the stepping leg.

Polka Step. The **polka step** is done to an uneven rhythm with an upbeat tempo. From a position with the feet together and the weight on the left foot, hop left, raise the right knee slightly, and step right forward. Move the left foot to the right, taking some weight off the left, and step forward with the right. The process is repeated starting with a hop on the right foot.

Schottische Step.   The **schottische step** is done to an even rhythm and a moderate tempo. Step forward on the right foot, step forward left, step forward right, hop right (step, step, step, hop). The next schottische step starts with the left foot.

Step-Close.   The **step-close** is done to an even rhythm and a slow tempo. Step sideways to the right while at the same time pointing the left toe to the left side with the left heel raised and the leg straight. Then slowly draw the left foot to the right, taking the weight on to the right foot (step-draw-close). The process is repeated with the same foot leading or reversed to the opposite side.

Slip Step.   The **slip step** is done to an uneven beat and a fast tempo. It is a sideward slide. Slide the right foot to the side, slide the left foot to close to the right. Repeat. The slip step may be repeated in the opposite direction or continued in the same direction.

Step-Hop.   The **step-hop** is done to an even rhythm and a moderate tempo. Step forward on the right foot and hop on the right, then step forward on the left foot and hop on the left. Repeat.

Two-Step.   The **two-step** is done to an uneven beat (quick, quick, slow) and a moderately fast tempo. Step forward with the left foot on count one. Then bring the right foot up to the left on the second half of count one. Now step forward on the left again on count two. Use key words: step-close-step-hold.

Waltz Run.   The **waltz run step** is done to an even rhythm and either a slow or fast tempo. From a waltz position, the step consists of a continuous run, forward or backward. The first beat of each measure is accented with a slight stamp. There are three runs to each measure.

CONCEPT 29.3
The movement skill and expressive elements of structured dance activities should not be overlooked.

Terms

The following is a list of words commonly used in square dance terminology:

Allemande Left. The boy places his left hand in the left hand of his partner. They turn counterclockwise and back to place.

Circle Eight Hands Around. Two couples join hands and walk clockwise around the set.

Corner. Person to left of the boy and to the right of the girl in a set.

Do-Si-Do. Partners face each other, walk forward, pass right shoulders, go around each other, and walk backward to place.

Elbow Swing. Partners join right elbows, swing around once, and return to place.

Forward and Back. Dancer takes three steps to the center of the set and back to place.

Grand Right and Left. Partners face and clasp right hands in a handshake; they walk in the direction in which they are facing, alternating right- and left-hand clasps with each dancer they meet.

Honor Your Partner or Corner. The boy bows and the girl curtsies to the person named in the call.

Ladies Chain. The girls walk forward and clasp right hands, pass right shoulders with girl of opposite couple, give left hand to opposite boy as he turns counterclockwise once around to face center of the set again.

Partner. The person with whom you are dancing. Girls stand to the boy's right.

Promenade. Couples assume a skating position (right hand to right hand and left hand to left hand) and walk around the set.

Right-Hand Star. Four people walk to center of the set, turn right sides to center and join right hands, walk clockwise once around. Reverse the movement for a left-hand star.

Right and Left Through. Two couples face, walk forward, and pass right shoulders with the opposite dancer. Each boy then takes the girl's left hand with his left hand, places his right hand around the girl's waist, turns her around, repeats the first movement, and returns to the original position.

Sets. Square dances are done in sets of four couples. The head couple (couple 1) is the couple nearest the caller or the music. The side couples (couples 2 and 4) are opposite one another; the foot couple (couple 3) is opposite the head couple.

Varsovienne Position.   Boy stands beside and to the left of the girl. His right hand is placed in her right hand over her right shoulder. Boy's left hand is in girl's left hand at waist level.

Formations

A variety of formations are used in folk dancing. Most use a circle or line formation. Most square dances use a square formation with four couples forming a set. Figure 29.1 provides a diagram of common folk and square dance formations.

CONCEPT 29.4
Successful teaching of structured dance activities requires careful preparation and a commitment to children's learning in an atmosphere of fun and personal enjoyment.

ETHNIC DANCES

True ethnic folk dances are generally introduced after singing rhythms or around the second or third grade. The dances found in this section are appropriate for children in the intermediate and upper elementary grades and have been classified as beginning, intermediate, or advanced level activities in Table 29.1. It will be necessary to listen to the musical accompaniment to each dance before presenting it to your students. A record source is provided at the end of the chapter for each of the folk dances found in this section. Participation in folk dance activities will

1. contribute to understanding and expressing rhythm through movement,
2. develop and reinforce a variety of dance steps,
3. facilitate development of auditory rhythmic abilities,
4. foster greater appreciation for other cultures,
5. serve as a means of integrating various social studies concepts into the physical education program,

6. provide opportunities for social contact in a wholesome environment among boys and girls, and
7. help develop the ability to use various folk dance steps to rhythmic accompaniment.

Turn Me Around

Movement Skills: Running, elbow swing, and pivoting.

Origin: England.

Record: RCA LPM-1624.

Formation: Double circle, partners facing each other, boys on the inside. Any number may participate.

Procedures: Partners hook right elbows and take seven slow running steps around. They release on the eighth beat, hook left elbows, and run slowly in the opposite direction. Partners join right hands, holding them high. The girl turns in place with four steps followed by the boy. The entire dance is then repeated from the beginning.

Greensleeves

Movement Skills: Walking, elbow swing, and promenade.

Origin: England.

Record: RCA EPA 4141, ERS "Folk Dances for Beginners."

Formation: Double circle formation with partners facing.

Procedures: Right and left across. In each set of six couples, the boys take their partner's right hand in their right hand and skip eight steps clockwise. Then they drop right hands, join left hands, and skip eight steps counterclockwise back to their original positions.

   Through the arch. Couples join inside hands and the head couple skips four steps backward under the joined hands of couple number two. Couple number two skips forward four steps. Repeat with couple number two skipping backward. Repeat through-the-arch movement.

   Promenade the file. Head couple joins inside hands and skips to the bottom of the line while the other five couples clap their hands.

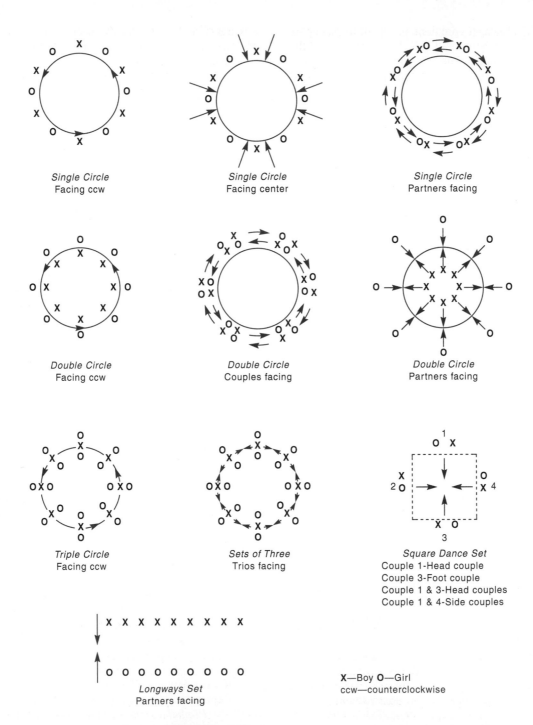

FIGURE 29.1 *Common folk and square dance formations.*

TABLE 29.1   *Selected Folk Dances Sequenced in Terms of Complexity*

Folk Dances (page number)	Suggested Progression for Children		
	Beginning Level	Intermediate Level	Advanced Level
Turn Me Around (567)	x		
Greensleeves (567)	x		
Seven Jumps (569)	x		
Glow Worm (569)	x		
Chimes of Dunkirk (569)	x		
Finger Polka (570)	x		
La Raspa (570)	x		
Ace of Diamonds (570)		x	
Oh Susanna (571)		x	
Girls' Jig (571)		x	
Patty-Cake Polka (571)		x	
Tinikling (571)			x
Mexican Clap Dance (572)			x
Hora (572)		x	
Virginia Reel (572)			x

New head couple. All partners, with both hands joined, turn each other around while moving up one place in file formation with the new head couple.

Seven Jumps

Movement Skills: Slide, skip, or step-hop balancing.

Origin: Denmark.

Record: RCA EPA 4138, Folkcraft 1163, ERS "Folk Dances from Near and Far."

Formation: Single circle facing inward. Any number may participate.

Procedures: All the children join hands and take seven sliding, skipping, or step-hop steps to the left. They turn and return with seven steps to the right during the chorus. On the first sustained note, they raise one leg off the ground and hold it there until the second sustained note sounds. Then they lower the leg and stand at attention (position 1). The chorus then begins again and seven slides (skips or step-hops) are taken to the left and then to the right. The following positions are added on succeeding sets of sustained notes:

Position 2. Repeat position 1 and lift the opposite leg.

Position 3. Repeat positions 1 and 2 and add a kneel on one leg.

Position 4. Repeat positions 1, 2, and 3, and add a kneel on the opposite leg.

Position 5. Repeat positions 1, 2, 3, and 4, and place one elbow on the floor.

Position 6. Repeat positions 1, 2, 3, 4, and 5, and place the other elbow on the floor.

Position 7. Repeat positions 1, 2, 3, 4, 5, and 6, and place the head on the floor.

Glow Worm

Movement Skills: Walking forward and backward to the beat of the music.

Origin: United States.

Record: RCA LPM-1623, ERS "Folk Dances from Near and Far."

Formation: Double circle of couples, boys on the inside. Any number may participate.

Procedures: Facing counterclockwise, all take four walking steps forward, followed by four walking steps backward. Partners then face each other. Girls take four walking steps forward, returning to their original position, while the boys take four walking steps diagonally left and forward to their new partner. The dance is repeated several times.

Chimes of Dunkirk

Movement Skills: Stamping, clapping, and turning to the beat of the music.

Origin: France.

Record: RCA LPM-1624, ERS "Folk Dances from Near and Far."

Formation: Double circle with partners facing each other, boys on the inside. Any number may participate.

Procedures: Everyone stamps their feet (right, left, right). Then they all clap their hands three times. Next, partners join both hands and turn clockwise in eight steps back to place. Then they join right hands and step forward on their right foot, back on their left, and repeat. Now they join both hands and walk clockwise around each other in eight counts, with the boys advancing forward to a new partner. The dance is repeated several times.

Finger Polka

Movement Skills: Skipping and elbow swing.

Origin: Sweden.

Record: Folkcraft F-1419, "Folk Dance Fundamentals."

Formation: Double circle of couples, partners' inside hands joined, facing counterclockwise, boys on the inside. Any number of couples may participate.

Procedures: Partners skip sixteen steps counterclockwise around the circle. Partners face each other with hands on hips and stamp their feet three times. They then clap their own hands three times and shake the right forefinger at their partner three times. Then they shake the left forefinger at their partner three times. Partners join right elbows and turn once around clockwise. The boy then moves counterclockwise around the circle to the first girl on his left and she becomes his new partner. The entire dance is repeated several times.

La Raspa

Movement Skills: Bleking step.

Origin: Mexico.

Record: RCA EPA-4139, Folkcraft F-1119A, ERS "Folk Dances from Near and Far."

Formation: Double circle of couples, partners facing each other, the boys on the inside. Any number of couples may participate.

Procedures: Bleking step and clap. Hop to the left and put the right foot forward; hop to the right and put the left foot forward; hop to the left and put the right foot forward; pause and clap hands together twice. Repeat. Start each set of bleking steps by reversing the initial foot movement.

Elbow swing and clap. Join left elbows and swing counterclockwise, using eight skipping steps. Partners finish the swing facing each other and clapping their own hands once. Repeat this procedure, swinging clockwise. The boys move counterclockwise around the circle to a new partner and the dance is repeated.

Ace of Diamonds

Movement Skills: Complex hopping patterns, elbow swing, and sliding.

Origin: Denmark.

Record: RCA LPM-1622.

Formation: Double circle of couples, partners facing each other, boys on the inside. Any number of couples may participate.

Procedures: Children face their partners, clap their own hands, and place their right heels forward on the floor. They then hook right elbows and walk around each other with six walking steps. The same procedure is repeated, extending the left foot and hooking the left elbow.

The children then hop slowly on the left foot, placing the right heel forward and repeat, hopping on the right foot and placing the left heel forward. The same pattern is repeated four more times but quickly, starting with the right foot. The entire pattern is then repeated, first slowly and then quickly from the beginning.

The children now join hands to form a single circle and slide sixteen steps counterclockwise.

Oh Susanna

Movement Skills: Walking, grand right and left, and promenade.

Origin: United States.

Record: RCA 45-6178, ERS "Folk Dances from Near and Far."

Formation: Single circle with partners facing the center, girls to the right of the boys, eighteen to twenty-four per circle.

Procedures: Ladies to the center. Four steps to the center of the circle, curtsy, and back to place.

Gents to the center. Same as above, except boys bow. The above calls are repeated.

Grand right and left. Partners face, join right hands, step past partner to person behind him, join left hands and repeat the procedure, stopping with the last person, who becomes the new partner. (When holding right hands, right shoulders should pass. When holding left hands, left shoulders should pass.)

Promenade. Boys put their new partners on the right, join right hand to right and left hand to left, face counterclockwise, and skip sixteen steps around the circle.

The entire dance is repeated several times.

Girls' Jig

Movement Skills: Slide, skip, and hop.

Origin: Ireland.

Record: RCA LPM 1623.

Formation: Double line with partners facing (girls in one line, boys in the other). Any number may participate.

Procedures: Partners stand facing with hands on hips, take four skip steps forward and four skip steps back. Repeat this movement. Hop on left foot while tapping right toe four times. Then take four slide steps to the right. Repeat this movement starting with the right foot. Repeat the whole movement pattern in its entirety.

Partners take four skip steps forward and back. Repeat this movement. Partners hop on the left foot, tap right toe and heel two times, then take four slide steps to the right. Repeat this movement, starting with the right foot. The dance is repeated.

Patty-Cake Polka

Movement Skills: Hopping, heel-toe-point, coordinated clapping, sliding, and stepping.

Origin: Poland.

Record: Columbia 52007.

Formation: Double circle of couples facing each other, boys on the inside, hands joined. Any number may participate.

Procedures: Partners join hands. The boys hop on the right foot and place the left heel to the side. They hop again on the right foot and place the left toe behind the right heel (girls perform the same steps, hopping on the left foot and stepping with the right foot). Couples then slide three steps and step counterclockwise around the circle. Repeat this procedure using the opposite footwork and slide clockwise.

Clap three times with partner, using right hands. Then rest one count, clap left hands three times, rest one count, clap both hands three times, rest one count, clap own hands three times, and rest one count. Repeat.

Hook right elbows and swing around clockwise one time. Boys now move counterclockwise around the circle and move to a new partner. The entire dance is now repeated.

Tinikling

Movement Skills: Rhythmical hopping and jumping.

Origin: Philippines.

Record: Kimbo KEA 8095-C and KEAAA 9015-C, ERS, "Folk Dances for People Who Love Folk Dances."

Equipment: Two poles about ten feet long and two 2-foot by 4-foot wood blades three feet long. No record is necessary, but any record with a distinct 3/4 rhythm will do nicely (such as "Alley Cat," ATCA 45-6226).

Formation: Single file at each set of poles with a beater at the end of each set.

Procedures: The two beaters at each end of the poles strike them together once and then strike them apart twice on the 2 by 4s. This same beating pattern is repeated throughout the entire dance.

Several steps may be performed:

1. *Side step.* The children stand with hands on hips outside a set of imaginary poles. Side step to right (over first pole) with right foot, bring left alongside. With right foot, take one more step to the right (over the second pole). The children are now standing on the right foot. The same pattern is repeated, this time having the children start with the left foot. The rhythm pattern is

Right. Step, together, step
Left. Step, together, step
Right. Step, together, step, and so on.
After the side step has been mastered over the imaginary poles, use the real pole in the 3/4 rhythmical pattern.

2. *Forward and back.* Children stand facing the pole with hands on hips. They step forward with left foot, following the same rhythm pattern as side step:

Forward. Step, together, step
Back. Step, together, step
Forward. Step, together, step

3. *Straddle step.* Children stand between imaginary poles with hands on hips and feet together. On the first beat, straddle jump to side, and then bring feet together and bounce twice.

Mexican Clap Dance

Movement Skills: Step-swing, balance step, and clapping.

Origin: Mexico.

Record: Folkcraft 1093, ERS "Folk Dances for People Who Love Folk Dancing."

Formation: Double circle of couples, boys on the inside. Any number of couples may participate.

Procedures: Step, swing opposite leg over, and clap. The boy steps to his left with his left foot and swings his right leg across his left leg. He then steps right and swings his left leg across his right leg. He again steps to his left, swings his right leg across his left, and holds this position while clapping his hands twice. The girl performs the same movement, only starting with a step to the right and swinging her left leg across. The procedure is repeated, but with the footwork reversed.

Balance and clap. The boy, keeping hands joined with his partner, steps away from his partner with his left foot, steps back toward her with his left foot, and again steps away from her with his left foot and holds that position, clapping his hands twice. The girl performs the same movement, except that she steps with the right foot. Repeat this procedure, stepping forward on the first step.

Walk and turn. Partners join inside hands and face counterclockwise around the circle. As they walk around the circle, the girl turns counterclockwise under the boy's arm, using two walking steps. The boy now performs the same movement. Next, they both perform the same movement together. Everybody claps their hands twice and the boy moves counterclockwise to the next girl. She becomes his new partner and the dance is repeated.

Hora

Movement Skills: Modified grapevine step.

Origin: Israel.

Record: Folkcraft 1106, RCA EPA-4140, ERS "Folk Dances from Near and Far."

Formation: Single circle, hands joined. Any number may participate.

Procedures: The modified grapevine step must first be learned. It consists of a step sideways on the left foot, followed by crossing the right foot behind the left, stepping left again, and hopping at the same time on the same foot while swinging the right foot in front of the left. The same procedure is repeated to the right.

First practice the step in a line formation without the music. Stand with your back to the children while demonstrating. As the step is mastered, increase the tempo and have good performers help others individually. After the children have mastered the step, form a circle and try it to the music. It is composed entirely of grapevine steps to the left and to the right.

Virginia Reel

Movement Skills: Hands around, do-si-do, grand right and left, and walking.

Origin: United States.

Record: Folkcraft, RCA EPA LPM-1623, RCA 45-6180.

TABLE 29.2   *Selected Square Dances Sequenced in Terms of Complexity*

Square Dances (page number)	Suggested Progression for Children		
	Beginning Level	Intermediate Level	Advanced Level
Oh Johnny (574)	X		
Red River Valley (574)	X		
Take a Little Peek (574)	X		
Birdie in the Cage (575)	X		
Duck for the Oyster (575)	X		
Pop Goes the Weasel (575)		X	
Texas Star (575)		X	
Ladies Chain (576)		X	
Corner of the World (576)		X	
Farmer's Daughter (576)		X	
Heads and Sides (577)			X
Snake Chain (577)			X
Inside Out and Outside In (577)			X
Grand Square (577)			X

Formation: Two lines of couples facing each other, boys in one line, girls in the other. Four to eight couples per set.

Procedures: Forward and back. The two lines walk forward three steps and bow and then back four steps to place.

Right hand around. The two lines walk forward, grasp right hands, and walk around each other and back to place.

Left hand around. Repeat as above, but with the left hand.

Both hands around. Repeat as above, but with both hands.

Do-si-do with right shoulder. The two lines walk forward and do-si-do, passing right shoulders first, then moving back to place.

Do-si-do with left shoulder. Repeat as above, but with left shoulders passing first.

Head couple down the set. Head couple joins hands and slides eight short steps down the center to the foot of the line and back again with eight more steps.

Reel. The head boy then proceeds to do a grand right and left (see page 566 for a concise explanation) down the girls' line while the head girl does the same down the boys' line. They meet, join hands, and slide back up the set to their places.

Peel off. The boys' and girls' lines take a quarter turn left and right, respectively, and follow the head couple down the outside of the set to the foot.

Form an arch. At the foot of the set, the head couple forms an arch while the other couples join hands and pass through. Couple one now stays at the foot of the set and couple two becomes the head couple.

The dance is repeated so that all couples have an opportunity to be the head couple.

SQUARE DANCES

Uniquely North American in origin, square dances are a popular form of folk dancing and generally use a square (or "set") as their basic formation. The square dance activities contained in this section and listed in Table 29.2 are appropriate for most children in the upper elementary grades and beyond. Square dancing should be introduced after other folk dances have been mastered. The basic steps in teaching dance that were discussed earlier should be carefully followed when teaching a square dance. Several have a number of different formations that will require practice separately and without the music prior to putting it all together. Practice in square dance activities will help children to

1. develop improved auditory rhythmic abilities,
2. combine skillful movement with music,
3. listen to directions and respond in an appropriate manner,
4. work cooperatively with a partner and a small group in a common endeavor,
5. develop an appreciation for the pioneer cultures of the United States and Canada, and
6. participate in wholesome opportunities for social contact among groups of boys and girls.

Oh Johnny

Movement Skills: Elbow swing, allemande left, do-si-do, and promenade.

Record: RCA LE 3000

Formation: Four-couple square.

Procedures: All join hands and circle the ring. All join hands and circle right.

Stop where you are and give your honey a swing. Boys elbow swing with their partners twice around.

Swing that gal behind you. Boys elbow swing their corner twice around.

Go back home and swing your own. Boys elbow swing their partners twice around.

Allemande left with the corner gal. Left hand to left and walk counterclockwise twice around.

Do-si-do your own. Boys do-si-do their own partners.

All promenade your corner maid. Everyone promenades his corner and sings "Oh Johnny, Oh Johnny, Oh." Repeat the dance with a new partner.

Red River Valley

Movement Skills: Elbow swing, do-si-do, and right-hand star.

Record: RCA LE 3000, Folkcraft 1056.

Formation: Four-couple square with eight per set.

Procedures: All join hands in the valley and circle to the left and to the right. The children all hold hands and circle left four steps and then right four steps.

Swing the girl in the valley. Boys elbow swing with their corner around twice.

Now swing that Red River gal. Boys elbow swing with their own partners around twice.

And you circle to the left and to the right. All couples walk left four steps and then right four steps.

Ladies star in the valley. Girls perform a right hand star and walk around once clockwise.

Now swing with that Red River gal. Boys elbow swing with their own partners around twice.

Same couples to the left down the valley. Couples one and three walk to their left and join hands with the couples two and four.

And you circle to the left and to the right. All couples walk left four steps and then right four steps.

Now gents star in the valley. Boys perform a right-hand star, walking around once clockwise.

And you swing that Red River gal. Boys elbow swing with their partners around twice. Repeat the entire dance.

Take a Little Peek

Movement Skills: Walk and swing.

Record: "Honor Your Partner" (Album 1), ERS "Basic Square Dances."

Formation: Four-couple set.

Procedures: Square the sets.

First couple to the right of the ring. Couple number one moves to face couple number two.

Around that couple, take a little peek. Couple number one separates and moves to the outside of the person they are facing, looking at each other behind couple number two.

Back to the center and swing your sweet. Couple number one walks backward to the center of the set and does an elbow swing.

Around that couple and swing once more. Couple number one again peeks around couple number two.

Back to the center and circle up four. Couple number one walks backward to the center of the set and joins hands with couple number two.

Swing your own round and round. Bounce that pretty girl off the ground as you whirl her round the town. Couple number one swings, with the boy whirling the girl in the air and setting her down in front of couple number three. Repeat action with couples three and four.

Couples two, three, and four repeat the entire dance.

Birdie in the Cage

Movement Skills: Balance, swing, and do-si-do.

Record: Any good square dance music.

Formation: Four-couple set.

Procedures: First couple balance, first couple swing. First couple balances and swings.

Lead right out to the right of the ring with four hands around. Couple number one moves to couple number two, forms a circle, and moves around clockwise.

Cage the bird with three hands around. Girl number one moves into the circle made by the other three dancers.

Bird hops out, crow hops in. Girl number one rejoins circle and boy number one moves to the center of the circle.

Ring up three and you're gone again. Boy number one rejoins the circle between two girls, forming a right-hand star moving clockwise.

Back to the left at any cost. Form a left-hand star and circle counterclockwise.

Do-si-do the gent you know. Do-si-do the partner, passing left shoulder.

Ladies go si, and gents go do. Do-si-do the partners, passing right shoulders.

Take your honey and away you go. Couple number one moves to couple number three and repeats dance. Repeat dance with couple number four. Other couples repeat entire dance.

Duck for the Oyster

Movement Skills: Duck through arches, circle four, swing.

Record: "Honor Your Partner" (Album 2), ERS "Basic Square Dances."

Formation: Four-couple set.

Procedures: Honor your partner. Boys bow, girls curtsy.

Swing your corner. Boys each perform an elbow swing with girl on the left.

First couple to the right of the ring. Couple number one moves to face couple number two.

With four hands around. Both couples join hands and circle one and one-half times around, with couple one ending up on the outside of the set.

Duck for the oyster. Couple number one goes through the arch formed by couple two and back. Do not drop hands.

Dive for the clam. Couple number two performs the preceding movement while couple number one forms the arch.

Dive for the sardine and take a full can. Couple number one goes through the arch formed by couple number two and moves on to face couple number three. Repeat the dance with couples three and four. Allow each couple to repeat the entire dance.

Pop Goes the Weasel

Movement Skills: Allemande, grand right and left, and promenade.

Record: RCA LPM 1623.

Formation: Four-couple set.

Procedures: Head couple moves to couple number two, joins hands, and circles left. The head couple "pops" under the arch made by couple two and moves on to couples three and four, repeating the movement. This is followed by an allemande left to original positions.

Couples then perform a two-hand swing. Couples two, three, and four repeat the procedure. The dance is concluded with a grand right and left and a promenade back to the original positions.

Texas Star

Movement Skills: Right-hand star, left-hand star, swing, and promenade.

Record: "Honor Your Partner" (Album 3), ERS "Advanced Beginning Square Dances."

Formation: Four-couple set.

Procedures: Ladies to the center and back. The ladies walk to the center, curtsy, and return to their positions.

Gents to the center and form a star. Boys each do a right-hand star clockwise around the center of the set.

Back to the left and don't get lost. Boys stop and perform a left-hand star counterclockwise around the center of the set.

Meet your honey and pass her by. Boys pass partners.

Catch the next girl on the fly. Boys place right arm around the waist of the first girl past their partner.

Gents swing out and ladies swing in to form that Texas star again. Boys back around, each keeping arm around a girl's waist. Girls grasp opposite right hands, moving clockwise.

Ladies swing out and right back in to form that Texas star again. Boys and girls circle a whole turn to the left. The boys pivot and do a right-hand star.

Swing your partner up and down. Boys swing present partners with an elbow swing.

Promenade home and around the town. Boys promenade present partner to original position. Repeat the entire dance.

Ladies Chain

Movement Skills: Chain through, swing, turn, and do-si-do.

Record: "Honor Your Partner" (Album 2).

Formation: Four-couple set.

Procedures: First couple to the right of the ring. Couple number one moves to face couple number two.

With right-hand star you step and sing. All join hands and circle once around to original position.

Ladies chain across the hall. Boys drop hands; girls retain right-hand grasp, turning one-half turn to face the opposite boy and placing right hand on right hip. The boy places his right hand on the girl's waist and backs around as the girl moves forward one complete turn.

Chain back through with a "Hi, you all." Repeat previous movement with boys turning girls.

Circle four and away you go. All join hands and circle once.

On to the next with a do-si-do. Couple number one moves to couple number three and couples two and four repeat the dance. Allow each couple to repeat the entire dance.

Corner of the World

Movement Skills: Balance and swing, right-hand star, allemande left, and grand right and left.

Record: "Honor Your Partner" (Album 1) or any good square dance music.

Formation: Four-couple set.

Procedures: One and three balance and swing. Couples one and three balance and do a right elbow swing.

Star by the right in the center of the ring. Couples one and three perform a right-hand star in the center of the set, turning once around the set.

Side couples whirl to the corner of the world. Boys turn left and girls turn right one turn, taking large steps.

Heads cross trail through, don't hesitate. Couples one and three move forward to face each other and pass right shoulder to right shoulder.

Left to the corner and don't be late. Face your partner, pass partner, and give your left hand to the person you are facing.

Swing your own for heaven's sake. Couples swing their own partners.

Star by the right in the center once more. Couples one and three perform a right-hand star in the center of the set.

Side couples whirl as you did before. The boys turn right and girls turn left.

Heads cross trail through across the land. Couples one and three return to original positions.

Left allemande and a right-and-left grand. Turn your corner partner with an allemande left and do a grand right and left, starting with your partner, right hand to right hand.

Meet your honey and promenade home. When you meet your partner, promenade to original position. Repeat dance with couples two and four going to the center of the set.

Farmer's Daughter

Movement Skills: Swing, promenade, allemande left, grand right and left, and do-si-do.

Record: RCA LE 3000 (or any acceptable square dance music).

Formation: Four-couple sets.

Procedures: First gent leads out to the right. Boy of couple number one walks to couple number two.

Shake hands with the farmer. Shake hands with boy number two.

Shake hands with the daughter. Shake hands with girl number two.

Swing the daughter. Boy one and girl two perform an elbow swing.

Now run home and swing your own and everybody swing. Repeat.

Heads and Sides

Movement Skills: Swing, do-si-do, and promenade.

Record: "Honor Your Partner" (Album 1).

Formation: Four-couple set.

Procedures: First gent lead out to the right. Boy of couple number one walks to couple number two.

Shake hands with the farmer. Shake hands with boy number two.

Shake hands with the daughter. Shake hands with girl number two.

Swing the daughter. Boy one and girl two perform an elbow swing.

Now run home and swing your own and everybody swing your daughter. Boy number one returns to his original position and everybody swings their partners. Repeat the movement with boy one moving to couples three and four.

Honor your partner. Boys bow and girls curtsy.

Honor your corner. Same movement except with corner partners.

Allemande left your corner. Allemande left with the corner partners.

And a grand right and left. All do a grand right and left.

Meet your partner and do-si-do. When partners meet, do a do-si-do.

Step right up and swing her high and low. Everybody swings their partner.

And promenade home. All promenade partners to original positions. Remaining couples repeat entire dance.

Snake Chain

Movement Skills: Arches, circles, and swing.

Record: RCA CE 3000 (or any acceptable square dance music).

Formation: Any number of couples form a single line.

Procedures: Single line of couples holding hands and standing side by side with the girl on the right. The head couple leads the rest of the dancers through a series of square dance movements. They can create circles within circles (in serpentine fashion), move through arches formed by the other dancers, swing partners, do-si-do partners, and so forth. Be sure to select a head couple that is imaginative. Allow other couples to be the head couple. Work in small groups of four to six people.

Inside Out and Outside In

Movement Skills: Dishrag turn and shuffle step, allemande left, and grand right and left.

Record: Any good square dance music.

Formation: Four-couple set.

Procedures: Couples one and three, forward and back. Couples one and three move forward three steps. Ladies curtsy and men bow. All move back four steps.

Forward again on the same old track. Repeat movement.

One dive in for an inside out and an outside in. Couple number three forms an arch and couple number one ducks through the arch. Couple number one forms an arch and couple number three backs through the arch.

Bow your back and do it again. Repeat previous movement.

Forward up and take your opposite girl. Couples one and three move forward facing each other.

Turn to the side with a dishrag whirl. Take both hands of the person you are facing (boy one and girl two; boy three and girl one), turn under your arms toward the outside of the set, and face side couples two and four.

Inside out and outside in. Inside couple, boy three and girl one, duck through arch of couple two. Boy one and girl three duck through arch of couple number four. Repeat this movement with couples number two and four backing through arches to original positions.

Bow your back and do it again. Repeat previous movement.

Allemande left with your left hand. Boys give their left hand to lady in front of them (their original corner).

Right to your honey and a right and left grand. Extend left hand to next person met after passing partners. Proceed around set, alternating hands.

Meet your honey and promenade. Meet your partner and move to gent's home position. Repeat dance.

Grand Square

Movement Skills: Grand square, ladies chain, half promenade, and right and left through.

Record: Any good square dance.

Formation: Four-couple set.

Procedures: Grand square couples one and three walk four steps forward; partners face and walk four steps back away from each other; face opposites and walk four steps back; face each other and walk four steps forward to original positions.

At the same time, couples two and four face partners and walk four steps back away from each other; face opposites and walk four steps in; face center and walk four steps to their partner; face opposite and walk four steps back to original positions.

Reverse grand square. Couples one and three repeat action of couples two and four; couples two and four repeat actions of one and three.

Right and left through. Couples one and three walk across set, passing right shoulders; boy takes partner and turns her in place; couples repeat steps, back to place. Couples two and four repeat this movement. Head couples walk to the couple on their right and perform a right and left through and back to place. Side couples walk to their right and perform a right and left through and return to position. All dancers repeat the grand square and reverse grand square.

Ladies chain. Head girl extends right hand to opposite girl and left hand to opposite boy and turn around in place. Side girls repeat their movement. Repeat with head couples turning to the right. Repeat with side couples turning right. Repeat grand square and reverse grand square.

Half-promenade. Couples one and three walk across set and boys pass left shoulders (girls to outside) and turn in place; return to original position with a right and left through. Side couples repeat this movement. Head couples walk to the right; half-promenade and back with a right and left through. Side couples repeat this movement. Repeat grand square and reverse grand square. Bow to your partner.

LINE DANCES

(Thanks to Gwynn Hamm, Department of Kinesiology, Indiana University for her valuable contributions to this section)

Since the 'Stroll' made its debut in the mid to late '50s, there has been a resurgence of line dancing, made possible with the advent of the "Hustle," a popular dance that took hold of America's youth during the early 1970s.

From that time to the present, line dancing has enjoyed enormous popularity, as seen in the number of persons who take to the floor when the music to the "Electric Slide" or "Boot Scootin' Boogie" is played.

There are several distinguishing characteristics that make line dances fun and easy to learn. First, everyone begins and ends on the same foot and moves in the same direction(s). The exception to this would be dances involving couples or partners. Second, dances are performed in sequences, each with its own specific number of counts. The sequences are repeated until the end of the song. Third, steps usually move forward, backward, and/or sideward, and include turns (1/4, 1/2, and whole) that provide additional variety and interest. Fourth, dances can be adapted to any age group—elementary through senior citizen. Fifth, dance steps can be reasonably mastered within the length of the musical selection, Sixth, line dances may be performed individually, without a partner. This particular characteristic can be a real advantage in presenting dance to certain elementary school children. The dances that follow are also listed in Table 29.3 and range from simple to complex and include contemporary as well as country line dances.

Bunny Hop

Movement Skills: Jumping.
Formation: Conga line; hands are placed on the waist or shoulders of the person in front.
Record: Michael Jackson: "Jam."
Procedures: Heel step; jump.

I. *Heel step*
Extend L heel diagonally front; replace it center
Counts 1, 2
Repeat actions of heel step L
Counts 3, 4
Repeat heel step with R foot twice
Counts 5, 6, 7, 8

II. *Jumps*
Jump forward
Counts 1, hold 2
Jump backward
Counts 3, hold 4
Jump forward three times
Counts 5, 6, 7, hold 8

Dance repeats from the beginning until the music ends.

Heel step may also be performed with hops; hop onto the R foot as heel extends front, hop as heel is replaced.

TABLE 29.3   *Selected Line Dances Sequenced in Terms of Complexity*

Folk Dances (page number)	Beginning Level	Intermediate Level	Advanced Level
Bunny Hop (578)	x		
Alley Cat (579)	x		
The Slide (580)	x		
The Slide #2 (580)	x		
Amos Moses (580)	x		
Electric Slide (580)	x		
Continental Walk (580)		x	
Hully Gully (581)		x	
Bus Stop (581)		x	
Four-Corner Stomp (581)		x	
Jive Talkin' (581)		x	
Boot Scootin' Boogie (#1) (582)		x	
Boot Scootin' Boogie (#2) (582)		x	
Honky Tonk Stomp (582)			x
Waltz Around Texas (582)			x
Six Shooter (583)			x
Slappin' Leather (583)			x
Sugartown (583)			x
Achy Breaky (584)			x

Alley Cat

Movement Skills: Touch step, kick (hitch), jump turn.
Formation: Open order, with everyone facing the music.
Record: "Car Wash."
Procedures:

Touch R toe in front;	Step R foot in place (center)
Counts 1, 2	Counts 3, 4
Touch L toe in front;	Step L foot in place (center)
Counts 5, 6	Counts 7, 8
Touch R toe behind;	Step R foot in place (center)
Counts 1, 2	Counts 3, 4
Touch L toe behind;	Step L foot in place (center)
Counts 5, 6	Counts 7, 8
Kick R foot forward;	Step R foot in place (center)
Count 1	Count 2
Kick L foot forward;	Step L foot in place (center)
Count 3	Count 4
Repeat above counts 5 through 8;	
Clap hands one time;	Clap hands one time
Count 1, hold 2	Count 3, hold 4

Jump with 1/4 turn to R
Counts 5, 6, 7, 8

Dance repeats from the beginning until music ends.

The Slide

Movement Skills: Heel step, grapevine, 1/4 turn, walk.
Formation: Horizontal lines, with everyone facing the music.
Record: "Baby's Got Her Blue Jeans On."
Procedures:

R heel forward, step R in place (center) R heel forward, step R in place (center)
Counts 1, 2, 3, 4
L heel forward, step L in place (center) L heel forward, step L in place (center)
Counts 5, 6, 7, 8

R heel forward/center;	L heel forward/center
Counts 1, 2	Counts 3, 4

R grapevine step (R-L-R) ending with the weight on the R foot
Counts 5, 6, 7
1/4 turn to the R, with the L leg up (clap)

Count 8
Walk backwards L-R-L step together R
Counts 9, 10, 11, 12 (clap)

Dance repeats from the top.

The Slide #2

Movement Skills: Touch step, jazz square, jump turn.
Formation: Open order with everyone facing the music.
Record: "We Are Family."
Procedures:
Touch R foot to R side, in place, to R side, in place
Counts 1, 2, 3, 4
Touch L foot to L side, in place, to L side, in place
Counts 5, 6, 7, 8
Touch R foot to R side, in place
Counts 1, 2
Touch L foot to L side, in place
Counts 3, 4
Jazz Square—cross R foot over L (Count 5), step L
diagonal back (Count 6), step R side (Count 7), 1/4 turn to
R as both feet jump together (Count 8)

Dance repeats until the music ends.

Amos Moses

Movement Skills: Heel step, grapevine, stomp, clap.
Formation: Dancers in horizontal lines with all facing the
same direction.
Record: Jerry Reid: "Amos Moses."
Procedures: The dance consists of 10 counts.

I. Heel Step
Extend R heel diagonally front, step R in place (center)
Counts 1, 2
Extend L heel diagonally front, step L in place (center)
Counts 3, 4

II. Grapevine
Grapevine step R as you 1/4 turn to face L (Count 5) Cross
behind L (Count 6), Step R side as you make a 1/2 turn
(Count 7), Step L as you complete turn (Count 8), Step R
in place (Count 9), clap (Count 10).

Dance repeats from the beginning.

CONCEPT 29.5
Country and western line dance and square dances
are uniquely North American and reflect the pioneer
ancestry of many Americans.

Electric Slide

Movement Skills: Step together step, touch- or grapevine step,
walk, rock step, 1/4 turn.
Formation: Horizontal lines, with all facing the music.
Record: "Electric Slide."
Procedures: The dance consists of 10 counts.
Step R, together L, step R, touch L
-or-
R grapevine step, touch L
Counts 1, 2, 3, 4
Step L, together R, step L, touch R
Counts 5, 6, 7, 8
Walk backwards R-L-R, touch L
Counts 1, 2, 3, 4
Rock step forward L, touch R
Counts 5, 6
Rock step backward R, touch L
Counts 7, 8
Step L, 1/4 turn to L as R foot scuffs through
Counts 9, 10
Variation: step together, step touch
-or-
on grapevine step, a 3-step turn can be used.

Continental Walk

Movement Skills: Walking step, grapevine, heel clicks, toe
touch, 1/4 turns.
Formation: Horizontal lines, with all facing the music.
Record: Janet Jackson: "Escapade."
Procedures: 1/4 turns.

I. Walks
Walk backwards R-L-R, touch L
Counts 1, 2, 3, 4
Walk forward L-R-L, touch R
Counts 5, 6, 7, 8
Repeat Counts 1–8

II. Grapevine
R grapevine step (R, cross front L, side R), touch L
Counts 1, 2, 3, 4
L grapevine step (L, cross front R, side L), touch R
Counts 5, 6, 7, 8
Step side R, touch L; Step side L, touch R
Counts 1, 2, 3, 4
Separate heels and click twice
Counts 5, 6
Hip sway R/L
Counts 7, 8

III. Toe Touch

Touch R front twice; Touch R back twice
Counts 1, 2, 3, 4
Touch R front/back
Counts 5, 6
Touch R side
Count 7
Kick R front as you 1/4 turn to L on L foot
Count 8
Repeat Toe touches with kick and 1/4 turn
Counts 9–16
You are now facing backward

Dance repeats from the beginning.

Hully Gully

Movement Skills: Grapevine, walk, step touch.
Formation: Dancers in horizontal lines facing the same direction.
Record: "Reggae Cowboy."
Procedures:

I. Grapevine

Grapevine R (R-L-R), kick L
Counts 1, 2, 3, kick 4
Grapevine L (L-R-L), kick R
Counts 5, 6, 7, kick 8

II. Walk, step touch

Step R forward, touch L, step L forward, touch R
Counts 1, 2, 3, 4
Walk forward R-L-R with 1/4 turn to R (wt. on R foot)
Counts 5, 6, 7, 8
Walk backward L-R-L, kick R
Counts 9, 10, 11, kick 12

Dance repeats from the beginning.

Bus Stop

Movement Skills: Step together, toe touch, 1/4 turn.
Formation: Dancers in horizontal line, with all facing the same direction.
Record: Fly Robbins: "Fly."
Procedures:

Step backward R, close L to R, step backward R, close L to R
Counts 1, 2, 3, 4
Step forward L, close R to L, step forward L, close R to L
Counts 5, 6, 7, 8
Right grapevine step (R-L-R) touch L
Counts 1, 2, 3, 4
Left grapevine step (L-R-L) touch R

Counts 5, 6, 7, 8
Step R, touch L, step L, touch R
Counts 1, 2, 3, 4
Slight jump (feet apart) to wide parallel; slight jump (feet together)
Counts 5, 6
Separate heels and click them
Counts 7, 8
Touch R front twice; touch R in back twice (weight on left foot)
Counts 1, 2, 3, 4
Touch R front once; touch R back once (weight on left foot)
Counts 5, 6
Touch R to side; step L and 1/4 turn to L
Counts 7, 8

Four-Corner Stomp

Movement Skills: Step-together-step-stomp (clap), walk, turn.
Formation: Dancers in horizontal lines, with all facing the same direction.
Record: Michael Jackson: "Black and White."
Procedures:

Step side L, close R, step L, stomp R (clap)
Counts 1, 2, 3, 4 (clap)
Step side R, close L, step R, stomp L (clap)
Counts 5, 6, 7, 8 (clap)
Repeat step-together-step-stomp (clap) to the L and R
Counts 1–8 (clap)
Walk forward on L foot, circle hips to R
Counts 1, 2
Walk forward on R foot, circle hips to L
Counts 3, 4
Walk forward on L foot, circle hips to R
Counts 5, 6
Walk forward on R and 1/4 turn to R, ending with weight on R foot
Counts 7, 8

Dance repeats from the beginning.

Jive Talkin'

Movement Skills: Heel step, two-step, grapevine, hip sway.
Formation: Dancers in horizontal lines, with all facing the same direction.
Record: "Hustle."
Procedures:

Heel Step

Extend R heel forward, step R in place, repeat heel step L, step L in place
Counts 1, 2, 3, 4

Two-step

Step forward R, close L, step R hold
Counts 1, 2, 3, hold 4
Step forward L, close R, step L hold
Counts 5, 6, 7, hold 8

Grapevine

Grapevine Step R (R-L-R), kick L foot
Counts 1, 2, 3, kick 4
Grapevine Step L (L-R-L), kick R foot
Counts 5, 6, 7, kick 8

Grapevine with turn

Grapevine step R (R-L-R—1/2 turn to face back wall) with weight on the R foot
Counts 1, 2, 3, 4
Step L, R
Counts 5, 6
Hip sway R, L
Counts 7, 8

Dance repeats from the beginning.

Boot Scootin' Boogie (#1)

Movement Skills: Grapevine, walk, hop.
Formation: Horizontal lines, with all facing the music.
Record: "Boot Scootin' Boogie."
Procedures:
(Starting position: Weight on the L foot)
Step onto R foot, hop hop
Step L forward, together R, step L, stomp R
Walk backward, R-L-hop R (with L leg up)
L grapevine step (L-R-L) hop L
R grapevine step (R-L-R) hop R, 1/4 turn to R, hop hop

Dance repeats from the top.

Boot Scootin' Boogie (#2)

Movement Skills: Grapevine, walk, hop (scoot), fan, step touch.
Formation: Same as #1.
Record: "Boot Scootin' Boogie."
Procedures:
Lift R foot (Count 1), cross R in front of L ("cut") (Count 2), Extend R foot
(Count 3), Step R in place (Count 4)
L foot fans (toe goes to the side and back front—weight on heel)
Counts 5, 6, 7, 8
Scoot, scoot (forward) on R foot
Grapevine L (L-R-L kick/clap R)
Counts 1, 2, 3, kick/clap 4

Grapevine R (R-L-R kick/clap L)
Counts 5, 6, 7, kick/clap 8
1 1/4 turn to L (L-R-L-R, ending with weight on R)
Counts 1, 2, 3, 4
Scoot, scoot (forward) on R foot
Step L, together R, step L, touch R (moving forward)
Step side R, touch L, Step side L, touch R
Step back R, touch L (or hitch), step forward L, stomp R

Honky Tonk Stomp

Movement Skills: Heel clicks, stomp, grapevine, 1/2 turns.
Formation: Dancers in horizontal lines, with all facing the same direction.
Record: "Elvira."
Procedures:

Heel Clicks

Heels apart, heels together, heels apart, heels together
Counts 1, 2, 3, 4

Heel Step

R heel forward, R toe back
Counts 5, 6, 7, 8
R heel forward, step R in place (center) Counts 1, 2
L foot stomps twice Counts 3, 4
L heel forward, step L in place (center) Counts 5, 6
R foot stomps twice   Counts 7, 8

Grapevine

Grapevine R (R-L-R kick L)
Counts 1, 2, 3, 4
Grapevine L (L-R-L kick R) 1/2 turn
Counts 5, 6, 7, 8
Grapevine R (R-L-R kick L)
Counts 1, 2, 3, 4
Grapevine L (L-R-L stomp R)
Counts 5, 6, 7, 8

Dance repeats from the beginning.

Waltz Around Texas

Movement Skills: Triplet (waltz) step, grapevine turn.
Formation: Dancers in horizontal lines, with all facing the same direction.
Record: Bob Willard & The Texas Playboys: "Waltz Around Texas."
Procedures:

Triplet Step

Triplet moving and facing R (R-L-R)
Counts 1, 2, 3

Triplet moving and facing L (L-R-L)
Counts 1, 2, 3
Triplet forward (R-L-R); Triplet backward (L-R-L)
Counts 1, 2, 3, 4, 5, 6

Triplet Grapevine Turn

Triplet turn R (R-L-R Counts 1, 2, 3), cross L in front
(Count 1), step R side (Count 2), cross behind with L
(Count 3), step R side (Count 1), step L in place (Count 2),
step R in place (Count 3)
Triplet turn L (L-R-L Counts 1, 2, 3), cross R in front
(Count 1), step L side (Count 2), cross behind with R
(Count 3), step L side (Count 1), step R in place (Count 2),
step L in place (Count 3)
Triplet forward R-L-R; L-R-L (Counts 1–6)
Triplet backward L-R-L; R-L-R (Counts 1–6)

Dance repeats from the beginning.

Six Shooter

Movement Skills: Heel swivels, stomp, 4-step turn, step
together, step touch.
Formation: Dancers in horizontal lines, with all facing the
same direction.
Record: Bob Willis: "Six Shooter."
Procedures:

Heel swivels

Swivel heels to L and back center (Counts 1, 2)
Stomp twice with R foot (Counts 3, 4)
R heel front, "cut," R heel front, step R in place
Counts 5, 6, 7, 8
L heel front, "cut," L heel front, touch L toe back
Counts 1, 2, 3, 4

4-step turn

One whole turn toward the L (L-R-L-R)
Counts 5, 6, 7, 8
Step L side, close R, step R side, close L
Counts 1, 2, 3, 4
3 step turn R-L-R, hold
Counts 5, 6, 7, hold 8 with weight on R
Step forward L, close R, step L, 1/2 turn to L with weight
on L
Counts 1, 2, 3, 4
Step R forward, close L, step R, together L
Counts 5, 6, 7, 8

Dance repeats from the beginning.

Slappin' Leather

Movement skills: Grapevine, heel swivels, toe touch.

Formation: Line.
Record: "Rhinestone Cowboy."
Procedures:

Heel swivels

Heels swivels to R, center, L, center
Counts 1, 2, 3, 4
R toe touch side, in place, side, in place
Counts 5, 6, 7, 8
L toe touch side, in place, side, in place
Counts 1, 2, 3, 4
R heel front and tap twice; tap back twice
Counts 5, 6, 7, 8
R heel front, side, back, side
Counts 1, 2, 3, 4
1/4 turn to L slap R toe front; slap R toe to R hand
Counts 5, 6
Grapevine R (R-L-R), kick/clap L; Grapevine L,
kick/clap R
Counts 1, 2, 3, 4; 5, 6, 7, 8
Walk back R-L-R, L leg hitch
Counts 1, 2, 3, hitch 4
Step L forward, close R, step L, together R
Counts 5, 6, 7, 8

Dance repeats from the beginning.

Sugartown

Movement Skills: Grapevine, step-together-step touch, pivot.
Formation: Dancers in horizontal lines, with all facing the
same direction.
Record: "Sugartown."
Procedures:
Grapevine R (R-L-R) kick or scuff L
Counts 1, 2, 3, kick 4
Grapevine L (L-R-L) kick or scuff R
Counts 5, 6, 7, kick 8
Walk backward R-L-R scuff L
Counts 1, 2, 3, scuff 4
Step forward L, close R, step forward L, together R
Counts 5, 6, 7, 8
Step R diagonal forward, touch L toe
Counts 1, 2
Step L diagonal back, touch R toe
Counts 3, 4
Step R diagonal back, touch L toe
Counts 5, 6
Step forward, touch R toe
Counts 7, 8
Step R with 1/4 turn to R, touch L toe side
Counts 1, 2

⬤ **TEACHING TIPS** ▶

Selected Record Sources

The following companies were cited as record sources for the dance activities on the preceding pages. On request they will send a complete catalog of their folk, square, and line dance records and tapes and will place you on their mailing list:

- Bowman Records, 622 Radier Drive, Glendale, CA 91201.

- Columbia Records, Educational Department, 1473 Barnum Avenue, Bridgeport, CT 06601.

- Educational Activities, Box 392, Freeport, NY 11520.

- Educational Record Sales, 157 Chambers Street, New York, NY 10007.

- Folkcraft Record Company, 1159 Broad Street, Newark, NJ 07714.

- Kimbo Educational Records, P.O. Box 477, Long Beach, NJ 07740.

- Radio Corporation of America, RCA Victor Educational Records, 155 East 24th Street, New York, NY 10010.

Cross L over R, touch R toe side
Counts 3, 4
1/2 turn (pivot)
Counts 5, 6
L hip side, R hip side
Counts 7, 8
Step L forward, close R, step L, together R
Counts 1, 2, 3, 4

Dance repeats from the beginning.

Achy Breaky

Movement Skills: Grapevine, 1/4 turn, 1/2 turn.
Formation: Line.
Record: Billy Ray Cyrus: "Achy Breaky."
Procedures:

Grapevine R (R-L-R hold); Hip sway L-R-L hold
Counts 1, 2, 3, hold 4; 5, 6, 7, hold 8
R toe back (Count 1), side (Count 2), front with 1/4 turn to L, (Count 3), take weight onto L as you continue into 1/2 turn, step back on R foot (Count 4)
Step back L-R with weight on R with 1/4 turn to L (L leg up) lower L in place;
step back R-L-R stomp L
Counts 5, 6, 7, 8, 9, 10, 11, 12
Hip sway L-R-L hold
Counts 1, 2, 3, hold 4
1/4 turn to R, stomp/clap; 1/2 turn to L, stomp/clap
Counts 5, 6, 7, 8
Grapevine R (R-L-R) stomp L
Counts 9, 10, 11, stomp 12

SUMMARY

This chapter focused on structured dance, namely ethnic folk dance, square dance, and line dance. Participation in these activities is an excellent way to help children become not only more skillful and expressive movers but also more cooperative social learners. The very nature of structured dance activities is social. Working in cooperative rhythmic unison, and coming into close physical contact with members of the opposite sex is "big time stuff" for elementary school children. Although structured dance activities should not be engaged in solely for the social learning element, they do provide an excellent way for boys and girls to come into contact with each other in a socially acceptable manner.

Careful preparation is the key to success in teaching folk and square dances. Preplan by knowing your students' movement capabilities, social maturity, and behavioral consistency. Careful attention to the music and the steps in presenting and teaching a new dance is also very important. Folk dance is part of our cultural heritage. Children should have the opportunity to learn more about the many cultures of the world through dance.

COMPLEMENTARY READINGS

Harris, Jane A., Anne M. Pittman, and M. S. Waller. (1994). *Dance Awhile*: *Handbook of Folk, Square, Contra, and Social Dance*. New York: MacMillan College Publishing.

Miller-Berryman, S., ed. (1991). Multicultural dance—The spirit of cultural tradition. *JOPERD* 62:33–48.

Ray, O. M. (1992). *Encyclopedia of Line Dances: The Steps That Came and Stayed.* Reston, VA: AAHPERD.

Weiller, K. H. (1992). The social-emotional component of physical education for children. *JOPERD* 63:50–53.

SUPPLEMENTARY READINGS

Joyce, M. (1994). *Dance Technique for Children.* Mountain View, CA: Mayfield.

Pila, R. (1995). *Experiences in Movement with Music, Activities and Theory.* Albany, NY: Delmar Publishers.

VIDEOS

Learn Country Line Dancin', Volumes 1, 3, 5. McDonald, Judi. Plymouth, MN: Simitar Entertainment Productions. (about 30 min. each).

Line Dancing is It! Puckett, D. Byron, CA: Front Row Experience. (28 min.).

Dances of the World. England/Korea/Appalachia/Mexico/ Puerto Rico/Poland/France/Russia/Ireland/Folk Games. Reston, VA: AAHPERD. (Order separately or as a complete set, 25–60 min. each).

AUDIO RESOURCES

Folk Dance

All-American Dance Winners. Educational Activities, Inc., Box 392, Freeport, NY 11520.

American Folk Dances. Imperial Records, 137 North Western Ave., Los Angeles, CA 90053.

And the Beat Goes on for Physical Education. Kimbo Educational Activities Record Company, P.O. Box 477, Long Branch, NJ 07740 (KEA 5020-C).

Ball Gymnastics. Kimbo Educational Activities Record Company, Box 477, Long Branch, NJ 07740 (KIM 4031C).

Baltic Dances. Imperial Records, 137 North Western Ave., Los Angeles, CA 90053.

Contemporary Tinikling Activities. Kimbo Educational Activities Record Company, P.O. Box 477, Long Branch, NJ 07740 (KEA 8095-C).

First Folk Dances. Michael Herman, RCA Victor, 124 East 24th Street, New York, NY 10010.

Folk Dance Funfest. Educational Dance, David McKay Company, 119 W. 40th Street, New York, NY 10010 (FD-1, FD-2, FD-3, FD-4).

Holiday Time Album. No. 302, Bowmar Records, 622 Rodier Drive, Glendale, CA 91201.

Jewish Folk Dances, Vols. I and II. Ultra Records, New York, NY. Also available from Michael Herman, Box 201, Flushing, NY 11352.

Keep on Steppin'. Educational Activities, Inc., Box 392, Freeport, NY 11520.

Library of International Dances. Folkcraft Record Company, 1159 Broad Street, Newark, NJ 07714.

Russian Folk Dances. Imperial Records, 137 North Western Ave., Los Angeles, CA 90053.

Scandinavian Folk Dance Album. Michael Herman, Box 201, Flushing, NY 11352.

Tinikling. Kimbo Educational Activities Record Company, Box 477, Long Branch, NJ 07740 (KEA 9015-C).

Square Dance

Square Dances (with calls). Bedford, L. Imperial Records, 137 North Western Ave., Los Angeles, CA 90053.

Get Ready to Square Dance. Educational Activities, Inc., Box 392, Freeport, NY 11520 (AR68).

Square Dances (without calls). Imperial Records, 137 North Western Ave., Los Angeles, CA 90053.

Honor Your Partner. Square Dance Associates, 102 N. Columbus Avenue, Freeport, NY 11520.

Up-Beat Square Dances. Educational Activities, Inc., Box 392, Freeport, NY 11520 (AR32, AR33, AR46).

Texas Square Dance Music (without calls). Henlee Record Company, 2402 Harris, Austin, TX 78767.

FUNDAMENTAL MOVEMENT SKILLS
TOTAL BODY/CLASS OBSERVATION CHART

Class _____   Grade _____   Observer _____

Mark the proper overall stage rating (I, E, M, S)* for each skill in the space provided. *I. initial stage E. elementary stage M. mature stage S. sport-skill stage **NAME**	STABILITY SKILLS								LOCOMOTOR SKILLS										MANIPULATIVE SKILLS							
	Static Balance	Dynamic Balance	Body Rolling	Dodging	Springing/Landing	Axial Movements	Inverted Supports	Transitional Supports	Running	Jump for Distance	Jump for Height	Jump from Height	Hopping	Skipping	Sliding	Galloping	Leaping	Climbing	Throwing	Catching	Kicking	Trapping	Dribbling	Volleying	Striking	Ball Rolling

FUNDAMENTAL MOVEMENT SKILLS
BODY SEGMENT/CLASS OBSERVATION CHART

Class _____ Grade _____ Observer _____

Mark the proper stage (I, E, M, S)* for each body segment. Then give an overall rating in the space provided.

*I. initial stage
E. elementary stage
M. mature stage
S. sport-skill stage

NAME

Leg Action	Trunk Action	Arm Action	Overall Rating	Leg Action	Trunk Action	Arm Action	Overall Rating	Leg Action	Trunk Action	Arm Action	Overall Rating	Leg Action	Trunk Action	Arm Action	Overall Rating	Leg Action	Trunk Action	Arm Action	Overall Rating

PHYSICAL EDUCATION PROGRESS REPORT

Dear Parent:
The skills checked have been assessed for this 9-week period. More than one check in a row indicates progress from one stage to another.

Child's Name _____   Grade _____   Class _____

	1ST 9 Wks.				2ND 9 Wks.				3RD 9 Wks.				4TH 9 Wks.				STAGE OF DEVELOPMENT
	Initial Stage	Elementary Stage	Mature Stage	Sport-Skill Stage	Initial Stage	Elementary Stage	Mature Stage	Sport-Skill Stage	Initial Stage	Elementary Stage	Mature Stage	Sport-Skill Stage	Initial Stage	Elementary Stage	Mature Stage	Sport-Skill Stage	Initial (Beginning) Elementary (Primary) Mature (Intermediate) Sport Skill (Advanced)
Stability skills: Maintaining balance in static and dynamic situations																	Comments
One-Foot Balance																	
Beam Walk																	
Body Rolling																	
Dodging																	
Landing																	
Locomotor skills: Giving force to the body through space																	Comments
Running																	
Jumping																	
Hopping																	
Skipping																	
Leaping																	
Manipulative skills: Giving force to and receiving force from objects																	Comments
Throwing																	
Catching																	
Kicking																	
Dribbling																	
Striking																	

PARENT COMMENTS

_____   _____
PARENT SIGNATURE   DATE

_____   _____
PARENT SIGNATURE   DATE

_____   _____
PARENT SIGNATURE   DATE

BASKETBALL SKILLS RATING CHART

Class _____   Grade _____   Entry Assessment Date _____   Exit Assessment Date _____

Observe during drill or play situations. Mark entry rating in upper left corner and exit ratings in lower right corner of each square.	PASSING/CATCHING SKILLS				DRIBBLING/PIVOTING SKILLS				GOAL-SHOOTING SKILLS				ASSOCIATED SKILLS		KEY
	Chest Pass	Bounce Pass	Two-handed Pass	Baseball Pass	Stationary Dribble	Moving Dribble	Cross-over Dribble	Pivoting	Push Shot	Jump Shot	Lay-up Shot	Free Throw	Guarding	Rebounding	A: Advanced—Correct technique, plus good control and force production.
															I: Intermediate—Correct technique but lacks control or force production.
															B: Beginning—Inconsistent use of correct technique.
															COMMENTS:

SOFTBALL SKILLS RATING CHART

Class _____   Grade _____   Entry Assessment Date _____   Exit Assessment Date _____

Observe during drill or play situations. Mark entry rating in upper left corner and exit rating in lower right corner of each square.	THROWING SKILLS				FIELDING SKILLS			BATTING SKILLS		ASSOCIATED SKILLS			KEY
	Overhand	Sidearm	Underhand	Pitching	High Fly	Low Fly	Grounder	Batting	Bunting	Base Running	Base Playing	Base Stealing	A: Advanced—Correct technique plus good control and force production.
													I: Intermediate—Correct technique but lacks control or force production.
													B: Beginning—Inconsistent use of correct technique.
													COMMENTS:

SOCCER SKILLS RATING CHART

Class _____   Grade _____   Entry Assessment Date _____   Exit Assessment Date _____

Observe during drill or play situations. Mark entry rating in upper left corner and exit rating in lower right corner of each square.	KICKING SKILLS				TRAPPING SKILLS					DRIBBLING SKILLS		VOLLEYING SKILLS		ASSOCIATED SKILLS			KEY
	Instep Kick	Push Pass	Outside-of-Foot Kick	Punting	Sole Trap	Shin Trap	Foot Trap	Thigh Trap	Chest Trap	Inside-of-Foot Dribble	Outside-of-Foot Dribble	Juggling	Heading	Goal Keeping	Screening/Blocking	Tracking	A: Advanced— Correct technique, plus good control and force production.

I: Intermediate— Correct technique but lacks control or force production.

B: Beginning— Inconsistent use of correct technique. |
																	COMMENTS:

VOLLEYBALL SKILLS RATING CHART

Class _____   Grade _____   Entry Assessment Date _____   Exit Assessment Date _____

Observe during drill or play situations. Mark rating in upper left corner of box for entry assessments, and lower right corner for exit assessments.	VOLLEYBALL SKILLS				SERVING SKILLS		ASSOCIATED SKILLS		KEY
	Overhand	Set-up	Bump	Dig	Underhand	Overhead	Blocking	Spiking	A: Advanced—Correct technique plus good control and force production. I: Intermediate—Correct technique but lacks control or force production. B: Beginning—Inconsistent use of correct technique.
									COMMENTS:

The following position papers may be obtained free of charge or for a nominal fee from the respective organization.

National Association for Sport and Physical Education
1900 Association Drive
Reston, VA 22091

- Appropriate Practice in Physical Education
- Assessing Physical Fitness
- Checklist for Elementary School Physical Education
- Children's Physical Education Teacher Preparation: The Specialist
- Content Standards for School Physical Education
- Developmentally Appropriate Physical Education for Children
- Developmentally Appropriate Practice in Movement Programs for Young Children Ages 3–5
- Fit to Achieve
- Guidelines for Coaching Education: Youth Sports
- Guidelines for Elementary School Physical Education
- Guidelines to Middle School Physical Education
- Looking at Physical Education from a Developmental Perspective: A Guide to Teaching
- Making a Case for Quality Daily Physical Education (12 min. video)
- Movement Programs for Young Children
- National Youth Fitness Summit Report
- Physical Education and Physical Fitness
- Physical Education for Children: Preparation of the Teacher Specialist
- Program Appraisal Checklist for Elementary School PE Programs
- Required: Quality Daily Physical Education
- Shape of the Nation 1993: Survey of State Physical Education Requirements
- Standards for Beginning Physical Education Teachers
- The Physically Educated Person

National Association for the Education of Young Children
1834 Connecticut Avenue N.W.
Washington, DC 20009

- Good Teaching Practices for 4- and 5-Year-Olds
- Guidelines for Appropriate Curriculum and Assessment in Programs Serving Children Ages 3 Through 8
- Reaching Potentials: Appropriate Curriculum and Assessment for Young Children
- Teaching Young Children to Resist Bias
- Testing Young Children: Concerns and Cautions

American Academy of Pediatrics
141 Northwest Point Blvd.
P.O. Box 927
Elk Grove Village, IL 60009

- Better Health Through Fitness
- Caring for Your Baby and Young Child: Birth to Age 5
- Child Sexual Abuse
- Sport and Your Child
- Your Child's Growth: Developmental Milestones

National Strength and Conditioning Association
P.O. Box 81410
Lincoln, NE 68501

- Anaebolic Drug Use by Athletes
- Pre-Pubescent Strength Training
- Strength Training for Female Athletes

American Heart Association
National Center
7320 Greenville Avenue
Dallas, TX 75231

- About Your Heart and Blood Pressure
- About Your Heart and Diet
- About Your Heart and Exercise
- Jump Rope for Heart

A

AAU Physical Fitness Test, 192, 193, 194
Academic concept learning, 77–78
Accent (rhythm element), 174, 540
Accident report, 249–251
Active listening, 216
Activity concept learning, 75, 77
Adapted physical education, 102–103
Aerobic dance, 176
Aerobic endurance, 501–503
Aerobic exercise
    activities for, 501–505
    definition of, 63
Affective growth, 14, 84–99
Agility, definition of, 64
Aims, definition of, 6
American Alliance for Health, Physical
        Education, Recreation and Dance
        (AAHPERD), 5, 204
Anaerobic exercise, 63
Apparatus skills. *See* Equipment skills
Arthritis, 109
Assessment
    computer applications for, 194
    entry level, 149, 182
    exit level, 182
    fitness, 190–194
    motor, 183–190
    observational, 183–184
    performance, 184
    process, 183–184
    product, 184
    self-referenced, 182
    tests of, 184–190, 191–194
    See also specific skill themes
Asthma, 108–109
Attention deficit disorder, 116
Attitude formation, 92–94
Attractive nuisance, 245–246
Auditory discrimination, 532–533
Auditory impairment, 105–106
Auditory memory, 533–534
Auditory perception activities, 530–534
Autism, 115
Axial movements, 28, 259

B

Backward roll, 359–360
    See also Body rolling skills
Balance, 64
    concepts of, 265
    dynamic, 28, 261
    sequence of, 28
    static, 28, 261
    See also Stability skills
Balance beam skills, 376–378
Balance board activities, 390
Ball activities, 391–392
Balloon activities, 390–391
Ball rolling, 324–327
    assessment of, 352
    exploratory activities for, 341
    guided discovery activities for, 342
Basketball activities
    history of, 412
    lead-up games, 426–429
    practice conditions for, 422–423
    rules for, 429–430
    skill drills, 423–426
    warm-up activities, 423
Basketball skills
    assessment of, 430–432
    catching, 415–416
    dribbling, 417–419
    free throw shooting, 421
    goal shooting, 419–422
    jump shot, 420–421
    lay-up shot, 420–421
    passing, 413–415
    pivoting, 418–419
    sequencing of, 412–413
    theme development of, 412
Beam walk, 261–265
    assessment of, 276
Beanbag activities, 392–393
Beat, underlying, 174, 540
    See also Rhythm
Behavioristic learning theory, 236–237
Belonging, sense of, 86
Body awareness
    activities for, 516–519

definition of, 79
Body composition, 63–64
Body image, 118–119
Body rolling skills, 265, 356–357
    assessment of, 276
    backward, 359–360
    developmental stages of, 266–267
    exploratory activities for, 270
    forward, 265–267, 357–359
    guided-discovery activities for, 271
    objectives of, 357
    sideways, 357
Brain damage, characteristics of, 112
Bulletin boards, 162

C

Cardiovascular endurance, 62–63
Cardiovascular limitations, 106
Cargo net skills, 378–380
Catching, 317, 319–320
    assessment of, 351
    in basketball, 415–416
    in disc sports, 404–406
    exploratory activities for, 333
    guided discovery activities for, 334
Cephalocaudal development, 25
Cerebral palsy, 106–108
Character education, 92–94
Chinese jump rope, 396
Club programs, 142
Cognitive concept learning, components of
    academic concept learning, 77–78
    fitness concept learning, 77
    movement concept learning, 76–77
    multisensory learning, 78
    perceptual-motor learning, 78–79
    skill concept learning, 75–76
Cognitive concept learning, definition of,
        11–13, 73
Cognitive learning theory, 74
Cognitive maps, 73
Combative activities, 505–507, 508–510
Command teaching, 237
Communication
    improvement of, 214–216

nonverbal, 212–213
physical distance and, 214–215
techniques for, 227
verbal, 208–212
Community representative, 202–203
Competence, 86–87
Compliance, 234
Concept learning. *See* Cognitive concept
    learning
Conceptual framework, 127–128
Conditioning exercises, 505–508
Consistency, reasons for, 224–225
Cooperative games, 170
Cooperative learning, 91
Coordination, 64
Corporal punishment (spanking), 222
Counseling, 202
Creative dance, 174–175
    creative rhythmic expression, 555–556
    dance making, 559–560
    imitative, 556–558
    interpretative, 558–559
Creative rhythmic expression, 555–556
Creativity
    definition of, 555
    tips on fostering, 554
Critical thinking, 73–74
Cultural norms, definition of, 91
Curricular balance, 133–134
Curriculum
    design of, 131–135
    developmental model of, 136–139
    extended, 139–142
    steps in planning, 125–136
Cystic fibrosis, 109

D

Daily fitness programs, 141
Dance, 172–176
    aerobic, 176
    creative, 174–175, 555–561
    folk, 174–175, 563–585
    objectives of, 179
    selection of, 176
    social, 175–176
Dance activities
    creative, 556–560
    dance making, 559–560
    folk dances, 567–573
    fundamental rhythmic activities, 541–545
    imitative dances, 556–558
    interpretative dances, 558–559
    line dances, 578–584
    singing, 545–554

square dances, 573–578
Dance making, 559–560
Demonstrations, public, 144
Depth perception
    activities for, 527–528
    definition of, 527
Development
    definition of, 24, 25
    transactional model of, 24–25
    See also Motor development
Developmental physical education, 7–9,
        103–104
    components of, 9–15
    conceptual framework for, 137
    goals of, 7, 127
Developmental Sequence of Fundamental
        Motor Skills Inventory (DSFMSI),
        186
Differentiation, 29
Directional awareness
    activities for, 522–525
    definition of, 81
Disabilities
    emotional, 113–115
    inclusion of children with, 104
    learning, 115–117
    legislation for children with, 101,
        247–248
    mental, 110–113
    physical, 104–110
    programs for children with, 102–104
    special needs of children with, 118–119
Discipline, 220
    planning for, 226–227
    punishment, 222–223
    requirements for, 226–228
    self-control techniques, 223–226
    teacher control techniques, 220–222
Discovery teaching, 239–240
Disc sport skills
    assessment of, 408–409
    catching, 404–406
    sequencing of, 400–402
    skill drills for, 407–408
    theme development of, 400
    throwing, 400–404
    warm-up activities for, 406–407
Distance messages, 214–215
Dodging, 267–270
    assessment of, 276
    exploratory activities for, 272
    guided-discovery activities for, 273
Dribbling, 324–325
    assessment of, 352
    in basketball, 417–419

exploratory activities for, 339
guided discovery activities for, 340
in soccer, 444–445
Dynamic systems, 24

E

Eager movers, definition of, 68–70
Early childhood
    developmental model for, 137–138
    growth in, 18–21
    motor development in, 29–32
Ecological Task Analysis (ETA), 190
Educational gymnastics,
        definition of, 177
Effort, definition of, 76–77
Emergency care policy, 252
Emotional disorders, 113–115
Endurance, 62–63, 505
    activities for, 506–510
Enthusiasm
    for students, 213–214
    for subject matter, 213–214
Epilepsy, 108
Equipment
    placement and use of, 161
    selection of, 160–161
Equipment skills
    assessment of, 397
    balance beam skills, 376–378
    horizontal ladder skills, 380–382
    inner tube skills, 382–384
    large equipment skills, 375–389
    parachute skills, 387–389
    rope-climbing skills, 378–380
    safety considerations for, 375
    small equipment skills, 390–397
    springboard skills, 382–386
    teaching tips for, 389
    turning bar skills, 386–387
    vaulting skills, 384–386
Error correction, 212
Ethnic dances. *See* Folk dances
Exercise, affects of (on growth), 22–23
Exploratory teaching, 239
Extended curriculum, 139–142
Extracurricular activity policy, 252–253

F

Facilities
    indoor, 159–160
    organization of, 158–160
    outdoor, 160
Facility report, 251–252

Feedback, 210
    functions of, 211
    tips on using, 211
    types of, 210–211
Field day, 143
Figure-ground perception
    activities for, 529–530
    definition of, 529
Fine motor manipulation, 41
Finger plays, 546–548
Fit movers, definition of, 58
Fitness activities
    aerobic activities, 501–505
    flexibility activities, 510–513
    strength/endurance activities, 505–510
Fitness assessment, 190–194
    computer applications for, 194
    guidelines for, 190–191
    tests of, 191–194
Fitness awards, 191
Fitness concept learning, 75, 77
Fitness development
    benefits of, 67
    principles of, 66–68
Fitnessgram, 192, 193–194
Fitness homework, 68
Fitness profile, 501–502
Fitness programs, daily, 184
Fitness testing. *See* Fitness assessment
FITT principle, 67–68
Flexibility
    activities for, 510–513
    definition of, 63
Folk dances, 174–175
    ethnic dances, 567–573
    formations for, 568
    history of, 564
    line dances, 578–584
    record sources for, 584
    square dances, 573–578
    steps used in, 565–566
    teaching of, 564–565
    terms used in, 566–567
Formations, 163–165
Form perception
    activities for, 528–529
    definition of, 528
Forward roll, 265–267, 357–359
    See also Body rolling skills
Frisbee. *See* Disc sport skills
Fundamental Movement Pattern
        Assessment Instrument (FMPAI),
        185–189
Fundamental movement phase, 43–45
Fundamental movement skills, 11, 37

G

Galloping, 289–291
    assessment of, 313
    exploratory activities for, 307
    guided discovery activities for, 308
Games, 168–172
    ability levels for, 171–172
    cooperative, 170
    formal, 170
    lead-up, 170–171
    locomotor, 309–312
    low-level, 169–170
    manipulative, 347–350
    modification of, 172
    objectives of, 179
    official sport, 171
    selection of, 171–172
    skill challenge, 170
    stability, 272–275
    types of, 168–171
Gestures, 213
Goals
    definition of, 6
    setting, 96, 125
Gross motor manipulation, 40
Growth, 18
    in early childhood, 18–21
    factors affecting, 22–23
    in later childhood, 21–22
Gym helpers, 166
Gymnastics. *See* Equipment skills; Stunt
        skills; Tumbling skills
Gym shows, 143–144

H

Handstand skills, 370–371
Headstand skills, 367–369
Heart disease, 106
Homework, 50–54, 68
Hoop activities, 393–394
Hopping, 283, 288–289
    assessment of, 313
    exploratory activities for, 303
    guided discovery activities for, 304
Horizontal ladder skills, 380–382
Hyperactivity, 116–117

I

Illness, affects of (on growth), 23
Imitative dances, 556–558
Individual differences, 216–217
Individuality, principle of, 68

Individualized education program (IEP),
        101, 118
Informed movers, definition of, 65–66
Inner tube skills, 382–384
Instructional aids, 161–162
Insurance, 253
Integration (motor development process), 29
Intensity (rhythm element), 174, 541
Interpretative dances, 558–559
Interscholastic programs, 142
Intramural programs, 141–142
Inverted support skills
    handstand, 370–371
    headstand, 367–369
    transitional, 369–370
Isokinetic strength, 62
Isometric strength, 62
Isotonic strength, 62

J

James, William (on self-perception), 85
Jumping
    assessment of, 313
    exploratory activities for, 297, 299, 301
    guided discovery activities for, 298, 300,
        302
    from a height, 286–288
    horizontal, 283–285
    vertical, 285–286
Jump rope activities, 394–395

K

Kicking, 320–322
    assessment of, 351
    exploratory activities for, 335
    guided discovery activities for, 336
    in soccer, 435–441
Kwashiorkor, 22
Kyphosis, 110

L

Ladder, horizontal, 380–382
Ladder tournament, 144–146
Laterality, definition of, 81
Lawsuits. *See* Legal liability
Leaping, 279, 282–283
    assessment of, 313
    exploratory activities for, 295
    guided discovery activities for, 296
Learning
    definition of, 78
    See also Cognitive concept learning

Learning disabilities, 115–117
Learning-through-movement, 6, 15
Learning-to-move, 6, 15
Legal liability, 244
    conditions leading to, 247–249
    conditions of, 244–247
    reduction of, 249–253
Lesson plan, daily, 151
    discipline and, 226–227
    evaluation of, 157–158
    format of, 153–155
    implementation of, 156–159
Liability. *See* Legal liability
Limitation method, 241–242
Line dances
    history of, 578
    record sources for, 584
    selected dances, 578–584
    steps used in, 565–566
    teaching of, 564–565
Listening skills, 216
    activities for, 531–532
Locomotor games, 309–312
Locomotor skills
    assessment of, 312–313
    development activities for, 292–308
    hopping, 283, 288–289, 303–304
    jumping, 283–288, 297–302
    leaping, 279, 282–283, 295–296
    running, 279–282, 293–294
    sequencing of, 279
    skipping, 289, 291–292, 305–306
    sliding and galloping, 289–291, 307–308
    theme development of, 280
Lordosis, 110

M

Malfeasance, 245
Malpractice, 246
Manipulation, definition of, 40–41
Manipulative skills
    assessment of, 350–352
    ball rolling, 324–327, 341–342, 352
    catching, 317, 319–320, 333–334, 351
    development activities for, 330–346
    dribbling, 324–325, 339–340, 352
    games, 347–350
    kicking, 320–322, 335–336, 351
    sequencing of, 316–317
    striking, 327–329, 343–344, 352
    theme development of, 316
    throwing, 317–319, 331–332, 351
    trapping, 322–324, 337–338, 351
    volleying, 329–330, 345–346, 352

Mental retardation
    causes of, 112–113
    classifications of, 111
    definition of, 110
    teaching tips for, 111–112
Misfeasance, 245
Mission statement, 125–127
Moral dilemmas, 94, 96
Moral growth, 94, 96, 97
Motivational techniques, 69, 502
Motor assessments
    computer applications for, 194
    process assessments, 183–184
    product assessments, 184
    tests of, 184–190
Motor development, 9, 24
    in early childhood, 29–32
    in later childhood, 32–34
    phases of, 43–46
    readiness in, 28–29
    sequence of, 25–28
    variability in, 47–51
Movement, types of, 46–47
Movement concept learning, 76–77
Movement pattern, definition of, 37
Movement phrases, 41
Movement skill homework, 50–54
Movement skills, 9, 36–37
    environmental factors influencing,
        41–43
    factors in learning, 231–235
    learning levels of, 47–51, 231–233
    phases of, 43–46
    types of, 37–41
Movement skill themes. *See* Skill themes
Movers, types of, 36, 58, 65–66, 68–70
Multisensory learning, 78
Myelination, 18

N

Naturalistic observation, 215
Negligence, 244–245
    defenses against, 246–247
    See also Legal liability
Neuromuscular limitations, 106–108
Nonfeasance, 245
Noon-hour programs, 139, 141
Norms, definition of, 191
Nutrition, 22

O

Obesity, 63–64, 66
Objective localization, 80

Objectives, 6
    behavioral, 130
    benchmark, 131–132
    general curricular, 128–129
    specific curricular, 129–130
    terminal, 131
One-foot balance, 261–265
    assessment of, 276
Organizations, fitness (list of), 59
Osgood-Schlatter's condition, 109
Otitis media, 21
Overload principle, 66

P

Parachute skills, 387–389
Perceived competence, 86–87
Perception, 516
Perceptual motor activities
    auditory perception activities, 530–534
    body awareness activities, 516–519
    directional awareness activities,
        522–525
    spatial awareness activities, 519–522
    tactile/kinesthetic perception activities,
        534–536
    temporal awareness activities,
        525–527
    visual perception activities, 527–530
Perceptual-motor learning,
        13, 78–82, 516
Perceptual-motor process, 79–80
Performance-related fitness,
        58, 61, 64–65
Physical education. *See* Developmental
        physical education
Physical fitness, 9–10, 58
    components of, 10–12, 58–65
    testing of, 191–194
Physically educated, definition of, 6
Piaget, Jean, 74
Planning, 147–166
Play, significance of, 29–31
Play day, 143
Poems, 549–551
Policies, written, 252–253
Postural deviations, 109–110
Power, definition of, 65
President's Challenge Physical Fitness
        Program, 192–193, 194
Professional growth, 203–204
Professional journals, 203
Proficiency barrier, 45
Proximodistal development, 25
Punishment, 222–223

R

Readiness, 28–29
Recess, 139, 141
Reciprocal teaching, 238
Record-keeping, 249–252
Remedial physical education, 82, 102
Reports
    accident, 249–251
    facility, 251–252
    supply/equipment, 251
Resolution 97 (Congressional), 5
Rhymes, 549–551
Rhythm, 173
    elements of, 174, 540–541
    fundamentals of, 540–545
    singing, 174
Rhythm activities
    application activities, 543–545
    discovery activities, 541–542
    finger plays, 546–548
    rhymes and poems, 549–551
    singing dances, 551–554
Rhythmic pattern, 174, 540
Role models, 226
Rope-climbing skills, 378–380
Round-robin tournaments, 144–145
Routines, establishing, 224
Rules, establishing, 224
Running, 279–282
    assessment of, 313
    exploratory activities for, 293
    guided discovery activities for, 294

S

Scoliosis, 110
Scope and sequence chart, 131, 133
    example of, 149–150
Secular trends, 23
Security, 89–90
Self-acceptance, 87–88
Self-assessment, 96
    guidelines for, 228
Self-concept, 14, 85–86
    components of, 86–89
    importance of, 89–91
Self-control techniques, 223–226
Self-encouragement, 95–96
Self-esteem, 85
Self-study, 215–216
Self-testing activities, 176–177
    objectives of, 179
    presentation of, 178
    selection of, 178–179
    types of, 177–178

Sensitive period, 29
Singing dance activities
    finger plays, 546–548
    rhymes and poems, 549–551
    singing dances, 551–554
Singing rhythms, 174, 545–554
Skill charts, 162
Skill concept learning, 75–76
Skillful movers, definition of, 36
Skill themes, 9–10
    basketball skills, 411–433
    disc sport skills, 399–410
    large equipment skills, 375–389
    locomotor skills, 278–314
    manipulative skills, 315–353
    small equipment skills, 390–397
    soccer skills, 434–457
    softball skills, 458–479
    stability skills, 258–277
    stunt skills, 362–372
    tumbling skills, 355–362
    volleyball skills, 480–497
Skipping, 289, 291–292
    assessment of, 313
    exploratory activities for, 305
    guided discovery activities for, 306
Sliding, 289–291
    assessment of, 313
    exploratory activities for, 307
    guided discovery activities for,
        308
Small group teaching, 238
Soccer activities
    history of, 435
    lead-up games, 450–452
    rules for, 453
    skill drills, 448–449
    warm-up activities, 447–448
Soccer skills
    assessment of, 453–456
    dribbling, 444–445
    heading, 446–447
    juggling, 446–447
    kicking, 435–441
    sequencing of, 435–437
    trapping, 441–444
    volleying, 446–447
Socialization
    definition of, 14–15
    reasons for, 91–94
Softball activities, 461, 468
    lead-up games, 471–475
    rules for, 475–476
    skill drills, 469–471
    warm-up activities, 468–469

Softball skills
    assessment of, 476–479
    fielding, 464–466
    hitting, 466–468
    pitching, 463–464
    sequencing of, 459–461
    theme development of, 459
    throwing, 460–464
Space, definition of, 80
Spatial awareness, 76–77, 79–80
    activities for, 519–522
Specialized movement phase, 45–46
Specialized movement skills, 37
Speed, definition of, 64–65
Sports day, 143
Sportsmanship, 95
Spotting, 356
Springboard skills, 382–386
Springing skills, 360–362
Squad leaders, 165–166
Squads, 162, 165
Square dances
    formations for, 568
    history of, 564
    record sources for, 584
    selected dances, 573–578
    steps used in, 565–566
    teaching of, 564–565
    terms used in, 566–567
Stability, 259
    movement categories of, 259–260
Stability skills
    application activities for, 271–275
    assessment of, 276–277
    beam walk, 261–263
    development activities for, 270–273
    dodging, 267–270
    forward roll, 265–267
    games, 272–275
    one-foot balance, 261–262, 264
    sequencing of, 260–262
    theme development of, 260
Status, 90–91
Stilt activities, 390
Strength, muscular
    activities for, 505–510
    definition of, 61–62, 505
Stretch rope activities, 395–397
Striking, 327–329
    assessment of, 352
    exploratory activities for, 343
    guided discovery activities for, 344
Stunt skills, 355
    assessment of, 371–372
    inverted support skills, 367–371

safety considerations for, 356
sequencing of, 355
spotting for, 356
teaching tips for, 357
theme development for, 355
upright support skills, 362–367
Subjective localization, 79–80
Supply/equipment report, 251
Support skills
  handstand, 370–371
  headstand, 367–369
  individual, 363–366
  inverted, 367–371
  partner, 364, 366–367
  transitional, 369–370
  upright, 362–367

T

Tactile discrimination, 534–536
Tactile/kinesthetic perception activities,
  534–536
Task card, 161
Task teaching, 237–238
Teachers
  conveyance of enthusiasm by, 213–214
  developmental stages of, 204–205
  responsibilities of, 201–204
  traits of, 206–208
Teaching episodes, 155
Teaching styles, 231
  child-centered, 238–240
  direct styles, 236–238, 241
  factors influencing, 231–235
  indirect styles, 238–241
  selection of, 235
  teacher centered, 236–238
Tempo, 174, 540
Temporal awareness, 81
  activities for, 525–527

Test of Gross Motor Development (TGMD),
  186, 190
Throwing, 317–319
  assessment of, 351
  in disc sports, 400–404
  exploratory activities for, 331
  guided discovery activities for,
    332
  in softball, 460–464
Time-out, 221–222
Title IX, 248
Tournaments, 144–146
Transactional model of development,
  24–25
Trapping, 320, 322–324
  assessment of, 351
  exploratory activities for, 337
  guided discovery activities for, 338
  in soccer, 441–444
Tumbling skills, 355
  assessment of, 371–372
  body rolling, 356–360
  safety considerations for, 356
  sequencing of, 355
  spotting for, 356
  springing, 360–362
  teaching tips for, 357
  theme development for, 355
Turning bar skills, 386–387

U

Ultimate, rules for, 408
Underlying beat, 174, 540
  See also Rhythm
Uniqueness, 88–89
Unit plans, 151
Upright support skills
  individual supports, 363–366
  partner supports, 364, 366–367

V

Value base, 125–126
Values education, 92–94
Vaulting skills, 384–386
Virtue, sense of, 89
Visual aids, 162
Visual impairment, 104–105
Visual perception activities,
  527–530
Volleyball activities, 482, 488–489
  history of, 481
  lead-up games, 490–494
  rules for, 494
  skill drills, 489–490
  warm-up activities, 489
Volleyball skills
  assessment of, 494–496
  passing, 483–486
  sequencing of, 481–482
  serving, 486–488
  theme development of, 481
Volleying, 329–330
  assessment of, 352
  exploratory activities for, 345
  guided discovery activities for,
    346
  in soccer, 446–447
  in volleyball, 483–486

W

Wand activities, 397
Worthiness, sense of, 87

Y

Yearly plans, 151–152
YMCA Youth Fitness Test, 192, 193

This activity index is organized under the following four major headings:

- DANCE ACTIVITIES
- FUNDAMENTAL MOVEMENT ACTIVITIES
- GAMES AND SPORTS ACTIVITIES
- SELF-TESTING ACTIVITIES

DANCE ACTIVITIES

Creative Dance Activities
  Activity Progression Charts
    Finger plays, 546
    Rhymes and poems, 549
    Singing dances, 551
    Creative dances, 556
  Imitative Dance Activities, 556–558
    Imitating objects
    Imitating events
  Interpretive Dance Activities, 558–559
    Interpreting action words
    Interpreting feelings and moods
    Interpreting art
    Interpreting action sequences
    Interpreting pendular movements
    Interpreting special holidays
  Dance Making Activities, 559–560
    Name dances
    Rhyme dances
    Slogan dances
    Menu dances
Folk and Square Dance Activities
  Activity Progression Charts
    Folk dances, 567–573
      Turn me around
      Greensleeves
      Seven jumps
      Glow worm
      Chimes of Dunkirk
      Finger polka
      La raspa
      Ace of diamonds
      Oh Susanna
      Girls' jig
      Patty-cake polka

Tinikling
Mexican clap dance
Hora
Virginia reel
Square dances, 573–578
  Oh Johnny
  Red River valley
  Take a little peek
  Birdie in the cage
  Duck for the oyster
  Pop goes the weasel
  Texas star
  Ladies' chain
  Corner of the world
  Farmer's daughter
  Heads and sides
  Snake chain
  Inside out and outside in
  Grand square
Line dances, 578–584
  Bunny hop
  Alley Cat
  The slide
  The slide #2
  Amos Moses
  Electric slide
  Continental walk
  Hully gully
  Bus stop
  Four-corner stomp
  Jive talkin'
  Boot scootin' boogie
  Honky tonk stomp
  Waltz around Texas
  Six shooter
  Slappin' leather
  Sugartown
  Achy breaky
Fundamental Dance Activities
  Discovering Rhythm Activities, 541–542
    In beat
    Body talk
    Copycat
    The accent
    Echo

Names in rhythm
Conversations
Applying Rhythm Activities, 543–545
  Sound compositions
  Tampering with the element
  Conducting the beats
  Percussion instrument stories
  Orchestration
Singing Dance Activities
  Finger Plays, 546–548
    Here is the beehive
    This little clown
    I'm a little teapot
    Over the hills
    Row, row, row
    Dig a little hole
    Ten fingers
    Little fish
    Bunny
    If I were a bird-1
    If I were a bird-2
    Two little
    Flowers
    Left and right
  Rhymes and Poems, 549–551
    My hands
    The noble Duke of York
    Choo-choo
    Windy weather
    Funny clown
    My little puppy
    How creatures move
    Jack-in-the-box
    Stormy days
    Follow-the-leader rhymes
    Drawing numerals in space
    Head, shoulders, baby
  Singing Dances, 551–554
    Mulberry bush
    Ten little jingle bells
    Lobby loo
    Blue bird
    Ten little Indians
    Farmer in the dell
    How do you do, my partner?
    Round and round the village

I see you
A-hunting we will go
Did you ever see a lassie?

FUNDAMENTAL MOVEMENT ACTIVITIES

Locomotor Activities, 278–314
    Skill application, 308–312
    Skill development, 292–308
Manipulative Activities, 315–353
    Skill application, 346–350
    Skill development, 330–346
Stability Activities, 258–277
    Skill application, 271–275
    Skill development, 270–271

GAMES AND SPORTS ACTIVITIES

Low-level Game Activities
    Activity Progression Charts
        Locomotor games, 309
        Manipulative games, 347
        Stability games, 273
    Locomotor Games, 309–312
        Crows and cranes
        Squirrels in the trees
        Colors
        Magic carpet
        Back-to-back
        Hunter
        Spaceship
        Touch and follow
        Where's my partner?
        Whistle stop
        Frog in the sea
        Crossing the brook
        Jump the shot
        Jack be nimble
    Manipulative Games, 347–350
        Clean your yard
        Hot potato
        Teacher ball
        Moon shot
        Spud
        Keep away
        Tunnel ball
        Roll it out
        Kick-away
        Cross the line
        Balloon volleying
        Kick the can
        Corner kickball
        Guard the castle
        Target bombardment

Stability Games, 272–275
    Beanbag balance tag
    Super beanbag balance tag
    Circle freeze tag
    Mirror touch tag
    Animal tag
    Amoeba tag
    Fly trap
    Opposites
    Circle tug-of-war
    Silly Simon
    Circle-point dodgeball
    Team-point dodgeball
    Engineer and caboose dodgeball
Sport Skill Games and Drills
    Activity Progression Charts
        Basketball, 425
        Disc sports, 402
        Soccer, 437
        Softball, 461
        Volleyball, 482
    Basketball Lead-up Games, 426–429
        Five passes
        Circle keep away
        Hands up
        Dribble-pivot-pass
        Base basketball
        Twenty-one
        Around the world
        Six-hole basketball
        Nine-court basketball
        Sideline basketball
        Half-court basketball
        Backline basketball
    Basketball Skill Drills, 423–426
        Wall pass
        Partner pass
        Over-under
        Keep away
        Overhead pass
        Line passing
        Star passing
        Stationary dribble
        Dribble and look
        Line dribble
        Line-dribble pass
        Wander dribble
        Directional dribble
        Chair dribble
        Dribble and weave
        Pivot drill
        Pivot wall pass
        Partner pivot
        Four-point pivot
        Pivot keep away

Center guard
Spot shot
Two-column free throw shooting
Pass and shoot
Dribble and shoot
Pass, pivot, and shoot
Block that shot
Rebound ball
Disc Skill Drills, 407–408
    Flat throw
    Bullseye
    Hoop throw
    Throw for distance
    Disc bowl
    Bird shoot
    Distance/accuracy throw
    Hover
    Curve
    Throw around
    Throw and catch
    Mobile throw and catch
    Keep away
    Gunner
    Self-throw and catch
    Self-throw, run, and catch
    Partner guts
    Team guts
    Skip it
    Freestyle
Soccer Lead-up Games, 450–452
    Circle soccer
    Line soccer
    Soccer keep away
    Sideline soccer
    Pin kickball
    Soccer kickball
    Team keep away
    Crab soccer
    Zone soccer
    Six-a-side soccer
    Regulation soccer
Soccer Skill Drills, 448–449
    Wall kick
    Target kick
    Partner pass
    Circle pass
    Criss-cross passing
    Distance kick
    Accuracy kick
    Partner punting
    Partner trapping
    Toss and trap
    Circle trap
    Follow the leader
    Shadow

One-on-one-double kick
Dribble shuttle
Obstacle dribble relay
Push-pass relay
Volley drill
Circle volley
Keep-it-up
Partner keep-it-up
One-on-one
Three-on-three
Three-on-three change
Softball Lead-up Games, 471–475
Team distance throw
Toss-up
Circle overtake
Throw softball
Around the bases
Base-running overtake
Throw around
Home-run derby
Ground-ball pursuit
Line-ball pepper
Softball pop-up
500
Three-pitch softball
Milk-carton softball
Tee ball
Whiffle ball
Softball Skill Drills, 469–471
Wall toss
Vertical toss and catch
Partner toss and catch
Exchange throwing
Over/under exchange throwing
Alternate over/under
Stretch and catch
One-bounce drill
Fly ball drill
Fly ball/pick-off drill
Around the horn
Throwing/catching shuttle
Run, throw, catch
Fielding grounders
Grounder exchange
Grounder/fly ball exchange
Partner throw-out
Strong-side throw-out
Weak-side throw-out
Grounder shuttle
Speed base running
Around the bases
Base-runner pick-off
Base reverse
Suspended-ball batting
Swinging ball batting

Tee batting
Batting practice
Pepper
Pepper pick
Fungo batting
Volleyball Lead-up Games, 490–494
Ten volleys
Block volley
Balloon volleyball
One bounce
One-line volleyball
High ball
Deck tennis
Newcomb
Shower service ball
Serve, pass, and catch
Bump game
Modified volleyball
Volleyball
Volleyball Skill Drills, 489–490
Volley and catch
Self-volley
Bump and catch
Bump it up
Over-under
High wall volley
Low wall volley
Partner toss
Partner volley
Spot
Partner set
Three-person set
One-two-three over
Circle volley
Bounce volley
Partner wall volley
Bump and run
Wall serve
Over-net serve
Alley serve
Net recovery

SELF-TESTING ACTIVITIES

Fitness Activities
Activity Progression Charts
Aerobic activities, 503
Strength/endurance activities, 506, 509
Flexibility activities, 511
Aerobic Activities, 501–505
Partner tag
Monster tag
Shadow
Shipwreck
Rabbit and turtle

Freeze and melt
Red, white, blue
Circle chase
Circle change
Beanbag drop
Line touch
Rhythmical running
Rhythmical rope jumping
Aerobic rhythm exercise
Hit the deck
Capture the flag
Take the point
Run for distance
Run for time
Combative Activities, 508–510
One-person pull
One-person push
Rooster fight
Hand push
Hand wrestle
Back-to-back tug
Knee slap
Club knock
Leg wrestle
Breaking arms
Drake fight
Elbow struggle
Back-to-back lift
Back-to-back push
Stepping on toes
All-four ankle drag
Ball wrestle
American wrestle
Flexibility Activities, 510–513
Back and Trunk Stretching Activities, 510–512
Side stretch
Windshield wiper
Trunk circles
Simon says
Knee lifts
Ankle pull
Bicycle
Knee arch
Drawbridge
Willow bend
Arm and Shoulder Stretching Activities, 512
Arm circles
Star burst
Giraffe
Chicken hawk
Greet yourself
Towel stretch
Towel dislocate

Leg Stretching Activities, 513
  Toe-toucher
  Straddle stretch
  Center stretch
  Fencer's lunge
  Heel drop
  Heel stretch
  Angle circles
Strength/Endurance Activities, 505–510
Arm and Shoulder Activities, 507
  Seal crawl
  Coffee grinder
  Spread-eagle walk
  Modified pull-ups
  Bent-knee push-ups
  Push-ups
Abdominal Activities, 507–508
  Shoulder curl
  Half-curl
  Half-V-sits
  Bent-knee sit-ups
  Alternate-knee-touch sit-ups
  V-sits
Lower Back Activities, 508
  Alternate leg lifts
  Double leg lifts
  Back arch
  Rocking horse
Leg Activities, 508
  Rabbit hop
  Blast off
  Sprinter
  Heel lifts
  Heel drops
  Pogo jumps
  Squat thrusts
Equipment Activities
  Activity Progression Charts
    Balance beam, 377
    Rope-climbing skills, 379
    Horizontal ladder skills, 381
    Inner tube/springboard skills, 383
    Springboard vaulting skills, 385
    Turning bar skills, 387
    Selected small apparatus activities, 391
  Small Equipment Skills
    Balance-boards and Stilts Activities, 390
    Balloon Activities, 390–391
    Ball Activities, 391–392
    Beanbag Activities, 392–393
    Hoop Activities, 393–394
    Jump Rope Activities, 394–395
    Stretch Rope Activities, 395–397
    Chinese Jump Rope, 396
    Wand Activities, 397

Large Equipment
  Balance-Beam Skills, 376–378
    Beam stand
    Balance and touch
    Beam walk
    Walk-turn-walk
    Double-turn walk
    Walk and touch
    Toe walk
    Dip walk
    Crouch walk
    Cat walk
    Knee touch
    Full turn
    Step over
    Go through
    Over and through
    Beanbag pickup
    Beanbag balance
    Knee scale
    Front scale
    V-seat
    V-seat to knee scale
    Partner pass
    Partner scale
    Toss and catch
  Rope-Climbing and Cargo Net Skills, 378–380
    Head touch
    Back lift
    Heel pivot
    Straight pull
    Nose touch
    Nose-to-rope touch
    Jump and grasp
    Jump and hold
    Swing and hold
    Tarzan and Jane
    Rope pull-ups
    Leg hold
    Rope climb
    Bell ringer
    Double-rope hold
    Double-rope swing
    Double-rope candle stand
    Double-rope pullover
  Horizontal Ladder Skills, 380–382
    Straight hang
    Single-knee lift
    Double-knee lift
    Leg lift
    Trunk twister
    Bicycle hang
    Hang and swing
    Half chin

    Flexed-arm hang
    Chin-ups
    Side-rail travel
    Single-rung travel
    Monkey rung travel
    Super monkey travel
    Inverted push-ups
    Inverted hang
    Inverted swing
    Pull through
    Skin the cat
    Pull to top
  Inner Tube/Springboard Skills, 382–386
    Sit and bounce
    Walk around
    Stand and bounce
    Center jump
    Ins and outs
    Half-turn bounce
    Bounce and touch
    Bounce and squat
    Bouncing bunny
    Bounce and roll
    Tuck jump
    Toe jump
    Knee bounce
    Full-turn bounce
    Partner bounce
    Around the world
    Feet to seat
    Bounce and kick
    Jump and half-turn
    Star bounce
    Jump and full turn
    Bounce and knee straddle
    Bounce and ankle straddle
    Bounce and jackknife
    Bounce and toe straddle
    Double spin
    Double reverse spin
    Double spin plus
  Springboard/Vaulting Skills, 384–386
    Squat mount
    Free mount
    Running squat mount
    Running free mount
    Jump and land
    Jump and turn
    Upright springs
    Jump and roll
    Jump, turn, and roll
    Squat vault
    Flank vault
    Straddle mount
    Straddle vault

Shoot squat vault
Turning Bar Skills, 386–387
    Straight hang
    Single toe point
    Double toe point
    Double knee raise
    Hanging walk
    Bicycle hang
    Hang and swing
    Pivot swing
    Change grips
    L-seat
    Straight swing
    Toe toucher
    Swing and drop
    Swing and clap
    Swing and turn
    Bar travel
    Monkey travel
    Knee hang
    Knee swing
    Pull through and drop
    Skin the cat
    Bird's nest
Parachute Skills, 387–389
    Number chase
    Smash-a-chute
    Parachute soccer
    Chute the bacon
    Big top
    Pass the ball
    Steal the ball
    Chute dribble
    Simon says
    Team popcorn
    Roll through
    Poison parachute
    Colors
    Mousetrap
    Huddle
    Jacks
    Parachute golf
    Heads in the basket
Auditory Perception Activities
    Listening Skills, 531–532
        Traditional games
        Hot and cold
        Clap clap
        Poems
        Music
        Bounce bounce
        Active animals
        Hands
        Echo
        Listening walk

It is I
Tape recorder sounds
Voice recording
Freeze and melt
Marching
Auditory Discrimination, 532–533
    Close your eyes
    Musical instruments
    What does it sound like?
    What is it?
    Where is the bell?
    Keep off
    Sound targets
    Bounce off
    Match the cans
Auditory Memory, 533–534
    A trip to the zoo
    Story telling
    Action rhymes
    Instrument playing
    Silly hat
    Horse race
    The winner is . . .
    Lost and found
Tactile/Kinesthetic Perception Activities
    Tactile Discrimination and Matching,
        534–536
        Collections
        Texture paintings
        Collages
        Creative movement
        Mystery bag
        Tag an object
        Geometric shapes
        Shape trace
        Heavy and light
        Sandpaper sort
        Touch tag
        Search
    Tactile/Kinesthetic Memory, 536
        Where is it?
        Guess who?
        Put in order
        Memory ball
        Sandpaper numbers and letters
Visual Perception Activities
    Depth Perception Skills, 527–528
        Bowling
        Targets
        Hoops
        Jumping
        Balance beam
        Boxes
    Form perception, 528–529
        Shape walking

Tracing
Making things
Body shapes
Shape tag
Stepping shapes
Matching shapes
Beanbag toss
Shadow pantomime
Figure-Ground Perception, 529–530
    Discrimination
    Sorting
    Attention
    Ladder maze
    Target toss
    Eggshell walk
    Rope walk
    Paddle balance
    Rope maze
    Candyland
    Hidden objects
    Finger fixation
    Pencil-wall fixation
    Paper-punch pictures
Perceptual-Motor Activities
    Body Awareness Activities, 516–519
        Locating the large body parts
        Locating the small body parts
        Move and listen
        Partner practice
        Body-part differentiation
        Where can you bend?
        Paired parts
        Put-together people
        Mirror activities
    Directional Awareness Activities,
        522–525
        Clock games
        Swinging-ball activities
        Directional commands
        Over, under, and around
        Walking-board activities
        Unilateral, bilateral, and cross-lateral
            activities
        Throwing activities
        Chalkboard activities
        Ladder activities
        Twist-board activities
        Creeping and walking activities
        Ball activities
    Spatial Awareness Activities, 519–522
        Big and small
        Maze walk
        Rope walking
        Back space
        Obstacle course

Body space
Other space
Near and far
Map activities
Miscellaneous activities
Temporal Awareness Activities, 525–527
Ball activities
Rhythmic movement
My beat
Free flow
Moving-target toss
Balloon-volleying activities

Miscellaneous large-motor temporal
activities
Miscellaneous fine-motor temporal
activities
Stunts and Tumbling Activities
Activity Progression Charts
Body rolling, 358
Springing, 361
Upright supports, 363–364
Inverted support skills, 368
Body-Rolling Skills, 356–360
Sideways rolling

Forward rolling
Backward rolling
Springing Skills, 360–362
Upright springing
Inverted springing
Upright Support Skills, 362–367
Individual supports/Partner supports
Inverted Support Skills,
367–371
Headstand skills
Transitional supports
Handstand skills

This developmental skills index is organized under the following four major topic headings:

- EQUIPMENT SKILLS
- FUNDAMENTAL MOVEMENT SKILLS
- SPORT SKILLS
- STUNTS AND TUMBLING SKILLS

EQUIPMENT SKILLS

Balance-Beam Skills, 376–378
  Beam stand
  Balance and touch
  Beam walk
  Walk-turn-walk
  Double-turn walk
  Walk and touch
  Toe walk
  Dip walk
  Crouch walk
  Cat walk
  Knee touch
  Full turn
  Step over
  Go through
  Over and through
  Beanbag pickup
  Beanbag balance
  Knee scale
  Front scale
  V-seat
  V-seat to knee scale
  Partner pass
  Partner scale
  Toss and catch
Rope-Climbing and Cargo Net Skills, 378–380
  Head touch
  Back lift
  Heel pivot
  Straight pull
  Nose touch
  Nose-to-rope touch
  Jump and grasp

Jump and hold
Swing and hold
Tarzan and Jane
Rope pull-ups
Leg hold
Rope climb
Bell ringer
Double-rope hold
Double-rope swing
Double-rope candle stand
Double-rope pullover
Horizontal Ladder Skills, 380–382
  Straight hang
  Single-knee lift
  Double-knee lift
  Leg lift
  Trunk twister
  Bicycle hang
  Hang and swing
  Half chin
  Flexed-arm hang
  Chin-ups
  Side-rail travel
  Single-rail travel
  Single-rung travel
  Monkey rung travel
  Super monkey travel
  Inverted push-ups
  Inverted hang
  Inverted swing
  Pull through
  Skin the cat
  Pull to top
Inner Tube and Springboard Skills, 382–386
  Sit and bounce
  Walk around
  Stand and bounce
  Center jump
  Ins and outs
  Half-turn bounce
  Bounce and touch
  Bounce and squat
  Bouncing bunny
  Bounce and roll
  Tuck jump
  Toe jump

Knee bounce
Full-turn bounce
Partner bounce
Around the world
Feet to seat
Bounce and kick
Jump and half-turn
Star bounce
Jump and full turn
Bounce and knee straddle
Bounce and ankle straddle
Bounce and jackknife
Bounce and toe straddle
Double spin
Double reverse spin
Double spin plus
Springboard/Vaulting Skills, 384–386
  Squat mount
  Free mount
  Running squat mount
  Running free mount
  Jump and land
  Jump and turn
  Upright springs
  Jump and roll
  Jump, turn, and roll
  Squat vault
  Flank vault
  Straddle mount
  Straddle vault
  Shoot squat vault
Turning Bar Skills, 386–387
  Straight hang
  Single toe point
  Double toe point
  Double knee raise
  Hanging walk
  Bicycle hang
  Hang and swing
  Pivot swing
  Change grips
  L-seat
  Straight swing
  Toe toucher
  Swing and drop
  Swing and clap

Swing and turn
Bar travel
Monkey travel
Knee hang
Knee swing
Pull through and drop
Skin the cat
Bird's nest

FUNDAMENTAL MOVEMENT SKILLS

Locomotor Skills, 278–314
   Skill sequencing, 279
   Developing a locomotor skill theme, 280
   Skill development activities, 292–308
   Skill application activities, 308–312
   Assessing progress, 312–313
Running and Leaping, 279–283
   Running, 280
   Leaping, 282
   Verbal description
   Visual description
   Teaching tips
   Concepts children should know
   Exploratory activity ideas
   Guided-discovery activity ideas
Jumping and Hopping, 283–289
   Horizontal jumping, 283
   Vertical jumping, 285
   Jumping from a height, 286
   Hopping, 288
   Verbal description
   Visual description
   Teaching tips
   Concepts children should know
   Exploratory activity ideas
   Guided-discovery activity ideas
Skipping, Sliding, Galloping, 289–292
   Skipping, 291
   Sliding and galloping, 289
   Verbal description
   Visual description
   Teaching tips
   Concepts children should know
   Exploratory activities
   Guided-discovery activities
Manipulative Skills, 315–353
   Skill sequencing, 316–317
   Developing a manipulative skill theme, 316
   Skill development activities, 329
   Skill application activities, 330
   Assessing progress, 350–352

Throwing and Catching, 317–320
   Throwing, 317
   Catching, 319
   Verbal description
   Visual description
   Teaching tips
   Concepts children should know
   Exploratory activity ideas
   Guided-discovery activity ideas
Kicking and Trapping, 320–324
   Kicking, 321
   Trapping, 322
   Verbal descriptions
   Visual descriptions
   Teaching tips
   Concepts children should know
   Exploratory activity ideas
   Guided-discovery activity ideas
Dribbling and Ball Rolling, 324–327
   Dribbling, 324
   Ball rolling, 325
   Verbal description
   Visual description
   Teaching tips
   Concepts children should know
   Exploratory activity ideas
   Guided-discovery activity ideas
Striking and Volleying, 327–330
   Striking, 327
   Volleying, 329
   Verbal descriptions
   Visual descriptions
   Teaching tips
   Concepts children should know
   Exploratory activity ideas
   Guided-discovery activity ideas
Stability Skills, 258–277
   Developing a stability skill theme, 260
   Skill sequencing, 259–261
   Skill development activities, 270–272
   Skill application activities, 271–275
   Assessing progress, 276–277
Dynamic and Static Balance, 261–265
   Beam walk, 262–263
   One-foot balance, 264
   Verbal descriptions
   Visual descriptions
   Teaching tips
   Concepts children should know
Body Rolling, 265–267
   Forward roll, 265
   Verbal description
   Visual description
   Teaching tips
   Concepts children should know

Exploratory activity ideas
Guided-discovery activity ideas
Dodging, 267–270
   Verbal description
   Visual description
   Teaching tips
   Concepts children should know
   Dodging
   Exploratory activity ideas

SPORTS SKILLS

Basketball Skills, 411–422
   Skill sequencing progression chart, 413
   Developmental activities progression chart, 425
   Warm-up activities, 423
   Skill drills, 423–426
   Lead-up games, 426–429
   Basic rules, 429–430
   Assessing progress, 430–432
Passing and Catching Skills, 413–416
   Chest pass, 413–414
   Bounce pass, 414
   One-handed overarm pass, 414–415
   Two-handed overarm pass, 415
   Catching, 415–416
   Verbal description
   Visual description
   Teaching tips
   Concepts children should know
Dribbling and Pivoting Skills, 417–419
   Stationary dribble, 417
   Moving dribble, 417
   Crossover dribble, 418
   Pivoting, 418
   Verbal descriptions
   Visual descriptions
   Teaching tips
   Concepts children should know
Goal Shooting Skills, 419–422
   One-hand push shot, 420
   Jump shot, 420
   Lay-up shot, 420
   Free throw shooting, 421
   Verbal description
   Visual description
   Teaching tips
   Concepts children should know
Disc Sport Skills, 399–406
   Skill sequencing progression chart, 401
   Developmental activities progression chart, 402
   Warm-up activities, 406–407
   Skill drills, 407–408

Basic rules, 408
    Assessing progress, 408–409
Throwing Skills, 400–404
    Backhand throw, 401–402
    Forehand throw, 401–403
    Overhand throw, 403
    Verbal description
    Visual description
    Teaching tips
    Concepts children should know
Catching Skills, 404–406
    Sandwich catch, 404–405
    Two-handed clap catch, 404–405
    One-handed catch, 405–406
    Verbal description
    Visual description
    Teaching tips
    Concepts children should know
Soccer Skills, 434–447
    Skill sequencing progression chart, 436
    Developmental activities progression
        chart, 437
    Warm-up activities, 447–448
    Skill drills, 448–449
    Soccer lead-up games, 450–452
    Basic rules, 453
    Assessing progress, 453–456
Kicking Skills, 435–441
    Instep kick, 435–438
    Push pass, 438–439
    Outside of foot kick, 438–439
    Punting, 439–440
    Verbal description
    Visual description
    Teaching tips
    Concepts children should know
Trapping Skills, 441–444
    Shin trap, 441
    Sole-of-foot trap, 441–442
    Inside-of-foot trap, 442
    Inside-of-thigh trap, 442
    Chest trap, 443
Dribbling Skills, 444–445
    Inside-of-foot, 444
    Outside-of-foot, 444–445
    Verbal description
    Visual description
    Teaching tips
    Concepts children should know
Volleying Skills, 446–447
    Juggling, 446
    Heading, 446
    Verbal descriptions
    Visual descriptions
    Teaching tips

Concepts children should know
Softball Skills, 458–468
    Skill sequencing progression chart, 460
    Developmental activities progression
        chart, 461
    Warm-up activities, 468–469
    Skill drills, 469–471
    Lead-up games, 471–475
    Basic rules, 475–476
    Assessing progress, 476–478
Throwing Skills, 460–464
    Overhand throw, 461–462
    Underhand throw, 462
    Sidearm throw, 462
    Pitching, 463
    Verbal description
    Visual description
    Teaching tips
    Concepts children should know
Fielding Skills, 464–466
    Fly ball, 464
    Line drive, 465
    Ground ball, 465
    Verbal descriptions
    Visual descriptions
    Teaching tips
    Concepts children should know
Hitting Skills, 466–468
    Batting, 466
    Bunting, 467
    Verbal descriptions
    Visual descriptions
    Teaching tips
    Concepts children should know
Volleyball Skills, 480–488
    Skill sequencing progression chart, 482
    Developmental activities progress chart,
        482
    Warm-up activities, 489
    Skill drills, 489–490
    Lead-up games, 490–494
    Basic rules, 494
    Assessing progress, 494–496
Volleying Skills, 483–486
    Overhead pass, 483
    Bump, 483
    Set, 484
    Dig, 484
Serving Skills, 486–488
    Underhand serve, 486
    Overhead serve, 487
    Verbal description
    Visual description
    Teaching tips
    Concepts children should know

STUNTS AND TUMBLING SKILLS

    Skill sequencing, 355
    Safety considerations, 356
    Spotting, 356
Body-Rolling Skills, 356–360
Sideways Rolling Skills, 357
    Soldier log roll
    Rocket log roll
    Sideways roll
Forward Rolling Skills, 357–359
    Look back
    Tip over
    Back rocker
    Roll-up
    Forward roll
    Consecutive forward rolls
    Step-roll
    Reach-over roll
    Dive roll
    Partner dive roll
    Straddle roll
    Eskimo roll
Backward Rolling Skills, 359–360
    Back rocker
    Back tucker
    Rabbit ears
    Snail balance
    Back shoulder roll
    Rock-back shoulder roll
    Forearm sit and roll
    Forearm rock and roll
    Backward roll
    Consecutive back rolls
    Forward-backward roll combination
    Back straddle roll
    Back extension roll
Inverted Support Skills, 367–371
Headstand Skills, 367–369
    Head balance
    Greet the elbows
    Tripod
    One-knee tripod
    Half-headstand
    Three-quarter headstand
    Headstand
    Kick-up headstand
    Headstand to a roll
    Drag headstand
    Forearm stand
Transitional Support Skills, 369–370
    One leg up
    Side switch
    Half-cartwheel
    Cartwheel

Consecutive cartwheels
Olympic cartwheel
Heel-click cartwheel
One-hand cartwheel
Roundoff
Running roundoff
Handstand Skills,
    370–371
Swing-up
Mule kick
Wall stand
Partner-aided handstand
Handstand
Springing Skills, 360–362
Upright springing
Rocket ship
Knee lifter
Butt kicker
Toe toucher
Half-turn
Three-quarter turn
Full turn
Straddle jump
Star jump
Knee straddle
Ankle straddle
Toe straddle

Inverted Springing, 362
Low mat roll
Mat headspring
Headspring
Neck spring
Knee-neck spring
Partner handspring
Front handspring
Upright Support Skills, 362–367
Individual Supports, 364–366
Rocker
Thread the needle
Coffee grinder
Corkscrew
Turk stand
Egg seat
Egg roll
Seal crawl
Nose dive
Fishhawk dive
Wicket walk
Stump walk
Bear dance
V-seat
Candle stand
Heel click
Greet the toe

Human ball
Inchworm
Knee dip
Knee spring
Hitch kick
Pirouette
Straight fall
Shoot through
Front scale
Side scale
Partner Supports, 366–367
Butter churn
Partner walk
Two-person rocker
Wheelbarrow
Wring the dishrag
Chinese get up
Leapfrog
Chest balance
Thigh stand-in
Front swan
Back swan
Hand-knee shoulder stand
Hand-foot and foot-hand stand
Hand-to-foot stand
Shoulder stand-out